English – French
French – English
Word to Word Dictionary

Féquière Vilsaint
France Robert-Dubois

EDUCA VISION

Authors: Féquière Vilsaint, France Robert-Dubois
Cover and layout design: Nathalie Jn Baptiste
© Copyright 2008, Educa Vision
Coconut Creek, FL

For information, please contact:

Educa Vision Inc.,
7550 NW 47th Avenue
Coconut Creek, FL 33073
Telephone: 954-968-7433
Fax: 954-970-0330
E-mail: educa@aol.com
Web: www.educavision.com

ISBN 13: 978-1-58432-480-5
ISBN 10: 1-58432-480-5

PREFACE

The English French Dictionary is a practical instrument to help both English and French learners of the other language to improve their language skills and clarify issues of orthography. It contains 27,000 word entries and expressions, many with multiple meanings.

We depart dramatically from our previous edition by first using a word frequency list of the English language to select frequent entries in common English communication. Second, we added special vocabulary from secondary-school content fields such as social sciences, physical sciences, biological sciences, mathematics, language arts etc. The result is a comprehensive list of English entries with French equivalents in all areas covered in school curricula.

LIST OF ABREVIATIONS
LISTE D'ABRÉVIATIONS

	English	French
a.	adjective	adjectif
adv.	adverb	adverbe
art.	article	article
conj.	conjunction	conjonction
interj.	interjection	interjection
n.	name	nom
pos.	possessive adjective	adjectif possessif
prep.	preposition	préposition
pron.	pronoun	pronom
v.	verb	verbe

English – French
Word to Word Dictionary

Section 1

A

a.m: *adv.* du matin
a: *art.* un; une
aback: *adv.* to be taken
- = vi être décontenancé
abacus: *n.* abaque; boulier
abandon: *vt.* abandonner; laisser
abandonment: *n.* abandon
abase: *vt.* avilir; humilier
abasement: *n.* avilissement m;humiliation
abash: *vt.* couvrir de honte
abate: *vt.* baisser; vi baisser; se calmer
abatement: *n.* baisse; réduction
abbess: *n.* abbesse
abbey: *n.* abbaye
abbot: *n.* abbé
abbreviate: *vt.* abréger; raccourcir
abbreviation: *n.* abréviation
abdicate: *vt.* abdiquer; renoncer à
abdication: *n.* abdication; renonciation
abdomen: *n.* abdomen
abdominal: *adj.* abdominal
abduct: *vt.* kidnapper; enlever
abduction: enlèvement; abduction
abductor: *n.* abducteur
abed: *adv.* au lit
aberrant: *adj.* aberrant
aberration: *n.* aberration
abet: *vt.* to aid and
- = être complice de
abeyance: *n.* suspension
abhor: *vt.* abhorrer; exécrer
abhorrence: *n.* exécration; horreur
abhorrent: *adj.* exécrable
abide: *vt.* supporter; souffrir
abilities: *pl.* talents
ability: *n.* capacité; aptitude
abiotic: *adj.* abiotique
abject: *adj.* misérable; abject; méprisable; -ly *adv.* = misérablement

abjuration: *n.* renonciation; abandon; abjuration; reniement
abjure: *vt.* abjurer; renoncer à
ablative: *n.* ablatif
ablaze: *adj.* enflammé
able: *adj.* capable; to be - = pouvoir
able-bodied: *adj.* robuste
ablution: *n.* ablution
ably: *adv.* habilement
abnegation: *n.* renoncement
abnormal: *adj.* anormal
abnormality: *n.* anomalie
aboard: *adv.* à bord
abode: *n.* domicile
abolish: *vt.* abolir; supprimer
abolition: *n.* abolition; suppression
abominable: *adj.* abominable
abomination: *n.* abomination
aboriginal: *adj.* aborigène
aborigines: *npl.* aborigènes
abort: *vi.* avorter
abortion: *n.* avortement
abortive: *adj.* raté
abound: *vi.* abonder;
- with abonder en
about: *prep.* au sujet de; vers
above: *prep.* au-dessus de; *adv.* au-dessus
aboveboard: *adj.* franc
abrade: *v.* éroder; abraser
abrasion: *n.* écorchure
abrasive: *adj.* abrasif
abreast: *adv.* de front
abridge: *vt.* abréger; raccourcir; résumer
abridgment: *n.* abrégement m; version abrégée
abroad: *adv.* à l'étranger; to go - se rendre à l'étranger
abrogate: *vt.* abroger
abrogation: *n.* abrogation
abrupt: *adj.* abrupt; brusque
abrupt;: *adv.* abruptement
abscess: *n.* abcès

abscond: *vi.* s'enfuir
absence: *n.* absence
absent: *adj.* absent; *vi.* s'absenter
absentee: *n.* absent
absenteeism: *n.* absentéisme
absent-minded: *adj.* distrait
absolute temperature: température absolue
absolute value: valeur absolue
absolute zero: zéro absolu
absolute: *adj.* absolu
absolution: *n.* absolution
absolutism: *n.* absolutisme
absolve: *vt.* absoudre
absorb: *vt.* absorber
absorbent cotton: *n.* coton hydrophile
absorbent: *adj.* absorbant
absorption: *n.* absorption
abstain: *vi.* s'abstenir
abstemious: *adj.* sobre
abstemiousness: *n.* sobriété
abstinence: *n.* abstinence
abstinent: *adj.* abstinent
abstract: *adj.* abstrait; *n.* abrégé
abstraction: *n.* abstraction; extraction
abstractly: *adv.* abstraitement
abstruse: *adj.* abstrus; obscur
absurd: *adj.* absurde
absurdity: *n.* absurdité
abundance: *n.* abondance
abundant: *adj.* abondant
abuse: *n.* abus m; injures fpl; mauvais traitements
abuse: *vt.* abuser de; insulter; maltraiter
abusive: *adj.* injurieux; -ly = *adv.* injurieusement
abut: *vi.* être contigu
abysmal: *adj.* abominable
abyss: *n.* abîme
acacia: *n.* acacia
academic background: formation universitaire

academic: *adj.* universitaire; scolaire; théorique; académique
academician: *n.* académicien
academy: *n.* académie
accede: *vi.* accéder
accelerate: *vt.* accélérer
acceleration: *n.* accélération
accelerator: *n.* accélérateur
accent: *n.* accent m; *vt.* accentuer
accentuate: *vt.* accentuer
accentuation: *n.* accentuation
accept: *vt.* accepter
acceptability: *n.* acceptabilité
acceptable: *adj.* acceptable
acceptance: *n.* acceptation
access path: chemin d'accès
access provider: fournisseur d'accès
access something (to): avoir accès; accéder; à qch
access: *n.* accès
accessible: *adj.* accessible
accession: *n.* augmentation; accession
accessioning of serials: bulletinage
accessioning: enregistrement (mention visant à garder trace d'une opération)
accessory: *n.* accessoire m; (law) complice
accident: *n.* accident m; hasard
accidental: *adj.* accidentel; -ly = *adv.* par hasard
acclaim: *vt.* acclamer
acclamation: *n.* acclamation
acclimate: *vt.* acclimater
accommodate: *vt.* loger; accommoder
accommodating: *adj.* obligeant
accommodations: *npl.* logement
accompaniment: *n.* accompagnement
accompanist: *n.* accompagnateur
accompany: *vt.* accompagner
accomplice: *n.* complice
accomplish: *vt.* accomplir

accomplished: *adj.* accompli
accomplishment: *n.* accomplissement
accord: *n.* accord
accordance n: in - = with conformément à
according: *prep.* selon; - as = selon que; -ly = *adv.* en conséquence
accordion: *n.* accordéon
accost: *vt.* accoster
account book: livre de comptes
account number: numéro de compte
account: *n.* compte
accountability: *n.* responsabilité
accountable: *adj.* responsable
accountancy: *n.* comptabilité
accountant: *n.* comptable
accounting system: plan comptable
accounts department: service comptable
accounts payable book: livre des effets à payer
accounts receivable book: livre des effets à recevoir
accrue: *vi.* s'accumuler; revenir
accumulate: *vt.* accumuler; *vi.* s'accumuler
accumulation: *n.* accumulation
accuracy: *n.* exactitude
accurate: *adj.* exact; -ly = *adv.* exactement
accursed: *adj.* maudit
accusation: *n.* accusation
accusative: *n.* accusatif
accusatory: *adj.* accusateur
accuse: *vt.* accuser
accused: *n.* accusé
accuser: *n.* accusateur
accustom: *vt.* accoutumer
accustomed: *adj.* accoutumé
ace: *n.* as
acerbic: *adj.* acerbe
acetate: *n.* acétate
ache: *n.* douleur

ache: *vi.* faire mal
achieve: *vt.* réaliser; obtenir; réussir à; parvenir à
achievement: *n.* réalisation; exploit
acid dissociation constant: constante de dissociation acide
acid: *adj.* acide; aigre
acidity: *n.* acidité
acknowledge: *vt.* reconnaître; admettre
acknowledgement of order: accusé de réception de commande
acknowledgment: *n.* reconnaissance
acme: *n.* apogée
acne: *n.* acné
acorn: *n.* gland
acoustics: *n.* acoustique
acquaint: *vt.* informer; aviser
acquaintance: *n.* connaissance
acquiesce: *vi.* acquiescer; consentir
acquiescence: *n.* consentement
acquiescent: *adj.* consentant
acquire: *vt.* acquérir
acquisition policy: politique d'acquisition
acquisition: *n.* acquisition
acquit: *vt.* acquitter
acquittal: *n.* acquittement
acre: *n.* acre
acrid: *adj.* âcre; acerbe
acrimonious: *adj.* acrimonieux
acrimony: *n.* acrimonie
acronym: *n.* acronyme
across: *adv.* en travers; d'un côté à l'autre
act of god: un cas de force majeure; une catastrophe naturelle
act: *vt.* jouer; agir; jouer la comédie
acting: *adj.* intérimaire
action replay: *n.* répétition
action: *n.* action; combat
activate: *vt.* activer
activation energy: énergie d'activation

active listener: interlocuteur attentif
active voice: voix active
active: *adj.* actif; -ly = *adv.*
activement
activity series: série d'activité
activity: *n.* activité
actor: *n.* acteur
actress: *n.* actrice
actual yield: produit actuel
actual: *adj.* réel; concret; -ly = *adv.*
en fait; réellement
actuary: *n.* actuaire
acumen: *n.* perspicacité
Acute angle: angle aigu
Acute triangle: triangle aigu
acute: *adj.* aigu; perspicace;
- accent = accent aigu
acuteness: *n.* finesse; intensité
ad lib: *vt.* improviser
ad nauseam: *adv.* à saturation
ad: *n.* annonce
adage: *n.* adage
adamant: *adj.* inflexible
adapt: *vt.* adapter; ajuster
adaptability: *n.* adaptabilité
adaptable: *adj.* adaptable
adaptation: *n.* adaptation
adaptor: *n.* adaptateur
add: *vt.* ajouter; - up additionner
addendum: *n.* addendum
adder: *n.* vipère
addict: *n.* intoxiqué
addiction: *n.* dépendance
addictive: *adj.* qui crée une
dépendance
add-in: extension logicielle
addition: *n.* addition
additional: *adj.* additionnel
additive inverse: élément opposé
additive: *n.* additif
address file: fichier d'adresses
address: *vt.* adresser; s'adresser à
addressing machine: une machine à
adresser

adduce: *vt.* mentionner; citer
adenoids: *npl.* végétations
adept: *adj.* expert
adequacy: *n.* suffisance f capacité
adequate: *adj.* adéquat; suffisant; -ly
= *adv.* convenablement; suffisamment
adhere: *vi.* adhérer
adherence: *n.* adhérence
adherent: *n.* adhérent; partisan
adhesion: *n.* adhérence f; adhésion
adhesive tape: sparadrap m;
papier m collant
adhesive: *adj.* adhésif
adhesiveness: *n.* adhérence
adiabatic demagnetization:
démagnétisation adiabatique
adiabatic: *adj.* adiabatique
adieu: *adv.* adieu; adieux
adipose: *adj.* adipeux
adjacent: *adj.* adjacent; contigu
adjectival: *adj.* adjectival; -ly *adv.* =
adjectivalement
adjective: *n.* adjectif
adjoin: *vi.* être contigu
adjoining: *adj.* contigu
adjourn: *vt.* reporter; remettre
adjournment: *n.* ajournement
adjudicate: *vt.* décider; juger
adjunct: *n.* subalterne; annexe
adjust: *vt.* ajuster; adapter
adjustable: *adj.* ajustable; adaptable
adjustment: *n.* ajustement; réglage
adjutant: *n.* adjudant
administer: *vt.* administrer; distribuer
administration: *n.* administration;
gouvernement
administrative: *adj.* administratif
administrator: *n.* administrateur
admirable: *adj.* admirable;
-bly *adv.* = admirablement
admiral: *n.* amiral
admiralship: *n.* amirauté
admiralty: *n.* ministère de la Marine
admiration: *n.* admiration

admire: *vt.* admirer
admirer: *n.* admirateur
admiringly: *adv.* avec admiration
admissible: *adj.* admissible
admission: *n.* admission; entrée
admit: *vt.* admettre
admittance: *n.* admission
admittedly: *adv.* il est vrai (que)
admixture: *n.* mélange
admonish: *vt.* admonester; réprimander
admonition: *n.* admonestation; conseil
admonitory: *adj.* admonestation
ado: *n.* agitation
adolescence: *n.* adolescence
adopt: *vt.* adopter
adopted: *adj.* adoptif
adoption: *n.* adoption
adoptive: *adj.* adoptif
adorable: *adj.* adorable
adorably: *adv.* adorablement
adoration: *n.* adoration
adore: *vt.* adorer
adorn: *vt.* orner
adornment: *n.* ornement
adrift: *adv.* à la dérive
adroit: *adj.* adroit; habile
adroitness: *n.* adresse
adsorption: *n.* adsorption
adulation: *n.* adulation
adulatory: *adj.* adulateur
adult: *adj.* adulte
adulterate: *vt.* falsifier; *adj.* falsifié
adulteration: *n.* falsification
adulterer: *n.* adultère
adulteress: *n.* adultère
adulterous: *adj.* adultère
adultery: *n.* adultère
advance: *vt.* avancer; *vi.* avancer
advanced: *adj.* avancé
advancement: *n.* avancement
advantage: *n.* avantage m; to affectingly

advantageous: *adj.* avantageux; affectionate
advantageousness: *n.* avantage
-advent: *n.* venue
adventitious: *adj.* accidentel
adventure: *n.* aventure
adventurer: *n.* aventurier
adventurous: *adj.* aventureux
adverb: *n.* adverbe
adverbial: *adj.* adverbial
adversary: *n.* adversaire
adverse: *adj.* défavorable
adversity: *n.* adversité; malheur
advertise: *vt.* faire de la publicité
advertisement: une publicité; une annonce
advertising agency: une agence de publicité
advertising department: le service publicité
advertising media: les supports publicitaires; les médias
advertising: la publicité
advertising; deceptive: la publicité mensongère
advice: *n.* conseil; avis
advisability: *n.* opportunité
advisable: *adj.* prudent; conseillé
advise: *vt.* conseiller; aviser
advisedly: *adv.* de manière avisée
advisory: *adj.* consultatif
advocacy: *n.* défense
advocate: *n.* avocat
aerial: *n.* antenne
aerobics: *npl.* aérobic
aerometer: *n.* aéromètre
aeroplane: *n.* avion
aerosol: *n.* aérosol
aerostat: *n.* aérostat
afar: *adv.* au loin
affability: *n.* affabilité
affable: *adj.* affable
affair: *n.* affaire
affect: *vt.* toucher; affecter

affectation: *n.* affectation
affected: *adj.* affecté
affection: *n.* affection
affidavit: *n.* déclaration sous serment
affiliate: *vt.* affilier
affiliation: *n.* affiliation
affinity: *n.* affinité
affirm: *vt.* affirmer; déclarer
affirmation: *n.* affirmation
affirmative: *adj.* affirmatif
affix: *vt.* coller; apposer
afflict: *vt.* affliger
affliction: *n.* affliction
affluent: *adj.* riche; abondant
afflux: *n.* afflux; affluence
afford: *vt.* fournir; to be able to
affray: *n.* rixe
affront: *n.* affront; injure
affront: *vt.* affronter; insulter
aflame: *adv.* en flammes
afloat: *adv.* à flot
afore: *prep.* avant; *adv.* d'abord
afraid: *adj.* apeuré
afresh: *adv.* à nouveau
Africa: *n.* Afrique
African: *n.* Africain; *adj.* Africain
after: *prep.* après
afterbirth: *n.* placenta
after-crop: *n.* deuxième récolte
after-effects: *npl.* répercussions
afterlife: *n.* vie après la mort
aftermath: *n.* conséquences
afternoon: *n.* après-midi
afterpains: *npl.* tranchées utérines
after-sales service: service
après-vente
aftershave: *n.* après-rasage
aftertaste: *n.* arrière-goût
afterward(s): *adv.* ensuite
afterword: *n.* postface
again: *adv.* à nouveau
against: *prep.* contre
agate: *n.* agate
age: *n.* âge; vieillesse; under mineur

age: *vt.* vieillir
aged: *adj.* âgé
agency: *n.* agence
agenda: *n.* ordre du jour
agent: *n.* agent
agent; clearing: un agent en douane
agent; commission: un
commissionnaire
agent; forwarding: un transitaire
agent; sole: un agent exclusif
agglomerate: *vt.* agglomérer
agglomeration: *n.* agglomération
aggrandisement: *n.* avancement
aggravate: *vt.* aggraver; énerver
aggravation: *n.* aggravation;
énervement
aggregate: *n.* agrégat
aggregation: *n.* agrégation
aggression: *n.* agression
aggressive: *adj.* agressif
aggressor: *n.* agresseur
aggrieved: *adj.* offensé
aghast: *adj.* horrifié
agile: *adj.* agile; adroit
agility: *n.* agilité; adresse
agitate: *vt.* agiter
agitation: *n.* agitation
agitator: *n.* agitateur
ago: *adv.* how long -? = il y a
combien de temps?
agog: *adj.* en émoi; impatient
agonising: *adj.* atroce; angoissant
agony: *n.* douleur atroce; angoisse
agrarian: *adj.* agraire
agree: *vt.* convenir; être d'accord
agreeable: *adj.* agréable; -bly *adv.* =
agréablement; - with = conforme à
agreeableness: *n.* caractère agréable
agreed: *adj.* convenu
agreement: *n.* accord
agricultural: *adj.* agricole
agriculture: *n.* agriculture
agriculturist: *n.* agriculteur
ahead: *adv.* en avant; à l'avance;

sur l'avant
aid: *vt.* aider; secourir
AIDS: SIDA
ail: *vt.* affliger
ailing: *adj.* souffrant
ailment: *n.* maladie
aim: *vt.* pointer; viser; aspirer à
aimless: *adj.* sans but
air balloon: ballon
air cushion: coussin d'air
air force: armée de l'air
air freshener: appareil de conditionnement d'air
air gun: carabine à air comprimé
air isole: trou d'aération
air pump: compresseur
air resistance: résistance de l'air
air terminal: aérogare
air waybill: une lettre de transport aérien
air: *n.* air m
air: *vt.* aérer
aîrborne: *adj.* aéroporté
air-conditioned: *adj.* climatisé
aircraft: *n.* avion
airiness: *n.* aération; ventilation
airless: *adj.* mal aéré; mal ventilé
airlift: *n.* pont aérien
airline: *n.* ligne aérienne
airmail: par avion
airplane: *n.* avion
airport: *n.* aéroport
airsick: *adj.* to be - = avoir le mal de l'air
airstrip: *n.* piste d'atterrissage
airtight: *adj.* hermétique
airy: *adj.* aéré; léger
aisle: *n.* nef d'église
ajar: *adj.* entrouvert
akimbo: *adj.* les poings sur les hanches
akin: *adj.* ressemblant
alabaster: *n.* albâtre
alacrity: *n.* vivacité

alarm bell: sonnette d'alarme
alarm clock: réveil
alarm: *n.* alarme
alarm: *vt.* alarmer; inquiéter
alarmist: *n.* alarmiste
alas: *adv.* hélas
albeit: *conj.* bien que
album: *n.* album
alchemist: *n.* alchimiste
alchemy: *n.* alchimie
alcohol: *n.* alcool
alcoholic: *adj.* alcoolisé; alcoo-lique
alcove: *n.* alcôve
aldehyde: *n.* aldéhyde
alder: *n.* aulne
ale: *n.* bière
alehouse: *n.* taverne; brasserie
alert: *adj.* vigilant; vif; alerte
alertness: *n.* vigilance; vivacité
algebra: *n.* algèbre
algebraic expression: expression algébrique
algebraic: *adj.* algébrique
alias: *adj.* alias
alibi: *n.* alibi
alien: *adj.* étranger; étranger; extra-terrestre
alienate: *vt.* aliéner
alienation: *n.* aliénation
alight: *vi.* mettre pied à terre
align: *vt.* aligner
alike: *adj.* semblable; égal; *adv.* de la même façon
alimentary: *n.* digestif
alimony: *n.* pension alimentaire
alive: *adj.* en vie; vivant; actif
alkali metals: métaux alcalins
alkali: *n.* alcali
alkaline: *adj.* alcalin
alkene: *n.* alcène
alkyne: *n.* alkyne
all clear: feu vert
all right: *adv.* bien
all: *adj.* tout; *adv.* totalement; at once

allay: *vt.* apaiser
allegation: *n.* allégation
allege: *vt.* alléguer
allegiance: *n.* loyauté; fidélité
allegorical: *adj.* allégorique;
-ly *adv.* = allégoriquement
allegory: *n.* allégorie
allegro: *n.* allegro
allele: *n.* allèle
allergic: *adj.* allergique
allergy: *n.* allergie
alleviate: *vt.* alléger
alleviation: *n.* allègement
alley: *n.* ruelle
alliance: *n.* alliance
allied: *adj.* allié
alligator: *n.* alligator
alliteration: *n.* allitération
all-night: *adj.* ouvert toute la nuit
allocate: *vt.* allouer
allocation: *n.* allocation
allot: *vt.* assigner
allotropes: *n.* allotropes
allow: *vt.* permettre; accorder; for
tenir compte de
allowable: *adj.* admissible; permis
allowance: *n.* allocation; concession
alloy: *n.* alliage
all-round: *adj.* complet
allspice: *n.* piment de la Jamaïque
allude: *vi.* faire allusion à
allure: *n.* charme; attrait
allurement: *n.* attrait
alluring: *adj.* attrayant; -ly
allusion: *n.* allusion
allusive: *adj.* allusif; -ly
alluvial: *adj.* alluvial
ally: *n.* allié
ally: *vt.* allier
almanac: *n.* almanach
almighty: *adj.* omnipotent; tout-
puissant
almond tree: amandier
almond: *n.* amande

almond-milk: *n.* lait d'amandes
almost: *adv.* presque
alms: *n.* aumône
aloft: *prep.* en l'air; en haut
alone: *adj.* seul; *adv.* seul; to leave -
= laisser tranquille
along: *adv.* le long de
aloof: *adj.* distant
aloud: *adj.* à voix haute
alpha particle: particule alpha
alphabet: *n.* alphabet
alphabetical: *adj.* alphabétique
alpine: *adj.* alpin
already: *adv.* déjà
also: *adv.* aussi
altar: *n.* autel
altarpiece: *n.* retable
alter: *vt.* modifier
alteration: *n.* modification
altercation: *n.* altercation
alternate: *adj.* alterné
alternate: *vt.* alterner
alternating: *adj.* alterné
alternation: *n.* alternance
alternative: *n.* alternative
alternator: *n.* alternateur
although: *conj.* bien que; malgré
altitude: *n.* altitude
altogether: *adv.* complètement
alum: *n.* alun
aluminium: *n.* aluminium
aluminous: *adj.* alumineux
always: *adv.* toujours
amalgam: *n.* amalgame
amalgamate: *vt.* amalgamer; *vi.*
s'amalgamer
amalgamation: *n.* amalgamation
amanuensis: *n.* copiste
amaryllis: *n.* amaryllis
amass: *vt.* accumuler; amasser
amateur: *n.* amateur
amateurish: *adj.* d'amateur
amatory: *adj.* amoureux; galant
amaze: *vt.* stupéfier

amazement: *n.* stupéfaction
amazing: *adj.* stupéfiant
amazon: *n.* amazone
ambassador: *n.* ambassadeur
ambassadress: *n.* ambassadrice
amber: *n.* ambre m; *adj.* ambré
ambidextrous: *adj.* ambidextre
ambient: *adj.* ambiant
ambiguity: *n.* ambiguïté
ambiguous: *adj.* ambigu; *adv.* de manière ambiguë
ambition: *n.* ambition
ambitious: *adj.* ambitieux; *adv.* ambitieusement
amble: *vi.* marcher tranquillement
ambulance: *n.* ambulance
ambush: *n.* embuscade; to lie in être embusqué
ameliorate: *vt.* améliorer
amelioration: *n.* amélioration
amenable: *adj.* responsable
amend: *vt.* modifier; amender
amendable: *adj.* réparable; corrigible
amendment: *n.* modification; amendement
amends: *npl.* compensation
amenities: *npl.* commodités
America: *n.* Amerique
American: *adj.* Américain
amethyst: *n.* améthyste
amiability: *n.* amabilité
amiable: *adj.* aimable
amiableness: *n.* amabilité
amiably: *adv.* aimablement
amicable: *adj.* amical
amicably: *adv.* amicalement
amino acid: acid aminé
ammonia: *n.* ammoniaque
ammunition: *n.* munitions
amnesia: *n.* amnésie
amnesty: *n.* amnistie
amongst: *prep.* entre; parmi
amoral: *adj.* amoral
amorous: *adj.* amoureux

amorously: *adv.* amoureusement
amorphous: *adj.* informe
amount: *n.* montant m; quantité
ampere: *n.* ampère
amphibian: *n.* amphibie
amphibious: *adj.* amphibie
amphitheatre: *n.* amphithéâtre
ample: *adj.* spacieux; abondant; gros
ampleness: *n.* abondance
amplification: *n.* amplification
amplifier: *n.* amplificateur
amplify: *vt.* amplifier
amplitude: *n.* amplitude
amply: *adv.* amplement
amputate: *vt.* amputer
amputation: *n.* amputation
amulet: *n.* amulette
amuse: *vt.* distraire; divertir
amusement: *n.* distraction; divertissement
amusing: *adj.* divertissant
anachronism: *n.* anachronisme
anaemia: *n.* anémie
anaemic: *adj.* anémique
anaesthetic: *n.* anesthésique
analog: *adj.* analogique
analogous: *adj.* analogue
analogy: *n.* analogie
analyse: *vt.* analyser
analysis: *n.* analyse
analyst: *n.* analyste
analytical bibliography: bibliographie analytique
analytical: *adj.* analytique
anarchic: *adj.* anarchique
anarchist: *n.* anarchiste
anarchy: *n.* anarchie
anatomical: *adj.* anatomique
anatomise: *vt.* disséquer
anatomy: *n.* anatomie
ancestor: *n.* ancêtre
ancestral: *adj.* ancestral
ancestry: *n.* ascendance
anchor: *n.* ancre

anchor: *vi.* jeter l'ancre
anchorage: *n.* ancrage
anchovy: *n.* anchois
ancient: *adj.* ancien; antique
ancillary: *adj.* auxiliaire
and: *conj.* et
anecdotal: *adj.* anecdotique
anecdote: *n.* anecdote
anemia: *n.* anémie
anemone: *n.* anémone
anesthesia: *n.* anesthésie
anew: *adv.* de nouveau
angel: *n.* ange
angelic: *adj.* angélique
anger: *n.* colère
anger: *v.* mettre en colère; irriter
angle: *n.* angle
angle: *vi.* pêcher à la ligne
angled: *adj.* anguleux
angler: *n.* pêcheur à la ligne
anglicism: *n.* anglicisme
angling: *n.* pêche à la ligne
angrily: *adv.* avec colère
angry: *adj.* en colère; irrité
anguish: *n.* angoisse
angular momentum: moment
angulaire
angular: *adj.* angulaire
angularity: *n.* caractère anguleux
animal: *n.* animal; *adj.* animal
animate: *vt.* animer; *adj.* vivant
animated: *adj.* animé
animation: *n.* animation
animosity: *n.* animosité
animus: *n.* haine
anise: *n.* anis
aniseed: *n.* graine d'anis
ankle: *n.* cheville f; -bone =
astra-gale
annals: *n.* annales
annex: *vt.* annexer
annexation: *n.* annexion
annihilate: *vt.* annihiler; anéantir
annihilation: *n.* anéantissement

anniversary: *n.* anniversaire
annotate: *vt.* annoter
annotated entry: notice analytique
annotation: *n.* annotation
announce: *vt.* annoncer
announcement: *n.* annonce
announcer: *n.* présentateur
annoy: *vt.* ennuyer
annoyance: *n.* ennui
annoying: *adj.* ennuyeux
annual: *adj.* annuel
annually: *adv.* annuellement
annuity: *n.* rente viagère
annul: *vt.* annuler; abroger
annulment: *n.* annulation
annunciation: *n.* annonciation
anode: *n.* anode
anodyne: *adj.* calmant
anoint: *vt.* oindre
anomalous: *adj.* anormal
anomaly: *n.* anomalie; irrégularité
anonymity: *n.* anonymat
anonymous: *adj.* anonyme
anonymously: *adv.* anonymement
anorexia: *n.* anorexie
another: *adj.* un autre;
one - = l'un l'autre
answer: *vt.* répondre à
answerable: *adj.* responsable
answering machine: répondeur
téléphonique
ant: *n.* fourmi
antagonise: *vt.* provoquer
antagonism: *n.* antagonisme; rivalité
antagonist: *n.* antagoniste
antarctic: *adj.* antarctique
anteater: *n.* fourmilier
antecedent: *pl.* antécédents
antechamber: *n.* antichambre
antedate: *vt.* antidater
antelope: *n.* antilope
antenna: *n.* antenne
anterior: *adj.* antérieur; précédent
anthem: *n.* hymne

anthill: *n.* fourmilière
anthology: *n.* anthologie
anthracite: *n.* anthracite
anthropology: *n.* anthropologie
antiaircraft: *adj.* antiaérien
antibiotic: *n.* antibiotique
antibody: *n.* anticorps
anticipate: *vt.* prévoir
anticipation: *n.* attente; prévision
anticlockwise: *adv.* dans le sens contraire des aiguilles d'une montre
antidote: *n.* antidote
antifreeze: *n.* antigel
antimony: *n.* antimoine
antipathy: *n.* antipathie
antipodes: *npl.* antipodes
antiquarian: *n.* antiquaire
antiquated: *adj.* vieux; suranné
antique: *n.* meuble ancien
antiquity: *n.* antiquité
antiseptic: *adj.* antiseptique
antisocial: *adj.* antisocial
antithesis: *n.* antithèse
antler: *n.* corne
anvil: *n.* enclume
anxiety: *n.* anxiété; désir
anxious: *adj.* anxieux
apace: *adv.* rapidement
apart: *adv.* séparément
apartment house: immeuble
apartment: *n.* appartement
apathetic: *adj.* apathique
apathy: *n.* apathie
ape: *n.* singe
aperture: *n.* ouverture
apex: *n.* sommet; apex
aphorism: *n.* aphorisme
apiary: *n.* rucher
apiece: *adv.* chacun; chacune
aplomb: *n.* aplomb
Apocalypse: *n.* Apocalypse
apocrypha: *npl.* apocryphes
apocryphal: *adj.* apocryphe
apologetic: *adj.* d'excuse

apologise: *vt.* excuser
apologist: *n.* apologiste
apology: *n.* apologie; défense
apoplexy: *n.* apoplexie
apostle: *n.* apôtre
apostolic: *adj.* apostolique
apostrophe: *n.* apostrophe
apotheosis: *n.* apothéose
appal: *vt.* horrifier; atterrer
appalling: *adj.* horrible
apparatus: *n.* appareil
apparel: *n.* vêtements
apparent: *adj.* évident; apparent
apparently: *adv.* apparemment
apparition: *n.* apparition; vision
appeal: *vi.* faire appel
appealing: *adj.* attrayant
appear: *vi.* paraître
appearance: *n.* apparence
appease: *vt.* apaiser
appellant: *n.* appelant
append: *vt.* annexer
appendage: *n.* appendice
appendicitis: *n.* appendicite
appendix: *n.* appendice
appertain: *vi.* appartenir (à)
appetising: *adj.* appétissant
appetite: *n.* appétit
appetizer: *n.* amuse-gueule
applaud: *vt.* applaudir
applause: *n.* applaudissements
apple pie: tourte aux pommes
apple tree: pommier
apple: *n.* pomme
appliance: *n.* appareil
applicability: *n.* applicabilité
applicable: *adj.* applicable
applicant: *n.* demandeur; postulant; déposant; candidat
application form: formulaire à remplir pour demander
application: *n.* demande; réservation
applied: *adj.* appliqué
apply for: demander; postuler à

apply: *vt.* appliquer; s'adresser
appoint at: nommer
appointee: *n.* personne nommée
appointment: *n.* rendez-vous;
nomination
apportion: *vt.* répartir
apportionment: *n.* répartition
apposite: *adj.* approprié; juste
apposition: *n.* apposition
appraisal: *n.* tri; triage; évaluation;
estimation; prisée
appraise: *vt.* évaluer
appreciable: *adj.* appréciable;
sensible
appreciably: *adv.* sensiblement
appreciate: *vt.* apprécier;
être conscient de
appreciation: *n.* appréciation
appreciative: *adj.* reconnaissant
apprehend: *vt.* appréhender
apprehension: *n.* appréhension
apprehensive: *adj.* appréhensif
apprentice: *n.* apprenti
apprenticeship: *n.* apprentissage
apprise: *vt.* informer
approach: *vi.* (s') approcher
approbation: *n.* approbation
appropriate: *adj.* approprié; adéquat
appropriate: *vt.* s'approprier
approval: *n.* approbation; accord
approval; on: sous condition
approve: *vt.* approuver
approximate: *adj.* approximatif
approximate: *vi.* s'approcher
approximately: *adv.*
approximativement
approximation: *n.* approximation
apricot: *n.* abricot
April: *n.* avril
apron: *n.* tablier
apse: *n.* abside
apt: *adj.* idéal; susceptible
aptitude: *n.* aptitude
aqualung: *n.* scaphandre autonome

aquarium: *n.* aquarium
Aquarius: *n.* Verseau
aquatic: *adj.* aquatique
aqueduct: *n.* aqueduc
aquiline: *adj.* aquilin
arabesque: *n.* arabesque
arable: *adj.* arable
arbiter: *n.* arbitre
arbitrariness: *n.* caractère arbitraire
arbitrary: *adj.* arbitraire
arbitrate: *vt.* arbitrer
arbitration: *n.* arbitrage
arbitrator: *n.* arbitre
arbour: *n.* tonnelle
arcade: *n.* galerie
arch: *n.* arc; *adj.* malicieux
archaic: *adj.* archaïque
archangel: *n.* archange
archbishop: *n.* archevêque
archbishopric: *n.* archevêché
archeological: *adj.* archéologique
archeology: *n.* archéologie
archer: *n.* archer
archery: *n.* tir à l'arc
architect: *n.* architecte
architectural: *adj.* architectural
architecture: *n.* architecture
archive group: fonds d'archives
archives administration:
archivistique
archives: *npl.* archives
archivist: *n.* archiviste
archly: *adv.* malicieusement
archway: *n.* arcade; voûte
arctic: *adj.* arctique
ardent: *adj.* ardent
ardently: *adv.* ardemment
ardour: *n.* ardeur
arduous: *adj.* ardu; difficile
area: *n.* région; domaine
arena: *n.* arène
arguably: *adv.* peut-être; sans doute
argue: *vi.* se disputer
argument: *n.* argument; dispute

argumentation: *n.* argumentation
argumentative: *adj.* raisonneur
aria: *n.* aria
arid: *adj.* aride
aridity: *n.* aridité
Aries: *n.* Bélier
aright: *adv.* correctement;
to set - = rectifier
arise: *vi.* se lever; survenir
aristocracy: *n.* aristocratie
aristocrat: *n.* aristocrate
aristocratic: *adj.* aristocratique
arithmetic sequence: suite
arithmétique
arithmetic: *n.* arithmétique
arithmetical: *adj.* arithmétique
ark: *n.* arche
arm: *n.* bras; arme
arm: *vt.* armer
armament: *n.* armement
armchair: *n.* fauteuil
armed: *adj.* armé
armful: *n.* brassée
armhole: *n.* emmanchure
armistice: *n.* armistice
armour: *n.* armure
armoured car: voiture blindée
armoury: *n.* arsenal
armpit: *n.* aisselle
armrest: *n.* accoudoir
army: *n.* armée
aroma: *n.* arôme
aromatic: *adj.* aromatique
around: *prep.* autour de; *adv.* autour
arouse: *vt.* éveiller; exciter
arraign: *vt.* traduire en justice
arraignment: *n.* accusation; procès
criminel
arrange: *vt.* arranger; organiser
arrangement: *n.* arrangement
arrant: *adj.* fieffé
array: *n.* série
arrears: *npl.* arriéré; retard
arrest: *n.* arrestation
arrest: *vt.* arrêter
arrival: *n.* arrivée
arrive: *vi.* arriver
arrogance: *n.* arrogance
arrogant: *adj.* arrogant
arrogate: *vt.* s'arroger
arrogation: *n.* usurpation
arrow: *n.* flèche
arsenal: *n.* arsenal
arsenic: *n.* arsenic
arson: *n.* incendie criminel
art gallery: musée d'art
art school: école des beaux-arts
art: *n.* art
arterial: *adj.* artériel
artery: *n.* artère
artesian well: puits artésien
artful: *adj.* malin; astucieux
artfulness: *n.* astuce; habileté
arthritis: *n.* arthrite
artichoke: *n.* artichaut
article: *n.* article
articulate: *vt.* articuler
articulated: *adj.* articulé
articulation: *n.* articulation
artifice: *n.* artifice
artificial intelligence: intelligence
artificielle
artificial: *adj.* artificiel
artificiality: *n.* caractère artificiel
artificially: *adv.* artificiellement
artillery: *n.* artillerie
artisan: *n.* artisan
artist: *n.* artiste
artistic: *adj.* artistique
artistry: *n.* habileté
artless: *adj.* naturel; simple
artlessness: *n.* simplicité; naturel
as: *conj.* comme; pendant que
asbestos: *n.* asbeste; amiante
ascend: *vi.* monter
ascendancy: *n.* ascendant
ascension: *n.* ascension
ascent: *n.* montée

ascertain: *vt.* établir
ascetic: *adj.* ascétique
ascribe: *vt.* attribuer
asexual reproduction: reproduction asexuée
Ash Wednesday: mercredi des Cendres
ash: *n.* frêne; cendre
ashamed: *adj.* honteux
ashbin: *n.* poubelle
ashore: *adv.* à terre; to go - = débarquer
ashtray: *n.* cendrier
Asia: *n.* Asie
Asian: *n. adj.* Asiatique
aside: *adv.* de côté
ask: *vt.* demander
askance: *adv.* avec méfiance
askew: *adv.* de côté
asleep: *adj.* endormi
asparagus: *n.* asperge
aspect: *n.* aspect
aspen: *n.* tremble
aspersion: *n.* calomnie
asphalt: *n.* asphalte
asphyxia: *n.* asphyxie
asphyxiate: *vt.* asphyxier
asphyxiation: *n.* asphyxie
aspirant: *n.* aspirant
aspirate: *n.* aspirée
aspirate: *vt.* aspirer
aspiration: *n.* aspiration
aspire: *vi.* aspirer; désirer
aspirin: *n.* aspirine
ass: *n.* âne
assail: *vt.* assaillir; attaquer
assailant: *n.* assaillant; agresseur
assassin: *n.* assassin
assassinate: *vt.* assassiner
assassination: *n.* assassinat
assault: *n.* assaut; agression
assault: *vt.* agresser
assemblage: *n.* assemblage

assemble: *vt.* assembler; *vi.* s'assembler
assembly line: chaîne de montage
assembly: *n.* assemblée
assent: *n.* assentiment
assent: *vi.* donner son assentiment
assert: *vt.* soutenir; affirmer
assertion: *n.* assertion
assertive: *adj.* péremptoire
assess: *vt.* évaluer
assessment: *n.* évaluation
assessor: *n.* assesseur
assets: *npl.* biens
assiduous: *adj.* assidu
assign: *vt.* assigner
assignation: *n.* rendez-vous; cession
assignment: *n.* cession; mission
assimilate: *vt.* assimiler
assimilation: *n.* assimilation
assist: *vt.* assister; aider; secourir
assistance: *n.* assistance; aide; secours
assistant: *n.* aide; assistant
associate: *adj.* associé; *n.* associé
associate: *vt.* associer
association: *n.* association
assonance: *n.* assonance
assorted: *adj.* assorti
assortment: *n.* assortiment
assuage: *vt.* calmer; adoucir
assume: *vt.* assumer; supposer
Assumption: *n.* Assomption
assumption: *n.* supposition
assurance: *n.* assurance
assure: *vt.* assurer
assuredly: *adv.* assurément
asterisk: *n.* astérisque
astern: *adv.* en poupe
asthma: *n.* asthme
asthmatic: *adj.* asthmatique
astonish: *vt.* surprendre; stupéfier
astonishing: *adj.* stupéfiant
astonishment: *n.* surprise; stupéfaction

astound: *vt.* ébahir
astray: *adv.* to go - = s'égarer;
to lead - = détourner du droit chemin
astride: *adv.* à califourchon
astringent: *adj.* astringent
astrologer: *n.* astrologue
astrological: *adj.* astrologique
astrology: *n.* astrologie
astronaut: *n.* astronaute
astronomer: *n.* astronome
astronomical unit: unité astronomique
astronomical: *adj.* astronomique
astronomy: *n.* astronomie
astute: *adj.* malin
asylum: *n.* asile; refuge
at: *prep.* à; en
atheism: *n.* athéisme
atheist: *n.* athée
athlete: *n.* athlète
athletic: *adj.* athlétique
atlas: *n.* atlas
ATM: distributeur automatique
atmosphere: *n.* atmosphère
atmospheric pressure: pression atmosphérique
atmospheric: *adj.* atmosphérique
atom bomb: bombe atomique
atom: *n.* atome
atomic mass unit: unite de masse atomique
atomic number: nombre atomique
atomic solid: solide atomique
atomic: *adj.* atomique
atone: *vt.* expier
atonement: *n.* expiation
atop: *adv.* en haut
atrocious: *adj.* atroce
atrocity: *n.* atrocité; énormité
atrophy: *n.* atrophie
attach: *vt.* joindre
attaché: *n.* attaché
attached document: fichier joint; pièce jointe

attachment: *n.* attachement
attack: *n.* attaque
attack: *vt.* attaquer
attacker: *n.* attaquant
attain: *vt.* atteindre; obtenir
attainable: *adj.* accessible
attempt: *n.* essai; tentative
attempt: *vt.* essayer
attend: *vt.* servir; assister à
attendance: *n.* service; assistance; présence
attendant: *n.* serviteur
attention: *n.* attention; soin
attentive: *adj.* attentif
attentively: *adv.* attentivement
attenuate: *vt.* atténuer
attest: *vt.* attester
attic: *n.* grenier
attire: *n.* atours
attitude: *n.* attitude
attorney: *n.* avocat
attract: *vt.* attirer
attraction: *n.* attraction; attrait
attractive: *adj.* attrayant
attribute: *n.* attribut
attribute: *vt.* attribuer
attrition: *n.* usure
auburn: *adj.* auburn
auction sale: vente aux enchères
auction site: site de vente aux enchères
auction: *n.* vente aux enchères
auctioneer: *n.* commissaire-priseur
audacious: *adj.* audacieux; téméraire
audaciously: *adv.* audacieusement
audacity: *n.* audace; témérité
audible: *adj.* audible
audience: *n.* audience; auditoire
audio tapes: cassettes audio
audit: *n.* audit
audit: *vt.* vérifier
auditor: *n.* vérificateur de comptes; auditeur
auditory: *adj.* auditif

augment: *vt.* augmenter
augmentation: *n.* augmentation
august: *adj.* auguste; majestueux
August: *n.* août
aunt: *n.* tante
aura: *n.* aura
auspicious: *adj.* favorable; propice
austere: *adj.* austère; sévère
austerity: *n.* austérité
authentic: *adj.* authentique
authenticate: *vt.* légaliser
authenticity: *n.* authenticité
author affiliation: affiliation d'auteur
author catalogue: catalogue-auteurs
author heading: en-tête auteur
author: *n.* auteur
authoress: *n.* femme auteur
authorisation: *n.* autorisation
authorise: *vt.* autoriser
authoritarian: *adj.* autoritaire
authoritative: *adj.* autoritaire
authority: *n.* autorité
authorization: *n.* autorisation
authorize: *v.* autoriser
author's point of view: point de vue de l'auteur
author's purpose: but de l'auteur
author's tone: ton de l'auteur
authorship: *n.* paternité
auto: *n.* voiture
autobiographical: *adj.* autobiographique
autobiography: *n.* autobiographie
autocrat: *n.* autocrate
autocratic: *adj.* autocratique
autograph: *n.* autographe
automate: *v.* automatiser
automated feature: fonction automatisée
automated: *adj.* automatisé
automatic debiting: prélèvement automatique
automatic teller machine (ATM): guichet (bancaire) automatique
automatic: *adj.* automatique
automation: *n.* automatisation
automaton: *n.* automate
autonomy: *n.* autonomie
autopsy: *n.* autopsie
autumn: *n.* automne
autumnal: *adj.* automnal
auxiliary verb: verbe auxiliaire
auxiliary: *adj.* auxiliaire
available: *adj.* disponible
avalanche: *n.* avalanche
avarice: *n.* avarice
avaricious: *adj.* avare
avenge: *vt.* venger
avenue: *n.* avenue
aver: *vt.* affirmer; déclarer
average: *vt.* atteindre la moyenne de
aversion: *n.* aversion; dégoût
avert: *vt.* détourner; écarter
aviary: *n.* volière
avoid: *vt.* éviter; échapper à
avoidable: *adj.* évitable
await: *vt.* attendre
awake: *vt.* réveiller; *vi.* se réveiller; *adj.* éveillé
awakening: *n.* réveil
award: *n.* prix; décision
award: *vt.* attribuer
aware: *adj.* conscient; au courant
awareness: *n.* conscience
away game: *n.* match à l'extérieur
away: *adv.* absent; loin
awe: *n.* peur; crainte
awful: *adj.* horrible; terrible
awhile: *adv.* un moment
awkward: *adj.* gauche; maladroit; délicat
awkwardness: *n.* maladroitesse; difficulté
awl: *n.* alêne
awning: *n.* taud
awry: *adv.* de travers

axe: *n.* hache
axe: *vt.* licencier; supprimer
axiom: *n.* axiome
axis: *n.* axe
axle: *n.* axe
azeotrope: *n.* azéotrope

B

baa: *n.* bêlement
babble: *vi.* bavarder; babiller
babbler: *n.* bavard
babbling: *n.* bavardage; babillage
babe; baby: *n.* bébé; enfant en bas-âge; nourrisson
baboon: *n.* babouin
baby carriage: voiture d'enfant
baby linen: layette
babyhood: *n.* petite enfance
babyish: *adj.* enfantin; puéril
baby-sit: *v.* garder les enfants
baby-sitter: *n.* baby-sitter
bachelor: *n.* célibataire
bachelorship: *n.* célibat
back cover: quatriène de couverture
back issue: un ancien numéro
back number: vieux numéro
back payment: rappel de salaire
back up a file: sauvegarder un fichier
back: *n.* dos; *adv.* en arrière; à l'arrière
backbite: *vt.* médire
backbiter: *n.* détracteur
backbone: *n.* colonne vertébrale; épine dorsale
backdate: *vt.* antidater
backdoor: *n.* porte de derrière
backer: *n.* partisan
backgammon: *n.* (jeu de) jacquet
background image: image d'arrière-plan; fond d'image
background: *n.* milieu; origines; contextes; arrière-plan; fond
backlash: *n.* réaction violente
backlog: *n.* accumulation de travail en retard
backpack: *n.* sac à dos
backpacker: *n.* randonneur
backside: *n.* derrière
backup copy: copie de sauvegarde
back-up lights: *npl.* (auto) feux de marche arrière

backward: *adj.* rétrograde; retardé; lent; *adv.* en arrière
backward-compatible (software): (logiciel) à compatibilité descendante
bacon: *n.* lard
bacteria: *n.* bactérie
bad: *adj.* mauvais; de mauvaise qualité; méchant; malade
badge: *n.* symbole; signe; plaque
badger: *n.* blaireau
badger: *vt.* harceler
badly: *adv.* mal
badminton: *n.* badminton
badness: *n.* mauvaise qualité; méchanceté
baffle: *vt.* déconcerter; confondre
bag: *n.* sac m; valise
baggage: *n.* bagages; équipement
bagpipe: *n.* cornemuse
bail: *n.* mise en liberté sous caution; caution
bail: *v.* mettre en liberté sous caution; mettre en dépôt
bailiff: *n.* huissier; régisseur
bait: *n.* appât; amorce
bait: *vt.* tourmenter; appâter
baize: *n.* serge
bake: *vt.* faire cuire au four
baker: *n.* boulanger
bakery: *n.* boulangerie
baking powder: levure
baking: *n.* cuisson; fournée
balance sheet: bilan
balance: *n.* balance; équilibre; solde d'un compte
balance: *vt.* peser; peser le pour et le contre; solder; équilibrer
balcony: *n.* balcon
bald: *adj.* chauve
baldness: *n.* calvitie
bale: *n.* balle
bale: *vt.* emballer; écoper
baleful: *adj.* sinistre; funeste; maléfique

ball: *n.* balle; boule; ballon
ballad: *n.* ballade
ballast: *n.* lest m
ballast: *vt.* lester
ballerina: *n.* ballerine
ballet: *n.* ballet
ballistic: *adj.* balistique
balloon: *n.* montgolfière; aérostat
ballot: *n.* scrutin; vote
ballpoint (pen): *n.* stylo à bille
ballroom: *n.* salle de bal
balm; balsam: *n.* baume
balmer series: balmer; série de
balmy: *adj.* balsamique; parfumé; doux
balot: *vi.* voter au scrutin
balustrade: *n.* balustrade
bamboo: *n.* bambou
bamboozle: *vt.* embobiner
ban: *n.* interdiction
ban: *vt.* interdire
banal: *adj.* banal
banana: *n.* banane
band: *n.* bande; reliure; courroie de transmission; orchestre
bandage: *n.* bande; bandage
bandaid: *n.* pansement; adhésif
bandit: *n.* bandit
bandstand: *n.* kiosque à musique
bandy: *vt.* avoir des mots
bandy-legged: *adj.* aux jambes arquées
bang: *n.* coup violent; claquement; détonation
bang: *vt.* frapper violemment; claquer
bangle: *n.* bracelet
banish: *vt.* bannir; exiler; chasser; expatrier
banishment: *n.* exil; bannissement
banisters: *npl.* rampe d'escalier
banjo: *n.* banjoam
bank account: compte en banque
bank card: carte bancaire
bank statement: relevé de compte

bank: *n.* rive; remblai; banque; banc; digue

bank: *vt.* déposer de l'argent à la banque

bank; merchant: une banque d'affaires

bank; overseas: une banque d'outremer

banker: *n.* banquier

banking: *n.* opérations bancaires

banknote: *n.* billet de banque

bankrupt: *adj.* failli; failli

bankruptcy: *n.* banqueroute; faillite

bankruptcy; to file a petition: déposer le bilan

banner: *n.* bannière; calicot; oriflamme; étendard

banquet: *n.* banquet

bantering: *n.* badin

baptise: *vt.* baptiser

baptism: *n.* baptême

baptismal: *adj.* de baptême; baptismal

baptistery: *n.* baptistère

bar code: code barres

bar graph: diagramme à barres

bar: *n.* bar; barre; obstacle

bar: *vt.* empêcher; interdire; exclure

barb: *n.* barbe

barbarian: *n.* barbare; *adj.* barbare; cruel

barbaric: *adj.* barbare

barbarism: *n.* barbarisme; barbarie

barbarity: *n.* barbarie; atrocité

barbarous: *adj.* barbare; cruel

barbecue: *n.* barbecue

barber: *n.* coiffeur (pour hommes)

bard: *n.* barde; poète

bare: *adj.* nu; dépouillé; simple; pur

bare: *vt.* dénuder; découvrir

barefaced: *adj.* éhonté; impudent

barefooted: *adj.* aux pieds nus

bareheaded: *adj.* nu-tête

barelegged: *adj.* aux jambes nues

barely: *adv.* à peine; tout juste

bareness: *n.* nudité

bargain prices: prix de soldes

bargain sale: vente en soldes

bargain: *n.* affaire; contrat; marché; occasion

bargain: *vi.* conclure un marché; négocier

barge: *n.* péniche

baritone: *n.* baryton

bark: *n.* écorce; aboiement

bark: *vi.* aboyer

barley: *n.* orge

barmaid: *n.* serveuse

barman: *n.* barman

barn: *n.* grange; étable

barnacle: *n.* anatife; bernacle

barometer: *n.* baromètre

baron: *n.* baron

baroness: *n.* baronne

baronial: *adj.* de baron

barracks: *npl.* caserne

barrage: *n.* barrage; torrent

barrel organ: orgue de Barbarie

barrel: *n.* tonneau; fût; canon de fusil

barrelled: *adj.* (firearms) à canons

barren: *adj.* stérile; infertile; improductif

barricade: *n.* barricade; barrière

barricade: *vt.* barricader; barrer

barrier: *n.* barrière; obstacle

barring: *adv.* excepté; sauf

barrow: *n.* brouette

bartender: *n.* barman

barter: *vi.* faire du troc

barter: *vt.* troquer; échanger

base: *n.* base; partie inférieure; pied; point de départ

base: *vt.* fonder sur

baseball: *n.* baseball

baseless: *adj.* sans fondement; injustifié

baseline: *n.* accroche

basement: *n.* sous-sol

baseness: *n.* bassesse; vilenie
bash: *vt.* frapper
bashful: *adj.* timide; modeste
basic: *adj.* fondamental; de base
basilisk: *n.* basilic
basin: *n.* cuvette; lavabo
basis: *n.* base; fondement
bask: *vi.* se prélasser
basket: *n.* panier; corbeille
basketball: *n.* basket-ball
bass viol: viole de gambe
bass voice: voix de basse
bass: *n.* contrebasse
bassoon: *n.* basson
bastard: *n.* bâtard; *adj.* bâtard
bastardy: *n.* bâtardise
baste: *vt.* arroser la viande de son jus; bâtir
basting: *n.* bâti; jus (de viande); rossée
bastion: *n.* bastion
bat: *n.* chauve-souris
batch: *n.* fournée
bath: *n.* bain
bathe: *vt.* se baigner
bathing suit: maillot de bain
bathos: *n.* platitudes
bathroom: *n.* salle de bain
bathtub: *n.* baignoire
baton: *n.* matraque
battalion: *n.* bataillon
batter: *n.* pâte à frire
batter: *vt.* battre; frapper; martyriser
battering ram: bélier
battery: *n.* pile; batterie
battle array: ordre de bataille
battle: *n.* bataille; combat
battle: *vi.* se battre; combattre
battlefield: *n.* champ de bataille
battlement: *n.* remparts
battleship: *n.* cuirassé
bauble: *n.* babiole; marotte; colifichet
bawdy: *adj.* paillard
bawl: *vi.* brailler; gueuler

bay window: fenêtre en saillie
bay: *n.* baie; laurier
bay: *vi.* aboyer; hurler
bayonet: *n.* baïonnette
bazaar: *n.* bazar
be: *vi.* être
beach: *n.* plage
beacon: *n.* phare; signal lumineux
bead: *n.* perle
beagle: *n.* beagle
beak: *n.* bec
beaker: *n.* gobelet
beam: *n.* rayon; poutre
beam: *vi.* rayonner; resplendir
bean: *n.* haricot
beansprouts: *npl.* germes de soja
bear: *n.* ours
bear: *vi.* se diriger
bear: *vt.* porter; supporter; produire
bearable: *adj.* supportable
beard: *n.* barbe
bearded: *adj.* barbu
bearer: *n.* porteur; arbre fructifère
bearing: *n.* relation; maintien; port
beast: *n.* bête; brute
beastliness: *n.* bestialité; brutalité
beastly: *adj.* bestial; brutal; abominable
beat: *n.* battement; pulsation
beat: *vt.* battre; palpiter
beatific: *adj.* béatifique; béat
beatify: *vt.* béatifier; sanctifier
beating: *n.* correction; raclée; battement
beatitude: *n.* béatitude
beautiful: *adj.* beau; belle; magnifique
beautify: *vt.* embellir; décorer
beauty: *n.* beauté; institut de beauté
beaver: *n.* castor
because: *conj.* parce que
beckon: *vi.* faire signe
become: *vt.* convenir; aller à
becoming: *adj.* convenable; seyant

bed: *n.* lit
bedclothes: *npl.* couvertures et draps
bedding: *n.* literie
bedecked: *adj.* orné
bedlam: *n.* maison de fous; chahut
bed-post: *n.* colonne de lit
bedraggled: *adj.* dépenaillé; embrousaillé
bedridden: *adj.* cloué au lit; grabataire
bedroom: *n.* chambre
bedspread: *n.* dessus-de-lit
bedtime: *n.* heure d'aller au lit
bee: *n.* abeille
beech: *n.* hêtre
beef: *n.* viande de boeuf
beefburger: *n.* hamburger
beefsteak: *n.* bifteck
beehive: *n.* ruche
beeline: *n.* ligne droite
beer: *n.* bière
beeswax: *n.* cire
beet: *n.* betterave
beetle: *n.* scarabée
befall: *vi.* arriver; survenir
befit: *vt.* convenir à
before: *prep.* avant; devant
beforehand: *adv.* à l'avance; au préalable
befriend: *vt.* traiter en ami; aider
befuddle: *adj.* embrouillé
beg: *vt.* mendier; solliciter; supplier
beget: *vt.* engendrer
beggar: *n.* mendiant
begin: *vt.* commencer
beginner: *n.* débutant
beginning: *n.* commencement; début; origine
begrudge: *vt.* donner à contrecoeur; envier
beguile: *v.* leurrer; captiver
behalf: *n.* faveur; intérêt
behave: *vi.* se comporter; se conduire
behavior: *n.* conduite; comportement

behead: *vt.* décapiter
behemoth: *n.* béhémoth; mastodonte; hippopotame
behind: *prep.* derrière; *adv.* derrière; par-derrière; en arrière
behold: *vt.* voir; contempler; observer
behove: *vi.* (impers) incomber à
beige: *adj.* beige
being: *n.* existence; être
belated: *adj.* tardif
belch: *n.* éructation; rot
belch: *vi.* éructer; vomir
belfry: *n.* beffroi; clocher
Belgian: *n. adj.* Belge
Belgium: *n.* Belgique
belie: *vt.* démentir; tromper
belief: *n.* foi; croyance; conviction; opinion; credo
believable: *adj.* croyable
believe: *vt.* croire; penser; croire
believer: *n.* croyant; adepte; partisan
belittle: *vt.* rabaisser
bell: *n.* cloche
bellicose: *adj.* belliqueux
belligerence: *n.* agressivité; belligérance
belligerent: *adj.* belligérant
bellow: *n.* beuglement; mugissement
bellow: *vi.* beugler; mugir; hurler
belly: *n.* ventre
bellyful: *n.* ventrée; ras-le-bol
belong: *vi.* appartenir à
belongings: *npl.* affaires
beloved: *adj.* chéri; bien-aimé
below: *adv.* en dessous; en bas; *prep.* sous; au-dessous de; en dessous
belt: *n.* ceinture
beltway: *n.* périphérique
bemoan: *vt.* déplorer; pleurer
bemused: *adj.* déconcerté
bench marking: évaluation des performances (d'une machine; d'une installation; d'un site)
bench: *n.* banc

bend: *n.* courbe
bend: *vt.* courber; plier; incliner
beneath: *adv.* au-dessous; *prep.* sous; au-dessous de
benediction: *n.* bénédiction
benefactor: *n.* bienfaiteur
benefice: *n.* bénéfice; bénéfice ecclésiastique
beneficent: *adj.* bienfaisant
beneficial: *adj.* profitable; salutaire; utile
beneficiary: *n.* bénéficiaire
benefit night: soirée de bienfaisance
benefit: *n.* intérêt; avantage; profit; bienfait
benefit: *vt.* profiter à; bénéficier
benevolence: *n.* bienveillance; générosité
benevolent: *adj.* bienveillant; de bienfaisance
benign: *adj.* bienveillant; doux; affable; bénin
bent: *n.* penchant
benzine: *n.* benzine
bequeath: *vt.* léguer
bequest: *n.* legs
bereave: *vt.* priver
bereavement: *n.* perte; deuil
beret: *n.* béret
berry: *n.* baie
berserk: *adj.* fou furieux
berth: *n.* couchette
beseech: *vt.* supplier; implorer; conjurer
beside(s): *prep.* à côté de; excepté; *adv.* de plus; en outre
besiege: *vt.* assiéger; assaillir
best: *adj.* le meilleur; la meilleure; *adv.* le mieux; *n.* le meilleur; le mieux
bestial: *adj.* bestial; brutal
bestiality: *n.* bestialité; brutalité
bestow: *vt.* accorder; conférer; consacrer
bestseller: *n.* best-seller

bet: *n.* pari
bet: *vt.* parier
beta particle: particule beta
beta radioactivity: rayonnement
betray: *vt.* trahir
betrayal: *n.* trahison
betroth: *vt.* promettre en mariage
betrothal: *n.* fiançailles
betting: *n.* pari
between: *prep.* entre; *adv.* au milieu
bevel: *n.* biseau
beverage: *n.* boisson
bevy: *n.* bande; groupe
beware: *vi.* prendre garde
bewilder: *vt.* déconcerter; dérouter
bewilderment: *n.* perplexité
bewitch: *vt.* ensorceler; enchanter
beyond: *prep.* au-delà de; au-dessus de; plus de; sauf; *adv.* au‑delà; plus loin
bias: *n.* préjugé; tendance; inclination
bib: *n.* bavoir
Bible: *n.* Bible
biblical: *adj.* biblique
bibliographic entry: notice bibliographique
bibliography: *n.* bibliographie
bicarbonate of soda: bicarbonate de soude
bicker: *vi.* se chamailler
bicycle: *n.* bicyclette
bid: *n.* offre; tentative
bid: *vt.* ordonner; commander; offrir
bidder: *n.* enchérisseur
bidding: *n.* ordre; enchère; offre
bide: *vt.* attendre; supporter
biennial: *adj.* biennal; bisannuel
bifocals: *npl.* verres à double foyer
bifurcated: *adj.* divisé en deux branches
big: *adj.* grand; gros; important
bigamist: *n.* bigame
bigamy: *n.* bigamie
bigheaded: *adj.* frimeur

bigness: *n.* grandeur; grosseur
bigot: *n.* fanatique
bigoted: *adj.* fanatique
bike: *n.* vélo
bikini: *n.* bikini
bilberry: *n.* airelle
bile: *n.* bile
bilingual: *adj.* bilingue
bilious: *adj.* bilieux
bill of exchange: lettre de change
bill of lading: connaissement
bill: *n.* addition; billet
billboard advertising: publicité sur panneaux
billboard: *n.* panneau d'affichage
billboard: *n.* panneau; support d'affichage
billet: *n.* logement
billfold: *n.* portefeuille
billiard table: table de billard
billion: *n.* milliard
billy: *n.* matraque
bimolecular reaction: réaction bimoléculaire
bin: *n.* coffre
binary compound: composé binaire
bind: *vt.* attacher; lier; entourer; relier
binder: *n.* relieur
binding: *n.* reliure
binge: *n.* beuverie; bringue
bingo: *n.* loto
binoculars: *npl.* jumelles
biochemistry: *n.* biochimie
biodiversity: *n.* diversité biologique
biographer: *n.* biographe
biographical sketch: résumé biographique
biographical: *adj.* biographique
biography: *n.* biographie
biological: *adj.* biologique
biology: *n.* biologie
biome: *n.* biome
biotic: *adj.* biotique
biped: *n.* bipède

birch: *n.* bouleau
bird: *n.* oiseau
bird's-eye view: vue d'ensemble
bird-watcher: ornithologue
birth certificate: extrait de naissance
birth control: limitation des naissances
birth: *n.* naissance
birthday: *n.* anniversaire
birthplace: *n.* lieu de naissance
birthright: *n.* droit de naissance
biscuit: *n.* biscuit
bisect: *vt.* couper en deux
bishop: *n.* évêque
bison: *n.* bison
bit: *n.* morceau; peu
bitch: *n.* chienne
bite: *vt.* mordre
bitter: *adj.* amer; âpre; cuisant; acerbe; glacial
bitterness: *n.* amertume; rancoeur
bitumen: *n.* bitume
bizarre: *adj.* étrange; bizarre
blab: *vi.* jacasser; lâcher le morceau
black ice: verglas
black market: marché noir
black pudding: boudin
black sheep: brebis galeuse
black: *adj.* noir; obscur
blackberry: *n.* mûre
blackbird: *n.* merle
blackboard: *n.* tableau
blacken: *vt.* noircir; ternir
blackleg: *n.* jaune (pendant une grève)
blacklist: *n.* liste noire
blackmail: *n.* chantage
blackness: *n.* couleur noire; obscurité; noirceur
blacksmith: *n.* forgeron
blackthorn: *n.* épine noire
bladder: *n.* vessie
blade: *n.* lame
blame: *vt.* blâmer; faute

blameless: *adj.* irréprochable
blanch: *vt.* blanchir
bland: *adj.* affable; suave; doux; apaisant
blank check: chèque en blanc
blank: *adj.* blanc; vide; déconcerté
blanket: *n.* couverture
blare: *vi.* retentir
blase: *adj.* blasé
blaspheme: *vt.* blasphémer
blasphemous: *adj.* blasphématoire
blasphemy: *n.* blasphème
blast: *n.* souffle d'air; explosion
blast: *vt.* faire sauter
blast-on lancement: mise à feu
blatant: *adj.* flagrant
blaze: *n.* flamme
blaze: *vi.* flamber; resplendir
bleach: *vt.* blanchir; décolorer
bleached: *adj.* blanchi; décoloré
bleachers: *npl.* gradins
bleak: *adj.* morne; lugubre; glacial; désolé
bleakness: *n.* froid; austérité
bleary (-eyed): *adj.* larmoyant
bleat: *n.* bêlement
bleat: *vi.* bêler
bleed: *vt.* saigner
bleeding: *n.* saignement
bleeper: *n.* bip
blemish: *n.* tâche; infamie
blemish: *vt.* gâter; ternir
blend: *vt.* mélanger
bless: *vt.* bénir
blessing: *n.* bénédiction; bienfait
blight: *vt.* détruire
blind aide: côté faible de quelqu'un
blind spot: angle mort
blind: *adj.* aveugle; *n.* aveugle
blind: *vt.* aveugler; éblouir
blinders: *npl.* oeillères
blindfold: *vt.* bander les yeux de
blindly: *adv.* à l'aveuglette; aveuglément

blindness: *n.* cécité
blink: *vi.* clignoter
blinkers: *npl.* clignotants
bliss: *n.* bonheur extrême; félicité
blissful: *adj.* heureux; béat; bienheureux
blissfulness: *n.* bonheur extrême; félicité
blister: *n.* ampoule; cloque
blister: *vi.* se couvrir de cloques
blitz: *n.* bombardement aérien
blizzard: *n.* tempête de neige
bloated: *adj.* gonflé; boursouflé; bouffi
blob: *n.* goutte; tache
bloc: *n.* bloc
block: *n.* bloc; encombrement; blocage; pâté de maisons
block: *vt.* bloquer
blockade: *n.* blocus
blockage: *n.* obstruction
blockbuster: *n.* grand succès
blockhead: *n.* lourdaud; sot; crétin
blond: *adj.* blond
blood donor: donneur de sang
blood group: groupe sanguin
blood poisoning: empoisonnement du sang
blood pressure: pression artérielle
blood test: analyse de sang
blood transfusion: transfusion sanguine
blood vessel: veine; vaisseau sanguin
blood: *n.* sang
bloodhound: *n.* limier
bloodily: *adv.* cruellement
bloodiness: *n.* cruauté
bloodless: *adj.* exangue; anémié; sans effusion de sang
bloodshed: *n.* effusion de sang; carnage
bloodshot: *adj.* injecté de sang
bloodstream: *n.* système sanguin
bloodsucker: *n.* sangsue; vampire

bloodthirsty: *adj.* sanguinaire
bloody: *adj.* sanglant; ensanglanté; cruel
bloom: *n.* fleur
bloom: *vi.* éclore; fleurir
blossom: *n.* fleur
blot: *n.* tache
blot: *vt.* tacher; sécher; effacer
blotchy: *adj.* marbré; couvert de taches
blotting pad: buvard
blotting paper: papier buvard
blouse: *n.* chemisier
blow: *n.* coup
blow: *vi.* souffler; sonner
blowout: *n.* éclatement
blowpipe: *n.* sarbacane
blubber: *n.* blanc de baleine
blubber: *vi.* pleurnicher
bludgeon: *n.* gourdin; matraque
blue: *adj.* bleu
bluebell: *n.* campanule
bluebottle: *n.* bleuet; mouche bleue
blueness: *n.* bleu
blueprint: *n.* projet
bluff: *n.* esbrouffe
bluff: *vt.* faire de l'esbrouffe
bluish: *adj.* bleuâtre
blunder: *n.* gaffe
blunder: *vi.* faire une gaffe; rougir
blunt: *adj.* émoussé; obtus; direct
blunt: *vt.* émousser
bluntly: *adv.* carrément; sans ménagements
bluntness: *n.* brusquerie; rudesse
blur: *n.* image floue
blur: *vt.* brouiller
blurt out: *vt.* laisser échapper
blush: *n.* rougeur; fard à joues
blustery: *adj.* de tempête; violent
boa: *n.* boa
boar: *n.* verrat
board of directors: conseil d'administration

board: *n.* planche; conseil
board: *vt.* monter à bord de
boarder: *n.* pensionnaire
boarding card: carte d'embarquement
boarding house: internat; pension de famille
boarding school: pensionnat
boast: *n.* vantardise; rodomontade
boast: *vi.* se vanter
boastful: *adj.* vantard
boat: *n.* bateau; canot; barque
boating: *n.* canotage; promenade en bateau
bobsleigh: *n.* bobsleigh
bode: *vt.* présager; augurer
bodice: *n.* corsage
bodily adj: *adv.* physiquement
body: *n.* corps m; cadavre
body-building: culturisme
bodyguard: *n.* garde du corps
bodywork: *n.* (auto) carrosserie
bog: *n.* marécage
boggy: *adj.* marécageux
bogus: *adj.* faux
boil: *n.* furoncle; ébullition
boil: *vi.* bouillir
boiled egg: oeuf à la coque
boiled potatoes: *npl.* pommes de terre à l'eau
boiler: *n.* casserole; chaudière
boiling point: point d'ébullition
boisterous: *adj.* bruyant; turbulent; tumultueux
bold: *adj.* audacieux; téméraire; osé; hardi
boldness: *n.* intrépidité; audace; effronterie
bolster: *n.* traversin
bolster: *vt.* soutenir
bolt: *n.* verrou
bolt: *vt.* verrouiller; fermer au verrou
bomb: *n.* bombe
bombard: *vt.* bombarder

bombardier: *n.* bombardier
bombardment: *n.* bombardement
bombshell: *n.* bombe
bond holder: obligataire
bond: *n.* lien; attache; engagement;
obligation
bond: *vi.* bondir; sauter
bondage: *n.* esclavage;
asservissement
bone: *n.* os
bone: *vt.* désosser
boneless: *adj.* désossé; sans os
bonfire: *n.* feu (de joie)
bonnet: *n.* bonnet
bonny: *adj.* joli
bonus: *n.* prime
bony: *adj.* osseux
boo: *vt.* huer
booby trap: mine
book jacket: jacquette
book mobile: bibliothèque itinérante
book of specifications: cahier des
charges
book plate: ex-libris
book: *n.* livre
book: *vt.* obliger à rendre des
comptes.
bookbinder: *n.* relieur de livres
bookcase: *n.* bibliothèque
bookkeeper: *n.* comptable
bookkeeping entries: écritures
comptables bookkeeping or accounts
department: service de comptabilité
bookkeeping: *n.* comptabilité
bookkeeping; double-entry:
comptabilité en partie double
bookkeeping; single-entry:
comptabilité en partie simple
bookmaking: *n.* prise des paris
bookmarker: *n.* signet
bookseller: *n.* libraire
bookstore: *n.* librairie
bookworm: *n.* rat de bibliothèque
boom: *n.* grondement; essor

boom: *vi.* gronder
boon: *n.* bienfait; aubaine; faveur
boor: *n.* rustre; brute
boorish: *adj.* rustre; rustique
boost: *n.* stimulation
boost: *vt.* stimuler
booster: *n.* propulseur
boot: *n.* botte; coffre
booth: *n.* cabine; baraque
bootleg: *v.* vendre illégalement;
pirater
bootlegger: *n.* pirate
booty: *n.* butin
booze: *n.* alcool
booze: *vi.* se saôuler
border: *n.* bord; bordure; lisière;
frontière
border: *vt.* border; avoisiner
borderline: *n.* limite
bore: *n.* perceuse; calibre; raseur
bore: *vt.* forer; percer; ennuyer
boredom: *n.* ennui
boring: *adj.* ennuyeux
born: *adj.* né; originaire
borrow: *vt.* emprunter
borrower: *n.* emprunteur
bosom friend: ami intime
bosom: *n.* sein; poitrine
boss: *n.* chef; patron
botanical: *adj.* botanique
botanist: *n.* botaniste
botany: *n.* botanique
botch: *vt.* cochonner
bother: *n.* ennui; problème
bother: *vt.* ennuyer; déranger
bottle: *n.* bouteille
bottle: *vt.* mettre en bouteille
bottleneck: *n.* embouteillage; goulot
bottle-opener: *n.* ouvre-bouteille
bottom note: note de bas de page
bottom: *n.* fond; fondement; *adj.* du
bas; dernier
bottomless: *adj.* sans fond;
insondable; inépuisable

boùgh: *n.* branche; rameau
boulder: *n.* gros galet
bounce: *n.* bond; rebond
bounce: *vi.* rebondir; bondir; faire des bonds
bound by law (to be): être légalement tenu
bound: *n.* limite; saut; répercussion
boundary: *n.* limite; frontière
boundless: *adj.* illimité; infini
bounteous: *adj.* abondant; prodigue; généreux; bienfaisant
bounty: *n.* libéralité; générosité
bouquet: *n.* bouquet
bourgeois: *adj.* bourgeois
bout: *n.* attaque; accès; combat
bovine: *adj.* bovin
bow tie: noeud papillon
bow: *n.* arc; archet; noeud
bow: *n.* salut; révérence
bow: *vt.* incliner; baisser
bowel: *n.* intestin
bowl: *n.* bol; saladier; boule
bowl: *vi.* jouer aux boules
bowling alley: bowling
bowling green: terrain de boules
bowling: *n.* boules
bowstring: *n.* corde (d'arc)
box office: guichet
box: *n.* boîte; caisse; loge
box: *vt.* mettre en boîte; boxer
boxed text: pavé; encadré
boxer: *n.* boxeur
boxing gloves: gants de boxe
boxing ring: ring
boxing: *n.* boxe
box-seat: *n.* place à côté du siège du cocher
boy: *n.* garçon
boycott: *n.* boycottage
boycott: *vt.* boycotter
boyfriend: *n.* petit ami
boyish: *adj.* d'enfant; puéril; de garçon

bra: *n.* soutien-gorge
brace: *n.* attache; bretelle; appareil dentaire
bracelet: *n.* bracelet
bracing: *adj.* vivifiant; tonifiant
bracken: *n.* fougère
bracket: *n.* tranche; parenthèse
brag: *n.* fanfaronnade
brag: *vi.* se vanter; fanfaronner
braid: *n.* tresse
braid: *vt.* tresser
brain: *n.* cerveau; tête
brain: *vt.* assommer; défoncer le crâne à
brainchild: *n.* invention personnelle
brainless: *adj.* stupide
brainwash: *vt.* faire un lavage de cerveau à
brainwave: *n.* idée lumineuse
brainy: *adj.* intelligent
brake fluid: liquide de frein
brake light: feu de stop
brake: *n.* frein
brake: *vi.* freiner
bramble: *n.* ronce
bran: *n.* son
branch line: ligne d'embranchement
branch: *n.* branche; ramification
branch: *vi.* se ramifier
branching: *n.* ramification
brand: *n.* marque; marque au fer
brand: *vt.* marquer au fer
brandish: *vt.* brandir
brand-new: *adj.* flambant-neuf
brandy: *n.* cognac
brash: *adj.* grossier; impertinent
brass: *n.* cuivre
brassiere: *n.* soutien-gorge
brat: *n.* môme; gosse
bravado: *n.* bravade
brave: *adj.* courageux; brave; vaillant; brave
brave: *vt.* braver

bravery: *n.* bravoure; courage; magnificence
brawl: *n.* bagarre; rixe
brawl: *vi.* se bagarrer
brawn: *n.* muscle; fromage de tête
bray: *n.* braiment
bray: *vi.* braire
braze: *vt.* souder au laiton
brazen: *adj.* de cuivre; impudent; effronté
brazier: *n.* crochet; brasero
breach of copyright: violation de droit d'auteur
breach: *n.* rupture; brèche; violation
bread: *n.* pain
breadbox: *n.* panière
breadcrumbs: *npl.* chapelure
breadth: *n.* largeur
breadwinner: *n.* soutien de famille
break: *n.* cassure; rupture
break: *vt.* casser; briser; violer; interrompre
breakage: *n.* casse
breakdown: *n.* panne; dépression nerveuse
breakdown: une ventilation (des coûts)
breakfast: *n.* petit déjeuner
breakfast: *vi.* déjeuner
breaking: *n.* bris; violation; fracture
breakthrough: *n.* percée; innovation
breakwater: *n.* digue
breast: *n.* poitrine; sein
breastbone: *n.* sternum
breastplate: *n.* pectoral; plastron
breaststroke: *n.* brasse
breath: *n.* haleine; respiration; souffle
breathe: *vt.* respirer; exhaler
breathing space: moment de répit
breathing: *n.* respiration; souffle
breathless: *adj.* ors d'haleine
breathtaking: *adj.* stupéfiant
breed: *n.* race; espèce

breed: *vt.* élever
breeder: *n.* éleveur
breeding: *n.* élevage; éducation
breeze: *n.* brise
breezy: *adj.* frais
brethren: *npl.* frères
brevet: *vt.* faire breveter
breviary: *n.* bréviaire
brevity: *n.* brièveté; concision
brew: *n.* infusion
brew: *vt.* faire infuser; brasser; comploter
brewer: *n.* brasseur
brewery: *n.* brasserie
briar: *n.* ronce; églantier
bribe: *n.* pot-de-vin
bribe: *vt.* acheter; soudoyer
bribery: *n.* corruption
bric-à-brac: *n.* bric-à-brac
brick: *n.* brique
brick: *vt.* bâtir en briques
bricklayer: *n.* maçon
bridal: *adj.* de noces; nuptial
bride: *n.* mariée
bridegroom: *n.* marié
bridesmaid: *n.* demoiselle d'honneur
bridge: *n.* pont; arête du nez; chevalet
bridle: *n.* bride; frein
bridle: *vt.* brider; réfréner
brief: *adj.* bref; concis; succint
brief: *n.* affaire; résumé
briefcase: *n.* serviette
briefly: *adv.* brièvement; en peu de mots
brigade: *n.* brigade
brigadier: *n.* général de brigade
brigand: *n.* bandit; brigand
bright: *adj.* clair; brillant; éclatant
brighten: *vt.* faire briller
brightness: *n.* éclat; brillant
brilliance: *n.* éclat
brilliant: *adj.* éclatant; génial
brim: *n.* bord

brimful: *adj.* plein jusqu'au bord
bring: *vt.* apporter; amener; persuader
brink: *n.* bord
brisk: *adj.* vif; rapide; frais
brisket: *n.* poitrine de boeuf
briskly: *adj.* vivement; rapidement
bristle: *n.* poil; soie
bristle: *vi.* se hérisser
bristly: *adj.* hérissé
brittle: *adj.* cassant; fragile
broach: *vt.* aborder
broad: *adj.* large
broadbean: *npl.* eves
broadcast data: diffuser des données
broadcast: *n.* émission
broadcast: *vt.* diffuser; émettre
broadcasting: *n.* radiodiffusion; émission de télévision
broaden: *vt.* élargir
broadly: *adv.* généralement
broad-minded: *adj.* tolérant; aux idées larges
broadness: *n.* largeur
broadsheet: journal de grand format
broadside: *n.* flanc d'un navire; attaque cinglante
broadways: *adv.* en large; dans le sens de la largeur
brocade: *n.* brocart
broccoli: *n.* brocoli
brochure: *n.* brochure; dépliant
brogue: *n.* accent du terroir broil
brogue: *vt.* griller
broke; to be: être fauché
broken: *adj.* cassé; interrompu
broker: *n.* courtier
brokerage fee: droit de courtage
brokerage: *n.* courtage
bronchial: *adj.* des bronches
bronchitis: *n.* bronchite
bronze: *n.* bronze
bronze: *vt.* bronzer; brunir
brooch: *n.* broche
brood: *n.* couvée; nichée

brood: *vi.* couver; ruminer
brood-hen: *n.* couveuse
brook: *n.* ruisseau
broom: *n.* genêt; balai
broomstick: *n.* manche à balai
broth: *n.* bouillon de viande et de légumes
brothel: *n.* bordel
brother: *n.* frère
brotherhood: *n.* fraternité
brother-in-law: *n.* beau-frère
brotherly: *adj.* fraternel; *adv.* fraternellement
brow: *n.* sourcil; front; sommet
browbeat: *vt.* intimider
brown: *adj.* marron; brun; *n.* marron
brown: *vt.* brunir
browse mode: mode survol
browse: *vt.* parcourir; feuilleter
browser: navigateur; logiciel de navigation
bruise: *n.* bleu; ecchymose
bruise: *vt.* faire un bleu à
brunette: *n.* brune
brunt: *n.* choc
brush: *n.* brosse; pinceau; accrochage
brush: *vt.* brosser
brushwood: *n.* broussailles; brindilles
brusque: *adj.* brusode
brut: *adj.* brutal
brutalise: *vt.* brutaliser
brutality: *n.* brutalité
brute: *n.* brute; *adj.* bestial; féroce
brutish: *adj.* brutal; bestial; féroce
brutly: *adv.* brutalement
bubble: *n.* bulle
bubble: *vi.* faire des bulles; bouillonner; pétiller
bubblegum: *n.* bubble-gum
bucket: *n.* seau
buckle: *n.* boucle
buckle: *vt.* attacher; boucler
bucolic: *adj.* bucolique

bud: *n.* bourgeon; bouton
bud: *vi.* bourgeonner
Buddhism: *n.* Bouddhisme
budding: *adj.* en bouton
buddy: *n.* copain
budge: *vi.* bouger; remuer; céder
budgerigar: *n.* perruche
budget: *n.* budget
buff: *n.* mordu
buffalo: *n.* bison
buffer: *n.* tampon; polissoir; butoir
buffer: *v.* tamponner
buffet: *n.* buffet
buffet: *vt.* gifler; frapper
buffoon: *n.* bouffon
bug: *n.* punaise
bugbear: *n.* épouvantail; croque-mitaine
bug-free: sans bogue; sans erreur
build: *vt.* construire; bâtir
builder: *n.* constructeur; entrepreneur
building society: organisme de crédit immobilier
building: *n.* bâtiment; immeuble; édifice
built-in: *adj.* incorporé; intégré
bulb: *n.* bulbe; oignon
bulbous: *adj.* bulbeux
bulge: *n.* gonflement; renflement
bulge: *vi.* se renfler
bulk: *n.* masse; volume; grosseur; majeure partie
bulky: *adj.* volumineux; encombrant
bull: *n.* taureau
bulldog: *n.* bouledogue
bulldozer: *n.* bulldozer
bullet: *n.* balle
bulletin board: panneau d'affichage
bulletproof: *adj.* pare-balles; blindé
bullfight: *n.* corrida
bullfighter: *n.* torero
bullfighting: *n.* tauromachie
bullion: *n.* or en barre
bullock: *n.* bouvillon

bullring: *n.* arène
bull's-eye: *n.* centre de la cible
bully: *n.* tyran
bully: *vt.* tyraniser
bulwark: *n.* rempart
bum: *n.* clochard
bumblebee: *n.* bourdon
bump: *n.* heurt; secousse; bosse
bump: *vt.* heurter
bumpkin: *n.* rustre; plouc
bumpy: *adj.* cahoteux; bosselé
bun: *n.* petit pain; chignon
bunch: *n.* botte; groupe
bundle: *n.* paquet; liasse; ballot; fagot
bundle: *vt.* empaqueter; mettre en liasse
bung: *n.* bonde
bung: *vt.* boucher
bungalow: *n.* bungalow
bungle: *vt.* bousiller
bunion: *n.* oignon
bunk: *n.* couchette
bunker: *n.* abri; bunker
buoy: *n.* bouée
buoyancy: *n.* flottabilité; optimisme
buoyant: *adj.* flottable; gai; enjoué
burden: *n.* bête de somme
burden: *n.* charge; fardeau
burden: *vt.* charger
bureau: *n.* commode; bureau
bureaucracy: *n.* bureaucratie
bureaucrat: *n.* bureaucrate
burglar alarm: signal d'alarme; signal antivol
burglar: *n.* cambrioleur
burglary: *n.* cambriolage
burial place: lieu de sépulture
burial: *n.* enterrement; obsèques
burlesque: *n.* caricature; parodie; *adj.* burlesque; caricatural
burly: *adj.* robuste; de forte carrure
burn: *n.* brûlure
burn: *vt.* brûler; incendier; mettre le feu à

burner: *n.* brûleur
burning: *adj.* brûlant
burrow: *n.* terrier
burrow: *vi.* se terrer
bursar: *n.* intendant
burst: *vi.* éclater
bury: *vt.* enterrer; inhumer
bus: *n.* autobus
bush: *n.* buisson
bushy: *adj.* touffu; plein de buissons
busily: *adv.* activement; avec empressement
business connections: relations d'affaires
business letter: lettre d'affaires
business trip: voyage d'affaires
business: *n.* entreprise; commerce; affaires; activité
businesslike: *adj.* sérieux
businessman: *n.* homme d'affaires
businesswoman: *n.* femme d'affaires
bus-stop: *n.* arrêt d'autobus
bust: *n.* buste
bustle: *n.* remue-ménage; animation
bustle: *vi.* s'affairer; s'activer
bustling: *adj.* animé
busy: *adj.* occupé; actif
busybody: *n.* mouche du coche
but: *conj.* mais; sauf; excepté; seulement
butcher shop: boucherie
butcher: *n.* boucher
butcher: *vt.* abattre; massacrer
butchery: *n.* boucherie; carnage
butler: *n.* majordome
butt: *n.* butte; mégot
butt: *vt.* donner un coup de tête à
butter: *n.* beurre
butter: *vt.* beurrer
buttercup: *n.* bouton d'or
butterfly: *n.* papillon
buttermilk: *n.* babeurre
buttocks: *npl.* fesses
button: *n.* bouton

button: *vt.* boutonner
buttonhole: *n.* boutonnière
buttress: *n.* contre-fort; soutien
buttress: *vt.* soutenir
buxom: *adj.* bien en chair
buy: *vt.* acheter
buyer: *n.* acheteur
buzz: *n.* bourdonnement; murmure
buzz: *vi.* bourdonner
buzzard: *n.* buse
buzzer: *n.* interphone
by: *prep.* à côté de; près de; par; de
bygone: *adj.* passé
by-law: *n.* arrêté municipal
bypass: *n.* route de contournement
by-product: *n.* sous-produit
by-road: *n.* chemin de traverse
bystander: *n.* spectateur; badaud
byte: *n.* (computing) octet
byword: *n.* proverbe; dicton

C

cab: *n.* taxi
cabbage: *n.* chou
cabin: *n.* cabine; cabane
cabinet: *n.* conseil des ministres
cabinet-maker: *n.* ébéniste
cable car: téléphérique
cable television: télévision par cable
cable: *n.* (mar) câble
caboose: *n.* coquerie
cabstand: *n.* station de taxis
cache: *n.* cachette
cackle: *n.* caquetage; jacasserie
cackle: *vi.* caqueter; jacasser
cactus: *n.* cactus
cadence: *n.* cadence
cadet: *n.* cadet
cadge: *vt.* taper
café: *n.* café
cafeteria: *n.* cafétéria
caffeine: *n.* caféine
cage effect: effet de cage
cage: *n.* cage; prison
cage: *vt.* mettre en cage; emprisonner
cagey: *adj.* circonspect
cajole: *vt.* cajoler
cake: *n.* gâteau
calamitous: *adj.* calamiteux; catastrophique
calamity: *n.* calamité; désastre
calculable: *adj.* calculable
calculate: *vt.* calculer; compter
calculation: *n.* calcul
calculator: *n.* calculatrice
calendar: *n.* calendrier
calf: *n.* veau; vachette; mollet
calibre: *n.* calibre
calisthenics: *npl.* gymnastique rythmique
call: *vt.* appeler; appeler au téléphone; convoquer
caller: *n.* visiteur
calligraphy: *n.* calligraphie
calling: *n.* profession; vocation

callous: *adj.* dur; insensible
calm: *n.* calme; tranquillité; *adj.* calme; tranquille
calm: *vt.* calmer; apaiser
calmness: *n.* calme; tranquillité
calorie: *n.* calorie
calorimetry: *n.* calorimétrie
calumny: *n.* calomnie
Calvary: *n.* Calvaire
calve: *vi.* vêler; mettre bas
camel: *n.* chameau
cameo: *n.* camée
camera: *n.* appareil photographique; caméra
cameraman: *n.* cameraman; cadreur
camomile: *n.* camomille
camouflage: *n.* camouflage
camp: *n.* camp
camp: *vi.* camper
campaign: *n.* campagne
campaign: *vi.* faire campagne
campaigner: *n.* militant; candidat en campagne électorale
camper: *n.* campeur
camphor: *n.* camphre
campsite: *n.* camping
can opener: ouvre-boîte
canal: *n.* conduit; canal
cancel an order; to: annuler une commande
cancel: *vt.* annuler
cancellation: *n.* annulation
cancer: *n.* cancer
cancerous: *adj.* cancéreux
candid: *adj.* candide; simple; sincère
candidate: *n.* candidate
candied: *adj.* confit
candle: *n.* bougie; cierge
candlelight: *n.* lueur d'une bougie
candlestick: *n.* bougeoir
candour: *n.* candeur; sincérité
candy: *n.* bonbon
cane: *n.* canne; bâton
canine: *adj.* canin

canister: *n.* boîte métallique
cannabis: *n.* cannabis
cannibal: *n.* cannibale; anthropophage
cannibalism: *n.* cannibalisme
cannon: *n.* canon
cannonball: *n.* boulet de canon
canny: *adj.* rusé; prudent
canoe: *n.* canoë
canon: *n.* canon
canonisation: *n.* canonisation
canonise: *vt.* canoniser
canopy: *n.* baldaquin; marquise
cantankerous: *adj.* acariâtre; atrabilaire
canteen: *n.* cantine
canter: *n.* petit galop
canvas: *n.* toile
canvass: *vt.* sonder; examiner; débattre
canvasser: *n.* prospecteur; démarcheur
canyon: *n.* canyon
cap: *n.* casquette
capability: *n.* capacité; aptitude; faculté
capable: *adj.* capable
capacitate: *vt.* rendre capable
capacity: *n.* capacité; aptitude; potentiel
cape: *n.* cap; promontoire
caper: *n.* cabriole; gambade
caper: *vi.* cabrioler; gambader
capillary: *adj.* capillaire
capital punishment: peine de mort; peine capitale
capital: *adj.* capital; principal; *n.* capital; capitale; majuscule
capitalise: *vt.* capitaliser
capitalism: *n.* capitalisme
capitalist: *n.* capitaliste
capitalization: mise en majuscules
capitulate: *vi.* capituler
capitulation: *n.* capitulation

caprice: *n.* caprice
capricious: *adj.* capricieux
capsize: *vt.* chavirer
capsule: *n.* capsule
captain: *n.* capitaine
captaincy: *n.* grade de capitaine; statut de capitaine
captivate: *vt.* captiver
captivation: *n.* fascination
captive: *n.* captif; prisonnier
captivity: *n.* captivité
capture data (to): saisir des données
capture: *n.* capture
capture: *vt.* prendre; capturer
car hire: location de voiture
car wash: station de nettoyage pour voitures
car: *n.* voiture; automobile; wagon
carafe: *n.* carafe
caramel: *n.* caramel
carat: *n.* carat
caravan: *n.* caravane
caraway: *n.* cumin
carbohydrate: *n.* hydrate de carbone
carbon copy: copie carbone; double carbone
carbon paper: papier carbone
carbon: *n.* carbone
carbonise: *vt.* carboniser
carboxylic acid: acide carboxylique
carbuncle: *n.* escarboucle; furoncle; tumeur maligne
carburettor: *n.* carburateur
carcass: *n.* cadavre
card catalogue: fichier de bibliothèque
card game: jeu de cartes
card index files: fichier
card table: table de jeu
card (to): mettre en fiches
card: *n.* carte
cardboard: *n.* carton
cardiac: *adj.* cardiaque

cardinal: *adj.* cardinal; principal; *n.* cardinal
care: *n.* soin; souci
care: *vi.* se soucier de; être concerné par
career: *n.* carrière; cours; aller à toute vitesse
carefree: *n.* insouciant
careful: *adj.* soigneux; consciencieux; prudent
careless: *adj.* insouciant; négligent; indolent
carelessness: *n.* négligence; indifférence
caress: *n.* caresse
caress: *vt.* caresser
caretaker: *n.* gardien; concierge
car-ferry: *n.* ferry
cargo: *n.* cargaison de navire
caricature: *n.* caricature
caricature: *vt.* caricaturer
caries: *n.* carie
caring: *adj.* aimant; humanitaire
carnage: *n.* carnage
carnal: *adj.* charnel; sensuel
carnation: *n.* oeillet
carnival: *n.* carnaval
carnivorous: *adj.* carnivore
carnot cycle: cycle de carnot
carol: *n.* chant de Noël
carpenter: *n.* charpentier
carpentry: *n.* charpenterie
carpet: *n.* tapis m
carpet: *vt.* recouvrir d'un tapis; moquetter
carpeting: *n.* moquette
carping: *n.* chicaneries; *adj.* malveillant
carriage: *n.* port; voiture; wagon
carriage-free: *adj.* franco de port
carrier pigeon: pigeon voyageur
carrier: *n.* porteur; transporteur
carrion: *n.* charogne
carrot: *n.* carotte

carry out: mener à bien; réaliser
carry: *vt.* porter; transporter; conduire
cart: *n.* charrette; chariot; charrier
cartel: *n.* cartel
carthorse: *n.* cheval de trait
cartilage: *n.* cartilage
cartload: *n.* charretée
carton: *n.* pot; boîte
cartoon: *n.* dessin animé
cartridge: *n.* cartouche
cartulary: *n.* chatrier
carve: *vt.* tailler; sculpter; ciseler
carving knife: couteau à découper
carving: *n.* sculpture
cascade: *n.* cascade
case files: dossiers documentaires
case: *n.* boîte; valise; cas; étui; enveloppe
casebound book: livre à couverture cartonnée
cash book: livre de caisse
cash card: carte bancaire
cash dispenser: distributeur automatique de billets
cash on delivery: paiement comptant à la livraison
cash with order: paiement comptant à la commande
cash: *n.* espèces
cash: *vt.* encaisser
cash; to be in: être en fonds
cash; to be out of: être à court d'argent
cash; to: toucher; encaisser
cashier: *n.* caissier
cashmere: *n.* cashemire
casing: *n.* chambranle; enveloppe
casino: *n.* casino
cask: *n.* tonneau; fût
casket: *n.* cercueil
casserole: *n.* cocotte
cassette player: *n.* lecteur de cassettes; magnétophone

cassette: *n.* cassette
cassock: *n.* soutane
cast iron: fonte
cast steel: acier fondu
cast: *n.* coup; moule
cast: *vt.* jeter; lancer; couler
castanets: *npl.* castagnettes
castaway: *n.* réprouvé; paria
caste: *n.* caste
castigate: *vt.* punir sévèrement
casting vote: voix prépondérante
castle: *n.* château
castor oil: huile de ricin
castrate: *vt.* castrer
castration: *n.* castration
casual: *adj.* accidentel; fortuit
casualty: *n.* victime
cat: *n.* chat
cataclysmic: *adj.* cataclysmique
catalogue entry: notice catalographique
catalogue: *n.* catalogue
catalogue: *v.* cataloguer
cataloguing: *n.* catalogage
catalysis: *n.* catalyse
catalyst: *n.* catalyseur
cataplasm: *n.* cataplasme
catapult: *n.* catapulte
cataract: *n.* cataracte
catarrh: *n.* rhume; catarrhe
catastrophe: *n.* catastrophe
catcall: *n.* sifflet
catch: *n.* prise; capture
catch: *vt.* attraper; saisir; prendre; surprendre
catching: *adj.* contagieux; communicatif
catchphrase: *n.* rengaine; slogan
catchy: *adj.* qui attire l'attention; accrocheur
catechise: *vt.* cathéchiser; interroger
catechism: *n.* catéchisme
categorical: *adj.* catégorique
categorise: *vt.* classer par catégories

category: *n.* catégorie
cater: *vi.* approvisionner en nourriture
caterer: *n.* fournisseur; traiteur
catering: *n.* restauration
caterpillar: *n.* chenille
catgut: *n.* boyau de chat
catharsis: *n.* catharsis
cathedral: *n.* cathédrale
cathode: *n.* cathode
Catholic: *n.* catholique; *adj.* catholique
Catholicism: *n.* catholicisme
cattle show: exposition bovine
cattle: *n.* bétail
caucus: *n.* réunion d'un comité électoral
cauliflower: *n.* chou-fleur
caulk: *n.* mastic
caulk: *v.* mastiquer; calfater
causal: *adj.* causal
causality: *n.* causalité
cause: *n.* cause; raison; motif
cause: *vt.* causer
causeway: *n.* chaussée
caustic: *adj.* caustique
caution: *n.* prudence; précaution
cautionary: *adj.* d'avertissement
cautious: *adj.* prudent; circonspect
cavalcade: *n.* cavalcade; cortège
cavalier: *adj.* cavalier
cavalry: *n.* cavalerie
cave: *n.* grotte; caverne
caveat: *n.* avertissement; mise en garde
cavern: *n.* caverne
cavernous: *adj.* caverneux
cavil: *n.* point de détail
cavity: *n.* cavité
cease at: *v.* cesser; arrêter
ceasefire: *n.* cessez-le-feu
ceaseless: *adj.* incessant; continuel
cedar: *n.* cèdre
cede: *vt.* céder

ceiling: *n.* plafond
celebrate: *vt.* célébrer; fêter
celebration: *n.* tete
celebrity: *n.* célébrité
celery: *n.* céleri
celestial: *adj.* céleste; divin
celibacy: *n.* célibat
celibate: *adj.* célibataire
cell: *n.* cellule
cellar: *n.* cave; cellier
cello: *n.* violoncelle
cellophane: *n.* cellophane
cellular: *adj.* cellulaire
cellulose: *n.* cellulose
cement: *n.* ciment
cement: *vt.* cimenter
cemetery: *n.* cimetière
cenotaph: *n.* cénotaphe
censor: *n.* censeur; critique
censorious: *adj.* sévère; critique
censorship: *n.* censure
censure: *n.* censure; critique
censure: *vt.* censurer; condamner;
critiquer
census: *n.* recensement
cent: *n.* centime
centenarian: *n.* centenaire
centenary: *n.* centenaire; *adj.*
centenaire
centennial: *adj.* centenaire
center of mass: centre de masse
centigrade: *n.* centigrade
centilitre: *n.* centilitre
centimetre: *n.* centimètre
centipede: *n.* mille-pattes
central problem: problème central
central processing unit: unité
centrale (ordinateur)
central: *adj.* central
centralise: *vt.* centraliser
centre: *n.* centre
centre: *vt.* centrer; concentrer
centrifugal: *adj.* centrifuge
centripetal force: force centripète

century: *n.* siècle
ceramic: *adj.* en céramique
cereals: *npl.* céréales
cerebral: *adj.* cérébral
ceremonial: *n.* cérémonial; rituel;
adj. cérémoniel; officiel
ceremonious: *adj.* cérémonieux
ceremony: *n.* cérémonie
certain: *adj.* certain; sûr
certainty: *n.* certitude; conviction
certificate: *n.* certificat; acte
certification: *n.* authentification
certified copy: copie authentique;
copie certifiée conforme
certified mail: *n.* envoi avec accusé
de réception
certify: *vt.* certifier; assurer
cervical: *adj.* cervical
cessation: *n.* cessation
cesspool: *n.* cloaque; fosse d'aisances
chafe: *vt.* irriter; frotter
chaff: *n.* menue paille
chaffinch: *n.* pinson
chagrin: *n.* dépit
chain carrier: porteur de chaîne
chain length: longueur de chaîne
chain of stores: une chaîne de
magasins
chain reaction: réaction en chaîne
chain: *n.* chaîne; série; suite
chain: *vt.* enchaîner; attacher avec
une chaîne
chainstore: *n.* grand magasin à
succursales
chair a meeting; to: présider une
réunion
chair: *n.* chaise
chair: *vt.* présider
chairman: *n.* président
chalice: *n.* calice
chalk: *n.* craie
challenge: *n.* défi
challenge: *vt.* défier
challenger: *n.* provocateur

challenging: *adj.* provocateur
chamber: *n.* pièce; chambre
chambermaid: *n.* femme de chambre
chameleon: *n.* caméléon
chamois leather: peau de chamois
champagne: *n.* champagne
champion: *n.* champion
champion: *vt.* défendre
championship: *n.* championnat
chance: *n.* hasard; chance; occasion
chancellor: *n.* chancelier
chancery: *n.* chancellerie
chandelier: *n.* lustre
change of state: état de change
change: *vt.* changer; transformer
changeable: *adj.* changeant; variable; inconstant
changeless: *adj.* constant; immuable
changing: *adj.* variable; changeant
channel: *n.* canal; chaîne
channel: *vt.* canaliser
chant: *n.* chant
chant: *vt.* scander
chaos: *n.* chaos
chaotic: *adj.* chaotique
chapel: *n.* chapelle
chaplain: *n.* chapelain
chapter: *n.* chapitre
char: *vt.* carboniser
character: *n.* caractère; personnage
characterise: *vt.* caractériser
characteristic: *adj.* caractéristique
characterless: *adj.* sans caractère
charade: *n.* charade
charcoal: *n.* charbon de bois
charge card: carte de crédit
charge interest; to: percevoir des intérêts
charge to an account; to: imputer à un compte (crédit)
charge: *n.* fardeau; accusation
charge: *vt.* charger; accuser
chargeable: *adj.* passible
charitable: *adj.* caritatif; charitable

charity: *n.* charité; bienfaisance; aumône
charlatan: *n.* charlatan
charm: *n.* charme; attrait
charm: vt charmer; enchanter
charming: *adj.* charmant
chart: *n.* carte de navigation; diagramme
charter flight: vol charter
charter party: une charte partie
charter: *n.* charte; privilège
charter: *vt.* affréter
chase: *n.* chasse
chase: *vt.* donner la chasse à; poursuivre
chasm: *n.* abîme
chaste: *adj.* chaste; pur; sobre
chasten: *vt.* châtier; corriger
chastise: *vt.* châtier; punir; corriger
chastisement: *n.* châtiment
chastity: *n.* chasteté; pureté
chat: *n.* petite conversation; bavardage
chat: *vi.* causer
chatter: *n.* bavardage; jacasserie
chatter: *vi.* bavarder; jacasser
chatterbox: *n.* moulin à paroles; pipelette
chatty: *adj.* bavard
chauffeur: *n.* chauffeur
chauvinist: *n.* chauvin
cheap: *adj.* bon marché; peu cher
cheapen: *vt.* baisser le prix de
cheaper: *adj.* moins cher
cheat: *n.* fraude; tricherie
cheat: *vt.* tromper; frauder
check box: case à cocher
check up: un bilan de santé
check: *n.* contrôle
check: *vt.* vérifier; contrôler; réprimer; enrayer; stopper; enregistrer
checklist: liste de contrôle
checkmate: *n.* échec et mat
checkout: *n.* caisse

checkpoint: *n.* poste de contrôle
checkroom: *n.* consigne
checkup: *n.* bilan de santé
cheek: *n.* joue; culot
cheekbone: *n.* pommette
cheer: *n.* gaieté; joie; applaudissement
cheer: *vt.* réconforter; égayer
cheerful: *adj.* gai; enjoué; joyeux
cheerfulness: *n.* gaieté; bonne humeur
cheese: *n.* fromage
chef: *n.* chef (de cuisine)
chemical bond: liaison chimique
chemical change: changement chimique
chemical properties: propriété chimique
chemical reaction: réaction chimique
chemical weathering: détérioration chimique
chemical: *adj.* chimique
chemist: *n.* chimiste; pharmacien
chemistry: *n.* chimie
cheque account: compte courant
cheque book: carnet de chèques
cheque stub: talon de chèque
cheque to bearer: chèque au porteur
cheque without cover: chèque sans provisions
cheque: *n.* chèque
cheque; certified: chèque certifié
cheque; crossed: un chèque barré
cheque; dud: un chèque en bois
cheque; to cross: a barrer un chèque
cheque; to stop: a faire opposition à un cheque
chequerboard: *n.* échiquier
chequered: *adj.* à carreaux
cherish: *vt.* chérir; aimer
cheroot: *n.* petit cigare
cherry: *n.* cerise; *adj.* vermeil
cherrytree: *n.* cerisier
cherub: *n.* chérubin

chess: *n.* échecs
chessboard: *n.* échiquier
chessman: *n.* pièce de jeu d'échecs
chest: *n.* poitrine; cage thoracique
chestnut tree: châtaigner
chestnut: *n.* châtaigne
chew: *vt.* mâcher; mastiquer
chewing gum: chewing-gum
chic: *adj.* chic
chicanery: *n.* chicane; chicanerie
chick: *n.* poussin; poulette
chicken: *n.* poulet
chickenpox: *n.* varicelle
chickpea: *n.* pois chiche
chicory: *n.* chicorée
chide: *vt.* gronder; réprimander
chief executive: directeur général
chief: *adj.* principal; en chef; *n.* chef
chieftain: *n.* chef
chiffon: *n.* mousseline de soie
chilblain: *n.* engelure
child: *n.* enfant
childbirth: *n.* accouchement
childhood: *n.* enfance
childish: *adj.* enfantin; puéril
childishness: *n.* enfantillage; puérilité
childless: *adj.* sans enfants
childlike: *adj.* d'enfant
chill: *adj.* froid; frais; fraîche; *n.* froid
chill: *vt.* refroidir; glacer
chilly: *adj.* froid; très frais
chime: *n.* carillon; harmonie
chime: *vi.* sonner; s'accorder
chimney: *n.* cheminée
chimpanzee: *n.* chimpanzé
chin: *n.* menton
china: *n.* porcelaine
chink: *n.* fente; tintement
chink: *vi.* tinter
chip: *n.* fragment; éclat; puce; frite
chip: *vt.* ébrécher; *vi.* s'ébrécher
chiropodist: *n.* pédicure
chirp: *n.* épiement; gazouillis
chirp: *vi.* pépier; gazouiller

chirping: *n.* chant des oiseaux
chisel: *n.* ciseau
chisel: *vt.* ciseler
chitchat: *n.* bavardage; papotage
chivalrous: *adj.* chevaleresque
chivalry: *n.* chevalerie
chives: *npl.* ciboulette
chlorine: *n.* chlore
chloroform: *n.* chloroforme
chnage: *n.* changement; modification; variété; change
chock-full: *adj.* plein à craquer; comble
chocolate: *n.* chocolat
choice: *n.* choix; préférence; assortiment; sélection
choir: *n.* choeur
choke: *vt.* étrangler; étouffer
cholera: *n.* choléra
choose: *vt.* choisir; élire
chop: *n.* côtelette
chop: *vt.* trancher; couper; hacher
chopper: *n.* hélicoptère
chopping block: billot
choral: *adj.* choral
chord: *n.* corde; accord
chore: *n.* corvée; travail routinier
chorist: *n.* choriste
chorus: *n.* choeur
Christ: *n.* Jésus-Christ
christen: *vt.* baptiser
christening: *n.* baptême
Christian: *adj.* chrétien; *n.* chrétien
Christianity: *n.* christianisme; chrétienté
Christmas card: carte de Noël
Christmas Eve: veille de Noël
Christmas: *n.* Noël
chromatography: *n.* chromatographie
chrome: *n.* chrome
chronic: *adj.* chronique
chronicle: *n.* chronique
chronicler: *n.* chroniqueur

chronological: *adj.* chronologique
chronologically: *adv.* chronologiquement; ordre chronologique
chronology: *n.* chronologie
chronometer: *n.* chronomètre
chrun: *vt.* baratter
chubby: *adj.* potelé
chuck: *vt.* lancer; jeter
chuckle: *vi.* rire; glousser
chug: *vi.* souffler; haleter
chum: *n.* copain; copine
chunk: *n.* gros morceau
church: *n.* église
churchyard: *n.* cimetière
churlish: *adj.* fruste; grossier; hargneux
churn: *n.* baratte
cider: *n.* cidre
cigar: *n.* cigare
cigarette case: étui à cigarettes
cigarette end: mégot
cigarette holder: fume-cigarette
cigarette: *n.* cigarette
cinder: *n.* braise
cinema: *n.* cinéma
cinnamon: *n.* cannelle
cipher: *n.* chiffre
circle graph: diagramme circulaire
circle: *n.* cercle; groupe
circle: *vt.* encercler; tourner autour de
circuit: *n.* circuit; tour; tournée
circuitous: *adj.* détourné; indirect
circular: *adj.* circulaire; *n.* circulaire
circulate: *vi.* circuler
circulation: *n.* circulation
circumcise: *vt.* circoncire
circumcision: *n.* circoncision
circumference: *n.* circonférence
circumflex: *n.* accent circonflexe
circumlocution: *n.* circonlocution
circumnavigate: *vt.* contourner
circumnavigation: *n.* circum-navigation

circumscribe: *vt.* circonscrire
circumspect: *adj.* circonspect
circumspection: *n.* circonspection
circumstance: *n.* circonstance;
situation
circumstantial: *adj.* circonstancié;
accessoire
circumstantiate: *vt.* détailler
circumvent: *vt.* circonvenir
circumvention: *n.* évitement;
tricherie
circus: *n.* cirque
cistern: *n.* citerne
citadel: *n.* citadelle
citation: *n.* citation
cite: *vt.* citer
citizen: *n.* citoyen
citizenship: *n.* citoyenneté
city: *n.* ville
civic: *adj.* civique
civil defence: défense passive
civil engineer: ingénieur des travaux
publics
civil law: droit civil
civil servant: fonctionnaire
civil war: guerre civile
civil: *adj.* civil; courtois
civilian: *n.* civil
civilisation: *n.* civilisation
civilise: *vt.* civiliser
civility: *n.* civilité; courtoisie
clad: *adj.* vêtu; habillé
claim: *n.* demande; réclamation
claim: *vt.* revendiquer; réclamer
claimant: *n.* demandeur
clairvoyant: *n.* voyant
clam: *n.* palourde
clamber: *vi.* grimper
clammy: *adj.* moite
clamour: *n.* clameur; cris
clamour: *vi.* vociférer; crier
clamp: *n.* attache
clamp: *vt.* serrer; imposer
clan: *n.* clan; groupe

clandestine: *adj.* clandestin
clang: *n.* bruit métallique
clang: *vi.* faire un bruit métallique
clap: *vi.* applaudir
clapping: *n.* applaudissements
claret: *n.* vin rouge de Bordeaux
clarification: *n.* clarification;
éclaircissement
clarify: *vt.* clarifier; éclaircir
clarinet: *n.* clarinette
clarity: *n.* clarté
clash: *n.* choc; affrontement
clash: *v.* heurter; s'entrechoquer
clasp: *n.* fermoir; boucle;étreinte
clasp: *vt.* agrafer; étreindre
class: *n.* classe; catégorie
class: *vt.* classer; classifier
classical: *adj.* classique; *n.* auteur
classique
classification scheme: cadre de
classement
classification: *n.* classification
classified advertisement: petite
annonce
classified catalogue: catalogue
systématique
classify: *vt.* classifier; classer
classmate: *n.* camarade de classe
classroom: *n.* salle de classe
clatter: *n.* cliquetis
clatter: *vi.* résonner; cliqueter
clause: *n.* proposition; clause
claw: *n.* griffe; serre; pince
claw: *vt.* griffer; agripper
clay: *n.* argile
clean: *adj.* propre; net
clean: *vt.* nettoyer
cleaning: *n.* nettoyage
cleanliness: *n.* propreté; pureté
cleanly: *adj.* propre; *adv.* proprement;
nettement
cleanness: *n.* propreté
cleanse: *vt.* nettoyer

clear: *adj.* clair; net; transparent; évident
clear: *vt.* clarifier; éclaircir; dégager; disculper
clearance: *n.* déblaiement; autorisation
clear-cut: *adj.* net
clearing bank: banque de dépôts
clearing house: chambre de compensation
clearly: *adv.* clairement; manifestement
cleaver: *n.* couperet
clef: *n.* clé
cleft: *n.* fissure; crevasse
clemency: *n.* clémence
clement: *adj.* clément
clenched: *adj.* serré
clergy: *n.* clergé
clergyman: *n.* ecclésiastique
clerical: *adj.* clérical; ecclésiastique
clerk: *n.* ecclésiastique; employé
clever: *adj.* intelligent; habile; astucieux
cliché: *n.* cliché
click: *vt.* claquer
client: *n.* client
cliff: *n.* falaise
climate: *n.* climat
climatic: *adj.* climatique
climax: *n.* point culminant; apogée
climb: *vt.* grimper; escalader
climber: *n.* alpiniste
climbing: *n.* alpinisme
clinch: *vt.* serrer fort
cling: *vi.* s'accrocher (à); se cramponner (à); adhérer; (se) coller
clinic: *n.* clinique
clink: *n.* tintement
clink: *vt.* faire tinter; tinter; résonner
clip: *n.* clip; pince
clip: *vt.* couper
clipping files: dossiers de coupures de presse

clipping: *n.* coupure
clique: *n.* clique
cloak: *n.* cape; prétexte
cloak: *vt.* masquer
cloakroom: *n.* vestiaire
clock: *n.* horloge
clockwork: *n.* mécanisme d'horloge; *adj.* précis
clod: *n.* motte (de terre)
clog: *n.* sabot
clog: *vi.* se boucher
cloister: *n.* cloître
close: *n.* fin; conclusion; *adj.* proche; étroit; ajusté dense; réservé
close: *vt.* fermer; clore; conclure; terminer
closed-access: en accès indirect
closely: *adv.* étroitement; de près
closeness: *n.* proximité; fidélité; exactitude; intimité; minutie
closet: *n.* placard
close-up: *n.* gros plan
closure: *n.* fermeture; clôture
clot: *n.* caillot; grumeau
cloth: *n.* tissu; chiffon; toile
clothe: *vt.* habiller; vêtir
clothes basket: panière à linge
clotheshorse: *n.* séchoir à linge
clothesline: *n.* corde à linge
clothespin: *n.* pince à linge
clothing: *n.* vêtements
cloud: *n.* nuage; nuée
cloud: *vt.* rendre trouble; assombrir
cloudiness: *n.* nébulosité; obscurité
cloudy: *adj.* nuageux; nébuleux; obscur; sombre; trouble
clout: *n.* coup de poing
clove: *n.* clou de girofle
clover: *n.* trèfle
clown: *n.* clown
club: *n.* matraque; club
clue: *n.* indice; indication; idée
clump: *n.* massif
clumsily: *adv.* gauchement

clumsiness: *n.* gaucherie
clumsy: *adj.* gauche; maladroit; lourd
cluster: *n.* bouquet; grappe; groupe
cluster: *vt.* grouper; *vi.* se rassembler
clutch: *n.* prise; embrayage
clutch: *vt.* empoigner; agripper
clutter: *vt.* encombrer
coach trip: excursion en car
coach: *n.* autocar; wagon; entraîneur
coach: *vt.* entraîner; donner des cours particuliers à
coagulate: *vt.* coaguler; agglutiner; *vi.* se coaguler; s'agglutiner
coal: *n.* charbon
coalesce: *vi.* s'unir; se fondre
coalfield: *n.* gisement charbonnier
coalition: *n.* coalition
coalman: *n.* charbonnier
coalmine: *n.* mine de charbon; houillère
coarse: *adj.* rude; grossier
coarsely: *adv.* grossièrement
coast: *n.* côte
coastal: *adj.* côtier
coastguard: *n.* gendarmerie maritime; garde-côte
coastline: *n.* littoral
coat hanger: cintre
coat: *n.* manteau; pelage; couche
coat: *vt.* enduire; revêtir
coating: *n.* revêtement
coax: *vt.* cajôler
cob: *n.* épi de maïs
cobbler: *n.* cordonnier
cobbles: *npl.* pavés ronds
cobweb site: site obsolète; non remis à jour
cobweb: *n.* toile d'araignée
cocaine: *n.* cocaïne
cock fighting: combat de coqs
cock: *n.* coq m
cock: *vt.* armer; dresser
cock-a-doodle-doo: cocorico
cockcrow: *n.* chant du coq

cockerel: *n.* jeune coq
cockle: *n.* coque
cockpit: *n.* cabine de pilotage
cockroach: *n.* cafard
cocktail: *n.* cocktail
cocoa: *n.* cacao
coconut: *n.* noix de coco
cocoon: *n.* cocon
cod: *n.* morue
code: *n.* code; indicatif
coding sheet: bordereau de saisie
cod-liver oil: huile de foie de morue
coefficient: *n.* coefficient
coercion: *n.* coercition; contrainte
coexistence: *n.* coexistence
coffee break: pause-café
coffee house: café
coffee table book: beau livre
coffee table: table basse
coffee: *n.* café
coffeepot: *n.* cafetière
coffer: *n.* coffre; caisse
coffin: *n.* cercueil
cog: *n.* dent d'engrenage
cogency: *n.* puissance; force
cogent: *adj.* convaincant; puissant
cognac: *n.* cognac
cognate: *adj.* apparenté
cognisance: *n.* connaissance; compétence
cognisant: *adj.* instruit; compétent
cognition: *n.* connaissance; cognition
cogwheel: *n.* roue dentée
cohabit: *vi.* cohabiter
cohabitation: *n.* cohabitation
cohere: *vi.* se tenir; être cohérent
coherence: *n.* cohérence
coherent: *adj.* cohérent; logique
cohesion: *n.* cohésion
cohesive: *adj.* cohésif
coil: *n.* rouleau m; bobine
coil: *vt.* enrouler
coin: *n.* pièce de monnaie
coin: *vt.* frapper

coincide: *vi.* coïncider
coincidence: *n.* coïncidence
coincident: *adj.* coïncident
coke: *n.* coke
colander: *n.* passoire
cold sore: bouton de fièvre
cold: *adj.* froid; indifférent; *n.* froid; rhume
cold-blooded: *adj.* insensible
coldness: *n.* froideur
cold-storage unit: chambre froide
coleslaw: *n.* salade de chou cru
colic: *n.* coliques
collaborate: *vi.* collaborer
collaboration: *n.* collaboration
collaborative work: oeuvre de collaboration
collapse: *n.* écroulement; évanouissement
collapse: *vi.* s'écrouler
collapsible: *adj.* pliant
collar: *n.* col
collarbone: *n.* clavicule
collate: *vt.* collationner; confronter
collateral: *adj.* concomitant; parallèle; *n.* nantissement
collateral: *n.* caution pour un prêt
collating: *n.* collationnement
collation: *n.* collation
colleague: *n.* collègue; confrère; consoeur
collect: *vt.* rassembler; collectionner
collecting: *n.* collecte
collection letter: lettre de recouvrement
collection: *n.* collection
collective work: oeuvre collective
collective: *adj.* collectif
collectively: *adv.* collectivement
collector: *n.* collectionneur
college: *n.* faculté
collide: *vi.* entrer en collision; se heurter

colligative property: propriété colligative
collision: *n.* collision; heurt
colloid: *n.* colloide
colloquial: *adj.* familier; parlé
colloquialism: *n.* expression familière
collusion: *n.* collusion
colon: *n.* deux-points; colon
colonel: *n.* colonel
colonial: *adj.* colonial
colonise: *vt.* coloniser
colonist: *n.* colon
colony: *n.* colonie
color: *n.* couleur
colossal: *adj.* colossal
colossus: *n.* colosse
colour television: télévision en couleur
colour: *n.* couleur; prétexte; drapeau
colour: *vt.* colorer
colour-blind: *adj.* daltonien
colourful: *adj.* coloré
colouring: *n.* teint; coloris
colourless: *adj.* sans couleur; incolore
colt: *n.* poulain
column: *n.* colonne
columnist: *n.* chroniqueur
coma: *n.* coma
comatose: *adj.* comateux
comb: *n.* peigne
comb: *vt.* peigner
combat: *n.* combat; single duel
combat: *vt.* combattre
combatant: *n.* combattant
combative: *adj.* combatif
combination reaction: réaction de combinaison
combination: *n.* combinaison; association
combine: *vt.* combiner
combustion: *n.* combustion

come: *vi.* venir; rencontrer par hasard; tomber sur

comedian: *n.* comédien; comique

comedienne: *n.* comédienne; comique

comedy: *n.* comédie

comet: *n.* comète

comfort: *n.* confort; aises; commodités; consolation

comfort: *vt.* réconforter; soulager; consoler

comfortable: *adj.* confortable; réconfortant

comfortably: *adv.* confortablement; agréablement

comforter: *n.* personne qui réconforte; édredon

comic strip: bande dessinée

comical: *adj.* comique

coming: *n.* venue; arrivée; *adj.* à venir

comma: *n.* virgule

command: *n.* ordre

command: *vt.* ordonner; commander

commander: *n.* commandant

commandment: *n.* commandement

commando: *n.* commando

commemorate: *vt.* commémorer

commemoration: *n.* commémoration

commence: *vt.* commencer

commencement: *n.* commencement

commend: *vt.* recommander; confier à; louer

commendable: *adj.* louable

commendably: *adv.* élogieusement

commendation: *n.* louange; recommandation

commensurate: *adj.* proportionné

comment: *n.* commentaire

comment: *vt.* commenter

commentary: *n.* commentaire; observation

commentator: *n.* commentateur

commerce: *n.* commerce; affaires; relations

commercial intelligence: veille commerciale

commercial: *adj.* commercial

commiserate: *vt.* compatir

commiseration: *n.* commisération; pitié

commissariat: *n.* intendance; ravitaillement

commission: *n.* commission

commissioner: *n.* commissionnaire; coursier

commit: *vt.* commettre; confier à; engager

commitment: *n.* engagement

committee: *n.* comité

commodity: *n.* produit; denrée

common law: droit coutumier

common noun: nom commun

common sense: bon sens

common: *adj.* commun; ordinaire

commoner: *n.* roturier

commonly: *adv.* communément; généralement

commonpl.ace: *n.* lieux communs; *adj.* banal

commotion: *n.* vacarme; perturbation

commune: *vi.* discuter avec sincérité

communicable: *adj.* communicable; transmissible

communicate: *vt.* communiquer; transmettre

communication: *n.* communication

communicative: *adj.* communicatif

communion: *n.* communion

communiqué: *n.* communiqué

communism: *n.* communisme

communist: *n.* communiste

community centre: centre social

community chest: fonds commun

community: *n.* communauté

community: *n.* communité

commutable: *adj.* interchangeable; permutable
commutation ticket: carte d'abonnement
commutative property of **addition**: propriété commutative de l'addition
commutative property of **multiplication**: propriété commutative de multiplication
commute: *vt.* échanger
compact disc: disque compact
compact: *adj.* compact; serré; dense; *n.* accord; contrat
companion: *n.* compagnon; compagne
companionship: *n.* camaraderie; compagnie
company: *n.* compagnie; fréquentation; société
comparable: *adj.* comparable
comparative: *adj.* comparatif
compare: *vt.* comparer
comparison: *n.* comparaison
compartment: *n.* compartiment
compass: *n.* boussole
compassion: *n.* compassion
compassionate: *adj.* compatissant
compatibility: *n.* compatibilité
compatible numbers: nombres compatibles
compatible: *adj.* compatible
compatriot: *n.* compatriote
compel: *vt.* contraindre; obliger; forcer
compelling: *adj.* irrésistible
compensate: *vt.* compenser
compensation: *n.* compensation; dédommagement
compère: *n.* animateur
compete: *vi.* rivaliser avec; faire concurrence à
competence: *n.* compétence; aptitude
competent: *adj.* compétent; suffisant

competition: *n.* compétition; concurrence
competitive intelligence: veille concurrentielle
competitive: *adj.* concurrentiel; compétitif
competitor: *n.* concurrent
compilation: *n.* compilation
compile: *vt.* compiler
complacency: *n.* suffisance
complacent: *adj.* suffisant
complain: *vi.* se plaindre; déposer une plainte
complaint: *n.* plainte; réclamation
complement: *n.* complément
complementary: *adj.* complémentaire
complete: *adj.* complet; achevé
complete: *vt.* achever; mener à bien; compléter
completion: *n.* achèvement
complex problem: problem complexe
complex sentence: phrase complexe
complex: *adj.* complexe
complexion: *n.* teint; aspect
complexity: *n.* complexité
compliance: *n.* conformité; soumission
compliant: *adj.* docile; soumis
complicate: *vt.* compliquer
complication: *n.* complication
complicity: *n.* complicité
compliment: *n.* compliment
compliment: *vt.* complimenter
complimentary: *adj.* flatteur; à titre gracieux
comply with; to: se conformer à
comply: *vi.* se soumettre; se plier; se conformer
component: *adj.* composant
compose: *vt.* composer; constituer
composed: *adj.* calme; posé
composer: *n.* auteur; compositeur

composite author: auteur collectif
composite number: nombre composé
composite work: oeuvre composite
composite: *adj.* composite; composé
composition: *n.* composition
compositor: *n.* compositeur
compost: *n.* compost
composure: *n.* maîtrise de soi; calme; sang-froid
compound sentence: phrase complexe
compound: *adj.* composé; *n.* composé
compound: *vt.* composer; combiner
compound-complex: complexe composé
comprehend: *vt.* comprendre; englober
comprehensible: *adj.* compréhensible
comprehension: *n.* compréhension; inclusion
comprehensive: *adj.* global; complet; compréhensif
compress: *n.* compresse
compress: *vt.* comprimer; concentrer
comprise: *vt.* comprendre; embrasser
compromise: *n.* compromis
compromise: *vt.* compromettre; *vi.* adopter un compromis
compte: m. calcul; chef d'accusation; comte
compton scattering: compton; effet
compulsion: *n.* contrainte; compulsion
compulsive: *adj.* compulsif
compulsory: *adj.* obligatoire
compunction: *n.* remords; scrupule
computable: *adj.* computable; calculable
computation: *n.* computation; calcul
compute: *vt.* calculer
computer artist: infographiste

computer literacy: culture informatique; maîtrise de l'outil informatique
computer programming: programmation
computer science: informatique
computer scientist: informaticien
computer: *n.* ordinateur
computer-aided animation: animation assistée par ordinateur
computer-aided design: conception assistée par ordinateur
computer-aided drawing: dessin assisté par ordinateur
computer-aided learning: apprentissage assisté par ordinateur
computer-aided manufacturing: fabrication assistée par ordinateur
computer-aided publication: publication assistée par ordinateur
computer-aided sound design: conception sonore assistée par ordinateur
computer-aided teaching: enseignement assisté par ordinateur
computer-aided translation: traduction assistée par ordinateur
computer-generated image: image de synthèse
computer-illiterate: qui est débutant en informatique; qui ne sait pas se servir d'un ordinateur
computerise: *vt.* traiter par ordinateur; informatiser
computerization: *n.* informatisation
computer-literate (to be): savoir se servir d'un ordinateur
comrade: *n.* camarade; compagnon; compagne
comradeship: *n.* camaraderie
con man: *n.* escroc
con: *n.* duperie
con: *vt.* duper
concave: *adj.* concave

concavity: *n.* concavité
conceal: *vt.* cacher; dissimuler
concealment: *n.* dissimulation; recel
concede: *vt.* concéder; accorder
conceit: *n.* vanité; trait d'esprit
conceited: *adj.* vaniteux; prétentieux
conceivable: *adj.* concevable
conceive: *vt.* concevoir; *vi.* concevoir
concentrate: *vt.* concentrer
concentration camp: camp de concentration
concentration: *n.* concentration
concentric: *adj.* concentrique
concept: *n.* concept
conception: *n.* conception
concern: *n.* affaire; souci
concern: *vt.* concerner; toucher
concerning: *prep.* en ce qui concerne; concernant
concert: *n.* concert
concerto: *n.* concerto
concession: *n.* concession
conciliate: *vt.* concilier
conciliation: *n.* conciliation
conciliatory: *adj.* conciliateur; conciliant
concise: *adj.* concis; succinct
conclude: *vt.* conclure; décider; déduire
conclusion: *n.* conclusion; déduction; fin
conclusive: *adj.* décisif; concluant
concoct: *vt.* confectionner; fabriquer
concoction: *n.* préparation; élaboration
concomitant: *adj.* concomitant
concord: *n.* entente; harmonie
concordance: *n.* accord
concordant: *adj.* concordant
concourse: *n.* rassemblement;carrefour; foule
concrete: *n.* béton
concrete: *vt.* bétonner
concubine: *n.* concubine

concur: *vi.* coïncider; s'entendre
concurrence: *n.* consentement; coïncidence; union
concurrently: *adv.* simultanément
concussion: *n.* commotion
condemn: *vt.* condamner; désapprouver
condemnation: *n.* condamnation
condensation: *n.* condensation
condense: *vt.* condenser
condescend: *vi.* condescendre; daigner
condescending: *adj.* condescendant
condescension: *n.* condescendance
condiment: *n.* condiment
condition: *n.* état
condition: *vt.* conditionner
conditional: *adj.* conditionnel; hypothétique
conditioned: *adj.* conditionné
conditioner: *n.* après-shampoing
conditioning: *n.* climatisation
condolences: *npl.* condoléances
condom: *n.* préservatif
condominium: *n.* condominium; copropriété
condone: *vt.* pardonner; fermer les yeux sur
conducive: *adj.* propice; opportun
conduct: *n.* conduite; comportement
conduct: *vt.* conduire; mener
conduction: *n.* conduction
conductor: *n.* receveur; chef d'orchestre; conducteur
conduit: *n.* conduit; tuyau
cone: *n.* cône
confection: *n.* sucrerie; confiserie; confection
confectioner: *n.* confiseur
confectioner's shop: *n.* confiserie; pâtisserie
confederacy: *n.* confédération
confederate: *adj.* confédéré; *n.* confédéré

confederate: *vi.* se confédérer
confer: *vt.* conférer
conference: *n.* conférence
confess: *vt.* confesser
confession: *n.* confession
confessional: *n.* confessionnal
confessor: *n.* confesseur
confidant: *n.* confident
confide: *vt.* confier
confidence trick: abus de confiance; escroquerie
confidence: *n.* confiance; assurance
confident: *adj.* confiant; assuré; sûr
confidential: *adj.* confidentiel
configuration: *n.* configuration
confine: *vt.* limiter; emprisonner
confinement: *n.* détention; alitement
confirm delivery: accusé de réception
confirm: *vt.* confirmer; ratifier
confirmation: *n.* confirmation; ratification; corroboration
confirmed: *adj.* invétéré; endurci
confiscate: *vt.* confisquer
confiscation: *n.* confiscation
conflagration: *n.* incendie; conflagration
conflict: *n.* conflit; lutte; dispute
conflicting: *adj.* contradictoire
confluence: *n.* confluence; rencontre
conform: *vt.* conformer; adapter
conformity: *n.* conformité; accord
confound: *vt.* confondre
confront: *vt.* confronter; affronter
confrontation: *n.* affrontement; confrontation
confuse: *vt.* confondre; embarrasser; embrouiller
confusing: *adj.* déroutant
confusion: *n.* confusion; désordre
congeal: *vt.* solidifier; congeler
congenial: *adj.* sympathique; similaire
congenital: *adj.* congénital

congested: *adj.* encombré; congestionné
congestion: *n.* encombrement; congestion
conglomerate: *adj.* aggloméré; *n.* conglomérat
conglomerate: *vt.* conglomérer; agglomérer
conglomeration: *n.* conglomération
congratulate: *vt.* complimenter; féliciter
congratulations: *npl.* félicitations
congratulatory: *adj.* de félicitation
congregate: *vt.* rassembler; réunir
congregation: *n.* assemblée; rassemblement
congress: *n.* congrès; conférence
congressman: *n.* membre du Congrès
congruent figures: figures congruentes
congruity: *n.* congruence
congruous: *adj.* congru; approprié
conical: *adj.* conique
conifer: *n.* conifère
coniferous: *adj.* conifère
conjecture: *n.* conjecture; supposition
conjecture: *vt.* conjecturer; supposer
conjugal: *adj.* conjugal
conjugate acid: acide conjugé
conjugate base: base conjugué
conjugate: *vt.* conjuguer
conjugation: *n.* conjugaison
conjunction: *n.* conjonction; union
conjuncture: *n.* conjoncture; occasion
conjure: *vt.* conjurer; exorciser
conjurer: *n.* magicien; illusionniste
connect: *vt.* relier; joindre; rattacher
connection: *n.* liaison; connexion
connivance: *n.* connivence
connive: *vi.* fermer les yeux (sur); être de connivence
connoisseur: *n.* connaisseur

connotative: *adj.* connotatif
conquer: *vt.* conquérir; vaincre
conqueror: *n.* vainqueur; conquérant
conquest: *n.* conquête
conscience: *n.* conscience
conscientious: *adj.* consciencieux; de conscience
conscious: *adj.* conscient; intentionnel
consciousness: *n.* conscience
conscript: *n.* conscrit
conscription: *n.* conscription
consecrate: *vt.* consacrer
consecration: *n.* consécration
consecutive: *adj.* consécutif
consensus: *n.* consensus
consent: *n.* consentement; assentiment
consent: *vi.* consentir
consequence: *n.* conséquence; importance
consequent: *adj.* consécutif
conservation of energy: conservation de l'énergie
conservation of mass: conservation de la masse
conservation: *n.* conservation
conservative: *adj.* conservateur
conservatory: *n.* conservatoire
conserve: *vt.* conserver
consider: *vt.* considérer; examiner; *vi.* penser; délibérer
considerable: *adj.* considérable; important
considerate: *adj.* prévenant; attentionné; prudent
consideration: *n.* considération; réflexion; estime; rémunération
considering: *conj.* étant donné que
consign: *vt.* confier; remettre; expédier
consignee: *n.* consignataire; destinataire
consignment: *n.* expédition; envoi

consignor: *n.* expéditeur
consist: *vi.* consister (en)
consistency: *n.* consistance; cohérence; constance
consistent: *adj.* constant; cohérent; compatible
consolable: *adj.* consolable
consolation: *n.* consolation; réconfort
consolatory: *adj.* consolateur
console: *vt.* consoler
consolidate: *vt.* consolider; grouper; *vi.* se consolider
consolidation: *n.* consolidation
consonant: *adj.* en accord; *n.* consonne
consort: *n.* consort; associé
conspicuous: *adj.* voyant; manifeste; notable
conspiracy: *n.* conspiration
conspirator: *n.* conspirateur
conspire: *vi.* conspirer
constancy: *n.* constance; fermeté d'âme; persévérance
constant: *adj.* constant; persévérant
constellation: *n.* constellation
consternation: *n.* consternation
constipated: *adj.* constipé
constipation: *n.* constipation
constituency: *n.* électorat; circonscription
constituent: *n.* composant; *adj.* constituant
constitute: *vt.* constituer; établir
constitution: *n.* constitution
constitutional: *adj.* constitutionnel
constrain: *vt.* contraindre; forcer; obliger
constraint: *n.* contrainte
constrict: *vt.* serrer; gêner
construct: *vt.* construire; bâtir
construction: *n.* construction
construe: *vt.* interpréter; analyser
consul: *n.* consul
consular: *adj.* consulaire

consulate: *n.* consulat
consulship: *n.* consulat
consult: *vt.* consulter; *vi.* (se) consulter
consultant: *n.* conseiller
consultation: *n.* consultation; délibération
consume: *vt.* consommer; dissiper; consumer; brûler
consumer goods: biens de consommation
consumer society: société de consommation
consumer: *n.* consommateur
consumerism: *n.* consumérisme
consumer-to-consumer auction: enchère de particulier à particulier
consummate: *adj.* accompli; consommé
consummate: *vt.* consommer; accomplir; perfectionner
consummation: *n.* consommation; perfection
consumption: *n.* consommation
contact lenses: lentilles de contact
contact: *n.* contact
contagious: *adj.* contagieux
contain: *vt.* contenir; renfermer; refréner
container: *n.* conteneur hermétique
container: *n.* récipient
containerization: *n.* mise en conteneurs
contaminate: *vt.* contaminer
contamination: *n.* contamination
contemplate: *vt.* contempler
contemplation: *n.* contemplation
contemplative: *adj.* contemplatif
contemporaneous: *adj.* contemporain
contempt: *n.* mépris; dédain
contemptible: *adj.* méprisable; vil
contemptuous: *adj.* méprisant; dédaigneux

contend: *vi.* combattre; lutter; *vt.* affirmer
content: *adj.* content; satisfait; *n.* contentement; table des matières
content: *vt.* contenter; satisfaire
contentedly: *adv.* avec contentement
contentious: *adj.* litigieux; querelleur
contentment: *n.* contentement; satisfaction
contest: *n.* concours; altercation
contest: *vt.* contester; discuter; disputer
contestant: *n.* concurrent
context clue: indice de contexte
context: *n.* contexte
contiguous: *adj.* contigu; voisin
continent: *adj.* continent; chaste; *n.* continent
continental: *adj.* continental
contingency: *n.* contingence; événement imprévu; éventualité
contingent: *n.* contingent; *adj.* contingent; éventuel
continual: *adj.* continuel
continually: *adv.* continuellement
continuation: *n.* continuation; reprise; suite
continue: *vt.* continuer
continuing education: formation continue; permanente
continuity: *n.* continuité
continuous spectrum: spectre continu
continuous: *adj.* continu
contort: *vt.* tordre; déformer
contortion: *n.* contorsion
contour: *n.* contour
contraband: *n.* contrebande; *adj.* de contrebande
contraception: *n.* contraception
contraceptive: *n.* contraceptif; *adj.* contraceptif
contract employee: personne travaillant en cdd

contract: *n.* contrat
contract: *vt.* contracter; *vi.* se contracter
contraction: *n.* contraction
contractor: *n.* entrepreneur
contradict: *vt.* contredire
contradiction: *n.* contradiction
contradictory: *adj.* contradictoire
contraption: *n.* gadget; bidule
contrariness: *n.* esprit de contradiction
contrary: *adj.* contraire; opposé; *n.* contraire
contrast: *n.* contraste
contrast: *vt.* contraster; mettre en contraste
contrasting: *adj.* contrasté; opposé
contravention: *n.* infraction
contributary: *adj.* contributif
contribute: *vt.* contribuer
contribution: *n.* contribution; cotisation
contributor: *n.* souscripteur; collaborateur
contributory: *adj.* contribuant
contrite: *adj.* contrit; repentant
contrition: *n.* contrition; repentir
contrivance: *n.* dispositif; invention
contrive: *vt.* inventer; combiner; trouver le moyen de
control room: salle des commandes
control tower: tour de contrôle
control: *n.* contrôle; maîtrise; autorité
control: *vt.* maîtriser; réguler; contrôler; gouverner
controversial: *adj.* polémique
controversy: *n.* polémique
contusion: *n.* contusion
conundrum: *n.* énigme
conurbation: *n.* conurbation
convalesce: *vi.* être en convalescence
convalescence: *n.* convalescence
convalescent: *adj.* convalescent
convection: *n.* convection

convene: *vt.* convoquer; réunir
convenience: *n.* commodité; convenance
convenient: *adj.* commode; pratique; qui convient
convent: *n.* couvent
convention: *n.* convention; contrat; assemblée
conventional: *adj.* conventionnel
converge: *vi.* converger
convergence: *n.* convergence
convergent boundary: limite convergente
convergent: *adj.* convergent
conversant: *adj.* au courant; compétent
conversation: *n.* conversation
converse: *vi.* converser
conversely: *adv.* inversement; réciproquement
conversion: *n.* conversion; transformation
convert: *vt.* convertir
convertible: *adj.* convertible
convex: *adj.* convexe
convexity: *n.* convexité
convey: *vt.* transporter; transmettre; communiquer
conveyance: *n.* transport; transfert; cession
conveyancer: *n.* notaire
convict: *n.* détenu
convict: *vt.* déclarer coupable
conviction: *n.* condamnation; conviction
convince: *vt.* convaincre; persuader
convincing: *adj.* convaincant
convincingly: *adv.* de façon convaincante
convivial: *adj.* jovial
conviviality: *n.* jovialité
convoke: *vt.* convoquer
convoy: *n.* convoi
convulse: *vt.* ébranler; convulser

convulsion: *n.* convulsion;
bouleversement; forte agitation
convulsive: *adj.* convulsif
coo: *vt.* roucouler
cook: *n.* cuisinier
cook: *vt.* cuire; falsifier; faire la
cuisine; cuisiner
cookbook: *n.* livre de cuisine
cooker: *n.* cuisinière
cookery: *n.* cuisine
cookie: *n.* gâteau m sec
cool: *adj.* frais; calme; *n.* fraîcheur
cool: *vt.* rafraîchir; refroidir
coolly: *adv.* fraîchement; de sang-
froid
coolness: *n.* fraîcheur; froideur; sang-
froid
cooperate: *vi.* coopérer
cooperation: *n.* coopération
cooperative: *adj.* coopératif
coordinate: *vt.* coordonner
coordinates: *n.* coordonnee;
ensemble
coordinating: *adj.* assorti
coordination: *n.* coordination
cop: *n.* flic
copartner: *n.* coassocié
cope: *vi.* se débrouiller
copier: *n.* photocopieuse
copious: *adj.* copieux;
abondantmment
copper: *n.* cuivre
coppice: *n.* taillis
copulate: *vi.* copuler
copy: *n.* copie; reproduction;
exemplaire
copy: *vt.* copier; imiter
copybook: *n.* cahier
copying machine: photocopieuse
copyist: *n.* copiste
copyright library: bibliothèque de
dépôt légal
copyright materials: documents
protégés par

copyright: *n.* droit d'auteur;
copyright
copywriter: *n.* rédacteur publicitaire
coral reef: récif de corail
coral: *n.* corail
cord: *n.* cordon; corde
cordial: *adj.* cordial; chaleureux
cordially: *adv.* cordialement
corduroy: *n.* velours côtelé
core: *n.* trognon; noyau; centre; coeur
cork: *n.* liège; bouchon
cork: *vt.* boucher
corkscrew: *n.* tire-bouchon
corn: *n.* maïs; grain; blé
corncob: *n.* épi de maïs
cornea: *n.* cornée
corned beef: corned-beef
corner: *n.* coin; angle
cornerstone: *n.* pierre angulaire
cornet: *n.* cornet
cornfield: *n.* champ de maïs
cornflakes: *npl.* flocons de maïs;
cornflakes
cornice: *n.* corniche
cornstarch: *n.* farine de maïs
corollary: *n.* corollaire
coronary: *n.* infarctus
coronation: *n.* couronnement
coroner: *n.* coroner
coronet: *n.* couronne
corporal: *n.* caporal
corporate author: collectivité-auteur
corporate sponsorship: mécénat
d'entreprise; parrainage
corporate: *adj.* en commun;
d'entreprise
corporation: *n.* corporation; société
par actions
corporeal: *adj.* corporel
corps: *n.* corps
corpse: *n.* cadavre
corpulent: *adj.* corpulent
corpuscle: *n.* corpuscule; électron
corral: *n.* corral

correct: *adj.* correct; juste
correct: *vt.* corriger; rectifier
correction: *n.* correction; rectification
corrective: *adj.* correcteur; correctif; *n.* rectificatif
correctly: *adv.* correctement
correctness: *n.* correction
correlation: *n.* corrélation
correlative: *adj.* corrélatif
correspond: *vi.* correspondre
correspondence: *n.* correspondance
correspondent: *adj.* correspondant; *n.* correspondant
corridor: *n.* couloir; corridor
corroborate: *vt.* corroborer
corroboration: *n.* corroboration
corroborative: *adj.* qui corrobore
corrode: *vt.* corroder
corrosion: *n.* corrosion
corrosive: *adj.* corrosif
corrugated iron: tôle ondulée
corrupt: *adj.* corrompu; dépravé
corrupt: *vt.* corrompre
corruptible: *adj.* corruptible
corruption: *n.* corruption; dépravation
corruptive: *adj.* qui corrompt
corset: *n.* corset; gaine
cortege: *n.* cortège
cosily: *adv.* confortablement; douillettement
cosmetic: *adj.* cosmétique; *n.* cosmétique
cosmic: *adj.* cosmique
cosmonaut: *n.* cosmonaute
cosmopolitan: *adj.* cosmopolite
cosset: *vt.* dorloter
cost effective: rentable
cost price: prix de revient
cost: *n.* prix; coût
cost: *vi.* coûter
costly: *adj.* coûteux; cher
costume: *n.* costume

cot: *n.* lit de camp
cottage: *n.* cottage
cotton candy: barbe à papa
cotton mill: filature de coton
cotton wool: coton hydrophile
cotton: *n.* coton
couch: *n.* canapé; divan
couchette: *n.* couchette
cough: *n.* toux
cough: *vi.* tousser
council: *n.* conseil
councillor: *n.* membre du conseil
counsel: *n.* conseil; avocat
counsellor: *n.* conseiller; avocat
count: *vt.* compter; dénombrer; calculer
countdown: *n.* compte à rebours
countenance: *n.* visage; aspect; mine
counter: *n.* comptoir; pion
counteract: *vt.* contrecarrer; neutraliser; contrebalancer
counterbalance: *n.* contrepoids
counterbalance: *vt.* contrebalancer; compenser
counterfeit: *adj.* faux
counterfeit: *vt.* contrefaire
counterfoil: *n.* talon
countermand: *vt.* annuler
counterpart: *n.* contrepartie; homologue
counterproductive: *adj.* qui va à l'encontre du but visé
countersign: *vt.* contresigner
countess: *n.* comtesse
countless: *adj.* innombrable
countrified: *adj.* rustique; campagnard
country house: maison de campagne
country: *n.* pays; patrie; campagne; région; *adj.* rustique; campagnard
countryman: *n.* campagnard; compatriote
county: *n.* comté
coup: *n.* coup d'État

coupé: *n.* coupé
couple: *n.* couple
couple: *vt.* unir; associer
couplet: *n.* distique; couplet
coupon: *n.* coupon; bon
courage: *n.* courage
courageous: *adj.* courageux
courier: *n.* messager; guide
course: *n.* cours; route; chemin; plat; marche à suivre
court: *n.* cour; tribunal
court: *vt.* courtiser; solliciter
courteous: *adj.* courtois; poli
courtesan: *n.* courtisane
courtesy: *n.* courtoisie
courthouse: *n.* palais de justice
courtly: *adj.* élégant; raffiné
court-martial: *n.* conseil de guerre
courtroom: *n.* salle de tribunal
courtyard: *n.* cour
cousin: *n.* cousin
cove: *n.* crique; anse
covenant: *n.* contrat; convention
covenant: *vi.* convenir; stipuler par contrat
cover letter: lettre explicative
cover: *n.* couverture; abri; prétexte
cover: *vt.* recouvrir; dissimuler; protéger
coverage: *n.* reportage; couverture
covering: *n.* couverture; couche
covert: *adj.* voilé; caché; secret
cover-up: *n.* dissimulation
covet: *vt.* convoiter
covetous: *adj.* avide; cupide
cow: *n.* vache
coward: *n.* lâche
cowardice: *n.* lâcheté
cowardly: *adj.* lâche; *adv.* lâchement
cowboy: *n.* cowboy
cower: *vi.* se tapir
cowherd: *n.* vacher
coy: *adj.* timide; coquet; évasif
coyness: *n.* timidité; modestie

cozy: *adj.* douillet
crab: *n.* crabe
crab-apple tree: pommier sauvage
crab-apple: *n.* pomme sauvage
crack: *n.* craquement; fente; fissur
crack: *vt.* fêler; craquer
cracker: *n.* pétard; biscuit salé
crackle: *vi.* crépiter; pétiller
crackling: *n.* crépitement; friture
cradle: *n.* berceau
cradle: *vt.* bercer
craft: *n.* habileté; métier manuel; barque
craftily: *adv.* astucieusement
craftiness: *n.* astuce; ruse
craftsman: *n.* artisan
craftsmanship: *n.* artisanat
crafty: *adj.* astucieux; rusé
crag: *n.* rocher escarpé
cram: *vt.* bourrer; fourrer; entasser
crammed: *adj.* bourré
cramp: *n.* crampe
cramp: *vt.* entraver
cramped: *adj.* à l'étroit
crampon: *n.* crampon
cranberry: *n.* canneberge
crane: *n.* grue
crash course: cours intensif; cours accéléré
crash helmet: casque
crash landing: atterrissage en catastrophe
crash programme: programme d'urgence
crash: *n.* fracas; collision
crash: *vi.* s'écraser
crass: *adj.* grossier; crasse
crate: *n.* caisse; cageot
crater: *n.* cratère
cravat: *n.* foulard; cravate
crave: *vt.* avoir extrêmement besoin de
craving: *n.* désir extrême; soif
crawfish: *n.* écrevisse

crawl: *vi.* ramper
crayfish: *n.* écrevisse
crayon: *n.* crayon de couleur
craze: *n.* manie; engouement
craziness: *n.* folie
crazy: *adj.* fou
creak: *vi.* grincer; craquer
cream: *n.* crème; *adj.* crème
creamy: *adj.* crémeux
crease: *n.* pli
crease: *vt.* froisser
create: *vt.* créer; causer
creation: *n.* création
creative: *adj.* créatif
creator: *n.* créateur
creature: *n.* créature
credence: *n.* créance; crédit
credibility: *n.* crédibilité
credible: *adj.* crédible
credit card: carte de crédit
credit: *n.* crédit; honneur; reconnaissance
credit: *vt.* croire; reconnaître; créditer
creditable: *adj.* estimable; honorable
creditor: *n.* créancier
credulity: *n.* crédulité
credulous: *adj.* crédulité
creed: *n.* credo
creek: *n.* ruisseau
creep: *vi.* ramper; avancer lentement
creeper: *n.* plante grimpante
creepy: *adj.* terrifiant; qui donne la chair de poule
cremate: *vt.* incinérer
cremation: *n.* incinération; crémation
crematorium: *n.* crématoire
crescent: *adj.* croissant; *n.* croissant de lune
cress: *n.* cresson
crest: *n.* crête
crested: *adj.* à crête
crestfallen: *adj.* découragé; abattu
crevasse: *n.* crevasse
crevice: *n.* fissure; lézarde

crew: *n.* bande; équipe; équipage
crew: *n.* équipage
crib: *n.* berceau; mangeoire
cricket: *n.* grillon
crime: *n.* crime délit
criminal: *adj.* criminel; *n.* criminel
criminality: *n.* criminalité
crimson: *adj.* cramoisi
cripple: *adj.* invalide
cripple: *vt.* estropier; paralyser
crisis: *n.* crise
crisp: *adj.* frais; croquant
crispness: *n.* croquant
criss-cross: *adj.* entrecroisé
criteria: *n.* critère
criterion: *n.* critère
critic: *n.* critique
critical mass: masse critique
critical point: point critique
critical: *adj.* critique; exigeant; sévère
criticise: *vt.* critiquer
criticism: *n.* critique
croak: *vi.* coasser; croasser
crochet: *n.* crochet
crochet: *vi.* faire du crochet
crockery: *n.* poterie
crocodile: *n.* crocodile
crony: *n.* copain de longue date
crook: *n.* escroc; filou
crooked: *adj.* tordu; malhonnête
crop: *n.* culture; récolte
crop: *vt.* récolter
cross section: section de capture
cross: *n.* croix; croisement
cross: *vt.* traverser; croiser
crossbar: *n.* barre transversale
crossbreed: *n.* hybride
cross-country: *n.* cross-country
cross-examine: *vt.* soumettre à un
crossfire: *n.* feux croisés
crossing: *n.* traversée; passage pour piétons
cross-purpose: *n.* malentendu

cross-reference: *n.* renvoi; référence
crossroad: *n.* carrefour
crosswalk: *n.* passage clouté
crotch: *n.* entre-jambes
crouch: *vi.* s'accroupir; se tapir
crow: *n.* corbeau; chant du coq
crow: *vi.* chanter victoire
crowd: *n.* foule; monde
crowd: *vt.* entasser
crown prince: prince héritier
crown: *n.* couronne; sommet
crown: *vt.* couronner
crucial: *adj.* crucial
crucible: *n.* creuset
crucifix: *n.* crucifix
crucifixion: *n.* crucifixion
crucify: *vt.* crucifier
crude: *adj.* brut; grossier
cruel: *adj.* cruel
cruelty: *n.* cruauté
cruet: *n.* huilier-vinaigrier
cruise: *n.* croisière
cruise: *vi.* croiser
cruiser: *n.* croiseur
crumb: *n.* miette
crumble: *vt.* émietter; effriter
crumple: *vt.* froisser
crunch: *n.* crise
crunch: *vt.* croquer
crunchy: *adj.* croquant
crusade: *n.* croisade
crush: *n.* cohue
crush: *vt.* écraser; opprimer
crust: *n.* croûte
crustaceous: *n.* crustacé
crusty: *adj.* croustillant; hargneux;
bourru
crutch: *n.* béquille
crux: *n.* coeur (d'une question)
cry: *n.* cri; sanglot
cry: *vt.* crier; pleurer
cryoscopy: *n.* cryométrie; cryoscopie
crypt: *n.* crypte
cryptic: *adj.* énigmatique

crystal lattice: réseau cristallin
crystal: *n.* cristal
crystal-clear: *adj.* clair comme de
l'eau de roche
crystalline: *adj.* cristallin; pur
crystallise: *vi.* se cristalliser; *vt.*
cristalliser
cub: *n.* petit
cube: *n.* cube
cubic: *adj.* cubique
cuckoo: *n.* coucou
cucumber: *n.* concombre
cuddle: *n.* étreinte; câlin
cuddle: *vt.* embrasser; *vi.* s'enlacer
cudgel: *n.* gourdin; trique
cue: *n.* queue de billard
cuff: *n.* manchette; revers de pantalon
culinary: *adj.* culinaire
cull: *vt.* sélectionner; éliminer
culminate: *vi.* culminer
culmination: *n.* point culminant
culpability: *n.* culpabilité
culpable: *adj.* coupable; blâmable
culprit: *n.* coupable
cult: *n.* culte
cultivate: *vt.* cultiver; améliorer;
perfectionner
cultivation: *n.* culture
cultural: *adj.* culturel
culture: *n.* culture
cumbersome: *adj.* encombrant;
lourd; pesant
cumulative: *adj.* cumulatif
cunning: *adj.* astucieux; rusé
cup: *n.* tasse; coupe
cupboard: *n.* placard
curable: *adj.* guérissable
curate: *n.* vicaire
curator: *n.* conservateur; curateur
curb: *n.* frein; bord du trottoir
curb: *vt.* freiner; juguler; modérer
curd: *n.* lait caillé
curdle: *vt.* cailler; figer
cure: *n.* remède; cure

cure: *vt.* guérir
curfew: *n.* couvre-feu
curie temperature: curie; température de
curing: *n.* salaison
curiosity: *n.* curiosité
curious: *adj.* curieux
curl: *n.* boucle de cheveux
curl: *vt.* boucler; friser
curling iron: fer à friser
curly: *adj.* frisé; bouclé
currant: *n.* raisin
currency: *n.* monnaie; circulation; cours
current account: compte courant
current bibliography: bibliographie courante
current: *adj.* courant; actuel; *n.* cours; tendance; courant
currently: *adv.* actuellement
curriculum vitae: curriculum vitae
curry: *n.* curry
curse: *n.* malédiction
curse: *vt.* maudire; *vi.* jurer
cursive: *n.* cursive; *adj.* crusif
cursor: *n.* curseur
cursory: *adj.* superficiel; hâtif
curt: *adj.* succinct; sec
curtail: *vt.* réduire; écourter
curtain rod: tringle à rideaux
curtain: *n.* rideau
curtsy: *n.* révérence
curtsy: *vi.* faire une révérence
curvature: *n.* courbure
curve: *n.* courbe
curve: *vt.* courber
cushion: *n.* coussin
custard: *n.* crème anglaise
custodian: *n.* gardien
custody: *n.* garde; emprisonnement
custom house: bureau de douane
custom: *n.* coutume; usage
customary: *adj.* habituel; coutumier; ordinaire

customer: *n.* client
customized: personnalisé; adapté
customs duty: droits de douane
customs entry: déclaration en douane
customs officer: douanier
customs tariffs: tarifs douaniers
customs unions: unions douanières
customs: *npl.* douane
cut: *vt.* découper; couper; tailler; réduire; blesser
cutback: *n.* réduction
cutburst: *n.* explosion
cute: *adj.* mignon
cutlery: *n.* couverts
cutlet: *n.* côtelette
cut-rate: *adj.* à prix réduit
cut-throat: *n.* assassin; *adj.* acharné
cutting: *n.* coupure; *adj.* coupant; tranchant
cutting-edge: à jour; dernier cri
cyanide: *n.* cyanure
cyber angel: ange du cyberespace
cyber auction: enchère electronique
cyberaddict: drogué du cyberespace
cycle: *n.* cycle; bicyclette
cycle: *vi.* aller à bicyclette
cycling: *n.* cyclisme
cyclist: *n.* cycliste
cyclone: *n.* cyclone
cygnet: *n.* jeune cygne
cylinder: *n.* cylindre; rouleau
cylindrical: *adj.* cylindrique
cymbals: *n.* cymbale
cynical: *adj.* cynique; sceptique; *n.* cynique
cynicism: *n.* cynisme
cypress: *n.* cyprès
cyst: *n.* kyste
czar: *n.* tsar

$\mathcal{D}$

dab: *n.* petit peu; touche
dabble: *vi.* barboter
daddy: *n.* papa
daddy-long-legs: *n.* cousin
daffodil: *n.* narcisse; jonquille
dagger: *n.* poignard
daily: *adj.* quotidien; *n.* quotidien
daintily: *adv.* délicatement
daintiness: *n.* élégance; délicatesse
dainty: *adj.* délicat; élégant
dairy farm: laiterie
dairy produce: produits laitiers
dairy: *n.* laiterie
daisy wheel: marguerite
daisy: *n.* marguerite
dale: *n.* vallée
dally: *vi.* traîner
dam: *n.* barrage
dam: *vt.* endiguer
damage: *n.* dommage; tort
damage: *vt.* endommager; faire du tort à
damask: *n.* damas; *adj.* damassé
dame: *n.* dame; fille
damn: *adj.* maudit
damn: *vt.* condamner
damnable: *adj.* maudit
damnation: *n.* damnation
damning: *adj.* accablant
damp: *adj.* humide; *n.* humidité
damp: *vt.* humidifier
dampen: *vt.* humidifier
dampness: *n.* humidité
damson: *n.* prune de Damas
dance hall: dancing
dance: *n.* danse; soirée dansante
dance: *vt.* danser
dancer: *n.* danseur
dandelion: *n.* pissenlit
dandruff: *n.* pellicules
dandy: *adj.* génial
danger: *n.* danger
dangerous: *adj.* dangereux

dangle: *vi.* pendre
dank: *adj.* humide
dapper: *adj.* soigné
dappled: *adj.* tacheté
dare: *vi.* oser; défier
daredevil: *n.* casse-cou
daring: *n.* audace; *adj.* audacieux
dark: *adj.* sombre; obscur; *n.* obscurité; ignorance
darken: *vt.* assombrir; obscurcir
darkness: *n.* obscurité
darkroom: *n.* chambre noire
darling: *adj.* chéri
darn: *vt.* repriser
dart: *n.* dard
darts: *n.* jeu de fléchettes
dash: *n.* goutte; tiret; trait
dash: *vi.* se dépêcher
dashboard: *n.* tableau de bord
dashing: *adj.* impétueux; élégant
dastardly: *adj.* infâme
data bank: banque de données
data base: base de données
data broadcasting: diffusion de données
data medium: support de données
data processing: traitement de données
data retrieval: extraction de données
data sharing: partage de données
data warehouse: entrepôt de données
data: *n.* données
database: *n.* base de données
date of maturity: date d'échéance
date: *n.* date; rendez-vous
date: *vt.* dater; sortir avec
dated: *adj.* démodé
dative: *n.* datif
daub: *vt.* barbouiller
daughter: *n.* fillet
daunting: *adj.* décourageant
dawdle: *vi.* traîner
dawn: *n.* aube
dawn: *vi.* se lever

day laborer: journalier
day: *n.* jour; journée
daybreak: *n.* aube
daycare: *n.* garderie
daylight: *n.* lumière du jour; lumière naturelle
daytime: *n.* journée; jour
daze: *vt.* étourdir
dazed: *adj.* étourdi
dazzle: *vt.* éblouir
dazzling: *adj.* éblouissant de mots
deacon: *n.* diacre
dead march: marche funèbre
dead: *adj.* mort; m*pl.* les morts
dead-drunk: *adj.* ivre-mort
deaden: *vt.* amortir
deadly: *adj.* mortel
deadness: *n.* inertie
deaf: *adj.* sourd
deafen: *vt.* assourdir
deaf-mute: *n.* sourd-muet
deafness: *n.* surdité
deal: *n.* accord; marché
dealer: *n.* commerçant; trafiquant
dean: *n.* doyen
dear: *adj.* cher
dearness: *n.* cherté
dearth: *n.* pénurie
death certificate: acte de décès
death penalty: peine de mart
death warrant: condamnation à mort
death: *n.* mort
deathbed: *n.* lit de mort
deathblow: *n.* coup mortel
debacle: *n.* débâcle
debar: *vt.* exclure
debase: *vt.* dégrader
debasement: *n.* dégradation
debatable: *adj.* discutable
debate: *n.* débat
debatge: *vt.* discuter; examiner
debauched: *adj.* débauché
debauchery: *n.* débauche
debenture: *n.* obligation

debilitate: *vt.* débiliter
debit note: note de débit
debit: *n.* débit
debit: *vt.* débiter
debt: *n.* dette
debtor: *n.* débiteur
debunk: *vt.* démystifier
decade: *n.* décennie
decadence: *n.* décadence
decaffeinated: *adj.* décaféiné
decagon: *n.* decagone
decanter: *n.* carafe
decapitate: *vt.* décapiter
decapitation: *n.* décapitation
decay: *n.* déclin; pourissement; carie
decay: *vi.* décliner; pourrir
deceased: *adj.* décédé
deceit: *n.* tromperie
deceitful: *adj.* trompeur
deceive: *vt.* tromper
December: *n.* décembre
decency: *n.* décence; pudeur
decent: *adj.* décent; bien; bon
deception: *n.* tromperie
deceptive: *adj.* trompeur
decibel: *n.* décibel
decide: *vt.* decider
decided: *adj.* décidé
decidedly: *adv.* décidément
deciduous: *adj.* à feuilles caduques
decimal notation: notation décimale
decimal: *adj.* décimal
decimate: *vt.* décimer
decipher: *vt.* déchiffrer
decision: *n.* décision; détermination
decision-maker: décideur
decisive: *adj.* décisif
deck: *n.* pont
deck: *vt.* orner
deckchair: *n.* chaise longue
declaim: *vt.* déclamer
declamation: *n.* déclamation
declaration: *n.* déclaration
declare: *vt.* déclarer

declension: *n.* déclinaison
decline: *n.* déclin; décadence
decline: *vt.* décliner; refuser
declivity: *n.* déclivité
declutch: *vi.* débrayer
decode: *vt.* décoder
decompose: *vt.* décomposer
decomposer: *n.* décomposeur
decomposition: *n.* décomposition
decor: *n.* décor; décoration
decorate: *vt.* décorer; orner
decoration: *n.* décoration
decorative: *adj.* décoratif
decorator: *n.* décorateur
decorous: *adj.* bienséant; convenable
decorum: *n.* décorum
decoy: *n.* leurre
decrease: *n.* diminution
decrease: *vt.* diminuer
decree: *n.* décret
decree: *vt.* décréter; ordonner
decrepit: *adj.* décrépit
decrepitude: *n.* vétusté; délabrement;
décrépitude
decry: *vt.* décrier
dedicate: *vt.* dédier; consacrer
dedication: *n.* dédicace; consacration
deduce: *vt.* déduire; conclure
deducible: qui peut se déduire
deduct: *vt.* déduire; soustraire
deduction: *n.* déduction
deed: *n.* action; exploit
deeds: *npl.* titres
deem: *vt.* juger; considérer
deep: *adj.* profond
deepen: *vt.* approfondir
deep-freeze: *n.* congélateur
deeply: *adv.* profondément
deepness: *n.* profondeur
deer: *n.* cerf
deface: *vt.* défigurer
defacement: *n.* défiguration
defamation: *n.* diffamation
defame: *v.* diffamer

default: *n.* défaut; manque
default: *vi.* manquer à ses
engagements
defaulter: *n.* défaillant
defeat: *n.* défaite
defeat: *vt.* vaincre; frustrer
defect: *n.* défaut
defection: *n.* désertion
defective: *adj.* défectueux
defend: *vt.* défendre; protéger
defendant: *n.* accusé
defense: *n.* défense; protection
defenseless: *adj.* sans défense
defensive: *adj.* défensif
defer: *vt.* déférer
deference: *n.* déférence
deferential: *adj.* respectueux
defiance: *n.* défi
defiant: *adj.* provocant
deficiency: *n.* défaut; manque
deficient: *adj.* insuffisant
deficit: *n.* déficit
defile: *vt.* souiller
definable: *adj.* définissable
define: *vt.* définir
definite: *adj.* sûr; précis
definition: *n.* définition
definitive: *adj.* définitif
deflagration: *n.* déflagration
deflate: *vt.* dégonfler
deflect: *vt.* dévier
deflower: *vt.* déflorer
deform: *vt.* déformer
deformity: *n.* déformité
defraud: *vt.* escroquer
defray: *vt.* payer
defrost: *vt.* dégivrer; décongeler
defroster: *n.* dégivreur
deft: *adj.* habile
defunct: *adj.* défunt
defuse: *vt.* désamorcer
degenerate: *adj.* dégénéré
degenerate: *vi.* dégénérer
degeneration: *n.* dégénération

degradation: *n.* dégradation
degrade: *vt.* dégrader
degree: *n.* degré; diplôme
dehydrated: *adj.* déshydraté
de-ice: *vt.* dégivrer
deign: *vi.* daigner
deity: *n.* divinité
dejected: *adj.* découragé
dejection: *n.* découragement
delay: *n.* retard
delay: *vt.* retarder
delectable: *adj.* délectable
delegate: *n.* délégué
delegate: *vt.* déléguer
delegation: *n.* délégation
delete: *vt.* effacer
deliberate: *adj.* délibéré
deliberate: *vt.* examiner
deliberation: *n.* délibération
deliberative: *adj.* délibérant
delicacy: *n.* délicatesse
delicate: *adj.* délicat
delicious: *adj.* délicieux; exquis
delight: *n.* délice; enchantement
delight: *vt.* enchanter; *vi.* adorer
delighted: *adj.* enchanté
delightful: *adj.* charmant
delineate: *vt.* décrire; délimiter
delineation: *n.* tracé
delinquency: *n.* délinquance
delinquent: *n.* délinquant
delirious: *adj.* délirant
delirium: *n.* délire
deliver: *vt.* livrer; délivrer; prononcer
deliverance: *n.* libération
delivery dates: délais de livraison
delivery note: bon de livraison
delivery: *n.* livraison; accouchement
delude: *vt.* tromper
deluge: *n.* déluge
delusion: *n.* tromperie; illusion
delve: *vi.* creuser; chercher
demagogue: *n.* démagogue
demand: *n.* demande

demand: *vt.* exiger; réclamer
demanding: *adj.* exigeant
demarcation: *n.* démarcation
demean: *vi.* s'abaisser
demeanor: *n.* conduite; comportement
demented: *adj.* dément
demise: *n.* disparition
democracy: *n.* démocratie
democrat: *n.* démocrate
democratic: *adj.* démocratique
demolish: *vt.* démolir
demolition: *n.* démolition
demon: *n.* démon; diable
demonstrable: *adj.* démontrable
demonstrate: *vt.* démontrer; prouver; *vi.* manifester
demonstration: *n.* démonstration; manifestation
demonstrative: *adj.* démonstratif
demonstrator: *n.* manifestant
demoralisation: *n.* démoralisation
demoralise: *vt.* démoraliser
demote: *vt.* rétrograder
demur: *vi.* émettre une objection; rechigner
demure: *adj.* réservé
den: *n.* antre
denatured alcohol: alcool dénaturé
denial: *n.* dénégation
denomination: *n.* valeur; dénomination
denominator: *n.* dénominateur
denote: *vt.* dénoter; indiquer
denouement: *n.* dénouement
denounce: *vt.* dénoncer
dense: *adj.* dense; épais
density: *n.* densité
dent: *n.* bosse
dent: *vt.* cabosser
dental: *adj.* dentaire
dentifrice: *n.* dentifrice
dentist: *n.* dentiste
dentistry: *n.* dentisterie

denture: *n.* dentier
denude: *vt.* dénuder; dépouiller
denunciation: *n.* dénonciation
deny: *vt.* nier
deodorant: *n.* déodorant
deodorise: *vt.* déodoriser
depart: *vi.* partir
department store: grand magasin
department: *n.* département; service
departure lounge: salle d'embarquement
departure: *n.* départ
depend: *vi.* dépendre
dependable: *adj.* fiable; sûr
dependant: *n.* personne à charge
dependency: *n.* dépendance
dependent variable: variable dépendante
dependent: *adj.* dépendant
depict: *vt.* dépeindre; décrire
depleted: *adj.* réduit
deplorable: *adj.* déplorable; lamentable
deplore: *vt.* déplorer; lamenter
deploy: *vt.* déployer
depopulated: *adj.* dépeuplé
depopulation: *n.* dépopulation
deport: *vt.* déporter; expulser
deportation: *n.* déportation; expulsion
deportment: *n.* comportement
deposit account: compte de dépôts
deposit slip: bordereau de versement
deposit: *n.* dépôt; caution
deposit: *vt.* déposer
deposition: *n.* déposition
depositor: *n.* déposant
depot: *n.* dépôt
deprave: *vt.* dépraver; corrompre
depraved: *adj.* dépravé
depravity: *n.* dépravation
deprecate: *vt.* désapprouver
depreciate: *vi.* se déprécier
depreciation: *n.* dépréciation

depredation: *n.* déprédation
depress: *vt.* déprimer
depressed: *adj.* déprimé
depression: *n.* dépression
deprivation: *n.* privation
deprive: *vt.* priver
deprived: *adj.* défavorisé
depth: *n.* profondeur
deputation: *n.* députation
depute: *vt.* députer; déléguer
deputise: *vi.* remplacer
deputy: *n.* remplaçant; adjoint
derail: *vt.* faire dérailler
deranged: *adj.* dérangé
derby: *n.* chapeau melon
derelict: *adj.* abandonné; en ruines
deride: *vt.* se moquer de
derision: *n.* dérision
derisive: *adj.* ridicule; moqueur
derivable: *adj.* déductible
derivation: *n.* dérivation
derivative work: oeuvre dérivée
derivative: *n.* dérivé
derive: *vt.* dériver
derogatory: *adj.* désobligeant
derrick: *n.* derrick
désagrément: *vt.* incommoder
descant: *n.* déchant
descend: *vi.* descendre
descendant: *n.* descendant
descent: *n.* descente
describe: *vt.* décrire
description: *n.* description
descriptive entry: notice descriptive
descriptive word: mot ou parole descriptif
descriptive: *adj.* descriptif
descry: *vt.* distinguer
desecrate: *vt.* profaner
desecration: *n.* profanation
desert: *n.* désert; *adj.* désert
desert: *vt.* abandonner; déserter
deserter: *n.* déserteur
desertion: *n.* désertion

deserve: *vt.* mériter
deservedly: *adv.* à juste titre
deserving: *adj.* méritant
déshabillé: *n.* déshabillé
desideratum: *n.* desideratum
design: *vt.* concevoir; dessiner; dessein; design; dessin
designate: *vt.* désigner
designation: *n.* désignation
designedly: *adv.* exprès; délibérément
designer: *n.* créateur; styliste
desirability: *n.* avantage; attrait
desirable: *adj.* désirable
desire: *n.* désir
desire: *vt.* désirer
desirous: *adj.* désireux
desist: *vi.* abandonner
desk: *n.* bureau
desktop computer: ordinateur de bureau
desktop publishing: édition électronique; micro-édition; édition assistée par ordinateur
desktop: *n.* bureau (à l'écran)
desolate: *adj.* désert; désolé
desolation: *n.* désolation
despair: *n.* désespoir
despair: *vi.* se désespérer
despairingly: *adj.* désespérément
desperado: *n.* bandit
desperate: *adj.* désespéré
desperation: *n.* désespoir
despicable: *adj.* méprisable
despise: *vt.* mépriser
despite: *prep.* malgré
despoil: *vt.* dépouiller
despondency: *n.* abattement
despondent: *adj.* abattu
despot: *n.* despote
despotic: *adj.* despotique
despotism: *n.* despotisme
dessert: *n.* dessert
destination: *n.* destination

destine: *vt.* destiner
destiny: *n.* destin; sort
destitute: *adj.* indigent
destitution: *n.* indigence
destroy: *vt.* détruire
destruction: *n.* destruction
destructive: *adj.* destructeur
desultory: *adj.* irrégulier; sans méthode
detach: *vt.* séparer; détacher
detachable: *adj.* détachable
detachment: *n.* détachement
detail: *n.* détail
detail: *vt.* détailler
detain: *vt.* retenir; détenir
detect: *vt.* détecter
detection: *n.* détection; découverte
detective: *n.* détective
detector: *n.* détecteur
detention: *n.* détention
deter: *vt.* dissuader
detergent: *n.* détergent
deteriorate: *vt.* détériorer
deterioration: *n.* détérioration
determination: *n.* détermination
determine: *vt.* déterminer; décider
determined: *adj.* déterminé
deterrent: *n.* force de dissuasion
detest: *vt.* détester
detestable: *adj.* détestable
dethrone: *vt.* détrôner
dethronement: *n.* détrônement
detonate: *vi.* détoner
detonation: *n.* détonation
detour: *n.* déviation
detract: *vi.* nuire à
detriment: *n.* détriment
detrimental: *adj.* préjudiciable
deuce: *n.* deux; égalité
devaluation: *n.* dévaluation
devastate: *vt.* dévaster
devastating: *adj.* dévastateur
devastation: *n.* dévastation
develop: *vt.* développer

development: *n.* développement
deviate: *vi.* dévier
deviation: *n.* déviation
device: *n.* mécanisme
devil: *n.* diable; démon
devilish: *adj.* diabolique
devious: *adj.* tortueux
devise: *vt.* inventer; concevoir
devoid: *adj.* dépourvu
devolve: *vt.* déléguer
devote: *vt.* consacrer
devoted: *adj.* dévoué
devotee: *n.* partisan
devotion: *n.* dévotion
devotional: *adj.* dévot
devour: *vt.* dévorer
devout: *adj.* dévot; pieux
dew: *n.* rosée
dewy: *adj.* couvert de rosée; ingénu
dexterity: *n.* dextérité
dexterous: *adj.* adroit; habile
diabetes: *n.* diabète
diabetic: *n.* diabétique
diabolic: *adj.* diabolique
diadem: *n.* diadème
diagnosis: *n.* diagnostic
diagnostic: *adj.* diagnostique; diagnostic
diagonal: *adj.* diagonal; *n.* diagonale
diagram: *n.* diagramme
dial code: code
dial tone: tonalité
dial: *n.* cadrant
dialect: *n.* dialecte
dialogue: *n.* dialogue
diamagnetism: *n.* diamagnétisme
diameter: *n.* diamètre
diametrical: *adj.* diamétral
diamond: *n.* diamant
diamond-cutter: tailleur de diamant
diaper: *n.* couche
diaphragm: *n.* diaphragme
diarrhoea: *n.* diarrhée
diary: *n.* journal

dice: *npl.* dés
dictate: *vt.* dicter
dictation: *n.* dictée
dictatorial: *adj.* dictatorial
dictatorship: *n.* dictature
diction: *n.* diction
dictionary: *n.* dictionnaire
didactic: *adj.* didactique
die: *n.* dé
die: *vi.* mourir
diehard: *n.* réactionnaire
dielectric constant: constante diélectrique
diesel: *n.* diesel
diet: *n.* diète; régime
diet: *vi.* être au régime
dietary: *adj.* diététique
differ: *vi.* différer
difference: *n.* différence
different: *adj.* différent
differentiate: *vt.* différencier
difficult: *adj.* difficile
difficulty: *n.* difficulté
diffidence: *n.* timidité; manque d'assurance
diffident: *adj.* timide; mal assuré
diffraction: *n.* diffraction
diffuse: *vt.* diffuser; répandre; *adj.* diffus
diffusion coefficien: coefficient de diffusion
diffusion: *n.* diffusion
dig: *n.* coup
dig: *vt.* creuser
digest: *vt.* digérer
digestible: *adj.* digestible
digestion: *n.* digestion
digestive: *adj.* digestif
digger: *n.* excavatrice
digit: *n.* chiffre
digital: *adj.* digital; numérique
digitization: *n.* numérisation
digitize: *v.* numériser
dignified: *adj.* digne

dignitary: *n.* dignitaire
dignity: *n.* dignité
digress: *vi.* faire une digression
digression: *n.* digression
dike: *n.* digue
dilapidated: *adj.* délabré
dilapidation: *n.* délabrement
dilate: *vt.* dilater; se dilater
dilation: *n.* dilatation
dilemma: *n.* dilemme
diligence: *n.* assiduité
diligent: *adj.* assidu
dilute: *vt.* diluer
dilution: *n.* dilution
dim: *adj.* indistinct; faible; sombre
dim: *vt.* affaiblir; troubler
dime: *n.* pièce de dix cents
dimension: *n.* dimension
dimensional analysis: analyse dimensionelle
diminish: *vt.* diminuer
diminution: *n.* diminution
diminutive: *n.* diminutif
dimly: *adv.* indistinctement; faiblement
dimmed: *adj.* grisé; estompé
dimmer: *n.* interrupteur d'intensité
dimple: *n.* fossette
din: *n.* vacarme
dine: *vi.* dîner
dinghy: *n.* canot pneumatique
dingy: *adj.* sale; miteux
dining room: salle à manger
dinner time: heure du dîner
dinner: *n.* dîner
dinosaur: *n.* dinosaure
diocese: *n.* diocèse
dip: *vt.* tremper
diphtheria: *n.* diphtérie
diphthong: *n.* diphtongue
diploma: *n.* diplôme
diplomacy: *n.* diplomatie
diplomat: *n.* diplomate
diplomatic: *adj.* diplomatique

dipole moment: moment dipolaire
dipsomania: *n.* dipsomanie
dipstick: *n.* (auto) jauge
dire: *adj.* atroce; affreux
direct quotation: citation au style direct
direct reaction: réaction directe
direct: *adj.* direct
direct: *vt.* diriger
direction: *n.* direction; instruction
directly: *adj.* directement; immédiatement
director: *n.* directeur; administrateur
directory: *n.* annuaire
dirt: *n.* saleté
dirtiness: *n.* saleté
dirty: *adj.* sale
disability: *n.* incapacité; infirmité
disable (a system): *v.* désactiver
disabled: *adj.* infirme
disabuse: *vt.* détromper
disadvantage: *n.* désavantage
disadvantageous: *adj.* désavantageux
disaffected: *adj.* mécontent
disagree: *vi.* ne pas être d'accord
disagreeable: *adj.* désagréable
disagreement: *n.* désaccord; disallow
disagreement: *vt.* rejeter
disappear: *vi.* disparaître
disappearance: *n.* disparition
disappoint: *vt.* décevoir
disappointed: *adj.* déçu
disappointing: *adj.* décevant
disappointment: *n.* déception
disapproval: *n.* désapprobation
disapprove: *vt.* désapprouver
disarm: *vt.* désarmer
disarmament: *n.* désarmement
disarray: *n.* désordre
disaster: *n.* désastre
disastrous: *adj.* désastreux
disband: *vt.* disperser
disbelief: *n.* incrédulité
disbelieve: *vt.* ne pas croire

disburse: *vt.* débourser
discard: *vt.* jeter
discern: *vt.* discerner; percevoir
discernible: *adj.* perceptible
discerning: *adj.* perspicace
discernment: *n.* perspicacité
discharge: *n.* décharge
discharge: *vt.* décharger; régler; remplir
disciple: *n.* disciple
discipline: *n.* discipline
discipline: *vt.* discipliner
disclaim: *vt.* nier
disclaimer: *n.* dénégation
disclose: *vt.* révéler
disclosure: *n.* révélation
disco: *n.* discothèque
discoloration: *n.* décoloration
discolour: *vt.* décolorer
discomfort: *n.* incommodité
disconcert: *vt.* déconcerter
disconnect: *vt.* débrancher
disconsolate: *adj.* inconsolable
discontent: *n.* mécontentement; *adj.* mécontent
discontented: *adj.* mécontent
discontinue: *vt.* interrompre
discord: *n.* discorde
discordant: *adj.* discordant
discount rate: taux d'escompte
discount: *n.* escompte; remise
discount: vt escompter
discourage: *vt.* décourager
discouraged: *adj.* découragé
discouragement: *n.* découragement
discouraging: *adj.* décourageant
discourse: *n.* discours
discourteous: *adj.* discourtois
discourtesy: *n.* manque de courtoisie
discover: *vt.* découvrir
discovery: *n.* découverte
discredit: *vt.* discréditer
discreditable: *adj.* peu honorable
discreet: *adj.* discret

discrepancy: *n.* contradiction
discrete: *adj.* séparé; distinct
discretion: *n.* discrétion
discretionary: *adj.* discrétionnaire
discriminate: *vt.* distinguer; discriminer
discrimination: *n.* discrimination
discursive: *adj.* discursif
discuss: *vt.* discuter
discussion: *n.* discussion
disdain: *n.* dédain; mépris
disdain: *vt.* dédaigner
disdainful: *adj.* dédaigneux; méprisant
disease: *n.* maladie
diseased: *adj.* malade
disembark: *vt.* débarquer
disembarkation: *n.* débarquement
disenchant: *vt.* désenchanter
disenchanted: *adj.* désenchanté
disenchantment: *n.* désenchantement
disengage: *vt.* dégager
disentangle: *vt.* démêler
disfigure: *vt.* défigurer
disgrace: *n.* honte; scandale
disgrace: *v.* déshonorer
disgraceful: *adj.* honteux; scandaleux
disgruntled: *adj.* mécontent
disguise: *n.* déguisement
disguise: *vt.* déguiser
disgust: *n.* dégoût
disgust: *vt.* dégoûter
disgusting: *adj.* dégoûtant
dish: *n.* plat; assiette
dish: *vt.* servir dans un plat
dishcloth: *n.* torchon à vaisselle
dishearten: *vt.* démoraliser
dishevelled: *adj.* ébouriffé
dishonest: *adj.* malhonnête
dishonesty: *n.* malhonnêteté
dishonour: *n.* déshonneur
dishonour: *vt.* déshonorer
dishonourable: *adj.* déshonorable
dishtowel: *n.* torchon à vaisselle

dishwarmer: *n.* chauffe-plats
dishwasher: *n.* lave-vaisselle; plongeur
disillusion: *vt.* désillusionner
disillusioned: *adj.* désillusionné
disincentive: *n.* élément dissuasif
disinclination: *n.* aversion
disinclined: *adj.* peu enclin
disinfect: *vt.* désinfecter
disinfectant: *n.* désinfectant
disinherit: *vt.* déshériter
disintegrate: *vi.* se désintégrer
disinterested: *adj.* désintéressé
disjointed: *adj.* déréglé; décousu
disk: *n.* disque; disquette
diskette: *n.* disque; disquette
dislike: *n.* aversion
dislike: *vt.* ne pas aimer
dislocate: *vt.* disloquer
dislocation: *n.* dislocation
dislodge: *vt.* déloger
disloyal: *adj.* déloyal
disloyalty: *n.* déloyauté
dismal: *adj.* triste; lugubre
dismantle: *vt.* démonter
dismay: *n.* consternation
dismember: *vt.* démembrer
dismiss: *vt.* renvoyer; écarter; licencier
dismissal: *n.* renvoi; rejet; licenciement
dismount: *vt.* désarçonner; descendre
disobedience: *n.* désobéissance
disobedient: *adj.* désobéissant
disobey: *vt.* désobéir
disorder: *n.* désordre
disorderly: *adj.* en désordre; confus
disorganisation: *n.* désorganisation
disorganised: *adj.* désorganisé
disorientated: *adj.* désorienté
disown: *vt.* renier
disparage: *vt.* dénigrer
disparaging: *adj.* désobligeant
disparity: *n.* disparité

dispassionate: *adj.* impartial; calme
dispatch: *n.* envoi; dépêche
dispatch: *vt.* envoyer
dispel: *vt.* dissiper
dispensary: *n.* dispensaire
dispense: *vt.* dispenser; distribuer
disperse: *vt.* disperser
dispirited: *adj.* démoralisé
displace: *vt.* déplacer
display area: zone d'affichage
display: *n.* exposition; déploiement
display: *vt.* exposer; faire preuve
displeased: *adj.* mécontent
displeasure: *n.* mécontentement
disposable: *adj.* à jeter
disposal authorization: visa d'élimination
disposal list: bordereau d'élimination
disposal: *n.* disposition
dispose: *vt.* disposer
disposed: *adj.* disposé
disposition: *n.* disposition
dispossess: *vt.* déposséder
disproportionate: *adj.* disproportionné
disproportionation reaction: réaction de dismutation
disprove: *vt.* réfuter
dispute: *n.* dispute; controverse
dispute: *vt.* mettre en cause; litige
disqualify: *vt.* exclure; disqualifier
disquiet: *n.* inquiétude
disquieting: *adj.* inquiétant
disquisition: *n.* dissertation
disregard: *n.* dédain
disregard: *vt.* ne pas tenir compte de; mépriser
disreputable: *adj.* de mauvaise réputation
disrespect: *n.* irrévérence
disrespectful: *adj.* irrespectueux
disrobe: *vt.* dévêtir
disrupt: *vt.* interrompre
disruption: *n.* interruption

dissatisfaction: *n.* mécontentement
dissatisfied: *adj.* mécontent
dissect: *vt.* disséquer
dissection: *n.* dissection
disseminate: *vt.* disséminer
dissension: *n.* dissension
dissent: *n.* dissension
dissent: *vi.* être en dissension
dissenter: *n.* dissident
dissertation: *n.* thèse
dissident: *n.* dissident
dissimilar: *adj.* dissemblable
dissimilarity: *n.* dissemblance
dissimulation: *n.* dissimulation
dissipate: *vt.* dissiper
dissipation: *n.* dissipation
dissociate: *vt.* dissocier
dissociation constant: constante de dissociation
dissociation energy: énergie de dissociation
dissociation: *n.* dissociation
dissolute: *adj.* dissolu
dissolution: *n.* dissolution
dissolve: *vt.* dissoudre; *vi.* se dissoudre
dissonance: *n.* dissonance
dissuade: *vt.* dissuader
distance: *n.* distance
distance: *vt.* distancer
distant: *adj.* distant
distaste: *n.* dégoût
distasteful: *adj.* désagréable
distend: *vt.* distendre
distil: *vt.* distiller
distillation: *n.* distillation
distillery: *n.* distillerie
distinct: *adj.* distinct
distinction: *n.* distinction
distinctive: *adj.* distinctif
distinctness: *n.* clarté
distinguish: *vt.* distinguer; discerner
distort: *vt.* déformer
distorted: *adj.* déformé

distortion: *n.* distortion
distract: *vt.* distraire
distracted: *adj.* distrait
distraction: *n.* distraction; confusion
distraught: *adj.* éperdu
distress: *n.* souffrance; détresse
distress: *vt.* désoler; affliger
distressing: *adj.* affligeant
distribute: *vt.* distribuer; répartir
distribution: *n.* distribution
distributor: *n.* distributeur
district attorney: procureur de la république
district: *n.* district
distrustful: *adj.* méfiant
disturb: *vt.* déranger
disturbance: *n.* dérangement; trouble
disturbed: *adj.* troublé
disturbing: *adj.* troublant
disuse: *n.* désuétude
disused: *adj.* abandonné
ditch: *n.* fossé
dither: *vi.* hésiter
ditto: *adv.* idem
ditty: *n.* chansonnette
diuretic: *adj.* diurétique
dive: *vi.* plonger
diver: *n.* plongeur
diverge: *vi.* diverger
divergence: *n.* divergence
divergent: *adj.* divergent
diverse: *adj.* divers; différent
diversion: *n.* diversion
diversity: *n.* diversité
divert: *vt.* dévier; divertir
divest: *vt.* dénuder; dépouiller
divide: *vt.* diviser; *vi.* se diviser
dividend: *n.* dividende
divine: *adj.* divin
diving board: plongeoir
diving: *n.* plongeon
divinity: *n.* divinité
divisible: *adj.* divisible
division: *n.* division

divisor: *n.* diviseur
divorce: *n.* divorce
divorce: *vi.* divorcer
divorced: *adj.* divorcé
divulge: *vt.* divulguer
dizziness: *n.* vertige
dizzy: *adj.* pris de vertige
do: *vt.* faire
docile: *adj.* docile
dock: *n.* dock
dock: *vi.* entrer aux docks
docker: *n.* docker
dockyard: *n.* chantier m naval
doctor: *n.* docteur
doctrinal: *adj.* doctrinal
doctrine: *n.* doctrine
document: documenter; relater; montrer en détails
document: *n.* document
documentary evidence: pièces justificatives
documentary interview: interview-document
documentary sequence: chaîne documentaire
documentary: *adj.* documentaire
documentation: *n.* documentation; documents
dodge: *vt.* esquiver
doe: *n.* biche
dog kennel: refuge pour chiens
dog: *n.* chien
dogged: *adj.* tenace
dogmatic: *adj.* dogmatique
do-it-yourself: *n.* bricolage
doleful: *adj.* lugubre; triste
doll: *n.* poupée
dollar: *n.* dollar
dolphin: *n.* dauphin
domain: *n.* domaine
dome: *n.* dôme
domestic: *adj.* domestique
domesticate: *vt.* domestiquer
domestication: *n.* domestication

domesticity: *n.* domesticité
domicile: *n.* domicile
dominance: *n.* domination; prépondérance; dominance
dominant: *adj.* dominant
dominate: *vi.* dominer
domination: *n.* domination
domineer: *vi.* dominer
domineering: *adj.* autoritaire
dominion: *n.* domination
dominoes: *npl.* domino
donate: *vt.* donner; faire don de
donation: *n.* donation
donkey: *n.* âne
donor: *n.* donneur; donateur
doodle: *vi.* gribouiller
doom: *n.* sort
door handle: poignée de porte
door: *n.* porte
doorbell: *n.* sonnette
doorman: *n.* portier
doormat: *n.* paillasson
doorplate: *n.* plaque
doorstep: *n.* pas de porte
doorway: *n.* entrée
dormant: *adj.* latent; dormant
dormer window: lucarne
dormitory: *n.* dortoir
dormouse: *n.* loir
dosage: *n.* dose; dosage
dose: *n.* dose
dose: *vt.* doser; donner une dose à
dossier: *n.* dossier
dot: *n.* point
dote: *vi.* adorer
dotingly: *adv.* avec adoration
double bed: lit m à deux places
double chin: double menton
double entry: comptabilité en partie double
double negative: double négation
double room: *n.* chambre pour deux
double: *adj.* double; *n.* double
double: *vt.* doubler

double-breasted: *adj.* croisé
double-dealing: *n.* duplicité
double-edged: *adj.* à double tranchant
double-lock: *vt.* fermer à double tour
doubly: *adv.* doublement
doubt: *n.* doute
doubt: *vt.* douter de
doubtful: *adj.* douteux
doubtless: *adv.* indubitablement
dough: *n.* pâte
douse: *vt.* éteindre
dove: *n.* colombe
dovecot: *n.* colombier
dowdy: *adj.* mal habillé
down payment: acompte
down: *n.* duvet; *prep.* en bas
downcast: *adj.* démoralisé; baissé
downfall: *n.* ruine
downhearted: *adj.* découragé
downhill: *adv.* en descendant
download: *v.* télécharger
downloading: *n.* téléchargement
downpour: *n.* grosse averse
downright: *adj.* manifeste
downsizing: *n.* micronisation; diminution des effectifs
downstairs: *adv.* en bas
down-to-earth: *adj.* pratique; terre à terre
downtown: *adv.* dans le centre; en ville
downward(s): *adv.* vers le bas
dowry: *n.* dot
doze: *vi.* somnoler
dozen: *n.* douzaine
dozy: *adj.* somnolent
drab: *adj.* gris; morne
draft: *n.* brouillon; traite
drag: *n.* drague; ennui
drag: *vt.* tirer
dragnet: *n.* seine; filet
dragon: *n.* dragon
dragonfly: *n.* libellule

drain: *n.* tuyau d'écoulement
drain: *vt.* drainer; vider
drainage: *n.* drainage
drainboard: *n.* égouttoir
drainpipe: *n.* tuyau d'écoulement
drake: *n.* canard mâle
dram: *n.* petit verre
drama: *n.* drame
dramatic: *adj.* dramatique
dramatise: *vt.* dramatiser
dramatist: *n.* dramaturge
drape: *vt.* draper
drastic: *adj.* radical
draught: *n.* courant d'air
draughts: *npl.* jeu de dames
draughtsman: *n.* dessinateur industriel
draughty: *adj.* exposé aux courants d'air
draw: *vt.* tirer; dessiner
drawback: *n.* désavantage; inconvénient
drawer: *n.* tiroir; tireur
drawing board: planche à dessin
drawing room: salon
drawing: *n.* dessin
drawl: *vi.* parler d'une voix traînante
dread: *n.* terreur
dread: *vt.* redouter; craindre
dreadful: *adj.* horrible
dream: *n.* rêve
dream: *vi.* rêver
dreary: *adj.* triste; morne
dredge: *vt.* draguer
drench: *vt.* tremper
dress: *n.* robe
dress: *vt.* habiller; panser
dresser: *n.* buffet
dressing gown: peignoir
dressing room: loge; garde-robe
dressing table: coiffeuse
dressing: *n.* pansement; sauce
dressmaker: *n.* couturier
dressy: *adj.* élégant

dribble: *vi.* tomber goutte à goutte
dried: *adj.* séché
drift: *n.* amoncellement; courant; sens
drift: *vi.* aller à la dérive
driftwood: *n.* bois flottant
drill: *n.* perceuse; exercice
drill: *vt.* percer
drink: *n.* boisson
drink: *vt.* boire
drinkable: *adj.* potable; buvable
drinker: *n.* buveur
drinking bout: bcuvcrie
drinking water: eau potable
drip: *n.* goutte; goutte-à-goutte
drip: *vi.* goutter
dripping: *n.* graisse
drive: *n. n.* promenade en voiture; allée; entrée; (for disk) lecteur; unité
drive: *vt.* conduire; pousser
drivel: *n.* imbécilités
drivel: *vi.* baver; dire des imbécilités
driver: *n.* conducteur;chauffeur
driveway: *n.* allée; entrée
driving instructor: moniteur d'auto-école
driving licence: permis de conduire
driving school: auto-école
driving test: examen du permis de conduire
driving: *n.* conduite
drizzle: *vi.* bruiner
droll: *adj.* drôle
drone: *n.* bourdonnement
droop: *vi.* tomber
drop: *n.* goutte
drop: *vt.* laisser tomber
drop-down menu: menu déroulant
drop-out: *n.* marginal
dropper: *n.* compte-gouttes
dross: *n.* scories
drought: *n.* sécheresse
drown: *vt.* noyer
drowsiness: *n.* somnolence

drowsy: *adj.* somnolent
drudgery: *n.* corvée
drug addict: drogué
drug: *n.* drogue
drug: *vt.* droguer
druggist: *n.* pharmacien
drugstore: *n.* pharmacie
drum majorette: majorette
drum: *n.* tambour
drum: *vi.* jouer du tambour
drummer: *n.* batteur
drumstick: *n.* baguette de tambour
drunk: *adj.* ivre
drunkard: *n.* ivrogne
drunken: *adj.* ivre
drunkenness: *n.* ivresse
dry rot: pourriture
dry: *adj.* sec
dry: *vt.* faire sécher; sécher
dry-cleaning: nettoyage à sec
dryer: *n.* séchoir
dry-goods store: *n.* mercerize
dryness: *n.* sécheresse
dual: *adj.* double
dual-purpose: *adj.* à double emploi
dubbed: *adj.* doublé
dubious: *adj.* douteux
duck: *n.* canard
duck: *vt.* plonger
duckling: *n.* caneton
dud: *adj.* nul; faux
due: *adj.* dû; due; *n.* droit; chose due
duel: *n.* duel
duet: *n.* duo
dull: *adj.* terne; insipide; gris
dull: *vt.* ternir; atténuer
duly: *adv.* dûment; en temps voulu
dumb: *adj.* muet
dumbbell: *n.* haltère
dumbfounded: *adj.* interloqué
dummy: *n.* mannequin; prête-nom
dump: *n.* tas
dump: *vt.* jeter; laisser tomber
dumping: *n.* dumping

dumpling: *n.* boulette de pâte
dumpy: *adj.* boulot
dunce: *n.* cancre
dune: *n.* dune
dung: *n.* fumier
dungarees: *npl.* salopette
dungeon: *n.* donjon; cachot
dupe: *n.* dupe
dupe: *vt.* duper
duplex: *n.* duplex
duplicate: *n.* duplicata; copie
duplicate: *vt.* dupliquer
duplicity: *n.* duplicité
durability: *n.* durabilité
durable: *adj.* durable
duration: *n.* durée
duress: *n.* contrainte
during: *prep.* pendant
dusk: *n.* crépuscule
dust jacket: jacquette
dust: *n.* poussière
dust: *vt.* épousse-ter
duster: *n.* chiffon
dusty: *adj.* poussiéreux
duteous: *adj.* fidèle; loyal
dutiful: *adj.* obéissant; soumis
duty paid: dédouané
duty: *n.* devoir; obligation
duty-free: *adj.* hors taxe
dwarf: *n.* nain; naine
dwarf: *vt.* rapetisser
dwell: *vi.* habiter; vivre
dwelling: *n.* habitation; domicile
dwindle: *vi.* diminuer
dye: *n.* teinture
dye: *vt.* teindre
dyeing: *n.* teinturerie; teinture
dyer: *n.* teinturier
dye-works: *npl.* teinturerie
dying: *adj.* mourant; agonisant
dynamic: *adj.* dynamique
dynamics: *n.* dynamique
dynamite: *n.* dynamite
dynamiter: *n.* dynamiteur

dynamo: *n.* dynamo
dynasty: *n.* dynastie
dysentery: *n.* dysenterie
dyspepsia: *n.* dyspepsie
dyspeptic: *adj.* dyspeptique

ς

eager: *adj.* enthousiaste; ardent
eagerness: *n.* enthousiasme; ardeur; désir
eagle: *n.* aigle
eagle-eyed: *adj.* aux yeux d'aigle
eaglet: *n.* aiglon
ear: *n.* oreille; ouïe
earache: *n.* mal d'oreille
eardrum: *n.* tympan
early: *adj.* premier
earmark: *vt.* désigner
earn: *vt.* gagner
earnest: *adj.* sérieux
earnestness: *n.* sérieux
earnings: *npl.* revenus
earphones: *npl.* écouteurs
earring: *n.* boucle d'oreille
earth: *n.* terre
earthen: *adj.* de terre
earthenware: *n.* poterie
earthquake: *n.* tremblement de terre
earthworm: *n.* ver de terre
earthy: *adj.* terreux; truculent
earwig: *n.* perce-oreille
ease: *n.* aise facilité
ease: *vt.* apaiser; soulager
easel: *n.* chevalet
easily: *adv.* facilement
easiness: *n.* facilité
east: *n.* est; orient
Easter: *n.* Pâques
easterly: *adj.* d'est
eastern: *adj.* de l'est; oriental
eastward(s): *adv.* vers l'est
easy chair: fauteuil
easy: *adj.* facile; commode
eat: *vt.* manger
eatable: *adj.* comestible; mangeable
eavesdrop: *vt.* espionner; écouter discrètement
ebb: *n.* reflux
ebb: *vi.* refluer; décliner
ebony: *n.* ébène

ebullience: *n.* exubérance
ebullient: *adj.* exubérant
ebullioscopy: *n.* ébulliométrie
eccentric: *adj.* excentrique
eccentricity: *n.* excentricité
ecclesiastic: *adj.* ecclésiastique
echo: *n.* écho
echo: *vi.* résonner
eclectic: *adj.* éclectique
eclecticism: *n.* éclectisme
eclipse: *n.* éclipse
eclipse: *vt.* éclipser
ecologist: *n.* écologiste
ecology: *n.* écologie
economic: *adj.* économique
economical: *adj.* économique
economise: *vt.* économiser
economist: *n.* économiste
economy: *n.* économie
ecosystem: *n.* écosystème
ecstasy: *n.* extase
ecstatic: *adj.* extatique
eczema: *n.* eczéma
eddy: *n.* tourbillon
eddy: *vi.* tourbillonner
edge: *n.* fil; pointe; bord; acrimonie
edge: *vt.* border; affiler
edging: *n.* bordure
edgy: *adj.* nerveux
edible: *adj.* mangeable; comestible
edict: *n.* édit; décret
edification: *n.* édification
edify: *vt.* édifier
edit: *vt.* diriger; rédiger; couper
edition: *n.* édition
editor: *n.* directeur; rédacteur
editorial: *adj.* rédactionnel; *n.* éditorial
educate: *vt.* éduquer; instruire
education: *n.* éducation; instruction
educational: *adj.* éducatif; pédagogique
edutainment software: logiciel ludo-éducatif; ludacticiel

eel: *n.* anguille
eerie: *adj.* inquiétant; surnaturel
efface: *vt.* effacer
effect: *n.* effet; réalité
effect: *vt.* effectuer
effective: *adj.* efficace; effectif
effectiveness: *n.* efficacité
effectual: *adj.* efficace
effeminacy: *n.* caractère efféminé
effeminate: *adj.* efféminé
effervescence: *n.* effervescence
effete: *adj.* stérile; faible
efficacious: *adj.* efficace
efficacy: *n.* efficacité
efficiency: *n.* efficacité
efficient: *adj.* efficace
effigy: *n.* effigie
effort: *n.* effort
effortless: *adj.* sans effort
effrontery: *n.* effronterie
effusion: *n.* épanchement;
écoulement; fuite; débordement;
effusion
effusive: *adj.* chaleureux; expansif
egg: *n.* oeuf
eggcup: *n.* coquetier
eggplant: *n.* aubergine
eggshell: *n.* coquille d'oeuf
egoism: *n.* égoïsme
egoist: *n.* égoïste
egregious: *adj.* flagrant
eiderdown: *n.* édredon
eight: *adj.* huit
eighteen: *adj.* dix-huit
eighteenth: *adj.* dix-huitième
eighth: *adj.* huitième
eightieth: *adj.* quatre-vingtième
eighty: *adj.* quatre-vingt
either: *pron.* n'importe lequel;
n'importe laquelle; *conj.* ou; soit
ejaculate: *vi.* s'exclamer; éjaculer
ejaculation: *n.* exclamation;
éjaculation
eject: *vt.* éjecter; expulser

ejection: *n.* éjection; expulsion
ejector seat: siège éjectable
eke: *vt.* augmenter; prolonger
elaborate: *adj.* élaboré; compliqué
elaborate: *vt.* élaborer
elaboration: *n.* élaboration
elapse: *vi.* s'écouler
elastic: *adj.* élastique
elasticity: *n.* élasticité
elated: *adj.* exultant
elation: *n.* exultation
elbow: *n.* coude
elbow: *vt.* pousser du coude
elbow-room: espace; liberté; latitude
elder: *n.* sureau; *adj.* aimé
elderly: *adj.* d'un âge avancé
eldest: *adj.* aîné
elect: *vt.* élire; choisir
election: *n.* élection; choix
electioneering: *n.* propagande
électorale
elective: *adj.* facultatif; électif
elector: *n.* électeur
electoral: *adj.* électoral
electorate: *n.* électorat
electric blanket: couverture
électrique
electric cooker: cuisinière électrique
electric fire: radiateur électrique
electrical: *adj.* électrique
electrician: *n.* électricien
electricity: *n.* électricité
electrify: *vt.* électriser
electrolisys: *n.* électrolyse
electrolyte: *n.* électrolyte
electromagnet: *n.* électro-aimant
electromagnetic radiation: radiation
électromagnétique
electromagnetic waves: ondes
électromagnétiques
electron affinity: affinité
électronique
electron scavenger reaction:
réaction de capture

electron: *n.* électron
electronegativity: *n.* électronégativité
electronic publishing: édition électronique
electronic source: source électronique
electronic: *adj.* électronique
electropositive: *adj.* électropositif
elegance: *n.* élégance
elegant: *adj.* élégant
elegy: *n.* élégie
element: *n.* élément
elementary reaction: réaction élémentaire
elementary: *adj.* élémentaire
elephant: *n.* éléphant
elephantine: *adj.* lourd
elevate: *vt.* élever; hausser
elevation: *n.* élévation; hauteur
elevator: *n.* ascenseur
eleven: *adj.* onze
eleventh: *adj.* onzième
elf: *n.* elfe
elicit: *vt.* tirer; obtenir
eligibility: *n.* éligibilité
eligible: *adj.* éligible
eliminate: *vt.* éliminer; écarter
elk: *n.* élan
ellipsis: *n.* ellipse; point de suspension
elliptical: *adj.* elliptique
elm: *n.* orme
elocution: *n.* élocution
elocutionist: *n.* professeur d'élocution
elongate: *vt.* allonger
elope: *vi.* s'échapper; s'enfuir
elopement: *n.* fugue; évasion
eloquence: *n.* éloquence
eloquent: *adj.* éloquent
else: *pron.* autre
elsewhere: *adv.* ailleurs
elucidate: *vt.* élucider; expliquer
elucidation: *n.* élucidation; explication

elude: *vt.* éluder; éviter
elusive: *adj.* insaisissable
emaciated: *adj.* émacié
e-mail: *n.* courrier éléctronique; courriel
emanate: *vi.* émaner
emancipate: *vt.* émanciper; affranchir
emancipation: *n.* émancipation; affranchissement
embalm: *vt.* embaumer
embankment: *n.* talus; quai
embargo: *n.* embargo
embark: *vt.* embarquer
embarkation: *n.* embarcation
embarrass: *vt.* embarrasser
embarrassed: *adj.* embarrassé
embarrassing: *adj.* embarrassant
embarrassment: *n.* embarras
embassy: *n.* ambassade
embed: *vt.* enchâsser; intégrer
embellish: *vt.* embellir; orner
embellishment: *n.* ornement
ember: *n.* braise
embezzle: *vt.* détourner
embezzlement: *n.* détournement de fonds
embitter: *vt.* rendre amer
emblem: *n.* emblème
emblematical: *adj.* emblématique; symbolique
embodiment: *n.* incorporation; incarnation
embody: *vt.* incorporer; incarner
embrace: *n.* étreinte
embrace: *vt.* étreindre; comprendre
embroider: *vt.* broder
embroidery: *n.* broderie
embroil: *vt.* impliquer
embryo: *n.* embryon
emendation: *n.* correction
emerald: *n.* émeraude
emerge: *vi.* émerger; apparaître
emergency cord: sonnette d'alarme
emergency exit: sortie de secours

emergency landing: atterrissage forcé

emergency meeting: réunion extraordinaire

emergency: *n.* urgence

emery: *n.* émeri

emigrant: *n.* émigré

emigrate: *vi.* émigrer

emigration: *n.* émigration

eminence: *n.* hauteur; éminence; excellence

eminent: *adj.* élevé; éminent; distingué

emission: *n.* émission

emit: *vt.* émettre

emotion: *n.* émotion

emotional: *adj.* émotionnel; ému

emotive: *adj.* émotif

emperor: *n.* empereur

emphasis: *n.* emphase

emphasise: *vt.* souligner; accentuer

emphatic: *adj.* emphatique

empire: *n.* empire

employ: *vt.* employer

employee: *n.* employé

employer: *n.* employeur

employment: *n.* emploi; travail

emporium: *n.* grand magasin

empress: *n.* impératrice

emptiness: *n.* vide; futilité

empty: *adj.* vide; vain

empty: *vt.* vider

empty-handed: *adj.* les mains vides

emulate: *vt.* imiter

emulsion: *n.* émulsion

en route: *adv.* en route

enable: *vt.* permettre

enact: *vt.* promulguer; représenter

enamel: *n.* émail

enamel: *vt.* émailler

enamour: *vt.* s'éprendre de

encamp: *vi.* camper

encampment: *n.* campement

encase: *vt.* entourer

enchant: *vt.* enchanter

enchanting: *adj.* enchanteur

enchantment: *n.* enchantement

encircle: *vt.* encercler

enclose: *vt.* entourer; inclure; joindre

enclosure: *n.* clôture; enceinte

encompass: *vt.* comprendre

encore: *adv.* encore

encounter: *n.* rencontre; combat

encounter: *vt.* rencontrer

encourage: *vt.* encourager

encouragement: *n.* encouragement

encroach: *vi.* empiéter

encroachment: *n.* empiètement

encrusted: *adj.* incrusté

encryption software: logiciel de cryptage

encryption: chiffrement; cryptage

encumber: *vt.* embarrasser

encumbrance: *n.* embarras

encyclical: *adj.* encyclique

encyclopedia: *n.* encyclopédie

end point: extrémité

end: *n.* fin; extrémité; bout

end: *vt.* terminer; conclure

endanger: *vt.* mettre en danger

endear: *vt.* faire aimer

endearing: *adj.* attachant

endearment: *n.* expression de tendresse

endeavour: *n.* effort

endeavour: *vi.* s'efforcer; tenter

endemic: *adj.* endémique

ending: *n.* fin; conclusion; dénouement; terminaison

endive: *n.* endive

endless: *adj.* infini; perpétuel

endorse: *vt.* endosser; approuver

endorsement: *n.* endos; approbation

endorser: *n.* endosseur

endothermic: *adj.* endothermique

endow: *vt.* doter

endowment: *n.* dotation

endurable: *adj.* supportable

endurance: *n.* endurance; patience
endure: *vt.* supporter
endways; endwise: *adv.* debout
enemy: *n.* ennemi
energetic: *adj.* énergique; vigoureux
energy level diagram: diagramme des niveaux d'énergie
energy pyramid: énergie pyramide
energy transfer: transfer d'énergie
energy: *n.* énergie; force
enervate: *vt.* débiliter
enfeeble: *vt.* affaiblir
enfold: *vt.* envelopper
enforce: *vt.* mettre en vigueur
enforced: *adj.* forcé
enfranchise: *vt.* émanciper
engage: *vt.* aborder; engager
engaged: *adj.* fiancé; occupé
engagement: *n.* engagement;combat; fiançailles
engaging: *adj.* attrayant
engender: *vt.* engendrer; produire
engine driver: *n.* conducteur
engine: *n.* moteur; locomotive
engineer: *n.* ingénieur; mécanicien
engineering: *n.* ingénierie
England: *n.* Angleterre
English: *n.* Anglais; *adj.* Anglais
engrave: *vt.* graver
engraving: *n.* gravure
engrossed: *adj.* absorbé
engulf: *vt.* submerger
enhance: *vt.* améliorer; réhausser
enhanced version (of a software): version améliorée (d'un logiciel)
enhancement: *n.* amélioration
enigma: *n.* énigme
enjoy: *vt.* aimer; jouir de
enjoyable: *adj.* agréable; amusant
enjoyment: *n.* plaisir; jouissance
enlarge: *vt.* agrandir; étendre; dilater
enlargement: *n.* agrandissement; extension; dilatation
enlighten: *vt.* éclairer

enlightened: *adj.* éclairé
enlistment: *n.* recrutement
enliven: *vt.* animer; égayer
enmity: *n.* inimitié; haine
enormity: *n.* énormité; atrocité
enormous: *adj.* énorme
enough: *adv.* suffisamment; assez
enounce: *vt.* déclarer
enquire: *vi.* inquire
enrage: *vt.* rendre furieux
enrapture: *vt.* enchanter; enthousiasmer
enrich: *vt.* enrichir; orner
enrichment: *n.* enrichissement
enrol: *vt.* enrôler inscrire
enrolment: *n.* inscription
ensign: *n.* drapeau; porte-étendard; pavillon
enslave: *vt.* asservir
ensue: *vi.* s'ensuivre
ensure: *vt.* assurer
entail: *vt.* impliquer; entraîner
entangle: *vt.* emmêler; embrouiller
entanglement: *n.* emmêlement
enter data (to): entrer des données
enter key: touche entrée
enter: *vt.* entrer dans; inscrire
enterprise: *n.* entreprise
enterprising: *adj.* entreprenant
entertain: *vt.* divertir; recevoir; avoir
entertainer: *n.* artiste
entertaining: *adj.* divertissant; amusant
entertainment: *n.* divertissement; passe-temps
enthalpy: *n.* enthalpie
enthralled: *adj.* captivé
enthralling: *adj.* captivant
enthrone: *vt.* introniser
enthusiasm: *n.* enthousiasme
enthusiast: *n.* enthousiaste
enthusiastic: *adj.* enthousiaste
entice: *vt.* tenter; séduire
entire: *adj.* entier; complet; parfait

entirety: *n.* intégralité
entitle: *vt.* intituler; conférer un droit à
entitled: *adj.* intitulé
entity: *n.* entité
entourage: *n.* entourage
entrails: *npl.* entrailles
entrance examination: examen d'entrée
entrance fee: droit d'inscription
entrance hall: vestibule
entrance ramp: bretelle d'accès
entrance: *n.* entrée; admission
entrant: *n.* participant; candidat
entrap: *vt.* piéger
entreat: *vt.* implorer; supplier
entreaty: *n.* supplication; prière
entrepreneur: *n.* entrepreneur
entropy: *n.* entropie
entrust: *vt.* confier
entry form: feuille d'inscription
entry phone: interphone
entry: *n.* entrée
entwine: *vt.* entrelacer
enumerate: *vt.* énumérer
enunciate: *vt.* énoncer
enunciation: *n.* énonciation
envelop: *vt.* envelopper
envelope: *n.* enveloppe
enviable: *adj.* enviable
envious: *adj.* envieux
environment: *n.* environnement
environmental: *adj.* relatif à l'environnement
envisage: *vt.* envisager
envoy: *n.* envoyé
envy: *n.* envie
envy: *vt.* envier
enzyme: *n.* enzyme
ephemeral: *adj.* éphémère
epic: *adj.* épique; *n.* récit épique
epidemic: *adj.* épidémique; *n.* épidémie
epilepsy: *n.* épilepsie

epileptic: *adj.* épileptique
epilogue: *n.* épilogue
Epiphany: *n.* Epiphanie
episcopacy: *n.* épiscopat
episcopal: *adj.* épiscopal
episcopalian: *n.* épiscopalien
episode: *n.* épisode
epistle: *n.* épître
epistolary: *adj.* épistolaire
epithet: *n.* épithète
epitome: *n.* modèle; résumé
epitomise: *vt.* incarner; résumer
epoch: *n.* époque
equable: *adj.* uniforme
equal: *adj.* égal; semblable; *n.* égal
equal: *vt.* égaler
equalise: *vt.* égaliser
equaliser: *n.* point égalisateur
equality: *n.* égalité
equally: *adv.* également
equanimity: *n.* équanimité
equate: *vt.* comparer; assimiler
equation: *n.* équation
equator: *n.* équateur
equatorial: *adj.* équatorial
equestrian: *adj.* équestre
equilateral triangle: triangle équilatéral
equilateral: *adj.* équilatéral
equilibrium constant: constante d'équilibre
equilibrium: *n.* équilibre
equinox: *n.* équinoxe
equip: *vt.* équiper
equipment: *n.* équipement
equitable: *adj.* équitable; impartial
equity: *n.* équité; justice; impartialité
equivalence point: point d'équivalence
equivalent fractions: fractions équivalentes
equivalent ratio: rapport équivalent
equivalent: *adj.* équivalent
equivocal: *adj.* équivoque; ambigu

equivocate: *vt.* équivoquer; user d'équivoques
equivocation: *n.* faux-fuyants
era: *n.* ère
eradicate: *vt.* supprimer; extirper
eradication: *n.* suppression; extirpation
erase: *vt.* effacer; gommer
eraser: *n.* gomme
erect: *adj.* droit; debout
erect: *vt.* ériger; élever
erection: *n.* érection; structure
ermine: *n.* hermine
erode: *vt.* éroder; ronger
erosion: *n.* érosion
erotic: *adj.* érotique
err: *vi.* se tromper
errand boy: garçon de courses; messager
errand: *n.* message; commission
erratic: *adj.* changeant; irrégulier
erroneous: *adj.* erroné; faux
error: *n.* erreur
erudite: *adj.* érudit
erudition: *n.* érudition
erupt: *vi.* entrer en éruption; faire éruption
eruption: *n.* éruption
escalate: *vi.* monter en flèche; s'intensifier
escalation: *n.* montée en flèche; intensification
escalator: *n.* escalier roulant
escapade: *n.* fredaine
escape: *n.* évasion; fuite
escape: *vt.* éviter; échapper à
escapism: *n.* évasion de la réalité
eschew: *vt.* fuir; éviter
escort: *n.* escorte
escort: *vt.* escorter
esoteric: *adj.* ésotérique
especial: *adj.* spécial
espionage: *n.* espionnage
esplanade: *n.* esplanade

espouse: *vt.* épouser
essay: *n.* essai
essence: *n.* essence
essential: *n.* essentiel; *adj.* essentiel; principal
establish: *vt.* établir; fonder; démontrer
establishment: *n.* établissement; fondation; institution
estate: *n.* état; domaine; biens
esteem: *n.* estime; considération
esteem: *vt.* estimer; apprécier
esthetic: *adj.* esthétique
estimate: *vt.* estimer; évaluer
estimation: *n.* estimation; évaluation
estrange: *vt.* éloigner; séparer
estranged: *adj.* séparé
estrangement: *n.* séparation; distance
estuary: *n.* estuaire
etch: *vt.* graver à l'eau forte
etching: *n.* gravure à l'eau forte
eternal: *adj.* éternel; perpétuel
eternity: *n.* éternité
ether: *n.* éther
ethical: *adj.* éthique; moral
ethnic: *adj.* ethnique
ethos: *n.* génie; esprit
etiquette: *n.* étiquette
etymological: *adj.* étymologique
etymologist: *n.* étymologiste
etymology: *n.* étymologie
Eucharist: *n.* Eucharistie
eulogy: *n.* éloge
eunuch: *n.* eunuque
euphemism: *n.* euphémisme
euro: *n.* euro
Europe: *n.* Europe
European: *n.* Européen; *adj.* européen
evacuate: *vt.* évacuer
evacuation: *n.* évacuation
evade: *vt.* éviter; échapper à
evaluate: *vt.* évaluer
evangelical: *adj.* évangélique

evangelist: *n.* évangéliste
evaporate: *vt.* faire évaporer;
s'évaporer; se volatiliser
evaporated milk: lait condensé
evaporation: *n.* évaporation
evasion: *n.* dérobade
evasive: *adj.* évasif
eve: *n.* veille
even: *adj.* égal; uni; pair
even: *vt.* égaliser; unir
even-handed: *adj.* impartial;
équitable
evening class: cours du soir
evening dress: robe du soir; tenue de
soirée
evening: *n.* soir; soirée
evenness: *n.* égalité; uniformité;
régularité; impartialité
event: *n.* événement; épreuve
eventful: *adj.* mouvementé
eventual: *adj.* final
eventuality: *n.* éventualité
ever: *adv.* toujours; jamais; déjà
evergreen: *adj.* à feuilles
persistantes; *n.* arbre à feuilles
persistantes
everlasting: *adj.* éternel
evermore: *adv.* toujours
every: *adj.* chacun; chacune; where
partout
evict: *vt.* expulser
eviction: *n.* expulsion
evidence: *n.* évidence; témoignage;
preuve
evidence: *vt.* témoigner de
evident: *adj.* évident; manifeste
evil: *adj.* mauvais; malveillant; *n.* mal
evil-minded: *adj.* malintentionné
evocative: *adj.* évocateur
evoke: *vt.* évoquer
evolution: *n.* évolution
evolve: *vt.* développer
ewe: *n.* brebis
exacerbate: *vt.* exacerber

exact: *adj.* exact
exact: *vt.* exiger
exacting: *adj.* exigeant
exaction: *n.* exaction; extorsion
exactly: *adj.* exactement
exactness; exactitude: *n.* exactitude
exaggerate: *vt.* exagérer
exaggeration: *n.* exagération
exalt: *vt.* exalter; élever
exaltation: *n.* exaltation; élévation
exalted: *adj.* exalté; élevé
examination: *n.* examen
examine: *vt.* examiner
examiner: *n.* examinateur
example: *n.* exemple
exasperate: *vt.* exaspérer; irriter
exasperation: *n.* exaspération;
irritation
excavate: *vt.* exhumer; creuser
excavation: *n.* excavation
exceed: *vt.* excéder; dépasser
exceedingly: *adv.* trop; extrêmement
excell: *vt.* surpasser; exceller
excellence: *n.* excellence; supériorité
excellency: *n.* excellence
excellent: *adj.* excellent
except: *vt.* excepter; exclure; *prep.*
excepté; à l'exception de
exception: *n.* exception
exceptional: *adj.* exceptionnel
excerpt: *n.* extrait
excess: *n.* excès
excessive: *adj.* excessif
exchange rate: taux de change
exchange: *n.* échange; change
exchange: *vt.* échanger; permuter
excise: *n.* taxe
excitability: *n.* excitabilité
excitable: *adj.* excitable
excite: *vt.* exciter; animer;
enthousiasmer; stimuler
excited: *adj.* animé; enthousiaste;
excité

excitement: *n.* animation; enthousiasme
exciting: *adj.* passionnant; stimulant
exclaim: *vi.* s'exclamer
exclamation mark: *n.* point d'exclamation
exclamation: *n.* exclamation
exclamatory: *adj.* exclamatif
exclude: *vt.* exclure
exclusion: *n.* exclusion; exception
exclusive: *adj.* exclusif
excommunication: *n.* excommunion
excrement: *n.* excrément
excruciating: *adj.* atroce; horrible
exculpate: *vt.* disculper; justifier
excursion: *n.* excursion; digression
excusable: *adj.* excusable
excuse: *n.* excuse
excuse: *vt.* excuser; pardonner
execute: *vt.* exécuter
execution: *n.* exécution
executioner: *n.* bourreau
executive board: directoire
executive committee: comité de direction
executive: *n.* (business) cadre; *adj.* exécutif
executor: *n.* exécuteur testamentaire
exemplary: *adj.* exemplaire
exemplify: *vt.* exemplifier
exempt: *adj.* exempt
exemption: *n.* exemption
exercise book: cahier
exercise: *n.* exercice
exercise: *vt.* exercer; montrer
exert: *vt.* employer; exercer
exertion: *n.* effort
exhale: *vt.* exhaler; expirer
exhaust: *n.* échappement
exhaust: *vt.* épuiser
exhausted: *adj.* épuisé
exhaustion: *n.* épuisement
exhaustive: *adj.* exhaustif; complet
exhibit: *n.* (law) pièce à conviction

exhibit: *vt.* exhiber; montrer
exhibition: *n.* exposition; présentation
exhilarating: *adj.* stimulant; grisant
exhilaration: *n.* joie f intense
exhort: *vt.* exhorter
exhortation: *n.* exhortation
exhume: *vt.* exhumer; déterrer
exil m;: *vt.* exiler; déporter
exist: *vi.* exister
existence: *n.* existence
existent: *adj.* existant
existing: *adj.* actuel; présent
exit ramp: bretelle d'accès
exit: *n.* sortie
exit: *vi.* sortir
exodus: *n.* exode
exonerate: *vt.* disculper; décharger
exoneration: *n.* disculpation; décharge
exorbitant: *adj.* exorbitant; excessif
exorcise: *vt.* exorciser
exorcism: *n.* exorcisme
exothermic: *adj.* exothermique
exotic: *adj.* exotique
expand: *vt.* étendre; dilater
expanse: *n.* étendue
expansion: *n.* expansion
expansive: *adj.* expansif
expatriate: *vt.* expatrier
expect: *vt.* attendre; espérer; penser
expectance: *n.* attente; espoir
expectant mother: femme enceinte
expectant: *adj.* d'attente
expectation: *n.* expectative; attente
expediency: *n.* convenance; opportunité
expedient: *adj.* opportun; *n.* expédient
expedite: *vt.* accélérer; expédier
expedition: *n.* expédition
expeditious: *adj.* expéditif
expel: *vt.* expulser
expend: *vt.* dépenser; utiliser

expendable: *adj.* jetable; consommable
expenditure: *n.* dépense
expense account: frais de représentation
expense: *n.* dépense; coût
expensive: *adj.* cher; coûteux
experience: *n.* expérience; pratique
experience: *vt.* ressentir; éprouver; connaître
experienced: *adj.* expérimenté
experiment: *n.* expérience
experiment: *vi.* expérimenter
experimental: *adj.* expérimental
expert: *adj.* expert
expertise: *n.* compétences
expiration: *n.* expiration
expire: *vi.* expirer
explain: *vt.* expliquer
explanation: *n.* explication
explanatory: *adj.* explicatif
expletive: *adj.* explétif
explicable: *adj.* explicable
explicit: *adj.* explicite
explode: *vt.* faire exploser; *vi.* exploser
exploit: *n.* exploit
exploit: *vt.* exploiter
exploitation: *n.* exploitation
exploration: *n.* exploration
exploratory: *adj.* exploratoire
explore: *vt.* explorer; examiner; sonder
explorer: *n.* explorateur
explosion: *n.* explosion
explosive: *n.* explosif; *adj.* explosif
exponent: *n.* exposant
exponential form: forme exponentielle
exponential growth: croissance exponentielle
export: *vt.* exporter
exportation: *n.* exportation
exporter: *n.* exportateur

expose: *vt.* exposer; dévoiler
exposed: *adj.* exposé
exposition: *n.* exposition; interprétation
expostulate: *vi.* faire des remonstrances
exposure meter: photomètre
exposure: *n.* exposition; temps de pose; cliché
expound: *vt.* exposer; interpréter
express: *adj.* exprès; *n.* exprès
express: *vt.* exprimer
expression: *n.* expression; locution
expressionless: *adj.* inexpressif
expressive: *adj.* expressif
expressly: *adv.* expressément
expressway: *n.* autoroute
expropriate: *vt.* exproprier
expropriation: *n.* expropriation
expulsion: *n.* expulsion
expurgate: *vt.* expurger
exquisite: *adj.* exquis
extant: *adj.* existant
extempore: *adv.* à l'improviste
extemporise: *vi.* improviser
extend: *vt.* étendre; élargir; *vi.* s'étendre
extension: *n.* extension
extensive: *adj.* étendu; important
extent: *n.* extension
extenuate: *vt.* atténuer
extenuating: *adj.* atténuant
exterior: *adj.* extérieur; *n.* extérieur
exterminate: *vt.* exterminer; supprimer
extermination: *n.* extermination; suppression
extern: *adj.* externe
external: *adj.* externe
extinct: *adj.* disparu; éteint
extinction coefficient: coefficient d'extinction
extinction: *n.* extinction
extinguish: *vt.* éteindre; supprimer

extinguisher: *n.* extincteur
extirpate: *vt.* extirper
extol: *vt.* louer; exalter
extort: *vt.* extorquer; arracher
extortion: *n.* extorsion
extortionate: *adj.* exorbitant
extra: *adv.* particulièrement; *n.* supplément
extract: *n.* extrait
extract: *vt.* extraire
extraction: *n.* extraction; origine
extracurricular: *adj.* périscolaire
extradite: *vt.* extrader
extradition: *n.* (law) extradition
extramarital: *adj.* extérieur au mariage
extramural: *adj.* extra-muros
extraneous: *adj.* superflu; sans rapport
extraordinarily: *adv.* extraordinairement
extraordinary: *adj.* extraordinaire
extravagance: *n.* extravagance; gaspillage
extravagant: *adj.* extravagant; exorbitant; gaspilleur
extreme: *adj.* extrême; suprême; ultime; *n.* extrême
extremist: *adj.* extrémiste; *n.* extrémiste
extremity: *n.* extrémité
extricate: *vt.* extirper; démêler
extrinsical: *adj.* extrinsèque
extrovert: *adj.* extraverti
exuberance: *n.* exubérance
exuberant: *adj.* exubérant
exude: *vi.* exsuder
exult: *vi.* exulter; triompher
exultation: *n.* exultation
eye contact: contact visuel
eye: *n.* oeil
eye: *vt.* regarder; observer; lorgner
eyeball: *n.* globe oculaire
eyebrow: *n.* sourcil

eyelash: *n.* cil
eyelid: *n.* paupière
eyesight: *n.* vue
eyesore: *n.* monstruosité
eyetooth: *n.* canine
eyewitness: *n.* témoin oculaire
eyrie: *n.* aire; nid d'aigle

F

fable: *n.* fable; légende
fabric: *n.* tissu
fabricate: *vt.* fabriquer; inventer
fabrication: *n.* fabrication; invention
fabulous: *adj.* fabuleux
facade: *n.* façade
face cream: crème pour le visage
face powder: poudre de riz
face value: valeur nominale
face: *n.* visage; figure; surface; façade; mine; apparence
face: *vt.* faire face à; affronter
face-lift: *n.* lifting
facet: *n.* facette
facetious: *adj.* facétieux; plaisant; spirituel
facial: *adj.* facial
facile: *adj.* facile; superficiel
facilitate: *vt.* faciliter
facilitator: *n.* facilitateur
facility: *n.* facilité; équipement; infrastructure
facing: *n.* revers; *prep.* en face de
facsimile: *n.* fac-similé
fact: *n.* fait; réalité
faction: *n.* faction; dissension
factor: *n.* facteur
factory outlet: magasin de vente directe d'usine
factory: *n.* usine
factual: *adj.* factuel; basé sur les faits
faculty: *n.* faculté; corps enseignant
fad: *n.* engouement
fade: *vi.* se faner; perdre son éclat
fail: *vt.* échouer à; omettre; manquer à ses engagements envers
failing: *n.* défaut
failure rate: taux de panne
failure: *n.* échec; panne; raté; faillite; manquement
faint: *n.* évanouissement; *adj.* faible
faint: *vi.* s'évanouir; défaillir

fainthearted: *adj.* timide; timoré; pusillanime
faintness: *n.* faiblesse; légèreté
fair play: *n.* fair-play; franc-jeu
fair: *adj.* beau; blond; clair; favorable; juste; équitable; considérable; passable; *n.* foire
fairly: *adv.* équitablement; absolument
fairness: *n.* beauté; justice
fairy tale: conte de fées; histoire à dormir debout
fairy: *n.* fée
faith: *n.* foi; croyance; fidélité
faithful: *adj.* fidèle; loyal
faithfulness: *n.* fidélité; loyauté
fake web site: site truqué; faux site
fake: *n.* falsification; imposteur; *adj.* faux
fake: *vt.* feindre; falsifier
falcon: *n.* faucon
falconry: *n.* fauconnerie
fall due; to: arriver à échéance
fall: *n.* chute; automne
fall: *vi.* tomber; s'effondrer; diminuer; baisser
fallacious: *adj.* fallacieux; trompeur
fallacy: *n.* erreur; sophisme; tromperie
fallibility: *n.* faillibilité
fallible: *adj.* faillible
fallout shelter: abri antiatomique
fallout: *n.* retombées
fallow: *adj.* en jachère; *n.* daim
false alarm: fausse alerte
false statement: fausse déclaration
false: *adj.* faux
falsehood: *n.* mensonge; fausseté
falsify: *vt.* falsifier
falsity: *n.* fausseté
falter: *vi.* vaciller; faiblir
faltering: *adj.* chancelant
fame: *n.* réputation; renommée; notoriété

famed: *adj.* célèbre
familiar: *adj.* familier; domestique
familiarise: *vt.* familiariser
familiarity: *n.* familiarité
family background: milieu familial
family business: affaire de famille
family doctor: médecin de famille
family: *n.* famille
famine: *n.* famine; disette
fammished: *adj.* affamé
famous: *adj.* célébre; fameux
fan belt: courroie de ventilateur
fan: *n.* éventail; ventilateur; jeune admirateur
fan: *vt.* éventer; attiser
fanatic: *adj.* fanatique; *n.* fanatique
fanaticism: *n.* fanatisme
fanciful: *adj.* fantasque; capricieux
fancy goods: *npl.* nouveautés
fancy: *n.* fantaisie; imagination; caprice
fancy: *vt.* avoir envie de; s'imaginer
fancydress hall: bal masqué
fanfare: *n.* fanfare
fang: *n.* croc
fantastic: *adj.* fantastique; excentrique
fantasy: *n.* imagination
far: *adv.* loin; *adj.* lointain; éloigné
faraway: *adj.* lointain
farce: *n.* farce
farcical: *adj.* grotesque
fare: *n.* prix (du voyage); tarif
farewell: *n.* adieu
farm: *n.* ferme; exploitation agricole
farm: *vt.* cultiver
farmer: *n.* fermier; agriculteur
farmhouse: *n.* ferme
farming: *n.* agriculture
farmland: *n.* terres arables
farmyard: *n.* cour de ferme
far-reaching: *adj.* d'une grande portée; considérable

farther: *adv.* plus loin; *adj.* plus éloigné
farthest: *adv.* le plus lointain; le plus loin; au plus
fascinate: *vt.* fasciner; captiver
fascinating: *adj.* fascinant
fascination: *n.* fascination; charme
fascism: *n.* fascisme
fashion show: défilé de mode
fashion: *n.* manière; façon; forme; coutume; mode; style
fashion: *vt.* façonner; confectionner
fashionable: *adj.* à la mode; chic
fast breeder reactor: surgénérateur
fast food: restauration rapide
fast: *n.* jeûne; *adj.* rapide; ferme; stable; *adv.* rapidement; fermement; solidement
fast: *vi.* jeûner
fastener: *n.* attache; fermoir
fastenn: *vt.* attacher; fixer; attribuer
fastidious: *adj.* minutieux; méticuleux
fat: *adj.* gros; gras; *n.* graisse
fatal: *adj.* mortel; néfaste
fatalism: *n.* fatalisme
fatalist: *n.* fataliste
fatality: *n.* accident mortel; fatalité
fatally: *adv.* mortellement
fate: *n.* destin; sort
fateful: *adj.* fatidique
father: *n.* père
fatherhood: *n.* paternité
father-in-law: *n.* beau-père
fatherland: *n.* patrie
fatherly: *adj.* paternel
fathomm: *n.* brasse (mesure)
fathomm: *vt.* sonder; pénétrer
fatigue: *n.* fatigue
fatigue: *vt.* fatiguer; lasser
fatten: *vt.* engraisser
fatty: *adj.* gras; graisseux
fatuous: *adj.* imbécile; stupide; niais
faucet: *n.* robinet

fault: *n.* défaut; faute; délit; faille
faultfinder: *n.* chicaneur
faultless: *adj.* irréprochable
faulty: *adj.* défectueux
fauna: *n.* faune
faux pas: impair
favorites folder: dossier de favoris
favour: *n.* faveur; approbation avantage
favour: *vt.* favoriser; préférer
favourable: *adj.* favorable; propice
favoured: *adj.* favorisé
favourite: *n.* favori m; *adj.* favori
favouritism: *n.* favoritisme
fawn: *n.* faon
fawn: *vi.* flatter servilement
fawningly: *adv.* d'une flatterie servile
fax: *n.* télécopieur; fax; télécopie; fax
fax: *vt.* envoyer par fax; télécopier
fear: *n.* crainte
fear: *vt.* craindre
fearful: *adj.* effrayant; craintif; peureux
fearless: *adj.* intrépide; courageux
fearlessness: *n.* intrépidité
feasibility: *n.* faisabilité
feasible: *adj.* faisable; réalisable
feast: *n.* festin; banquet; fête
feast: *vi.* banqueter
feat: *n.* exploit; prouesse
feather bed: lit de plumes
feather: *n.* plume
feature film: long métrage
feature: *n.* caractéristique; trait
feature: *vi.* figurer
February: *n.* février
federal: *adj.* fédéral
federalist: *n.* fédéraliste
federate: *vt.* fédérer
federation: *n.* fédération
fed-up: *adj.* to be fed-up = en avoir marre
fee: *n.* honoraires; frais
feeble: *adj.* faible; frêle

feebleness: *n.* faiblesse
feebly: *adv.* faiblement
feed: *n.* nourriture f; alimentation
feed: *vt.* nourrir; alimenter
feedback: *n.* réaction; répercussion
feel: *n.* sensation; toucher
feel: *vt.* sentir; toucher; croire
feeler: *n.* antenne; tentative
feeling: *n.* sensation; sentiment
feelingly: *adv.* avec émotion
fees: tarifs; droits (à acquitter); honoraires
feign: *vt.* inventer; feindre; simuler
feline: *adj.* félin
fellow citizen: concitoyen
fellow countryman: compatriote
fellow feeling: sympathie
fellow men: semblables
fellow student: copain de fac
fellow traveller: compagnon (compagne) de voyage
fellow: *n.* homme; type; membre
fellowship: *n.* camaraderie; association
felon: *n.* criminel
felony: *n.* crime
felt: *n.* feutre
felt-tip pen: feutre
female: *n.* femelle; *adj.* de sexe féminin; femelle
feminine: *adj.* féminin
feminist: *n.* féministe
fen: *n.* marais
fence: *n.* barrière; clôture
fence: *vt.* clôturer
fencing: *n.* escrime
fender: *n.* pare-chocs
fennel: *n.* fenouil
ferment: *n.* agitation
ferment: *vi.* fermenter
fern: *n.* fougère
ferocious: *adj.* féroce
ferocity: *n.* férocité
ferret: *n.* furet

ferret: *vt.* fureter
ferry: *n.* bac; ferry
ferry: *vt.* transporter
fertile: *adj.* fertile; fécond
fertilise: *vt.* fertiliser
fertiliser: *n.* engrais
fertility: *n.* fertilité; fécondité
fervent: *adj.* fervent; ardent
fervid: *adj.* ardent; véhément
fervor: *n.* ferveur; ardeur
fester: *vi.* suppurer; s'envenimer
festival: *n.* fête; festival
festive: *adj.* de fête
festivity: *n.* fête; réjouissances
fetch: *vt.* aller chercher
fetching: *adj.* charmant; séduisant
fête: *n.* fête
fetid: *adj.* fétide; nauséabond
fetus: *n.* foetus
feud: *n.* rivalité; dissension
feudalism: *n.* féodalité
fever: *n.* fièvre
feverish: *adj.* fiévreux
few: *adj.* peu
fewer: *adj.* moins (de); *adv.* moins
fewest: *adj.* le moins (de)
flagstop: *n.* arrêt facultatif
fiancé: *n.* fiancé
fiancée: *n.* fiancée
fib: *n.* bobard
fib: *vi.* raconter des bobards
fibre: *n.* fibre
fibreglass: *n.* fibre de verre
fickle: *adj.* volage; inconstant
fiction: *n.* fiction; invention
fictional: *adj.* fictif
fictitious: *adj.* fictif; imaginaire
fiddle: *n.* violon; combine
fiddle: *v.* jouer du violon
fiddler: *n.* violoneux
fidelity: *n.* fidélité; loyauté
fidget: *vi.* s'agiter; s'impatienter
fidgety: *adj.* agité; remuant

field day: jour de grandes
manoeuvres
field search: recherche par champ
field: *n.* champ; étendue; domaine
fieldmouse: *n.* mulot
fieldwork: *n.* recherches sur le terrain
fiend: *n.* démon; mordu
fiendish: *adj.* diabolique
fierce: *adj.* féroce; violent; acharné;
furieux
fierceness: *n.* férocité; fureur
fiery: *adj.* ardent; fougueux
fifteen: *adj.* quinze
fifteenth: *adj.* quinzième
fifth: *adj.* cinquième
fiftieth: *adj.* cinquantième
fifty: *adj.* cinquante
fig: *n.* figue
fight: *n.* bataille; combat; lutte
fight: *vt.* se battre; combattre; lutter
fighter: *n.* combattant; lutteur;
chasseur
fighting: *n.* combat
fig-leaf: *n.* feuille de figuier
figurative language: langage figuré;
langage figuratif
figurative: *adj.* figuratif
figure: *n.* figure; forme; silhouette;
image; chiffre
figure: *vi.* figurer; avoir du sens
figurehead: *n.* figure de proue
filament: *n.* filament; fibre
filch: *vt.* chiper
filcher: *n.* voleur
file cabinet: armoire de classement
file card: fiche (de classeur)
file clerk: préposé au classement
file compatible: compatible du point
de vue des fichiers
file copy: exemplaire d'archives
file management: gestion ou tenue
de fichiers
file number: cote (d'un document
dans un fichier)

file: *n.* file; liste; colonne; rangée; lime; dossier; fichier
file: *vt.* classer; archiver
file: *vt.* enregistrer; limer; classer; déposer
file-swapping software: logiciel permettant les échanges de fichiers
filing by subject: classement idéologique
filing cabinet: armoire de classement
filing cabinet: *n.* classeur
filing clerk: préposé au classement
filing tray: corbeille pour la correspondance à classer
filing tray: une corbeille à classement
filing: *n.* classement
fill in a document (to): remplir un document
fill in the blanks (to): remplir les blancs
fill in; fill out a form: remplir un formulaire
fill: *vt.* remplir
fillet steak: filet de boeuf
fillet: *n.* filet
filling station: station-service
fillip: *n.* coup de fouet
filly: *n.* pouliche
film library: cinémathèque
film star: vedette de cinéma
film: *n.* pellicule; film; cello-phane
film: *vt.* filmer
filmstrip: *n.* film
filter: un filtre
filter: *vt.* filtrer
filtering software: logiciel de filtrage; de contrôle d'accès
filtering tool: outil de filtrage
filter-tipped: *adj.* à bout filtre
filthiness: *n.* immondice; ordure; saleté; crasse
filthy: *adj.* crasseux; dégoûtant
fin: *n.* nageoire

final draft: manuscrit corrigé; final
final: *adj.* dernier; définitif
finale: *n.* finale
finalise: *vt.* parachever; rendre définitif
finalist: *n.* finaliste
finance: *n.* finance
financial year: l'exercice financier
financial: *adj.* financier
find: *n.* trouvaille
find: *vt.* trouver; découvrir
findings: *npl.* résultats; conclusions; verdict
fine arts: *npl.* beaux arts
fine: *adj.* fin; pur; aigu; raffiné; beau; délicat; subtil; élégant; *n.* amende
fine: *vt.* infliger une amende
finely: *adv.* magnifiquement
finery: *n.* parure
finesse: *n.* finesse subtilité
finger: *n.* doigt
finger: *vt.* toucher; manier
fingernail: *n.* ongle
fingerprint: *n.* empreinte digitale
fingertip: *n.* bout du doigt
finicky: *adj.* pointilleux; difficile
finish: *vt.* finir; terminer; achever
finishing line: ligne d'arrivée
finishing school: école privée
finite: *adj.* fini
fir: *n.* sapin
fire alarm: alarme d'incendie
fire department: pompiers
fire engine: voiture de pompiers
fire escape: escalier de secours
fire extinguisher: extincteur
fire station: caserne de pompiers
fire: *n.* feu; incendie
fire: *v.* met-tre le feu à; incendier; tirer
firearm: arme à feu
fireball: *n.* boule de feu
firefly: *n.* luciole
fireman: *n.* pompier

fireplace: *n.* cheminée
fireplace: *n.* cheminée; foyer
fireproof: *adj.* ignifugé
fireside: *n.* coin du feu
firewall: pare-feu; mur coupe-feu
firewater: *n.* eau de vie
firewood: *n.* bois de chauffage
fireworks: *npl.* feu d'artifice
firing squad: peloton d'exécution
firing: *n.* fusillade
firm: *adj.* ferme
firm: *adj.* ferme; solide; constant
firmament: *n.* firmament
firmness: *n.* fermeté; résolution
first aid: premiers secours
first law of thermodynamics:
première loi de thermodynamique
first name: *n.* prénom
first: *adj.* premier; *adv.* d'abord
first-aid kit: trousse de premiers
secours
first-class: *adj.* de première classe; de
première catégorie
first-hand: *adj.* de première main
first-rate: *adj.* de première qualité
fiscal: *adj.* fiscal
fish farm: entreprise de pisciculture
fish: *n.* poisson
fish: *v.* pêcher
fishbone: *n.* arête
fisherman: *n.* pêcheur
fishing line: ligne de pêche
fishing rod: canne à pêche
fishing tackle: attirail de pêche
fishing: *n.* pêche
fishseller: *n.* poissonnier ère
fishstore: *n.* poissonnerie
fishy: *adj.* suspect
fissure: *n.* fissure; crevasse
fist: *n.* poing
fit tree: figuier
fit: *n.* accès; attaque; crise; *adj.* en
forme; capable; adapté à; qui convient
fit: *vt.* aller à; ajuster; adapter

fitment: *n.* meuble encastré
fitness: *n.* forme physique; aptitude
fitted carpet: moquette
fitted kitchen: cuisine encastrée
fitter: *n.* monteur
fitting: *adj.* qui convient; approprié;
juste
fitting: *n.* accessoire; *npl.*
installations
five pot: billet de cinq dollars
five: *adj.* cinq
fix: *vt.* fixer; établir
fixation: *n.* obsession
fixings: *npl.* garniture; accessoires
fixture: *n.* rencontre
fizz: *vi.* pétiller
fizzy: *adj.* gazeux
flabbergasted: *adj.* abasourdi
flabby: *adj.* mou; molle; flasque
flaccid: *adj.* flasque; mou; molle
flag: *n.* drapeau
flair: *n.* flair; talent
flak: *n.* tir antiaérien; critiques
flake: *n.* flocon m; paillette
flake: *vi.* s'effriter; s'écailler
flaky: *adj.* floconneux; friable
flamboyant: *adj.* flamboyant;
ostentatoire
flame: *n.* flamme; ardeur
flamingo: *n.* flamant
flammable: *adj.* inflammable
flank: *n.* flanc
flank: *vt.* flanquer
flannel: *n.* flanelle
flap: *n.* battement; rabat
flap: *vti.* battre
flare: *n.* flamme
flare: *vi.* luire; briller
flash cube: cube de flash
flash photolysis: photolyse éclair
flash screen: écran d'accueil
flash: *n.* éclair
flash: *v.* clignoter
flashback: *n.* souvenir; retour

flashbulb: *n.* ampoule de flash
flashlight: *n.* lampe f de poche
flashy: *adj.* tape-à-l'oeil; voyant
flask: *n.* flasqu; flacon
flat: *adj.* plat; fixe (rate)
flat: *adj.* plat; uniforme; insipide; *n.* plaine; plat
flatness: *n.* égalité; monotonie
flatten: *vt.* aplanir; aplatir
flatter: *vt.* flatter
flattering: *adj.* flatteur
flattery: *n.* flatterie
flatulence: *n.* flatulence
flaunt: *vt.* étaler; afficher
flavour: *n.* saveur
flavour: *vt.* parfumer; assaisonner
flavoured: *adj.* savoureux; parfumé
flavourless: *adj.* insipide
flaw: *n.* défaut; imperfection
flawless: *adj.* parfait
flax: *n.* lin
flea bite: piqûre de puce
flea: *n.* puce
fleck: *n.* petite tache; particule
flee: *vt.* fuir de
fleece: *n.* toison
fleece: *vt.* tondre
fleet: *n.* flotte
fleeting: *adj.* fugace; fugitif
flesh wound: blessure superficielle
flesh: *n.* chair
fleshy: *adj.* charnu
flex: *n.* cordon
flex: *vt.* fléchir
flexibility: *n.* flexibilité
flexible: *adj.* flexible; souple
flick: *n.* petit coup
flick: *vt.* donner un petit coup
flicker: *vt.* vaciller; trembloter
flier: *n.* aviateur
flight attendant: steward; hôtesse de l'air
flight deck: cabine de pilotage
flight: *n.* vol; fuite; volée; envolée

flimsy: *adj.* léger; fragile
flinch: *vi.* sourciller
fling: *vt.* lancer; jeter
flint: *n.* silex
flip: *vt.* lancer
flippant: *adj.* désinvolte; cavalier
flipper: *n.* nageoire
flirt: *n.* charmeureuse
flirt: *vi.* flirter
flirtation: *n.* flirt
flit: *vi.* voler; voleter
float: *n.* flotteur; char
float: *vt.* faire flotter; lancer
flock: *n.* troupeau; volée; foule
flock: *vi.* affluer
flog: *vt.* fustiger
flogging: *n.* fustigation; flagellation
flood: *n.* inondation; marée haute; déluge
flood: *vt.* inonder
flooding: *n.* inondation
floodlight: *n.* projecteur
floor lamp: lampadaire
floor show: spectacle de cabaret
floor: *n.* sol; plancher; étage
floor: *vt.* parqueter; déconcerter
floorboard: *n.* planche
flop: *n.* four; fiasco
floppy: *adj.* lâche; *n.* disquette
flora: *n.* flore
floral: *adj.* floral
florescence: *n.* floraison
florid: *adj.* fleuri
florist: *n.* fleuriste
florist's (shop): boutique de fleuriste
flotilla: *n.* flotille
flounder: *n.* flet
flounder: *vi.* patauger
flour: *n.* farine
flourish: *n.* fioriture; fioriture
flourish: *vi.* fleurir; prospérer
flourishing: *adj.* florissant
flout: *vt.* mépriser; se moquer de
flow chart: organigramme

flow: *vi.* couler; circuler; monter
flower show: exposition de fleurs
flower: *n.* fleur
flower: *vi.* fleurir
flowerbed: *n.* parterre de fleurs
flowerpot: *n.* pot de fleurs
flowery: *adj.* fleuri
fluctuate: *vi.* fluctuer
fluctuation: *n.* fluctuation
fluency: *n.* aisance
fluent: *adj.* coulant; facile
fluff: *n.* peluchex
fluid: *adj.* fluide; *n.* fluide
fluidity: *n.* fluidité
fluke: *n.* veine
fluoride: *n.* fluorure
flurry: *n.* rafale; agitation
flush: *n.* rougeur; éclat
flush: *vt.* to flush out = nettoyer à grande eau; *vi.* rougir
flushed: *adj.* rouge
fluster: *vt.* énerver
flustered: *adj.* énervé
flute: *n.* flûte
flutter: *n.* agitation; émoi
flutter: *vi.* voleter; s'agiter
flux: m. écoulement; flot; flux
fly: *n.* mouche
fly: *vt.* piloter; transporter par avion
flying saucer: soucoupe volante
flypast: *n.* défilé aérien
flysheet: *n.* feuille volante
fo: *n.* poulain
foam rubber: caoutchouc mousse
foam: *vi.* écumer
foams: *n.* écume
foamy: *adj.* écumeux
focus: *n.* foyer; centre
fodder: *n.* fourrage
foe: *n.* ennemi; adversaire
fog light: feu de brouillard
fog: *n.* brouillard
foggy: *adj.* brumeux
foible: *n.* point faible

foil: *n.* papier d'aluminium; fleuret
foil: *vt.* déjouer
fold: *n.* pli; parc à moutons
fold: *vt.* plier
folder: *n.* chemise; dépliant
folding chair: chaise pliante
folding: *adj.* pliant
foliage: *n.* feuillage
foliation: *n.* foliotage; numérotation des feuillets
folio: *n.* folio
folk song: chant folklorique
folk: *n.* gens
folklore: *n.* folklore
folktale: *n.* conte
follow: *vt.* suivre
follower: *n.* serviteur; disciple; partisan; adhérent; admirateur
following: *adj.* suivant; *n.* partisans
folly: *n.* folie; extravagance
foment: *vt.* fomenter
fond: *adj.* affectueux
fondle: *vt.* caresser
fondness: *n.* prédilection; affection
font size: corps
font style: style
font: *n.* police de caractères
food chain: chaîne alimentaire
food mixer: mixer
food poisoning: intoxication alimentaire
food processor: robot ménager
food web (food cycle): réseau alimentaire
food: *n.* nourriture
foodstuffs: *npl.* produits alimentaires
fool: *n.* imbécile; idiot
fool: *vt.* duper
foolhardy: *adj.* téméraire
foolish: *adj.* idiot; insensé
foolproof: *adj.* infaillible
foolscap: *n.* papier ministre
foot note: note de bas de page
foot: *n.* pied; patte

footage: *n.* métrage
football: *n.* football; ballon de football
footballer: *n.* footballeur
footbrake: *n.* frein à pied
footbridge: *n.* passerelle
foothills: *npl.* contreforts
foothold: *n.* prise (pour le pied)
footing: *n.* prise (pour le pied); statut; situation; plan
footlights: *npl.* feux de la rampe
footman: *n.* valet de pied; soldat d'infanterie
footpath: *n.* sentier
footprint: *n.* empreinte (de pas)
footsore: *adj.* aux pieds endoloris
footstep: *n.* pas
footwear: *n.* chaussures
for free: gratuitement
for: *prep.* pour; en raison de; pendant; *conj.* car
foray: *n.* incursion
forbid: *vt.* interdire; défendre; empêcher
forbidding: *adj.* menaçant; sévère
force constant: constante de force
force: *n.* force; puissance; vigueur; violence; forces armées
force: *vt.* forcer; obliger; contraindre; imposer
forced march: marche forcée
forced: *adj.* forcé
forceful: *adj.* énergique
forceps: *n.* forceps
forcible: *adj.* énergique; vigoureux; puissant
ford: *n.* gué
ford: *vt.* passer à gué
fore: to the fore = en évidence
forearm: *n.* avant-bras
foreboding: *n.* pressentiment
forecast: *n.* prévision
forecast: *vt.* prévoir
forecourt: *n.* avant-cour

forefather: *n.* aïeul; ancêtre
forefinger: *n.* index
forefront n: in the forefront of = au premier plan de
forego: *vt.* renoncer à; s'abstenir de
foregone: *adj.* passé; anticipé
foreground: *n.* premier plan
forehead: *n.* front
foreign exchange: devises
foreign: *adj.* étranger
foreigner: *n.* étranger
foreleg: *n.* patte de devant
foreman: *n.* contremaître; (law) premier juré
foremost: *adj.* principal
forenoon: *n.* matinée
forensic: *adj.* médico-légal
forerunner: *n.* précurseur; signe avant-coureur
foresee: *vt.* prévoir
foreshadow: *vt.* présager
foresight: *n.* prévoyance; prescience
forest: *n.* forêt
forestall: *vt.* anticiper; prévenir
forester: *n.* garde forestier
forestry: *n.* sylviculture
foretaste: *n.* avant-goût
foretell: *vt.* prédire
forethought: *n.* prévoyance f; préméditation
foretitle: avant-titre
forever: *adv.* toujours; un temps infini
forewarn: *vt.* avertir; prévenir
foreword: *n.* préface
forfeit: *n.* amende; confiscation
forfeit: *vt.* perdre
forge: *n.* forge; usine métallurgique
forge: *n.* fourrage
forge: *vt.* forger; contrefaire
forge: *vt.* fourrager; fouiller
forger: *n.* faussaire
forgery: *n.* contrefaçon
forget: *vt.* oublier

forgetful: *adj.* étourdi; négligent
forgetfulness: *n.* étourderie; négligence
forget-me-not: *n.* myosotis
forgive: *vt.* pardonner
forgiveness: *n.* pardon; indulgence
fork: *n.* fourchette; fourche
fork: *vi.* bifurquer
forked: *adj.* fourchu
fork-lift truck: chariot élévateur
forlorn: *adj.* malheureux; abandonné
form: *n.* forme; formule; formulaire; formalité
form: *vt.* former
formal: *adj.* formel; méthodique; cérémonieux
formality: *n.* formalité; cérémonie
format: *n.* format
format: *vt.* formater
formation: *n.* formation
formative: *adj.* formateur
formatting: *n.* formatage
former: *adj.* ancien; antérieur; précédent
formidable: *adj.* effrayant; terrible
formula: *n.* formule
formulate: *vt.* formuler
forsake: *vt.* abandonner; renoncer à
fort: *n.* fort
forte: *n.* fort
forthcoming issue: un numéro à paraître
forthcoming: *adj.* prochain; sociable
forthright: *adj.* franc
forthwith: *adv.* immédiatement; tout de suite
fortieth: *adj.* quarantième
fortification: *n.* fortification
fortify: *vt.* fortifier; renforcer
fortitude: *n.* stoïcisme; courage
fortnight: *n.* quinze jours; deux semaines
fortress: *n.* forteresse
fortuitous: *adj.* fortuit; imprévu

fortunate: *adj.* chanceux
fortunately: *adv.* heureusement
fortune: *n.* chance; sort; fortune
fortune-teller: *n.* diseuse de bonne aventure
forty: *adj.* quarante
forum: *n.* forum; tribune
forward: *adj.* avancé; précoce; présomptueux
forward: *vt.* transférer; faire suivre; transmettre; promouvoir; expédier
forwardess: *n.* précocité; effronterie
fossil fuels: combustible fossile
fossil: *n.* fossile
foster child: enfant adoptif
foster father: père adoptif
foster mother: mère adoptive
foster: *vt.* encourager
foul: *adj.* infect; ignoble; vil; déloyal; *n.* copie illisible
fouly: *n.* jeu déloyal; meurtre
found: *vt.* fonder; créer; établir; édifier; fondre
foundation: *n.* foundation; fondement
founder: *n.* fondateur
foundling: *n.* enfant trouvé
foundry: *n.* fonderie
fountain: *n.* fontaine
fountainhead: *n.* source; origine
four: *adj.* quatre
fourfold: *adj.* quadruple
fouriertransform series: fourier; série de transformée de
four-poster (bed): lit à baldaquin
foursome: *n.* groupe de quatre personnes
fourteen: *adj.* quatorze
fourteenth: *adj.* quatorzième
fourth: *adj.* quatrième; *n.* quart
fowl: *n.* volaille
fox: *n.* renard; rusé
foyer: *n.* vestibule
frac: *n.* rixe

fraction: *n.* fraction
fractional distillation: rectification
fractionating column: colonne à plateaux
fracture: *n.* fracture
fracture: *vt.* fracturer
fragile: *adj.* fragile; frêle
fragility: *n.* fragilité; faiblesse; délicatesse
fragment: *n.* fragment
fragmentary: *adj.* fragmentaire
fragrance: *n.* parfum
fragrant: *adj.* parfumé; odorant
frail: *adj.* frêle; fragile
frailty: *n.* fragilité; faiblesse
frame of mind: état d'esprit
frame: *n.* charpente; châssis; armature; cadre; structure; monture
frame: *vt.* encadrer; concevoir; construire; former
framework: *n.* charpente; structure; cadre
France: *n.* France
franchise: *n.* droit de vote; franchise
frank: *adj.* franc; direct
frankly: *adv.* franchement
frankness: *n.* franchise
frantic: *adj.* frénétique; effréné
fraternal: *adj.* fraternel
fraternity: *n.* fraternité
fraternize: *vi.* fraterniser
fratricide: *n.* fratricide
fraud: *n.* fraude; tromperie
fraudulence: *n.* caractère frauduleux
fraudulent: *adj.* frauduleux
fraught: *adj.* accablé; tendu
fray: *n.* rixe; bagarre; querelle
freak: *n.* caprice; phénomène
freckle: tache de rousseur
freckled: *adj.* couvert de taches de rousseur
free access: libre-accès; accès direct
free acquisition: acquisition à titre gratuit

free carrier: franco transporteur
free energy: énergie libre
free gift: prime
free kick: coup franc
free of charge: gratuit; gratuitement
free radical: radical libre
free software: logiciel gratuit; libre
free trade: libre échange
free will: libre arbitre
free: *adj.* libre; autonome; gratuit; dégagé
free: *vt.* affranchir; libérer; débarrasser
freedom: *n.* liberté
free-for-all: *n.* mêlée générale
freehold: *n.* propriété libre
freelance: *adj.* indépendant
freely: *adv.* librement; franchement; libéralement
freemason: *n.* franc-maçon
freemasonry: *n.* franc-maçonnerie
freepost: *n.* port payé
free-range: *adj.* de plein air
freethinker: *n.* libre-penseur
freethinking: *n.* libre pensée
freeway: *n.* autoroute
freewheel: *vi.* rouler en roue libre
freeze (froze; frozen): *vi.* (se) bloquer
freeze: *vi.* geler; congeler; geler
freeze-dried: *adj.* lyophilisé
freezer: *n.* congélateur
freezing point: point de congélation
freezing: *adj.* gelé
freight (airborne): le fret aérien
freight (sea): transport maritime
freight (seaborne): le fret maritime
freight train: *n.* train de marchandises
freight: *n.* cargaison; fret
freighter: *n.* affréteur
French bean: *n.* haricot vert
French fries: *npl.* frites
French window: porte-fenêtre

frenzied: *adj.* fou; frénétique
frenzy: *n.* frénésie; folie
frequency factor: facteur de fréquence
frequency: *n.* fréquence
frequent: *adj.* fréquent
frequent: *vt.* fréquenter
fresco: *n.* fresque
fresh water: eau douce
fresh: *adj.* frais; nouveau; récent
freshen: *vt.* rafraîchir
freshly: *adv.* nouvellement; récemment
freshman: *n.* nouveau; nouvelle
freshness: *n.* fraîcheur
fret: *vi.* s'agiter; se tracasser
friar: *n.* moine
friction: *n.* friction
Friday: *n.* vendredi
friend: *n.* ami
friendless: *adj.* sans amis
friendliness: *n.* amitié; bienveillance
friendship: *n.* amitié
frieze: *n.* frise
frigate: *n.* frégate
fright: *n.* peur; frayeur
frighten: *vt.* effrayer
frightened: *adj.* effrayé; apeuré
frightening: *adj.* effrayant
frightful: *adj.* épouvantable; effroyable
frigid: *adj.* froid; glacé; frigide
fringe benefits: avantages en nature
fringe: *n.* frange
frisk: *vt.* fouiller
frisky: *adj.* vif; fringant
frivolity: *n.* frivolité
frivolous: *adj.* frivole; léger
frizz: *vt.* friser
frizzle: *vt.* grésiller
frizzy: *adj.* frisé
frock: *n.* robe
frog: *n.* grenouille
frolic: *vi.* folâtrer; gambader

frolicsome: *adj.* folâtre; gai
from: *prep.* de; depuis; à partir de
front cover: couverture
front door: porte d'entrée
front page: première page
front: *adj.* de devant; premier
front: *n.* avant; devant; façade
frontal: *adj.* de front
frontier: *n.* frontière
front-wheel drive: *n.* (auto) traction avant
frost: *n.* gel; gelée
frost: *vt.* geler
frostbite: *n.* engelure
frostbitten: *adj.* gelé
frosted: *adj.* gelé; givré
frosty: *adj.* glacial; givré
froth: *n.* écume
froth: *vi.* écumer
frothy: *adj.* mousseux; écumeux
frown: *vt.* froncer les sourcils
frozen: *adj.* gelé
frugal: *adj.* frugal; économique
fruit juice: jus de fruit
fruit salad: salade de fruits
fruit tree: arbre fruitier
fruit: *n.* fruit
fruiterer: *n.* fruitier
fruitful: *adj.* fécond; fertile; fructueux; utile
fruitfulness: *n.* fertilité; caractère fructueux
fruition: *n.* réalisation
fruitless: *adj.* stérile; infécond
frustrate: *vt.* contrecarrer
frustrated: *adj.* frustré
frustration: *n.* frustration
fry: *vt.* frire
frying pan: poêle
fuchsia: *n.* fuchsia
fudge: *n.* caramel mou
fuel tank: réservoir à carburant
fuel: *n.* combustible; carburant
fugitive: *adj.* fugitif; *n.* fugitif

fugue: *n.* fugue
fulcrum: *n.* pivot
fulfill: *vt.* accomplir; réaliser
fulfillment: *n.* accomplissement
full moon: pleine lune
full text search: recherche en texte intégral; en plein texte
full text: texte intégral; plein texte
full: *adj.* plein; rempli; complet
full-blown: *adj.* complet
full-length: *adj.* en pied; de long métrage
fullness: *n.* plénitude; abondance
full-page display: affichage pleine page
full-scale: *adj.* grandeur nature; total; complet
full-screen: plein écran; écran complet
full-time: *adj.* à plein temps
fully: *adv.* pleinement; entièrement
fully-fledged: *adj.* diplômé; qualifié
fulsome: *adj.* exagéré
fumble: *vi.* manier gauchement; farfouiller
fume: *vi.* exhaler des vapeurs; rager; fumer
fumigate: *vt.* fumiger
fun: *n.* amusement; plaisir
function: *n.* fonction
function: *v.* fonctionner
functional group: groupe fonctionel; opérationel
fund: *n.* fonds
fund: *vt.* financer
fund: *vt.* financer
fundamental: *adj.* fondamental
funding: *n.* financement
funeral service: service funèbre
funeral: *n.* enterrement
funereal: *adj.* funèbre; lugubre
fungus: *n.* champignon; moisissure
funnel: *n.* entonnoir; cheminée
funny: *adj.* amusant; curieux

fur coat: manteau de fourrure
fur: *n.* fourrure
furious: *adj.* furieux; déchaîné
furlong: *n.* mesure de longueur (220 yards = 201 mètres); furlong
furnace: *n.* fourneau; chaudière
furnish: *vt.* meubler; fournir; pourvoir
furnishings: *npl.* ameublement
furniture: *n.* meubles
furrow: *n.* sillon
furrow: *vt.* sillonner
furry: *adj.* à poil
further education: formation f postscolaire
further: *adj.* supplémentaire; plus lointain; *adv.* plus loin; plus avant; en outre; de plus
further: *vt.* faire avancer; favoriser; promouvoir
furthermore: *adv.* de plus
furthest: *adv.* le plus loin; le plus éloigné
furtive: *adj.* furtif; secret
fury: *n.* fureur; furie; colère
fuse box: boîte à fusibles
fuse: *n.* fusible; amorce
fuse: *vt.* fondre; faire sauter; vifondre; sauter
fusion: *n.* fusion
fuss: *n.* tapage; histoires
fussy: *adj.* tatillon; chipoteur
futile: *adj.* futile; vain
futility: *n.* futilité
future: *adj.* futur; *n.* futur; avenir
fuzzy: *adj.* flou; confus; crépu

$\mathcal{G}$

gab: *n.* (film) bavardage
gabble: *n.* charabia
gabble: *vi.* baragouiner
gable: *n.* pignon
gadget: *n.* gadget
gaffe: *n.* gaffe; bévue
gag: *n.* bâillon; blague
gag: *vt.* bâillonner
gaiety: *n.* gaieté
gaily: *adv.* gaiement
gain: *n.* gain; bénéfice
gain: *vt.* gagner; atteindre
gait: *n.* démarche; maintien
gala: *n.* gala
galaxy: *n.* galaxie
gale: *n.* grand vent
gall bladder: vésicule biliaire
gall: *n.* bile; fiel
gallant: *adj.* galant
gallery: *n.* galerie
galley: *n.* galère; cuisine
gallon: *n.* gallon
gallop: *n.* galop
gallop: *vi.* galoper
gallows: *n.* potence
gallstone: *n.* calcul biliaire
galore: *adv.* en abondance
galvanise: *vt.* galvaniser
gambit: *n.* stratagème
gamble: *n.* risque; pari
gamble: *vi.* jouer; spéculer
gambler: *n.* joueur
gambling: *n.* jeu d'argent
game software: logiciel de jeux; ludiciel
game: *n.* jeu; divertissement; partie; gibier
game: *vi.* jouer
gamekeeper: *n.* garde-chasse
gameware: logiciel de jeux; ludiciel
gaming: *n.* jeu m d'argent
gamma radioactivity: rayonnement gamma

gammon: *n.* jambon
gamut: *n.* gamme
gander: *n.* jars
gang: *n.* gang; bande
gangrene: *n.* gangrène
gangster: *n.* gangster
gangway: *n.* passerelle
gap: *n.* trou; vide; intervalle; écart
gape: *vi.* être bouche bée; bâiller
gaping: *adj.* béant
garage: *n.* garage
garbage can: poubelle
garbage man: éboueur
garbage: *n.* ordures
garbled: *adj.* confus
garden hose: tuyau d'arrosage
garden: *n.* jardin
gardener: *n.* jardinier
gardening: *n.* jardinage
gargle: *vi.* se gargariser
gargoyle: *n.* gargouille
garish: *adj.* tapageur
garland: *n.* guirlande
garlic: *n.* ail
garment: *n.* vêtement
garnish: *n.* garniture
garnish: *vt.* garnir; décorer
garret: *n.* mansarde
garrison: *n.* garnison
garrison: *vt.* mettre en garnison; protéger d'une garnison
garrote: *vt.* étrangler; garrotter
garrulous: *adj.* locace; bavard
garter: *n.* jarretelle
gas burner: brûleur à gaz
gas constant per mole: constante des gaz parfaits
gas cylinder: bouteille de gaz
gas fire: radiateur à gaz
gas mask: masque à gaz
gas meter: compteur à gaz
gas pedal: accélérateur
gas ring: brûleur à gaz
gas station: *n.* poste d'essence

gas tap: robinet de gaz
gas: *n.* gaz; essence
gaseous: *adj.* gazeux
gash: *n.* entaille; fente
gash: *vt.* entailler
gasket: *n.* joint d'étanchéité
gasoline: *n.* gazoline
gasp: *n.* halètements
gasp: *vi.* haleter
gassy: *adj.* gazeux
gastric: *adj.* gastrique
gastronomic: *adj.* gastronomique
gasworks: *npl.* usine à gaz
gate: *n.* porte; portail
gateway: *n.* passerelle; interface
gather: *vt.* rassembler; ramasser; comprendre
gathering: *n.* réunion; récolte
gauche: *adj.* gauche; maladroit
gaudy: *adj.* criard
gauge: *n.* calibre; écartement
gauge: *vt.* mesurer; calibrer
gaunt: *adj.* décharné
gauze: *n.* gaze
gay: *adj.* gai; vif; homosexuel
gaze: *n.* regard
gaze: *vi.* contempler; considérer
gazelle: *n.* gazelle
gazette: *n.* gazette
gazetteer: *n.* répertoire géographique
gear shift: levier de vitesse
gear wheel: roue d'engrenage
gear: *n.* équipement; matériel; appareil; affaires; vitesse
gearbox: *n.* boîte de vitesses
gel: *n.* gel
gelatine: *n.* gélatine
gelignite: *n.* gélignite
gem: *n.* pierre précieuse; perle
gender: *n.* genre
gene: *n.* gène
genealogical: *adj.* généalogique
genealogy: *n.* généalogie
general election: élections générales

general library: bibliothèque encyclopédique
general meeting: l'assemblée générale
general office: secrétariat général
general partner: associé gérant
general partnership: une société en nom collectif
general: *adj.* général; commun; usuel; *n.* général
generalisation: *n.* généralisation
generalise: *vt.* généraliser
generality: *n.* généralité; majeure partie
generate: *vt.* engendrer; produire; causer
generation: *n.* génération
generator: *n.* générateur
generic: *adj.* générique
generosity: *n.* générosité; libéralité
generous: *adj.* généreux
genetics: *npl.* génétique
genii: *adj.* cordial; doux
genitals: *npl.* organes génitaux
genitive: *n.* génitif
genius: *n.* génie
genotype: *n.* génotype
genre: *n.* genre
genteel: *adj.* distingué
gentle: *adj.* doux; modéré
gentleman: *n.* gentleman
gentleness: *n.* douceur
gently: *adv.* doucement
gentry: *n.* aristocratie
gents: *n.* toilettes pour hommes
genuflexion: *n.* génuflexion
genuine: *adj.* authentique; sincère
genus: *n.* genre
geographer: *n.* géographe
geographical: *adj.* géographique
geography: *n.* géographie
geological: *adj.* géologique
geologist: *n.* géologue
geology: *n.* géologie

geometric: *adj.* géométrique
geometrical isomer: isomère géométrique
geometry: *n.* géométrie
geranium: *n.* géranium
geriatric: *n.* malade gériatrique; *adj.* gériatrique
germ: *n.* germe
German: *n.* Allemand; *adj.* allemand
Germany: *n.* Allemagne
germinate: *vi.* germer
gerund: *n.* nom verbal
gesticulate: *vi.* gesticuler
gesture: *n.* geste
get: *vt.* avoir; obtenir; atteindre; gagner; attraper
geyser: *n.* geyser; chauffe-eau
ghastly: *adj.* affreux; sinistre
gherkin: *n.* cornichon
ghost: *n.* fantôme; spectre
ghostly: *adj.* spectral
giant: *n.* géant
gibberish: *n.* charabia; sornettes
gibe: *n.* moquerie
gibe: *vi.* se moquer
giblets: *npl.* abattis (de volaille)
giddiness: *n.* vertige
giddy: *adj.* vertigineux
gift voucher: bon-cadeau
gift: *n.* cadeau; don; talent
gifted: *adj.* talentueux; doué
gigantic: *adj.* gigantesque
giggle: *vi.* rire bêtement
gild: *vt.* dorer
gilding: *n.* dorure
gill: *n.* quart de pinte
gilt-edged: *adj.* de premier ordre
gilt-edged: doré sur tranche
gimmick: *n.* truc
gin: *n.* gin
ginger: *n.* gingembre
gingerbread: *n.* pain d'épice
ginger-haired: *adj.* roux
giraffe: *n.* girafe

girder: *n.* poutre
girdle: *n.* gaine; ceinture
girl: *n.* fine
girlfriend: *n.* amie; petite amie
girlish: *adj.* de fille
giro cheque: chèque postal britannique
giro: *n.* virement
girth: *n.* sangle; circonférence
gist: *n.* essence
give: *vt.* donner; offrir; prononcer; faire; consacrer
gizzard: *n.* gésier
glacial: *adj.* glacial
glacier: *n.* glacier
glad: *adj.* joyeux; content
gladden: *vt.* réjouir
gladiator: *n.* gladiateur
glamorous: *adj.* attrayant; séduisant
glamour: *n.* attrait; séduction
glance: *n.* regard
glance: *vi.* regarder; jeter un coup d'oeil
glancing: *adj.* oblique
gland: *n.* glande
glare: *n.* éclat; regard féroce
glare: *vi.* éblouir; briller; lancer des regards indignés
glaring: *adj.* éclatant; évident; furieux
glass: *n.* verre; longue-vue; miroir; *adj.* en verre
glassware: *n.* verrerie
glassy: *adj.* vitreux; cristallin
glaze: *vt.* vitrer; vernisser
glazier: *n.* vitrier
gleam: *n.* rayon
gleam: *vi.* rayonner; briller
gleaming: *adj.* brillant
glean: *vt.* glaner
glee: *n.* joie; exultation
glen: *n.* vallée
glib: *adj.* facile; volubile
glide: *vi.* glisser; planer

gliding: *n.* vol plané
glimmer: *n.* lueur
glimmer: *vi.* luire
glimpse: *n.* aperçu; vision
glimpse: *vt.* entrevoir
glint: *vi.* briller; scintiller
glisten: *vi.* luire; briller
glitter: *vi.* luire; briller
gloat: *vi.* exulter
global: *adj.* global; mondial
globe: *n.* globe; sphère
gloominess: *n.* obscurité; mélancolie; tristesse
gloomy: *adj.* sombre; obscur; triste; mélancolique
glorification: *n.* glorification
glorify: *vt.* glorifier; célébrer
glorious: *adj.* glorieux; illustre
glory: *n.* gloire; célébrité
gloss: *n.* glose; lustre
gloss: *vt.* gloser; interpréter; lustrer
glossary: *n.* glossaire
glossy: *adj.* lustré; brillant
glove compartment: boîte à gants
glove: *n.* gant
glow: *vi.* rougeoyer; rayonner
glower: *vi.* lancer des regards noirs
glue: *n.* colle
glue: *vt.* coller
gluey: *adj.* gluant; visqueux
glum: *adj.* abattu; triste
glut: *n.* surabondance
glutinons: *adj.* glutineux
glutton: *n.* glouton
gluttony: *n.* gloutonnerie
glycerine: *n.* glycérine
gnarled: *adj.* noueux
gnaw: *vt.* ronger
gnome: *n.* gnome
go: *vi.* aller; s'en aller; partir; disparaître; se perdre
goad: *n.* aiguillon
goad: *vt.* aiguillonner; stimuler

go-ahead: *adj.* entreprenant; *n.* feu vert
goal: *n.* but; objectif
goalkeeper: *n.* gardien de but
goalpost: *n.* poteau de but
goat: *n.* chèvre
goatherd: *n.* chevrier
gobble: *vt.* engloutir; avaler
go-between: *n.* intermédiaire
goblet: *n.* coupe
goblin: *n.* lutin
God: *n.* Dieu
godchild: *n.* filleul
goddaughter: *n.* filleule
goddess: *n.* déesse
godfather: *n.* parrain
godforsaken: *adj.* perdu
godhead: *n.* divinité
godless: *adj.* impie; athée
godlike: *adj.* divin
godliness: *n.* piété; dévotion; sainteté
godly: *adj.* pieux; dévot; religieux; droit
godmother: *n.* marraine
godsend: *n.* don du ciel
godson: *n.* filleul
goggle-eyed: *adj.* aux yeux exorbités de surprise
goggles: *npl.* lunettes; lunettes de plongée
going: *n.* départ; sortie; progrès
gold: *n.* or
golden: *adj.* doré; d'or; excellent
goldfish: *n.* poisson rouge
gold-plated: *adj.* plaqué or
goldsmith: *n.* orfèvre
golf ball: balle de golf
golf club: club de golf
golf course: terrain de golf
golf: *n.* golf
golfer: *n.* golfeur
gondolier: *n.* gondolier
gone: *adj.* parti; perdu; passé; fini; mort; disparu

gong: *n.* gong
Good Friday: *n.* Vendredi Saint
good nature: bon caractère
good: *adj.* bon; bienveillant; favorable; valable; *adv.* bien; *n.* bien; avantage; marchandise
goodbye!: *excl.* au revoir!
goodies: *npl.* gourmandises
good-looking: *adj.* beau
good-natured: *adj.* qui a bon caractère
goodness: *n.* bonté; qualité
goods; consumer: biens de consommation
goods; flawed: marchandises présentant un défaut
goods; to clear: dédouaner les marchandises
goodwill: *n.* bienveillance
goose: *n.* oie
gooseberry: *n.* groseille à maquereau
goosebumps: *npl.* chair de poule
goose-step: *n.* pas de l'oie
gore: *n.* sang
gore: *vt.* blesser d'un coup de corne
gorge: *n.* gorge
gorge: *vt.* engloutir; avaler
gorgeous: *adj.* merveilleux
gorilla: *n.* gorille
gorse: *n.* ajonc riz
gory: *adj.* sanglant
goshawk: *n.* autour
gospel: *n.* évangile
gossamer: *n.* gaze; toile d'araignée
gossip: *n.* commérages; cancans
gossip: *vi.* cancaner; faire des commérages
gothic: *adj.* gothique
gout: *n.* goutte
govern: *vt.* gouverner; diriger
governess: *n.* gouvernante
government: *n.* gouvernement; administration publique
governor: *n.* gouverneur

gown: *n.* toge; robe; robe de chambre
grab: *n.* poigne; compréhension; prise
grab: *vt.* saisir; empoigner; comprendre
grabber-hand: main de saisie
grace: *n.* grâce; faveur; pardon; grâces
grace: *vt.* orner; honorer
graceful: *adj.* gracieux
gracious: *adj.* gracieux; favorable
gradation: *n.* gradation
grade crossing: passage à niveau
grade school: école primaire
grade: *n.* grade; degré; classe
grade: *v.* calibrer
gradient: *n.* (rail) rampe
gradual: *adj.* graduel
graduate school: université de 3e cycle
graduate studies: études de 3e cycle
graduate: *vi.* graduer; obtenir son diplôme
graduation: *n.* graduation; remise des diplômes
graffiti: *n.* graffiti
graft: *n.* greffe
graft: *vt.* greffer
grain: *n.* grain; graine; céréales
gram: *n.* gramme
grammar checker: logiciel de vérification; correction grammaticale
grammar: *n.* grammaire
grammatical: *adj.* grammatical
granary: *n.* grenier
grand piano: piano à queue
grand: *adj.* grandiose; magnifique
grandad: *n.* pépé
grandchild: *n.* petit-fils; petite-fille
grandchildren: *npl.* petits-enfants
granddaughter: *n.* petite-fille
grandeur: *n.* grandeur; pompe
grandfather: *n.* grand-père
grandiose: *adj.* grandiose

grandma: *n.* mémé
grandmother: *n.* grand-mère
grandparents: *npl.* grands-parents
grandson: *n.* petit-fils
grandstand: *n.* tribune
granite: *n.* granit
granny: *n.* mamie
grant a discount, to: accorder une remise
grant: *n.* bourse; allocation
grant: subvention; bourse d'études
grant: *vt.* accorder
granulate: *vt.* granuler
granule: *n.* granule
grape: *n.* grain de raisin
grapefruit: *n.* pamplemousse
graph: *n.* graphe; graphique
graphic: *adj.* graphique; pittoresque
graphics digitizer: convertisseur numérique de graphiques
graphics software: logiciel graphique; de graphisme; grapheur
graphics: *n.* art graphique; graphiques
grapnel: *n.* grappin
grasping: *adj.* avide
grass snake: couleuvre
grass: *n.* herbe
grasshopper: *n.* sauterelle
grassland: *n.* prés
grass-roots: *adj.* populaire; de base
grassy: *adj.* herbeux
grate: *n.* grille
grate: *vt.* râper; grincer
grateful: *adj.* reconnaissant
gratefulness: *n.* gratitude; reconnaissance
gratification: *n.* satisfaction
gratify: *vt.* satisfaire; faire plaisir à
gratifying: *adj.* réjouissant
grating: *n.* grillage; grincement; *adj.* grinçant; énervant
gratis: *adv.* gratis; gratuitement

gratitude: *n.* gratitude; reconnaissance
gratuitous: *adj.* gratuit; volontaire
gratuity: *n.* gratification
grave digger: fossoyeur
grave: *n.* tombe; *adj.* grave; sérieux
gravel: *n.* gravier
gravestone: *n.* pierre tombale
graveyard: *n.* cimetière
gravit te: *vi.* graviter
gravitation: *n.* gravitation
gravity: *n.* gravité
gravy: *n.* jus de viande; sauce
gray: *adj.* gris
graze: *vt.* paître; effleurer
grease: *n.* graisse
grease: *vt.* graisser
greaseproof: *adj.* (papier) sulfurisé
greasy: *adj.* gras
great: *adj.* grand; important; fort
greatcoat: *n.* pardessus
great-grandfather: *n.* arrière-grand-père
great-grandmother: *n.* arrière-grand-mère
greatness: *n.* grandeur; importance; pouvoir; noblesse
greedily: *adv.* avidement
greediness: *n.* avidité; gloutonnerie
greedy: *adj.* avide; glouton
green belt: zone verte
green card: carte verte
green room: foyer des artistes
green: *adj.* vert; inexpérimenté; *n.* vert; verdure
greenback: *n.* (US) billet
greenery: *n.* verdure
greengrocer: *n.* marchand de fruits et légumes
greenhouse: *n.* serre
greenish: *adj.* verdâtre
greenness: *n.* verdure; manque d'expérience
greet: *vt.* saluer; accueillir

greeting card: carte de voeux
greeting: *n.* salutation; accueil
gregarious: *adj.* sociable; grégaire
grenade: *n.* grenade
grenadier: *n.* grenadier
grey: *adj.* gris; *n.* gris
grey-haired: *adj.* aux cheveux gris
greyhound: *n.* lévrier
greyish: *adj.* grisâtre; grisonnant
greyness: *n.* couleur grise; grisaille
grid: *n.* grille; réseau
gridiron: *n.* gril; terrain de foot-ball américain
grief: *n.* chagrin; douleur; peine
grievance: *n.* grief; doléance
grieve: *vt.* peiner; affliger
grievous: *adj.* douloureux; grave; atroce
griffin: *n.* griffon
grill: *n.* gril m; grillade
grill: *vt.* faire griller; interroger; cuisiner
grille: *n.* grille
grim: *adj.* peu engageant; sinistre
grimace: *n.* grimace; moue
grime: *n.* saleté
grimy: *adj.* crasseux
grin: *n.* grimace; sourire
grin: *vi.* grimacer; sourire
grind: *vt.* moudre; piler; broyer; affûter; aiguiser
grinder: *n.* moulin; rémouleur; molaire
grip: *n.* prise poignée; sac de voyage
grip: *vt.* saisir; agripper
gripping: *adj.* passionnant
grisly: *adj.* horrible; sinistre
gristle: *n.* cartilage
gristly: *adj.* cartilagineux
grit: *n.* gravillon; cran
groan: *n.* gémissement; grognement
groan: *vi.* gémir; grogner
grocer: *n.* épicier
groceries: *npl.* épicerie; provisions

grocer's (shop): *n.* épicerie
groggy: *adj.* sonné; étourdi
groin: *n.* aine
groom: *n.* palefrenier; valet; marié
groom: *vt.* panser; préparer
groove: *n.* rainure
grope: *vt.* chercher à tâtons; *vi.* tâtonner
gross: *adj.* gros; corpulent; épais; grossier; brut
grotesque: *adj.* grotesque
grotto: *n.* grotte
ground floor: rez-de-chaussée
ground staff: personnel au sol
ground: *n.* terre; sol; terrain; territoire; fondement; raison fondamentale; fond
ground: *vt.* retenir au sol; fonder; mettre une prise de terre
grounding: *n.* connaissances de base
groundless: *adj.* sans fondement
groundwork: *n.* travaux de préparation
group: *n.* groupe
group: *vt.* regrouper
groupware: *n.* logiciel de travail en groupe; collecticiel
grouse: *n.* grouse; coq de bruyère
grouse: *vi.* grogner
grove: *n.* bosquet
grovel: *vi.* se trainer; ramper
grow: *vt.* cultiver; faire pousser
grower: *n.* cultivateur; producteur
growing: *adj.* croissant; grandissant
growl: *n.* grognement
growl: *vi.* grogner
grown-up: *n.* adulte
growth factor: facteur de croissance
growth: *n.* croissance; augmentation; poussée
grub street: le monde du journalisme
grub: *n.* asticot
grubby: *adj.* sale
grudge: *n.* rancune

grudge: *vt.* accorder à contrecoeur
grudgingly: *adv.* à contrecoeur
gruel: *n.* gruau
gruelling: *adj.* difficile; pénible
gruesome: *adj.* horrible
gruff: *adj.* brusque
gruffness: *n.* brusquerie
grumble: *vi.* grogner; grommeler
grumpy: *adj.* ronchon; grincheux
grunt: *n.* grognement
grunt: *vi.* grogner
guarantee: *n.* garantie
guarantee: *vt.* garantir
guard: *n.* garde; garde
guard: *vt.* garder; défendre
guarded: *adj.* prudent; surveillé
guardian: *n.* tuteur; gardien
guardianship: *n.* tutelle
guardroom: *n.* corps de garde
guerilla warfare: guérilla
guerrilla: *n.* guérillero
guess: *n.* conjecture
guess: *vt.* deviner; supposer
guest room: chambre d'amis
guffaw: *n.* éclat de rire
guidance: *n.* guidage; direction
guide dog: chien d'aveugle
guide: *n.* guide
guide: *vt.* guider; diriger
guidebook: *n.* guide
guidelines: *npl.* directives; lignes directrices
guild: *n.* association; corporation
guile: *n.* astuce
guileless: *adj.* candide
guillotine: *n.* guillotine
guillotine: *vt.* guillotiner
guilt: *n.* culpabilité
guiltless: *adj.* innocent
guilty: *adj.* coupable
guinea pi: cochon d'Inde; cobaye
guise: *n.* apparence
guitar: *n.* guitare
gulf: *n.* golfe; abîme

gull: *n.* mouette
gullet: *n.* oesophage
gullibility: *n.* crédulité
gullilble: *adj.* crédule
gully: *n.* ravine
gum tree: gommier
gum: *n.* gomme; gencive
gum: *vt.* coller
gun carriage: affût de canon
gun: *n.* pistolet; fusil
gunboat: *n.* canonnière
gunfire: *n.* coups de feu
gunman: *n.* homme armé
gunmetal: *n.* bronze à canon
gunner: *n.* artilleur
gunnery: *n.* artillerie gunpoint
gunpowder: *n.* poudre à canon
gunshot: *n.* coup de feu
gunsmith: *n.* armurier
gurgle: *vi.* gargouiller
guru: *n.* gourou
gush: *n.* jaillissement
gush: *vi.* jaillir; bouillonner
gushing: *adj.* jaillissant; très exubérant
gusset: *n.* soufflet
gust: *n.* rafale; bouffée
gusto: *n.* plaisir; délectation
gusty: *adj.* venteux
gut: *n.* intestin; coeur au ventre
gut: *vt.* vider
gutter press: la presse à scandale
gutter: *n.* gouttière; caniveau
guttural: *adj.* guttural
guy: *n.* mec; type
guzzle: *vt.* bouffer; engloutir; avaler
gymnasium: *n.* gymnase
gymnast: *n.* gymnaste
gymnastic: *adj.* gymnastique
gynaecologist: *n.* gynécologue
gypsy: *n.* gitan
gyrate: *vi.* tourner

H

haberdasher: *n.* mercier
haberdashery: *n.* mercerie
habit: *n.* habitude
habitable: *adj.* habitable
habitat: *n.* habitat
habitual: *adj.* habituel
hack: *n.* coupure; entaille
hack: *vt.* entailler; couper
hacker: *n.* pirate informatique
hackneyed: *adj.* rebattu
haddock: *n.* aiglefin
haemorrhage: *n.* hémorragie
haemorrhoids: *npl.* hémorroïdes
hag: *n.* sorcière
haggard: *adj.* exténué; défait
haggle: *vi.* marchander
hail: *n.* grêle f
hail: *vt.* saluer; *vi.* grêler
hailstone: *n.* grêlon
hair remover: crème dépilatoire
hair: *n.* cheveux; poil
hairbrush: *n.* brosse pour cheveux
haircut: *n.* coupe à cheveux
hairdresser: *n.* coiffeur
hairdryer: *n.* séchoir à cheveux
hairless: *adj.* chauve; sans poils
hairnet: *n.* filet à cheveux
hairpin bend: virage en épingle à cheveux
hairpin: *n.* épingle à cheveux
hairspray: *n.* laque à cheveux
hairstyle: *n.* coiffure
hairy: *adj.* chevelu; poilu
hale: *adj.* vigoureux
half: *n.* moitié; *adj.* demi; *adv.* à moitié
half-caste: *adj.* métis
half-hearted: *adj.* peu enthousiaste
half-hour: *n.* demi-heure
half-life: *n.* demi-vie
half-moon: *n.* demi-lune
half-price: *adj.* à moitié prix
half-reaction: *n.* demi-réaction

half-time: *n.* mi-temps
halfway: *adv.* à mi-chemin
hall: *n.* vestibule
hallmark: *n.* marque
hallow: *vt.* consacrer; sanctifier
hallucination: *n.* hallucination
halo: *n.* halo
halogen: *n.* halogène
halt: *n.* arrêt; halte
halt: *vi.* s'arrêter
halting: *adj.* hésitant; boiteux; heurté
halve: *vt.* couper en deux
ham: *n.* jambon
hamlet: *n.* hameau
hammer: *n.* marteau
hammer: *vt.* marteler
hammock: *n.* hamac
hamper: *n.* panier
hamper: *vt.* embarrasser; entraver
hamstring: *vt.* couper les jarrets à
hand: *n.* main; ouvrier; aiguille
hand: *vt.* donner; passer
handbag: *n.* sac à main
handbell: *n.* sonnette
handbook: *n.* manuel
handbrake: *n.* frein à main
handcuff: *n.* menotte
handful: *n.* poignée
handicap: *n.* handicap
handicapped: *adj.* handicapé
handicraft: *n.* artisanat
handiwork: *n.* travail manuel
handkerchief: *n.* mouchoir
handle with care: attention; fragile
handle: *n.* manche; queue; anse; poignée
handle: *n.* surnom; pseudonyme; alias
handle: *vt.* manier; traiter; prendre
handlebars: *npl.* guidon
handling operations: opérations de manutention
handling: *n.* maniement; traitement
handlist: *n.* index

handrail: *n.* garde-fou
handshake: *n.* poignée de mains
handsome: *adj.* beau
handwriting: *n.* écriture
handwritten: *adj.* autographe
handy: *adj.* pratique; adroit
hang: *vt.* accrocher; pendre
hanger: *n.* cintre
hanger-on: *n.* parasite
hangings: *npl.* tapisserie
hangman: *n.* bourreau
hangover: *n.* gueule de bois
hang-up: *n.* complexe
hanker: *vi.* avoir envie
haphazard: *adj.* fortuit
hapless: *adj.* malheureux
happen: *vi.* se passer
happening: *n.* événement
happily: *adv.* heureusement;
gaiement
happiness: *n.* bonheur
happy: *adj.* heureux
harangue: *n.* harangue
harangue: *vt.* haranguer
harass: *vt.* harceler; tourmenter
harbinger: *n.* précurseur
harbour: *n.* port
harbour: *vt.* héberger; entretenir;
nourrir
hard drive: unité de disque dur
hard: *adj.* dur; pénible; sévère; rigide
hardback (book): livre cartonné; à
couverture rigide
harden: *v.* durcir
hard-hearted: *adj.* au coeur dur;
insensible
hardiness: *n.* robustesse
hardly: *adv.* à peine
hardness: *n.* dureté; difficulté;
sévérité
hardship: *n.* épreuves
hard-up: *adj.* fauché; sans le sou
hardware: *n.* matériel; hardware;
quincaillerie

hardwearing: *adj.* résistant
hardy: *adj.* fort; robuste; résistant
hare: *n.* lièvre
hare-brained: *adj.* écervelé
hare-lipped: *adj.* qui a un bec de
lièvre
haricot: *n.* haricot blanc
harlequin: *n.* arlequin
harm: *n.* mal; tort
harm: *vt.* faire du mal à; nuire à
harmful: *adj.* nuisible
harmless: *adj.* inoffensif
harmonic oscillator: oscillateur
harmonique
harmonic: *adj.* harmonique
harmonious: *adj.* harmonieux
harmonise: *vt.* harmoniser
harmony: *n.* harmonie
harness: *n.* harnais
harness: *vt.* harnacher
harp: *n.* harpe
harpist: *n.* harpiste
harpoon: *n.* harpon
harpsichord: *n.* clavecin
harrow: *n.* herse
harry: *vt.* harceler; dévaster
harsh: *adj.* dur; austère; rude
harshness: *n.* aspérité; dureté;
austérité
harvest: *n.* récolte; moisson
harvest: *vt.* récolter; moissonner
harvester: *n.* moissonneur
hash (sign): caractère #; dièse
hash noise: bruit parasite
hashing: *n.* hachage
hassock: *n.* agenouilloir
haste: *n.* hâte
hasten: *vt.* accélérer; hâter
hastily: *adv.* à la hâte;
précipitamment
hasty: *adj.* hâtif; irréfléchi
hat: *n.* chapeau
hatbox: *n.* carton à chapeau
hatch: *n.* écoutille

hatch: *vt.* couver; faire éclore; tramer
hatchet: *n.* hachette
hatchway: *n.* écoutille
hate: *n.* haine
hate: *vt.* haïr; détester
hateful: *adj.* odieux; détestable
hatred: *n.* haine
hatter: *n.* chapelier
haughtily: *adv.* hautainement
haughtiness: *n.* orgueil; hauteur
haughty: *adj.* hautain; orgueilleux
haul: *n.* prise; butin; trajet
haul: *vt.* tirer
haulier: *n.* camionneur
haunch: *n.* hanche
haunt: *n.* repaire
haunt: *vt.* hanter; fréquenter
have: *vt.* avoir; posséder
haven: *n.* refuge
haversack: *n.* sac à dos
havoc: *n.* ravages
hawk: *n.* faucon
hawk: *vi.* chasser au faucon
hawthorn: *n.* aubépine
hay fever: rhume des foins
hay: *n.* foin
hayloft: *n.* fenil
hayrick: *n.* meule de foin
hazard: *n.* risque; danger
hazard: *vt.* risquer
hazardous: *adj.* risqué; dangereux
haze: *n.* brume
hazel: *n.* noisetier; *adj.* noisette
hazelnut: *n.* noisette
hazy: *adj.* brumeux
head office: siège social
head storekeeper: chef magasinier
head: *n.* tête; chef; esprit
head: *vt.* conduire
headache: *n.* mal de tête
headdress: *n.* coiffe
headland: *n.* promontoire
headlight: *n.* phare
headline: *n.* titre

headlong: *adv.* à toute allure
headmaster: *n.* directeur
headphones: *npl.* écouteurs
headquarters: *npl.* quartier général; siège social
headroom: *n.* hauteur
headstrong: *adj.* têtu
headwaiter: *n.* maître d'hôtel
headway: *n.* progrès
heady: *adj.* capiteux
heal: *vt.* guérir
health: *n.* santé
healthiness: *n.* bonne santé
healthy: *adj.* en bonne santé; sain
heap: *n.* tas
heap: *vt.* entasser
hear: *vt.* entendre; écouter
hearing aid: audiophone
hearing: *n.* ouïe
hearsay: *n.* rumeur
hearse: *n.* corbillard
heart attack: crise cardiaque
heart failure: arrêt cardiaque
heart: *n.* coeur
heartbreaking: *adj.* à fendre le coeur
heartburn: *n.* acidité gastrique
heartfelt: *adj.* sincère
hearth: *n.* foyer
heartily: *adv.* sincèrement; cordialement
heartiness: *n.* cordialité; sincérité
heartless: *adj.* cruel
hearty: *adj.* cordial
heat capacity: capacité calorifique
heat latent: chaleur latente
heat of reaction: chaleur de réaction
heat of vaporization: chaleur de vaporisation
heat: *n.* chaleur
heat: *vt.* chauffer
heater: *n.* radiateur
heathen: *n.* païen; *adj.* sauvage; barbare
heather: *n.* bruyère

heating: *n.* chauffage
heatwave: *n.* onde de chaleur
heave: *n.* effort
heave: *vt.* lever; tirer
heaven: *n.* ciel
heavenly: *adj.* divin
heavily: *adv.* lourdement
heaviness: *n.* lourdeur
heavy: *adj.* lourd; pesant;
considérable
heckle: *vt.* interrompre
hectic: *adj.* agité
hedge: *n.* haie
hedge: *vt.* entourer d'une haie
hedgehog: *n.* hérisson
heed: *vt.* tenir compte de; *n.* soin;
attention
heedless: *adj.* inattentif; étourdi
heel: *n.* talon
hefty: *adj.* costaud; puissant
heifer: *n.* génisse
height: *n.* hauteur; altitude
heighten: *vt.* rehausser; augmenter;
intensifier
heinous: *adj.* atroce
heir: *n.* héritier
heiress: *n.* héritière
heirloom: *n.* héritage
helicopter: *n.* hélicoptère
hell: *n.* enfer
hellish: *adj.* infernal
helm: *n.* (mar) barre
helmet: *n.* casque
help: *n.* aide; secours
help: *vt.* aider; secourir
helper: *n.* aide
helpful: *adj.* utile; qui rend service
helping: *n.* portion
helpless: *adj.* impuissant
helter-skelter: *adv.* n'importe
comment; en désordre
he-m: *n.* dur; mâle
hem: *n.* ourlet
hem: *vt.* ourler

hemisphere: *n.* hémisphère
hemp: *n.* chanvre
hen: *n.* poule
henceforth: *adv.* dorénavant
henchman: *n.* acolyte
hen-house: *n.* poulailler
hepatitis: *n.* hépatite
herald: *n.* héraut
heraldry: *n.* héraldique
herb: *n.* herbe
herbaceous: *adj.* herbacé
herbalist: *n.* herboriste
herbivore: *n.* herbivore
herbivorous: *adj.* herbivore
herd: *n.* troupeau
here: *adv.* ici
hereabout(s): *adv.* dans les environs
hereafter: *adv.* plus tard; ci-après
hereby: *adv.* par la présente
hereditary: *adj.* héréditaire
heredity: *n.* hérédité
heresy: *n.* hérésie
heretic: *adj.* hérétique
heritage: *n.* patrimoine; héritage
hermetic: *adj.* hermétique
hermit: *n.* ermite
hermitage: *n.* ermitage
hernia: *n.* hernie
hero: *n.* héros
heroic: *adj.* héroïque
heroine: *n.* héroïne
heroism: *n.* héroïsme
heron: *n.* héron
herring: *n.* hareng
hers: *pron.* le sien; la sienne
herself: *pron.* elle-même
hesitant: *adj.* hésitant
hesitate: *vi.* hésiter
hesitation: *n.* hésitation
heterogeneous mixture: mélange
hétérogène
heterogeneous: *adj.* hétérogène
heterosexual: *adj.* hétérosexuel
heterozygous: *adj.* heterozygote

hew: *vt.* tailler; couper
heyday: *n.* apogée
hiatus: *n.* hiatus
hibernate: *vi.* hiberner
hiccup: *n.* hoquet
hiccup: *vi.* avoir le hoquet
hickory: *n.* noyer d'Amérique
hide a view (to): masquer une zone d'affichage
hide: *n.* cuir; peau
hide: *vt.* cacher
hideaway: *n.* cachette
hideous: *adj.* hideux; horrible
hiding-place: *n.* cachette
hierarchical notation: notation hiérarchique
hierarchy: *n.* hiérarchie
hieroglyphic: *adj.* hiéroglyphique; *n.* hiéroglyphe
hi-fi: *n.* hi-fi
higgiedy-piggledy: *adv.* pêle-mêle
high altar: maître-autel
high chair: chaise haute
high school: lycée
high water: marée haute
high: *adj.* haut; élevé
higher education: enseignement supérieur
high-handed: *adj.* tyrannique
highlands: *npl.* terres montagneuses
highlight: *n.* point fort
highlight: *v.* souligner
highlighting feature: fonction de surlignage
highly: *adj.* extrêmement; hautement
highness: *n.* hauteur; altesse
high-strung: *adj.* nerveux; tendu
highway: *n.* grande route
hijack: *vt.* détourner
hijacker: *n.* pirate de l'air
hike: *vi.* faire une randonnée
hilarious: *adj.* hilarant; hilare
hill: *n.* colline
hillock: *n.* petite colline

hillside: *n.* coteau
hilly: *adj.* montagneux
hilt: *n.* poignée
him: *pron.* lui; le
himself: *pron.* lui-même; soi
hind: *adj.* derrière; *n.* biche
hinder: *vt.* gêner; entraver
hindmost: *adj.* dernier
hindquarter: *n.* arrière-train
hindrance: *n.* gêne; obstacle
hinge: *n.* charnière; gond
hint: *n.* allusion; insinuation
hint: *vt.* insinuer; suggérer
hip: *n.* hanche
hippopotamus: *n.* hippopotame
hire: *n.* location
hire: *vt.* louer
his: *pron.* son; sa; ses; le sien; la sienne
Hispanic: *adj.* hispanique
hiss: *vt.* siffler
historian: *n.* historien
historical document: document historique
historical: *adj.* historique
history: *n.* histoire
histrionic: *adj.* théâtral
hit: *n.* coup; succès
hit: *vt.* frapper; atteindre; heurter
hitch: *n.* noeud; anicroche
hitch: *vt.* accrocher
hitchhike: *vi.* faire du stop
hitherto unpublished: inédit
hitherto: *adv.* jusqu'à présent; jusqu'ici
hive: *n.* ruche
hoard: *n.* stock; trésor caché
hoard: *vt.* accumuler; amasser
hoarfrost: *n.* givre
hoarse: *adj.* rauque
hoarseness: *n.* voix rauque
hoax: *n.* canular
hoax: *vt.* faire un canular à
hobble: *vi.* boitiller

hobby: *n.* passe-temps
hobbyhorse: *n.* cheval de bataille
hobo: *n.* vagabond
hockey: *n.* hockey
hodge-podge: *n.* confusion
hoe: *n.* binette
hoe: *vt.* biner
hog: *n.* porc
hoist: *n.* grue
hoist: *vt.* hisser
hoisting device: appareil de levage
hold: *n.* prise; pouvoir
hold: *vt.* tenir; détenir; contenir
holder: *n.* détenteur; titulaire; porteur (d'un document)
holding: *n.* possession
holdup: *n.* hold-up
hole: *n.* trou
holiday: *n.* jour de congé; jour férié
holiness: *n.* sainteté
hollow: *adj.* creux; *n.* creux
hollow: *vt.* creuser; vider
holly: *n.* (bot) houx
hollyhock: *n.* rose trémière
holocaust: *n.* holocauste
holster: *n.* étui de révolver
holy water: eau bénite
holy week: semaine sainte
holy: *adj.* saint; bénit; sacré
homage: *n.* hommage
home address: domicile
home computer: ordinateur familial; domestique
home page: page d'accueil
home trade: le commerce intérieur
home: *n.* maison; patrie; domicile
homeless: *adj.* sans abri
homeliness: *n.* simplicité
homemade: *adj.* fait maison
homeopathist: *n.* homéopathe
homeopathy: *n.* homéopathie
homesick: *adj.* nostalgique; qui a le mal du pays

homesickness: *n.* nostalgie; mal du pays
hometown: *n.* ville natale
homeward: *adj.* vers chez soi; vers son pays
homework: *n.* devoirs
homicid: *adj.* homicide
homicide: *n.* homicide
homogeneous mixture: mélange homogène
homogeneous: *adj.* homogène
homosexual: *adj.* homosexuel; *n.* homosexuel
homozygous: *adj.* homozygote
honest: *adj.* honnête
honesty: *n.* honnêteté
honey: *n.* miel
honeycomb: *n.* rayon de miel
honeymoon: *n.* lune de miel
honeysuckle: *n.* (bot) chèvrefeuille
honorary: *adj.* honoraire
honour: *n.* honneur
honour: *vt.* honorer
honourable: *adj.* honorable
honourably: *adv.* honorablement
hood: *n.* capot; capuche
hoodlum: *n.* truand
hoof: *n.* sabot
hook: *n.* crochet; hameçon
hook: *vt.* accrocher
hooked: *adj.* crochu
hooligan: *n.* vandale
hoop: *n.* cerceau
hooter: *n.* sirène
hop: *n.* (bot) houblon; saut
hop: *vi.* sauter
hope: *n.* espoir; espérance
hope: *vi.* espérer
hopeful: *adj.* plein d'espoir; prometteur
hopefulness: *n.* bon espoir
hopeless: *adj.* désespéré
horde: *n.* horde
horizon: *n.* horizon

horizontal axis: axe horizontal
horizontal: *adj.* horizontal
hormone: *n.* hormone
horn: *n.* corne
horned: *adj.* à cornes
hornet: *n.* frelon
horny: *adj.* calleux
horoscope: *n.* horoscope
horrendous: *adj.* horrible
horrible: *adj.* horrible
horribly: *adv.* horriblement;
énormément
horrific: *adj.* horrible; affreux
horrify: *vt.* horrifier
horror film: film d'horreur
horror: *n.* horreur
hors d'oeuvre: hors-d'oeuvre
horse chestnut: marron d'lnde
horse race: course de chevaux
horse: *n.* cheval
horse-breaker: *n.* dresseur de
chevaux
horsefly: *n.* taon
horseman: *n.* cavalier
horsemanship: *n.* équitation
horsepower: *n.* cheval-vapeur;
puissance en chevaux
horseradish: *n.* raifort
horseshoe: *n.* fer à cheval
horsewoman: *n.* cavalière
horticulture: *n.* horticulture
horticulturist: *n.* horticulteur
hose-pipe: *n.* tuyau
hosiery: *n.* bonneterie
hospitable: *adj.* hospitalier
hospitably: *adv.* avec hospitalité
hospital: *n.* hôpital
hospitality: *n.* hospitalité
host: *n.* hôte; hostie
hostage: *n.* otage
hostess: *n.* hôtesse
hostile: *adj.* hostile
hostility: *n.* hostilité

hot link: lien dynamique; lien
populaire; très demandé
hot: *adj.* chaud; épicé
hotbed: *n.* foyer
hotdog: *n.* hot-dog
hotel: *n.* hôtel
hotelier: *n.* hôtelier
hotheaded: *adj.* exalté
hothouse: *n.* serre
hot-line: ligne d'assistance
téléphonique
hotlist: *n.* favoris; liens favoris
hotly: *adv.* violemment
hotplate: *n.* plaque chauffante
hound: *n.* chien de chasse
hour: *n.* heure
hourglass: *n.* sablier
hourly: *adv.* toutes les heures
house: *n.* maison; maisonnée
house: *vt.* loger; éberger; abriter
houseboat: *n.* péniche; housebreaker;
cambrioleur
housebreaking: *n.* cambriolage
household: *n.* famille; ménage
householder: *n.* propriétaire; chef de
famille
housekeeper: *n.* gouvernante
housekeeping: *n.* travaux ménagers
houseless: *adv.* sans abri
house-warming party: pendaison de
crémaillère
housewife: *n.* ménagère
housework: *n.* travaux ménagers
housing development: urbanisation
housing: *n.* logement
hovel: *n.* taudis
hover: *vi.* planer
how: *adv.* comme; comment
however: *adv.* de quelque manière
que; cependant; néanmoins
howl: *n.* hurlement
howl: *vi.* hurler
hub: *n.* centre; moyeu
hubbub: *n.* vacarme

hubcap: *n.* enjoliveur
hue: *n.* teinte; nuance
hug: *n.* étreinte
hug: *vt.* étreindre
huge: *adj.* énorme
hulk: *n.* (mar) carcasse ponton
hull: *n.* (mar) coque
hum: *vi.* chantonner
human: *adj.* humain
humane: *adj.* humain
humanise: *vt.* humaniser
humanist: *n.* humaniste
humanitarian: *adj.* humanitaire
humanities (the): les sciences humaines
humanity: *n.* humanité
humanly: *adv.* humainement
humble: *adj.* humble; modeste
humble: *vt.* humilier
humbleness: *n.* humilité
humbly: *adv.* humblement
humbug: *n.* blagues
humdrum: *adj.* monotone
humid: *adj.* humide
humidity: *n.* humidité
humiliate: *vt.* humilier
humiliation: *n.* humiliation
humility: *n.* humilité
hummingbird: *n.* colibri
humorist: *n.* humoriste
humorous: *adj.* humoristique
humour: *n.* sens de l'humour; humour
humour: *vt.* complaire à
hump: *n.* bosse
hunch: *n.* intuition
hundred: *adj.* cent; *n.* centaine
hundredth: *adj.* centième
hundredweight: *n.* quintal
hunger strike: grève de la faim
hunger: *n.* faim
hunger: *vi.* avoir faim
hungrily: *adv.* avidement
hungry: *adj.* qui a faim; affamé

hunt: *n.* chasse
hunt: *vt.* chasser; poursuivre; chercher
hunter: *n.* chasseur
hunting: *n.* chasse
huntsman: *n.* chasseur
hurdle: *n.* haie
hurl: *vt.* lancer avec violence; jeter
hurricane: *n.* ouragan
hurried: *adj.* fait à la hâte; précipité
hurry: *n.* hâte
hurry: *vt.* presser; *vi.* se presser; se dépêcher
hurt: *n.* mal
hurt: *vt.* faire mal à; blesser
hurtful: *adj.* blessant
husband: *n.* mari
husbandry: *n.* agriculture
husk: *n.* coque
huskiness: *n.* voix rauque; *adj.* rauque
hustings: *n.* plate-forme électorale
hustle: *vt.* pousser avec force; bousculer
hut: *n.* cabane; hutte
hutch: *n.* clapier
hyacinth: *n.* jacinthe
hybrid orbital: hybride orbitaire
hydrant: *n.* bouche d'incendie
hydration: *n.* hydratation
hydraulic: *adj.* hydraulique
hydrocarbon: *n.* hydrocarbure
hydroelectric: *adj.* hydroélectrique
hydrofoil: *n.* hydroptère
hydrogen: *n.* hydrogène
hydrogenation: *n.* hydrogénation
hydrophobia: *n.* hydrophobie
hydroxide ion: ion hydroxyde
hyena: *n.* hyène
hygiene: *n.* hygiène
hygienic: *adj.* hygiénique
hymn: *n.* hymne
hyperbole: *n.* hyperbole
hypermarket: *n.* hypermarché

hyphen: *n.* trait d'union
hyphenated word: mot composé
hypochondria: *n.* hypocondrie
hypochondriac: *adj.* hypocondriaque
hypocrisy: *n.* hypocrisie
hypocrite: *adj.* hypocrite; *n.* hypocrite
hypocritic: *adj.* hypocrite
hypothesis: *n.* hypothèse
hypothetical: *adj.* hypothétique
hysteric: *adj.* hystérique
hysterics: *npl.* hystérie; crise de nerfs

I

ice cream: glace
ice rink: patinoire
ice skating: patinage sur glace
ice: *n.* glace
ice: *vt.* glacer; geler
ice-axe: *n.* piolet
iceberg: *n.* iceberg
ice-bound: *adj.* fermé par les glaces
icebox: *n.* glacière
icicle: *n.* stalactite; glaçon
iconoclast: *n.* iconoclaste
icy: *adj.* glacé
idea: *n.* idée
ideal gas: gaz parfait
ideal: *adj.* idéal
idealist: *n.* idéaliste
idenitical: *adj.* identique
identification: *n.* identification
identifier: *n.* identificateur
identify: *vt.* identifier
identity: *n.* identité
ideology: *n.* idéologie
idiom: *n.* expression idiomatique
idiomatic: *adj.* idiomatique
idiosyncrasy: *n.* idiosyncrasie
idiot: *n.* imbécile
idiotic: *adj.* idiot; bête
idle: *adj.* désoeuvré; au repos; inutile
idleness: *n.* paresse; oisiveté
idler: *n.* paresseux
idly: *adv.* oisivement; paresseusement; vainement
idol: *n.* idole
idolatry: *n.* idôlatrie
idolise: *vt.* idôlatrer
idyllic: *adj.* idyllique
igneous rock: roche ignée
ignite: *vt.* allumer; enflammer
ignition key: clé de contact
ignition: *n.* ignition; allumage
ignoble: *adj.* infâme; bas
ignominious: *adj.* ignominieux
ignominy: *n.* ignominie; infamie

ignoramus: *n.* ignorant
ignorance: *n.* ignorance
ignorant: *adj.* ignorant
ignore: *vt.* ne pas tenir compte de
ill feeling: rancoeur
ill: *adj.* malade; *n.* mal; dommage
ill-advised: *adj.* malavisé
illegal: *adj.* illégal
illegality: *n.* illégalité
illegible: *adj.* illisible
illegibly: *adv.* illisiblement
illegitimacy: *n.* illégitimité
illegitimate: *adj.* illégitime
illicit: *adj.* illicite
illiterate: *adj.* analphabète; illettré
illness: *n.* maladie
illogical: *adj.* illogique
ill-timed: *adj.* inopportun
ill-treat: *vt.* maltraiter
illuminate: *vt.* illuminer
illuminated: *adj.* enluminé
illumination: *n.* illumination
illusion: *n.* illusion
illusory: *adj.* illusoire
illustrate: *vt.* illustrer
illustration: *n.* illustration
illustrative: *adj.* qui illustre
illustrious: *adj.* illustre
ill-will: *n.* malveillance
image map: image cliquable
image processing: traitement de l'image
image: *n.* image
imagery: *n.* images
imaginable: *adj.* imaginable
imaginary: *adj.* imaginaire
imagination: *n.* imagination
imaginative: *adj.* imaginatif
imagine: *vt.* imaginer
imbalance: *n.* déséquilibre
imbecile: *adj.* imbécile; idiot
imbibe: *vt.* boire; imbiber; absorber
imbue: *vt.* imprégner
imitate: *vt.* imiter

imitation: *n.* imitation
imitative: *adj.* imitatif
immaculate: *adj.* immaculé
immaterial: *adj.* insignifiant
immature: *adj.* pas mûr
immeasurable: *adj.* incommensurable
immeasurably: *adv.* immensément
immediate: *adj.* immédiat
immense: *adj.* immense; énorme
immensity: *n.* immensité
immerse: *vt.* immerger
immersion: *n.* immersion
immigrant: *n.* immigrant
immigration: *n.* immigration
imminent: *adj.* imminent
immiscible: *adj.* immicible
immobile: *adj.* immobile
immobility: *n.* immobilité
immoderate: *adj.* immodéré; excessif
immodest: *adj.* immodeste
immoral: *adj.* immoral
immorality: *n.* immoralité
immortal: *adj.* immortel
immortalise: *vt.* immortaliser
immortality: *n.* immortalité
immune: *adj.* immunisé
immunise: *vt.* immuniser
immunity: *n.* immunité
immutable: *adj.* immuable
imp: *n.* lutin
impact: *n.* impact
impair: *vt.* diminuer; affaiblir
impale: *vt.* empaler
impalpable: *adj.* impalpable
impart: *vt.* communiquer
impartial: *adj.* impartial
impartiality: *n.* impartialité
impassable: *adj.* impraticable; infranchissable
impasse: *n.* impasse
impassive: *adj.* impassible
impatience: *n.* impatience
impatient: *adj.* impatient

impeach: *vt.* mettre en accusation
impeccable: *adj.* impeccable
impecunious: *adj.* impécunieux
impede: *vt.* empêcher; entraver
impediment: *n.* obstacle
impel: *vt.* pousser
impending: *adj.* imminent
impenetrable: *adj.* impénétrable
impenitent: *adv.* impénitent
imperative: *adj.* impératif
imperceptible: *adj.* imperceptible
imperceptibly: *adv.* imperceptiblement
imperfect: *adj.* imparfait; *n.* (grammar) imparfait
imperfection: *n.* imperfection; défaut
imperial: *adj.* impérial
imperialism: *n.* impérialisme
imperious: *adj.* impérieux
impermeable: *adj.* imperméable
impersonal: *adj.* impersonel
impersonate: *vt.* se faire passer pour; imiter
impertinence: *n.* impertinence
impertinent: *adj.* impertinent
imperturbable: *adj.* imperturbable
impervious: *adj.* imperméable; indifférent
impetuosity: *n.* impétuosité
impetuous: *adj.* impétueux
impetus: *n.* élan
impiety: *n.* impiété
impinge (on): *vi.* affecter; empiéter (sur)
impious: *adj.* impie
implacable: *adj.* implacable
implacably: *adv.* implacablement
implant: *vt.* implanter
implausible: *adj.* implausible
implement: *n.* outil; ustensile
implementation: *n.* mise en oeuvre; application
implicate: *vt.* impliquer
implication: *n.* implication

implicit: *adj.* implicite
implied: *adj.* implicite
implore: *vt.* supplier
imply: *vt.* supposer
impolite: *adj.* impoli
impoliteness: *n.* impolitesse
impolitic: *adj.* maladroit; impolitique
import quotas: contingents d'importation
import: *n.* importation
import: *vt.* importer
importance: *n.* importance
important: *adj.* important
importation: *n.* importation
importer: *n.* importateur
importun: *adj.* importun
importune: *vt.* importuner
importunity: *n.* importunité
impose: *vt.* imposer
imposing: *adj.* imposant
imposition: *n.* imposition
impossibility: *n.* impossibilité
impossible event: évènement impossible
impossible: *adj.* impossible
impostor: *n.* imposteur
impotence: *n.* impotence
impotent: *adj.* impotent
impound: *vt.* confisquer
impoverish: *vt.* appauvrir
impoverished: *adj.* appauvri
impoverishment: *n.* appauvrissement
impracticability: *n.* impraticabilité
impracticable: *adj.* impraticable
impratical: *adj.* peu pratique
imprecation: *n.* imprécation; malédiction
imprecise: *adj.* imprécis
impregnable: *adj.* inexpugnable
impregnate: *vt.* imprégner; féconder
impregnation: *n.* fécondation; imprégnation
impress: *vt.* impressionner
impression: *n.* impression; édition

impressionable: *adj.*
impressionnable
impressive: *adj.* impressionnant
imprint: *n.* empreinte
imprint: *vt.* imprimer; marquer
imprison: *vt.* emprisonner
imprisonment: *n.* emprisonnement
improbability: *n.* improbabilité
improbable: *adj.* improbable
improbable: *adj.* improbable
impromptu: *adj.* impromptu
improper: *adj.* indécent; déplacé
impropre: *adv.* indécemment; de
manière déplacée; improprement
impropriety: *n.* impropriété;
inconvenance
improve: *vt.* améliorer; *vi.* s'améliorer
improvement: *n.* amélioration
improvident: *adj.* imprévoyant
improvise: *vt.* improviser
imprudence: *n.* imprudence
imprudent: *adj.* imprudent
impudence: *n.* impudence
impudent: *adj.* impudent
impugn: *vt.* attaquer; contester
impulse: *n.* impulsion
impulsive: *adj.* impulsif
impunity: *n.* impunité
impure: *adj.* impur
impurity: *n.* impureté
in: *prep.* dans; en
inability: *n.* incapacité
inaccessible: *adj.* inaccessible
inaccuracy: *n.* inexactitude
inaccurate: *adj.* inexact
inaction: *n.* inaction
inactive: *adj.* inactif
inactivity: *n.* inactivité
inadequate: *adj.* inadéquat
inadmissible: *adj.* inadmissible
inadvertently: *adv.* par inadvertance
inalienable: *adj.* inaliénable
inane: *adj.* inepte
inanimate: *adj.* inanimé

inapplicable: *adj.* inapplicable
inappropriate: *adj.* impropre
inappropriate: *adj.* inopportun
inasmuch: *adv.* attendu que
inasulate: *vt.* isoler; insonoriser
inattentive: *adj.* inattentif
inaudible: *adj.* inaudible
inaugural: *adj.* inaugural
inaugurate: *vt.* inaugurer
inauguration: *n.* inauguration
in-between: *adj.* intermédiaire
inborn: *adj.* inné
incalculable: *adj.* incalculable
incandescent: *adj.* incandescent
incantation: *n.* incantation
incapable: *adj.* incapable
incapacitate: *vt.* mettre dans
l'incapacité
incapacity: *n.* incapacité
incarcerate: *vt.* incarcérer
incarnate: *adj.* incarné
incarnation: *n.* incarnation
incautious: *adj.* imprudent
incendiary: *n.* bombe incendiaire;
incendiaire
incense: *n.* encens
incense: *vt.* exaspérer
incentive: *n.* stimulant; prime; aide
inception: *n.* commencement
incessant: *adj.* incessant; continuel
incest: *n.* inceste
incestuous: *adj.* incestueux
inch: *n.* pouce
incidence: *n.* fréquence
incident: *n.* incident
incidental: *adj.* fortuit
incinerator: *n.* incinérateur
incipient: *adj.* naissant
incise: *vt.* inciser
incision: *n.* incision
incisive: *adj.* incisif
incisor: *n.* incisive
incite: *vt.* inciter; encourager
inclement: *adj.* inclément

inclination: *n.* inclination; propension
incline: *vt.* incliner; *vi.* s'incliner
inclined plane: plan incliné
include: *vt.* inclure; comprendre
including: *prep.* inclus; y compris
inclusion: *n.* inclusion
inclusive: *adj.* inclus; tout compris
incognito: *adv.* incognito
incoherence: *n.* incohérence
incoherent: *adj.* incohérent
income: *n.* revenu; recettes
incomparable: *adj.* incomparably
incompatibility: *n.* incompatibilité
incompatible: *adj.* incompatible
incompetence: *n.* incompétence
incompetent: *adj.* incompétent
incomplete: *adj.* incomplet
incomprehensibility: *n.* incompréhensibilité
incomprehensible: *adj.* incompréhensible
inconceivable: *adj.* inconcevable
inconclusive: *adj.* peu concluant
incongruity: *n.* incongruité
incongruous: *adj.* incongru
inconsequential: *adj.* inconséquent
inconsiderate: *adj.* sans considération; inconsidéré
inconsistency: *n.* inconsistance
inconsistent: *adj.* inconsistant
inconsolable: *adj.* inconsolable
inconspicuous: *adj.* discret
incontinence: *n.* incontinence
incontinent: *adj.* incontinent
incontrovertible: *adj.* indéniable
inconvenience: *n.* inconvénient
inconvenient: *adj.* incommode
incorporate: *vt.* incorporer
incorporated company: société constituée
incorporation: *n.* incorporation
incorrect: *adj.* incorrect; inexact
incorrigible: *adj.* incorrigible

incorruptibility: *n.* incorruptibilité
incorruptible: *adj.* incorruptible
increase: *n.* augmentation
increase: *vt.* augmenter
increasing: *adj.* croissant
incredible: *adj.* incroyable
incredulity: *n.* incrédulité
incredulous: *adj.* incrédule
increment: *n.* augmentation
incriminate: *vt.* incriminer
incrust: *vt.* incruster
incubate: *vi.* couver
incubator: *n.* couveuse
inculcate: *vt.* inculquer
incumbent: *adj.* en exercice; *n.* titulaire
incur: *vt.* encourir
incurability: *n.* incurabilité
incurable: *adj.* incurable
incursion: *n.* incursion
indebted: *adj.* endetté; redevable
indecency: *n.* indécence
indecent: *adj.* indécent
indecision: *n.* indécision; irrésolution
indecisive: *adj.* indécis; irrésolu
indecorous: *adj.* inconvenant
indeed: *adv.* vraiment
indefatigable: *adj.* infatigable
indefinite: *adj.* indéfini
indelible: *adj.* indélébile
indelicacy: *n.* indélicatesse
indelicate: *adj.* peu délicat
indemnify: *vt.* indemniser
indemnity: *n.* indemnité
indent: *vt.* bosseler; renfoncer; une commande à l'étranger
independence: *n.* indépendance
independent events: évènements indépendants
independent variable: variable indépendante
independent: *adj.* indépendant
indescribble: *adj.* indescriptible
indestructible: *adj.* indestructible

indeterminte: *adj.* indéterminé
index card: fiche
index finger: index
index: *n.* indice; index
index: *v.* indexer
indexed pages: pages indexées; référencées
indexed search: recherche indexée
indexed: *adj.* indexé
indexing: *n.* indexation
indicate: *vt.* indiquer
indication: *n.* indication; indice
indicative: *adj.* indicatif; *n.* (grammar) indicatif
indicator: *n.* indicateur
indict: *vt.* accuser
indictment: *n.* accusation
indifference: *n.* indifférence
indifferent: *adj.* indifférent
indigenous: *adj.* indigène
indigent: *adj.* indigent
indigestible: *adj.* indigeste
indigestion: *n.* indigestion
indignant: *adj.* indigné
indignation: *n.* indignation
indignity: *n.* indignité
indigo: *n.* indigo
indirect: *adj.* indirect
indiscreet: *adj.* indiscret
indiscretion: *n.* indiscrétion
indiscriminate: *adj.* sans discernement
indispensable: *adj.* indispensable
indisposed: *adj.* indisposé
indisposition: *n.* indisposition
indisputable: *adj.* indiscutable
indisputably: *adv.* indiscutablement
indistinct: *adj.* indistinct
indistinguishable: *adj.* indiscernable
individual: *adj.* individuel; *n.* individu
individuality: *n.* individualité
indivisible: *adj.* indivisible
indoctrinate: *vt.* endoctriner

indoctrination: *n.* endoctrinement
indolence: *n.* indolence
indolent: *adj.* indolent
indomitable: *adj.* indomptable
indoors: *adv.* à l'intérieur
indubitably: *adv.* indubitablement
induce: *vt.* persuader; causer; provoquer
inducement: *n.* encouragement; incitation
induction: *n.* induction
indulge: *vt.* céder à; *vi.* se permettre; se laisser aller
indulgence: *n.* indulgence
indulgent: *adj.* indulgent
industrial park: zone industrielle
industrial: *adj.* industriel
industrialise: *vt.* industrialiser
industrialist: *n.* industriel
industrious: *adj.* travailleur
industry: *n.* industrie
inebriated: *vt.* ivre
inebriation: *n.* ivresse
inedible: *adj.* non comestible
ineffable: *adj.* ineffable
ineffective: *adj.* inefficace
inefficiency: *n.* inefficacité
inefficient: *adj.* inefficace
ineligible: *adj.* inéligible
inept: *adj.* inepte; déplacé
ineptitude: *n.* ineptie
inequality: *n.* inégalité
inert: *adj.* inerte
inertia: *n.* inertie
inescapable: *adj.* inévitable
inestimable: *adj.* inestimable
inevitable: *adj.* inévitable
inevitably: *adv.* inévitablement
inexcusable: *adj.* inexcusable
inexhaustible: *adj.* inépuisable
inexorable: *adj.* inexorable
inexpedient: *adj.* imprudent
inexpensive: *adj.* bon marché
inexperience: *n.* inexpérience

inexperienced: *adj.* inexpérimenté
inexpert: *adj.* néophyte
inexplicable: *adj.* inexplicable
inexpressible: *adj.* indicible;
inexprimable
inextricably: *adv.* inextricablement
infallibility: *n.* infaillibilité
infallible: *adj.* infaillible
infamous: *adj.* vil; infâme
infamy: *n.* infamie
infancy: *n.* enfance
infant: *n.* bébé; enfant
infanticide: *n.* infanticide
infantile: *adj.* infantile
infantry: *n.* infanterie
infatuated: *adj.* fou
infatuation: *n.* folie; obsession
infect: *vt.* infecter
infection: *n.* infection
infectious: *adj.* contagieux;
infectieux
infer: *vt.* inférer
inference: *n.* inférence
inferior: *adj.* inférieur; *n.* subordonné
inferiority: *n.* infériorité
infernal: *adj.* infernal
inferno: *n.* enfer
infest: *vt.* infester
infidel: *n.* infidèle
infidelity: *n.* infidélité
infiltrate: *vi.* s'infiltrer
infinite: *adj.* infini
infinitive: *n.* (grammar) infinitif
infinity: *n.* infini; infinité
infirm: *adj.* infirme
infirmary: *n.* infirmerie
infirmity: *n.* infirmité
inflame: *vt.* enflammer
inflammation: *n.* inflammation
inflammatory: *adj.* inflammatoire
inflatable: *adj.* gonflable
inflate: *vt.* gonfler
inflation: *n.* inflation
inflection: *n.* inflexion

inflexibility: *n.* inflexibilité
inflexible: *adj.* inflexible
inflexibly: *adv.* inflexiblement
inflict: *vt.* infliger
influence: *n.* influence
influence: *vt.* influencer
influential: *adj.* influent
influenza: *n.* grippe
influx: *n.* afflux
infoglut: *n.* surabondance
d'informations; saturation
inform: *vt.* informer
informal: *adj.* informel; simple;
familier
informality: *n.* simplicité
informant: *n.* informateur
information broker: courtier en
informations
information highway: autoroute de
l'information; inforoute
information retrieval: recherche;
récupération d'information; recherche
documentaire
information: *n.* information
informative: instructif; savant
informed judgment: jugement fondé
infraction: *n.* infraction
infrared: *adj.* infrarouge
infrastructure: *n.* infrastructure
infrequent: *adj.* rare
infrigement of copyright:
contrefaçon; violation de droits
d'auteur
infringe: *vt.* enfreindre
infringement: *n.* infraction
infuriate: *vt.* rendre furieux
infuse: *vt.* infuser
infusion: *n.* infusion
ingenious: *adj.* ingénieux
ingenuity: *n.* ingéniosité
ingenuous: *adj.* ingénu; sincère
inglorious: *adj.* infamant
ingot: *n.* lingot
ingrained: *adj.* invétéré

ingratitude: *n.* ingratitude
ingredient: *n.* ingrédient
inhabit: *vt.* habiter
inhabitable: *adj.* habitable
inhabitant: *n.* habitant
inhale: *vt.* inhaler
inherent: *adj.* inhérent
inherit: *vt.* hériter
inheritance: *n.* héritage
inheritor: *n.* héritier
inhibit: *vt.* inhiber
inhibited: *adj.* inhibé
inhibition: *n.* inhibition
inhospitable: *adj.* inhospitalier
inhospitality: *n.* inhospitalité
inhuman: *adj.* inhumain
inhumanity: *n.* inhumanité; cruauté
inimical: *adj.* hostile; ennemi
inimitable: *adj.* inimitable
iniquitous: *adj.* inique; injuste
iniquity: *n.* iniquité; injustice
initial: *adj.* initial; *n.* initiale
initially: *adv.* au début
initiate: *vt.* commencer; initier
initiation: *n.* début; commencement; amorçage; initiation
initiative: *n.* initiative
inject: *vt.* injecter
injection: *n.* injection
injudicious: *adj.* peu judicieux
injunction: *n.* injonction; ordre
injure: *vt.* blesser
injury time: arrêts de jeu
injury: *n.* blessure; tort
injustice: *n.* injustice
ink: *n.* encre
inkling: *n.* soupçon
inkstand: *n.* encrier
inlaid: *adj.* incrusté
inland: *adj.* intérieur
in-laws: *npl.* belle-famille
inlay: *vt.* incruster
inlet: *n.* entrée; bras de mer
inmate: *n.* détenu

inmost: *adj.* le plus profond
inn: *n.* auberge; hôtel
innate: *adj.* inné
inner tube: chambre à air
inner: *adj.* intérieur
innermost: *adj.* le plus profond
innkeeper: *n.* aubergiste; hôtelier
innocence: *n.* innocence
innocent: *adj.* innocent
innocuous: *adj.* inoffensif
innovate: *vt.* innover
innovation: *n.* innovation
innuendo: *n.* allusion; insinuation
innumerable: *adj.* innombrable
inoculate: *vt.* inoculer
inoculation: *n.* inoculation
inoffensive: *adj.* inoffensif
inopportune: *adj.* inopportun
inordinately: *adv.* démesurément
inorganic compound: composé inorganique
inorganic: *adj.* inorganique
in-patient: *n.* patient hospitalisé
input: *n.* entrée; consommation
inquest: *n.* enquête
inquire: *vt.* demander
inquiry: *n.* demande de renseignements; enquête
inquisition: *n.* investigation
inquisitive: *adj.* curieux
inroad: *n.* incursion
insane: *adj.* fou; folle
insanity: *n.* folie
insatiable: *adj.* insatiable
inscribe: *vt.* inscrire; dédier
inscription: *n.* inscription; dédicace
inscrutable: *adj.* impénétrable
insect: *n.* insecte
insecticide: *n.* insecticide
insecure: *adj.* peu assuré
insecurity: *n.* insécurité
insemination: *n.* insémination
insensible: *adj.* inconscient; insensible

insensitive: *adj.* insensible
inseparable: *adj.* inséparable
insert: *vt.* introduire; insérer
insertion: *n.* insertion
inshore: *adj.* côtier
inside out: à l'envers; à fond
inside: *n.* intérieur; *adv.* à l'intérieur
insidious: *adj.* insidieux
insight: *n.* perspicacité
insignia: *npl.* insignes
insignificant: *adj.* insignifiant
insincere: *adj.* peu sincère
insincerity: *n.* manque de sincérité
insinuate: *vt.* insinuer
insinuation: *n.* insinuation
insipid: *adj.* insipide
insist: *vi.* insister
insistence: *n.* insistance
insistent: *adj.* insistant
insole: *n.* semelle intérieure
insolence: *n.* insolence
insolent: *adj.* insolent
insoluble: *adj.* insoluble
insolvency: *n.* insolvabilité
insolvent: *adj.* insolvable
insomnia: *n.* insomnie
insomuch: *conj.* à tel point
inspect: *vt.* examiner; inspecter
inspection copy: spécimen
inspection: *n.* inspection
inspection; on: sur vérification
inspector: *n.* inspecteur
inspiration: *n.* inspiration
inspirational speech: discours inspiré
inspire: *vt.* inspirer
instability: *n.* instabilité
install: *vt.* installer
installation: *n.* installation
installment: *n.* installation; versement
instalment plan: plan de vente à tempérament
instance: *n.* exemple

instant access: accès instantané
instant: *adj.* instantané; *n.* instant; moment
instantaneous: *adj.* instantané
instep: *n.* cou-de-pied
instigate: *vt.* inciter; susciter
instigation: *n.* incitation
instill: *vt.* instiller; inspirer
instinct: *n.* instinct
instinctive: *adj.* instinctif
institute: *n.* institut
institute: *vt.* instituer
institution: *n.* institution
instruct: *vt.* instruire
instruction: *n.* instruction
instructive: *adj.* instructif
instructor: *n.* professeur; moniteur
instrument of trade: un effet de commerce
instrument: *n.* instrument
instrumental: *adj.* instrumental
insubordinate: *adj.* insubordonné
insubordination: *n.* insubordination
insufferable: *adj.* insupportable
insufferably: *adv.* insupportablement
insufficiency: *n.* insuffisance
insufficient: *adj.* insuffisant
insular: *adj.* insulaire; borné
insulate: *v.* isoler
insulating tape: ruban isolant
insulation: *n.* isolation; insonorisation
insulin: *n.* insuline
insult: *n.* insulte
insult: *vt.* insulter
insulting: *adj.* insultant
insuperable: *adj.* insurmontable
insurance company: une compagnie d'assurance
insurance policy: police d'assurance
insurance: *n.* assurance
insure: *vt.* assurer
insured person: assuré
insurer: *n.* assureur

insurgent: *n.* insurgé; rebelle
insurmountable: *adj.* insurmontable
insurrection: *n.* insurrection
intact: *adj.* intact
intake: *n.* admission; consommation
integer: *n.* nombre entier relatif
integral: *adj.* intégrant; *n.* intégrale
integrate: *vt.* intégrer
integrated tool: outil intégré
integration: *n.* intégration
integrity: *n.* intégrité
intellect: *n.* intellect
intellectual work: oeuvre de l'esprit
intellectual: *adj.* intellectuel
intelligence: *n.* intelligence
intelligent: *adj.* intelligent
intelligentsia: *n.* intelligentsia
intelligible: *adj.* intelligible
intelligibly: *adv.* intelligiblement
intemperate: *adj.* immodéré
intend: *vt.* avoir l'intention de
intendant: *n.* intendant
intended: *adj.* voulu
intense: *adj.* intense
intensify: *vt.* intensifier
intensity: *n.* intensité
intensive care unit: service de soins intensifs
intensive: *adj.* intensif
intent: *adj.* résolu; attentif; *n.* intention; dessein
intention: *n.* intention; dessein
intentional: *adj.* intentionnel
inter: *vt.* enterrer
interaction: *n.* interaction
intercede: *vi.* intercéder
intercept: *vt.* intercepter
intercession: *n.* intercession
interchange: *n.* échange
intercom: *n.* interphone
intercourse: *n.* relations sexuelles
interest rate: taux d'intérêt
interest: *n.* intérêt
interest: *vt.* intéresser

interesting: *adj.* intéressant
interfacial tension: tension interfaciale
interfere: *vi.* s'ingérer
interference: *n.* ingérence; interférence
interim: *adj.* intérimaire
interior designer: décorateur d'intérieur
interior: *adj.* intérieur
interjection: *n.* interjection
interlock: *vi.* s'entremêler
interlocutor: *n.* interlocuteur
interloper: *n.* intrus
interlude: *n.* intermède
intermarriage: *n.* intermariage
intermediary: *n.* intermédiaire
intermediate: *adj.* intermédiaire
interment: *n.* enterrement
interminable: *adj.* interminable
intermingle: *vt.* entremêler; *vi.* s'entremêler
intermission: *n.* entracte; interruption
intermittent: *adj.* intermittent
intern: *n.* interne
internal: *adj.* intérieur; interne
international bibliography: bibliographie internationale
international: *adj.* international
Internet: *n.* Internet
internship: *n.* stage
interpersonal: *adj.* humain; de communication
interplay: *n.* interaction
interpose: *vt.* interposer
interpret: *vt.* interpréter
interpretation: *n.* interprétation
interpreter: *n.* interprète
interregnum: *n.* interrègne
interrelated: *adj.* en corrélation
interrogate: *vt.* interroger
interrogation: *n.* interrogatoire
interrogative: *adj.* interrogatif
interrupt: *vt.* interrompre

interruption: *n.* interruption
intersect: *vi.* se croiser
intersection: *n.* croisement
intersperse: *vt.* parsemer
intertwine: *vt.* entrelacer
interval: *n.* intervalle; mi-temps
intervene: *vi.* intervenir
intervention: *n.* intervention
interview: *n.* entrevue; interview
interview: *vt.* faire passer une entrevue à; interviewer
interviewer: *n.* interviewer
interweave: *vt.* entrelacer
intestate: *adj.* intestat
intestinal: *adj.* intestinal
intestine: *n.* intestin
intimacy: *n.* intimité
intimate: *n.* intime; *adj.* intime
intimate: *vt.* insinuer; laisser entendre
intimidate: *vt.* intimider
into: *prep.* dans; en
intolerable: *adj.* intolérable
intolerably: *adv.* intolérablement
intolerance: *n.* intolérance
intolerant: *adj.* intolérant
intonation: *n.* intonation
intoxicate: *vt.* enivrer
intoxication: *n.* ivresse
intractable: *adj.* intraitable
intransitive: *adj.* intransitif
intravenous: *adj.* intraveineux
in-tray: *n.* courrier à l'arrivée
intrepid: *adj.* intrépide
intrepidity: *n.* intrépidité
intricacy: *n.* complexité
intricate: *adj.* complexe; compliqué
intrigue: *n.* intrigue
intrigue: *vi.* intriguer
intriguing: *adj.* intrigant
intrinsic: *adj.* intrinsèque
introduce: *vt.* introduire
introduction: *n.* introduction
introductory: *adj.* d'introduction

introsection: *n.* introspection
introvert: *n.* introverti
intrude: *vi.* s'ingérer; s'immiscer
intruder: *n.* intrus
intrusion: *n.* intrusion
intuition: *n.* intuition
intuitive: *adj.* intuitif
inundate: *vt.* inonder
inundation: *n.* inondation
inure: *vt.* endurcir
invade: *vt.* envahir
invader: *n.* envahisseur
invalid word: mot erroné
invalid: *adj.* invalide; *n.* invalide
invalidate: *vt.* invalider; annuler
invaluable: *adj.* inappréciable
invariable: *adj.* invariable
invariably: *adv.* invariablement
invasion: *n.* invasion
invective: *n.* invective
inveigle: *vt.* persuader; entraîner
invent: *vt.* inventer
invention: *n.* invention
inventive: *adj.* inventif
inventor: *n.* inventeur
inventory: *n.* inventaire
inverse operations: operations inverses
inverse: *adj.* inverse
inversion: *n.* inversion
invert: *vt.* inverser
inverted commas: guillemets
invest: *vt.* investir
investigate: *vt.* faire des recherches sur; examiner
investigation: *n.* investigation; recherches
investigator: *n.* investigateur; chercheur
investment: *n.* investissement
inveterate: *adj.* invétéré
invidious: *adj.* adieux; désobligeant
invigilate: *vt.* surveiller
invigorating: *adj.* vivifiant

invincible: *adj.* invincible
invincibly: *adv.* invinciblement
inviolable: *adj.* inviolable
invisible: *adj.* invisible
invisibly: *adv.* invisiblement
invitation: *n.* invitation
invite: *vt.* inviter
inviting: *adj.* attrayant; tentant
invoice: *n.* facture
invoke: *vt.* invoquer
involuntarily: *adv.* involontairement
involuntary: *adj.* involontaire
involve: *vt.* impliquer; entraîner
involved: *adj.* compliqué; impliqué
involvement: *n.* implication; confusion
invulnerable: *adj.* invulnérable
inward: *adj.* intérieur; intime
iodine: *n.* iode
ionic bond: liaison ionique
ionic compound: composé ionique
ionic polymerization: polymérisation ionique
ionic scavenger: intercepteur ionique
ionization energy: énergie d'ionisation
ionization potential: potentiel d'ionisation
ionization: *n.* ionisation
irascible: *adj.* irascible
irate; ireful: *adj.* irrité
iris: *n.* iris
irksome: *adj.* fastidieux; ennuyeux
iron ore: minerai de fer
iron: *n.* fer
iron: *vt.* repasser
ironic: *adj.* ironique
ironie: *n.* repassage
ironing board: table à repasser
ironwork: *n.* ferronnerie
irony: *n.* ironie
irradiate: *vt.* irradier
irrational number: nombre irrationnel

irrational: *adj.* irrationnel
irreconcilable: *adj.* irréconciliable; inconciliable
irregular: *adj.* irrégulier
irregularity: *n.* irrégularité
irrelevant: *adj.* hors de propos
irreligious: *adj.* irréligieux
irreparable: *adj.* irréparable
irreplaceable: *adj.* irremplaçable
irrepressible: *adj.* irrépressible
irreproachable: *adj.* irréprochable
irresistible: *adj.* irrésistible
irresolute: *adj.* irrésolu
irresponsible: *adj.* irresponsable
irretrievably: *adv.* irréparablement
irreverence: *n.* irrévérence
irreverent: *adj.* irrévérencieux
irreversible reaction: réaction irréversible
irrigate: *vt.* irriguer
irrigation: *n.* irrigation
irritability: *n.* irritabilité
irritable: *adj.* irritable
irritant: *n.* irritant
irritate: *vt.* irriter
irritating: *adj.* irritant
irritation: *n.* irritation
Islam: *n.* Islam
island: *n.* île
islander: *n.* insulaire
isle: *n.* Ile
isolate: *vt.* isoler
isolation: *n.* isolement
isotope: *n.* isotope
issue: *n.* sujet; question
issue: *vt.* publier; distribuer; fournir
issuing bank: banque d'émission
isthmus: *n.* isthme
italic: *n.* italique
itch: *n.* démangeaison
itch: *v.* avoir des démangeaisons
item: *n.* article
itemise: *vt.* détailler
itinerant: *adj.* ambulant; itinérant

itinerary: *n.* itinéraire
itself: *pron.* lui-même; elle-même
ivory: *n.* ivoire
ivy: *n.* lierre

ℐ

jab: *vt.* planter; enfoncer
jabber: *vi.* baragouiner
jack plug: prise à fiche
jack: *n.* cric; valet
jackal: *n.* chacal
jackboots: *npl.* bottes de militaire
jackdaw: *n.* choucas
jacket: *n.* veste; couverture
jackknife: *vi.* se mettre en travers
jackpot: *n.* gros lot
jade: *n.* jade
jagged: *adj.* dentelé
jaguar: *n.* jaguar
jail: *n.* prison
jailbird: *n.* prisonnier
jailer: *n.* geôlier
jam: *n.* confiture embouteillage
jangle: *vi.* cliqueter
janitor: *n.* portier
January: *n.* janvier
jar: *n.* pot
jar: *vi.* se heurter; détonner; grincer
jargon: *n.* jargon
jasmine: *n.* jasmin
jaundice: *n.* jaunisse
jaunt: *n.* junte
jaunt: *n.* promenade
jaunty: *adj.* enjoué
javelin: *n.* javelot
jaw: *n.* mâchoire
jay: *n.* geai
jealous: *adj.* jaloux
jealousy: *n.* jalousie
jeer: *n.* raillerie; moquerie
jeer: *vi.* se moquer; railler
jelly: *n.* gelée
jellyfish: *n.* méduse
jeopardise: *vt.* risquer; mettre en péril
jerk: *n.* secousse
jerk: *vt.* donner une secousse à
jerky: *adj.* saccadé
jersey: *n.* jersey; tricot

jest: *n.* blague; plaisanterie
jester: *n.* bouffon
jestingly: *adv.* en plaisantant
Jesuit: *n.* jésuite
Jesus: *n.* Jésus
jet engine: moteur à réaction
jet: *n.* avion à réaction; jet; gicleur
jettison: *vt.* se défaire de
jetty: *n.* jetée
Jew: *n.* Juif
jewel: *n.* bijou
jeweller: *n.* bijoutier
jewellery store: bijouterie
jewellery: *n.* bijoux
jewish: *adj.* juif
jib: *n.* foc
jibe: *n.* raillerie; moquerie
jig: *n.* gigue
jigsaw: *n.* puzzle
jilt: *vt.* laisser tomber
jinx: *n.* porte-malheur
job: *n.* travail
jockey: *n.* jockey
jocular: *adj.* joyeux; facétieux
jog: *vi.* faire du jogging
join: *vt.* joindre; unir
joiner: *n.* menuisier
joinery: *n.* menuiserie
joint: *n.* articulation; *adj.* commun
jointly: *adv.* conjointement
joint-stock company: société par actions
joke: *n.* blague; plaisanterie
joke: *vi.* blaguer; plaisanter
joker: *n.* blagueur
jollity: *n.* gaieté
jolly: *adj.* gai; joyeux
jolt: *n.* secousse
jolt: *vt.* secouer
jostle: *vt.* bousculer
journal: *n.* revue
journalism: *n.* journalisme
journalist: *n.* journaliste
journey: *n.* voyage

journey: *vi.* voyager
jovial: *adj.* jovial; gai
joy: *n.* joie
joystick: *n.* manche à balai
jubilant: *adj.* réjoui
jubilation: *n.* jubilation
jubilee: *n.* jubilé
Judaism: *n.* judaïsme
judge: *n.* juge
judge: *vt.* juger
judgment: *n.* jugement
judicial: *adj.* judiciaire
judiciary: *n.* pouvoir judiciaire
judicious: *adj.* judicieux
judo: *n.* judo
jug: *n.* cruche
juggle: *vi.* jongler
juggler: *n.* jongleur
juice: *n.* jus; suc
juicy: *adj.* juteux
jukebox: *n.* juke-box
July: *n.* juillet
jumble: *n.* mélange; fouillis
jumble: *vt.* mélanger
jump: *n.* saut
jump: *vi.* sauter
jumper: *n.* pull; sauteur
jumpy: *adj.* nerveux
juncture: *n.* joncture
June: *n.* juin
jungle: *n.* jungle
junior: *adj.* plus jeune
juniper: *n.* genièvre
junk: *n.* cochonnerie; bric-à-brac
jurisdiction: *n.* juridiction
jurisprudence: *n.* jurisprudence
jurist: *n.* juriste
juror: *n.* juré
jury: *n.* jury
just: *adj.* juste
justice: *n.* justice
justifiably: *adv.* légitimement
justification: *n.* justification
justify: *vt.* justifier

just-in-time stock control: gestion de stock zéro
justly: *adv.* justement
justness: *n.* justesse
jute: *n.* jute
juvenile: *adj.* juvénile; pour enfants
juxtaposition: *n.* juxtaposition

K

kaleidoscope: *n.* kaléidoscope
kangaroo: *n.* kangourou
karate: *n.* karaté
kebab: *n.* brochette
keel: *n.* quille
keen: *adj.* aiguisé; vif; enthousiaste
keenness: *n.* enthousiasme
keep: *vt.* garder; conserver; tenir
keeper: *n.* gardien
keepsake: *n.* souvenir
keg: *n.* baril
kennel: *n.* niche
kernel: *n.* amande; noyau
kerosene: *n.* kérosène
ketone: *n.* cétone
kettle: *n.* bouilloire
kettle-drum: *n.* timbale
key ring: porte-clefs
key word: mot clé
key: *n.* clé; clef
keyboard: *n.* clavier
keyhole: *n.* trou de la serrure
keynote: *n.* tonique
keystone: *n.* clef de voûte
khaki: *n.* kaki
kick: *n.* coup de pied; plaisir
kick: *vi.* donner un coup de pied (à)
kid: *n.* gamin
kidnap: *vt.* kidnapper
kidnapper: *n.* kidnappeur
kidnapping: *n.* kidnapping
kidney: *n.* rein; rognon
kill: *v.* tuer
killer: *n.* assassin
killing: *n.* assassinat
kiln: *n.* four
kilo: *n.* kilo
kilobyte: *n.* kilo-octet
kilogram: *n.* kilogramme
kilometre: *n.* kilomètre
kin: *n.* parents
kind: *adj.* gentil; *n.* genre; sorte
kindergarten: *n.* jardin d'enfants

kind-hearted: *adj.* bon
kindle: *vt.* allumer; *vi.* s'allumer
kindliness: *n.* gentillesse; bonté
kindly: *adj.* bon; bienveillant
kindness: *n.* bonté
kindred: *adj.* apparenté
kinetic energy: énergie cinétique
kinetic theory of gas: théorie cinétique des gaz
kinetic: *adj.* cinétique
king: *n.* roi
kingdom: *n.* royaume
kingfisher: *n.* martin-pêcheur
kiosk: *n.* kiosque
kiss: *n.* baiser
kiss: *vt.* embrasser
kissing: *n.* baisers
kit: *n.* équipement
kitchen garden: potager
kitchen: *n.* cuisine
kite: *n.* cerf-volant
kitten: *n.* chaton
knack: *n.* don; chic
knapsack: *n.* sac à dos
knave: *n.* fripouille
knead: *vt.* pétrir
knee: *n.* genou
knee-deep: *adj.* jusqu'aux genoux
kneel: *vi.* s'agenouiller
knell: *n.* glas
knife: *n.* couteau
knight: *n.* chevalier
knit: *vt.* tricoter
knitter: *n.* tricoteur
knitting pin: aiguille à tricoter
knitwear: *n.* tricots
knob: *n.* bouton; noeud
knock: *n.* coup
knock: *vt.* cogner; frapper
knocker: *n.* heurtoir
knock-kneed: *adj.* aux genoux cagneux
knock-out: *n.* knock-out
knoll: *n.* butte

knot: *n.* noeud
knot: *vt.* nouer
knotty: *adj.* emmêlé; épineux
know: *vt.* savoir; connaître
know-all: *n.* je-sais-tout
know-how: *n.* savoir-faire
knowing: *adj.* entendu
knowledge: *n.* connaissances
knowledgeable: *adj.* bien informé
knuckle: *n.* articulation
kosher: *adj.* kascher

ℒ

label: *n.* étiquette
laboratory: *n.* laboratoire
labour union: syndicat
labour: *n.* travail
labour: *vi.* travailler
labourer: *n.* ouvrier
labourious: *adj.* laborieux; pénible
labyrinth: *n.* labyrinthe
lace: *n.* lacet; dentelle
lace: *vt.* lacer
lacerate: *vt.* lacérer
lack: *n.* manque
lack: *vt.* manquer
lackadaisical: *adj.* nonchalant
lackey: *n.* laquais
laconic: *adj.* laconique
lacquer: *n.* laque
ladder: *n.* échelle
ladle: *n.* louche
ladleful: *n.* louchée
lady: *n.* dame
ladybird: *n.* coccinelle
ladykiller: *n.* bourreau des coeurs
ladylike: *adj.* distingué
ladyship: *n.* madame
lag: *vi.* se laisser distancer
lager: *n.* bière blonde
lagoon: *n.* lagune
laidback: *adj.* décontracté
lair: *n.* repaire
lait: *n.* garçon
laity: *n.* laïcat
lake: *n.* lac
lamb: *n.* agneau
lamb: *vi.* agneler
lambswool: *n.* laine d'agneau
lame: *adj.* boiteux
lament: *vt.* se lamenter sur
lamentable: *adj.* lamentable; déplorable
lamentation: *n.* lamentation
laminated: *adj.* laminé
lamp: *n.* lampe

lampashade: *n.* abat-jour
lampoon: *n.* satire
lance: *n.* lance; bistouri
lance: *vt.* inciser
lancet: *n.* bistouri
land forces: armée de terre
land: *n.* pays; terre
land: *vt.* débarquer
landholder: *n.* propriétaire terrien
landing strip: piste d'atterrissage
landing: *n.* atterrissage
landlady: *n.* propriétaire
landlord: *n.* propriétaire
landlubber: *n.* marin d'eau douce
landmark: *n.* point de repère
landowner: *n.* propriétaire terrien
landscape: *n.* paysage
landslide: *n.* glissement de terrain
lane: *n.* allée; ruelle; file
language: *n.* langue; langage
languid: *adj.* languissant
languish: *vi.* languir
lank: *adj.* raide; plat
lanky: *adj.* grand et maigre
lantern: *n.* lanterne
lap: *n.* genoux
lap: *vt.* laper
lapdog: *n.* chien de salon
lapel: *n.* revers
laptop: *n.* ordinateur portable
larceny: *n.* vol
larch: *n.* mélèze
lard: *n.* saindoux
larder: *n.* garde-manger
large: *adj.* grand
large-scale: *adj.* à grande échelle
largesse: *n.* largesse
lark: *n.* alouette
larva: *n.* larve
laryngitis: *n.* laryngite
larynx: *n.* larynx
lascivious: *adj.* lascif
laser: *n.* laser
lash: *n.* coup de fouet

lash: *vt.* fouetter; attacher
lasso: *n.* lasso
last: *adj.* dernier; *n.* dernier
last: *vi.* durer
last-ditch: *adj.* ultime
lasting: *adj.* durable
last-minute: *adj.* de dernière minute
latch: *n.* loquet
latchkey: *n.* clef de porte d'entrée
late: *adj.* en retard; défunt
latecomer: *n.* retardataire
latent: *adj.* latent
lateral: *adj.* latérale
lathe: *n.* tour
lather: *n.* mousse
latitude: *n.* latitude
latrine: *n.* latrine
lattice: *n.* treillis
laudable: *adj.* louable
laudably: *adv.* louablement
laugh: *n.* rire
laugh: *vi.* rire; se moquer
laughable: *adj.* risible; dérisoire
laughing stock: risée
laughing: éclater de rire; *n.* éclatement
launch: *vt.* lancer; *vi.* se lancer
launching pad: rampe de lancement
launching: *n.* lancement
launder: *vt.* laver
laundrette: *n.* laverie automatique
laundry: *n.* lessive
laurel: *n.* laurier
lava: *n.* lave
lavatory: *n.* toilettes
lavender: *n.* lavande
lavish: *adj.* prodigue
law and order: ordre public
law court: tribunal
law of conservation of energy: loi de conservation d'énergie
law of conservation of mass: loi de conservation de masse
law school: faculté de droit

law suit: procès
law: *n.* loi; droit
law-abiding: *adj.* respectueux de la loi
lawful: *adj.* légal; légitime
lawless: *adj.* anarchique
lawlessness: *n.* anarchie
lawmaker: *n.* législateur
lawn: *n.* pelouse; gazon
lawnmower: *n.* tondeuse à gazon
lawyer: *n.* avocat; juriste
lax: *adj.* relâché
laxative: *n.* laxatif
laxity: *n.* relâchement; flou
lay: *vt.* coucher; mettre; pondre
layabout: *n.* paresseux
layer: *n.* couche
layette: *n.* layette
layman: *n.* laïc
layout: *n.* disposition; présentation
laze: *vi.* paresser
lazily: *adv.* paresseusement
laziness: *n.* paresse
lazy: *adj.* paresseux
lead: *n.* plomb
lead: *vt.* conduire; mener
leader: *n.* chef
leadership: *n.* direction
leading article: article de fond
leading: *adj.* principal; premier
leaf: *n.* feuille
leaflet: *n.* feuillet; prospectus; dépliant
leafy: *adj.* feuillu
league: *n.* ligue; lieue
leak: *n.* fuite
leak: *vi.* faire eau
leaky: *adj.* qui fuit
lean: *vt.* appuyer; *adj.* maigre
leap year: année bisextile
leap: *n.* saut
leap: *vi.* sauter
leapfrog: *n.* saute-mouton
learn: *vt.* apprendre

learned: *adj.* instruit
learner: *n.* élève; débutant
learning: *n.* érudition
lease: *n.* bail
lease: *vt.* louer
leasehold: *n.* bail
leash: *n.* laisse
least: *adj.* moindre
leather: *n.* cuir
leathery: *adj.* qui a l'aspect du cuir
leave: *n.* permission; congé
leave: *vt.* laisser
leaven: *n.* levain
leaven: *vt.* faire lever
leavings: *npl.* restes
lecherous: *adj.* lascif; lubrique
lecture: *n.* conférence
lecture: *vi.* faire une conférence
lecturer: *n.* conférencier
ledge: *n.* rebord
ledger: *n.* registre; un livre des comptes; le grand livre
lee: *n.* côté sous le vent
leech: *n.* sangsue
leek: *n.* poireau
leer: *vt.* regarder d'un oeil lascif
lees: *npl.* lie
leeward: *adj.* sous le vent
leeway: *n.* liberté d'action
left: *adj.* gauche
left-handed: *adj.* gaucher
left-luggage office: *n.* consigne
leftovers: *npl.* restes
leg: *n.* jambe; patte
legacy: *n.* héritage; legs
legal deposit: dépôt légal
legal document: acte authentique
legal holiday: jour férié
legal tender: monnaie légale
legal: *adj.* légal; légitime
legalise: *vt.* légaliser
legality: *n.* légalité; légitimité
legate: *n.* légat
legatee: *n.* légataire

legation: *n.* légation
legend: *n.* légende
legendary: *adj.* légendaire
legible: *adj.* lisible
legibly: *adv.* lisiblement
legion: *n.* légion
legislate: *vt.* légiférer
legislation: *n.* législation
legislative: *adj.* législatif
legislator: *n.* législateur
legislature: *n.* corps législatif
legitimacy: *n.* légitimité
legitimate: *adj.* légitime
legitimate: *vt.* légitimer
leisure: *n.* loisir
lemon tea: thé au citron
lemon tree: citronnier
lemon: *n.* citron
lemonade: *n.* limonade
lend money; to: prêter de l'argent
lend: *vt.* prêter
length: *n.* longueur; durée
lengthen: *vt.* allonger
lengthways: *adv.* dans le sens de la longueur
lengthy: *adj.* long
lenient: *adj.* indulgent
lens: *n.* lentille
Lent: *n.* Carême
lentil: *n.* lentille
leo: *n.* lion
leopard: *n.* léopard
leotard: *n.* justaucorps
leper: *n.* lépreux
leprosy: *n.* lèpre
lesbian: *n.* lesbienne
less: *adj.* moins; *adv.* moins
lessen: *vt.* diminuer
lesser: *adj.* moindre
lesson: *n.* leçon
lest: *conj.* de crainte que
let: *vt.* laisser; permettre; louer
lethal: *adj.* mortel
lethargic: *adj.* léthargique

lethargy: *n.* léthargie
letter bomb: lettre piégée
letter box: boite aux lettres
letter of credit: lettre de crédit
letter: *n.* lettre
lettering: *n.* inscription
lettuce: *n.* laitue
leukaemia: *n.* leucémie
level: *adj.* plat; égal; à niveau; *n.* niveau
level: *vt.* niveler
level-headed: *adj.* sensé
lever: *n.* levier
leverage: *n.* effet de levier; prise
levity: *n.* légèreté
levy: *n.* levée; prélèvement
levy: *vt.* prélever
lewd: *adj.* obscène
lexicon: *n.* lexique
liability: *n.* responsabilité
liable: *adj.* sujet (à); responsable
liaise: *vi.* effectuer une liaison
liaison: *n.* liaison
liar: *n.* menteur
libel: *n.* diffamation
libel: *vt.* diffamer
libellous: *adj.* diffamatoire
liberal: *adj.* libéral; généreux
liberality: *n.* libéralité; générosité
liberate: *vt.* libérer
liberation: *n.* libération
libertine: *n.* libertin
liberty: *n.* liberté
librarian: *n.* bibliothécaire
library: *n.* bibliothèque
libretto: *n.* livret
licence: *n.* licence; permis; permission
licentious: *adj.* licencieux
lichen: *n.* lichen
lick: *vt.* lécher
lid: *n.* couvercle
lie: *n.* mensonge
lie: *vi.* mentir; être allongé

lieutenant: *n.* lieutenant
life belt: gilet de sauvetage
life cycle: cycle vital
life jacket: gilet de sauvetage
life sentence: condamnation à perpétuité
life: *n.* vie
lifeboat: *n.* canot de sauvetage
lifeguard: *n.* maître nageur; garde du corps
lifeless: *adj.* mort; sans vie
lifelike: *adj.* naturel
lifeline: *n.* bouée de sauvetage
life-sized: *adj.* grandeur nature
lifespan: *n.* durée de vie
lifestyle: *n.* style de vie
life-support system: système de respiration artificielle
lifetime: *n.* durée de vie
lift: *vt.* lever
ligament: *n.* ligament
light bulb: ampoule
light pen: crayon optique
light year: année-lumière
light: *n.* lumière; *adj.* léger; clair
light: *vt.* allumer; éclairer
lighten: *vi.* s'éclaircir; éclairer; éclaircir; alléger
lighter: *n.* briquet
light-headed: *adj.* étourdi
lighthearted: *adj.* joyeux
lighthouse: *n.* phare
lighting: *n.* éclairage
lightly: *adv.* légèrement
lightning rod: paratonnerre
lightning: *n.* éclair
lightweight: *adj.* léger
ligneous: *adj.* ligneux
like terms: termes semblables
like: *adj.* pareil; *adv.* comme
like: *vt.* aimer
likelihood: *n.* probabilité
likely: *adj.* probable; vraisemblable
liken: *vt.* comparer

likeness: *n.* ressemblance
likewise: *adv.* pareillement
liking: *n.* goat
lilac: *n.* lilas
lily: *n.* lis
limb: *n.* membre
limber: *adj.* flexible; souple
lime: *n.* chaux; lime
limestone: *n.* pierre à chaux
limit: *n.* limite
limit: *vt.* limiter
limitation: *n.* limitation; restriction
limiting reagent: réactant limitatif
limitless: *adj.* illimité
limousine: *n.* limousine
limp: *n.* boitement; *adj.* mou
limp: *vi.* boiter
limpet: *n.* patelle
limpid: *adj.* limpide
linde process: linde; machine de
line: *n.* ligne; un produit; un article; ride
line: *vt.* rayer; rider
lineage: *n.* lignage
linear equation: equation linéaire
linear function: function linéaire
linear: *adj.* linéaire
lined: *adj.* rayé; ridé
linen: *n.* lin; linge de maison
liner: *n.* transatlantique
linesman: *n.* juge de ligne
linger: *vi.* trainer
lingerie: *n.* lingerie
lingering: *adj.* long
linguist: *n.* linguiste
linguistic: *adj.* linguistique
linguistics: *n.* linguistique
liniment: *n.* liniment
lining: *n.* doublure
link: *n.* chaînon; un lien
link: *vt.* relier
linnet: *n.* linotte
linoleum: *n.* linoléum
linseed: *n.* graine de lin

lint: *n.* peluche
lintel: *n.* linteau
lion: *n.* lion
lioness: *n.* lionne
lip salve: pommade pour les lèvres
lip: *n.* lèvre; bord
lipase: *n.* laps; défaillance
lipase: *vi.* expirer; se périmer; se relâcher
lip-read: *vi.* lire sur les lèvres
lipstick: *n.* rouge à lèvres
liqueur: *n.* liqueur
liquid: *adj.* liquide; *n.* liquide
liquidate: *vt.* liquider
liquidation: *n.* liquidation
liquidise: *vt.* liquéfier
liquor store: magasin de vins et spiritueux
liquor: *n.* spiritueux
liquorice: *n.* réglisse
lisp: *n.* zézaiement
lisp: *vi.* zézayer
list: *n.* liste
list: *vt.* faire une liste
listen: *vi.* écouter
listless: *adj.* indifférent
litany: *n.* litanie
liter: *n.* litre
literal: *adj.* littéral
literary device: modalite littéraire
literary form: forme litéraire
literary passage: passage litéraire
literary: *adj.* littéraire
literate: *adj.* cultivé
literature: *n.* littérature
lithe: *adj.* agile
lithograph: *n.* lithographie
lithography: *n.* lithographie
litigation: *n.* litige
litigious: *adj.* litigieux
litre: *n.* litre
litter: *n.* litière; ordures
litter: *vt.* joncher
little: *adj.* petit

liturgy: *n.* liturgie
live: *adj.* vivant
live: *vi.* vivre; habiter
livelihood: *n.* moyens de subsistance
liveliness: *n.* vivacité
lively: *adj.* vif
liven up: *vt.* animer
liver: *n.* foie
livery: *n.* livrée
livestock: *n.* bétail
livid: *adj.* livide; furieux
living room: salle de séjour
living: *n.* vie; *adj.* vivant
lizard: *n.* lézard
load: *n.* charge
load: *vt.* charger
loaded: *adj.* chargé
loaf: *n.* pain
loafer: *n.* paresseux
loam: *n.* terreau
loan: *n.* prêt
loathe: *vt.* détester
loathing: *n.* aversion
loathsome: *adj.* répugnant
lobby: *n.* vestibule
lobe: *n.* lobe
lobster: *n.* langouste
local anaesthetic: anesthésique local
local government: administration municipale; administration locale
local: *adj.* local
localise: *vt.* localiser
locality: *n.* localité
locally: *adv.* localement
locate: *vt.* localiser
location: *n.* situation
lock: *n.* serrure
lock: *vt.* fermer à clé
locker: *n.* casier
locket: *n.* médaillon
lockout: *n.* grève patronale
locksmith: *n.* serrurier
lock-up: *n.* cellule
locomotive: *n.* locomotive

locust: *n.* sauterelle
lodge: *n.* loge du gardien
lodge: *vi.* se loger
lodger: *n.* locataire
loft: *n.* grenier
log: *n.* bûche
logbook: *n.* journal de bord
logic: *n.* logique
logical: *adj.* logique
logo: *n.* logo
loll: *vi.* se prélasser
lollipop: *n.* sucette
loneliness: *n.* solitude
lonely: *adj.* seul; solitaire
long jump: saut en longueur
long wave: grandes ondes
long: *adj.* long
longevity: *n.* longévité
long-haired: *adj.* aux cheveux longs
longing: *n.* désir
longitude: *n.* longitude
longitudinal: *adj.* longitudinal
long-range: *adj.* à longue portée
long-term: *adj.* à long terme
long-winded: *adj.* prolixe
look: *n.* aspect; regard
look: *vi.* regarder; sembler
looking glass: miroir
look-out: *n.* sentinelle; vigie
loom: *n.* métier â tisser
loom: *vi.* menacer
loop: *n.* boucle
loophole: *n.* échappatoire
loose: *adj.* lâché; desserré
loose: *vt.* perdre
loosen: *vt.* lâcher; desserrer
loot: *n.* butin
loot: *vt.* piller
lop: *vt.* élaguer
lopsided: *adj.* de travers; déséquilibré
loquacious: *adj.* loquace
loquacity: *n.* loquacité
lord: *n.* seigneur
lore: *n.* savoir

loss: *n.* perte
lot: *n.* sort; lot
lotion: *n.* lotion
lottery: *n.* loterie
loud: *adj.* fort; bruyant
loudspeaker: *n.* haut-parleur
lounge: *n.* salon
louse: *n.* (*pl.* lice) pou
lout: *n.* vaurien
lovable: *adj.* sympathique
love letter: lettre d'amour
love: *n.* amour
love: *vt.* aimer
loveliness: *n.* beauté
lovely: *adj.* beau
lover: *n.* amant
love-sick: *adj.* fou amoureux
loving: *adj.* affectueux
low: *adj.* bas
low: *vi.* meugler
low-cut: *adj.* décolleté
lower extreme: point inférieur
lower quartile: quartile inférieur
lower: *adj.* plus bas
lower: *vt.* baisser
lowest: *adj.* le plus bas
lowland: *n.* plaine
lowliness: *n.* humilité
lowly: *adj.* humble
lowly: *adj.* minable
low-water: *n.* basse mer
loyal: *adj.* loyal; fidèle
loyalty: *n.* loyauté; fidélité
lozenge: *n.* pastille
lubricant: *n.* lubrifiant
lubricate: *vt.* lubrifier
lucid: *adj.* lucide
luck: *n.* chance
luckily: *adv.* heureusement; par chance
luckless: *adj.* malchanceux
lucky: *adj.* chanceux; qui a de la chance
lucrative: *adj.* lucratif

ludricrous: *adj.* absurde
lug: *vt.* traîner
luggage: *n.* bagages
lugubrious: *adj.* lugubre; triste
lukewarm: *adj.* tiède
lull: *n.* répit
lull: *vt.* bercer
lullaby: *n.* berceuce
lumbago: *n.* lumbago
lumber room: débarras
lumberjack: *n.* bûcheron
luminous: *adj.* lumineux
lump sum: somme globale
lump: *n.* bosse; grosseur; morceau
lump: *vt.* réunir
lunacy: *n.* folie
lunar: *adj.* lunaire
lunatic: *adj.* fou; folle
lunch: *n.* déjeuner
lung: *n.* poumon
lurch: *n.* embardée
lure: *n.* leurre; attrait
lure: *vt.* séduire; attirer
lurid: *adj.* criard; horrible
lurk: *vi.* être tapi
luscious: *adj.* délicieux
lush: *adj.* luxuriant
lust: *n.* luxure; sensualité; désir
lust: *vi.* désirer
luster: *n.* lustre
lustful: *adj.* luxurieux; voluptueux
lustily: *adv.* vigoureusement
lusty: *adj.* fort; vigoureux
lute: *n.* luth
luxuriance: *n.* exubérance; luxuriance
luxuriant: *adj.* exubérant; luxuriant
luxuriate: *vi.* pousser de manière exubérante
luxurious: *adj.* luxueux
luxury: *n.* luxe
lymph: *n.* lymphe
lynch: *vt.* lyncher
lynx: *n.* linx

lyrical: *adj.* lyrique
lyrics: *npl.* paroles

M

macaroni: *n.* macaronis
macaroon: *n.* macaron
mace: *n.* massue; macis
macerate: *vt.* macérer
machination: *n.* machination
machine gun: mitrailleuse
machine: *n.* machine
machinery: *n.* machinerie; mécanisme
mackerel: *n.* maquereau
mad: *adj.* fou; folle; furieux; insensé
Madam: *n.* madame
madden: *vt.* rendre fou; rendre furieux
madder: *n.* garance
madhouse: *n.* asile de fous
madman: *n.* fou
madness: *n.* folie
magazine: *n.* magazine; revue
maggot: *n.* asticot
magic: *n.* magie
magician: *n.* magicien
magisterial: *adj.* magistral
magistracy: *n.* magistrature
magistrate: *n.* magistrat
magnanimity: *n.* magnanimité
magnanimous: *adj.* magnanime
magnet: *n.* aimant
magnetic field: champs magnétique
magnetic susceptibility: susceptibilité magnétique
magnetic: *adj.* magnétique
magnetism: *n.* magnétisme
magnificence: *n.* magnificence
magnificent: *adj.* magnifique
magnify: *vt.* grossir; exagérer
magnifying glass: loupe
magnitude: *n.* magnitude
magpie: *n.* pie
mahogany: *n.* acajou
maid: *n.* bonne
maiden name: nom de jeune fille
maiden: *n.* jeune fille

mail coach: malle-poste
mail train: train-poste
mail: *n.* courrier
mailbox: *n.* boîte aux lettres
mailing list: fichier-clientèle
mail-order business: la vente par correspondance
mail-order: vente par correspondance
maim: *vt.* mutiler
main author: auteur principal
main event: action principale
main idea: idée principale
main line: *n.* grande ligne
main point: point clé
main street: rue principale
main: *adj.* principal; essentiel
mainland: *n.* continent
mainly: *adv.* principalement; essentiellement
maintain: *vt.* maintenir; soutenir
maintenance: *n.* entretien
maize: *n.* maïs
majestic: *adj.* majestueux
majesty: *n.* majesté
major events: évènement principal
major: *adj.* majeur; *n.* commandant
majority: *n.* majorité
make: *n.* marque
make: *vt.* faire
make-believe: *n.* invention
makeshift: *adj.* improvisé; de fortune
make-up remover: démaquillant
make-up: *n.* maquillage
malaise: *n.* malaise
malaria: *n.* malaria
malcontent adj: *n.* mécontent
male: *adj.* mâle; *n.* mâle
malevolence: *n.* malveillance
malevolent: *adj.* malveillant
malfunction: *n.* mauvais fonctionnement
malice: *n.* méchanceté
malicious: *adj.* méchant

malign: *adj.* nocif
malign: *vt.* calomnier
malignant: *adj.* malfaisant
mall: *n.* centre commercial
malleable: *adj.* malléable
mallet: *n.* maillet
mallow: *n.* mauve
malnutrition: *n.* malnutrition
malpractice: *n.* malversation
malt: *n.* malt
maltreat: *vt.* maltraiter
mammal: *n.* mammifère
mammoth: *adj.* gigantesque
man: *n.* homme
manacle: *n.* entrave menottes
manage: *vt.* diriger; réussir; *vi.* réussir; gérer administrer
manageable: *adj.* maniable
management: *n.* direction
manager: *n.* directeur
manageress: *n.* directrice
managerial: *adj.* directorial
managing director: directeur général
manaliness: *n.* virilité; courage
mandarin: *n.* mandarine; mandarin
mandat: *vt.* ordonner; commander; mettre en ordre
mandate: *n.* mandat
mandatory: *n.* obligatoire
mane: *n.* crinière
manfully: *adv.* vaillamment
manger: *n.* mangeoire
mangle: *n.* essoreuse
mangle: *vt.* mutiler
mangy: *adj.* miteux
manhandle: *vt.* altraiter; manutentionner
manhood: *n.* âge d'homme; virilité
man-hour: *n.* heure de main d'oeuvre
mania: *n.* manie
maniac: *n.* maniaque
manic: *adj.* obsessionnel
manicure: *n.* manucure
manifest: *adj.* manifeste

manifest: *vt.* manifester
manifestation: *n.* manifestation
manifesto: *n.* manifeste
manipulate: *vt.* manipuler
manipulation: *n.* manipulation
mankind: *n.* humanité
manlike: *adj.* viril; d'homme
manly: *adj.* viril
man-made: *adj.* artificiel
manner: *n.* manière; attitude
manoeuvre: *n.* manoeuvre
manpower: *n.* main-d'oeuvre
mansion: *n.* château
manslaughter: *n.* homicide
involontaire
mantelpiece: *n.* manteau de cheminée
manual: *adj.* manuel
manufacture: *n.* fabrication
manufacture: *vt.* fabriquer
manufacturer: *n.* fabricant
manure: *n.* fumier; engrais
manuscript: *n.* manuscrit
many: *adj.* beaucoup de
map: *n.* cartel; plan
March: *n.* mars
margin: *n.* marge
marine: *adj.* marin
mark: *n.* marque
mark: *vt.* marquer
market a product; to: distribuer un produit
market: *n.* marché
market: *v.* commercialiser
marriage: *n.* mariage
marry: *v.* épouser
masculine: *adj.* masculin
mask: *n.* masque
mask: *v.* masquer
mason: *n.* maçon
mass action law: principe d'action de masse
mass media: mass media
mass production: la production en série

mass: *n.* masse; messe
master copy: original
master: *n.* maitre
master: *v.* maîtriser
match: *n.* allumette; match
match: *v.* assortir
mate: *n.* compagnon; compagne
material: *n.* matière; tissu
maternity: *n.* maternité
mathematical reasoning: raisonnement mathématique
matter: *n.* matière; affaire
mattress: *n.* matelas
mature: *adj.* mûr
mature: *v.* mûrir
maturity: *n.* maturité
maximum: *adj.* maximum
May: *n.* mai
maybe: *adv.* peut-être
meal: *n.* repas
mean free path: libre parcours moyen
mean: *adj.* méchant
mean: *v.* signifier; vouloir dire
meaning: *n.* sens; signification
means of conveyance: moyens de transport
measure: *n.* mesure
measure: *vt.* mesurer
meat: *n.* viande
mechanic: *n.* mécanicien
mechanical: *adj.* mécanique
mechanism: *n.* mécanisme
medal: *n.* médaille
media: *n.* média
median: *n.* médiane
medical: *adj.* médical
medication: *n.* médicaments
méditation: *n.* méditation
meditative: *adj.* méditatif
medium wave: ondes moyennes
medium: *n.* milieu; médium; *adj.* moyen
medley: *n.* mélange

meek: *adj.* docile
meekness: *n.* docilité
meet: *vt.* rencontrer
meeting: *n.* réunion; congrès
megaphone: *n.* mégaphone
meiosis: *n.* méiose
melancholy: *n.* mélancolie
mellow: *adj.* moelleux; doux
mellow: *vi.* mûrir
mellowness: *n.* moelleux
melodious: *adj.* mélodieux
melody: *n.* mélodie
melon: *n.* melon
melt: *vt.* faire fondre; *vi.* fondre
melting point: point de fusion
member: *n.* membre
membership: *n.* adhésion
membrane: *n.* membrane
memento: *n.* mémento
memo: *n.* note de service
memoir: *n.* mémoire
memorable: *adj.* mémorable
memorandum of association: acte constitutif
memorandum: *n.* mémorandum; note de service
memorial: *n.* monument commémoratif; mémorial
memorise: *vt.* mémoriser
memory aids: aide mémoire
memory: *n.* mémoire souvenir
menace: *n.* menace
menace: *vt.* menacer
menacing: *adj.* menaçant
menagerie: *n.* ménagerie
mend: *vt.* réparer; raccommoder
mending: *n.* réparation; raccommodage
menial: *adj.* vil
meningitis: *n.* méningite
menopause: *n.* ménopause
menstruation: *n.* menstruation
mental image: image mentale
mental: *adj.* mental

mentality: *n.* mentalité
mentally: *adv.* mentalement
mention: *n.* mention
mention: *vt.* mentionner
menu: *n.* menu
mercantile: *adj.* commercial
mercenary: *adj.* mercenaire; *n.* mercenaire
merchandise: *n.* marchandise
merchant marine: marine marchande
merchant: *n.* négociant
merchantman: *n.* navire marchand
merciful: *adj.* miséricordieux
merciless: *adj.* impitoyable
mercury: *n.* mercure
mercy: *n.* pitié
mere: *adj.* simple
merge: *vt.* fusionner
merger: *n.* fusion
meridian: *n.* méridien
merit: *n.* mérite
merit: *vt.* mériter
meritorious: *adj.* méritoire
mermaid: *n.* sirène
merrily: *adv.* joyeusement
merriment: *n.* divertissement; réjouissance
merry: *adj.* joyeux
merry-go-round: *n.* manège
mesh: *n.* maille
mesmerise: *vt.* hypnotiser
mess: *n.* désordre; confusion; mess
message: *n.* message
messenger: *n.* messager
metabolism: *n.* métabolisme
metal: *n.* métal
metallurgy: *n.* métallurgie
metamorphic rock: roche métamorphique
metamorphosis: *n.* métamorphose
metaphor: *n.* métaphore
metaphorical: *adj.* métaphorique
metaphysical: *adj.* métaphysique

metaphysics: *n.* métaphysique
mete (out): *vt.* distribuer
meteor: *n.* météore
meteorological: *adj.* météorologique
meteorology: *n.* météorologie
meter: *n.* compteur
method: *n.* méthode
methodical: *adj.* méthodique
metre: *n.* mètre
metric system: système métrique
metric: *adj.* métrique
metropolis: *n.* métropole
metropolitan: *adj.* métropolitain
mettle: *n.* courage
mettlesome: *adj.* courageux
mew: *vi.* miauler
mezzanine: *n.* mezzanine
microbe: *n.* microbe
microchip: *n.* microprocesseur; puce
microfiche: *n.* microfiche
microfilm: *n.* microfilm
microphone: *n.* microphone
microscope: *n.* microscope
microscopic: *adj.* microscopique
microwave: *n.* four à micro-ondes
mid: *adj.* demi
midday: *n.* midi
middle name: deuxième prénom
middle: *adj.* moyen; du milieu; *n.* milieu
middleman: *n.* intermédiaire
middleweight: *n.* poids moyen
middling: *adj.* moyen; passable
midge: *n.* moucheron
midget: *n.* nain
midnight: *n.* minuit
midriff: *n.* diaphragme; estomac
midst: *n.* milieu
midsummer: *n.* milieu de l'été
midway: *adv.* à mi-chemin
midwife: *n.* sage-femme
midwifery: *n.* obstétrique
might: *n.* force
mighty: *adj.* fort; puissant

migraine: *n.* migraine
migrate: *vi.* émigrer
migration: *n.* émigration
migratory: *adj.* migratoire
mike: *n.* micro
mild: *adj.* doux; modéré
mildew: *n.* moisissure; mildiou
mildness: *n.* douceur
mile: *n.* mile
mileage: *n.* kilométrage
milestone: *n.* borne
milieu: *n.* milieu
militant: *adj.* militant
military: *adj.* militaire
militate: *vi.* militer
militia: *n.* milice
milk: *n.* lait
milk: *vt.* traire; exploiter
milkshake: *n.* milk-shake
milky: *adj.* laiteux
mill: *n.* moulin
mill: *vt.* moudre
millennium: *n.* millénaire
millet: *n.* millet
millier: *n.* meunier
milligram: *n.* milligramme
millilitre: *n.* millilitre
millimetre: *n.* millimètre
milliner: *n.* chapelier
millinery: *n.* chapellerie
million: *n.* million
millionaire: *n.* millionaire
millionth: *adj.* millionième
millstone: *n.* meule
mime: *n.* mime
mimic: *vt.* mimer
mimicry: *n.* mimique
mince: *vt.* hacher
mind: *n.* esprit
mind: *vt.* prendre soin de
minded: *adj.* disposé
mindful: *adj.* soucieux; attentif
mindless: *adj.* insouciant

mine: *pron.* le mien; la mienne; les miens; les miennes
mine: *vi.* exploiter la mine
minefield: *n.* champ de mines
miner: *adj.* minéral
miner: *n.* mineur
mineralogy: *n.* minéralogie
minesweeper: *n.* dragueur de mines
mingle: *vt.* mêler
miniature: *n.* miniature
minimal: *adj.* minime
minimise: *vt.* minimiser
minimum: *n.* minimum
mining: *n.* exploitation minière
minion: *n.* larbin
minister: *n.* ministre
minister: *vt.* servir
ministerial: *adj.* ministériel
ministry: *n.* ministère
mink: *n.* vison
minnow: *n.* vairon
minor: *adj.* mineur
minority: *n.* minorité
minstrel: *n.* ménestrel
mint: *n.* menthe
mint: *vt.* frapper la monnaie
minus: *adv.* moins
minute: *adj.* minuscule
minute: *n.* minute
miracle: *n.* miracle
miraculous: *adj.* miraculeux
mirage: *n.* mirage
mire: *n.* bourbe
mirky: *adj.* trouble; ténébreux
mirror: *n.* miroir
mirth: *n.* allégresse
mirthful: *adj.* joyeux
misadventure: *n.* mésaventure
misanthropist: *n.* misanthrope
misapply: *vt.* mal appliquer
misapprehension: *n.* méprise
misbehave: *vi.* se conduire mal
misbehaviour: *n.* mauvaise conduite
miscalculate: *vt.* mal calculer

miscarriage: *n.* fausse couche
miscarry: *vi.* faire une fausse couche; échouer
miscellaneous: *adj.* divers; varié
miscellany: *n.* mélange; assortiment
mischief: *n.* mal; tort
mischievous: *adj.* mauvais; espiègle
misconception: *n.* méprise
misconduct: *n.* mauvaise conduite
misconstrue: *vt.* mal interpréter
miscount: *vt.* mal compter
miscreant: *n.* scélérat
misdeed: *n.* méfait
misdemeanour: *n.* délit
misdirect: *vt.* mal diriger
miser: *n.* avare mf
miserable: *adj.* malheureux
miserly: *adj.* mesquin; avare
misery: *n.* malheur; misère
misfit: *n.* inadapté
misfortune: *n.* infortune
misgiving: *n.* doute
misgovern: *vt.* mal gouverner
misguided: *adj.* malencontreux; malavisé
mishandle: *vt.* maltraiter; mal s'y prendre avec; malmener
mishap: *n.* mésaventure
misinform: *vt.* mal renseigner
misinterpret: *vt.* mal interpréter
misjudge: *vt.* méjuger
mislay: *vt.* égarer
mislead: *vt.* induire en erreur
mismanage: *vt.* mal administrer
mismanagement: *n.* mauvaise administration
misnomer: *n.* nom inapproprié
misogynist: *n.* misogyne
misplace: *vt.* égarer
misprint: *n.* coquille
misprint: *vt.* mal imprimer
misrepresent: *vt.* mal représenter
miss: *n.* missel
miss: *vt.* rater; s'ennuyer de

misshapen: *adj.* déformé
missile: *n.* missile
missing: *adj.* perdu; absent
mission: *n.* mission
missionary: *n.* missionnaire
misspent: *adj.* gaspillé
mist: *n.* brouillard
mistake: *n.* mépris; erreur
mistake: *vt.* confondre
mistletoe: *n.* gui
mistress: *n.* maîtresse
mistrust: *n.* méfiance
mistrust: *vt.* se méfier de
mistrustful: *adj.* méfiant
misty: *adj.* brumeux
misunderstand: *vt.* mal comprendre
misunderstanding: *n.* malentendu
misuse: *vt.* faire un mauvais usage de; abuser de
mitigate: *vt.* atténuer
mitigation: *n.* atténuation
mitosis: *n.* mitose
mitre: *n.* mitre
mittens: *npl.* moufles
mix: *vt.* mélanger
mixed: *adj.* mélangé; mixte
mixed-up: *adj.* confus
mixer: *n.* mixeur
mixture: *n.* mélange
mix-up: *n.* confusion
moan: *n.* gémissement
moan: *vi.* gémir; se plaindre
moat: *n.* fossé
mob: *n.* foule; masse
mobile home: caravane
mobile: *adj.* mobile
mobilise: *vt.* mobiliser
mobility: *n.* mobilité
moccasin: *n.* mocassin
mock: *vt.* se moquer de
mockery: *n.* moquerie
mode: *n.* mode
model: *n.* modèle
model: *vt.* modeler

moderate: *adj.* modéré
moderate: *vt.* modérer
moderation: *n.* modération
modern: *adj.* moderne
modernise: *vt.* moderniser
modest: *adj.* modeste
modesty: *n.* modestie
modicum: *n.* minimum
modification: *n.* modification
modify: *vt.* modifier
modulate: *vt.* moduler
modulation: *n.* modulation
module: *n.* module
mogul: *n.* magnat
mohair: *n.* mohair
moist: *adj.* humide
moisten: *vt.* humidifier
moisture: *n.* humidité
molality: *n.* molalité
molar volume: volume molaire
molar: *n.* molaire
molarity: *n.* molarité
molasses: *npl.* mélasse
mold: *n.* moissure
mole fraction: fraction molaire
mole: *n.* taupe
molecular beam: faisceau moléculaire
molecular compound: composé moléculaire
molecular formula: formule moléculaire
molecular sieves: zéolithes
molecular speed: vitesses moléculaires
molecule: *n.* molécule
molehill: *n.* taupinière
molest: *vt.* importuner
mollify: *vt.* apaiser
mollusc: *n.* mollusque
mollycoddle: *vt.* dorloter
molten: *adj.* fondu
mom: *n.* maman
moment of inertia: moment d'inertie

moment: *n.* moment
moment: quantité de mouvement
momentarily: *adv.* momentanément
momentary: *adj.* momentané
momentous: *adj.* capital
momentum: *n.* vitesse f; élan
monarch: *n.* monarque
monarchy: *n.* monarchie
monastery: *n.* monastère
monastic: *adj.* monastique
Monday: *n.* lundi
monetary: *adj.* monétaire
money order: mandat postal
money supply: masse monétaire
money: *n.* argent; pièce de monnaie
mongol: *n.* (mad) mongolien
mongrel: *adj.* bâtard; *n.* bâtard
monitor: *n.* moniteur
monk: *n.* moine
monkey: *n.* singe
monochrome: *adj.* monochrome
monocle: *n.* monocle
monologue: *n.* monologue
monomolecular reaction:
monomoléculaire; réaction
monopolise: *vt.* monopoliser
monopoly: *n.* monopole
monosyllable: *n.* monosyllabe
monotonous: *adj.* monotone
monotony: *n.* monotonie
monsoon: *n.* mousson
monster: *n.* monstre
monstrosity: *n.* monstruosité
monstrous: *adj.* monstrueux
montage: *n.* montage
month: *n.* mois
monthly: *adj.* mensuel
monument: *n.* monument
monumental: *adj.* monumental
moo: *vi.* meugler
mood: *n.* humeur
moodiness: *n.* mauvaise humeur
moody: *adj.* de mauvaise humeur;
lunatique

moon phase: phase lunaire
moon: *n.* lune
moonbeams: *npl.* rayons de lune
moonlight: *n.* clair de lune
moor: *n.* lande
moor: *vt.* amarrer
moorland: *n.* lande
moose: *n.* élan; orignal
mop: *n.* lavette
mop: *vt.* éponger
mope: *vi.* se morfondre
moped: *n.* vélomoteur
moral: *adj.* moral
morale: *n.* moral
moralise: *vt.* moraliser
moralist: *n.* moraliste
morality: *n.* moralité
morass: *n.* marais
morbid: *adj.* morbide
more: *adv.* plus
moreover: *adv.* de plus; en outre
morgue: *n.* morgue
morning: *n.* matin
moron: *n.* imbécile
morose: *adj.* morose
morphine: *n.* morphine
morse curve: morse; formule de
morse: *n.* morse
morsel: *n.* bouchée; morceau
mortal: *adj.* mortel; *n.* mortel
mortality: *n.* mortalité
mortar: *n.* mortier
mortgage company: banque de prêts
hypothécaires
mortgage: *n.* hypothèque
mortgage: *vt.* hypothéquer
mortgager: *n.* débiteur hypothécaire
mortification: *n.* mortification
mortify: *vt.* mortifier
mortuary: *n.* morgue
mosaic: *n.* mosaïque
mosque: *n.* mosquée
mosquito: *n.* moustique
moss: *n.* mousse

mossy: *adj.* moussu
most: *pron.* la plupart de
moth: *n.* papillon de nuit; mite
mothball: *n.* boule de naphtaline
mother tongue: langue maternelle
mother: *n.* mère
motherhood: *n.* maternité
mother-in-law: *n.* belle-mère
motherless: *adj.* sans mère
motherly: *adj.* maternel
mother-of-pearl: *n.* nacre
mother-to-be: *n.* future maman
motif: *n.* motif
motion picture: film
motion: *n.* mouvement
motionless: *adj.* immobile
motivated: *adj.* motivé
motivation: *n.* motivation
motive: *n.* motif
motley: *adj.* bigarré
motor vehicle: automobile
motor: *n.* moteur
motorbike: *n.* moto
motorboat: *n.* canot à moteur
motorcycle: *n.* motocyclette
mottled: *adj.* marbré; tacheté
motto: *n.* devise
mould: *n.* moule
mould: *vt.* mouler
moulder: *vi.* s'effriter
mouldy: *adj.* moisi
moult: *vi.* muer
mound: *n.* monticule
mount: *n.* mont
mount: *vt.* gravir
mountain: *n.* montagne
mountaineer: *n.* alpiniste
mountaineering: *n.* alpinisme
mountainous: *adj.* montagneux
mourn: *vt.* pleurer
mourner: *n.* personne en deuil
mournful: *adj.* triste
mourning: *n.* deuil
mouse: *n.* souris

mouth organ: harmonica
mouth: *n.* bouche; embouchure
mouthful: *n.* bouchée
mouthpiece: *n.* bec; microphone
mouthwash: *n.* eau dentifrice
mouthwatering: *adj.* appétissant
movable: *adj.* mobile
move: *n.* mouvement
move: *vt.* déplacer; toucher; émouvoir
movement: *n.* mouvement
movie camera: caméra
movie: *adj.* touchant; émouvant
movie: *n.* film
mow: *vt.* tondre
mower: *n.* tondeuse
much: *pron.* beaucoup; *adv.*
beaucoup; très
muck: *n.* saleté
mucous: *adj.* muqueux
mucus: *n.* mucus
mud: *n.* boue
muddle: *n.* confusion; désordre
muddle: *vt.* confondre; embrouiller
muddy: *adj.* boueux
mudguard: *n.* garde-boue
muffle: *vt.* assourdir
mug: *n.* tasse
muggy: *adj.* lourd; étouffant
mulberry: *n.* mûre
mule: *n.* mulet; mule
mull: *vt.* méditer
multifarious: *adj.* divers
multiple meanings: significations
multiples
multiple: *adj.* multiple
multiplication: *n.* multiplication
multiply: *vt.* multiplier
multitude: *n.* multitude
mumble: *vt.* grommeler
mummy: *n.* momie
mumps: *npl.* oreillons
munch: *vt.* mâcher
mundane: *adj.* banal
municipal: *adj.* municipal

municipality: *n.* municipalité
munificence: *n.* munificence
munitions: *npl.* munitions
mural: *n.* mural
murder: *n.* assassinat; meurtre; homicide volontaire
murder: *vt.* assassiner
murderer: *n.* assassin; meurtrier
murderess: *n.* meurtrière
murderous: *adj.* meurtrier
murky: *adj.* obscur; glauque
murmur: *n.* murmure
murmur: *vt.* murmurer
muscle: *n.* muscle
muscular: *adj.* musculaire
muse: *vi.* méditer; rêver
museum: *n.* musée
mushroom: *n.* champignon
music: *n.* musique
musical: *adj.* musical; mélodieux
musician: *n.* musicien
musk: *n.* musc
muslin: *n.* mousseline
mussel: *n.* moule
mustache: *n.* moustache
mustard: *n.* moutarde
muster: *vt.* rassembler
musty: *adj.* moisi
mutation: *n.* mutation
mute: *adj.* muet; silencieux
muted: *adj.* assourdi
mutilate: *vt.* mutiler
mutilation: *n.* mutilation
mutiny: *n.* mutinerie
mutiny: *vi.* se mutiner; se révolter
mutter: *n.* grommellement
mutter: *vi.* grommeler; marmonner
mutton: *n.* mouton (viande)
mutual: *adj.* mutuel; réciproque
muzzle: *n.* muselière; museau
muzzle: *vt.* museler
myriad: *n.* myriade
myrrh: *n.* myrrhe
myrtle: *n.* myrte

myself: *pron.* moi-même
mysterious: *adj.* mystérieux
mystery: *n.* mystère
mystic: *adj.* mystique
mystify: *vt.* mystifier; laisser perplexe
mystique: *n.* mystique
myth: *n.* mythe
mythology: *n.* mythologie

N

nab: *vt.* coincer; pincer
nag: *n.* bourrin
nag: *vt.* harceler
nagging: *adj.* persistant; *n.* harcèlement
nail brush: brosse à ongles
nail polish: vernis à ongles
nail scissors: ciseaux à ongles
nail: *n.* ongle; clou
nail: *vt.* clouer
nailfile: *n.* lime à ongles
naive: *adj.* naïf
naked: *adj.* nu; dénudé; pur; simple
name catalogue: catalogue onomastique
name: *n.* nom; réputation
name: *vt.* nommer; mentionner
nameless: *adj.* anonyme
namely: *adv.* à savoir
namesake: *n.* homonyme
nanny: *n.* nourrice
nap: *n.* sieste; somme
napalm: *n.* napalm
nape: *n.* nuque
napkin: *n.* serviette
narcissus: *n.* narcisse
narcotic: *adj.* narcotique; *n.* narcotique
narrate: *vt.* narrer; raconter
narrative: *adj.* narratif; *n.* narration
narrow: *adj.* étroit
narrow: *vt.* resserrer; limiter
nasty: *adj.* méchant; mauvais; sale
natal: *adj.* natal
nation: *n.* nation
national archives: archives nationales
national: *adj.* national
nationalism: *n.* nationalisme
nationalist: *adj.* nationaliste; *n.* nationaliste
nationality: *n.* nationalité
nationalize: *vt.* nationaliser

nationwide: *adj.* au niveau national
native language: langue maternelle
native: *adj.* natal; *n.* autochtone
Nativity: *n.* Nativité
natural gas: gaz naturel
natural selection: sélection naturelle
natural: *adj.* naturel
naturalise: *vt.* naturaliser
naturalist: *n.* naturaliste
nature: *n.* nature; sorte
naught: *n.* zéro
naughty: *adj.* méchant
nausea: *n.* nausée; envie de vomir
nauseate: *vt.* donner des nausées à
nauseous: *adj.* écoeurant
nautical: *adj.* nautique
nave: *n.* nef (d'église)
navel: *n.* nombril
navigate: *vi.* naviguer
navigation: *n.* navigation
navy: *n.* marine
Nazi: *n.* nazi
neap tide: marée morte
near: *prep.* près de; *adv.* près; à côté; *adj.* proche
nearby: *adj.* proche
nearly: *adv.* presque
near-sighted: *adj.* myope
nebulous: *adj.* nébuleux
necessarily: *adv.* nécessairement
necessary: *adj.* nécessaire
necessitate: *vt.* nécessiter
necessity: *n.* nécessité
neck: *n.* cou
neck: *vi.* se bécoter
necklace: *n.* collier
necktie: *n.* cravate
nectar: *n.* nectar
need: *n.* besoin; pauvreté
need: *vt.* avoir besoin de; nécessiter
needle: *n.* aiguille
needless: *adj.* superflu; inutile
needlework: *n.* couture
needy: *adj.* nécessiteux; pauvre

negation: *n.* négation
negative: *adj.* négatif; *n.* négative; négation; négatif
neglect: *n.* négligence
neglect: *vt.* négliger
negligee: *n.* négligé; déshabillé
negligence: *n.* négligence; manque de soin
negligent: *adj.* négligent
negligible: *adj.* négligeable
negotiate: *vt.* négocier
negotiation: *n.* négociation
Negress: *n.* Noire
Negro: *adj.* noir; *n.* Noir
neigh: *n.* hennissement
neigh: *vi.* hennir
neighbor: *n.* voisin
neighbor: *vt.* être voisin de
neighborhood: *n.* voisinage
neighbouring: *adj.* voisin
neighbourly: *adj.* sociable
neither: *conj.* ni; aucun; ni l'un ni l'autre
neon light: lumière au néon
neon: *n.* néon
nephew: *n.* neveu
nepotism: *n.* népotisme
nerve: *n.* nerf; courage; toupet
nerve-racking: *adj.* exaspérant
nervous breakdown: dépression nerveuse
nervous: *adj.* nerveux
nest egg: économies
nest: *n.* nid; nichée
nestle: *vt.* se blottir
net: *adj.* soigné; net; propre
net: *n.* filet
netting: *n.* filet
nettle: *n.* ortie
network: *n.* réseau
neurosis: *n.* névrose
neurotic: *adj.* névrosé; *n.* névrosé
neuter: *adj.* neutre
neutral: *adj.* neutre

neutralise: *vt.* neutraliser
neutrality: *n.* neutralité
neutron bomb: bombe à neutrons
neutron: *n.* neutron
never: *adv.* jamais
never-ending: *adj.* interminable
nevertheless: *adv.* cependant; néanmoins
new: *adj.* neuf; nouveau; dernier
newborn: *adj.* nouveau-né
newcomer: *n.* nouveau venu
new-fangled: *adj.* moderne
news agency: agence de presse
news flash: flash d'information
news: *npl.* nouvelles; informations
newscaster: *n.* présentateur
newsdealer: *n.* marchand de journaux
newsletter: *n.* bulletin
newspaper: *n.* journal
newsreel: *n.* actualités
next: *adj.* prochain; *adv.* ensuite; après
nib: *n.* pointe
nibble: *vt.* mordiller
nice: *adj.* gentil; agréable; joli
nice-looking: *adj.* beau
niche: *n.* niche
nick: *n.* entaille
nick: *vt.* faucher
nickel: *n.* nickel; (US) pièce de cinq centimes
nickname: *n.* surnom
nickname: *vt.* surnommer
niece: *n.* nièce
niggling: *adj.* insignifiant
night school: cours du soir
night shift: équipe de nuit
night: *n.* nuit
nightclub: *n.* boîte de nuit
nightfall: *n.* tombée de la nuit
nightly: *adv.* tous les soirs; toutes les nuits; *adj.* nocturne
nightmare: *n.* cauchemar
night-time: *n.* nuit

nihilist: *n.* nihiliste
nimble: *adj.* léger; agile; souple
nine: *adj.* neuf; *n.* neuf
nineteen: *adj.* dix-neuf
nineteenth: *adj.* dix-neuvième
ninetieth: *adj.* quatre-vingt-dixième
ninety: *adj.* quatre-vingt-dix
ninth: *adj.* neuvième
nip: *vt.* pincer; mordre
nipple: *n.* mamelon; tétine
nit: *n.* lente
nitrogen: *n.* nitrogène
no: *adv.* non; *adj.* aucun; pas de
nobility: *n.* noblesse
noble: *adj.* noble; *n.* noble
nobleman: *n.* noble
nobody: *pron.* personne
nocturnal: *adj.* nocturne
nod: *n.* signe de tête
nod: *vi.* faire un signe de la tête; somnoler
noise: *n.* bruit
noisily: *adv.* bruyamment
noisiness: *n.* bruit; tapage
noisy: *adj.* bruyant
nominal: *adj.* nominal
nominate: *vt.* nommer
nomination: *n.* nomination
nominative: *n.* nominatif
nominee: *n.* candidat
nonalcoholic: *adj.* non alcoolisé
non-aligned: *adj.* non-aligné
nonchalant: *adj.* nonchalant
noncommittal: *adj.* réservé
nonconformist: *n.* nonconformiste
nondescript: *adj.* quelconque
none: *pron.* aucun; personne
nonentity: *n.* nullité
nonetheless: *adv.* cependant
nonexistent: *adj.* inexistant
nonfiction: *n.* ouvrages non romanesques
nonplussed: *adj.* perplexe

nonpolar covalent bond: liaison non-polaire covalente
non-print media: médium non imprimé
nonrenewable resource: ressource non-renouvelable
nonsense: *n.* absurdité
nonsensical: *adj.* absurde
nonsmoker: *n.* non-fumeur
nonstick: *adj.* anti-adhérent
nonstop: *adj.* direct; *adv.* sans s'arrêter
nonverbal cue: signal non verbal
noodles: *npl.* nouilles
noon: *n.* midi
noose: *n.* noeud coulant
nor: *conj.* ni
normal melting point: point de fusion normal
normal: *adj.* normal
normality: *n.* normalité
North America: Amérique du Nord
North Pole: pôle Nord
north: *n.* nord; *adj.* du nord
northeast: *n.* nord-est
northerly; northern: *adj.* du nord
northward(s): *adv.* vers le nord
northwest: *n.* nord-ouest
nose: *n.* nez
nosebleed: *n.* saignement de nez
nosedive: *n.* piqué
nostalgia: *n.* nostalgie
nostril: *n.* narine
not: *adv.* pas; non
notable: *adj.* notable
notably: *adv.* notamment
notary: *n.* notaire
notch: *n.* cran; dent
notch: *vt.* denteler
note: *n.* note; billet; mot; marque
note: *vt.* noter; marquer; remarquer
notebook: *n.* carnet
noted: *adj.* célèbre; connu
notepad: *n.* bloc-notes

notepaper: *n.* papier à lettres
nothing: *n.* rien
notice of tender: appel d'offres
notice of transfer: avis de virement
notice: *n.* notice; avis
notice: *vt.* remarquer
noticeable: *adj.* visible
notification: *n.* notification
notify: *vt.* notifier
notion: *n.* notion; opinion; idée
notoriety: *n.* notoriété
notorious: *adj.* notoire
notwithstanding: *conj.* quoique
nougat: *n.* nougat
nought: *n.* zéro
noun: *n.* nom; substantif
nourish: *vt.* nourrir; alimenter
nourishing: *adj.* nourrissant
novel: *n.* roman
novelist: *n.* romancier
novelty: *n.* nouveauté
November: *n.* novembre
novice: *n.* novice; débutant
now: *adv.* maintenant
nowadays: *adv.* de nos jours; à l'heure actuelle
nowhere: *adv.* nulle part
noxious: *adj.* nocif
nozzle: *n.* douille
nuance: *n.* nuance
nuclear fission: fission nucléaire
nuclear fusion: fusion nucléaire
nuclear reaction: réaction nucléaire
nuclear: *adj.* nucléaire
nucleon: *n.* nucléon
nucleus: *n.* noyau
nude: *adj.* nu
nudge: *vt.* donner un coup de coude à
nudist: *n.* nudiste
nudity: *n.* nudité
nuisance: *n.* ennui; gêne
nuke: *n.* bombe atomique
nuke: *vt.* atomiser
null: *adj.* nul

nullify: *vt.* annuler; invalider
numb: *adj.* engourdi
numb: *vt.* engourdir
number: *n.* numéro; nombre; quantité
number: *vt.* numéroter; compter
numberplate: *n.* plaque d'immatriculation
numbness: *n.* engourdissement
numeral: *n.* chiffre
numerator: *n.* numérateur
numeric: *adj.* numérique
numerous: *adj.* nombreux
nun: *n.* religieuse
nunnery: *n.* couvent
nupti: *adj.* nuptial
nurse: *n.* infirmière
nurse: *vt.* soigner; ménager
nursery rhyme: comptine
nursery school: école maternelle
nursery: *n.* crèche; chambre d'enfant
nursing home: maison de repos
nurture: *vt.* élever; soigner
nut shell: coquille de noix
nut: *n.* noix
nutcrackers: *npl.* casse-noix; casse-noisettes
nutmeg: *n.* noix de muscade
nutritious: *adj.* nutritif
nylon: *n.* nylon; *adj.* en nylon

O

oak: *n.* chêne
oar: *n.* rame
oasis: *n.* oasis
oat: *n.* avoine
oath: *n.* serment
obedience: *n.* obéissance
obedient: *adj.* obéissant
obese: *adj.* obèse
obesity: *n.* obésité
obey: *vt.* obéir
obituary: *n.* nécrologie
object: *n.* objet
object: *vt.* objecter
objection: *n.* objection
objectionable: *adj.* désagréable
objective: *adj.* objectif; *n.* objectif
objectivity: *n.* objectivité
obligation: *n.* obligation
obligatory: *adj.* obligatoire
oblige: *vt.* obliger; rendre service à
obliging: *adj.* obligeant
oblique: *adj.* oblique
obliterate: *vt.* effacer
oblivion: *n.* oubli
oblivious: *adj.* oublieux
obnoxious: *adj.* odieux
oboe: *n.* hautbois
obscene: *adj.* obscène
obscenity: *n.* obscénité
obscure: *adj.* obscur
obscure: *vt.* obscurcir
obscurity: *n.* obscurité
observance: *n.* observation; observance
observant: *adj.* observateur; respectueux
observation: *n.* observation
observatory: *n.* observatoire
observe: *vt.* observer
observer: *n.* observateur
observingly: *adv.* attentivement
obsess: *vt.* obséder
obsessive: *adj.* obsédant

obsolete: *adj.* désuet
obstacle: *n.* obstacle
obstinate: *adj.* obstiné
obstruct: *vt.* obstruer; entraver
obstruction: *n.* obstruction; encombrement
obtain: *vt.* obtenir
obtainable: *adj.* disponible
obtrusive: *adj.* importun
obtuse angle: angle obtus
obtuse triangle: triangle obtus
obtuse: *adj.* obtus
obvious: *adj.* évident
occasion: *n.* occasion
occasion: *vt.* occasionner; causer
occasional: *adj.* occasionnel
occupant; occupier: occupant; locataire
occupation: *n.* occupation; emploi
occupy: *vt.* occuper
occur: *vi.* se produire; arriver
occurrence: *n.* incident
ocean basin: bassin océanique
ocean: *n.* océan
ocean-goin: *adj.* de haute mer
oceanic: *adj.* océanique
ochre: *n.* ocre
octave: *n.* octave
October: *n.* octobre
octopus: *n.* poulpe
odd jobs: petits travaux
odd: *adj.* impair; étrange; quelconque
oddity: *n.* singularité; particularité
oddness: *n.* étrangeté; singularité
odds: *npl.* chances
odious: *adj.* odieux
odometer: *n.* odomètre
odorous: *adj.* odorant
odour: *n.* odeur; parfum
of course: *adv.* bien sûr
of: *prep.* de; à
off: *adj.* éteint; fermé; annulé; en congé

offend: *vt.* offenser; blesser; choquer; pécher
offender: *n.* délinquant
offense: *n.* offense; injure
offensive: *adj.* offensant; injurieux
offer: *n.* offre
offer: *vt.* offrir
offering: *n.* offrande; offre
offhand: *adj.* désinvolte; *adv.* soudainement
office automation: bureautique
office buildin: immeuble de bureaux
office equipment: machines de bureau
office hours: heures de bureau
office worker: employé de bureau
office: *n.* bureau; poste; fonctions; service
officer: *n.* officier; fonctionnaire
official appraisal: expertise
official: *adj.* officiel; *n.* employé
officiate: *vi.* officier
officious: *adj.* officieux
off-line backup: sauvegarde externe
offline: *adv.* hors ligne
off-peak: *adj.* aux heures creuses
off-season: *adv.* hors-saison
offset: *vt.* compenser; décaler
offshoot: *n.* ramification
offshore: *adj.* côtier
offside: *adj.* hors jeu
offspring: *n.* progéniture; descendance
offstage: *adv.* en coulisses
off-the-rack: *adj.* prêt-à-porter
often: *adv.* souvent
ogle: *vt.* lorgner
oil filter: filtre à huile
oil painting: peinture à l'huile
oil rig: derrick
oil tanker: pétrolier
oil well: puits pétrolifère
oil: *n.* huile
oil: *vt.* huiler

oilcan: *n.* burette d'huile; bidon d'huile
oilfield: *n.* gisement pétrolifère
oily: *adj.* huileux; gras
ointment: *n.* onguent
old age: vieillesse
old: *adj.* vieux
old-fashioned: *adj.* démodé
olive oil: huile d'olive
olive: *n.* olivier; olive
omelette: *n.* omelette
omen: *n.* augure; présage
ominous: *adj.* menaçant
omission: *n.* omission; négligence
omit: *vt.* omettre
omnipotence: *n.* omnipotence
omnipotent: *adj.* omnipotent; tout-puissant
on: *prep.* sur; dessus; en; pour; *adj.* allumé; branché; ouvert; de service
once: *adv.* une fois
oncoming: *adj.* qui arrive
one: *adj.* un; une
one-day excursion: billet d'aller-retour valable une journée
one-man concern: une entreprise individuelle
one-man: *adj.* individuel
onerous: *adj.* lourd; (law) dur
oneself: *pron.* soi-même
one-sided: *adj.* partial
one-to-one: *adj.* face à face
ongoing: *adj.* continu; en cours
onion: *n.* oignon
on-line adj: *adv.* en ligne
on-line backup: sauvegarde en ligne
onlooker: *n.* spectateur
only: *adj.* seul; unique; *adv.* seulement
onset; onslaught: *n.* début; attaque
onus: *n.* obligation
onward(s): *adv.* en avant
ooze: *vi.* suinter
opaque: *adj.* opaque

open: *adj.* ouvert; public; déclaré; sincère; franc
open: *vt.* ouvrir; commencer
open-access: en accès libre; direct
opening: *n.* ouverture; débouché; inauguration; commencement
open-minded: *adj.* aux idées larges
openness: *n.* clareté; franchise; sincérité
opera house: théâtre de l'opéra
opera: *n.* opéra
operate: *vi.* fonctionner; opérer
operation: *n.* fonctionnement; opération
operational: *adj.* opérationnel
operative: *adj.* actif; en vigueur
operator: *n.* opérateur; téléphoniste
ophthalmic: *adj.* ophtalmique
opine: *vt.* être d'avis
opinion poll: sondage
opinion: *n.* opinion; jugement
opinionated: *adj.* entêté
opponent: *n.* opposant; adversaire
opportune: *adj.* opportun
opportunist: *n.* opportuniste
opportunity: *n.* occasion
oppose: *vt.* s'opposer à
opposing: *adj.* opposé
opposite integer: nombre entier relatif opposé
opposite: *adj.* opposé; contraire; *n.* contraire
opposition: *n.* opposition; résistance
oppress: *vt.* opprimer
oppression: *n.* oppression
oppressive: *adj.* oppressif
oppressor: *n.* oppresseur
optical: *adj.* optique
optician: *n.* opticien
optimist: *n.* optimiste
optimistic: *adj.* optimiste
option: *n.* option
optional: *adj.* optionnel; facultatif
opulent: *adj.* opulent

or: *conj.* ou
oracle: *n.* oracle
oral direction: direction verbale
oral presentation: présentation orale
oral: *adj.* oral; verbal
orange: *n.* orange
orator: *n.* orateur
orbit: *n.* orbite
orchard: *n.* verger
orchestra: *n.* orchestre
orchestral: *adj.* orchestral
orchid: *n.* orchidée
ordain: *vt.* ordonner
ordeal: *n.* épreuve
order form: bon de commande
order of events: séquence des évènements
order of operations: ordre des opérations
order: *n.* ordre; commande
order: *vt.* commander
ordered pair: couple ordonné
orderly: *adj.* ordonné; réglé
ordinarily: *adv.* ordinairement
ordinary: *adj.* ordinaire
ordination: *n.* ordination
ordnance: *n.* artillerie
ore: *n.* minerai
organ: *n.* organe; orgue
organic compound: composé organique
organic: *adj.* organique
organisation: *n.* organisation
organise: *vt.* organiser
organism: *n.* organisme
organist: *n.* organiste
orgasm: *n.* orgasme
orgy: *n.* orgie
oriental: *adj.* oriental
orifice: *n.* orifice
origin: *n.* origine
original: *adj.* original; originel
originality: *n.* originalité

originate: *vi.* provenir (de); être originaire (de)
ornament: *n.* ornement
ornament: *vt.* ornementer; décorer
ornamental: *adj.* ornemental
ornate: *adj.* ornementé
orphan: *adj.* orphelin; *n.* orphelin
orphanage: *n.* orphelinat
orthodox: *adj.* orthodoxe
orthodoxy: *n.* orthodoxie
orthography: *n.* orthographe
orthopaedic: *adj.* orthopédique
oscillate: *vi.* osciller
osmometry: *n.* osmométrie
osmosis: *n.* osmose
osmotic pressure: pression osmotique
osprey: *n.* balbuzard pêcheur
ostensibly: *adv.* selon les apparences
ostentatious: *adj.* ostentatoire
osteopath: *n.* ostéopathe; ostracise
osteopath: *vt.* frapper d'ostracisme
ostrich: *n.* autruche
other: *pron.* autre
otherwise: *adv.* autrement
otter: *n.* loutre
oufitter: *n.* confectionneur
ounce: *n.* once
our: *adj.* nôtre
ours: *pron.* le nôtre; la nôtre; les nôtres
ourselves: *pron.* nous-mêmes
oust: *vt.* évincer; déposséder
out: *adv.* dehors; éteint
outback: *n.* intérieur
outbreak: *n.* éruption; explosion
outcast: *n.* paria
outcome: *n.* résultat
outcry: *n.* protestations
outdated: *adj.* démodé; périmé
outdo: *vt.* surpasser
outdoor: *adj.* de plein air
outer space: espace
outer: *adj.* extérieur

outermost: *adj.* extrême; le plus à l'extérieur
outfit: *n.* tenue; équipement
outgoing: *adj.* extroverti; sortant
outgrow: *vt.* devenir plus grand que
outhouse: *n.* dépendances
outing: *n.* excursion
outlandish: *adj.* bizarre
outlaw: *n.* hors-la-loi
outlaw: *vt.* proscrire
outlay: *n.* dépenses; frais
outlet: *n.* sortie; débouché
outline: *n.* contour; grandes lignes
outlive: *vt.* survivre à
outlook: *n.* perspective
outlying: *adj.* distant; éloigné
outmoded: *adj.* démodé
outnumber: *vt.* être plus nombreux que
out-of-date: *adj.* périmé; démodé
out-patient: *n.* patient(e) en consultation externe
outpost: *n.* avant-poste
output: *n.* production; rendement; sortie
outrage: *n.* outrage
outrage: *vt.* outrager
outrageous: *adj.* outrageant; atroce
outright: *adv.* absolument; complètement; *adj.* absolu; complet
outrun: *vt.* gagner de vitesse; distancer
outset (from the): *n.* commencement
outshine: *vt.* éclipser
outside: *n.* surface; extérieur; apparence; *adv.* dehors; prep en dehors de
outsider: *n.* étranger
outsize: *adj.* grande taille
outskirts: *npl.* périphérie; alentours
outspoken: *adj.* franc
outstanding: *adj.* exceptionnel; en suspens
outstretch: *vi.* s'étendre

outstrip: *vt.* devancer; surpasser
out-tray: *n.* courrier au départ
outward: *adj.* extérieur; vers
l'extérieur; d'aller
outweigh: *vt.* peser plus lourd que;
l'emporter sur
outwit: *vt.* être plus spirituel que
oval: *adj.* ovale
ovary: *n.* ovaire
oven: *n.* four
ovenproof: *adj.* allant au four
over: *prep.* sur; dessus; plus de;
pendant; *adj.* fini; en trop; en plus;
again à nouveau
overall reaction: réaction globale
overall: *adj.* total; *adv.* dans
l'ensemble
overawe: *vt.* impressionner
overbalance: *vi.* perdre l'équilibre
overbearing: *adj.* despotique
overboard: *adv.* (mar) par-dessus
bord
overbook: *vt.* surréserver
overcast: *adj.* couvert
overcharge: *vt.* surcharger; faire
payer un prix excessif à
overcharged; to be: être surfacturé
overcome: *vt.* vaincre; surmonter
overconfident: *adj.* trop confiant
overcrowded: *adj.* bondé surpeuplé
overdraft: *n.* découvert
overdrawn: *adj.* à découvert
overdress: *vi.* s'habiller trop
élégamment
overdue: *adj.* en retard; arriéré
overeat: *vi.* trop manger
overestimate: *vt.* surestimer
overflow: *n.* inondation; surplus
overflow: *vt.* déborder de; *vi.*
déborder
overgrown: *adj.* envahi
overgrowth: *n.* végétation
envahissante
overhang: *vt.* surplomber

overhaul: *n.* révision
overhaul: *vt.* réviser
overhead: *adv.* en l'air; au-dessus
overheads: les frais généraux
overhear: *vt.* entendre par hasard
overjoyed: *adj.* fou de joie
overkill: *n.* matraquage
overland: *adv.* par voie de terre
overlap: *vi.* se chevaucher
overleaf: *adv.* au dos
overload: *vt.* surcharger
overlook: *vt.* dominer; donner sur;
oublier; laisser passer
overnight: *adv.* pendant la nuit; *adj.*
de nuit
overpass: *n.* pont surélevé
overpowering: *adj.* écrasant
overpowerr: *vt.* dominer; écraser
overrate: *vt.* surévaluer
overrcoat: *n.* pardessus
overrdo: *vi.* exagérer
override: *vt.* outrepasser
overriding: *adj.* prédominant
overrun: *vt.* envahir; infester;
dépasser
overseas: *adv.* à l'étranger; outremer; *adj.* étranger
oversee: *vt.* inspecter; surveiller
overseer: *n.* contremaître
overshadow: *vt.* éclipser
oversight: *n.* oubli; erreur
oversleep: *vi.* se réveiller en retard
overspilll: *n.* excédent de population
overstate: *vi.* exagérer
overstep: *vt.* dépasser
overt: *adj.* ouvert; public
overtake: *vt.* doubler
overthrow: *n.* renversement; ruine;
déroute
overthrow: *vt.* renverser; détruire
overtime: *n.* heures supplémentaires
overtone: *n.* harmonique; connotation
overture: *n.* ouverture
overturn: *vt.* renverser

overweight: *adj.* trop lourd
overwhelm: *vt.* écraser; submerger
overwhelming: *adj.* écrasant; irrésistible
overwork: *vi.* se surmener; trop travailler
owe: *vt.* devoir; être redevable de
owl: *n.* chouette
own: *adj.* propre
own: *vt.* posséder
owner: *n.* propriétaire
ownership: *n.* possession
ox: *n.* bœuf
oxidize: *vt.* oxyder
oxygen mask: masque à oxygène
oxygen tent: tente à oxygène
oxygen: *n.* oxygène
oyster: *n.* huître
ozone: *n.* ozone

℗

pa: *n.* papa
pace: *n.* pas; allure
pace: *vt.* arpenter; *vi.* marcher
pacemaker: *n.* meneur de train
pacifical: *adj.* pacifique
pacification: *n.* pacification
pacify: *vt.* pacifier
pack: *n.* paquet; jeu de cartes; bande
pack: *vt.* empaqueter; remplier; *vi.* faire ses valises
package tour: voyage organisé
package: *n.* paquet; accord
packer: *n.* manutentionnaire
packet: *n.* paquet
packing: *n.* emballage
pact: *n.* pacte
pad: *n.* bloc; coussinet; tampon; plateforme; piaule
pad: *vt.* rembourrer
padding: *n.* rembourrage
paddle steamer: vapeur à roues
paddle: *n.* pagaie
paddle: *vi.* ramer
paddock: *n.* paddock
paddy: *n.* rizière
pagan: *n.* païen; *adj.* païen
page format: disposition
page: *n.* page
pageant: *n.* grand spectacle
pageantry: *n.* pompe
pail: *n.* seau
pain: *n.* douleur; mal; peine
pain: *vt.* peiner
pained: *adj.* peiné
painful: *adj.* douloureux; pénible
painkiller: *n.* analgésique
painless: *adj.* indolore; sans peine
painstaking: *adj.* soigneux
paint: *vt.* peindre
paintbrush: *n.* pinceau
painter: *n.* peintre
painting: *n.* peinture; tableau
paintwork: *n.* peinture

pair: *n.* pair
pajamas: *npl.* pyjamas
palate: *n.* palais
pale: *adj.* pâle; clair
palette: *n.* palette
paling: *n.* palissade
pall: *n.* nuage
pall: *vi.* perdre sa saveur
pallet: *n.* palette
palliative: *adj.* palliatif
pallid: *adj.* pâle
pallor: *n.* pâleur
pally: *n.* copain; copine; pote
Palm Sunday: Dimanche des Rameaux
palm: *n.* palme; palmier
palmistry: *n.* chiromancie
palpable: *adj.* palpable; évident
palpitation: *n.* palpitation
paltry: *adj.* dérisoire; mesquin
pamper: *vt.* gâter; dorloter
pamphlet: *n.* pamphlet; brochure
pan: *n.* casserole; poêle
panacea: *n.* panacée
panache: *n.* panache
pancake: *n.* crêpe
pandemonium: *n.* pandémonium
pane: *n.* vitre
panel: *n.* panneau; comité
panelling: *n.* lambrissage
pang: *n.* angoisse; tourment
panic: *n.* panique
panicky: *adj.* paniqué; affolé
panic-stricken: *adj.* pris de panique
pannsy: *n.* pensée
panther: *n.* panthère
panties: *npl.* culotte
pantihose: *n.* collant
pantry: *n.* placard
pants: *npl.* slip; pantalon
papacy: *n.* papauté
papal: *adj.* papal
paper bag: sac en papier
paper clip: trombone

paper: *n.* papier; journal; exposé; étude
paper: *vt.* garnir de papier; tapisser
paperback: *n.* livre de poche
paperweight: *n.* presse-papiers
paperwork: *n.* paperasserie
paprika: *n.* paprika
par: *n.* équivalence; égalité; pair
parable: *n.* parabole
parachute: *n.* parachute
parachute: *vi.* sauter en parachute
parade: *n.* parade; défilé
parade: *vt.* faire défiler; faire parader; *vi.* défiler; parader; se pavaner
paradise: *n.* paradis
paradox: *n.* paradoxe
paradoxical: *adj.* paradoxal
paragon: *n.* modèle absolu
paragraph: *n.* paragraphe
parallel lines: lignes parallèles
parallel reactions: réactions parallèles
parallel: *adj.* parallèle; *n.* parallèle
parallel: *vt.* mettre en parallèle; comparer
parallelogram: *n.* parallélogramme
paralyse: *vt.* paralyser
paralysis: *n.* paralysie
paralytical: *adj.* paralytique
paramagnetism: *n.* paramagnétisme
paramount: *adj.* suprême; supérieur
paranoid: *adj.* paranoïaque
paraphernalia: *n.* affaires; attirail
paraphrase: *n.* paraphrase
parasite: *n.* parasite
parasol: *n.* parasol
paratrooper: *n.* parachutiste
parcel: *n.* paquet; parcelle
parcel: *vt.* empaqueter; emballer
parch: *vt.* dessécher
parched: *adj.* desséché
parchement: *n.* parchemin
pardon: *n.* pardon

pardon: *vt.* pardonner
parent: *n.* parent
parentage: *n.* parenté; origine
parental: *adj.* parental
parenthesis: *n.* parenthèse
parish: *n.* paroisse; *adj.* paroissial
parishioner: *n.* paroissien
parity: *n.* parité
park: *n.* parc
park: *vt.* garer; *vi.* se garer
parking lot: parking
parking meter: parcomètre
parking: *n.* stationnement
parlance: *n.* langage
parliament: *n.* parlement
parliamentary: *adj.* parlementaire
parlour: *n.* parloir; salon
parody: *n.* parodie
parody: *vt.* parodier
parricide: *n.* parricide
parrot: *n.* perroquet
parrticipate: *vi.* participer (à)
parry: *vt.* parer
parsley: *n.* persil
parsnip: *n.* navet
part: *n.* partie; part; raie
part: *vt.* séparer; diviser; *vi.* se séparer; se diviser
partial pressure: pression partielle
partial: *adj.* partial
participant: *n.* participant
participation: *n.* participation
participle: *n.* participe
particle: *n.* particule
particular: *adj.* particulier; singulier
parting: *n.* séparation; raie
partisan: *n.* partisan
partition: *n.* partition; séparation
partition: *vt.* diviser en plusieurs parties; partager
partner: *n.* associé
partnership: *n.* association; société
partnership; limited: une société en commandite

partnership; to enter into: former une société en nom collectif
partridge: *n.* perdrix
part-time: *adv.* à mi-temps; à temps partiel
party: *n.* parti; fête
pass: *n.* permis; passage
pass: *vt.* passer; dépasser; adopter; transmettre; passer
passable: *adj.* passable; praticable
passage: *n.* passage; traversée; couloir
passbook: *n.* livret
passenger: *n.* passager
passer-by: *n.* passant
passing: *adj.* passager
passion: *n.* passion; amour; emportement
passionate: *adj.* passionné
passive voice: voix passive
passive: *adj.* passif
passkey: *n.* passe-partout
Passover: *n.* Pâque juive
passport control: contrôle des passeports
passport: *n.* passeport
password: *n.* mot de passe
past: *adj.* passé; *n.* prétérit; passé; *prep.* au-delà de; après
pasta: *n.* pâtes
paste: *n.* pâte; colle
paste: *vt.* coller
pasteurised: *adj.* pasteurisé
pastime: *n.* passe-temps; divertissement
pastor: *n.* pasteur
pastoral: *adj.* pastoral
pastry: *n.* pâtisserie
pasture: *n.* pâture
pasty: *adj.* pâteux; pâle
pat: *vt.* tapoter
patch: *n.* pièce; tache; terrain
patch: *vt.* rapiécer
pâté: *n.* pâté

patent leather: cuir verni
patent: *adj.* breveté; évident
paternal: *adj.* paternel
paternity: *n.* paternité
path: *n.* chemin; sentier
pathetic: *adj.* pathétique; lamentable
pathological: *adj.* pathologique
pathology: *n.* pathologie
pathway: *n.* sentier
patience: *n.* patience
patient: *adj.* patient; *n.* patient
patio: *n.* patio
patriarch: *n.* patriarche
patriot: *n.* patriote
patriotic: *adj.* patriotique
patriotism: *n.* patriotisme
patrol: *n.* patrouille
patrol: *vi.* patrouiller
patroll car: voiture de patrouille
patrolman: *n.* agent de police
patron: *n.* protecteur; client
patronage: *n.* patronage; clientèle
patronise: *vt.* patronner; protéger
patter: *n.* trottinement; bavardage
patter: *vi.* trottiner
pattern: *n.* motif; modèle
paunch: *n.* panse; ventre
pauper: *n.* pauvre
pause: *n.* pause
pause: *vi.* faire une pause; hésiter
pave: *vt.* paver; carreler
pavement: *n.* trottoir
pavilion: *n.* pavillon
paving atone: pavé
paw: *n.* patte
paw: *vt.* tripoter
pawnshop: *n.* bureau de prêteur sur gages
pay day: jour de paie
pay envelope: enveloppe de paie
pay: *n.* paie; salaire
pay: *vt.* payer; - back = *vt.* rembourser
payable: *adj.* payable

payee: *n.* bénéficiaire
paymaster: *n.* caissier
payment at sight: paiement à vue
payment received: pour acquit
payment: *n.* paiement
pay-phone: *n.* téléphone public
payroll: *n.* liste des employés; les salaires
pea: *n.* pois
peace: *n.* paix
peaceful: *adj.* paisible; pacifique
peach: *n.* pêche
peacock: *n.* paon
peak hours; peak period: heures de pointe
peak: *n.* pic; maximum
peanut: *n.* cacahuète
pear: *n.* poire
pearl: *n.* perle
peasant: *n.* paysan
peat: *n.* tourbe
pebble: *n.* caillou; galet
peck: *n.* coup de bec
peck: *vt.* picoter
pecking order: hiérarchie
peculiar: *adj.* étrange; singulier
peculiarity: *n.* particularité; singularité
pedal: *n.* pédale
pedal: *vi.* pédaler
pedant: *n.* pédant
pedantic: *adj.* pédant
peddler: *n.* colporteur
pedestal: *n.* piédestal
pedestrian: *n.* piéton; *adj.* pédestre
pediatrics: *n.* pédiatrie
pedigree: *n.* généalogie; pedigree; *adj.* de race
peek: *vi.* regarder à la dérobée
peel: *n.* peau; pelure
peel: *vt.* peler; éplucher; *vi.* peler
peer: *n.* pair
peerless: *adj.* incomparable
peeved: *adj.* fâché

peevish: *adj.* maussade; ronchon
peg: *n.* cheville; piquet
peg: *vt.* cheviller
pelican: *n.* pélican
pellet: *n.* boulette
pelt: *n.* fourrure
pelt: *vt.* arroser; *vi.* pleuvoir à verse
pen: *n.* stylo; plume; enclos
penal: *adj.* pénal
penalty: *n.* peine; sanction amende
penance: *n.* pénitence
pencil case: trousse
pencil: *n.* crayon
pendant: *n.* pendentif
pending: *adj.* pendant
pendulum: *n.* pendule
penetrate: *vt.* pénétrer
penguin: *n.* pingouin
penicillin: *n.* pénicilline
peninsula: *n.* péninsule
penis: *n.* pénis
penitence: *n.* pénitence
penitent: *adj.* pénitent
penitentiary: *n.* pénitencier
penknife: *n.* canif
pennant: *n.* fanion
penniless: *adj.* sans le sou
penny: *n.* penny
penpal: *n.* correspondant
pension: *n.* pension
pension: *vt.* pensionner
pensive: *adj.* pensif
pentagon: *n.* pentagone
Pentecost: *n.* Pentecôte
penthouse: *n.* appartement situé sur le toit d'un immeuble
pent-up: *adj.* repri; refoulé
penultimate: *adj.* pénultième; avant-dernier
people: *n.* peuple; nation; gens
people: *vt.* peupler
pep: *n.* énergie
pepper: *n.* poivre
pepper: *vt.* poivrer

peppermint: *n.* menthe poivrée
per annum: *adv.* par an
per capita: par habitant
per: *prep.* par
perceive: *vt.* percevoir
percent yield: pourcentage de rendement
percent: *n.* pourcent
percentage: *n.* pourcentage
perception: *n.* perception; notion
perch: *n.* perche
perchance: *adv.* par hasard
percolate: *vt.* filtrer
percolator: *n.* percolateur
percussion: *n.* percussion
perdition: *n.* perte; ruine
peremptory: *adj.* péremptoire; décisif
perennial: *adj.* perpétuel
perfect square: carré parfait
perfect: *adj.* parfait; idéal
perfect: *vt.* parfaire; perfectionner
perfection: *n.* perfection
perforate: *vt.* perforer
perforation: *n.* perforation
perform: *vt.* exécuter; effectuer
performance: *n.* exécution; accomplissement; rendement; représentation
performer: *n.* exécutant
perfume: *n.* parfum
perfume: *vt.* parfumer
perhaps: *adv.* peut-être
peril: *n.* péril; danger
perilous: *adj.* dangereux
perimeter: *n.* périmètre
period: *n.* période; époque; régies
periodic law: loi périodique
periodical: *adj.* périodique
periodical: *n.* journal
peripheral: *adj.* périphérique; *n.* unité périphérique
perish: *vi.* périr
perishable: *adj.* périssable

perjure: *vt.* parjurer
perjury: *n.* parjure
perk: *n.* extra; à-côté
perky: *adj.* animé; plein d'entrain
perm: *n.* permanente
permanent: *adj.* permanent
permeability: *n.* perméabilité
permissible: *adj.* permis
permission: *n.* permission
permissive: *adj.* permissif
permit: *n.* permis
permit: *vt.* permettre
permitivity: *n.* permittivité
permutation: *n.* permutation
perpendicular: *adj.* perpendiculaire; *n.* perpendiculaire
perpetrate: *vt.* perpétrer; commettre
perpetual: *adj.* perpétuel
perpetuate: *vt.* perpétuer; éterniser
perplex: *vt.* confondre; laisser perplexe
persecute: *vt.* persécuter; importuner
persecution: *n.* persécution
perseverance: *n.* persévérance
persevere: *vi.* persévérer
persist: *vi.* persister
persistence: *adj.* persistance
persistent: *adj.* persistant
person: *n.* personne
personable: *adj.* attrayant
personage: *n.* personnage
personal assistant: secrétaire de direction
personal column: annonces personnelles
personal computer: ordinateur individuel
personal: *adj.* personnel
personality: *n.* personnalité
personification: *n.* personnification
personify: *vt.* personnifier
personnel: *n.* personnel
perspective: *n.* perspective; perspiration

perspective: *vi.* transpirer
persuade: *vt.* persuader
persuasion: *n.* persuasion
persuasive passage: séquence persuasive
persuasive: *adj.* persuasif
pert: *adj.* plein d'entrain
pertaining to: *prep.* relatif à
pertinent: *adj.* pertinent
pertness: *n.* impertinence; entrain
perturb: *vt.* perturber
perusal: *n.* lecture
peruse: *vt.* lire; examiner attentivement
pervade: *vt.* pénétrer; traverser
perverse: *adj.* pervers; dépravé
pervert: *vt.* pervertir; corrompre
pessimist: *n.* pessimiste
pest: *n.* insecte nuisible; casse-pieds
pester: *vt.* importuner; fatiguer
pestilence: *n.* peste
pet: *n.* animal domestique; préféré
pet: *vt.* gâter; *vi.* se peloter
petal: *n.* pétale
petite: *adj.* menue
petition: *n.* pétition
petition: *vt.* présenter une pétition à; supplier
petrified: *adj.* pétrifié
petroleum: *n.* pétrole
petticoat: *n.* jupon
pettiness: *n.* insignifiance
petty cash: argent destiné aux dépenses courantes
petty officer: second maître
petty: *adj.* mesquin; insignifiant
petulant: *adj.* pétulant
pew: *n.* banc
pewter: *n.* étain
pH: potentiel Hydrogène
phantom: *n.* fantôme
Pharisee: *n.* Pharisien
pharmaceutical: *adj.* pharmaceutique

pharmacist: *n.* pharmacien
pharmacy: *n.* pharmacie
phase diagram: diagramme en phase
phase equilibrium: équilibre de phase
phase rule: règle des phases
phase: *n.* phase
pheasant: *n.* faisan
phenomenal: *adj.* phénoménal
phenomenon: *n.* phénomène
phenotype: *n.* phénotype
phial: *n.* fiole
philanthropic: *adj.* philanthropique
philanthropist: *n.* philanthrope
philanthropy: *n.* philanthropie
philologist: *n.* philologue
philology: *n.* philologie
philosopher: *n.* philosophe
philosophical: *adj.* philosophique
philosophise: *vi.* philosopher
philosophy: *n.* philosophie
phlegmatical: *adj.* flegmatique
phobia: *n.* phobie
phone book: annuaire
phone box: cabine téléphonique
phone call: coup de téléphone
phone: *n.* téléphone
phone: *vt.* téléphoner à
phosphorus: phosphore
photo: *n.* photo
photochemistry: *n.* photochimie
photocopier: *n.* photocopieuse
photocopy: *n.* photocopie
photoelectric effect: effet photoélectrique
photograph: *n.* photographie
photograph: *vt.* photographier
photographer: *n.* photographe
photographic: *adj.* photographique
photography: *n.* photographie
photosensitization: *n.* photosensibilisation
photosynthesis: *n.* photosynthèse
phrase book: guide de conversation

phrase: *n.* phrase; locution
phrase: *vt.* exprimer
physical change: changement physique
physical education: éducation physique
physical property: propriété physique
physical: *adj.* physique
physician: *n.* médecin
physicist: *n.* physicien
physiological: *adj.* physiologique
physiologist: *n.* physiologiste; physiologue
physiology: *n.* physiologie
physiotherapy: *n.* physiothérapie
physique: *n.* physique
pianist: *n.* pianiste
pichet: *n.* piquet
pick: *n.* pic; choix
pick: *vt.* choisir; cueillir; gratter
pickaxe: *n.* pic
pickle: *n.* saumure
pickle: *vt.* saumurer
pickpocket: *n.* pickpocket
pickup: *n.* fourgonnette
picnic: *n.* pique-nique
pictorial: *adj.* pictural; illustré
picture book: livre d'images
picture caption: sous-titre
picture clue: indice pictoral
picture dictionary: dictionnaire à l'image
picture: *n.* image; peinture
picturesque: *adj.* pittoresque
pie chart: graphique à secteurs; camembert
pie: *n.* gâteau; tarte; pâté en croûte
piece work: travail à la pièce
piece: *n.* morceau; pièce; tranche
piece: *vt.* raccommoder
piecemeal: *adv.* petit à petit; *adj.* partiel
pier: *n.* jetée

pierce: *vt.* percer; transpercer
piercing: *adj.* perçant
piety: *n.* piété; dévotion
pig: *n.* cochon
pigeon: *n.* pigeon
pigeonhole: *n.* casier
piggy bank: tirelire
pigheaded: *adj.* têtu
pigsty: *n.* porcherie
pigtail: *n.* natte
pike: *n.* brochet; pique
pile: *n.* tas; pile; amas; poil
pile: *vt.* entasser; empiler
pile-up: *n.* carambolage
pilfer: *vt.* chaparder
pilgrim: *n.* pèlerin
pilgrimage: *n.* pèlerinage
pill: *n.* pilule
pillage: *vt.* piller; mettre à sac
pillar: *n.* pilier
pillion: *n.* siège arrière
pillow case: taie d'oreiller
pillow: *n.* oreiller
pilot light: témoin
pilot: *n.* pilote
pilot: *vt.* piloter; mener
pimp: *n.* proxénète; maquereau
pimple: *n.* bouton
pin: *n.* épingle; goupille
pin: *vt.* épingler; goupiller
pinafore: *n.* tablier
pinball: *n.* flipper
pincers: *n.* tenailles
pinch: *n.* pincement; pincée
pinch: *vt.* pincer; faucher; *vi.* serrer
pincushion: *n.* pelote à épingles
pine: *n.* pin
pine: *vi.* languir
pineapple: *n.* ananas
ping: *n.* tintement
pink: *adj.* rose; *n.* rose
pinnacle: *n.* sommet
pinpoint: *vt.* préciser; souligner
pint: *n.* pinte

pioneer: *n.* pionnier
pious: *adj.* pieux; dévot
pip: *n.* pépin
pipe cleaner: cure-pipe
pipe dream: rêve impossible
pipe: *n.* tube; tuyau; pipe
pipeline: *n.* canalisation; oléoduc; gazoduc
piper: *n.* joueur de cornemuse
place of issue: lieu d'émission
place: *n.* endroit; lieu; place
plagiarism: *n.* plagiat
plain: *n.* plaine; *adj.* simple
plan: *n.* plan
plane: *n.* avion
planet: *n.* planète
planning: *n.* planification
plant: *n.* plante
plastic: *n.* plastique
plate tectonics: tectonique des plaques
plate: *n.* assiette
play: *n.* pièce (theater)
play: *v.* jouer
pleasure: *n.* plaisir
pleb: *n.* flegme
plot: *n.* scène; intrigue
plot: *vt.* tracer
plug: *n.* prise; bouchon
plug: *v.* brancher; boucher
plumber: *n.* plombier
plural noun: nom pluriel
plural: *n.* pluriel
plus: *prep.* plus
pocket: *n.* poche
pocketknife: *n.* canif
poem: *n.* poème
poetry: *n.* poésie
point of view: point de vue
point: *n.* point; pointe
point: *vt.* indiquer
poise: aplomb; sang-froid
poison: *n.* poison
poison: *vt.* empoisonner

poisonous: *adj.* toxique; vénéneux; venimeux
polar covalent bond: liaison polaire covalente
polarisability: *n.* polarisabilité
pole: *n.* poteau
police officer: agent de police
police station: commissariat de police
police: *n.* police
policy: *n.* politique; police (insurance)
polite: *adj.* poli
political: *adj.* politique
politics: *npl.* politique
pollution: *n.* pollution
polyhedron: *n.* polyhèdre
polymer: *n.* polymère
polymorphism: *n.* polymorphisme
polynomial: *n.* polynome
pond: *n.* étang
pony: *n.* poney
pool: *n.* piscine; billard
poor: *adj.* pauvre
pope: *n.* pape
population: *n.* population
pork: *n.* porc
port of loading: port d'embarquement
portrait: *n.* portrait
position: *n.* position
position: *vt.* placer
positive integer: nombre entier relatif positif
positive: *adj.* positif; sûr; certain
possessive pronoun: pronom possessif
possessive: *adj.* possessif
possible: *adj.* possible
post office: poste
post: *n.* poste
postcard: *n.* carte postale
posture: *n.* posture
pot: *n.* casserole

potential energy: énergie potentielle
pottery: *n.* poterie
poultry: *n.* volaille
pound: *n.* livre
pour: *v.* verser; pleuvoir à torrents
powder: *n.* poudre
power failure: panne de courant
power: *n.* pouvoir; courant; puissance
practical: *adj.* pratique
prawn: *n.* crevette
pray: *vi.* prier
prayer book: livre de messe
prayer: *n.* prière
preach: *vt.* prêcher
preacher: *n.* prédicateur
preamble: *n.* préambule
precarious: *adj.* précaire; incertain
precaution: *n.* précaution
precautionary: *adj.* préventif
precede: *vt.* précéder
precedence: *n.* précédence
precedent: *adj.* précédent
precinct: *n.* limite; enceinte; circonscription
precious: *adj.* précieux
precipice: *n.* précipice
precipitate: *adj.* précipité
precipitate: *vt.* précipiter
precise: *n.* précis; exact
precision: *n.* précision; exactitude
preclude: *vt.* exclure; empêcher
precocious: *adj.* précoce; prématuré
precodition: *n.* condition
preconceive: *vt.* préconcevoir
preconception: *n.* préjugé; idée préconçue
precursor: *n.* précurseur
predator: *n.* prédateur
predecessor: *n.* prédécesseur
predict: *vt.* prédire
predictable: *adj.* prévisible
prediction: *n.* prédiction
predilection: *n.* prédilection
predominant: *adj.* prédominant

predominate: *vt.* prédominer
preen: *vt.* nettoyer
prefab: *n.* maison préfabriquée
preface: *n.* préface
prefer: v préférer
preferably: *adv.* de préférence
preference: *n.* préférence
preferential: *adj.* préférentiel
preferment: *n.* promotion; préférence
prefix: *vt.* préfixer; préfixe
pregnancy: *n.* grossesse
pregnant: *adj.* enceinte
prehistoric: *adj.* préhistorique
prejudice: *n.* préjudice; tort; préjugé
prejudice: *vt.* préjudicier à; faire du tort à
prejudiced: *adj.* qui a des préjugés; partial
prejudicial: *adj.* préjudiciable
preliminary: *adj.* préliminaire
prelude: *n.* prélude
premarital: *adj.* préconjugal
premature: *adj.* prématuré
premeditation: *n.* préméditation
premises: *npl.* locaux
premium: *n.* prix; indemnité; prime
premonition: *n.* pressentiment; prémonition
preoccupied: *adj.* préoccupé; absorbé
prepaid: *adj.* port payé
preparation: *n.* préparation
preparatory: *adj.* préparatoire
prepare: *vt.* préparer
preponderance: *n.* prépondérance
preposition: *n.* préposition
prepositional phrase: locution prépositive
preposterous: *adj.* ridicule; absurde
prerequisite: *n.* condition requise
prerogative: *n.* prérogative
prescribe: *vt.* prescrire
prescription: *n.* prescription; ordonnance
presence: *n.* présence

present: *n.* cadeau; *adj.* présent; actuel
present: *vt.* offrir; donner; présenter
presentable: *adj.* présentable
presentation: *n.* présentation
present-day: *adj.* actuel
presenter: *n.* présentateur
presentiment: *n.* pressentiment; prémonition
preservation: *n.* préservation
preservative: *n.* préservatif
preserve: *n.* conserve; confiture
preserve: *vt.* préserver; conserver; faire des conserves de
preside: *vi.* présider; diriger
presidency: *n.* présidence
president: *n.* président
presidential: *adj.* présidentiel
press agency: agence de presse
press conference: conférence de presse
press: *n.* presse; pressoir; pression
press: *vt.* appuyer sur; serrer; pressurer; *vi.* se presser
pressing: *adj.* pressant; urgent
pressure cooker: autocuiseur
pressure group: groupe de pression
pressure: *n.* pression
pressurised: *adj.* pressurisé
prestige: *n.* prestige
presumable: *adj.* vraisemblable
presumably: *adv.* vraisemblableent
presume: *vt.* présumer; supposer
presumption: *n.* présomption
presumptuous: *adj.* présomptueux
presuppose: *vt.* présupposer
pretence: *n.* prétexte; simulation; prétention
pretend: *vi.* prétendre; faire semblant
pretender: *n.* prétendant
pretension: *n.* prétention
pretentious: *adj.* prétentieux
preterrite: *n.* prétérit
pretext: *n.* prétexte

pretty: *adj.* joli; mignon
prevail: *vi.* prévaloir; prédominer
prevailing: *adj.* dominant
prevalent: *adj.* prédominant
prevent: *vt.* prévenir; empêcher; éviter
prevention: *n.* prévention
preventive: *adj.* préventif
preview: *n.* avant-première
previous: *adj.* précédent; antérieur
prewar: *adj.* d'avant-guerre
prewrite: *n.* pre-écriture
prey: *n.* proie
price list: tarif
price: *n.* prix
priceless: *adj.* inappréciable
prick: *n.* piqûre; pointe
prick: *vt.* piquer; exciter
prickle: *n.* picotement; épine
prickly: *adj.* épineux
priclamation: *n.* proclamation; décret
pride: *n.* orgueil; vanité; fierté
priest: *n.* prêtre
priestess: *n.* prêtresse
priesthood: *n.* sacerdoce; prêtrise
priestly: *adj.* sacerdotal
priggish: *adj.* affecté; bégueule
prim: *adj.* prude; affecté
primacy: *n.* primauté
primarily: *adv.* principalement; surtout
primary: *adj.* primaire; principal; premier
prime minister: premier ministre
prime number: nombre premier
prime: *n.* commencement; *adj.* premier; principal; excellent
prime: *vt.* amorcer
primeval: *adj.* primitif
priming: *n.* amorçage
primitive: *adj.* primitif
primrose: *n.* primevère
prince: *n.* prince
princes: *n.* princesse

principal: *adj.* principal; *n.* principal; commettant
principality: *n.* principauté
principle: *n.* principe
print: *n.* impression; estampe; caractères imprimés
print: *vt.* imprimer
printed matter: imprimés
printer: *n.* imprimeur; imprimante
printing: *n.* impression
prior knowledge: connaissance préalable
prior: *adj.* antérieur; précédent; *n.* prieur
priority: *n.* priorité
priory: *n.* prieuré
prirmate: *n.* primate
prism: *n.* prisme
prison: *n.* prison
prisoner: *n.* prisonnier
privacy: *n.* intimité
private archives: archives privées
private eye: détective privé
private: *adj.* privé; secret; particulier
privet: *n.* troène
privilege: *n.* privilège
prize: *n.* prix
prize: *vt.* apprécier; évaluer
prize-giving: distribution des prix
prizewinner: *n.* gagnant
pro: *prep.* pour
probability: *n.* probabilité; vraisemblance
probable: *adj.* probable; vraisemblable
probation: *n.* essai; probation
probationary: *adj.* d'essai
probe: *n.* sonde; enquête
probe: *vt.* sonder; *vi.* faire des recherches
problem: *n.* problème
problematical: *adj.* problématique
procedure: *n.* procédure

proceed: *vi.* procéder; provenir; poursuivre
proceedings: *n.* procédure; procédé; procès
process data: traiter ou analyser des données
process: *n.* processus; procédé
procession: *n.* procession
proclaim: *vt.* proclamer; promulguer
procrastinate: *vt.* différer; retarder
proctor: *n.* censeur
procure: *vt.* procurer
procurement: *n.* obtention
prod: *vt.* pousser
prodigal: *adj.* prodigue
prodigious: *adj.* prodigieux
prodigy: *n.* prodige
produce dealer: revendeur
produce: *vt.* produire; créer; fabriquer
producer: *n.* producteur
product: *n.* produit; oeuvre; fruit
production line: chaîne de fabrication
production: *n.* production; produit
productive: *adj.* productif
productivity: *n.* productivité
profane: *adj.* profane
profess: *vt.* professer; exercer; déclarer
profession: *n.* profession
professional: *adj.* professionnel
professor: *n.* professeur
proficiency: *n.* capacité
proficient: *adj.* compétent
profile: *n.* profil
profit margins: marges bénéficiaires
profit: *n.* bénéfice; profit; avantage
profit: *vi.* profiter
profitability: *n.* rentabilité
profitable: *adj.* profitable; avantageux
program: *n.* programme
progress: *n.* progrès

progress: *v.* progresser
prohibit: *v.* interdire
project: *n.* project
project: *v.* projeter
promenade: *n.* promenade
promise: *n.* promesse
promise: *v.* promettre
promissory note: billet à ordre
prompt cash sale: achat comptant
prompt cash: comptant d'usage
pronoun: *n.* pronom
proof: *n.* preuve
proofread: *vt.* corriger
propaganda: *n.* propagande
property: *n.* propriété
proportion: *n.* proportion
proposal: *n.* proposition; demande en mariage
prose: *n.* prose
prosecuted; to be: être poursuivi
prosperous: *adj.* prospère
prostitute: *n.* prostituée
prostitution: *n.* prostitution
prostrate: *adj.* prostré
protagonist: *n.* protagoniste
protect: *vt.* protéger; abriter
protection: *n.* protection
protective: *adj.* protecteur
protector: *n.* protecteur
protégé: *n.* protégé
protein: *n.* protéine
protest: *n.* protestation
protest: *vi.* protester
Protestant: *n.* protestant
protester: *n.* manifestant; protestataire
protist: *n.* protiste
protocol: *n.* protocole
proton: *n.* proton
prototype: *n.* prototype
protracted: *adj.* prolongé
protractor: *n.* rapporteur
protrude: *vi.* déborder; ressortir
proud: *adj.* fier; orgueilleux

prove: *vt.* prouver; justifier; *vi.* s'avérer; se révéler
proverb: *n.* proverbe
proverbial: *adj.* proverbial
provide: *vt.* fournir; prévoir
provided: *conj.* provided that = pourvu que
providence: *n.* providence
province: *n.* province; compétence
provincial: *adj.* provincial
provision: *n.* provision; disposition
provisional: *adj.* provisoire
provisions: *n.* dispositions
proviso: *n.* stipulation
provocation: *n.* provocation
provocative: *adj.* provocateur
provoke: *vt.* provoquer
prow: *n.* proue
prowess: *n.* prouesse
prowl: *vi.* rôder
prowler: *n.* rôdeur
proximity: *n.* proximité
proxy: *n.* procuration; délégué
prudence: *n.* prudence
prudent: *adj.* prudent; circonspect
prudish: *adj.* prude
prune: *n.* pruneau
prune: *vt.* tailler
prussic acid: acide prussique
pry: *vi.* espionner
psalm: *n.* psaume
pseudonym: *n.* pseudonyme
psyche: *n.* psyché
psychiatric: *adj.* psychiatrique
psychiatrist: *n.* psychiatre
psychiatry: *n.* psychiatrie
psychic: *adj.* psychique
psychoanalysis: *n.* psychanalyse
psychoanalyst: *n.* psychanaliste
psychologie: *adj.* psychologique
psychologist: *n.* psychologue
psychology: *n.* psychologie
pub: *n.* pub
puberty: *n.* puberté

public archives: archives publiques
public opinion: opinion publique
public school: école privée
public transport: transport en commun
public: *adj.* public; commun; *n.* public
publican: *n.* patron de pub
publication: *n.* publication; édition
publicise: *vt.* faire de la publicité pour
publicity: *n.* publicité
publish: *vt.* publier
publisher: *n.* éditeur
publishing: *n.* édition
pucker: *vt.* plisser
pudding: *n.* pudding; dessert
puddle: *n.* flaque d'eau
puerile: *adj.* puéril
puff pastry: pâte feuilletée
puff: *n.* souffle; bouffée
puff: *vt.* souffler; dégager; *vi.* souffler; bouffer
puffy: *adj.* bouffi; gonflé
pull: *n.* tirage; secousse
pull: *vt.* tirer; arracher
pulley: *n.* poulie
pulp: *n.* pulpe
pulpit: *n.* chaire
pulsate: *vi.* palpiter
pulse: *n.* pouls; légumes
pulverise: *vt.* pulvériser
pumice: *n.* pierre ponce
pummel: *vt.* marteler
pump: *n.* pompe
pump: *vt.* pomper; puiser
pumpkin: *n.* citrouille
pun: *n.* jeu de mots
pun: *vi.* faire des jeux de mots
punch: *n.* coup de poing; poinçon; punch
punch: *vt.* cogner; perforer; poinçonner
punctual: *adj.* ponctuel; exact

punctuate: *vt.* ponctuer
punctuation: *n.* ponctuation
pundit: *n.* expert
pungent: *adj.* piquant; âcre; mordant
punish: *vt.* punir
punishment: *n.* châtiment; punition; peine
punk: *n.* punk; minable
punt: *n.* bateau plat
puny: *adj.* chétif; maigrelet
pup: *n.* chiot
pup: *vi.* avoir des chiots; mettre bas
pupil: *n.* élève; pupille
puppet: *n.* marionnette
purchase: *n.* achat; acquisition
purchase: *vt.* acheter
purchaser: *n.* acheteur
pure: *adj.* pur
purée: *n.* purée
purge: *vt.* purger
purification: *n.* purification
purify: *vt.* purifier
purist: *n.* puriste
puritan: *n.* puritain
purity: *n.* pureté
purl: *n.* maille à l'envers
purple: *adj.* pourpre; violet
purpose: *n.* intention; but; dessein
purposeful: *adj.* résolu
purr: *vi.* ronronner
purse: *n.* sac à main; porte-monnaie
purser: *n.* commissaire de bord
pursue: *vi.* poursuivre; suivre
pursuit: *n.* poursuite; occupation
purveyor: *n.* fournisseur
push: *n.* poussée; impulsion; effort; énergie
push: *vt.* pousser; presser
pusher: *n.* trafiquant de drogues
push-up: *n.* pompe
put: *vt.* mettre; poser; proposer; obliger
putrid: *adj.* putride
putt: *n.* putt

putt: *vt.* putter
putty: *n.* mastic
puzzle: *n.* énigme; casse-tête
puzzling: *adj.* étrange; mystérieux
pyjamas: *npl.* pyjama
pylon: *n.* pylône
pyramid: *n.* pyramide
pyrolysis: *n.* pyrolyse
python: *n.* python

Q

quack: *n.* canard; charlatan
quack: *vi.* cancaner
quadrangle: *n.* quadrilatère
quadrant: *n.* quadrant
quadrilateral: *adj.* quadrilatéral
quadruped: *n.* quadrupède
quadruple: *adj.* quadruple
quadruplet: *n.* quadruplé
quagmire: *n.* marécage
quail: *n.* caille
quaint: *adj.* désuet; bizarre
quake: *vi.* trembler
qualification: *n.* qualification; diplôme
qualified: *adj.* qualifié; diplômé
qualify: *vt.* qualifier; modérer; *vi.* se qualifier
quality: *n.* qualité
quandary: *n.* incertitude; doute
quantitative: *adj.* quantitatif
quantity: *n.* quantité
quantum number: nombre quantique
quantum theory: théorie quantique
quantum yield: rendement quantique
quantum: *n.* quantum pluriel
quarantine: *n.* quarantaine
quarrel: *n.* dispute; querelle
quarrel: *vi.* se disputer; se quereller
quarrelsome: *adj.* querelleur
quarry: *n.* carrière
quarter: *n.* quart
quarter: *vt.* diviser en quatre
quarterly: *adj.* trimestriel; *adv.* tous les trimestres
quartermaster: *n.* intendant
quartet: *n.* quartette; quatuor
quartile: *n.* quartile
quartz: *n.* quartz
quash: *vt.* écraser; annuler
quay: *n.* quai
queasy: *adj.* qui a des nausées; écoeurant

queen: *n.* reine; dame
queer: *adj.* extrange; pédale
quell: *vt.* étouffer; apaiser
quench: *vt.* assouvir; éteindre
quenching reaction: réaction de stabilisation
query: *n.* question
query: *vt.* demander
quest: *n.* recherche
question mark: point d'interrogation
question: *n.* question; sujet; doute
question: *vt.* douter de; mettre en question; questionner
questionable: *adj.* discutable; douteux
questioner: *n.* interrogateur
questionnaire: *n.* questionnaire
quibble: *vi.* chicaner
quick: *adj.* rapide; vif; prompt
quicken: *vt.* presser; accélérer; *vi.* s'accélérer
quicksand: *n.* sables mouvants
quicksilver: *n.* mercure
quick-witted: *adj.* à l'esprit vif
quiet: *adj.* calme; silencieux
quietness: *n.* calme; tranquillité; silence
quilt: *n.* édredon
quinine: *n.* quinine
quintet: *n.* quintette
quintuple: *adj.* quintuple
quintuplet: *n.* quintuplé
quip: *n.* sarcasme
quip: *vt.* railler
quirk: *n.* particularité
quit: *adj.* quitte
quit: *vt.* arrêter de; quitter; *vi.* abandonner; démissionner
quite: *adv.* assez; complètement; absolument
quits: *adj.* quitte
quiver: *vi.* trembler
quixotic: *adj.* donquichottesque
quiz: *n.* concours; examen

quiz: *vt.* interroger
quizzical: *adj.* railleur
quota: *n.* quota
quote: *vt.* citer
quotient: *n.* quotient

R

rabbi: *n.* rabbi; rabbin
rabbit hutch: clapier
rabbit: *n.* lapin
rabble: *n.* cohue
rabid: *adj.* forcené; enragé
rabies: *n.* rage
race: *n.* course; race
race: *vt.* faire une course avec; *vi.*
courir; faire une course; aller très
vite; foncer
racer: *n.* cheval de course
racial: *adj.* racial; *n.* raciste
raciness: *n.* vivacité
racing: *n.* courses
racism: *n.* racisme
rack: *n.* casier; étagère
rack: *vt.* soumettre au supplice du
chevalet; tourmenter
racket: *n.* vacarme; raquette
rack-rent: *n.* loyer démesuré
racy: *adj.* piquant; plein de verve
radiance: *n.* rayonnement; éclat
radiant: *adj.* rayonnant; radieux
radiate: *vi.* rayonner; irradier
radiation: *n.* irradiation
radiator: *n.* radiateur
radical reactions: réactions
radicalaires
radical scavenger: intercepteur
radicalaire
radical: *adj.* radical
radicalism: *n.* radicalisme
radio: *n.* radio
radioactive dating: datation
radioactive series: séries radioactives
radioactive: *adj.* radioactif
radiolysis: *n.* radiolyse
radish: *n.* radis
radius: *n.* radius
raffle: *n.* tombola
raffle: *vt.* mettre en tombola
raft: *n.* radeau; train de flottage
rafter: *n.* chevron

rag: *n.* lambeau; loque
ragamuffin: *n.* va-nu-pieds; galopin
rage: *n.* rage; fureur
rage: *vi.* être furieux; faire rage
ragged: *adj.* déguenillé
raging: *adj.* furieux; déchaîné; enragé
ragman: *n.* chiffonnier
raid: *n.* raid
raid: *vt.* faire un raid sur
raider: *n.* raider; pillard
rail: *n.* rambarde; garde-fou
rail: *vt.* entourer d'une barrière
raillery: *n.* taquinerie
railroad; railway: *n.* chemin de fer
raiment: *n.* vêtements
rain: *n.* pluie
rain: *vi.* pleuvoir
rainbow: *n.* arc-en-ciel
raincoat: *n.* imperméable
rainwater: *n.* eau de pluie
rainy: *adj.* pluvieux
raise: *vt.* lever; soulever; ériger; édifier; élever
raisin: *n.* raisin sec
rake: *n.* râteau; libertin
rake: *vt.* ratisser
rakish: *adj.* libertin; débauché
rally: *vt.* rallier; *vi.* se rallier
ram: *n.* bélier; navire bélier
ram: *vt.* enfoncer
ramble: *n.* excursion à pied; randonnée
ramble: *vi.* errer; faire une randonnée
rambler: *n.* excursionniste
ramification: *n.* ramification
ramify: *vi.* se ramifier
ramp: *n.* rampe
rampant: *adj.* exubérant
rampart: *n.* terre-plein; rempart
ramrod: *n.* baguette; refouloir
ramshackle: *adj.* délabré
ranch: *n.* ranch
rancid: *adj.* rance
rancour: *n.* rancoeur

random access: accès aléatoire
random: *adj.* fortuit; fait au hasard; at random = au hasard
range: *n.* rangée; ordre; portée; chaîne
range: *vt.* ranger; classer; *vi.* s'étendre
ranger: *n.* garde forestier
rank: *adj.* exubérant; fétide; flagrant; *n.* rang; classe; grade
rankle: *vi.* rester sur le coeur
rankness: *n.* exubérance; odeur rance
ransack: *vt.* saccager; piller
ransom: *n.* rançon
rant: *vi.* déclamer
rap: *n.* petit coup sec
rap: *vi.* donner un coup sec
rapacious: *adj.* rapace
rapacity: *n.* rapacité
rape: *n.* viol; rapt; colza
rape: *vt.* violer
rapid: *adj.* rapide
rapidity: *n.* rapidité
rapier: *n.* rapière
rapist: *n.* violeur
rapt: *adj.* extasié; absorbé
rapture: *n.* ravissement; extase
rapturous: *adj.* de ravissement
rare: *adj.* rare
rarity: *n.* rareté
rascal: *n.* vaurien
rash: *adj.* imprudent; téméraire
rash: *n.* vague; éruption
rashness: *n.* imprudence
rasp: *n.* rape
rasp: *vt.* râper
raspberry: *n.* framboise
rat: *n.* rat
rate of reaction: vitesse de réaction
rate: *n.* taux; prix; cours; classe; vitesse
rate: *vt.* estimer; évaluer
rather: *adv.* plutôt; quelque peu
ratification: *n.* ratification

ratify: *vt.* ratifier
rating: *n.* estimation; classement; indice
ratio: *n.* rapport
ration: *adj.* rationnel; raisonnable
ration: *n.* ration; vivres
rational numbers: nombres rationnels
rationality: *n.* rationalité
rattan: *n.* rotin
rattle: *n.* fracas; cliquetis
rattle: *vi.* s'entrechoquer; cliqueter; *vt.* faire s'entrechoquer
rattlesnake: *n.* serpent à sonnettes
ravage: *n.* ravage
ravage: *vt.* ravager; piller; dévaster
rave: *vi.* délirer
raven: *n.* corbeau
ravenous: *adj.* vorace
ravine: *n.* ravin
ravish: *vt.* enchanter; ravir
ravishing: *adj.* enchanteur
raw data: données brutes
raw: *adj.* cru; brut; novice
rawboned: *adj.* décharné; maigre
rawness: *n.* crudité; inexpérience
ray: *n.* rayon; (fish) raie
raze: *vt.* raser
razor blade: lame de rasoir
razor: *n.* rasoir
reach: *n.* portée
reach: *vt.* atteindre; arriver à; *vi.* s'étendre; porter
react: *vi.* réagir
reactant: *n.* réactif
reaction mechanism: mécanisme réactionnel
reaction order: ordre d'une réaction
reaction path: chemin réactionnel
reaction: *n.* réaction
read: *vt.* lire
readability: *n.* lisibilité; clarté
readable: *adj.* lisible
reader: *n.* lecteur

readily: *adv.* volontiers; facilement
readiness: *n.* bonne volonté; empressement
reading room: salle de lecture
reading strategy: stratégie de lecture
reading: *n.* lecture
readjust: *vt.* réajuster; réadapter
ready: *adj.* prêt; enclin; disposé
real estate: biens immobiliers
real: *adj.* réel; vrai
realisation: *n.* réalisation
realise: *vt.* se rendre compte de; réaliser
reality: *n.* réalité
realm: *n.* royaume
ream: *n.* rame de papier
reap: *vt.* moissonner
reappear: *vi.* réapparaître
rear: *n.* arrière; derrière
rear: *vt.* élever; dresser
rearmament: *n.* réarmement
reason: *n.* raison; cause
reason: *vt.* raisonner
reasonable: *adj.* raisonnable
reasonableness: *n.* bon sens; sagesse
reasonably: *adv.* raisonnablement
reasoning: *n.* raisonnement
reassure: *vt.* rassurer; réassurer
rebate: *n.* rabais
rebel: *n.* rebelle
rebel: *vi.* se rebeller
rebellion: *n.* rébellion
rebellious: *adj.* rebelle
rebound: *vi.* rebondir
rebuff: *n.* rebuffade
rebuff: *vt.* repousser
rebuild: *vt.* reconstruire
rebuke: *n.* réprimande
rebuke: *vt.* réprimander
rebut: *vt.* réfuter
recalcitrant: *adj.* récalcitrant
recall: *n.* retrait
recall: *vt.* se rappeler; retirer
recant: *vt.* rétracter; désavouer

recantation: *n.* rétractation
recapitulate: *vt.* récapituler
recapitulation: *n.* récapitulation
recapture: *n.* reprise
recede: *vi.* reculer
receipt: *n.* récépissé
receipt: *n.* reçu; réception
receivable: *adj.* recevable
receive: *vt.* recevoir; accueillir
receiver: *n.* récepteur
recent: *adj.* récent; neuf
receptacle: *n.* récipient
reception: *n.* réception
recess: *n.* vacance; renfoncement; recoin
recession: *n.* recul; récession
recessive: *adj.* recessif
recipe: *n.* recette
recipient: *n.* destinataire
reciprocal: *adj.* réciproque
reciprocate: *vi.* rendre la pareille
reciprocity: *n.* réciprocité
recital: *n.* récit; récital
recite: *vt.* réciter; exposer; énumérer
reckless: *adj.* téméraire
reckon: *vt.* compter; calculer; *vi.* calculer
reckoning: *n.* compte; calcul
reclaimable: *adj.* remboursable
recline: *vt.* reposer; *vi.* être allongé
recluse: *n.* reclus
recognise: *vt.* reconnaître
recognition: *n.* reconnaissance
recoil: *vi.* reculer
recollect: *vt.* se rappeler; se souvenir de
recollection: *n.* souvenir
recommence: *vt.* recommencer
recommend: *vt.* recommander
recommendation: *n.* recommandation
recompense: *n.* récompense
recompense: *vt.* récompenser
reconcilable: *adj.* conciliable

reconcile: *vt.* réconcilier
reconciliation: *n.* réconciliation
recondite: *adj.* abstrus; obscur
reconsider: *vt.* reconsidérer
reconstruct: *vt.* reconstruire
record: *n.* rapport; registre; disque; record
record: *vt.* enregistrer; consigner par écrit
recorder: *n.* magnétophone; archiviste
recount: *vt.* raconter
recourse: *n.* recours
recover: *vt.* retrouver; reprendre; récupérer; *vi.* se remettre; se rétablir
recoverable: *adj.* récupérable
recovery: *n.* guérison; reprise
recreation: *n.* détente; récréation
recriminate: *vi.* récriminer
recrimination: *n.* récrimination
recruit: *n.* recrue
recruit: *vt.* recruter
recruiting: *n.* recrutement
rectangle: *n.* rectangle
rectangular: *adj.* rectangulaire
rectification: *n.* rectification
rectify: *vt.* rectifier
rectilinear: *adj.* rectiligne
rectitude: *n.* rectitude
rector: *n.* pasteur
recumbent: *adj.* couché; étendu
recur: *vi.* se reproduire
recurrence: *n.* répétition
recurrent: *adj.* répétitif
recurring themes: thème recurrent
red tape: *n.* paperasserie
red: *adj.* rouge; *n.* rouge
redden: *vt.* rougir
reddish: *adj.* rougeâtre
redeem: *vt.* racheter; rembourser
redeemable: *adj.* rachetable
Redeemer: *n.* Rédempteur
redemption: *n.* rachat
redeploy: *vt.* réaffecter

red-hot: *adj.* brûlant; ardent
redness: *n.* rougeur; rousseur
redolent: *adj.* parfumé; odorant
redouble: *vt.* redoubler
redox reaction: réaction de réduction-oxidation
reduce: *vt.* réduire; diminuer; abaisser
reducible: *adj.* réductible
reduction: *n.* réduction; baisse
redundancy: *n.* licenciement
redundant: *adj.* superflu; licencié
reed: *n.* roseau
reek: *n.* puanteur
reek: *vi.* empester; puer
reel: *n.* bobine; bande; dévidoir
reel: *vi.* chanceler
re-election: *n.* réélection
re-engage: *vt.* rengager
re-enter: *vt.* rentrer
re-estabilshment: *n.* rétablissement; restauration
re-establish: *vt.* rétablir; réhabiliter
ref: *n.* ris; récif
refectory: *n.* réfectoire
refer: *vt.* soumettre; renvoyer; se référer à; *vi.* se référer
referee: *n.* arbitre
reference: *n.* référence; allusion
refine: *vt.* raffiner; affiner
refinement: *n.* raffinement; raffinerie; culture
refinery: *n.* raffinerie
reflect: *vt.* réfléchir; refléter; *vi.* réfléchir
reflection: *n.* réflexion; pensée
reflector: *n.* réflecteur; cataphote
reflex: *adj.* réflexe
reform: *vt.* réformer; *vi.* se réformer
reformer: *n.* réformateur
reformist: *n.* réformiste
refract: *vt.* réfracter
refraction: *n.* réfraction
refresh: *vt.* rafraîchir

refreshment: *n.* rafraîchissement
refrigerator: *n.* glacière; réfrigérateur
refuel: *vi.* se ravitailler (en carburant)
refuge: *n.* refuge; asile
refuge: *n.* réfugié
refund: *n.* remboursement
refund: *vt.* rembourser
refurbish: *vt.* rénover
refus: *n.* refus
refuse: *n.* déchets
refuse: *vt.* refuser
refute: *vt.* réfuter
regain: *vt.* recouvrer; reprendre
regal: *adj.* royal
regale: *vt.* régaler
regalia: *n.* insignes
regard: *n.* considération; respect
regard: *vt.* considérer
regardless: *adv.* quand même; malgré tout
regatta: *n.* régate
regency: *n.* régence
regenerate: *adj.* régénéré
regenerate: *vt.* régénérer
regeneration: *n.* régénération
regent: *n.* régent
regime: *n.* régime
regiment: *n.* régiment
region: *n.* région
register: *n.* registre
register: *vt.* enregistrer
registered- letter: lettre recommandée
registrar: *n.* officier d'état civil
registration: *n.* enregistrement
registry: *n.* enregistrement
regressive: *adj.* régressif
regret: *n.* regret
regret: *vt.* regretter
regretful: *adj.* plein de regrets
regular polygon: polygone régulier
regular: *adj.* régulier; ordinaire; *n.* habitué

regularity: *n.* régularité
regulate: *vt.* régler; réglementer
regulation: *n.* règlement; réglementation
regulator: *n.* régulateur
rehabilitate: *vt.* réhabiliter
rehabilitation: *n.* réhabilitation
rehearsal: *n.* répétition
rehearse: *vt.* répéter; raconter
reign: *n.* règne
reign: *vi.* régner
reimburse: *n.* remboursement
reimburse: *vt.* rembourser
rein: *n.* rêne
rein: *vt.* contenir
reindeer: *n.* renne
reinforce: *vt.* renforcer
reinstate: *vt.* réintégrer
reinsure: *vt.* réassurer
reissue: *n.* réédition
reiterate: *vt.* réitérer
reject: *vt.* rejeter
rejection: *n.* refus; rejet
rejoice: *vt.* réjouir; *vi.* se réjouir
rejoicing: *n.* réjouissance
relapse: *n.* rechute
relapse: *vi.* retomber
relate: *vt.* relater; rapprocher; *vi.* se rapporter
related: *adj.* apparenté
relation: *n.* rapport; parent
relationship: *n.* lien de parenté; relation; rapport
relative density: densité relative
relative: *adj.* relatif; *n.* parent
relax: *vt.* relâcher; détendre; *vi.* se relâcher; se détendre
relaxation: *n.* relâchement; détente
relay: *n.* relais
relay: *vt.* retransmettre
release: *n.* libération; décharge
release: *vt.* libérer; relâcher
relegate: *vt.* reléguer
relegation: *n.* relégation

relent: *vi.* s'adoucir
relentless: *adj.* implacable
relevant: *adj.* pertinent
reliability: *n.* fiabilité; exactitude
reliable: *adj.* fiable; digne de confiance
reliance: *n.* confiance
relic: *n.* relique
relief: *n.* soulagement; secours
relieve: *vt.* soulager; alléger; secourir
religion: *n.* religion
religious: *adj.* religieux
relinquish: *vt.* abandonner; renoncer à
relish: *n.* saveur; goat; attrait
relish: *vt.* savourer; se délecter de
reluctance: *n.* répugnance
reluctant: *adj.* peu disposé
rely: *vi.* compter sur; avoir confiance en
remain: *vi.* rester; demeurer
remainder: *n.* reste; restant
remark: *n.* remarque; observation
remark: *vt.* (faire) remarquer; (faire) observer
remarkable: *adj.* remarquable; notable
remarkably: *adv.* remarquablement
remarry: *vi.* se remarier
remedial: *adj.* de rattrapage
remedy: *n.* remède; recours
remedy: *vt.* remédier à
remember: *vt.* se souvenir de; se rappeler
remembrance: *n.* mémoire; souvenir
remind: *vt.* rappeler
reminiscence: *n.* réminiscence
remiss: *adj.* négligent
remission: *n.* rémission
remit: *vt.* remettre; pardonner; *vi.* diminuer
remittance: *n.* remise
remnant: *n.* reste; restant
remodel: *vt.* remodeler

remonstrate: *vi.* protester
remorse: *n.* remords
remorseless: *adj.* implacable
remote access: accès à distance
remote: *adj.* lointain; éloigné
remoteness: *n.* éloignement;
isolement
removable: *adj.* amovible
removal: *n.* suppression;
déménagement
remove: *vt.* enlever; *vi.* déménager
remunerate: *vt.* rémunérer
remunertion: *n.* rémunération
render: *vt.* rendre; remettre; traduire;
(law) rendre
rendezvous: *n.* rendez-vous; point de
ralliement
renew: *n.* renouvellement
renew: *vt.* renouveler
renewable resource: ressource
renouvelable
rennet: *n.* présure
renounce: *vt.* renoncer à
renovate: *vt.* rénover
renovation: *n.* rénovation
renown: *n.* renommée; célébrité
renowned: *adj.* célèbre renommé
rent: *n.* loyer; location
rent: *vt.* louer
renunciation: *n.* renonciation
reopen: *vt.* rouvrir
reorganisation: *n.* réorganisation
repair: *n.* réparation
repairable: *adj.* réparable
reparation: *n.* réparation
repartee: *n.* répartie; réplique
repatriate: *vt.* rapatrier
repay: *vt.* rembourser; rendre;
récompenser
repayment: *n.* remboursement
repeal: *n.* abrogation; annulation
repeal: *vt.* abroger; annuler
repeat: *vt.* répéter
repeatedly: *adv.* à plusieurs reprises

repeater: *n.* montre à répétition
repeating decimal: décimal indéfini
repel: *vt.* repousser; rebuter
repellent: *n.* insectifuge
repent: *vi.* se repentir
repentance: *n.* repentir
repentt: *adj.* repentant
repertory: *n.* répertoire
repetition: *n.* répétition; réitération
replace: *vt.* replacer; remplacer
replant: *vt.* replanter
replenish: *vt.* remplir de nouveau
replete: *adj.* rempli; rassasié
reply: *n.* réponse
reply: *vi.* répondre
report: *n.* rapport; compte rendu;
rumeur
report: *vt.* rapporter; relater; rendre
compte de
reporter: *n.* journaliste
repose: *n.* repos
repose: *vi.* (se) reposer
reposes: *vt.* reprendre possession de
repository: *n.* dépôt
reprehend: *vt.* condamner
reprehensible: *adj.* répréhensible
represent: *vt.* représenter
representation: *n.* représentation
representative: *adj.* représentatif; *n.*
représentant
repress: *vt.* réprimer; contenir
repression: *n.* répression
repressive: *adj.* répressif
reprieve: *n.* sursis
reprieve: *vt.* accorder un sursis ou un
répit à
reprimand: *n.* blâme; réprimande
reprimand: *vt.* réprimander; blâmer
reprint: *vt.* réimprimer
reprisal: *n.* représailles
reproach: *n.* reproche; opprobre
reproach: *vt.* reprocher
reproachul: *adj.* réprobateur
reproduce: *vt.* reproduire

reproduction: *n.* reproduction
reptile: *n.* reptile
republic: *n.* république
republican: *adj.* républicain; *n.* républicain
republicanism: *n.* républicanisme
repudiate: *vt.* renier
répugnance: *n.* répugnance; dégoût
repugnant: *adj.* répugnant
repulse: *vt.* repousser; rejeter
repulsion: *n.* répulsion
repulsive: *adj.* répulsif
reputable: *adj.* honorable
reputation: *n.* réputation
repute: *n.* renom
request: *n.* demande; requête
request: *vt.* demander; solliciter; prier
require: *vt.* demander; nécessiter; exiger
requirement: *n.* besoin; exigence
requisite: *adj.* nécessaire; indispensable; *n.* objets nécessaires
requisition: *n.* demande; (mil) réquisition
requite: *vt.* rembourser
reread: *vt.* relire
rescind: *vt.* annuler; abroger
rescue: *n.* secours; délivrance
rescue: *vt.* sauver; secourir
research: *n.* recherche
research: *vt.* faire des recherches
resemblance: *n.* ressemblance
resemble: *vt.* ressembler à
resent: *vt.* être contrarié par; irrité par
resentful: *adj.* plein de ressentiment
resentment: *n.* ressentiment
reservation: *n.* réserve; réservation
reserve: *n.* réserve
reserve: *vt.* réserver
reservedly: *adv.* avec réserve
reservoir: *n.* réservoir
reside: *vi.* résider
residence: *n.* résidence; séjour

resident: *adj.* résidant; *n.* résident
residuary: *adj.* restant
residue: *n.* reste; résidu
residuum: *n.* résidu
resign: *vt.* démissionner de; renoncer à; céder; se résigner à; *vi.* démissionner
resignation: *n.* démission
resin: *n.* résine
resinous: *adj.* résineux
resist: *vt.* résister; s'opposer
resistance: *n.* résistance
resolute: *adj.* résolu
resolution: *n.* résolution
resolve: *vt.* résoudre; *vi.* (se) résoudre; (se) décider
resonance structure: structure de résonnance
resonance: *n.* résonance
resonant: *adj.* résonant
resort: *n.* lieu de vacances; recours
resort: *vi.* recourir
resound: *vi.* résonner
resource: *n.* ressource; expédient
respect: *n.* respect; égard; rapport
respect: *vt.* respecter
respectability: *n.* respectabilité
respectable: *adj.* respectable; considérable
respectful: *adj.* respectueux
respecting: *prep.* en ce qui concerne
respective: *adj.* respectif
respirator: *n.* respirateur
respiratory: *adj.* respiratoire
respite: *n.* répit; sursis
respite: *vt.* repousser; différer
resplendence: *n.* resplendissement; splendeur
resplendent: *adj.* resplendissant
respond: *vi.* répondre; réagir
respondent: *n.* défendeur
response: *n.* réponse; réaction
responsibility: *n.* responsabilité
responsible: *adj.* responsable

responsive: *adj.* sensible à; réceptif
rest room: toilettes
rest: *n.* repos; pause
rest: *vt.* laisser reposer; appuyer; *vi.*
se reposer; reposer
rest: *vt.* réparer
restatement: *n.* réaffirmation
resting place: lieu de repos
restitution: *n.* restitution
restive: *adj.* rétif; récalcitrant; agité
restless: *adj.* agité; instable
restoration: *n.* restauration
restorative: *adj.* fortifiant
restore: *vt.* restituer; restaurer
restrain: *vt.* retenir; contenir
restraint: *n.* contrainte; entrave
restrict: *vt.* restreindre; limiter
restriction: *n.* restriction
restrictive: *adj.* restrictif
result: *n.* résultat
result: *vi.* résulter
resume: *vt.* reprendre
resurrection: *n.* résurrection
resuscitate: *vt.* réanimer
retail outlet: point de vente
retail trade: commerce de détail
retail: *n.* vente au détail
retail: *vt.* vendre au détail; détailler
retain: *vt.* retenir; conserver
retainer: *n.* serviteur
retake: *vt.* reprendre
retaliate: *vi.* se venger
retaliation: *n.* représailles
retardation: *n.* retard
retarded: *adj.* retardé
retch: *vi.* avoir des haut-le-coeur
retell: *vt.* redire
retention: *n.* rétention
retentive: *adj.* qui retient bien
reticence: *n.* réticence
reticule: *n.* réticule
retina: *n.* rétine
retire: *vt.* mettre à la retraite; *vi.* se
retirer; prendre sa retraite

retired: *adj.* retraité; à la retraite
retirement: *n.* isolement; retraite
retort: *n.* réplique
retort: *vt.* rétorquer
retouch: *vt.* retoucher
retrace: *vt.* retracer
retract: *vt.* rétracter; retirer
retrain: *vt.* recycler
retraining: *n.* recyclage
retreat: *n.* repli
retreat: *vi.* se retirer
retribution: *n.* châtiment;
récompense
retrievable: *adj.* récupérable;
réparable
retrieve data: restituer des données
retrieve: *vt.* récupérer; recouvrer
retriever: *n.* chien d'arrêt
retrograde: *adj.* rétrograde
retrospective bibliography:
bibliographie rétrospective
retrospective: *adj.* rétrospectif
return: *n.* retour; renvoi
return: *vt.* rendre; restituer; renvoyer
reunion: *n.* réunion
reunite: *vt.* réunir; *vi.* se réunir
reveal: *vt.* révéler
revel: *vi.* faire la fête
revelation: *n.* révélation
reveller: *n.* fêtard
revelry: *n.* fête
revenge: *n.* vengeance
revenge: *vt.* venger
revengeful: *adj.* vindicatif
revenue: *n.* revenu; rente
reverberate: *vt.* réverbérer; *vi.*
résonner; retentir; se réverbérer
reverberation: *n.* répercussion;
réverbération
revere: *n.* inverse; contraire; revers
revere: *vt.* renverser; annuler; *vi.* faire
marche arrière
revere: *vt.* révérer; vénérer
reverence: *n.* vénération

reverence: *vt.* révérer
reverend: *adj.* révérend; vénérable; *n.* curé
reverent: *adj.* révérenciel; respecteux
reversal: *n.* renversement; annulation
reversible: *adj.* révocable; réversible
reversion: *n.* retour; réversion
revert: *vi.* revenir; retourner
review: *vt.* revoir; passer en
reviewer: *n.* critique
revile: *vt.* vilipender
revise: *vt.* réviser; mettre à jour
reviser: *n.* réviseur
revision: *n.* révision
revisit: *vt.* retourner voir
revival: *n.* reprise; renouveau
revive: *vt.* ranimer; raviver; *vi.* reprendre connaissance; reprendre
revocation: *n.* révocation
revoke: *vt.* révoquer; annuler
revolt: *n.* révolte
revolt: *vi.* se révolter
revolting: *adj.* exécrable
revolution: *n.* révolution
revolutionary: *adj.* révolutionnaire; *n.* révolutionnaire
revolve: *vt.* retourner; *vi.* tourner
revolving: *adj.* tournant
revue: *n.* revue; examen
revulsion: *n.* écoeurement
reward: *n.* récompense
reward: *vt.* récompenser
rhapsody: *n.* rhapsodie
rhetoric: *adj.* rhétorique; *n.* rhétorique
rhetorical strategy: stratégie rhétorique
rheumatic: *adj.* rhumatisant
rheumatism: *n.* rhumatisme
rhinoceros: *n.* rhinocéros
rhomboid: *n.* rhomboïd
rhombus: *n.* rhombe
rhubarb: *n.* rhubarbe
rhyme: *n.* rime; vers

rhyme: *vi.* rimer
rhythm: *n.* rythme
rhythmical: *adj.* rythmique
rib: *n.* côte
ribald: *adj.* paillard
ribbon: *n.* ruban; lambeaux
rice: *n.* riz
rich: *adj.* riche; somptueux; abondant
richness: *n.* richesse; abondance
rickets: *n.* rachitisme
rickety: *adj.* rachitique
rid: *vt.* débarrasser; se débarrasser de
riddle: *n.* énigme; crible
riddle: *vt.* cribler
ride: *n.* promenade à cheval ou en voiture
ride: *vi.* monter à cheval; aller en voiture
rider: *n.* cavalier
ridge: *n.* arête; crête; chaîne
ridge: *vt.* rider; strier
ridicule: *n.* ridicule; raillerie
ridicule: *vt.* ridiculiser
ridiculous: *adj.* ridicule
riding chool: manège
riding habit: tenue d'amazone
riding: *n.* équitation; monte
rife: *adj.* répandu; abondant
riffraff: *n.* racaille
rifle: *n.* fusil
rifle: *vt.* dévaliser; piller; strier; rayer
rifleman: *n.* fusilier
rift valley: rift
rig: gréement; plate-forme de forage
rig: *vt.* équiper; truquer; gréer
rigging: *n.* gréement
right cylinder: cylindre droit
right rectangular prism: prisme rectangulaire droit
right triangle: triangle droit
right: *adj.* droit; bien; juste; *adv.* bien; correctement; *n.* justice; raison
right: *vt.* redresser
righteous: *adj.* droit; vertueux

righteousness: *n.* droiture;vertu
rigid: *adj.* rigide; sévère; strict
rigidity: *n.* rigidité; sévérité
rigmarole: *n.* galimatias
rigorous: *adj.* rigoureux
rigour: *n.* rigueur; sévérité
rim: *n.* bord; monture
ring: *n.* anneau; cercle; rond; bague; tintement de cloche
ring: *vt.* sonner; *vi.* sonner; retentir
ringer: *n.* carillonneur
ringleader: *n.* meneur
ringlet: *n.* anglaise
rink: *n.* patinoire
rinse: *vt.* rincer
riot: *n.* émeute
riot: *vi.* se livrer à une émeute
rioter: *n.* émeutier; *adj.* séditieux; dissolu
rip: *vt.* déchirer; fendre
ripe: *adj.* mûr
ripen: *vt.* mûrir
rise: *n.* hausse; augmentation; montée; lever; source
rise: *vi.* se lever; naître; monter; croître
rising: *n.* insurrection; levée; clôture
risk: *n.* risque; danger
risk: *vt.* risquer
risky: *adj.* risqué
rissole: *n.* rissole
rite: *n.* rite
ritual: *adj.* rituel; *n.* rituel
rival: *adj.* rival; *n.* rival
rival: *vt.* rivaliser avec; concurrencer
rivalry: *n.* rivalité
river: *n.* rivière
rivet: *n.* rivet
rivet: *vt.* riveter; river
rivulet: *n.* petit ruisseau
roach: *n.* blatte
road: *n.* route
roadsign: *n.* panneau de signalisation
roadstead: *n.* rade

roam: *vt.* parcourir; errer dans; *vi.* errer
roan: *adj.* rouan
roar: *n.* hurlement; rugissement; mugissement; grondement
roar: *vi.* hurler; rugir; mugir
roast beef: rôti de boeuf
roast: *vt.* rôtir; griller
rob: *vt.* voler
robber: *n.* voleur
robe: *n.* robe; peignoir de bain
robe: *vt.* revêtir d'une robe de cérémonie
robery: *n.* vol
robin: *n.* rouge-gorge
robust: *adj.* robuste
robustness: *n.* robustesse
rock crystal: cristal de roche
rock salt: sel gemme
rock: *n.* roche; rocher; roc
rock: *vt.* bercer; balancer; ébranler
rocket: *n.* fusée
rocky: *adj.* rocheux
rod: *n.* baguette; tringle; canne
rodent: *n.* rongeur
roe: *n.* chevreuil; oeufs
roebuck: *n.* chevreuil
rogation: *n.* rogations
roguish: *adj.* coquin
role: *n.* rôle
roll: *n.* roulement; rouleau; liste; catalogue; liasse; petit pain
roll: *vt.* rouler; étendre; enrouler
roller: *n.* rouleau; cylindre
rolling pin: rouleau à pâtisserie
romance: *n.* romance; roman; conte; fable
romantic: *adj.* romantique
romp: *vi.* jouer bruyamment
roof: *n.* toit; voûte
roof: *vt.* couvrir
roofing: *n.* toiture
rook: *n.* freux; tour

room: *n.* pièce; salle; place; espace; chambre
roominess: *n.* grande envergure
rooming house: pension
roomy: *adj.* spacieux
roost: *n.* perchoir
roost: *vi.* se percher
root word: racine d'un mot
root: *n.* racine; origine
rooted: *adj.* enraciné; ancré
rope: *n.* corde; cordage
rope: *vi.* attacher
ropemaker: *n.* cordier
rosary: *n.* rosaire
rose: *n.* rose
rosebed: *n.* massif de roses
rosebud: *n.* bouton de rose
rosebush: *n.* rosier
rosemary: *n.* romarin
rosette: *n.* rosette
rosewood: *n.* bois de rose
rosiness: *n.* couleur rosée
rosy: *adj.* rosé
rot: *n.* pourriture
rot: *vi.* pourrir
rotate: *vt.* faire tourner; *vi.* tourner
rotation: *n.* rotation
rotational constant: constante de rotation
rotten: *adj.* pourri; corrompu
rottenness: *n.* pourriture
rotund: *adj.* rond; replet; arrondi
rouble: *n.* rouble
rouge: *n.* rouge (à joues)
rough draft: brouillon
rough: *adj.* accidenté; inégal; rugueux; rude; brutal; brusque; houleux
roughcast: *n.* crépi
roughen: *vt.* rendre rugueux
roughness: *n.* rugosité; rudesse; brusquerie; agitation
round: *adj.* rond; circulaire; *n.* cercle; rond; tour

round: *vt.* contourner; arrondir
roundabout: *adj.* détourné; indirect; *n.* rond-point
roundness: *n.* rondeur
rouse: *vt.* réveiller; exciter
rout: *n.* déroute; débâcle
rout: *vt.* mettre en déroute
route: *n.* itinéraire; route
routine: *adj.* habituel; *n.* routine
rove: *vi.* vagabonder; errer
rover: *n.* vagabond; pirate
row: *n.* rangée; file
row: *vt.* (mar) ramer
rowdy: *n.* hooligan; voyou
rower: *n.* rameur
royal: *adj.* royal; princier
royalist: *n.* royaliste
royalty: *n.* royauté; droits d'auteur
rub: *n.* frottement; ennui; difficulté
rub: *vt.* frotter; irriter
rubber band: élastique
rubber: *n.* caoutchouc; gomme; préservatif
rubbish: *n.* détritus; ordures; bêtises; décombres
rubric: *n.* rubrique
ruby: *n.* rubis
rucksack: *n.* sac à dos
rudder: *n.* gouvernail
ruddiness: *n.* teint vif; rougeur
ruddy: *adj.* coloré; rouge
rude: *adj.* impoli; rude; brusque; grossier; primitif
rudeness: *n.* impolitesse; rudesse; insolence
rudiment: *n.* rudiments
rue: *n.* (bot) rue
rue: *vt.* regretter amèrement
rueful: *adj.* triste
ruffian: *n.* voyou; brute; *adj.* brutal
ruffle: *vt.* ébouriffer; déranger; rider
rug: *n.* tapis; carpette
rugged: *adj.* accidenté; déchiqueté; rude; robuste

ruin: *n.* ruine; perte; ruines
ruin: *vt.* ruiner; détruire
ruinous: *adj.* ruineux
rule: *n.* règle; règlement; pouvoir; domination
rule: *vt.* gouverner; dominer; décider; régler; diriger
ruler: *n.* dirigeant; règle
rules of conversation: règles de la conversation
rum: *n.* rhum
rumble: *vi.* gronder; tonner
ruminate: *vt.* ruminer
rummage: *vi.* fouiller
rumour: *n.* rumeur
rump: *n.* croupe
run: *n.* course; compétition; parcours; cours; série; mode; ruée
run: *vt.* diriger; organiser; faire couler; passer
runaway: *n.* fugitif; fuyard
rung: *n.* barreau; échelon
runner: *n.* coureur; concurrent; messager
running: *n.* course; direction
runway: *n.* piste de décollage
rupture: *n.* rupture; hernie
rural: *adj.* rural; champêtre
ruse: *n.* ruse; stratagème
rush: *n.* jonc; ruée; hâte
rush: *vt.* pousser vivement; *vi.* se précipiter; s'élancer
russet: *adj.* roux
rust: *n.* rouille
rust: *vi.* se rouiller
rustic: *adj.* rustique; *n.* paysan; rustaud
rustiness: *n.* rouille
rustle: *vi.* bruire; *vt.* faire bruire; froisser
rustling: *n.* vol de bétail; bruissement
rusty: *adj.* rouillé; roux
rut: *n.* rut; ornière
ruthless: *adj.* cruel; impitoyable

rye: *n.* seigle

$\mathcal{S}$

Sabbath: *n.* sabbat
sable: *n.* zibeline
sabotage: *n.* sabotage
sabre: *n.* sabre
saccharin: *n.* saccharine
sack: *n.* sac
sack: *vt.* mettre à sac; renvoyer
sacrament: *n.* sacrement; Eucharistie
sacramental: *adj.* sacramentel
sacred: *adj.* saint; sacré; inviolable
sacredness: *n.* caractère sacré
sacrifice: *n.* sacrifice
sacrifice: *vt.* sacrifier
sacrificial: *adj.* sacrificiel
sacrilege: *n.* sacrilège
sacrilegious: *adj.* sacrilège
sad: *adj.* triste; déprimé; attristant; regrettable
sadden: *vt.* attrister
saddle: *n.* selle; col
saddle: *vt.* seller
saddlebag: *n.* sacoche de selle
saddler: *n.* sellier
sadness: *n.* tristesse
safe: *adj.* sûr; en sécurité; sans danger; *n.* coffre-fort
safe-conduct: *n.* sauf-conduit
safeguard: *n.* sauvegarde
safeguard: *vt.* sauvegarder; protéger
safety belt: ceinture de sécurité
safety pin: épingle de nourrice
safety: *n.* sécurité; sûreté
saffron: *n.* safran
sage: *n.* sauge; sage; *adj.* sage
sago: *n.* sagou
sail: *n.* voile
sail: *vt.* piloter; *vi.* aller à la voile; naviguer
sailing: *n.* navigation
sailor: *n.* marin
saint: *n.* saint
sake: *n.* bien; égard; for God's sake = pour l'amour de Dieu

salad bowl: saladier
salad dressing: vinaigrette
salad oil: huile de table
salad: *n.* salade
salamander: *n.* salamandre
salary: *n.* salaire
sale: *n.* vente; solde
saleable: *adj.* vendable
sales executive: directeur commercial
sales policy: politique de vente
sales terms: conditions de vente
salesman: *n.* vendeur
saleswoman: *n.* vendeuse
salient: *adj.* saillant
saline: *adj.* salin
saliva: *n.* salive
sallow: *adj.* jaunâtre; cireux
sally: *n.* sortie; saillie
sally: *vi.* saillir
salmon trout: truite saumonée
salmon: *n.* saumon
saloon: *n.* bar
salt cellar: salière
salt: *n.* sel
salt: *vt.* saler
saltnness: *n.* salinité
saltpetre: *n.* salpêtre
salubrious: *adj.* salubre; sain
salubrity: *n.* salubrité
salutary: *adj.* salutaire
salutation: *n.* salutation
salute: *n.* salut
salute: *vt.* saluer
salvage: *n.* droit de sauvetage
salvation: *n.* salut
salve: *n.* baume; onguent
salver: *n.* plateau
salvo: *n.* salve
same: *adj.* même; identique
sameness: *n.* monotonie
sample: *n.* échantillon; prélèvement
sample: *vt.* goûter
sampler: *n.* échantillonneur; modèle
sanatorium: *n.* sanatorium

sanctify: *vt.* sanctifier
sanctimonious: *adj.* cagot
sanction: *n.* sanction
sanction: *vt.* sanctionner
sanctity: *n.* sainteté
sanctuary: *n.* sanctuaire; asile
sand: *n.* sable
sand: *vt.* sabler
sandal: *n.* sandale
sandbag: *n.* sac m de sable
sandpit: *n.* carrière de sable
sandstone: *n.* grès
sandy: *adj.* sablonneux; sableux
sane: *adj.* sain
sanguinary: *adj.* sanguinaire; sanglant
sanguine: *adj.* sanguin
sanitary towel: serviette hygiénique
sanity: *n.* santé mentale; raison
sap: *n.* sève
sap: *vt.* miner
sapient: *adj.* sage; prudent
sapling: *n.* jeune arbre
sapphire: *n.* saphir
sarcasm: *n.* sarcasme
sarcastic: *adj.* sarcastique; caustique
sarcophagus: *n.* sarcophage
sardine: *n.* sardine
sash window: fenêtre à guillotine
sash: *n.* écharpe; ceinture
sassy: *adj.* insolent
Satan: *n.* Satan
satanical: *adj.* satanique
satchel: *n.* cartable
satellite: *n.* satellite
satiate: *vt.* rassasier; assouvir
satin: *n.* satin; *adj.* en ou de satin
satire: *n.* satire
satirical: *adj.* satirique
satirist: *n.* écrivain satirique
satirize: *vt.* faire la satire de
satisfaction: *n.* satisfaction
satisfactorily: *adv.* d'une manière satisfaisante

satisfactory: *adj.* satisfaisant
satisfy: *vt.* satisfaire; convaincre
saturate: *vt.* saturer
Saturday: *n.* samedi
saturnine: *adj.* saturnien; sombre
satyr: *n.* satyre
sauce: *n.* sauce; assaisonnement
sauce: *vt.* assaisonner
saucepan: *n.* casserole
saucer: *n.* soucoupe
saucily: *adv.* avec impertinence
sauciness: *n.* impertinence; insolence
saucy: *adj.* impertinent
saunter: *vi.* flâner; se balader
sausage: *n.* saucisse
savage: *adj.* sauvage; barbare; *n.* sauvage
savageness: *n.* sauvagerie; barbarie
savagery: *n.* sauvagerie; barbarie
savannah: *n.* savane
save: *vt.* sauver; économiser; épargner; éviter; conserver
saveloy: *n.* cervelas
saver: *n.* libérateur; épargnant
saving: *adj.* économique; économe; *prep.* sauf; à l'exception
savings account: compte d'épargne
savings bank: caisse d'épargne
Saviour: *n.* Sauveur
savour: *n.* saveur; goût
savour: *vt.* déguster; savourer
savouriness: *n.* goût; saveur
savoury: *adj.* savoureux
saw: *n.* scie
saw: *vt.* scier
sawdust: *n.* sciure
sawfish: *n.* poisson scie
sawmill: *n.* scierie
sawyer: *n.* scieur
saxophone: *n.* saxophone
say: *vt.* dire
saying: *n.* dicton; proverbe
scab: *n.* gale; croûte
scabbard: *n.* gaine; fourreau

scabby: *adj.* galeux
scaffold: *n.* échafaud; échafaudage
scaffolding: *n.* échafaudage
scald: *n.* brûlure
scald: *vt.* échauder
scale: *n.* balance; échelle; gamme; écaille
scale: *vt.* escalader; écailler
scallion: *n.* échalote
scallop: *n.* feston
scallop: *vt.* festonner
scalp: *n.* cuir chevelu
scalp: *vt.* scalper
scamp: *n.* coquin
scamper: *vi.* galoper
scan: *vt.* scruter; explorer; scander
scandal: *n.* scandale; infamie
scandalise: *vt.* scandaliser
scandalous: *adj.* scandaleux
scantily: *adv.* pauvrement; insuffisamment
scantiness: *n.* insuffisance; pauvreté
scapegoat: *n.* bouc émissaire
scar: *n.* cicatrice
scar: *vt.* marquer d'une cicatrice
scarce: *adj.* rare
scarcity: *n.* rareté; pénurie
scare: *n.* peur; panique
scare: *vt.* effrayer
scarecrow: *n.* épouvantail
scarf: *n.* écharpe
scarlatina: *n.* scarlatine
scarlet: *n.* écarlate; *adj.* écarlate
scarp: *n.* escarpement
scatter plot: diagramme de dispersion
scatter: *vt.* éparpiller; disperser
scavenger: *n.* charognard; éboueur
scenario: *n.* scénario
scene: *n.* scène; lieu; spectacle; vue
scenery: *n.* vue; décor
scenic: *adj.* scénique
scent bottle: flacon â parfum
scent: *n.* parfum; odeur; odorat; piste

scent: *vt.* parfumer
scentless: *adj.* sans odeur; inodore
sceptic: *n.* sceptique
sceptical: *adj.* sceptique
scepticism: *n.* scepticisme
sceptre: *n.* sceptre
schedule: *n.* horaire; programme; liste
scheme: *n.* projet; plan; schéma; système; machination
scheme: *vt.* machiner; *vi.* intriguer
schemer: *n.* conspirateur; intrigant
schism: *n.* schisme
schismatic: *n.* schismatique
scholar: *n.* élève; érudit
scholarship: *n.* savoir; science; bourse (d'études)
scholastic: *adj.* scolaire
school: *n.* école
school: *vt.* instruire
schoolboy: *n.* écolier; élève
schoolgirl: *n.* écolière; élève
schooling: *n.* instruction; éducation
schoolmaster: *n.* instituteur; maître (d'école)
schoolmistress: *n.* institutrice; maîtresse (d'école)
schoolteacher: *n.* instituteur; professeur
schooner: *n.* goélette
sciatic: *n.* sciatique
science fiction: science-fiction
science: *n.* science
scientific method: méthode scientifique
scientific: *adj.* scientifique
scientist: *n.* scientifique
scimitar: *n.* cimeterre
scintillate: *vi.* scintiller; étinceler
scintillating: *adj.* brillant; scintillant
scission: *n.* scission; division
scissors: *npl.* ciseaux
scoff: *vi.* se moquer
scold: *vt.* réprimander; *vi.* grogner

scoop: *n.* louche; pelle; exclusivité
scoop: *vt.* évider; écoper; marquer; souligner
scooter: *n.* scooter; trottinette
scope: *n.* portée; envergure; étendue; zone de compétence; liberté d'action
scorch: *vt.* brûler; roussir; griller; *vi.* se brûler; roussir
score: *n.* score; marque; en-taille; rayure; titre; égard;
scoreboard: *n.* tableau (d'affichage)
scorn: *n.* dédain; mépris
scorn: *vt.* mépriser; dédaigner
scornful: *adj.* dédaigneux
scorpion: *n.* scorpion
scotch tape: scotch
scotch: *n.* whisky
scotch: *vt.* contrecarrer
scoundrel: *n.* vaurien
scour: *vt.* récurer; frotter; nettoyer; *vi.* battre la campagne
scourge: *n.* fouet; châtiment
scourge: *vt.* fouetter; châtier
scout: *n.* éclaireur; guetteur; reconnaissance
scout: *vi.* aller en reconnaissance
scowl: *n.* mine renfrognée
scowl: *vi.* se renfrogner
scragginess: *n.* décharnement; maigreur extrême; rugosité
scraggy: *adj.* rugueux; famélique
scramble: *n.* bousculade; ruée; ascension
scramble: *vi.* avancer â quatre pattes; grimper; se battre; se disputer
scrap: *n.* bout; restes; petit morceau; bagarre; ferraille
scrape: *n.* embarras; ennui
scrape: *vi.* racler; gratter; *vt.* érafler
scraper: *n.* racloir
scratch: *n.* égratignure
scratch: *vt.* griffer; égratigner; gratter; griffonner
scrawl: *n.* griffonnage

scrawl: *vi.* gribouiller
scream: *n.* cri perçant; hurlement
scream: *vi.* hurler; pousser des cris
screen capture: photo d'écran
screen display: affichage sur écran
screen: *n.* écran; paravent; rideau; écran de cheminée
screen: *vt.* abriter; cacher; projeter; passer au crible; sélectionner
screenplay: *n.* scénario
screw driver: tournevis
screw: *n.* vis
screw: *vt.* visser; extorquer; soutirer
scribble: *n.* gribouillage
scribble: *vt.* gribouiller
scribe: *n.* scribe
scrimmage: *n.* mêlée
script: *n.* scénario; script
scriptural: *adj.* biblique
Scripture: *n.* Écriture sainte
scroll: *n.* rouleau
scrub: *n.* broussailles; *adj.* mal soigné
scrub: *vt.* nettoyer â la brosse; récurer; annuler
scruple: *n.* scrupule
scrupulous: *adj.* scrupuleux
scrutinise: *vt.* étudier minutieusement; examiner
scrutiny: *n.* examen minutieux
scuffle: *n.* échauffourée; rixe
scuffle: *vi.* se bagarrer
scull: *n.* aviron
scullery: *n.* arrière-cuisine
sculpt: *v.* sculpter
sculptor: *n.* sculpteur
sculpture: *n.* sculpture
scum: *n.* écume; crasse; rebut
scurrilous: *adj.* injurieux; vil; ignoble
scurvy: *n.* scorbut; *adj.* vil; mesquin
scuttle: *n.* corbeille
scuttle: *vi.* courir précipitamment
scythe: *n.* faux

sea breeze: brise de mer
sea fight: combat naval
sea front: bord de mer
sea horse: hippocampe
sea plane: hydravion
sea: *n.* mer
seacoast: *n.* côte
seafood: *n.* fruits de mer
seagreen: *adj.* vert glauque
seagull: *n.* mouette
seal: *n.* sceau; phoque
seal: *vt.* cacheter, fermer
sealing wax: cire à cacheter
seam: *n.* couture
seam: *vt.* faire une couture
seamanship: *n.* habileté à naviguer
seamstress: *n.* couturière
seamy: *adj.* sordide
seaport: *n.* port de mer
sear: *vt.* cautériser
search: *n.* fouille; recherche; perquisition
search: *vt.* fouiller; inspecter; examiner; scruter; sonder
searchlight: *n.* projecteur
seashore: *n.* rivage; bord de mer
seasick: *adj.* sujet au mal de mer
seasickness: *n.* mal de mer
seaside: *n.* bord de mer
season ticket: carte d'abonnement
season: *n.* saison; moment opportun; assaisonnement
season: *vt.* assaisonner; dessécher
seasonable: *adj.* opportun; à propos
seasonably: *adv.* de façon opportune; à propos
seasoning: *n.* assaisonnement
seat belt: ceinture de sécurité
seat: *n.* siège; place; derrière; fond
seat: *vt.* (faire) asseoir; placer
seaward: *adj.* du large
seaweed: *n.* algue
seaworthy: *adj.* en état de naviguer
secede: *vi.* faire sécession; se séparer

secession: *n.* sécession; séparation
seclude: *vt.* éloigner; isoler
seclusion: *n.* solitude; isolement
second: *adj.* deuxième; *n.* second; seconde
second: *vt.* aider; seconder
secondary author: auteur secondaire
secondary school: collège d'enseignement secondaire
secondary source: source secondaire
secondary: *adj.* secondaire
secondhand: *n.* article d'occasion
secrecy: *n.* secret; discrétion
secret: *adj.* secret; *n.* secret
secretary: *n.* secrétaire
secrete: *vt.* cacher; (med) sécréter
secretion: *n.* sécrétion
secretive: *adj.* secret; dissimulé
sect: *n.* secte
sectarian: *n.* sectaire
section: *n.* section
sector: *n.* secteur
secular: *adj.* séculaire
secularise: *vt.* séculariser
secure: *adj.* sûr; en sûreté
secure: *vt.* mettre en sûreté; assurer
security: *n.* sécurité; sûreté; protection; caution
sedan chair: chaise à porteurs
sedan: *n.* berline
sedate: *adj.* calme; posé
sedateness: *n.* calme
sedative: *n.* sédatif
sedentary: *adj.* sédentaire
sedge: *n.* (bot) carex
sediment: *n.* sédiment; lie; dépôt
sedimentary rock: roche sédimentaire
sedition: *n.* sédition
seditious: *adj.* séditieux
seduce: *vt.* séduire; corrompre
seducer: *n.* séducteur
seduction: *n.* séduction
seductive: *adj.* séduisant

sedulous: *adj.* assidu
see: *vt.* voir; remarquer; découvrir
seed time: époque des semailles
seed: *n.* graine; semence
seed: *vi.* monter en graine
seedsman: *n.* grainetier
seedy: *adj.* minable
seek: *vt.* chercher; demander
seem: *vi.* paraître; sembler
seeming: *n.* apparence
seemliness: *n.* bienséance
seemly: *adj.* convenable; bienséant
seer: *n.* prophète
seesaw: *n.* bascule
seesaw: *vi.* osciller
seethe: *vi.* bouillir; bouillonner
segment: *n.* segment
seize: *vt.* saisir; attraper; opérer la saisie de
seizure: *n.* capture; saisie
seldom: *adv.* rarement; peu souvent
select: *adj.* choisi; sélectionné
select: *vt.* sélectionner; choisir
selection: *n.* sélection
self- styled: *adj.* autoproclamé
self: *n.* soi-même
self-command: maîtrise de soi
self-conceit: *n.* vanité
self-confident: *adj.* sûr de soi
self-control: maîtrise de soi; sang-froid
self-correct: auto-correction
self-defence: *n.* autodéfense
self-denial: *n.* abnégation de soi
self-evident: *adj.* évident; qui va de soi
self-governing: *adj.* autonome
self-ignition: auto-inflammation
self-inhibition: auto-inhibition
self-interest: *n.* intérêt personnel
selfish: *adj.* égoïste
selfishness: *n.* égoïsme
self-pity: *n.* apitoiement sur soi même
self-portrait: *n.* autoportrait

self-possession: *n.* sang-froid; assurance
self-reliant: *adj.* indépendant
self-respect: *n.* respect de soi
selfsame: *adj.* exactement le même; identique
self-satisfied: *adj.* suffisant
self-seeking: *adj.* égoïste
self-service: *adj.* libre-service
self-sufficient: *adj.* autosuffisant
self-taught: *adj.* autodidacte
self-willed: *adj.* obstiné; volontaire
sell: *vt.* vendre; attraper; *vi.* se vendre
seller: *n.* vendeur
sellff-employed: *adj.* indépendant
selling-off: *n.* liquidation
semantic context: contexte sémantique
semantics: *n.* sémantique
semblance: *n.* semblant; apparence
semen: *n.* sperme
semester: *n.* semestre
semicircle: *n.* demi-cercle
semicircular: *adj.* semi-circulaire
semicolon: *n.* point-virgule
semiconductor: *n.* semi-conducteur
seminary: *n.* séminaire
semitone: *n.* demi-ton
senate: *n.* sénat
senator: *n.* sénateur
senatorial: *adj.* sénatorial
send: *vt.* envoyer; expédier; adresser; émettre; pousser
sender: *n.* expéditeur
senile: *adj.* sénile
senility: *n.* sénilité
senior citizen: personne agée
senior: *n.* aîné; *adj.* aîné; supérieur
seniority: *n.* ancienneté
senna: *n.* (bot) séné
sensation: *n.* sensation
sense: *n.* sens; sensation; raison; bon sens; sentiment

senseless: *adj.* insensé; sans connaissance
senselessness: *n.* manque de bon
sensibility: *n.* sensibilité
sensible: *adj.* sensé; raisonnable; sensible
sensibly: *adj.* raisonnablement
sensitive: *adj.* sensible
sensual: *adj.* sensuel
sentence components: éléments de la phrase
sentence: *n.* phrase; condamnation
sentence: *vt.* condamner; prononcer une sentence contre
sententious: *adj.* sentencieux
sentient: *adj.* sensible
sentiment: *adj.* sentimental
sentiment: *n.* sentiment; opinion
sentinel: *n.* sentinelle
sentry box: guérite
separable: *adj.* séparable
separate: *adj.* séparé; distinct
separate: *vt.* séparer; *vi.* se séparer
separation: *n.* séparation
September: *n.* septembre
septennial: *adj.* septennal
sepulchre: *n.* sépulcre
sequel: *n.* conséquence; suite
sequence of events: chronologie des évènements
sequence: *n.* ordre; série
sequester: *vt.* séquestrer
sequestration: *n.* séquestration
seraglio: *n.* sérail
seraph: *n.* séraphin
serenade: *n.* sérénade
serenade: *vt.* jouer une sérénade pour
serene: *adj.* serein
serenity: *n.* sérénité
serf: *n.* serf; serve
serge: *n.* serge
sergeant: *n.* sergent; caporal-chef; brigadier

serial: *adj.* en série; *n.* feuilleton; téléroman
series: *n.* série
serious: *adj.* sérieux; grave (injury)
sermon: *n.* sermon
serpent: *n.* serpent
serpentine: *adj.* sinueux; *n.* serpentine
serum: *n.* sérum
servant: *n.* domestique
servant-girl: *n.* servante; bonne
serve: *vt.* servir; desservir; faire; accomplir
service station: station-service
service: *n.* service; office; entretien
service: *vt.* entretenir; réviser
serviceable: *adj.* utilisable; pratique
servile: *adj.* servile
servitude: *n.* servitude; esclavage
session: *n.* séance; session; réunion
set: *n.* jeu; service; ensemble; groupe; bande; *adj.* fixe; figé; prêt; déterminé
set: *vt.* mettre; poser; placer; fixer; déterminer
settee: *n.* canapé
setting: *n.* disposition; cadre; monture
settle: *vt.* poser; installer; arranger; régler; calmer
settlement: *n.* règlement; établissement; accord; résolution; colonie; colonisation
settler: *n.* colon; colonisateur
seven: *adj.* sept
seventeen: *adj.* dix-sept
seventeenth: *adj.* dix-septième
seventh: *adj.* septième
seventieth: *adj.* soixante-dixième
seventy: *adj.* soixante-dix
sever: *vt.* séparer
several: *adj.* plusieurs; *pron.* plusieurs
severance: *n.* séparation

severe: *adj.* sévère; rigoureux; austère; dur
severity: *n.* sévérité
sew: *vt.* coudre
sewer: *n.* égout
sewerage: *n.* système d'égouts; eaux d'égout
sewing machine: machine à coudre
sex: *n.* sexe
sexist: *adj.* sexiste
sextant: *n.* sextant
sexton: *n.* sacristain
sexual reproduction: reproduction sexuelle
sexual: *adj.* sexuel
sexy: *adj.* sexy
shabbily: *adv.* petitement; mesquinement
shabbiness: *n.* aspect décrépit ou miteux
shabby: *adj.* miteux
shackle: *vt.* enchaîner
shade: *n.* ombre; obscurité; nuance; abat-jour
shade: *vt.* ombrager; abriter; atténuer
shadiness: *n.* ombre; ombrage
shadow: *n.* ombre
shadowy: *adj.* ombragé; sombre; indistinct
shady: *adj.* ombreux; ombragé; sombre
shaft: *n.* flèche; fût; puits; arbre; rayon
shag: *n.* tabac; cormoran huppé
shaggy: *adj.* hirsute
shake: *n.* secousse; tremblement
shake: *vt.* secouer; agiter; trembler; chanceler;
shaking: *adj.* tremblant
shaky: *adj.* tremblant
shallowness: *n.* manque de profondeur; futilité
shalow: *adj.* peu profond; superficiel; futile

sham: *n.* imitation; imposture; *adj.* feint; simulé
sham: *vt.* feindre
shame: *n.* honte
shame: *vt.* faire honte à; déshonorer
shamefaced: *adj.* honteux; confus
shameful: *adj.* honteux; scandaleux
shameless: *adj.* effronté
shamelessness: *n.* effronterie; impudeur
shammy: *n.* (peau de) chamois
shampoo: *n.* shampooing
shampoo: *vt.* faire un shampooing
shamrock: *n.* trèfle
shank: *n.* jambe; hampe; tuyau (de pipe); canon
shanty town: bidonville
shanty: *n.* baraque
shape: *n.* forme; figure; modèle
shape: *vt.* former; façonner; modeler
shapeless: *adj.* informe
shapely: *adj.* bien proportionné
share: *n.* part; portion; action
share: *vt.* partager; répartir
shared cataloguing: catalogage en coopération; partagé
sharer: *n.* participant
shark: *n.* requin
sharp: *adj.* aigu; acéré; malin; fin; pénétrant; *n.* dièse
sharpen: *vt.* aiguiser; affûter
sharply: *adv.* brusquement; sévèrement; vivement; nettement
sharpness: *n.* tranchant; finesse; acuité; aigreur
shatter: *vt.* fracasser; détruire; *vi.* se fracasser
shave: *n.* rasage
shave: *vt.* raser; raboter; *vi.* se raser
shavel: *n.* pelle
shavel: *vt.* pelleter
shaver: *n.* rasoir électrique
shaving brush: blaireau
shaving: *n.* rasage

shawl: *n.* châle
shear stress: cisaillement; force de
shear: *vt.* tondre
sheath: *n.* fourreau
shed: *n.* hangar; cabane
shed: *vt.* verser; répandre; perdre
sheen: *n.* lustre
sheep: *n.* mouton
sheepfold: *n.* parc à moutons
sheepish: *adj.* penaud; timide
sheepishness: *n.* timidité; air penaud
sheep-run: *n.* patûrage pour moutons
sheepskin: *n.* peau de mouton
sheer: *adj.* pur; absolu; véritable
sheet anchor: ancre de veille
sheet iron: tôle
sheet lightning: éclairs en nappes
sheet: *n.* drap; plaque; feuille; écoute
sheeting: *n.* toile pour draps
shelf: *n.* étagère; écueil
shell: *n.* coquille; carcasse; écorce; obus
shell: *vt.* écosser; décortiquer; bombarder; *vi.* se décortiquer
shelter: *n.* abri; asile; refuge
shelter: *vt.* abriter; protéger; *vi.* s'abriter
shelve: *vt.* mettre au rancart
shelving: *n.* rayonnage
shepherd: *n.* berger
shepherdess: *n.* bergère
sherbet: *n.* sorbet
sheriff: *n.* shérif
sherry: *n.* xérès
shield: *n.* bouclier; écran protecteur
shield: *vt.* protéger
shift: *n.* changement; roulement
shift: *vi.* changer; se déplacer; *vt.* changer; bouger; transférer
shinbone: *n.* tibia
shine: *n.* éclat
shine: *vi.* briller; reluire; illuminer; *vt.* cirer
shingle: *n.* galets; zona

shining: *adj.* resplendissant; *n.* éclat
shiny: *adj.* brillant; reluisant
ship: *n.* bateau; navire; bâtiment
ship: *n.* vaisseau amiral
ship: *vt.* embarquer; transporter; expédier
shipbuilding: *n.* construction navale
shipmate: *n.* camarade de bord
shipment: *n.* cargaison; expédition
shipowner: *n.* armateur
shipper: *n.* expéditeur; agent d'expédition
shipping agent: agent maritime
shipping company: compagnie maritime
shipping department: service des expéditions
shipping documents: documents d'expédition
shipping order: commande de l'étranger
shipwreck: *n.* naufrage
shirt: *n.* chemise
shiver: *vi.* frissonner
shoal: *n.* banc (de poissons)
shock absorber: amortisseur
shock: *n.* choc; décharge; coup
shock: *vt.* bouleverser; choquer
shoddy: *adj.* de mauvaise qualité
shoe polish: cirage
shoe: *n.* chaussure; fer (à cheval)
shoe: *vt.* chausser; ferrer (un cheval)
shoeblack: *n.* cireur de chaussures
shoehorn: *n.* chausse-pied
shoelace: *n.* lacet de chaussure
shoemaker: *n.* cordonnier
shoestring: *n.* lacet de chaussure
shoot: *n.* pousse
shoot: *vt.* tirer; lancer; décocher; *vi.* pousser; bourgeonner; s'élancer
shooter: *n.* tireur
shooting: *n.* fusillade; tir
shop: *n.* magasin; atelier
shopfront: *n.* devanture

shopkeeper: *n.* commerçant
shoplifter: *n.* voleur à l'étalage
shopper: *n.* acheteur
shopping centre: centre commercial
shopping: *n.* courses
shop-soiled: défraîchi
shore: *n.* rivage; bord; côte
short: *adj.* court; bref; succinct; concis
shortcoming: *n.* insuffisance; défaut
shorten: *vt.* raccourcir; abréger
shortness: *n.* petitesse; brièveté
short-sighted: *adj.* myope
short-sightedness: *n.* myopie
shortwave: *n.* ondes courtes
shot: *n.* coup; décharge; plomb; prise
shotgun: *n.* fusil de chasse
shoulder: *n.* épaule; accotement
shoulder: *vt.* charger sur son épaule
shout: *n.* cri; acclamation
shout: *vi.* crier; *vt.* crier
shouting: *n.* cris
shove: *n.* poussée
shove: *vt.* pousser
show business: monde du spectacle
show: *n.* exposition; spectacle; manifestation; salon
show: *vt.* montrer; faire voir; présenter; prouver; expliquer
shower: *n.* averse; douche
shower: *vi.* pleuvoir
showery: *adj.* pluvieux
showroom: *n.* salle d'exposition
showy: *adj.* voyant; ostentatoire
shred: *n.* lambeau; parcelle
shred: *vt.* mettre en lambeaux
shrew: *n.* mégère; musaraigne
shrewd: *adj.* astucieux; perspicace
shrewdness: *n.* astuce
shriek: *n.* hurlement
shriek: *vt.* hurler
shrill: *adj.* aigu; strident
shrillness: *n.* ton aigu
shrimp: *n.* crevette; nabot; avorton

shrine: *n.* lieu saint
shrink: *vi.* rétrécir; se réduire; rapetisser
shrivel: *vi.* se ratatiner; se flétrir; *vt.* ratatiner
shroud: *n.* voile; linceul
shroud: *vt.* envelopper; voiler; ensevelir
shrub: *n.* arbuste
shrubbery: *n.* massif d'arbustes
shrug: *n.* haussement d'épaules
shrug: *vt.* hausser les épaules
shudder: *n.* frisson
shudder: *vi.* frissonner
shuffle: *vt.* mélanger; battre
shun: *vt.* fuir; éviter
shunt: *vt.* aiguiller
shut: *vt.* fermer; *vi.* fermer
shutter: *n.* volet
shuttle: *n.* navette
shuttlecock: *n.* volant
shy: *adj.* timide; réservé; embarrassé
shyness: *n.* timidité
sibling: *n.* enfants de mêmes parents
sibyl: *n.* sibylle
sick leave: congé de maladie
sick pay: indemnité de maladie
sick: *adj.* malade; écoeuré
sicken: *vt.* rendre malade; *vi.* tomber malade
sickle: *n.* faucille
sickliness: *n.* état maladif
sickly: *adj.* maladif
sickness benefits: assurance maladie
sickness: *n.* maladie
side: *n.* côté; flanc; camp; parti; *adj.* latéral; secondaire
sideboard: *n.* buffet
sidelight: *n.* veilleuse
sidelong: *adj.* oblique
sidewalk: *n.* trottoir
sideways: *adv.* de côté; obliquement
sidle: *vi.* avancer de côté; avancer furtivement

sieve: *n.* tamis; crible; passoire
sieve: *vt.* tamiser
sift: *vt.* tamiser; passer au crible; dégager
sigh: *n.* soupir
sigh: *vi.* soupirer; gémir
sight: *n.* vue; mire; spectacle; *adj.* aveugle
sightly: *adj.* séduisant
sightseeing: *n.* tourisme
sigma bond: liaison sigma
sign language: laguage des signes
sign: *n.* signe; indication; panneau; geste; trace
sign: *vt.* signer
signal lamp: lampe de signalisation
signal: *n.* signal; *adj.* insigne; remarquable
signaletic bibliography: bibliographie signalétique
signalise: *vt.* signaler
signalman: *n.* aiguilleur
signature: *n.* signature
signet: *n.* sceau
significance: *n.* importance
significant: *adj.* considérable
signify: *vt.* signifier
signpost: *n.* poteau indicateur
silence: *n.* silence
silence: *vt.* imposer le silence à
silent partner: un commanditaire; bailleur de fonds
silent: *adj.* silencieux
silex: *n.* silex
silicon chip: puce électronique
silk: *n.* soie
silken: *adj.* soyeux; satiné
silkiness: *n.* soyeux
silkworm: *n.* ver à soie
silky: *adj.* soyeux; satiné
sill: *n.* rebord; seuil
silliness: *n.* stupidité; bêtise; niaiserie
silly: *adj.* bête; stupide
silver: *n.* argent; *adj.* en argent

silversmith: *n.* orfèvre
silvery: *adj.* argenté
similar: *adj.* semblable; similaire
similarity: *n.* ressemblance
simile: *n.* comparaison
simmer: *vi.* cuire à feu doux; mijoter
simony: *n.* simonie
simper: *n.* sourire affecté
simper: *vi.* minauder
simple: *adj.* simple; naïf
simpleton: *n.* nigaud
simplicity: *n.* simplicité; naïveté
simplification: *n.* simplification
simplify: *vt.* simplifier
simply: *adv.* simplement; seulement
simulate: *vt.* simuler; feindre
simulation: *n.* simulation
simultaneous: *adj.* simultané
sin: *n.* péché
sin: *vi.* pécher
since: *adv.* depuis; *prep.* depuis; *conj.* depuis que; puisque
sincere: *adj.* sincère
sincerity: *n.* sincérité
sinecure: *n.* sinécure
sinew: *n.* tendon
sinewy: *adj.* usclé; tendineux
sinful: *adj.* coupable; honteux
sinfulness: *n.* corruption; péché
sing: *vt.* chanter; célébrer
singe: *vt.* roussir
singer: *n.* chanteur
singing: *n.* chant
single: *adj.* seul; unique; simple; célibataire; *n.* aller simple
single: *vt.* distinguer; séparer
singly: *adv.* séparément
singular noun: nom singulier
singular: *adj.* singulier; rare; *n.* singulier
singularity: *n.* singularité
sinister: *adj.* sinistre; de mauvais augure; funeste
sink: *n.* évier

sink: *vi.* couler; sombrer; baisser; *vt.*
couler; faire sombrer; ruiner
sinking fund: fonds d'amortissement
sinner: *n.* pécheur; pécheresse
sinuosity: *n.* sinuosité
sinuous: *adj.* sinueux
sinus: *n.* sinus
sip: *n.* petite gorgée
sip: *vt.* boire à petites gorgées
siphon: *n.* siphon
sipiritualist: *n.* spiritualiste
sir: *n.* monsieur
sire: *n.* étalon
siren: *n.* sirène
sirloin: *n.* aloyau (de boeuf)
sister: *n.* soeur
sisterhood: *n.* solidarité féminine
sister-in-law: belle-soeur
sisterly: *adj.* de soeur
sit: *vi.* s'asseoir; se trouver; *vt.* se
présenter à
site: *n.* emplacement; site
sit-in: *n.* sit-in; manifestation
sitting room: salle de séjour
sitting: *n.* séance; réunion; position
assise
situated: *adj.* situé
situation: *n.* situation
six: *adj.* six
sixteen: *adj.* seize
sixteenth: *adj.* seizième
sixth: *adj.* sixième
sixtieth: *adj.* soixantième
sixty: *adj.* soixante
size: *n.* taille; grandeur; volume;
dimension; ampleur; étendue
sizeable: *adj.* assez grand
skate: *n.* patin
skate: *vi.* patiner
skateboard: *n.* planche à roulettes;
skateboard
skating rink: patinoire
skating: *n.* patinage
skein: *n.* écheveau

skeleton key: passe-partout
skeleton: *n.* squelette
sketch: *n.* croquis; esquisse
sketch: *vt.* equisser;
faire un croquis de
skewer: *n.* broche; brochette
skewer: *vt.* embrocher
ski boot: chaussure de ski
ski: *n.* ski
ski: *vi.* skier
skid: *n.* dérapage
skid: *vi.* déraper
skier: *n.* skieur
skiing: *n.* ski
skilful: *adj.* adroit; habile
skilfulness: *n.* habileté
skill: *n.* habileté; adresse; dextérité
skilled: *adj.* adroit; qualifié
skim: *vt.* écrémer; effleurer
skimmed milk: lait écrémé
skimmer: *n.* écumoire
skin diving: plongée sous-marine
skin: *n.* peau
skin: *vt.* écorcher
skinned: *adj.* dépouillé
skinny: *adj.* maigre; efflanqué
skip: *n.* saut; bond; benne
skip: *vi.* sautiller; gambader; *vt.*
sauter; passer
skirmish: *n.* escarmouche; *vi.*
s'engager dans une escarmouche
skirt: *n.* jupe; bordure
skirt: *vt.* contourner
skit: *n.* parodie; satire
skittish: *adj.* espiègle; fantasque;
coquet; inconstant
skittle: *n.* quille
skulk: *vi.* se cacher; rôder
furtivement
skull: *n.* crâne
skullcap: *n.* calotte
sky: *n.* ciel
skylight: *n.* lucarne
skyrocket: *n.* fusée

skyscraper: *n.* gratte-ciel
slab: *n.* dalle
slack: *adj.* lâche; mou; indolent; négligent
slacken: *vt.* relâcher; ralentir; diminuer; *vi.* se relâcher; ralentir
slackness: *n.* manque d'énergie; ralentissement; laisser-aller
slag: *n.* scories
slam: *vt.* claquer violemment; *vi.* se refermer en claquant
slander: *n.* calomnie
slander: *vt.* calomnier; dire du mal de
slanderer: *n.* calomniateur
slanderous: *adj.* calomnieux
slang: *n.* argot
slant: *n.* inclinaison; point de vue
slant: *vi.* pencher; être incliné
slanting: *adj.* en pente; incliné
slap: *n.* claque; *adv.* en plein
slap: *vt.* donner une claque à; gifler
slash prices: casser les prix
slash: *n.* entaille
slash: *vt.* entailler
slate: *n.* ardoise
slating: *n.* recouvrement en ardoises
slaughter: *n.* carnage; massacre
slaughter: *vt.* abattre; massacrer
slaughterer: *n.* tueur; meurtrier
slaughterhouse: *n.* abattoir
slave: *n.* esclave
slave: *vi.* travailler comme un nègre
slaver: *n.* bave
slaver: *vi.* baver
slavery: *n.* esclavage
slavish: *adj.* servile; d'esclave
slavishness: *n.* servilité
slay: *vt.* tuer
slayer: *n.* tueur
sledge: *n.* traîneau
sledgehammer: *n.* marteau de forgeron
sleek: *adj.* lisse et brillant; luisant
sleep: *n.* sommeil

sleep: *vi.* dormir
sleeper: *n.* dormeur
sleepiness: *n.* envie de dormir
sleeping bag: sac de couchage
sleeping pill: somnifère
sleepless: *adj.* sans sommeil
sleepwalking: *n.* somnambulisme
sleepy: *adj.* qui a envie de dormir; endormi
sleet: *n.* neige fondue
sleeve: *n.* manche
slender: *adj.* svelte; mince; élancé; faible
slenderness: *n.* sveltesse; minceur; faiblesse
slice: *n.* tranche; spatule
slice: *vt.* couper
slide: *n.* glissade; coulisse; diapositive; toboggan
slide: *vi.* glisser; faire des glissades
sliding: *adj.* glissant; coulissant
slight: *adj.* léger; mince; petit; *n.* affront
slight: *vt.* manquer d'égards pour
slightly: *adv.* légèrement
slightness: *n.* fragilité; insignifiance
slim: *adj.* mince
slim: *vi.* maigrir
slime: *n.* vase; dépôt visqueux
sliminess: *n.* viscosité
slimming: *n.* amaigrissement
slimy: *adj.* visqueux; gluant
sling: *n.* fronde; écharpe
sling: *vt.* lancer
slink: *n.* glissade; faux pas; oubli; fiche
slink: *vi.* s'en aller furtivement; s'éclipser; *vi.* glisser; se faufiler; *vt.* glisser
slipper: *n.* pantoufle
slippery: *adj.* glissant
slipshod: *adj.* négligé
slipway: *n.* cale
slit: *n.* fente; incision

slit: *vt.* fendre; inciser
slobber: *n.* bave
sloe: *n.* prunelle
slogan: *n.* slogan
sloop: *n.* sloop
slop: *n.* fange; bouillon
slope formula: formule de pente
slope: *n.* inclinaison; pente; déclivité; versant
slope: *vt.* incliner
sloping: *adj.* en pente; incliné
sloppy: *adj.* négligé; peu soigné
sloth: *n.* paresse
slouch: *vi.* manquer de tenue; se tenir d'une façon négligée
slovenliness: *n.* négligence; manque de soin
slovenly: *adj.* négligé; sale; débraillé
slow worm: orvet
slow: *adj.* lent; lourd; ennuyeux
slowness: *n.* lenteur; lourdeur; manque d'intérêt
slug: *n.* lingot; limace; jeton; coup
sluggish: *adj.* paresseux; léthargique
sluggishness: *n.* paresse; mollesse
sluice: *n.* écluse
sluice: *vt.* lâcher les vannes
slum: *n.* taudis; quartier pauvre
slumber: *n.* sommeil paisible
slumber: *vi.* dormir paisiblement
slump: *n.* effondrement
slur: *n.* calomnie
slur: *vt.* dénigrer; calomnier; mal articuler
slush: *n.* neige fondante
slut: *n.* traînée
sly: *adj.* rusé
slyness: *n.* ruse; finesse
smack: *n.* léger goût; claque; gros baiser retentissant
smack: *vi.* sentir; embrasser bruyamment; *vt.* donner une claque à
small: *adj.* petit
smallish: *adj.* assez petit

smallness: *n.* petitesse
smalltalk: *n.* conversation banale
smart: *adj.* élégant; rapide; astucieux; vif
smartly: *adv.* astucieusement; vivement; avec élégance; habilement
smartness: *n.* astuce; vivacité; finesse
smash: *n.* fracas; coup violent
smash: *vt.* casser; briser; détruire; *vi.* se briser; se fracasser
smattering: *n.* connaissances superficielles
smear: *n.* frottis
smear: *vt.* enduire; salir
smell: *n.* odorat; odeur; mauvaise odeur
smell: *vt.* sentir
smelly: *adj.* malodorant
smelt: *n.* éperlan
smelt: *vt.* fondre
smelter: *n.* fondeur
smile: *n.* sourire
smile: *vi.* sourire
smirk: *vi.* sourire d'un air affecté
smite: *vt.* frapper
smith: *n.* forgeron
smithy: *n.* forge
smock: *n.* blouse
smoke shop: bureau de tabac
smoke: *n.* fumée; vapeur
smoke: *vt.* fumer
smokeless: *adj.* sans fumée
smoker: *n.* fumeur
smoky: *adj.* enfumé; qui fume
smooth: *adj.* lisse; uni; égal; doucereux; mielleux
smooth: *vt.* lisser; aplanir; adoucir
smoothly: *adv.* facilement; doucement
smoothness: *n.* douceur; aspect lisse; air doucereux
smother: *vt.* étouffer; réprimer
smoulder: *vi.* couver; se consumer

smudge: *n.* tache
smudge: *vt.* étaler
smug: *adj.* suffisant
smuggle: *vt.* passer en contrebande
smuggler: *n.* contrebandier
smuggling: *n.* contrebande
smut: *n.* saleté; trace de suie
smuttiness: *n.* suie; obscénité
smutty: *adj.* noirci; obscène
snack bar: snack-bar
snack: *n.* collation
snag: *n.* obstacle
snail: *n.* escargot
snake: *n.* serpent
snap fastener: bouton-pression
snap: *n.* claquement; photographie
snap: *vt.* casser net; *vi.* se casser net; claquer; mordre
snapdragon: *n.* gueule-de loup
snare: *n.* piège; collet
snarl: *vi.* gronder férocement
snatch: *n.* geste vif; vol; fragment
snatch: *vt.* saisir; s'emparer de
sneak: *n.* faux jeton
sneak: *vi.* se glisser furtivement
sneer: *vi.* parler d'un ton méprisant; ricaner
sneeringly: *adv.* d'un ton méprisant
sneeze: *vi.* éternuer
sniff: *vt.* renifler; *vi.* renifler
snigger: *vi.* ricaner
snip: *n.* petit coup de ciseaux; petit bout
snip: *vt.* donner de petits coups de ciseaux dans
snipe: *n.* bécassine
sniper: *n.* franc-tireur
snivel: *n.* pleurnicherie
snivel: *vi.* pleurnicher
sniveller: *n.* pleurnicheur
snobbish: *adj.* snob
snooze: *n.* petit somme
snooze: *vi.* faire un somme
snore: *vi.* ronfler

snorkel: *n.* tube respiratoire
snort: *vi.* renifler fortement
snout: *n.* museau; groin
snow: *n.* neige
snow: *vi.* neiger
snowball: *n.* boule de neige
snowboard: *n.* surf des neiges
snowdrop: *n.* perce-neige
snowflake: *n.* flocon de neige
snowman: *n.* bonhomme de neige
snowplough: *n.* chasse-neige
snowy: *adj.* neigeux; enneigé
snub: *vt.* repousser; rejeter
snub-nosed: *adj.* au nez retroussé
snuff: *n.* tabac à priser
snuffbox: *n.* tabatière
snuffle: *vi.* parler d'une voix nasillarde; nasiller; renifler
snug: *adj.* confortable; douillet; bien abrité
so: *adv.* si; tellement; aussi; ainsi
soak: *vi.* tremper; *vt.* faire tremper
soap bubble: bulle de savon
soap opera: feuilleton à l'eau de rose
soap powder: lessive
soap: *n.* savon
soap: *vt.* savonner
soapsuds: *n.* mousse de savon
soapy: *adj.* savonneux
soar: *vi.* monter en flèche
sob: *n.* sanglot
sob: *vi.* sangloter
sober: *adj.* sobre; sérieux
sobriety: *n.* sobriété; sérieux; calme
soccer: *n.* football
sociability: *n.* sociabilité
sociable: *adj.* sociable; liant
sociably: *adv.* sociablement
social background: milieu social
social work: assistance sociale
social worker: assistant social
social: *adj.* social; sociable
socialism: *n.* socialisme
socialist: *n.* socialiste

society: *n.* société; compagnie
sociologist: *n.* sociologue
sociology: *n.* sociologie
sock: *n.* chaussette
socket: *n.* prise de courant
sod: *n.* gazon
soda: *n.* soude; soda
sofa: *n.* canapé
soft: *adj.* doux; moelleux; aimable; gentil
soften: *vt.* ramollir; adoucir; atténuer
soft-hearted: *adj.* compatissant
softness: *n.* douceur; mollesse
soft-spoken: *adj.* à la voix douce
software: *n.* logiciel
soil: *n.* salissure
soil: *vt.* salir; souiller
sojourn: *n.* séjour
sojourn: *vi.* séjourner
solace: *n.* consolation
solace: *vt.* consoler; soulager
solar mass: masse solaire
solar system: système solaire
solar: *adj.* solaire
solder: *n.* soudure
solder: *vt.* souder
soldier: *n.* soldat
soldierly: *adj.* militaire
sole: *n.* plante du pied; semelle de chaussure; sole; *adj.* seul; unique
solecism: *n.* solécisme
solemn: *adj.* solennel
solemnise: *vt.* solenniser
solemnity: *n.* solennité
solicit: *vt.* solliciter; quémander
solicitation: *n.* sollicitation
solicitor: *n.* notaire
solicitous: *adj.* plein de sollicitude
solicitude: *n.* sollicitude
solid: *adj.* solide; compact; *n.* solide
solidify: *vt.* solidifier
solidity: *n.* solidité
soliloquy: *n.* soliloque
solitaire: *n.* solitaire

solitary: *adj.* solitaire; retiré; *n.* anachorète
solitude: *n.* solitude
solo: *n.* solo
solstice: *n.* solstice
solubility: *n.* solubilité
soluble: *adj.* soluble
solution: *n.* solution
solve: *vt.* résoudre
solvency: *n.* solvabilité
solvent: *adj.* solvable; *n.* solvant
some: *adj.* du; de la; de l'; des; quelques; quelconque
somebody: *pron.* quelqu'un
somehow: *adv.* d'une façon ou d'une autre
someplace: *adv.* quelque part
something: *pron.* quelque chose
sometime: *adv.* au cours de; un jour ou l'autre
sometimes: *adv.* quelquefois; parfois
somewhat: *adv.* quelque peu
somewhere: *adv.* quelque part
somnambulism: *n.* somnambulisme
somnambulist: *n.* somnambule
somnolence: *n.* somnolence; *adj.* somnolent
son: *n.* fils
song: *n.* chanson
son-in-law: *n.* gendre
sonnet: *n.* sonnet
sonochemistry: *n.* sonochimie
sonorous: *adj.* sonore
soon: *adv.* bientôt; dès que
sooner: *adv.* plus tôt; plutôt
soot: *n.* suie
soothe: *vt.* calmer; apaiser; flatter
soothsayer: *n.* devin
sop: *n.* pain trempé
sophism: *n.* sophisme
sophist: *n.* sophiste
sophistical: *adj.* sophistiqué
sophisticated: *adj.* sophistiqué
sophistry: *n.* sophistique

sophomore: *n.* étudiant de seconde année
soporific: *adj.* soporifique
sorcerer: *n.* sorcier
sorceress: *n.* sorcière
sorcery: *n.* sorcellerie
sordid: *adj.* sordide; sale
sordidness: *n.* bassesse; saleté
sore: *n.* plaie; blessure; *adj.* douloureux; sensible; contrarié
sorrel: *n.* oseille; *adj.* alezan; roux
sorrow: *n.* peine; chagrin
sorrow: *vi.* se lamenter
sorrowful: *adj.* triste; affligé
sorry: *adj.* désolé; navré; déplorable
sort: *n.* sorte; genre; espèce; race; manière
sort: *vt.* classer; trier
soul: *n.* âme; essence; personne
sound: *adj.* sain; solide; valide; *n.* son; bruit
sound: *vt.* sonner; *vi.* sonner; retentir; ressembler; sembler
sounding board: table d'harmonie; abat-voix
soundings: *npl.* sondage; (mar) fonds
soundness: *n.* santé; solidité
soundtrack: *n.* bande sonore
soup: *n.* soupe
sour: *adj.* aigre; acide; acerbe; revêche
sour: *vt.* aigrir; faire tourner; *vi.* s'aigrir; tourner
source: *n.* source; origine
sourness: *n.* acidité; aigreur; acrimonie
souse: *n.* soûlard
souse: *vt.* mariner; faire tremper
south: *n.* sud; *adj.* sud; du sud; au sud
southerly: *adj.* du sud; sud; méridional
southward(s): *adv.* vers le sud
southwester: *n.* vent du sud-ouest; suroît

souvenir: *n.* souvenir
sovereign: *adj.* souverain
sovereignty: *n.* souveraineté
sow: *n.* truie
sow: *vt.* semer; disperser
sowing time: époque des semailles
soy: *n.* soja
spa: *n.* station thermale
space: *n.* espace; intervalle
space: *vt.* espacer
spacecraft: *n.* vaisseau spatial
spaceman: *n.* astronaute
spacious: *adj.* spacieux; ample
spaciousness: *n.* dimensions spacieuses; espace
spade: *n.* bêche; pique
Spain: *n.* Espagne
span: *n.* envergure
span: *vt.* enjamber; embrasser
spangle: *n.* paillette
spangle: *vt.* orner de paillettes
spaniel: *n.* épagneul
Spanish: *adj.* espagnol; *n.* espagnol; Espagnol
spar: *n.* espar
spar: *vi.* s'entraîner
spare part: pièce de rechange
spare: *adj.* de trop; de réserve
spare: *vt.* épargner; ménager; éviter; se passer de
sparing: *adj.* limité; modéré; économe
spark plug: bougie
spark: *n.* étincelle
sparkle: *n.* scintillement; étincelle
sparkle: *vi.* étinceler; briller
sparrow: *n.* moineau
sparrowhawk: *n.* épervier
sparse: *adj.* clairsemé; épars
spasm: *n.* spasme
spasmodic: *adj.* spasmodique
spatial organization: organisation spatiale
spatter: *vt.* éclabousser; *vi.* gicler

spatula: *n.* spatule
spawn: *n.* frai
spawn: *vt.* pondre; engendrer
spawning: *n.* frai
speak: *vt.* parler; dire; *vi.* parler; s'entretenir; prendre la parole
speaker: *n.* haut-parleur; interlocuteur; orateur
spear: *n.* lance; harpon
spear: *vt.* transpercer d'un coup de lance
special issue: un hors-série
special: *adj.* spécial; particulier
speciality: *n.* spécialité
species: *n.* espèce
specific gravity: densité
specific heat capacity: capacité de chaleur spécifique
specific: *adj.* spécifique; *n.* remède spécifique
specifically: *adv.* spécifiquement; explicitement
specification: *n.* spécification
specify: *vt.* spécifier
specimen: *n.* spécimen; exemple
specious: *adj.* spécieux
speckle: *n.* grain; tache
speckle: *vt.* tacheter; moucheter
spectacle: *n.* spectacle
spectator: *n.* spectateur
spectral: *adj.* spectral; *n.* analyse spectrale
spectre: *n.* spectre
spectroscope: *n.* spectroscope
speculate: *vi.* spéculer; méditer
speculation: *n.* spéculation; conjecture; méditation
speculative: *adj.* spéculatif; méditatif
speculum: *n.* spéculum
speech: *n.* parole; discours; langage; élocution
speechify: *vi.* discourir; pérorer
speechless: *adj.* muet
speed limit: limitation de vitesse

speed: *n.* vitesse; rapidité
speed: *vt.* presser; accélérer; *vi.* se presser
speedboat: *n.* vedette
speedily: *adv.* rapidement; vite
speediness: *n.* rapidité; promptitude; célérité
speedometer: *n.* compteur de vitesse
speedway: *n.* piste de course
speedy: *adj.* rapide; prompt
spell: *n.* charme; sortilège; période
spell: *vt.* écrire; épeler; ensorceler; envoûter; s'écrire; s'épeler
spelling: *n.* ortographe
spend: *vt.* dépenser; passer; épuiser; gaspiller
spendthrift: *n.* dépensier
spent: *adj.* épuisé
sperm: *n.* sperme
spermaceti: *n.* spermaceti
spew: *vi.* vomir
sphere: *n.* sphère
spherical: *adj.* sphérique
spice: *n.* épice
spice: *vt.* épicer
spick-and-span: *adj.* impeccable; tiré à quatre épingles
spicy: *adj.* épicé
spider: *n.* araignée
spigot: *n.* clef de robinet
spike: *n.* pointe; clou
spike: *vt.* clouter
spill: *vt.* renverser; répandre; *vi.* se répandre
spin: *adj.* spinal
spin: *n.* tournoiement; tour (en voiture)
spin: *vt.* filer; inventer; fabriquer; faire tourner; *vi.* tourner
spinach: *n.* épinard
spindle: *n.* fuseau; broche
spine: *n.* colonne vertébrale; épine dorsale
spinet: *n.* (mus) épinette

spinner: *n.* fileur; fileuse
spinning wheel: rouet
spin-off: *n.* sous-produit
spinster: *n.* célibataire
spiral: *adj.* en spirale
spire: *n.* flèche; aiguille; tige
spirit lamp: lampe à alcool
spirit: *n.* esprit; âme; caractère
spirit: *vt.* encourager; animer
spirited: *adj.* vif; fougueux
spiritless: *adj.* sans entrain; abattu
spiritual: *adj.* spirituel
spirituality: *n.* spiritualité
spit: *n.* crachat; salive
spit: *vt.* cracher; crépiter
spite: *n.* dépit; rancune
spite: *vt.* vexer
spiteful: *adj.* rancunier; malveillant
spitefulness: *n.* méchanceté; rancune
spittle: *n.* salive; crachat
splash: *n.* éclaboussure; tache
splash: *vt.* éclabousser; faire gicler; *vi.* barboter
spleen: *n.* rate; spleen
splendid: *adj.* splendide; magnifique
splendour: *n.* splendeur; magnificence
splice: *vt.* (mar) épisser; abouter
splint: *n.* éclisse
splinter: *n.* éclat; esquille; écharde
splinter: *vt.* fendre en éclats
split: *n.* fente; rupture
split: *vt.* fendre; diviser; *vi.* se fendre
spoil: *vt.* abîmer; gâter; gâcher
spoiled: *adj.* abîmé; gâté
spoke: *n.* rayon (de roue)
spokesman: *n.* porte-parole
sponge: *n.* éponge
sponge: *vt.* éponger; *vi.* être un parasite
sponger: *n.* parasite
sponginess: *n.* spongiosité
spongy: *adj.* spongieux
sponsor: *n.* caution; parrain; marraine

sponsorship: *n.* parrainage
spontaneity: *n.* spontanéité
spool: *n.* bobine; rouleau
spoon: *n.* cuiller
spoonful: *n.* cuillerée
sporadical: *adj.* sporadique
sport: *n.* sport; jeu; divertissement; amusement
sports car: voiture de sport
sports jacket: veste sport
sportsman: *n.* sportif
sportswear: *n.* vêtements de sport
spot: *n.* tache; point; endroit; pois
spot: *vt.* apercevoir; tacher
spotless: *adj.* impeccable; immaculé
spotlight: *n.* feu de projecteur
spotted; spotty: *adj.* tacheté; à pois
spouse: *n.* époux; épouse
spout: *n.* bec; gargouille; jet
spout: *vi.* jaillir; gicler; déblatérer; *vt.* faire jaillir
sprain: *n.* entorse
sprain: *vt.* fouler
sprawl: *vi.* s'étaler
spray: *n.* spray; pulvérisation; embruns
spread: *n.* propagation; diffusion
spread: *vt.* étendre; étaler; répandre; propager; *vi.* s'étendre; se répandre
spree: *n.* fête
sprig: *n.* brin
sprightliness: *n.* vivacité; entrain
sprightly: *adj.* alerte; vif; fringant
spring tide: grande marée
spring: *n.* printemps; élasticité; ressort; saut; source
spring: *vi.* bondir; sauter; provenir; découler; émaner; naître
springiness: *n.* élasticité
springtime: *n.* printemps
springwater: *n.* eau de source
springy: *adj.* élastique
sprinkle: *vt.* arroser
sprinkling: *n.* arrosage

sprout: *n.* pousse; germe
sprout: *vi.* germer
spruce: *adj.* net; impeccable
spruce: *vi.* se mettre sur son trente-et-un
spruceness: *n.* élégance
spur: *n.* éperon; ergot (coq); stimulant
spur: *vt.* éperonner; stimuler
spurious: *adj.* faux; feint; falsifié; de contrefaçon
spurn: *vt.* repousser avec mépris
sputter: *vi.* postillonner; bredouiller; bafouiller
spy: *n.* espion
spy: *vt.* apercevoir; espionner; *vi.* espionner.
squabble: *n.* querelle; dispute
squabble: *vi.* se disputer; se quereller
squad: *n.* escouade; brigade; équipe
squadron: *n.* escadron
squalid: *adj.* misérable; sordide
squall: *n.* rafale; bourrasque
squall: *vi.* brailler
squally: *adj.* qui souffle en rafales
squalor: *n.* saleté; misère
squander: *vt.* gaspiller; dilapider
square brackets: crochets
square unit: unité carrée
square: *adj.* carré; catégorique; honnête; *n.* carré; place; équerre
square: *vt.* cadrer; mettre en
squareness: *n.* forme carrée
squash: *n.* squash
squash: *vt.* écraser
squat: *adj.* accroupi; trapu; courtaud
squat: *vi.* s'accroupir
squaw: *n.* squaw; femme peaurouge
squeak: *n.* cri; couinement
squeak: *vi.* grincer; crier
squeal: *vi.* pousser un cri aigu; couiner
squeamish: *adj.* impressionable; délicat

squeeze: *n.* pression; serrement de main; cohue
squeeze: *vt.* presser; tordre; comprimer
squid: *n.* calmar
squint: *adj.* atteint de strabisme; *n.* strabisme
squint: *vi.* loucher
squirrel: *n.* écureuil
squirt: *n.* giclée; jet
squirt: *vt.* faire gicler
stab: *n.* coup de couteau
stab: *vt.* poignarder
stabile: *adj.* stable
stabile: *n.* écurie
stabile: *vt.* mettre à l'écurie
stability: *n.* stabilité; solidité
stack: *n.* pile
stack: *vt.* empiler
stadium: *n.* stade
staff: *n.* personnel; bâton; soutien
stag: *n.* cerf
stage: *n.* étape; scène; théâtre; stade; estrade
stagger: *vi.* vaciller; tituber; hésiter; *vt.* stupéfier; échelonner
stagnant: *adj.* stagnant
stagnate: *vi.* stagner
stagnation: *n.* stagnation
staid: *adj.* posé; sérieux; guindé
stain: *n.* tache
stain: *vt.* tacher; ternir
stainless: *adj.* sans tache; immaculé
stair: *n.* marche
staircase: *n.* escalier
stake: *n.* pieu; enjeu
stake: *vt.* marquer; délimiter
stale: *adj.* rassis; rance
staleness: *n.* manque de fraîcheur; rance
stalk: *n.* tige; queue; trognon
stalk: *vi.* avancer d'un air majestueux
stall: *n.* stalle; stand; étalage
stall: *vt.* caler; *vi.* caler; atermoyer

stallion: *n.* étalon
stalwart: *n.* partisan fidèle
stamen: *n.* étamine
stamina: *n.* résistance
stammer: *n.* bégaiement
stammer: *vi.* bégayer
stamp: *n.* timbre; cachet; tampon; empreinte; estampille
stamp: *vt.* trépigner; timbrer; affranchir; tamponner; *vi.* trépigner
stampede: *n.* débandade
stand: *n.* position; support; étalage; état; tribune; stand
stand: *vi.* être debout; se tenir; se maintenir; *vt.* poser; résister; soutenir;
standard form: forme standard
standard: *n.* étendard; modèle; étalon; norme; *adj.* normal
standing: *adj.* permanent; fixe; établi; en pied; *n.* durée; importance; rang
standstill: *n.* arrêt; immobilisation
staple: *n.* agrafe; *adj.* principal; de base
staple: *vt.* agrafer
star: *n.* étoile; astérisque
starboard: *n.* tribord
starch: *n.* amidon
starch: *vt.* amidonner
stark: *adj.* raide; rigide; cru; *adv.* complètement
starling: *n.* étourneau
starry: *adj.* étoilé
start: *n.* début; ouverture; sursaut; départ; avance
start: *vt.* commencer; débuter; démarrer
starter: *n.* starter; démarreur
starting point: point de départ
startle: *vt.* faire sursauter
startling: *adj.* surprenant; alarmant
starvation: *n.* inanition; fai
starve: *vi.* mourir de faim
state: *n.* état; condition; pompe

state: *vt.* déclarer; exposer
stateliness: *n.* majesté; grandeur
stately: *adj.* majestueux; imposant
statement of invoices: relevé de factures
statement: *n.* déclaration; affirmation
statesman: *n.* homme d'État
statesmanship: *n.* qualité d'homme politique
static: *adj.* statique; *n.* parasites
station: *n.* station; place; position
station: *vt.* placer
stationary: *adj.* stationnaire; immobile
stationer: *n.* papetier
stationery: *n.* papeterie
statistical: *adj.* statistique
statistics: *npl.* statistiques
statuary: *n.* statuaire
statue: *n.* statue
stature: *n.* stature; taille
status: *n.* statut; condition légal
statute: *n.* statut; loi
stay: *n.* séjour
stay: *vi.* rester; demeurer
stead: *n.* place; lieu
steadfast: *adj.* ferme; résolu; inébranlable
steadily: *adv.* fermement; régulièrement
steadiness: *n.* fermeté; stabilité
steady: *adj.* stable; solide
steady-state: état quasistationnaire
steak: *n.* bifteck; steak
steal: *vt.* voler
stealth: *n.* discrétion
stealthily: *adv.* furtivement
stealthy: *adj.* furtif
steam distillation: entraînement à la vapeur
steam engine: locomotive à vapeur
steam: *n.* vapeur; buée
steam: *vt.* cuire à la vapeur; *vi.* fumer

steamer: *n.* bateau à vapeur; paquebot
steel: *n.* acier; *adj.* d'acier
steelyard: *n.* balance romaine
steep: *adj.* abrupt; excessif
steep: *vt.* tremper
steeple: *n.* clocher; flèche
steeplechase: *n.* steeple
steepness: *n.* raideur; escarpement
steer: *n.* bouvillon
steer: *vt.* conduire; diriger; gouverner; *vi.* tenir le gouvernail
steering wheel: volant
steering: *n.* direction
stellar: *adj.* stellaire
stem: *n.* tige; tronc; souche; pied; tuyau
stem: *vt.* endiguer
stench: *n.* odeur fétide
stencil: *n.* stencil; pochoir
stenographer: *n.* sténographe
stenography: *n.* sténographie
step: *n.* pas; marche; trace
step: *vi.* faire un pas; marcher
stepbrother: *n.* demi-frère
stepdaughter: *n.* belle-fille
stepfather: *n.* beau-père
stepmother: *n.* belle-mère
stepping stone: pierre de gué
stepsister: *n.* demi-soeur
stepson: *n.* beau-fils
stereo: *n.* stéréo
stereotype: *n.* stéréotype; stéréotyper
sterile: *adj.* stérile
sterility: *n.* stérilité
sterling: *adj.* de bon aloi; vrai; véritable; *n.* livres sterling
stern: *adj.* sévère; rigide; strict; *n.* poupe
stevedore: *n.* docker
stew: *n.* ragoût
stew: *vt.* faire cuire â l'étouffée
steward: *n.* intendant; steward
stewardess: *n.* hôtesse de l'air

stewardship: *n.* intendance
stick: *n.* bâton; canne; baguette
stick: *vt.* coller; piquer; planter; supporter; *vi.* tenir; se planter
stickiness: *n.* viscosité
stick-up: *n.* braquage; hold-up
sticky: *adj.* collant; poisseux
stiff neck: torticolis
stiff: *adj.* raide; rigide; inflexible; dur; entêté
stiffen: *vt.* raidir; renforcer; *vi.* se raidir
stiffness: *n.* raideur; rigidité; opiniâtreté
stifle: *vt.* étouffer
stifling: *adj.* suffocant
stigma: *n.* stigmate
stigmatise: *vt.* stigmatiser
stile: *n.* tourniquet
stiletto: *n.* stylet; talon aiguille
still: *adj.* silencieux; calme; *adv.* encore; toujours; quand même
still: *vt.* calmer; apaiser; faire taire
stillborn: *adj.* mort-né
stillness: *n.* calme; tranquillité
stilts: *npl.* échasses
stimulant: *n.* stimulant
stimulate: *vt.* stimuler
stimulation: *n.* stimulant; stimulation
stimulus: *n.* stimulant
sting: *n.* dard; piqûre; aiguillon
sting: *vt.* piquer; *vi.* brûler
stingily: *adv.* avec avarice
stinginess: *n.* mesquinerie; avarice
stingy: *adj.* mesquin; avare; pingre
stink: *n.* puanteur
stink: *vi.* puer
stint: *n.* tâche assignée
stipulate: *vt.* stipuler
stipulation: *n.* stipulation
stir: *n.* agitation; émoi
stir: *vt.* remuer; agiter; exciter; *vi.* remuer; bouger
stirrup: *n.* étrier

stitch: *n.* point; point de suture
stitch: *vt.* coudre
stoat: *n.* hermine
stock control card: fiche de stock
stock exchange: bourse
stock shortage: rupture de stock
stock: *n.* réserve; provision; action
stock: *vt.* approvisionner; stocker
stockade: *n.* prison militaire
stockbroker: *n.* agent de change
stockholder: *n.* actionnaire
stocking: *n.* bas
stoic: *adj.* stoïque; *n.* stoïque
stoicism: *n.* stoïcisme
stole: *n.* étole
stomach: *n.* estomac; ventre
stomach: *vt.* digérer; endurer
stone deaf: sourd comme un pot
stone: *n.* pierre; caillou; noyau; *adj.*
de pierre
stone: *vt.* lancer des pierres sur;
dénoyauter; empierrer
stoning: *n.* empierrement
stony: *adj.* pierreux; rocailleux; dur
stool: *n.* tabouret; rebord; appui
stoop: *n.* inclination en avant
stoop: *vi.* se baisser; se pencher
stop: *n.* arrêt; halte; pause; point
stop: *vt.* arrêter; interrompre;
boucher; *vi.* s'arrêter; cesser
stopover: *n.* escale; étape
stoppage: *n.* obstruction;
engorgement; suppression
stopwatch: *n.* chronomètre
storage: *n.* emmagasinage;
entreposage
store: *n.* provision; réserve; entrepôt;
magasin
store: *vt.* mettre en réserve;
accumuler; emmagasiner
storekeeper: *n.* marchand
storey: *n.* étage
stork: *n.* cigogne
storm: *n.* tempête; orage; assaut

storm: *vt.* prendre d'assaut; *vi.* faire
rage
stormily: *adv.* violemment
stormy: *adj.* orageux; houleux
story: *n.* histoire; récit; étage
stout: *adj.* corpulent; robuste;
vigoureux; solide
stoutness: *n.* vigueur; puissance;
corpulence
stove: *n.* poêle; cuisinière
stow: *vt.* ranger; mettre en place;
arrimer
straggle: *vi.* être disséminé
straggler: *n.* traînard
straight angle: angle droit
straight: *adj.* droit; direct; franc; *adv.*
droit; directement
straightaway: *adv.* immédiatement;
tout de suite
straighten: *vt.* redresser
straightforward: *adj.* honnête; franc;
direct
straightforwardness: *n.* honnêteté
strain: *n.* tension; effort; entorse;
contrainte; lignée; accent; ton
strain: *vt.* tendre; fouler; forcer;
mettre à l'épreuve; *vi.* peiner
strainer: *n.* passoire
strait: *n.* détroit; embarras; situation
critique
strait-jacket: *n.* camisole de force
strand: *n.* brin; rivage; rive
strange: *adj.* inconnu; étrange
strangeness: *n.* étrangeté; nouveauté
stranger: *n.* inconnu; étranger
strangle: *vt.* étrangler
strangulation: *n.* strangulation
strap: *n.* lanière; sangle; courroie
strap: *vt.* attacher avec une courroie
strapping: *adj.* robuste; charpenté
stratagem: *n.* stratagème
strategic: *adj.* stratégique
strategy: *n.* stratégie
stratum: *n.* strate

straw: *n.* paille
strawberry: *n.* fraise
stray: *adj.* perdu; errant
stray: *vi.* s'égarer; vagabonder
streak: *n.* raie; bande; filet
streak: *vt.* strier
stream: *n.* ruisseau; rivière; torrent
stream: *vi.* ruisseler
streamer: *n.* serpentin
stream-of-consciousness: courant de conscience
street: *n.* rue
streetcar: *n.* tramway
strength: *n.* force; puissance; vigueur; robustesse
strengthen: *vt.* fortifier; confirmer; renforcer
strenuous: *adj.* ardu; vigoureux
stress: *n.* pression; stress; tension; contrainte; importance
stretch: *n.* extension; étendue; période
stretch: *vt.* étendre; étirer; élargir; forcer; *vi.* s'étendre; s'étirer
stretcher: *n.* brancard
strew: *vt.* éparpiller; semer
strict: *adj.* strict; sévère; exact; rigoureux; précis
strictness: *n.* sévérité; rigueur
stride: *n.* grand pas
stride: *vi.* marcher à grandes enjambées
strife: *n.* conflit; lutte
strike: *n.* coup; grève; découverte
strike: *vt.* frapper; heurter; attaquer; rayer; *vi.* frapper; se mettre en grève; sonner
striker: *n.* gréviste
striking: *adj.* frappant; saisissant
string: *adj.* filandreux
string: *n.* ficelle; corde; cordon; rang; fibre
string: *vt.* munir d'une corde; enfiler; suspendre

stringent: *adj.* rigoureux
strip: *n.* bande; langue; bandelette
strip: *vt.* déshabiller; dévêtir; *vi.* se déshabiller
stripe: *n.* raie; rayure; coup de fouet
stripe: *vt.* rayer
strive: *vi.* s'efforcer; s'évertuer; lutter; se battre
stroke: *n.* coup; trait; course; caresse; apoplexie
stroke: *vt.* caresser
stroll: *n.* petit tour
stroll: *vi.* flâner
strong acid: acide fort
strong: *adj.* fort; vigoureux; robuste; puissant; intense
strongbox: *n.* coffre-fort
stronghold: *n.* forteresse
strophe: *n.* strophe
structural formula: formule structurelle
structure: *n.* structure; construction
struggle: *n.* lutte
struggle: *vi.* lutter; se battre; se démener
strum: *vt.* tapoter de
strut: *n.* démarche affectée
strut: *vi.* se pavaner
stub: *n.* souche; bout; talon
stubble: *n.* chaume; barbe de plusieurs jours
stubborn: *adj.* entêté; obstiné
stubbornness: *n.* entêtement; obstination
stucco: *n.* stuc
stud horse: étalon
stud: *n.* clou; crampon; écurie
student: *n.* étudiant
studio apartment: studio
studio: *n.* studio; atelier
studious: *adj.* studieux; sérieux
study: *n.* étude; études; méditation
study: *vt.* étudier; observer; *vi.* étudier; faire des études

stuff: *n.* matière; matériaux; étoffe
stuff: *vt.* rembourrer; remplir;
empailler
stuffing: *n.* rembourrage
stuffy: *adj.* mal aéré; collet monté
stumble: *n.* faux pas; trébuchement
stumble: *vi.* trébucher
stumbling block: hésitation; pierre
d'achoppement
stump: *n.* souche; moignon; bout
stun: *vt.* étourdir; stupéfier
stunner: *n.* personne ou chose
extraordinaire
stunt: *n.* cascade; coup de publicité
stunt: *vt.* empêcher de croître
stuntman: *n.* cascadeur
stupefy: *vt.* hébéter; stupéfier
stupendous: *adj.* prodigieux;
remarquable
stupid: *adj.* stupide
stupidity: *n.* stupidité
stupor: *n.* stupeur
sturdily: *adv.* fortement
sturdiness: *n.* force; robustesse;
résolution
sturdy: *adj.* vigoureux; robuste; fort;
hardi; résolu
sturgeon: *n.* esturgeon
stutter: *vi.* bégayer
sty: *n.* porcherie; taudis
stye: *n.* orgelet
style sheet: feuille de style
style: *n.* style; mode
style: *vt.* appeler; dénommer; créer;
dessiner
stylish: *adj.* élégant; qui a du chic
suave: *adj.* gentil; mélodieux;
adorable; *adv.* doux; sucré; *n.* bonbon
suave: *adj.* suave
subdivide: *vt.* subdiviser
subdivision: *n.* subdivision
subdue: *vt.* subjuguer; assujettir;
contenir; réfréner; adoucir

subject catalogue: catalogue-
matières
subject noun: nom sujet
subject: *adj.* soumis; sujet à
subject-heading: en-tête matière
subjection: *n.* sujétion
subjective: *adj.* subjectif
subjectivity: *n.* subjectivité
subjugate: *vt.* subjuguer; assujettir
subjugation: *n.* subjugation
subjunctive: *n.* subjonctif
sublet: *vt.* sous-louer
sublimate: *vt.* sublimer
sublimation: *n.* sublimation
sublime: *adj.* sublime; suprême; *n.*
sublime
sublimity: *n.* sublimité
submachine gun: mitraillette
submarine: *adj.* sous-marin; *n.* sous-
marin
submerge: *vt.* submerger
submersion: *n.* submersion
submission: *n.* soumission
submissive: *adj.* soumis; docile
submissiveness: *n.* docilité;
soumission
submit: *vt.* soumettre; *vi.* se
soumettre
subordinate: *adj.* subalterne;
inférieur
subordinate: *vt.* subordonner
subordination: *n.* subordination
subpoena: *n.* assignation à
comparaître
subscribe: *vi.* souscrire; *vt.* apposer;
signer
subscriber: *n.* souscripteur
subscription: *n.* souscription
subsequent: *adj.* ultérieur
subservient: *adj.* subordonné; utile
subside: *vi.* s'affaisser; baisser
subsidence: *n.* affaissement
subsidiary: *adj.* subsidiaire; *n.* filiale

subsidise: *vt.* subventionner; fournir des subsides à

subsidy: *n.* subvention; subside

subsist: *vi.* subsister; exister

subsistence: *n.* existence; subsistance

substance: *n.* substance; fond; essentiel

substantial: *adj.* considérable; réel; substantiel; solide

substantiate: *vt.* justifier

substantive: *n.* substantif

substitute: *n.* remplaçant

substitute: *vt.* substituer

substitution: *n.* substitution

substratum: *n.* substrat

subterfuge: *n.* subterfuge; faux fuyant

subterranean: *adj.* souterrain

subtitle: *n.* sous-titre

subtle: *adj.* subtile

subtlety: *n.* subtilité

subtly: *adv.* subtilement

subtract: *vt.* soustraire

subtraction: *n.* soustraction

suburb: *n.* banlieue

suburban: *adj.* de banlieue

subversion: *n.* subversion

subversive: *adj.* subversif

subvert: *vt.* subvertir; renverser

subway: *n.* métro

succeed: *vi.* réussir; succéder; avoir du succès; *vt.* succéder à; suivre

success: *n.* succès

successful: *adj.* couronné de succès; qui réussit

succession: *n.* succession

successive: *adj.* successif

successor: *n.* successeur

succinct: *adj.* succinct; concis

succulent: *adj.* succulent

succumb: *vi.* succomber

such: *adj.* tel; pareil

suck: *vt.* sucer; téter

suckle: *vt.* allaiter

suckling: *n.* nourrisson

suction: *n.* succion

sudden: *adj.* soudain; subit

suddenness: *n.* soudaineté

suds: *npl.* mousse de savon

sue: *vt.* poursuivre en justice; supaller

suede: *n.* daim

suet: *n.* graisse de rognon de boeuf

suffer: *vt.* souffrir; subir; tolérer; endurer; *vi.* souffrir

suffering: *n.* souffrance; douleur

suffice: *vi.* suffire; être suffisant

sufficiency: *n.* quantité suffisante; aisance

sufficient: *adj.* suffisant

suffix: *n.* suffixe

suffocate: *vt.* étouffer

suffocation: *n.* suffocation

suffrage: *n.* suffrage; vote

suffuse: *vt.* baigner; se répandre sur

sugar beet: betterave à sucre

sugar cane: canne à sucre

sugar lof: pain de sucre

sugar plum: bonbon

sugar: *n.* sucre

sugar: *vt.* sucrer

sugary: *adj.* sucré

suggest: *vt.* suggérer

suggestion: *n.* suggestion

suicidal: *adj.* suicidaire

suicide: *n.* suicide; suicidé

suit: *n.* procès; pétition; costume; tailleur; requête

suit: *vt.* convenir à; aller à; arranger; adapter

suitable: *adj.* qui convient; approprié

suitably: *adv.* convenablement

suitcase: *n.* valise

suite: *n.* suite; escorte; mobilier; cortège

suitor: *n.* plaideur; prétendant

sulkiness: *n.* bouderie

sulky: *adj.* boudeur; maussade

sullen: *adj.* maussade; sombre

sullenness: *n.* maussaderie; silence
sulphur: *n.* soufre
sulphurous: *adj.* sulfureux
sultan: *n.* sultane; raisin sec
sultry: *adj.* étouffant; chaud
sum: *n.* somme; total
sum: *vt.* résumer; récapituler; *vi.* résumer
summarily: *adv.* sommairement
summarize: *vt.* résumer; récapituler
summary: *adj.* résumé; *n.* résumé
summer: *n.* été
summerhouse: *n.* gloriette; pavillon de jardin
summit: *n.* sommet; cime
summon: *vt.* convoquer; citer à comparaître; sommer
summons: *n.* convocation; sommation
sumptuous: *adj.* somptueux
sun roof: toit ouvrant
sun: *n.* soleil
sunbathe: *vi.* prendre un bain de soleil; se faire bronzer
sunblock: *n.* écran total
sunburnt: *adj.* bronzé; hâlé
Sunday: *n.* dimanche
sundial: *n.* cadran solaire
sundry: *adj.* divers; différent
sunflower: *n.* tournesol
sunglasses: *npl.* lunettes de soleil
sunless: *adj.* sans soleil
sunlight: *n.* lumière du soleil
sunny: *adj.* ensoleillé; radieux
sunrise: *n.* lever de soleil
sunscreen: *n.* crème solaire
sunset: *n.* coucher de soleil
sunshade: *n.* parasol
sunshine: *n.* lumière du soleil; ensoleillement
sunstroke: *n.* insolation
suntan oil: huile solaire
suntan: *n.* bronzage
super: *adj.* sensationnel

superannuated: *adj.* en retraite
superannuation: *n.* retraite; pension de retraite
superb: *adj.* superbe
supercargo: *n.* subrécargue
supercilious: *adj.* hautain; dédaigneux
superficial: *adj.* superficiel
superfluity: *n.* surabondance; superfluité
superfluous: *adj.* superflu
superhuman: *adj.* surhumain
superintendent: *n.* directeur
superior: *adj.* supérieur; *n.* supérieur
superiority: *n.* supériorité
superlative: *adj.* superlatif; *n.* superlatif
supermarket: *n.* supermarché
supernatural: *n.* surnaturel
supernumerary: *adj.* surnuméraire
superpower: *n.* superpuissance
supersede: *vt.* remplacer; supplanter
supersonic: *adj.* supersonique
superstition: *n.* superstition
superstitious: *adj.* superstitieux
superstructure: *n.* superstructure
supertanker: *n.* gros pétrolier; supertanker
supervene: *vi.* survenir
supervise: *vt.* surveiller; superviser
supervision: *n.* surveillance
supervisor: *n.* surveillant
supine: *adj.* couché; étendu sur le dos; indolent
supper: *n.* diner
supplant: *vt.* supplanter
supple: *adj.* souple; flexible
supplement: *n.* supplément
supplementary: *adj.* supplémentaire
suppleness: *n.* souplesse
supplicate: *vt.* supplier
supplication: *n.* supplique; supplication
supplier: *n.* fournisseur

supply: *n.* approvisionnement; provision
supply: *vt.* fournir; approvisionner; suppléer à; remédier à
support: *n.* appui
support: *vt.* soutenir; supporter; appuyer
supportable: *adj.* supportable
supporter: *n.* partisan; supporter; adepte
supporting detail: détail à l'appui
suppose: *vt.* supposer
supposition: *n.* supposition
suppress: *vt.* supprimer
suppression: *n.* suppression
supremacy: *n.* suprématie
supreme: *adj.* suprême
surcharge: *n.* surtaxe
surcharge: *vt.* surcharger
sure: *adj.* sûr; certain; infaillible
sureness: *n.* certitude; sûreté
surety: *n.* certitude; caution
surf: *n.* ressac
surface tension: tension de surface
surface: *n.* surface
surface: *vt.* revêtir; *vi.* remonter à la surface
surfboard: *n.* planche
surfeit: *n.* excès
surge: *n.* vague; montée
surge: *vi.* déferler
surgeon: *n.* chirurgien
surgery: *n.* chirurgie
surgical: *adj.* chirurgical
surliness: *n.* air revêche; bourru
surly: *adj.* revêche; bourru
surmise: *n.* conjecture
surmise: *vt.* conjecturer
surmount: *vt.* surmonter
surmountable: *adj.* surmontable
surname: *n.* nom de famille
surpass: *vt.* surpasser; dépasser
surpassing: *adj.* sans pareil; incomparable

surplice: *n.* surplis
surplus: *n.* excédent; surplus; *adj.* en surplus
surprise: *n.* surprise
surprise: *vt.* surprendre
surprising: *adj.* surprenant
surrender: *n.* reddition
surrender: *vt.* rendre; céder; *vi.* se rendre
surreptitious: *adj.* subreptice
surrogate mother: mère porteuse
surrogate: *n.* substitut
surrogate: *vt.* remplacer
surround: *vt.* entourer; cerner; encercler
surroundings: *npl.* environs
survey: *n.* enquête; relevé (des plans)
survey: *vt.* examiner; inspecter; faire le relevé de
survive: *vi.* survivre; *vt.* survivre a
survivor: *n.* survivant
susceptibility: *n.* sensibilité
susceptible: *adj.* sensible
suspect: *n.* suspect
suspect: *vt.* soupçonner
suspend: *vt.* suspendre
suspense: *n.* incertitude; suspense
suspension bridge: pont suspendu
suspension: *n.* suspension
suspicion: *n.* soupçon
suspicious: *adj.* soupçonneux
suspiciousness: *n.* caractère soupçonneux
sustain: *vt.* soutenir; supporter; maintenir; subir
sustenance: *n.* subsistance
suture: *n.* suture
swab: *n.* tampon; prélèvement
swaddle: *vt.* emmailloter
swagger: *vi.* plastronner
swallow: *n.* hirondelle
swallow: *vt.* avaler
swamp: *n.* marais
swampy: *adj.* marécageux

swan: *n.* cygne
swap: *n.* échange
swap: *vt.* échanger
swarm: *n.* essaim; grouillement; nuée
swarm: *vi.* fourmiller; grouiller de monde; pulluler
swarthiness: *n.* teint basané
swarthy: *adj.* basané
swath: *n.* andain
swathe: *n.* bande
swathe: *vt.* emmailloter
sway: *n.* balancement; emprise; domination; puissance
sway: *vt.* balancer; *vi.* se balancer; osciller
swear: *vt.* jurer; faire prêter serment; *vi.* jurer
sweat: *n.* sueur
sweat: *vi.* suer; transpirer
sweater: *n.* pullover
sweep: *n.* coup de balai; grand geste; champ
sweep: *vt.* balayer; ramoner; *vi.* s'étendre
sweeping: *adj.* rapide
sweepstake: *n.* sweepstake
sweet: *adj.* sucré; doux; agréable
sweetbread: *n.* ris de veau
sweeten: *vt.* sucrer; adoucir; assainir; purifier
sweetener: *n.* édulcorant
sweetheart: *n.* petit ami; chéri
sweetmeats: *npl.* sucreries
sweetness: *n.* goût sucré; douceur
swell: *n.* houle; *adj.* génial; épatant
swell: *vi.* gonfler; enfler; augmenter; *vt.* gonfler; enfler; grossir
swelling: *n.* gonflement; boursouflure; tuméfaction
swelter: *vi.* étouffer de chaleur
swerve: *vi.* faire un écart; *vt.* dévier
swift: *adj.* rapide; prompt; vif; *n.* martinet
swiftly: *adv.* rapidement

swiftness: *n.* rapidité; promptitude
swill: *n.* pâtée
swill: *vt.* boire avidemment
swim: *n.* baignade
swim: *vi.* nager; *vt.* traverser à la nage
swimming pool: piscine
swimming: *n.* natation; nage; vertige
swimsuit: *n.* maillot de bain
swindle: *vt.* escroquer
swindler: *n.* escroc
swine: *n.* pourceau; porc
swing: *n.* balancement
swing: *vi.* se balancer; osciller; virer; *vt.* balancer; faire tourner; influencer
swinging door: porte battante
swinging: *adj.* rythmé
swirl: *n.* tourbillon
Swiss: *n. adj.* Suisse
switch: *n.* baguette; interrupteur; aiguille
switch: *vt.* changer de
switchboard: *n.* standard
swivel: *vt.* faire pivoter
swoon: *n.* évanouissement; défaillance
swoon: *vi.* s'évanouir
swoop: *n.* descente en piqué; descente; rafle
swoop: *vi.* fondre sur
sword: *n.* épée
swordfish: *n.* espadon
swordsman: *n.* tireur d'épée
sycamore: *n.* sycomore
sycophant: *n.* sycophante
syllabic: *adj.* syllabique
syllable: *n.* syllabe
syllabus: *n.* programme
syllogism: *n.* syllogisme
sylph: *n.* sylphe; sylphide
symbol: *n.* symbole
symbolic: *adj.* symbolique
symbolise: *vt.* symboliser
symmetrical: *adj.* symétrique
symmetry: *n.* symétrie

sympathetic: *adj.* compatissant
sympathise: *vi.* compatir
sympathy: *n.* compassion
symphony: *n.* symphonie
symptom: *n.* symptôme
synagogue: *n.* synagogue
synchronism: *n.* synchronisme
syndicate: *n.* syndicat
syndrome: *n.* syndrome
synod: *n.* synode
synonym: *n.* synonyme
synonymous: *adj.* synonyme
synopsis: *n.* synopsis; résumé
synoptical: *adj.* synoptique
syntax: *n.* syntaxe
synthesis: *n.* synthèse
synthesize: *vt.* synthétiser
syringe: *n.* seringue
syringe: *vt.* seringuer
system of equations: système d'équations
system: *n.* système
systematic: *adj.* systématique
systems analyst: analyste de systèmes

T

tab: *n.* patte; étiquette
tabernacle: *n.* tabernacle
table of contents: table des matières
table: *n.* table
table: *vt.* mettre en forme de tableau; ajourner
tablecloth: *n.* nappe
tablespoon: *n.* grande cuiller
tablet: *n.* tablette; comprimé
taboo: *adj.* tabou; *n.* tabou
taboo: *vt.* proscrire
tabular: *adj.* tabulaire
tacit: *adj.* tacite
taciturn: *adj.* taciturne
tack: *n.* broquette; bordée
tack: *vt.* clouer; *vi.* tirer des bordées
tackle: *n.* attirail; équipement; matériel; plaquage
tactician: *n.* tacticien
tactics: *npl.* tactique
tadpole: *n.* têtard
taffeta: *n.* taffetas
tag: *n.* ferret; étiquette
tag: *vt.* ferrer
tail: *n.* queue; basque
tail: *vt.* suivre; filer
tailgate: *n.* hayon arrière
tailor: *n.* tailleur
tailoring: *n.* métier de tailleur
tailor-made: *adj.* fait sur mesure
tailwind: *n.* vent arrière
taint: *n.* tache; souillure
taint: *vt.* infecter; polluer; vicier
tainted: *adj.* infecté; souillé
take: *vt.* prendre; saisir; apporter; emporter; conduire
takeoff: *n.* décollage
takeover: *n.* prise de contrôle
taking turns: tour de rôle
takings: *npl.* recette
talent: *n.* talent; don
talented: *adj.* talentueux
talisman: *n.* talisman

talk: *n.* conversation; discussion; entretien
talk: *vi.* parler; bavarder; causer
talkative: *adj.* loquace
talkshow: *n.* débat télévisé
tall: *adj.* grand; élevé; incroyable
tally chart: tableau de fréquence
talon: *n.* serre
tambourine: *n.* tambourin
tame: *adj.* apprivoisé; domestiqué
tame: *vt.* apprivoiser; domestiquer
tamper: *vi.* tripoter
tampon: *n.* tampon
tan: *n.* bronzage
tan: *vt.* bronzer
tang: *n.* saveur forte
tangent: *n.* tangente
tangerine: *n.* mandarine
tangible: *adj.* tangible
tangle: *vt.* enchevêtrer; embrouiller
tank: *n.* réservoir; citerne
tanker: *n.* pétrolier; camion-citerne
tanned: *adj.* bronzé
tantalising: *adj.* tentant
tantrum: *n.* accès de colère
tap: *n.* petite tape; robinet
tap: *vt.* taper doucement; exploiter; inciser
tape backup: sauvegarde sur bande
tape mesure: mètre à ruban
tape recorder: magnétophone
tape: *n.* ruban
tape: *vt.* enregistrer
taper: *n.* cierge
tapestry: *n.* tapisserie
tar: *n.* goudron
target: *n.* cible
tarif: *n.* tarif
tarmac: *n.* piste (d'aéroport)
tarnish: *vt.* ternir
tarpaulin: *n.* bâche (goudronnée)
tarragon: *n.* estragon
tart: *adj.* acidulé; *n.* tarte; tartelette
tartar: *n.* tartre

task: *n.* tâche
tassel: *n.* gland
taste: *n.* goût; saveur; pincée; penchant
taste: *vt.* sentir le goût de; goûter à; déguster; savourer
tasteful: *adj.* de bon goût
tasteless: *adj.* insipide; sans goût
tasty: *adj.* savoureux
tattoo: *n.* tatouage
tattoo: *vt.* tatouer
taunt: *n.* raillerie; sarcasme
taunt: *vt.* railler; accabler de sarcasmes
taut: *adj.* tendu
tautological: *adj.* tautologique
tautology: *n.* tautologie
tawdry: *adj.* tapageur; voyant; clinquant
tax authorities: services fiscaux
tax collector: percepteur
tax payer: contribuable
tax relief: dégrèvement fiscal
tax return: déclaration d'impôts
tax: *n.* impôt; contribution
tax: *vt.* imposer; mettre à l'épreuve
taxable: *adj.* imposable
taxation: *n.* imposition
tax-free: *adj.* exonéré d'impôts
taxi driver: chauffeur de taxi
taxi stand: station de taxis
taxi: *n.* taxi
tea: *n.* thé
teach: *vt.* enseigner; apprendre; *vi.* enseigner
teacher: *n.* professeur; instituteur
teaching: *n.* enseignement
teacup: *n.* tasse à thé
teak: *n.* teck
team: *n.* équipe
teamster: *n.* routier
teamwork: *n.* travail d'équipe
teapot: *n.* théière
tear gas: gaz lacrymogène

tear: *n.* larme
tear: *vt.* déchirer
tearful: *adj.* larmoyant
tease: *vt.* taquiner
teaspoon: *n.* petite cuiller
teat: *n.* tétine; mamelon
technic: *adj.* technique
technicality: *n.* technicité
technician: *n.* technicien
technique: *n.* technique
technological intelligence: veille
technologique
technological: *adj.* technologique
technology: *n.* technologie
teddy bear: ours en peluche
tedious: *adj.* ennuyeux; fastidieux
tedium: *n.* ennui; manque d'intérêt
teem: *vi.* grouiller
teenage: *adj.* adolescent
tee-shirt: *n.* T-shirt
teethe: *vi.* faire ses premières dents
teetotal: *adj.* antialcoolique; qui ne
boit jamais d'alcool
teetotaller: *n.* personne qui ne boit
jamais d'alcool
teleconferencing: *n.* téléconférence
telegram: *n.* télégramme
telegraph: *n.* télégraphe
telegraphic: *adj.* télégraphique
telegraphy: *n.* télégraphie
telepathy: *n.* télépathie
telephone booth: cabine
téléphonique
telephone call: appel téléphonique
telephone directory: annuaire
telephone number: numéro de
téléphone
telephone: *n.* téléphone
telescope: *n.* télescope
telescopic: *adj.* télescopique
televise: *vt.* téléviser
television set: téléviseur; poste de
télévision
television: *n.* télévision

telex: *n.* télex
telex: *vt.* envoyer par télex
tell: *vt.* dire; raconter
teller: *n.* caissier
telling: *adj.* révélateur
telltale: *adj.* dénonciateur
temper: *n.* colère
temper: *vt.* tempérer; modérer
temperament: *n.* tempérament
temperance: *n.* tempérance;
modération
temperate: *adj.* tempéré; modéré;
mesuré
temperature: *n.* température
tempest: *n.* tempête
tempestuous: *adj.* de tempête
template: *n.* gabarit
temple: *n.* temple; tempe
temporarily: *adv.* temporairement
temporary: *adj.* temporaire
tempt: *vt.* tenter
temptation: *n.* tentation
tempting: *adj.* tentant
ten: *adj.* dix
tenable: *adj.* défendable
tenacious: *adj.* tenace
tenacity: *n.* ténacité
tenancy: *n.* location
tenant: *n.* locataire
tend: *vt.* garder; surveiller; *vi.* avoir
tendance (à)
tendency: *n.* tendance
tender: *adj.* tendre; délicat; sensible
tenderness: *n.* tendresse
tendon: *n.* tendon
tenement: *n.* appartement
tenet: *n.* doctrine; principe
tennis court: court ou terrain de
tennis
tennis player: joueur de tennis
tennis racket: raquette de tennis
tennis shoes: chaussures de tennis
tenor: *n.* ténor; sens; substance
tense: *adj.* tendu; *n.* temps

tension: *n.* tension
tent pole: montant de tente
tent: *n.* tente
tentacle: *n.* tentacule
tenth: *adj.* dixième
tenuous: *adj.* ténu
tenure: *n.* titularisation
tepid: *adj.* tiède
term: *n.* terme; trimestre; mot; condition; clause
term: *vt.* appeler; nommer
terminal: *adj.* terminal; *n.* aérogare; terminal
terminate: *vt.* terminer
termination: *n.* fin; conclusion
termolecular reactions: réactions thermoléculaires
terrace: *n.* terrace
terrain: *n.* terrain
terrestrial: *adj.* terrestre
terrible: *adj.* terrible
terribly: *adv.* terriblement
terrier: *n.* terrier
terrific: *adj.* terrifiant; fantastique
terrify: *vt.* terrifier; épouvanter
territory: *adj.* territorial
territory: *n.* territoire
terror: *n.* terreur
terrorise: *vt.* terroriser
terrorism: *n.* terrorisme
terrorist: *n.* terroriste
terse: *adj.* concis; net
test pilot: pilote d'essai
test tube: éprouvette
test: *n.* essai; épreuve
test: *vt.* essayer; examiner
testament: *n.* testament
tester: *n.* contrôleur
testicles: *npl.* testicules
testify: *vt.* témoigner; déclarer sous serment
testimonial: *n.* certificat
testimony: *n.* témoignage
testy: *adj.* irritable

tetanus: *n.* tétanos
tether: *vt.* attacher
tethoscope: *n.* stéthoscope
text format: format texte
text: *n.* texte
textbook: *n.* manuel
textiles: *npl.* textile
textual: *adj.* textuel
texture: *n.* texture; (med) tissu
than: *adv.* que; de
thank: *vt.* remercier; dire merci à
thankful: *adj.* reconnaissant
thankfulness: *n.* reconnaissance
thankless: *adj.* ingrat
Thanksgiving: *n.* action de grâce
that: *pron.* cela; ça; ce; qui; que; celui-là; *conj.* que; afin que
thatch: *n.* chaume
thatch: *vt.* couvrir de chaume
thaw: *n.* dégel
thaw: *vi.* fondre; dégeler
theatre: *n.* théâtre
theatre-goer: *n.* habitué du théâtre
theatrical: *adj.* théâtral
theft: *n.* vol
them: *pron.* les; leur
theme: *n.* thème
themselves: *pron.* eux-mêmes; elles-mêmes
then: *adv.* alors; à cette époque; ensuite; en ce cas; *conj.* donc; en ce cas
theologian: *n.* théologien
theological: *adj.* théologique
theology: *n.* théologie
theorem: *n.* théorème
theoretical probability: probabilité théorique
theoretical yield: rendement théorique
theoretical: *adj.* théorique
theorise: *vt.* théoriser
theorist: *n.* théoricien
theory: *n.* théorie

therapeutics: *n.* thérapeutique
therapist: *n.* thérapeute
therapy: *n.* thérapie
there: *adv.* y; là
thereabout(s): *adv.* par là; près de là
thereafter: *adv.* par la suite; après
thereby: *adv.* de cette façon
therefore: *adv.* donc; par conséquent
thermal energy: énergie thermique
thermal printer: imprimante thermique
thermal: *adj.* thermal
thermodynamics: *n.* thermodynamiques
thermometer: *n.* thermomètre
thermostat: *n.* thermostat
thesaurus: *n.* trésor; dictionnaire de synonymes
these: *pron.* ceux-ci; celles-ci
thesis: *n.* thèse
they: *pron.* ils; elles
thick: *adj.* épais; gros; dense; obtus
thicken: *vi.* épaissir; grossir
thicket: *n.* fourré
thickness: *n.* épaisseur
thickset: *adj.* trapu; râblé
thick-skinned: *adj.* endurci; blindé
thief: *n.* voleur
thigh: *n.* cuisse
thimble: *n.* dé
thin: *adj.* mince; fin; maigre; clair
thin: *vt.* amincir; délayer; éclaircir
thing: *n.* chose; objet; truc
think: *vi.* penser; réfléchir; imaginer; *vt.* penser; croire; juger
thinker: *n.* penseur
thinking: *n.* pensée; réflexion; opinion
third person: troisième personne
third rate: *adj.* médiocre; de mauvaise qualité
third: *adj.* troisième; *n.* troisième
thirst: *n.* soif
thirsty: *adj.* assoiffé

thirteen: *adj.* treize
thirteenth: *adj.* treizième
thirtieth: *adj.* trentième
thirty: *adj.* trente
this: *adj.* ce; cet; cette; ces; *pron.* ceci; ce
thistle: *n.* chardon
thorn: *n.* épine; aubépine
thorny: *adj.* épineux
thorothough: *adj.* consciencieux; approfondi
thoroughbred: *adj.* pur-sang; de race
thoroughfare: *n.* rue; artère
those: *pron.* ceux-là; celles-la; *adj.* ces; ces.. là
though: *conj.* bien que; malgré le fait que; *adv.* pourtant
thought: *n.* pensée; réflexion; opinion; intention
thoughtful: *adj.* pensif
thoughtless: *adj.* étourdi; irréfléchi
thousand: *adj.* mille
thousandth: *adj.* millième
thrash: *vt.* battre; rouer de coups
thread: *n.* film; filetage
thread: *vt.* enfiler
threadbare: *adj.* râpé; élimé
threat: *n.* menace
threaten: *vt.* menacer
three: *adj.* trois
three-dimesional: à trois
threshold: *n.* seuil
thrifty: *adj.* économe
thrill: *n.* frisson
thrill: *vt.* faire frissonner
thriller: *n.* film ou roman à suspense
thrive: *vi.* prospérer; bien se développer
throat: *n.* gorge
throb: *vi.* palpiter; vibrer; lanciner
throne: *n.* trône
throng: *n.* foule
throng: *vi.* affluer
throttle: *n.* accélérateur

throttle: *vt.* étrangler
throughout: *prep.* partout dans; *adv.* partout
throw: *n.* jet; lancement
throw: *vt.* jeter; lancer; projeter
throwaway: *adj.* jetable
thrush: *n.* grive
thrust: *n.* poussée
thrust: *vt.* pousser violemment; enfoncer
thud: *n.* bruit sourd
thug: *n.* voyou
thumb: *n.* pouce
thumbtack: *n.* punaise
thump: *n.* coup de poing
thump: *vi.* frapper; cogner; *vt.* cogner à
thunder: *n.* tonnerre; *vi.* tonner
thunderbolt: *n.* foudre
thunderclap: *n.* coup de tonnerre
thunderstorm: *n.* orage
thundery: *adj.* orageux
Thursday: *n.* jeudi
thus: *adv.* ainsi; de cette manière
thwart: *vt.* contrecarrer
thyme: *n.* thym
thyroid: *n.* thyroïde
tiara: *n.* tiare
tic: *n.* tic
tick: *n.* tic-tac; instant
tick: *vt.* cocher
ticket: *n.* billet; ticket; étiquette; carte
tickle: *vt.* chatouiller
ticklish: *adj.* chatouilleux
tidal: *adj.* de la marée
tidal wave: raz-de-marée
tide: *n.* marée; afflux; cours
tidy: *adj.* rangé; en ordre; ordonné; soigné
tie line: segment conjugué
tie: *n.* attache
tie: *vt.* attacher; nouer
tier: *n.* gradin; étage
tiger: *n.* tigre

tight: *adj.* raide; tendu; serré; hermétique; *adv.* très fort
tighten: *vt.* reserrer; tendre
tightfisted: *adj.* avare
tightly: *adv.* très fort
tightrope: *n.* corde raide
tigress: *n.* tigresse
tile: *n.* tuile; carreau
tile: *vt.* couvrir de tuiles
tiled: *adj.* en tuiles; carrelé
till: *n.* caisse
till: *vt.* labourer; cultiver
tiller: *n.* barre du gouvernail
tilt: *vt.* pencher; *vi.* s'incliner
timber: *n.* bois de construction; arbres
time bomb: bombe à retardement
time lag: décalage
time line: chronologie
time off: temps libre
time scale: durée
time zone: fuseau horaire
time: *n.* temps; période; heure; moment
time: *vt.* fixer; chronométrer
timeless: *adj.* éternel
timely: *adj.* opportun
timer: *n.* sablier; minuteur
timid: *adj.* timide; timoré
timidity: *n.* timidité
timing: *n.* chronométrage
tin: *n.* étain; boîte
tinfoil: *n.* papier d'aluminium
tinge: *n.* teinte
tingle: *vi.* picoter; vibrer; frissonner
tingling: *n.* picotement; frisson
tinker: *n.* rétameur
tinkle: *vi.* tinter
tinplate: *n.* fer-blanc
tinsel: *n.* guirlande
tint: *n.* teinte
tint: *vt.* teinter
tinted: *adj.* teinté; fumé
tiny: *adj.* minuscule; tout petit

tip: *n.* pointe; bout; pourboire; conseil; tuyau

tip: *vt.* donner un pourboire à; pencher; effleurer

tip-off: *n.* avertissement

tipsy: *adj.* gai; éméché

tiptop: *adj.* excellent; de premier ordre

tirade: *n.* diatribe

tire pressure: *n.* pression des pneux

tire: *n.* pneu

tire: *vt.* fatiguer; *vi.* se fatiguer; se lasser

tired: *adj.* fatigué

tireless: *adj.* infatigable

tiresome: *adj.* ennuyeux; fatigant

tiring: *adj.* fatigant

tissue paper: papier de soie

tissue: *n.* tissu; mouchoir en papier

titbit: *n.* friandise; bon morceau

titillate: *vt.* titiller

title catalogue: catalogue par titres

title deed: titre de propriété

title page: page de titre

title: *n.* titre

titration: *n.* titration

titter: *n.* petit

titter: *vi.* rire sottement

titular: *adj.* titulaire

toad: *n.* crapaud

toadstool: *n.* champignon vénéneux

toast: *vt.* griller

toaster: *n.* grille-pain

tobacco pouch: blague à tabac

tobacco shop: bureau de tabac

tobacco: *n.* tabac

tobacconist: *n.* marchand

toboggan: *n.* toboggan; luge

today: *adv.* aujourd'hui

toddler: *n.* enfant qui commence à marcher

toddy: *n.* grog

toe: *n.* orteil; pointe

together: *adv.* ensemble; en même temps

toil: *n.* dur travail; labeur; peine

toil: *vi.* travailler dur; peiner; se donner du mal

toilet bag: trousse de toilette

toilet bowl: cuvette des toilettes

toilet paper: papier hygiénique

toilet: *n.* toilette; toilettes

token: *n.* signe; marque; souvenir; bon; jeton

tolerable: *adj.* tolérable; passable

tolerance: *n.* tolérance

tolerant: *adj.* tolérant

tolerate: *vt.* tolérer

toll: *n.* péage; nombre de victimes

toll: *vi.* sonner le glas

tomato: *n.* tomate

tomb: *n.* tombeau; tombe

tomboy: *n.* garçon manqué

tombstone: *n.* pierre tombale

tomcat: *n.* matou

tomorrow: *adv.* demain

ton: *n.* tonne

tone: *n.* ton; tonalité

tone: *vi.* s'harmoniser

tongue: *n.* langue

tongue-tied: *adj.* muet

tongue-twister: phrase difficile à prononcer

tonic: *n.* tonique

tonight: *adv.* ce soir

tonnage: *n.* tonnage

tonsil: *n.* amygdale

tonsure: *n.* tonsure

too: *adv.* aussi; trop

tool box: caisse à outils

tool: *n.* outil; ustensile

toot: *vi.* klaxonner

tooth: *n.* dent

toothache: *n.* rage de dents

toothbrush: *n.* brosse à dents

toothless: *adj.* édenté

toothpaste: *n.* dentifrice

toothpick: *n.* cure-dent
top floor: dernier étage
top: *n.* sommet; cime; haut; couvercle; étage supérieur; *adj.* du haut; premier
top: *vt.* dépasser; être au sommet
topaz: *n.* topaze
top-heavy: *adj.* instable; déséquilibré
topic sentence: phrase d'introduction
topic: *n.* sujet; *adj.* d'actualité
topless: *adj.* torse nu; aux seins nus
top-level: *adj.* au plus haut niveau
topmost: *adj.* le plus haut
topographical: *adj.* topographique
topography: *n.* topographie
topple: *vt.* renverser; *vi.* basculer
top-secret: *adj.* ultra-secret
topsy-turvy: *adv.* sens dessus dessous
torch: *n.* torche
torment: *n.* tourment
torment: *vt.* tourmenter
tornado: *n.* tornade
torrent: *n.* torrent
torrid: *adj.* torride
tortoise: *n.* tortue
tortoiseshell: *adj.* en écaille de tortue
tortuous: *adj.* tortueux; sinueux
torture: *n.* torture; *vt.* torturer
toss: *vt.* lancer; jeter; agiter; secouer
total: *adj.* total; global
totalitarian: *adj.* totalitaire
totality: *n.* totalité
totter: *vi.* chanceler
touch: *n.* toucher; contact; touche
touch: *vt.* toucher
touch-and-go: *adj.* incertain; précaire
touchdown: *n.* atterrissage; but
touched: *adj.* touché; timbré
touching: *adj.* touchant; attendrissant
touchstone: *n.* pierre de touche
touchwood: *n.* amadou
touchy: *adj.* susceptible

tough: *adj.* dur; pénible; résistant; fort
toughen: *vt.* durcir
toupee: *n.* postiche
tour: *n.* voyage; visite
tour: *vt.* visiter
touring: *n.* tourisme
tourism: *n.* tourisme
tourist office: office du tourisme
tourist: *n.* touriste
tournament: *n.* tournoi
tow: *n.* remorquage
tow: *vt.* remorquer
toward(s): *prep.* vers; dans la direction de; envers; à l'égard de
towel rack: porte-serviette
towel: *n.* serviette
towelling: *n.* tissu éponge
tower: *n.* tour
towering: *adj.* imposaint
town clerk: secrétaire de mairie
town hall: mairie
town: *n.* ville
towrope: *n.* câble de remorquage
toy: *n.* jouet
toyshop: *n.* magasin de jouets
trace: *n.* trace; piste
trace: *vt.* tracer; esquisser; retrouver
track: *n.* trace; empreinte; chemin; voie; piste
track: *vt.* suivre à la trace
tracksuit: *n.* survêtement
tract: *n.* étendue; région; brochure
traction: *n.* traction
trade courts: tribunaux de commerce
trade fair: foire commerciale
trade name: raison commerciale
trade union: syndicat
trade unionist: syndicaliste
trade: *n.* commerce; affaires; échange; métier
trade: *vi.* faire le commerce; commercer
trademark: *n.* marque de fabrique

trader: *n.* négociant
tradesman: *n.* fournisseur; commerçant
trading: *n.* commerce; *adj.* commercial
tradition: *n.* tradition
traditional: *adj.* traditionnel
traffic circle: *n.* rond-point
traffic jam: embouteillage
traffic: *n.* circulation; négoce
traffic: *vi.* faire le commerce
trafficker: *n.* trafiquant
tragedy: *n.* tragédie
tragic: *adj.* tragique
tragicomedy: *n.* tragi-comédie
trail: *n.* traînée; trace; queue
trail: *vt.* suivre la piste de; trainer; *vi.* trainer
trailer: *n.* remorque; caravane; bande-annonce
train: *n.* train
train: *vt.* entraîner; former
trained: *adj.* qualifié; diplômé
trainee: *n.* stagiaire
trainer: *n.* entraîneur
training: *n.* formation; entraînement
trait: *n.* trait
traitor: *n.* traître
tramp: *n.* clochard; putain
tramp: *vi.* marcher d'un pas lourd; *vt.* piétiner
trample: *vt.* piétiner
trampoline: *n.* trampoline
trance: *n.* transe; extase
tranquil: *adj.* tranquille
tranquillise: *vt.* tranquilliser
tranquilliser: *n.* tranquillisant
transact: *vt.* traiter
transaction: *n.* transaction; opération
transatlantic: *adj.* transatlantique
transcend: *vt.* transcender; dépasser; surpasser
transcription: *n.* transcription; copie

transfer: *n.* transfert; mutation; décalcomanie
transfer: *vt.* transférer; déplacer
transform: *vt.* transformer
transformation: *n.* transformation
transfusion: *n.* transfusion
transient: *adj.* transitoire; passager
transit: *n.* transit
transition state: état de transition
transition: *n.* transition; passage
transitional: *adj.* de transition
transitive: *adj.* transitif
translate: *vt.* traduire
translation: *n.* traduction
translator: *n.* tradvcteur
transmission: *n.* transmision
transmit: *vt.* transmettre
transmitter: *n.* transmetteur; émetteur
transparency: *n.* transparence; diapositive
transparent: *adj.* transparent
transpire: *vi.* transpirer; arriver
transplant: *n.* transplantation
transplant: *vt.* transplanter
transport: *n.* transport
transport: *vt.* transporter
transportation: *n.* moyen de transport
trap door: trappe
trap: *n.* piège
trap: *vt.* prendre au piège; bloquer
trapeze: *n.* trapèze
trash can: poubelle
trash: *n.* camelote; inepties
trashy: *adj.* sans valeur; de mauvaise qualité
travel agency: agence de voyages
travel agent: agent de voyages
travel sickness: mal de mer ou de l'air
travel: *n.* voyage
travel: *vi.* voyager; *vt.* parcourir
traveller: *n.* voyageur

traveller's check: *n.* chèque de voyage
travelling: *n.* voyages
travesty: *n.* parodie
trawler: *n.* chalutier
tray: *n.* plateau; tiroir
treacherous: *adj.* traître; perfide
treachery: *n.* traîtrise
tread: *n.* pas; bruit de pas; bande de roulement
tread: *vi.* marcher; écraser
treason: *n.* trahison
treasure: *n.* trésor
treasure: *vt.* conserver précieusement
treasurer: *n.* trésorier
treat: *n.* cadeau; plaisir
treat: *vt.* traiter; offrir
treatise: *n.* traité
treatment: *n.* traitement
treaty: *n.* traité
treble clef: clef de sol
treble: *adj.* triple
treble: *vt.* tripler
tree: *n.* arbre
trek: *n.* randonnée
trellis: *n.* treillis
tremble: *vi.* trembler
trembling: *n.* tremblement; frisson
tremendous: *adj.* terrible; énorme; formidable
tremor: *n.* tremblement
trench: *n.* fossé; tranchée
trend: *n.* tendance; direction; mode
trendy: *adj.* dernier cri
trepidation: *n.* vive inquiétude
trespass: *vt.* transgresser; violer
tress: *n.* boucle de cheveu; chevelure
trestle: *n.* tréteau; chevalet
trial: *n.* procès; épreuve; essai; peine
triangle: *n.* triangle
triangular: *adj.* triangulaire
tribal: *adj.* tribal
tribe: *n.* tribu
tribulation: *n.* tribulation

tribunal: *n.* tribunal
tributary: *adj.* tributaire; *n.* tributaire
tribute: *n.* tribut
trice: *n.* instant
trick: *n.* ruse; astuce; tour; blague; pli
trick: *vt.* attraper
trickery: *n.* supercherie
trickle: *n.* filet
trickle: *vi.* couler goutte à goutte
tricky: *adj.* délicat; difficile
tricycle: *n.* tricycle
trifle: *n.* bagatelle; vétille
trifle: *vi.* jouer; badiner
trifling: *adj.* futile; insignifiant
trigger: *n.* gâchette
trigger: *vt.* déclencher
trigonometry: *n.* trigonométrie
trill: *n.* trille
trill: *vi.* triller
trim: *adj.* net; soigné; bien tenu; en parfait état
trim: *vt.* arranger; tailler; orner
trinket: *n.* bibelot; babiole; colifichet
trip: *n.* faux pas; voyage
trip: *vt.* faire trébucher; *vi.* trébucher; faire un faux pas
tripe: *n.* tripes; bêtises
triple: *adj.* triple
triple: *vt.* tripler
triplicate: *n.* copie en trois exemplaires
tripod: *n.* trépied
trite: *adj.* banal; usé
triumph: *adj.* triomphal
triumph: *n.* triomphe
triumph: *vi.* triompher
triumphant: *adj.* triomphant; victorieux
trivial: *adj.* insignifiant; sans importance
triviality: *n.* banalité
trolley: *n.* chariot
trombone: *n.* trombone
troop: *n.* bande; *npl.* troupes

trooper: *n.* soldat de cavalerie
trophy: *n.* trophée
tropical: *adj.* tropical
tropism: *n.* tropisme
trot: *n.* trot
trot: *vi.* trotter
trouble: *n.* problème; ennui; difficulté; affliction; peine
trouble: *vt.* affliger; tourmenter
troubled: *adj.* inquiet; agité
troublemaker: *n.* agitateur
troubleshooter: *n.* médiateur
troublesome: *adj.* pénible
trough: *n.* abreuvoir; auge
troupe: *n.* troupe
trousers: *npl.* pantalon
trout: *n.* truite
trowel: *n.* truelle
truce: *n.* trêve
truck driver: routier
truck farm: jardin maraîcher
truck: *n.* camion; wagon
truculent: *adj.* brutal; agressif
trudge: *vi.* marcher lourdement
true: *adj.* vrai; véritable; sincère; exact
truelove: *n.* bien-aimé
truffle: *n.* truffe
truly: *adv.* vraiment; sincèrement
trump: *n.* atout
trumpet: *n.* trompette
trunk: *n.* malle; coffre; trompe
truss: *n.* botte
truss: *vt.* botteler; trousser
trust: *n.* confiance; trust; fidéicommis
trust: *vt.* avoir confiance en; confier à
trusted: *adj.* de confiance
trustee: *n.* fidéicommissaire; curateur; administrateur
trustful: *adj.* confiant
trustily: *adj.* fidèlement
trusting: *adj.* confiant
trustworthy: *adj.* digne de confiance

trusty: *adj.* fidèle; loyal; sûr
truth: *n.* vérité
truthful: *adj.* véridique; qui dit la vérité
truthfulness: *n.* véracité
try: *vt.* essayer; tâcher; chercher à; expérimenter; mettre à l'épreuve; tenter; juger
trying: *adj.* pénible; fatigant
tub: *n.* cuve; bac; baignoire
tuba: *n.* tuba
tube: *n.* tube; métro
tuberculosis: *n.* tuberculose
tubing: *n.* tuyaux
tuck: *vt.* mettre
tucker: *vt.* fatiguer
Tuesday: *n.* mardi
tuft: *n.* touffe; houppe
tug: *n.* remorqueur
tug: *vt.* remorquer
tuition: *n.* cours; enseignement
tulip: *n.* tulipe
tumble: *n.* chute; culbute
tumble: *vi.* tomber; faire une chute; se jeter; *vt.* renverser; culbuter
tumbledown: *adj.* délabré
tumbler: *n.* verre
tummy: *n.* ventre
tumor: *n.* tumeur
tumultuous: *adj.* tumultueux
tuna: *n.* thon
tune: *n.* air; accord; harmonie
tune: *vt.* accorder; syntoniser
tuneful: *adj.* mélodieux; harmonieux
tuner: *n.* syntoniseur
tunic: *n.* tunique
tunnel: *n.* tunnel
tunnel: *vt.* creuser un tunnel dans
turban: *n.* turban
turbine: *n.* turbine
turbulence: *n.* turbulence; agitation
turbulent: *adj.* turbulent; agité
tureen: *n.* soupière
turf: *n.* gazon

turf: *vt.* gazonner
turgid: *adj.* gonflé
turkey: *n.* dinde
turmoil: *n.* agitation; trouble
turn: *n.* tour; tournure; virage;
tendance
turn: *vi.* (se) tourner; devenir;
changer; se retourner; se changer
turncoat: *n.* renégat
turning: *n.* embranchement
turnip: *n.* navet
turn-off: *n.* sortie (d'autoroute);
embranchement
turnout: *n.* production
turnover: *n.* chiffre d'affaires
turnpike: *n.* barrière de péage
turnstile: *n.* tourniquet
turntable: *n.* platine
turpentine: *n.* (essence de)
térébenthine
turquoise: *n.* turquoise
turret: *n.* tourelle
turtle: *n.* tortue marine
turtledove: *n.* tourterelle
tusk: *n.* défense
tussle: *n.* lutte
tutor: *n.* professeur particulier;
directeur d'études
tutor: *vt.* enseigner; donner des cours
particuliers à
tuxedo: *n.* smoking
twang: *n.* vibration; ton nasillard
twelfth: *adj.* douzième
twelve: *adj.* douze
twentieth: *adj.* vingtième
twenty: *adj.* vingt
twice: *adv.* deux fois
twig: *n.* brindille
twig: *vi.* piger
twin: *n.* jumeau
twine: *n.* ficelle
twine: *vi.* s'enrouler; serpenter
twinge: *n.* élancement; remords
twinge: *vt.* élancer

twinkle: *vi.* scintiller; clignoter
twirl: *n.* tournoiement
twirl: *vt.* faire tournoyer; *vi.*
tournoyer
twist: *n.* torsion
twist: *vt.* tordre; tortiller; entortiller;
vi. serpenter
twit: *n.* crétin
twitch: *n.* tic
twitch: *vi.* avoir un mouvement
nerveux
twitter: *n.* gazouillis
twitter: *vi.* gazouiller
two: *adj.* deux
two-door: *adj.* à deux portes
two-faced: *adj.* hypocrite
twofold: *adj.* double; *adv.* au double
twosome: *n.* paire; couple
tycoon: *n.* magnat
type: *n.* type; caractère; exemple
type: *vi.* taper à la machine
typecast: *adj.* enfermé dans un rôle
typeface: *n.* police de caractère
typescript: *n.* texte dactylographié
typewriter: *n.* machine à écrire
typewritten: *adj.* dactylographié
typical: *adj.* typique
tyranny: *n.* tyrannie
tyrant: *n.* tyran
tyre: *n.* pneu

U

ubiquitous: *adj.* doué d'ubiquité
udder: *n.* pis
ugliness: *n.* laideur
ugly: *adj.* laid; inquiétant
ulcer: *n.* ulcère
ulterior: *adj.* ultérieur
ultimate: *adj.* final
ultimatum: *n.* ultimatum
ultramarine: *n.* outremer; *adj.* outremer
ultrasound: *n.* ultrason
umbilical cord: cordon ombilical
umbrella: *n.* parapluie
umpire: *n.* arbitre
umpteen: *adj.* un très grand nombre de; beaucoup de
unable: *adj.* incapable
unaccompanied: *adj.* non accompagné; seul
unaccomplished: *adj.* inaccompli; inachevé
unaccountable: *adj.* inexplicable
unaccountably: *adv.* inexplicablement
unaccustomed: *adj.* inaccoutumé; inhabituel
unacknowledged: *adj.* non reconnu; (resté) sans réponse
unacquainted: *adj.* qui ignore; qui n'a pas connaissance de
unadorned: *adj.* sans ornement
unadvlterated: *adj.* pur; sans mélange
unaffected: *adj.* sincère; non affecté
unaided: *adj.* sans aide
unaltered: *adj.* inchangé
unambitious: *adj.* sans ambition
unanimity: *n.* unanimité
unanimous: *adj.* unanime
unanswerable: *adj.* incontestable
unanswered: *adj.* sans réponse
unarmed: *adj.* non armé; désarmé

unassuming: *adj.* sans prétention; modeste
unattached: *adj.* indépendant; libre
unattainable: *adj.* inaccessible
unattended: *adj.* sans surveillance
unauthorised: *adj.* sans autorisation
unavitably: *adv.* inévitablement
unavoidable: *adj.* inévitable
unaware: *adj.* ignorant; inconscient
unawares: *adv.* à l'improviste; par mégarde
unbalnced: *adj.* déséquilibré; non soldé
unbearable: *adj.* insupportable
unbecoming: *adj.* malséant; déplacé; peu seyant
unbelievable: *adj.* incroyable
unbend: *vi.* se détendre
unbend: *vt.* redresser
unbiased: *adj.* impartial
unblemished: *adj.* sans tache; sans défaut
unborn: *adj.* à naître; pas encore né
unbreakable: *adj.* incassable
unbroken: *adj.* non brisé; intact
unbutton: *vt.* déboutonner
uncalled-for: *adj.* injustifié
uncanny: *adj.* mystérieux
unceasing: *adj.* incessant; continu
unceremonious: *adj.* brusque
uncertain: *adj.* incertain; douteux
uncertainty: *n.* incertitude
unchangeable: *adj.* immuable
unchanged: *adj.* inchangé
unchanging: *adj.* invariable; immuable
uncharitable: *adj.* peu charitable
unchecked: *adj.* non maîtrisé
unchristian: *adj.* peu chrétien
uncivil: *adj.* impoli; grossier
uncivilised: *adj.* barbare; non civilisé
uncle: *n.* oncle
uncomfortable: *adj.* inconfortable; incommode; désagréable

uncomfortably: *adv.* inconfortablement; mal; désagréablement
uncommon: *adj.* rare; extraordinaire
uncompromising: *adj.* intransigeant
unconcerned: *adj.* indifférent
unconditional: *adj.* inconditionnel; absolu
unconfined: *adj.* illimité; sans bornes
unconfirmed: *adj.* non confirmé
unconnected: *adj.* sans rapport
unconquerable: *adj.* invincible
unconscious: *adj.* inconscient
unconstrained: *adj.* non contraint; libre
uncontrollable: *adj.* irrésistible; qui ne peut être maîtrisé
unconvention: *adj.* peu conventionnel
unconvincing: *adj.* peu convaincant
uncork: *vt.* déboucher
uncorrected: *adj.* non corrigé
uncouth: *adj.* grossier
uncover: *vt.* découvrir
uncultivated: *adj.* inculte
uncut: *adj.* non taillé; intégral
undamaged: *adj.* non endommagé; indemne
undaunted: *adj.* intrépide
undecided: *adj.* indécis
undefiled: *adj.* pur; immaculé
undeniable: *adj.* indéniable; incontestable
under: *adv.* en dessous; *prep.* sous; au-dessous de
underage: *adj.* mineur
undercharge: *vt.* ne pas faire payer assez
underclothing: *n.* sous-vêtements
undercoat: *n.* première couche
undercover: *adj.* secret; clandestin
undercurrent: *n.* courant sous marin
undercut: *vt.* vendre moins cher que

underdeveloped: *adj.* sous-développé; insuffisamment développé
underdog: *n.* opprimé
underdone: *adj.* pas assez cuit
underestimate: *vt.* sous-estimer
undergo: *vt.* subir; supporter
undergradvate: *n.* étudiant en licence
underground: *n.* mouvement clandestin
undergrowth: *n.* broussailles; sous-bois
underhand: *adv.* en cachette; *adj.* secret; clandestin
underlie: *vi.* être à la base de
underline: *vt.* souligner
undermine: *vt.* saper
underpaid: *adj.* sous-payé
underprivileged: *adj.* défavorisé
underrate: *vt.* sous-estimer
undersecretary: *n.* sous-secrétaire
undershirt: *n.* maillot de corps
undershorts: *npl.* caleçon
underside: *n.* dessous
understand: *vt.* comprendre
understandable: *adj.* compréhensible
understanding: *n.* compréhension; intelligence; entendement; accord
understatement: *n.* affirmation en dessous de la vérité
undertake: *vt.* entreprendre
undertaking: *n.* entreprise; engagement
undervalue: *vt.* sous-estimer
underwater: *adj.* sous-marin; *adv.* sous l'eau
underwear: *n.* sous-vêtements; dessous
underworld: *n.* pègre
underwrite: *vt.* souscrire à; assurer contre
underwriter: *n.* assureur
undeserved: *adj.* immérité

undeserving: *adj.* peu méritant
undesirable: *adj.* peu souhaitable
undetermined: *adj.* indéterminé; indécis
undigested: *adj.* non digéré
undiminished: *adj.* non diminué
undisciplined: *adj.* indiscipliné
undisguised: *adj.* non déguisé
undismayed: *adj.* non découragé
undisputed: *adj.* incontesté
undisturbed: *adj.* non dérangé; paisible
undivided: *adj.* indivisé; entier
undo: *vt.* défaire; détruire
undoing: *n.* ruine
undoubted: *adj.* indubitable
undress: *vi.* se déshabiller
undue: *adj.* excessif; injuste
undulating: *adj.* ondulant
unduly: *adv.* trop; excessivement
undying: *adj.* éternel
unearth: *vt.* déterrer
unearthly: *adj.* surnaturel
uneasy: *adj.* inquiet; troublé; gêné
uneducated: *adj.* sans instruction
unemployed: *adj.* au chômage
unemployment: *n.* chômage
unending: *adj.* interminable
unenlightened: *adj.* peu éclairé
unenviable: *adj.* peu enviable
unequal: *adj.* inégal
unequalled: *adj.* inégalé
unerring: *adj.* infaillible
uneven: *adj.* inégal; impair
unexpected: *adj.* inattendu; inopiné
unexplored: *adj.* inexploré
unfailing: *adj.* infaillible; certain
unfair: *adj.* injuste; inéquitable
unfaithful: *adj.* infidèle
unfaithfulness: *n.* infidélité
unfaltering: *adj.* ferme; assuré
unfamiliar: *adj.* peu familier; peu connu
unfashionable: *adj.* démodé

unfasten: *vt.* détacher; défaire
unfathomable: *adj.* insondable; impénétrable
unfavourable: *adj.* défavorable
unfeeling: *adj.* insensible; impitoyable
unfinished: *adj.* inachevé; incomplet
unfold: *vt.* déplier; révéler; *vi.* s'ouvrir
unforeseen: *adj.* imprévu
unforgettable: *adj.* inoubliable
unforgivable: *adj.* impardonnable
unforgiving: *adj.* implacable
unfortunate: *adj.* malheureux
unfounded: *adj.* sans fondement
unfriendly: *adj.* inamical
unfruitful: *adj.* stérile; infructueux
unfurnished: *adj.* non meublé
ungainly: *adj.* gauche
ungentlemanly: *adj.* peu galant
ungovernable: *adj.* ingouvernable; indomptable
ungrateful: *adj.* ingrat; peu reconnaissant
ungrounded: *adj.* infondé
unhappily: *adv.* malheureusement
unhappiness: *n.* tristesse
unhappy: *adj.* malheureux
unharmed: *adj.* indemne; sain et sauf
unhealthy: *adj.* malsain; maladif
unheard-of: *adj.* inédit; sans précédent
unheeding: *adj.* insouciant; distrait
unhook: *vt.* décrocher; dégrafer
unhoped: *adj.* inespéré
unhurt: *adj.* indemne
unicorn: *n.* licorne
uniform: *adj.* uniforme; *n.* uniforme
uniformity: *adj.* uniformité
unify: *vt.* unifier
unimaginable: *adj.* inimaginable
unimpaired: *adj.* non diminué; intact
unimportant: *adj.* sans importance
uninformed: *adj.* mal informé

uninhabitable: *adj.* inhabitable
uninhabited: *adj.* inhabité; désert
uninjured: *adj.* indemne; sain et sauf
unintelligible: *adj.* inintelligible
unintelligibly: *adj.* inintelligiblement
unintentional: *adj.* involontaire
uninterested: *adj.* indifférent
uninteresting: *adj.* inintéressant
uninterrupted: *adj.* ininterrompu; continu
uninvited: *adj.* sans être invité
union catalogue: catalogue collectif
union: *n.* union; syndicat
unionist: *n.* syndicaliste
unique: *adj.* unique; exceptionnel
unison: *n.* unisson
unit factor: unité de facteur
unit: *adj.* inapte; impropre
unit: *n.* unité
unitarian: *n.* unitarien
unite: *vt.* unir; *vi.* s'unir
unitedly: *adv.* conjointement; ensemble
unity: *n.* unité; harmonie; accord
universal themes: thèmes universelles
universal: *adj.* universel
universe: *n.* univers
university: *n.* université
unjust: *adj.* injuste
unkempt: *adj.* négligé; débraillé
unkind: *adj.* peu aimable; méchant
unknowingly: *adv.* inconsciemment
unknown: *adj.* inconnu
unlawful: *adj.* illégal; illicite
unlawfulness: *n.* illégalité
unleash: *vt.* lâcher; déchaîner
unless: *conj.* à moins que; sauf
unlicensed: *adj.* illicite
unlike: *adj.* différent; dissemblable
unlikelihood: *n.* improbabilité
unlikely: *adj.* improbable; invraisemblable; *adv.* improbablement

unlimited: *adj.* illimité
unlisted: *adj.* ne figurant pas sur une liste/sur l'annuaire
unload: *vt.* décharger
unlock: *vt.* ouvrir; déverrouiller
unluckily: *adv.* malheureusement
unlucky: *adj.* malchanceux
unmangeable: *adj.* difficile; peu
unmannered: *adj.* mal élevé; impoli
unmannerly: *adj.* rustre
unmarried: *adj.* célibataire; qui n'est pas marié
unmask: *vt.* démasquer
unmentionable: *adj.* qu'il ne faut pas mentionner
unmerited: *adj.* immérité
unmindful: *adj.* oublieux; indifférent
unmistakable: *adj.* indubitable
unmitigated: *adj.* absolu
unmoved: *adj.* insensible; impassible
unnatural: *adj.* non naturel; pervers; affecté
unnecessary: *adj.* inutile; superflu
unneighbourly: *adj.* peu aimable avec ses voisins; peu sociable
unnoticed: *adj.* inaperçu
unnumbered: *adj.* innombrable
unobserved: *adj.* inaperçu
unobtainable: *adj.* impossible à obtenir; introuvable
unobtrusive: *adj.* discret
unoccupied: *adj.* inoccupé
unofficial: *adj.* non officiel
unorthodox: *adj.* hétérodoxe; peu orthodoxe
unpack: *vt.* défaire; déballer
unpaid: *adj.* non payé
unpalatable: *adj.* désagréable au goût
unparalleled: *adj.* incomparable; sans pareil
unpleasant: *adj.* désagréable
unpleasantness: *n.* caractère désagréable

unplug: *vt.* débrancher
unpolished: *adj.* non ciré; fruste; rude
unpopular: *adj.* impopulaire
unpractised: *adj.* inexpérimenté; inexercé
unprecedented: *adj.* sans précédent
unpredictable: *adj.* imprévisible
unprejudiced: *adj.* impartial
unprepared: *adj.* qui n'est pas préparé
unprofitable: *adj.* inutile; peu rentable
unprotected: *adj.* sans protection; exposé
unpublished: *adj.* inédit
unpunished: *adj.* impuni
unqualified: *adj.* non qualifié; inconditionnel
unquestionable: *adj.* incontestable; indiscutable
unquestioned: *adj.* incontesté; indiscuté
unravel: *vt.* débrouiller
unread: *adj.* qui n'a pas été lu; inculte
unreal: *adj.* irréel
unrealistic: *adj.* irréaliste
unreasonable: *adv.* déraisonnable
unreasonably: *adj.* déraisonnablement
unregarded: *adj.* négligé; dont on fait peu de cas
unrelated: *adj.* sans rapport; sans lien de parenté
unrelenting: *adj.* implacable
unreliable: *adj.* peu fiable
unremitting: *adj.* inlassable; constant
unrepentant: *adj.* impénitent
unreserved: *adj.* sans réserve; franc
unrest: *n.* agitation; troubles
unrestrained: *adj.* non contenu; non réprimé
unripe: *adj.* vert; pas mûr

unrivalled: *adj.* sans égal; sans pareil
unroll: *vt.* dérouler
unruliness: *n.* indiscipline; turbulence
unruly: *adj.* indiscipliné
unsafe: *adj.* dangereux; peu sûr
unsatisfactory: *adj.* peu satisfaisant
unsaturated: *adj.* non-saturé
unsavoury: *adj.* désagréable; insipide
unscathed: *adj.* indemne
unscrew: *vt.* dévisser
unscrupulous: *adj.* sans scrupules
unseasonable: *adj.* hors de saison; inopportun
unseemly: *adj.* inconvenant
unseen: *adj.* invisible; inaperçu
unselfish: *adj.* généreux
unsettle: *vt.* perturber
unsettled: *adj.* perturbé; instable; variable
unshaken: *adj.* inébranlable; ferme
unshaven: *adj.* non rasé
unsightly: *adj.* disgracieux; laid
unskilful: *adj.* maladroit; malhabile
unskilled: *adj.* inexpérimenté
unsociable: *adj.* insociable; sauvage
unspeakable: *adj.* ineffable; indicible
unstable: *adj.* instable
unsteadily: *adv.* d'un pas chancelant; d'une manière mal assurée
unsteady: *adj.* instable
unstudied: *adj.* naturel; spontané
unsuccessful: *adj.* infructueux; vain
unsuitable: *adj.* peu approprié; inopportun
unsure: *adj.* peu sûr
unsympathetic: *adj.* peu compatissant
untamed: *adj.* sauvage
untapped: *adj.* non exploité
untenable: *adj.* insoutenable
unthinkable: *adj.* inconcevable
unthinking: *adj.* irréfléchi; étourdi
untidiness: *n.* désordre

untidy: *adj.* en désordre; peu soigné

untie: *vt.* dénouer; défaire

until: *prep.* jusqu'à; *conj.* jusqu'à ce que

untimely: *adj.* intempestif

untiring: *adj.* infatigable

untold: *adj.* jamais révélé; indicible; incalculable

untouched: *adj.* intact

untoward: *adj.* fâcheux; inconvenant

untried: *adj.* qui n'a pas été essayé ou mis à l'épreuve

untroubled: *adj.* tranquille; paisible

untrue: *adj.* faux

untrustworthy: *adj.* indigne de confiance

untruth: *n.* mensonge; fausseté

unused: *adj.* neuf; inutilisé

unusual: *adj.* inhabituel; exceptionnel

unveil: *vt.* dévoiler

unwavering: *adj.* inébranlable

unwelcome: *adj.* importun

unwell: *adj.* indisposé; souffrant

unwieldy: *adj.* peu maniable

unwilling: *adj.* peu disposé

unwillingness: *n.* mauvaise grâce; mauvaise volonté

unwind: *vt.* dérouler; *vi.* se détendre

unwise: *adj.* imprudent

unwitting: *adj.* involontaire

unworkable: *adj.* impraticable

unworthy: *adj.* indigne

unwrap: *vt.* défaire

unwritten: *adj.* non écrit

up: *adv.* en haut; en l'air; levé; *prep.* au haut de; plus loin

upbringing: *n.* éducation

update: *vt.* mettre à jour

upheaval: *n.* bouleversement

uphill: *adj.* difficile; pénible; *adv.* en montant

uphold: *vt.* soutenir

upholstery: *n.* tapisserie

upkeep: *n.* entretien

uplift: *vt.* élever

upon: *prep.* sur

upper quartile: quartile supérieure

upper: *adj.* supérieur; élevé

upper-class: *adj.* aristocratique

upper-hand: *n.* dessus

uppermost: *adj.* le plus haut

upright: *adj.* droit; vertical; droit; honnête

uprising: *n.* soulèvement

uproar: *n.* tumulte; vacarme

uproot: *vt.* déraciner

upset: *n.* désordre; bouleversement; *adj.* vexé; bouleversé

upset: *vt.* renverser; déranger; bouleverser

upshot: *n.* résultat; aboutissement; conclusion

upside-down: *adv.* sens dessus dessous

upstairs: *adv.* en haut (d'un escalier)

upstart: *n.* parvenu

uptight: *adj.* très tendu

up-to-date: *adj.* à jour

upturn: *n.* amélioration

upward: *adj.* ascendant

urban: *adj.* urbain

urbane: *adj.* courtois

urchin: *n.* gamin

urge: *n.* impulsion; désir ardent

urge: *vt.* pousser

urgency: *n.* urgence

urgent: *adj.* urgent

urinal: *n.* urinoir

urinate: *vi.* uriner

urine: *n.* urine

urn: *n.* urne

us: *pron.* us

usage: *n.* utilisation; usage

use: *n.* usage; utilisation; emploi

use: *vt.* se servir de; utiliser

used: *adj.* usagé

useful: *adj.* utile

usefulness: *n.* utilité
useless: *adj.* inutile
uselessness: *n.* inutilité
user-friendly: *adj.* facile à utiliser
usher: *n.* huissier; placeur
usherette: *n.* ouvreuse
usual: *adj.* habituel; courant
usurer: *n.* usurier
usurp: *vt.* usurper
usury: *n.* usure
utensil: *n.* ustensile
uterus: *n.* utérus
utilise: *vt.* utiliser
utility bill: une facture des services
publics (gaz; électricité)
utility: *n.* utilité
utmost: *adj.* extrême; le plus grand;
dernier
utter: *adj.* complet; absolu; total
utter: *vt.* prononcer; proférer
U-turn: *n.* demi-tour

V

vacancy: *n.* chambre libre
vacant lot: *n.* terrain vague
vacant: *adj.* vacant; inoccupé
vaccinate: *vt.* vacciner
vaccination: *n.* vaccination
vaccine: *n.* vaccin
vacuous: *adj.* vide
vacuum bottle: thermos
vacuum: *n.* vide
vagin: *n.* vagin
vague: *adj.* vague
vain: *adj.* vain; inutile; vaniteux
valence electron: électron de valence
valet: *n.* valet de chambre
valiant: *adj.* courageux; brave
valid: *adj.* valide; valable
validity: *n.* validité
valley: *n.* vallée
valour: *n.* courage; bravoure
valuable: *adj.* précieux; de valeur
valuation: *n.* évaluation; estimation
value: *n.* valeur
value: *vt.* évaluer; tenir à; apprécier
valued: *adj.* précieux; estimé
valve: *n.* soupape
vampire: *n.* vampire
van: *n.* camionnette
vandal: *n.* vandale
vandalise: *vt.* saccager
vandalism: *n.* vandalisme
vanguard: *n.* avant-garde
vanilla: *n.* vanille
vanish: *vi.* disparaître; se dissiper
vanity case: vanity-case
vanity: *n.* vanité
vanquish: *vt.* vaincre
vantage point: position avantageuse
vaporization: *n.* vaporisation
vapour: *n.* vapeur
variable expression: expression
variable
variable: *n.* variable
variation: *n.* variation

varicose vein: varice
varied: *adj.* varié
variety show: spectacle de variétés
variety: *n.* variété
various: *adj.* divers; différent
varnish: *n.* vernis
varnish: *vt.* vernir
vary: *vt.* varier; *vi.* changer
vase: *n.* vase
vast: *adj.* vaste; immense
vat: *n.* cuve
vault: *n.* voûte; cave; caveau
veal: *n.* veau
vector: *n.* vecteur; trajectoire
veer: *vi.* virer
vegetable garden: potager
vegetable: *adj.* végétal; *n.* végétal
vegetarian: *n.* végétarien
vegetate: *vi.* végéter
vegetation: *n.* végétation
vehemence: *n.* véhémence; fougue
vehement: *adj.* véhément; violent
vehicle: *n.* véhicule
veil: *n.* voile
veil: *vt.* voiler; dissimuler
vein: *n.* veine; nervure; disposition
velocity: *n.* vitesse
velvet: *n.* velours
vending machine: distributeur automatique
vendor: *n.* vendeur
veneer: *n.* placage; vernis
venerable: *adj.* vénérable
venerate: *vt.* vénérer
veneration: *n.* vénération
venereal: *adj.* vénérien
venial: *adj.* véniel
venison: *n.* venaison
venom: *n.* venin
venomous: *adj.* vénéneux
vent: *n.* orifice; conduit
vent: *vt.* décharger
ventilate: *vt.* aérer
ventilation: *n.* ventilation; aération

ventilator: *n.* ventilateur
ventriloquist: *n.* ventriloque
venture: *n.* entreprise
venture: *vi.* s'aventurer; *vt.* risquer; hasarder
venue: *n.* lieu
veranda: *n.* véranda
verb: *n.* verbe
verbal: *adj.* verbal; oral
verbally: *adv.* verbalement
verbatim: *adv.* textuellement; mot pour mot
verbose: *adj.* verbeux
verdant: *adj.* verdoyant
verdict: *n.* verdict; jugement
verification: *n.* vérification
verify: *vt.* vérifier
veritable: *adj.* véritable
vermin: *n.* vermine
vermouth: *n.* vermouth
versatile: *adj.* doué de talents multiples; versatile
verse: *n.* vers; verset
versed: *adj.* versé
version: *n.* version
versus: *prep.* contre
vertebra: *n.* vertèbre
vertebral: *adj.* vertébral
vertebrate: *adj.* vertébré; *n.* vertébré
vertex: *n.* sommet
vertical axis: axe vertical
vertical: *adj.* vertical
vertigo: *n.* vertige
verve: *n.* verve; brio
very: *adj.* vrai; véritable; exactement; même; *adv.* très; fort; bien
vessel: *n.* récipient; vase; navire
vest: *n.* gilet
vestibule: *n.* vestibule
vestige: *n.* vestige
vestment: *n.* vêtement de cérémonie; chasuble
vestry: *n.* sacristie
veteran: *adj.* vétéran; *n.* vétéran

veterinarian: *n.* vétérinaire
veterinary: *adj.* vétérinaire
veto: *n.* véto
veto: *vt.* opposer son véto à
vex: *vt.* contrarier
vexed: *adj.* contrarié
via: *prep.* via; par
viaduct: *n.* viaduc
vial: *n.* fiole; ampoule
vibrate: *vi.* vibrer
vibration: *n.* vibration
vicarious: *adj.* par personne interposée
vice versa: vice versa
vice: *n.* vice; défaut; étau
vice-chairman: *n.* vice-président
vicinity: *n.* voisinage; proximité
vicious: *adj.* méchant
victim: *n.* victime
victimise: *vt.* prendre pour victime
victor: *n.* vainqueur
victorious: *adj.* victorieux
victory: *n.* victoire
video camera: caméra
video capture: capture vidéo
video tape: bande vidéo
video: *n.* vidéo; vidéocassette; magnétoscope
vie: *vi.* rivaliser
view: *n.* vue; perspective; opinion; panorama
view: *vt.* voir; examiner
viewer: *n.* téléspectateur
viewfinder: *n.* viseur
viewpoint: *n.* point de vue
vigil: *n.* veille; vigile
vigilance: *n.* vigilance
vigilant: *adj.* vigilant; attentif
vigorous: *adj.* vigoureux
vigour: *n.* vigueur; énergie
vile: *adj.* vil; infâme; exécrable
vilify: *vt.* diffamer
villa: *n.* pavillon; maison de campagne

village: *n.* village
villager: *n.* villageois
villain: *n.* scélérat
vindicate: *vt.* venger; défendre
vindication: *n.* défense; justification
vindictive: *adj.* vindicatif
vine: *n.* vigne
vinegar: *n.* vinaigre
vineyard: *n.* vignoble
vintage: *n.* millésime; époque
vinyl: *n.* vinyle
viola: *n.* viole
violate: *vt.* violer
violation: *n.* violation
violence: *n.* violence
violent: *adj.* violent
violet: *n.* violette
violin: *n.* violon
violinist: *n.* violiniste
violoncello: *n.* violoncelle
viper: *n.* vipère
virgin: *adj.* vierge
virginity: *n.* virginité
virile: *adj.* viril
virility: *n.* virilité
virtual: *adj.* virtuel; quasiment
virtue: *n.* vertu
virtuous: *adj.* virtueux
virulent: *adj.* virulent
virus checker: détecteur de virus
virus: *n.* virus
visa: *n.* visa
vis-à-vis: *prep.* vis-à-vis
viscous: *adj.* visqueux; gluant
visibility: *n.* visibilité
visible: *adj.* visible
visibly: *adv.* visiblement
vision: *n.* vision; vue
visit: *n.* visite
visit: *vt.* visiter
visitation: *n.* visite
visiting hours: heures de visite
visitor: *n.* visiteur; touriste
visor: *n.* visière

vista: *n.* vue; perspective
visual: *adj.* visuel
visualise: *vt.* s'imaginer
vital statistics: statistiques démographiques
vital: *adj.* vital; essentiel; indispensable
vitality: *n.* vitalité
vitamin: *n.* vitamine
vitiate: *vt.* vicier
vivacious: *adj.* vif
vivid: *adj.* vif; vivant; frappant
vivisection: *n.* vivisection
vocabulary: *n.* vocabulaire
vocal: *adj.* vocal
vocation: *n.* vocation; profession; métier
vocative: *n.* vocatif
vociferous: *adj.* bruyant
vogue: *n.* vogue; mode
voice: *n.* voix
voice: *vt.* exprimer
void: *adj.* vide; *n.* vide
volatile: *adj.* volatile; versatile
volcanic: *adj.* volcanique
volcano: *n.* volcan
volition: *n.* volonté
volley: *n.* volée; salve; grêle
volleyball: *n.* volley-ball
voltage: *n.* voltage
voluble: *adj.* volubile; loquace
volume: *n.* volume
voluntarily: *adv.* volontairement
voluntary: *adj.* volontaire
volunteer: *n.* volontaire
volunteer: *vi.* se porter volontaire
voluptuous: *adj.* voluptueux
vomit: *n.* vomissement
vomit: *vt.* vomir
voracious: *adj.* vorace
vortex: *n.* tourbillon
vote: *n.* vote; suffrage; voix
vote: *vt.* voter
voter: *n.* électeur

voting: *n.* vote
voucher: *n.* bon
vow: *n.* voeu
vow: *vt.* jurer
vowel: *n.* voyelle
voyage: *n.* voyage par mer; traversée
vulgar: *adj.* vulgaire; grossier
vulgarity: *n.* grossièreté; vulgarité
vulnerable: *adj.* vulnérable
vulture: *n.* vautour

W'

wad: *n.* tampon; bouchon; liasse
waddle: *vi.* se dandiner
wade: *vi.* patauger
wading pool: petit bassin (pour enfants)
wafer: *n.* gaufrette; plaque
waffle: *n.* gaufre
waft: *vt.* porter; apporter; *vi.* flotter
wag: *vt.* remuer
wage earner: salarié
wage: *n.* salaire
wager: *n.* pari
wager: *vt.* parier
waggle: *vt.* remuer
waggon: *n.* chariot; (rail) wagon
wagtchdog: *n.* chien de garde
wail: *n.* gémissement; plainte
wail: *vi.* gémir
waist: *n.* taille
waistline: *n.* taille
wait: *n.* attente; arrêt
wait: *vi.* attendre
waiter: *n.* serveur
waiting list: liste d'attente
waiting room: salle d'attente
waive: *vt.* renoncer à
wake: *n.* veillée; (mar) sillage
wake: *vi.* se réveiller; *vt.* réveiller
waken: *vt.* réveiller; *vi.* se réveiller
walk: *n.* promenade; marche
walk: *vi.* marcher; aller à pied
walker: *n.* marcheur
walkie-talkie: *n.* talkie-walkie
walking stick: canne
walking: *n.* marche à pied
walkout: *n.* grève surprise
walkover: *n.* victoire facile; gâteau
walkway: *n.* passage pour piétons
wall: *n.* mur; muraille; paroi
walled: *adj.* muré
wallet: *n.* portefeuille
wallflower: *n.* giroflée
wallow: *vi.* se vautrer

wallpaper: *n.* papier peint
walnut: *n.* noix; noyer
walrus: *n.* morse
waltz: *n.* valse
wan: *adj.* pâle
wand: *n.* baguette (magique)
wander: *vi.* errer; aller sans but
wane: *vi.* décroître
want: *n.* besoin; manque
want: *vt.* vouloir; demander; *vi.* manquer
wanting: *adj.* manquant; qui manque; qui fait défaut
wanton: *adj.* lascif; capricieux
war: *n.* guerre
wardrobe: *n.* garde-robe; penderie
warehouse: *n.* entrepôt; magasin
warehouseman: *n.* magasinier
warehousing: *n.* entreposage
warfare: *n.* guerre
warhead: *n.* ogive
warily: *adv.* avec circonspection
wariness: *n.* circonspection; prudence
warm: *adj.* chaud; chaleureux
warm: *vt.* réchauffer; *vi.* se réchauffer; s'échauffer; s'animer
warm-hearted: *adj.* affectueux
warmly: *adv.* chaudement; chaleureusement
warmth: *n.* chaleur
warn: *vt.* prévenir; avertir
warning light: voyant lumineux
warning: *n.* avertissement
warp: *vi.* se voiler; *vt.* voiler; fausser
warrant: *n.* garantie; mandat
warranty: *n.* garantie
warren: *n.* terrier
warrior: *n.* guerrier
warship: *n.* navire de guerre
wart: *n.* verrue
wary: *adj.* prudent; circonspect
wash: *n.* lavage; lessive
wash: *vt.* laver; *vi.* se laver
washable: *adj.* lavable**

washbowl: *n.* lavabo
washcloth: *n.* gant de toilette
washer: *n.* rondelle
washing machine: machine à laver
washing: *n.* linge à laver; lessive
washing-up: *n.* vaisselle
wash-out: *n.* fiasco
washroom: *n.* toilettes
wasp: *n.* guêpe
wastage: *n.* gaspillage; perte
waste paper: vieux papiers
waste pipe: tuyau d'échappement
waste: *n.* gaspillage; détérioration;
terre inculte; déchets
waste: *vt.* gaspiller; dévaster;
saccager; perdre; *vi.* se perdre
wasteful: *adj.* gaspilleur; prodigue
watch: *n.* montre; surveillance; garde
watch: *vt.* regarder; observer;
surveiller; faire attention à
watchful: *adj.* vigilant
watchmaker: *n.* horloger
watchman: *n.* veilleur de nuit;
gardien
watchtower: *n.* tour de guet
watchword: *n.* mot de passe; mot
d'ordre
water closet: W.C.
water cycle: cycle de l'eau
water heater: chauffe-eau
water level: niveau de l'eau
water line: ligne de flottaison
water main: conduite principale
d'eau
water: *n.* eau
water: *vt.* arroser; mouiller; *vi.*
pleurer; larmoyer
watercolour: *n.* aquarelle
waterfall: *n.* cascade
watering-can: *n.* arrosoir
waterlogged: *adj.* imprégné d'eau
watermark: *n.* filigrane
watermelon: *n.* pastèque
waterproof: *adj.* imperméable

watershed: *n.* moment critique
waterskiing: *n.* ski nautique
watertight: *adj.* étanche
waterworks: *npl.* usine hydraulique
watery: *adj.* aqueux; détrempé;
délavé
watt: *n.* watt
wave: *n.* vague; lame; onde
wave: *vi.* faire signe de la main;
onduler; *vt.* agiter
wavelength: *n.* longueur d'ondes
waver: *vi.* vaciller; osciller
wavering: *adj.* hésitant
wavy: *adj.* ondulé
wax paper: papier paraffiné
wax: *n.* cire
wax: *vt.* cirer; *vi.* croître
waxworks: *n.* musée de cire
way: *n.* chemin; voie; route; manière;
direction
waybill: une feuille de route; lettre de
voiture
waylay: *vt.* attaquer; arrêter au
passage
wayward: *adj.* capricieux
we: *pron.* nous
weak person: personne faible
weak: *adj.* faible
weaken: *vt.* affaiblir
weakness: *n.* faiblesse; point faible
wealth: *n.* richesse; abondance
wealthy: *adj.* riche
wean: *vt.* sevrer
weapon: *n.* arme
wear: *n.* usage; usure
wear: *vt.* porter; user; *vi.* s'user
weariness: *n.* lassitude; fatigue; ennui
wearisome: *adj.* fatigant
weary: *adj.* las; fatigué; ennuyeux
weasel: *n.* belette
weather forecast: prévisions
météorologiques
weather: *n.* temps
weather: *vt.* surmonter

weather-beaten: *adj.* ayant souffert des intempéries
weathercock: *n.* girouette
weathering: *n.* détérioration climatique
weave: *vt.* tisser; entrelacer
weaving: *n.* tissage
web: *n.* tissu; toile d'araignée; palmure
website: *n.* site web
wed: *vt.* épouser; *vi.* se marier
wedding day: jour du mariage
wedding dress: robe de mariée
wedding present: cadeau de mariage
wedding ring: alliance
wedding: *n.* mariage; noces
wedge: *n.* cale
wedge: *vt.* caler; enfoncer
wedlock: *n.* mariage
Wednesday: *n.* mercredi
wee: *adj.* petit
weed: *n.* mauvaise herbe
weed: *vt.* désherber
weedkiller: *n.* désherbant
weedy: *adj.* envahi par les mauvaises herbes
week: *n.* semaine
weekday: *n.* jour de semaine; jour ouvrable
weekend: *n.* week-end; fin de semaine
weekly: *adj.* de la semaine; hebdomadaire; *adv.* chaque semaine; par semaine
weep: *vt.* pleurer
weeping willow: saule pleureur
weigh: *vt.* peser
weight: *n.* poids
weightily: *adv.* pesamment
weightlifter: *n.* haltérophile
weighty: *adj.* lourd; important
weird: *adj.* bizarre
welcome: *adj.* opportun; *n.* accueil
welcome: *vt.* accueillir

weld: *n.* soudure
weld: *vt.* souder
welfare state: État-providence
welfare: *n.* bien-être; assistance sociale
well: *n.* source; fontaine; puits; *adj.* bien; bon; *adv.* bien
well-behaved: *adj.* bien élevé; sage
well-being: *n.* bien-être
well-bred: *adj.* bien élevé
well-built: *adj.* bien bâti; solide
well-deserved: *adj.* bien mérité
well-dressed: *adj.* bien habillé
well-known: *adj.* connu; célèbre
well-mannered: *adj.* poli; bien élevé
well-meaning: *adj.* bien intentionné
well-off: *adj.* aisé; dans l'aisance
well-to-do: *adj.* aisé; riche
well-wisher: *n.* admirateur
wench: *n.* jeune fille; jeune femme
west: *n.* ouest; occident; *adj.* ouest; de/à l'ouest; *adv.* vers/à l'ouest
westward: *adv.* vers l'ouest
wet suit: combinaison de plongée
wet: *adj.* mouillé; humide; *n.* humidité
wet: *vt.* mouiller
wetnurse: *n.* nourrice
whack: *n.* grand coup
whack: *vt.* donner un grand coup à
whale: *n.* baleine
wharf: *n.* quai
what: *pron.* que; quoi; que; qui; ce qui; ce que; *adj.* quel; quelle; *excl.* quoi! comment!
whatever: *pron.* quoi que; tout; n'importe quoi
wheat: *n.* blé
wheedle: *vt.* cajoler; câliner
wheel and axle: axe et roue
wheel: *n.* roue; volant; gouvernail
wheel: *vt.* tourner; pousser; rouler; *vi.* tourner en rond; tournoyer
wheelbarrow: *n.* brouette

wheelchair: *n.* fauteuil roulant
wheelclamp: *n.* sabot
wheeze: *vi.* respirer bruyamment
when: *adv.* quand; *conj.* quand
whenever: *adv.* quand; chaque fois que
where: *adv.* où; *conj.* où
whereabout(s): *adv.* où
whereas: *conj.* tandis que; attendu que
whereby: *pron.* par lequel (laquelle); au moyen duquel (de laquelle)
whereupon: *conj.* sur quoi; après quoi
wherever: *adv.* où que
wherewithal: *npl.* ressources
whet: *n.* blé
whet: *vt.* aiguiser
whether: *conj.* si
which: *pron.* lequel; laquelle; celui que; celui qui; ce qui; ce que; quoi
whiff: *n.* bouffée; odeur
while: *n.* moment; *conj.* pendant que; alors que; quoique
whim: *n.* caprice
whimper: *vi.* gémir; pleurnicher
whimsical: *adj.* capricieux; fantasque
whine: *n.* gémissement; plainte
whine: *vi.* gémir; se plaindre
whinny: *vi.* hennir
whip: *n.* fouet; cravache
whip: *vt.* fouetter; battre
whipped cream: crème fouettée
whirl: *vi.* tourbillonner; tournoyer; *vt.* faire tourbillonner; faire tournoyer
whirlpool: *n.* tourbillon
whirlwind: *n.* tornade
whisper: *vi.* chuchoter; murmurer
whispering: *n.* chuchotement; murmure
whistle: *n.* sifflement
whistle: *vi.* siffler
white elephant: bibelot

white lie: petit mensonge; mensonge innocent
white: *adj.* blanc; pâle; *n.* blanc; blanc d'oeuf
white-hot: *adj.* chauffé à blanc
whiten: *vt.* blanchir
whiteness: *n.* blancheur; pâleur
whitewash: *n.* blanc de chaux
whitewash: *vt.* blanchir à la chaux; disculper
whiting: *n.* merlan
whitish: *adj.* blanchâtre
who: *pron.* qui
whoever: *pron.* quiconque; qui que ce soit; quel que soit
whole: *adj.* tout; entier; intact; complet; sain; *n.* tout; ensemble
wholehearted: *adj.* sincère
wholemeal: *adj.* complet
wholesale: *n.* vente en gros
wholesome: *adj.* sain; salubre
wholewheat: *adj.* complet
wholly: *adv.* complètement
whom: *pron.* qui; que
whooping cough: coqueluche
whore: *n.* putain
why: *n.* pourquoi; *conj.* pourquoi; *excl.* eh bien!; tiens!
wick: *n.* mèche
wicked: *adj.* méchant; mauvais
wickedness: *n.* méchanceté; perversité
wicker: *n.* osier; *adj.* en osier
wide open: grand ouvert
wide: *adj.* large; ample; grand
wide-awake: *adj.* bien réveillé
widen: *vt.* élargir; agrandir
widespread: *adj.* très répandu
widow: *n.* veuve
widower: *n.* veuf
width: *n.* largeur
wield: *vt.* manier; brandir
wife: *n.* femme; épouse
wig: *n.* perruque

wiggle: *vt.* agiter; *vi.* s'agiter
wild life: faune
wild: *adj.* sauvage; féroce; désert; fou; furieux
wilderness: *n.* étendue déserte
wildly: *adv.* violemment; furieusement; follement
wilful: *adj.* délibéré; entêté
wilfulness: *n.* obstination
wiliness: *n.* ruse; astuce
will: *n.* volonté; testament
will: *vt.* vouloir
willing: *adj.* prêt; disposé
willingness: *n.* bonne volonté; empressement
willow: *n.* saule
willpower: *n.* volonté
wilt: *vi.* se fâner
wily: *adj.* astucieux
win: *vt.* gagner; conquérir; remporter
wince: *vi.* tressaillir
winch: *n.* treuil
wind: *n.* vent; souffle; gaz
wind: *vt.* enrouler; envelopper; donner un tour de; *vi.* serpenter
windfall: *n.* fruit abattu par le vent; aubaine
winding: *adj.* tortueux
windmill: *n.* moulin à vent
window box: jardinière
window cleaner: laveur de carreaux
window ledge: appui de fenêtre
window pane: *n.* carreau
window sill: rebord de fenêtre
window: *n.* fenêtre
windpipe: *n.* trachée artère
windscreen washer: lave-glace
windscreen wiper: essuie-glace
windshield: *n.* pare-brise
windy: *adj.* venteux
wine cellar: cave (à vin)
wine glass: verre à vin
wine list: carte des vins
wine merchant: négociant en vins

wine tasting: dégustation de vins
wine: *n.* vin
wing: *n.* aile
winged: *adj.* ailé
winger: *n.* ailier
wink: *n.* clin d'oeil; clignement
wink: *vi.* faire un clin d'oeil
winner: *n.* gagnant; vainqueur
winning post: poteau d'arrivée
winter sports: *npl.* sports d'hiver
winter: *n.* hiver
winter: *vi.* hiverner
wintry: *adj.* d'hiver; hivernal
wipe: *vt.* essuyer; effacer
wire: *n.* fil; télégramme
wire: *vt.* installer des fils électriques à; télégraphier
wiring: *n.* installation électrique
wiry: *adj.* effilé et nerveux
wisdom teeth: dents de sagesse
wisdom: *n.* sagesse; prudence
wise: *adj.* sage; avisé; judicieux; prudent
wisecrack: *n.* bon mot; plaisanterie
wish: *n.* souhait; désir
wish: *vt.* souhaiter; désirer
wishful: *adj.* désireux
wisp: *n.* brin; mince volute
wistful: *adj.* nostalgique; rêveur
wit: *n.* esprit; intelligence
witch: *n.* sorcière
witchcraft: *n.* sorcellerie
with: *prep.* avec; à; de; contre
withdraw: *vt.* retirer; rappeler; annuler; *vi.* se retirer
withdrawal slip: bordereau de remboursement
withdrawal: *n.* retrait
withdrawn: *adj.* réservé
wither: *vi.* se flétrir; se faner
withhold: *vt.* détenir; retenir; empêcher
within: *prep.* à l'intérieur de; *adv.* dedans; à l'intérieur

without: *prep.* sans
withstand: *vt.* résister à
witless: *adj.* sot; stupide
witness stand: barre des témoins
witness: *n.* témoin; témoignage
witness: *vt.* être témoin de; attester
witticism: *n.* mot d'esprit
wittily: *adv.* spirituellement
wittingly: *adv.* sciemment; à dessein
witty: *adj.* spirituel; plein d'esprit
wizard: *n.* magicien
wobble: *vi.* trembler
woe: *n.* malheur; affliction
woeful. *adj.* triste; malheureux
wolf: *n.* loup
woman: *n.* femme
womanish: *adj.* de femme
womanly: *adj.* féminin; de femme
womb: *n.* utérus
women's lib: *n.* mouvement de libération de la femme
wonder: *n.* merveille; miracle; émerveillement
wonder: *vi.* s'émerveiller
wonderful: *adj.* merveilleux
wondrous: *adj.* merveilleux
wont: *n.* coutume
woo: *vt.* faire la cour à
wood alcohol: alcool méthylique
wood carving: sculpture sur bois
wood engraving: gravure sur bois
wood: *n.* bois
woodcut: *n.* gravure sur bois
woodcutter: *n.* bûcheron
wooded: *adj.* boisé
wooden: *adj.* de bois; en bois
woodland: *n.* région boisée
woodlouse: *n.* cloporte
woodman: *n.* forestier; garde forestier
woodpecker: *n.* pic
woodwind: *n.* bois
woodwork: *n.* menuiserie; woodworm; ver du bois

wool: *n.* laine
woollen: *adj.* de laine
woollens: *npl.* lainages
woolly: *adj.* laineux; de laine
word choice: choix d'un mot
word origin: origine d'un mot
word processing: traitement de texte
word processor: machine à traitement de texte
word: *n.* mot; parole
word: *vt.* exprimer; rédiger
wordiness: *n.* verbosité
wording: *n.* formulation
wordy: *adj.* verbeux
work: *n.* travail; œuvre; ouvrage; emploi
work: *vi.* travailler; opérer; fonctionner; fermenter
workable: *adj.* exploitable
workaholic: *n.* drogué du travail
worker: *n.* travailleur; ouvrier
workforce: *n.* main-d'oeuvre
working-class: *adj.* ouvrier
workman: *n.* ouvrier; artisan
workmanship: *n.* exécution; qualité du travail
workmate: *n.* camarade de travail
workshop: *n.* atelier
world: *n.* monde; *adj.* du monde; mondial
worldliness: *n.* mondanité; attachement aux choses matrielles
worldly: *adj.* mondain; terrestre
worldwide: *adj.* mondial
worm: *n.* ver
worn-out: *adj.* épuisé; usé
worried: *adj.* inquiet
worry: *n.* souci
worry: *vt.* inquiéter
worrying: *adj.* inquiétant
worse: *adj.* pire; *n.* le pire
worship: *n.* culte; adoration
worship: *vt.* adorer; vénérer

worst: *adj.* le pire; *adv.* le plus mal;
n. le pire
worth: *n.* valeur; prix; mérite
worthily: *adv.* dignement; à juste titre
worthless: *adj.* sans valeur; inutile
worthwhile: *adj.* qui vaut la peine;
louable
worthy: *adj.* digne; louable
would-be: *adj.* soi-disant
wound: *n.* blessure
wound: *vt.* blesser
wrangle: *n.* dispute
wrangle: *vi.* se disputer
wrap: *vt.* envelopper
wrapping: *n.* couverture (de
protection)
wrath: *n.* colère
wreath: *n.* couronne; guirlande
wreck: *n.* naufrage; ruines;
destruction; épave
wreck: *vt.* causer le naufrage de;
démolir
wreckage: *n.* naufrage; épave; débris
wren: *n.* roitelet
wrench: *n.* clé; torsion violente
wrench: *vt.* tordre; forcer; tourner
violemment
wrest: *vt.* arracher
wrestle: *vi.* lutter
wrestling: *n.* lutte
wretched: *adj.* malheureux;
misérable
wriggle: *vi.* remuer; se tortiller
wrinkle: *n.* ride
wrinkle: *vt.* rider; *vi.* se rider
wrist: *n.* poignet
wristband: *n.* manchette de chemise
wristwatch: *n.* montre-bracelet
writ: *n.* écriture; assignation; acte
judiciaire
write: *vt.* écrire; composer
write-off: *n.* perte
writer: *n.* écrivain; auteur
writhe: *vi.* se tordre

writing conventions: conventions
littéraires
writing desk: bureau
writing paper: papier à lettres
writing: *n.* écriture; oeuvres; écrit
wrong: *n.* mal; tort; *adj.* mauvais;
mal; adv mal; inexactement
wrong: *vt.* faire du tort à; léser
wrong: *vt.* tordre; essorer; arracher
wrongful: *adj.* injuste
wrongly: *adv.* injustement
wry: *adj.* ironique; narquois

$\mathcal{X}$

x-axis: axe des abscisses
xenon: *n.* xénon
xenophobe: *n.* xénophobe
xenophobia: *n.* xénophobie
xenophobic: *adj.* xénophobique
x-ray: *n.* rayon x; radiographie
xylophone: *n.* xylophone

$\mathcal{Y}$

yacht: *n.* yacht
yachting: *n.* navigation de plaisance
yard: *n.* yard (0;914 m); cour
yardstick: *n.* critère d'évaluation
yarn: *n.* longue histoire; fil
yawn: *n.* bâillement
yawn: *vi.* bailler
yawning: *adj.* béant
yeah: *adv.* oui; ouais
year: *n.* année
yearbook: *n.* annuaire
yearling: *n.* animal âgé d'un an
yearly: *adj.* annuel; *adv.* annuellement
yearn: *vi.* languir
yearning: *n.* désir ardent
yeast: *n.* levure
yell: *n.* hurlement
yell: *vi.* hurler
yellow: *adj.* jaune; *n.* jaune
yellowish: *adj.* jaunâtre
yelp: *n.* jappement
yelp: *vi.* japper; glapir
yes: *adv.* oui; *n.* oui
yestersday: *adv.* hier; *n.* hier
yet: *conj.* pourtant; cependant; *adv.* encore
yew: *n.* if
yield: *n.* production; récolte; rendement
yield: *vt.* donner; produire; rapporter; *vi.* se rendre; céder
yoga: *n.* yoga
yoke: *n.* joug
yolk: *n.* jaune d'oeuf
yonder: *adv.* là-bas
you: *pron.* vous; tu; te; toi
young: *adj.* jeune
youngster: *n.* jeune
your: *adj.* ton; ta; tes; votre; vos
yours: *pron.* le tien; la tienne; les tiens; les tiennes; le/la vôtre; les vôtres

youth hostel: auberge de jeunesse
youth: jeunesse; adolescence
youthful: *adj.* jeune
youthfulness: *n.* jeunesse

Z

zany: *adj.* farfelu
zap: *vt.* flinguer
zeal: *n.* zèle; ardeur
zealous: *adj.* zélé
zebra: *n.* zèbre
zenith: *n.* zénith
zero: *n.* zéro
zero-point energy: point d'énergie zéro
zest: *n.* enthousiasme
zip code: code postale
zipper: *n.* fermeture éclair
zone: *n.* zone
zoo: *n.* zoo
zoom: *n.* zoom

French – English
Word to Word Dictionary

Section 2

A

à: *prép.* (in) to; at; on; by, per; aller l'école to go to school;
- neuf heures = at nine o'clock
a priori: *nm.* apriorism; adv a priori
abaissement: *nm.* fall, drop
abaisser: *vt.* to lower
abandon: *nm.* abandonment, desertion
abandonné: *adj.* deserted
abandonner: *vt.* to abandon, leave
abasourdi: *adj.* stunned
abasourdir: *vt.* to stun
abat-jour: *nm.* lampshade
abats: *nmpl.* giblets
abattement: *nm.* despondency; exhaustion
abattoir: *nm.* abattoir, slaughterhouse
abattre: *vt.* to shoot; slaughter
abattu: *adj.* despondent; exhausted
abbaye: *nf.* abbey
abbé: *nm.* abbot
abbesse: *nf.* abbess
abcès: *nm.* abscess
abdiquer: *vt.* and *vi.* to abdicate
abdomen: *nm.* abdomen
abdominal: *adj.* abdominal
abeille: *nf.* bee
aberrant: *adj.* aberrant; absurd
aberration: *nf.* aberration
abêtissant: *adj.* mindless
abêtissement: *nm.* mindlessness
abîme: *nm.* chasm
abîmer: *vt.* spoil, damage;
s'- vr. = to get spoiled ou damaged
abject: *adj.* abject
abjection: *nf.* abjectness
abjurer: *vt.* to abjure
ablatif: *nm.* ablative
ablation: *nf.* removal
abnégation: *nf.* abnegation
aboiement: *nm.* bark
abolir: *vt.* to abolish
abolition: *nf.* abolition

abominable: *adj.* abominable;
-ment = *adv.* abominably
abondamment: *adv.* abundantly
abondance: *nf.* abundance
abondant: *adj.* abundant, plentiful
abonder: *vi.* to be abundant ou plentiful
abonné: *nm.* subscriber
abonnement: *nm.* subscription
abonner: *vt.* - qn = to subscribe, take out a subscription (à to)
abord: *nm.* d'- = first (of all)
abordable: *adj* affordable
aborder: *vt.* to approach
aborigène: *nmf.* aborigine; *adj.* aboriginal
aboutir: *vi.* to succeed
aboutissement: *nm.* outcome; success
abrasif: *adj.* abrasive
abrégé: *nm.* summary; en - = briefly
abréger: *vt.* to shorten; abridge
abreuver: *vt.* to water
abreuvoir: *nm.* drinking trough
abréviation: *nf.* abbreviation
abri: *nm.* shelter
abricot: *nm.* apricot
abriter: *vt.* to shelter;
s'- vr. = to shelter
abroger: *vt.* to repeal
abrupt: *adj.* abrupt;
-ement = *adv.* abruptly
abruti: *nm.* idiot; *adj.* idiotic
abrutir: *vt.* to make stupid
abrutissant: *adj.* stunning; mindnumbing
abscisse: *nf.* (math) abscissa
absence: *nf.* absence
absent: *adj.* absent
absenter (s'): *vr.* to leave, go out
abside: *nf.* apse
absolu: *adj.* absolute; -ment = *adv.* absolutely; *nm.* absolute
absolution: *nf.* absolution

absolutisme: *nm.* absolutism
absorbant: *adj.* absorbent
absorber: *vt.* to absorb
absorption: *nf.* absorption
absoudre: *vt.* to absolve, abstenir (a')
vr. to abstain (from)
abstention: *nf.* abstention
abstentionniste: *nmf.* abstainer
abstinence: *nf.* abstinence
abstraction: *nf.* abstraction
abstrait: *adj.* abstract; -ement = *adv.*
in the abstract; *nm.* abstract;
abstract art
absurde: *adj.* absurd;
-ment = *adv.* absurdly
absurdité: *nf.* absurdity
abus: *nm.* abuse
abuser: *vt.* - de to exploit; abuse
abusif: *adj.* improper
académicien, -ne: *nmf.* academician
académie: *nf.* academy; learned
society
académique: *adj.* academic
acajou: *nm.* mahogany
acariâtre: *adj.* cantankerous
accablant: *adj.* overwhelming
accalmie: *nf.* lull, calm
accéder à: *vi.* to reach
accélérateur: *nm.* accelerator
accélération: *nf.* acceleration
accélérer: *vi.* to speed up, accelerate
accent: *nm.* accent
accentuation: *nf.* accentuation
accentué: *adj.* pronounced
accentuer: *vt.* to accentuate
acceptable: *adj.* acceptable
accepter: *vt.* to accept
accès: *nm.* access
accessible: *adj.* accessible
accessoire: *adj.* secondary;
-ment = *nm.* accessory
accident: *nm.* accident
accidentel: *adj.* accidental;
-lement = *adv.* accidentally

acclamations: *nfpl.* cheers;
acclamation
acclamer: *vt.* to acclaim, cheer
acclimater: *vt.* to acclimatise;
s'- = to become acclimatised
accolade: *nf.* embrace
accommodant: *adj.* accommodating
accommoder: *vt.* to prepare; adapt
accompagnateur: *nm.* -trice, *nf.*
(mils) accompanist; guide
accompagnement: *nm.*
accompaniment
accompagner: *vt.* to accompany
accomplir: *vt.* to achieve, accomplish
accomplissement: *nm.*
accomplishment
accord: *nm.* agreement
accordéon: *nm.* accordion
accorder: *vt.* to grant;
s'- = *vr.* to agree
accorder du crédit: to grant credit
accorder une remise: to grant a
discount
accoster: *vt.* to accost
accouchement: *nm.* (med) delivery
accoucher: *vi.* to give birth
accoudoir: *nm.* armrest
accouplement: *nm.* coupling; joining
accourir: *vi.* to run up (à, vers to)
accoutrement: *nm.* (pej) outfit, dress
accréditer: *vt.* to accredit
accroc: *nm.* tear, breach
accrocher: *vt.* to hang up (à on)
accroissement: *nm.* increase
accroître: *vt.* to increase
accroupir (s'): *vr.* to crouch
accueil: *nm.* welcome, reception
accueillant: *adj.* welcoming
accueillir: *vt.* to welcome
accumulateur: *nm.* battery
accumulation: *nf.* accumulation
accumuler: *vt.* to accumulate
accusateur: *nm.* accuser;
adj. accusing

accusatif: *nm.* accusative (case)
accusation: *nf.* accusation
accusé: *nm.* accused, defendant
accusé de réception de commande:
acknowledgement of order
accuser: *vt.* to accuse
ace bier: *vt.* to overwhelm
acerbe: *adj.* harsh; acrid
acétate: *nm.* acetate
acétone: *nf.* acetone
acharné: *adj.* bitter, fierce;
unrelenting
acharnement: *nm.* relentlessness;
determination
achat: *nm.* purchase
achat comptant: cash sale
acheminer, transporter: to convey
acheter: *vt.* to buy
acheteur: *nm.* buyer, purchaser
acheteur éventuel: potential buyer
achèvement: *nm.* completion
achever: *vt.* to finish; complete
acide: *adj.* acid
acidité: *nf.* acidity
acidulé: *adj.* acid, acidulous
acier: *nm.* steel
aciérie: *nf.* steelworks
acné: *nf.* acne
acompte: *nm.* deposit, downpayment
à-côté: *nm.* side issue
à-coup: *nm.* jolt
acoustique: *adj.* acoustic; *nf.*
acoustics
acquéreur: *nm.* buyer, purchaser
acquérir: *vt.* to buy, purchase
acquiescer: *vi.* to agree; acquiesce
acquis: *adj.* acquired; *nm.* experience
acquisition: *nf.* acquisition; purchase
acquit pour: payment received
acquittement: *nm.* payment;
(jur) acquittal
acquitter: *vt.* to acquit; pay
acre: *nf.* acre
âcre: *adj.* acrid

acrobate: *nmf.* acrobat
acrobatie: *nf.* acrobatics
acrobatique: *adj.* acrobatic
acrylique: *adj.* acrylic
acte: *nm.* act; deed
acte constitutif: memorandum of
association (M/A)
acteur, actrice: *nmf.* actor
actif: *nm.* assets; *adj.* active
actif circulant, de roulement:
current assets
action: *nf.* act, action; share
actionnaire: *nmf.* shareholder
actionner: *vt.* to activate; drive
activation d'énergie: activation
energy
activement: *adv.* actively
activer: *vt.* to speed up;
s'- *vr.* = to bustle about
activité: *nf.* activity; hustle and bustle
actualité: *nf.* current events
actuel: *adj.* current, present
acuité: *nf.* acuteness; shrillness
acuponcture: *nf.* acupuncture
adaptable: *adj.* adaptable
adaptateur: *nm.* adaptor
adaptation: *nf.* adaptation
adapter: *vt.* to adapt (à to)
additif: *nm.* additive
addition: *nf.* addition; bill
additionnel: *adj.* additional
additionner: *vt.* to add up
adepte: *nmf.* follower; enthusiast
adéquat: *adj.* suitable, appropriate
adhérence: *nf.* adhesion
adhérent: *nm.* member, adherent;
adj. adherent
adhérer: *vi.* to adhere, stick
adhésif: *adj.* adhesive
adhésion: *nf.* adherence; membership
adiabatique: *adj.* adiabatic
adjacent: *adj.* adjacent (à to)
adjectif: *nm.* adjective
adjoint: *nm.* assistant, deputy

adjudant: *nm.* warrant officer
adjudication: *nf.* sale by auction
adjuger: *vt.* to auction
admettre: *vt.* to admit; accept; assume
administrateur: *nm.* director, administrator
administrateur judiciaire: official receiver
administratif: *adj.* administrative
administration: *nf.* management; administration
administrer: *vt.* administrer, diriger, gérer
admirable: *adj.* admirable; -ment = *adv.* admirably, brilliantly
admiratif: *adj.* admiring
admiration: *nf.* admiration
admirativement: *adv.* admiringly
admirer: *vt.* to admire
admissible: *adj.* allowable
admission: *nf.* admission
adolescence: *nf.* adolescence
adolescent, -e: *nmf.* adolescent
adopter: *vt.* to adopt; pass
adoption: *nf.* adoption; passing
adorable: *adj.* adorable; -ment = *adv.* delightfully
adorer: *vt.* to adore, worship
adoucir: *vt.* to soften
adrénaline: *nf.* adrenalin
adresse: *nf.* address; skill
adresser: *vt.* to address; to send
adroit: *adj.* deft, skilful; -ement = *adv.* deftly, skilfully
adsorption: *nm.* adsorption
aduler: *vt.* to flatter
adulte: *nmf.* adult, grown-up; *adj.* adult, full-grown
adultère: *nm.* adultery
adverbe: *nm.* adverb
adverbial: *adj.* adverbial; -ement = *adv.* adverbially
adversaire: *nmf.* adversary, opponent

adversité: *nf.* adversity
aération: *nf.* ventilation
aérer: *vt.* to air
aérien adj.: *nf.* -ne air, airy; aerial
aérodrome: *nm.* aerodrome, air-field
aérodynamique: *adj.* aerodynamic; *nf.* aerodynamics
aérogare: *nf.* (air) terminal
aéroglisseur: *nm.* hovercraft
aéronautique: *adj.* aeronautic; *nf.* aeronautics
aéronaval: *adj.* air and sea
aéroport: *nm.* airport
aérosol: *nm.* aerosol
aérospatial: *adj.* aerospace
afame: *nf.* soul
affable: *adj.* affable
affaiblir: *vt.* to weaken
affaiblissement: *nm.* weakening
affaire: *nf.* matter
affaissement: *nm.* subsidence
affaisser: *vt.* to cause to subside
affamé: *adj.* starving
affamer: *vt.* to starve
affectation: *nf.* allocation (à to); affectation
affecté: *adj.* affected
affecter: *vt.* to affect
affectif: *adj.* emotional
affection: *nf.* affection
affectueusement: *adv.* affectionately
affectueux: *adj.* affectionate
affermir: *vt.* to strengthen; to make firm
affermissement: *nm.* strengthening
affichage: *nm.* bill posting
affiche: *nf.* poster
afficher: *vt.* to post ou put up
affiner: *vt.* to refine
affinité: *nf.* affinity
affinité électronique: electron affinity
affirmatif: *adj.* affirmative
affirmation: *nf.* assertion

affirmativement: *adv.* in the affirmative
affirmer: *vt.* to assert
affluent: *nm.* tributary
affluer: *vi.* to rush (à to)
afflux: *nm.* influx, rush
affolant: *adj.* alarming
affolement: *nm.* panic
affoler: *vt.* to throw into a panic
affranchir: *vt.* to frank, stamp; free
affranchissement: *nm.* stamping, franking; freeing
affréter: *vt.* to charter
affreusement: *adv.* horribly, dreadfully
affreux: *adj.* horrible; awful
affrontement: *nm.* confrontation
affronter: *vt.* to confront; s'- *vr.* = to confront one another
afin: *prép.* - de (in order) to; - que = in order that, so that
africain: *adj.* African
Afrique: *nf.* Africa
agaçant: *adj.* annoying
agacer: *vt.* to annoy, irritate
age: *nm.* age
agence: *nf.* agency; branch; offices
agence de publicité: advertising agency
agence, succursale: branch
agencement: *nm.* organisation, arrangement; equipment
agencer: *vt.* to arrange; equip
agenda: *nm.* diary
agenouiller (s'): *vr.* to kneel (down)
agent: *nm.* agent; policeman
agent de change: stockbroker
agent en douane: clearing agent
agent exclusif: sole agent
agent maritime: shipping agent
agglomération: *nf.* town, urban area
aggravant: *adj.* aggravating
aggravation: *nf.* worsening, aggravation; increase

aggraver: *vt.* to make worse; increase
agile: *adj.* agile, nimble; -ment = *adv.* nimbly
agilité: *nf.* agility
agir: *vi.* to act
agitateur: *nm.* agitator
agitation: *nf.* agitation
agiter: *vt.* to shake; wave
agneau: *nm.* lamb
agonie: *nf.* death throes
agrafe: *nf.* staple; hook
agrafer: *vt.* to staple (together); fasten up
agrafeuse: *nf.* stapler
agraire: *adj.* agrarian; land
agrandir: *vt.* to make bigger; widen; expand
agréable: *adj.* agreeable, pleasant; -ment = *adv.* agreeably, pleasantly
agresser: *vt.* to attack
agresseur: *nm.* attacker
agressif: *adj.* aggressive
agression: *nf.* attack
agressivement: *adv.* aggressively
agressivité: *nf.* aggressiveness
agricole: *adj.* agricultural
agriculteur: *nm.* farmer
agriculture: *nf.* agriculture, farming
agripper: *vt.* to grab
agronome: *nm.* agronomist
agronomie: *nf.* agronomy
agrumes: *nmpl.* citrus fruits
ahuri: *adj.* stunned; stupefied
ahurissant: *adj.* staggering
aide: *nf.* help; aid
aide-comptable: bookkeeper
aider: *vt.* to help
aigle: *nm.* eagle
aigre: *adj.* sour, bitter; -ment = *adv.* sourly
aigreur: *nf.* sourness; acidity
aigri: *adj.* bitter, embittered
aigu: *adj.* aiguëshrill; acute; sharp
aiguille: *nf.* needle

aiguillage: *nm.* shunting
aiguiller: *vt.* to direct; shunt
aiguiser: *vt.* to sharpen
ail: *nm.* garlic
ailé: *adj.* winged
aileron: *nm.* fin; aileron
ailleurs: *adv.* elsewhere; partout everywhere else
aimable: *adj.* kind; -ment = *adv.* kindly
aimant: *nm.* magnet
aimanter: *vt.* to magnetise
aimer: *vt.* to love
aimer bien: to like
aîné: *nm.* eldest ou oldest child; *adj.* elder, older; eldest, oldest
ainsi: *adv.* so, thus
air: *nm.* air
aire: *nf.* area
aise: *nf.* ease, comfort
aisé: *adj.* easy; well-off; -ment = *adv.* easily
aisselle: *nf.* armpit
ajournement: *nm.* adjournment
ajourner: *vt.* to adjourn; defer, postpone
ajout: *nm.* addition
ajouter: *vt.* to add
ajuster: *vt.* to adjust
alarmant: *adj.* alarming
alarme: *nf.* alarm
alarmer: *vt.* to alarm
albâtre: *nm.* alabaster
album: *nm.* album
albumine: *nf.* albumen
alcalin: *adj.* alkaline
alcaloïde: *nm.* alkaloid
alchimie: *nf.* alchemy
alchimiste: *nm.* alchemist
alcool: *nm.* alcohol
alcoolique: *adj.* alcoholic; *nmf.* drunkard
alcoolisme: *nm.* alcoholism
aléatoire: *adj.* uncertain; risky

alentours: *nmpl.* surroundings, on neighbourhood
alerte: *adj.* alert; agile; *nf.* alarm, allure, *nf.* speed; look. alert
alerter: *vt.* to alert; notify; warn
algèbre: *nf.* algebra
algébrique: *adj.* algebraic
algorithme: *nm.* algorithm
algue: *nf.* seaweed
alibi: *nm.* alibi
aliénation: *nf.* alienation
aliéner: *vt.* to alienate
alignement: *nm.* alignment; alignment; *adv.* alphabetically
aligner: *vt.* to align, line up
aliment: *nm.* food
alimentaire: *adj.* alimentary, food
alimentation: *nf.* feeding; diet; food
altérer; *vt.* to change, alter
alimenter: *vt.* to feed
alinéa: *nm.* paragraph
allée: *nf.* avenue; path
alléger: *vt.* to make lighter; alleviate
allégorie: *nf.* allegory
allégresse: *nf.* cheerfulness
alléguer: *vt.* to allege, put forward postponement
Allemagne: *nf.* Germany
Allemand: *adj.* German; *nm.* German
aller: *vi.* to go
allergie: *nf.* allergy
allergique: *adj.* allergic (à to)
alliage: *nm.* alloy
alliance: *nf.* wedding ring
allié: *nm.* ally; *adj.* allied
allier: *vt.* to combine
allô: hello!
allocation: *nf.* allocation; allowance

allongé: *adj.* être allongé to be lying (down)
allonger: *vt.* to lengthen; s'- vr. = to lengthen; lie down
allouer: *vt.* to allocate

allumage: *nm.* ignition
allumé: *adj.* on (TV)
allumer: *vt.* to light; turn ou switch
allumette: *nf.* match
allusion: *nf.* allusion (à to)
alluvions: *nfpl.* alluvium, alluvial
alors: *adv.* then
alouette: *nf.* lark
alourdir: *vt.* to make heavy; increase
alphabet: *nm.* alphabet
alphabétique: *adj.* alphabetical;
alpinisme: *nm.* mountaineering
alpiniste: *nmf.* mountaineer
altération: *nf.* alteration, change
altercation: *nf.* altercation
alternance: *nf.* alternation
alternatif: *adj.* alternate
alternative: *nf.* alternative
alternativement: *adv.* in turn,
alterner: *vt.* and *vi.* to alternate (avec with)
altitude: *nf.* altitude, height
altruisme: *nm.* altruism
aluminium: *nm.* aluminium
alvéole: *nf.* cell
amabilité: *nf.* kindness
amaigrir: *vt.* to make thinner
amaigrissant: *adj.* slimming
amalgamer: *vt.* to combine
amalgamme: *nm.* mixture, amalgam
amant: *nm.* lover
amarrer: *vt.* to moor
amas: *nm.* pile, heap
amasser: *vt.* to amass, pile up
amateur: *nm.* amateur; connaisseur
ambassade: *nf.* embassy
ambassadeur, -drice: *nmf.* ambassador
ambiance: *nf.* atmosphere
ambigu: *adj.* ambiguous
ambiguïté: *nf.* ambiguity
ambitieux: *adj.* ambitious
ambition: *nf.* ambition
ambivalence: *nf.* ambivalence

ambre: *nm.* amber
ambulance: *nf.* ambulance
ambulant: *adj.* travelling, mobile
amélioration: *nf.* improvement
améliorer: *vt.* to improve; s'- vr. = to improve
aménagement: *nm.* fitting out; adjustment; development
aménager: *vt.* to fit out; adjust; develop
amende: *nf.* fine
amendement: *nm.* amendment
amener: *vt.* to bring
amer: *adj.* bitter
amèrement: *adv.* bitterly
américain: *adj.* American
Américain: *nm.* American
Amérique: *nf.* America
amertume: *nf.* bitterness
ameublement: *nm.* furniture
ami: *nm.* friend
amiante: *nm.* asbestos
amibe: *nf.* amoeba
amical: *adj.* friendly; -ement = *adv.* in a friendly manner
amincir: *vt.* to thin (down)
amiral: *nm.* admiral
amitié: *nf.* friendship
ammoniac: *nm.* ammonia
amnésie: *nf.* amnesia
amnistie: *nf.* amnesty
amnistier: *vt.* to grant an amnesty to
amoindrir: *vt.* to weaken; reduce
amoindrissement: *nm.* weakening; reduction
amoncellement: *nm.* pile; accumulation
amorçage: *nm.* initiation
amorcer: *vt.* to bait; begin
amorphe: *adj.* apathetic
amortir: *vt.* to soften; deaden
amortissement: *nm.* paying off
amour: *nm.* love
amoureux: *adj.* in love (de with)

amovible: *adj.* detachable
ampère: *nm.* ampere, amp
amphibie: *adj.* amphibious
amphithéâtre: *nm.* amphitheatre
ample: *adj.* roomy; wide; -ment =
adv. amply, fully
ampleur: *nf.* fullness; range
amplifier: *vt.* to increase; amplify
amplitude: *nf.* amplitude; magnitude
ampoule: *nf.* bulb; phial; blister
amputation: *nf.* amputation
amputer: *vt.* to amputate
amusant: *adj.* amusing
amuse-gueule: *nm.* appetizer
amuser: *vt.* to amuse
amygdales: *nfpl.* tonsils
an: *nm.* year
anabolisant: *nm.* anabolic steroid
anachronisme: *nm.* anachronism
anagramme: *nm.* anagram
analgésique: *adj.* analgesic
analogice: *nf.* analogy
analogique: *adj.* analogical
analogue: *adj.* analogous (à to)
analphabète: *adj.* illiterate
analyse: *nf.* analysis; test
analyser: *vt.* to analyse
analyste: *nmf.* analyst; psychoanalyst
analytique: *adj.* analytical; -ment =
adv. analytically
ananas: *nm.* pineapple
anarchie: *nf.* anarchy
anarchiste: *nmf.* anarchist
anathème: *nm.* anathema
anatomie: *nf.* anatomy
anatomique: *adj.* anatomical; -ment
= *adv.* anatomically .
ancestral: *adj.* ancestral
ancêtre: *nm.* ancestor
anchois: *nm.* anchovy
ancien: *adj.* old; former
ancienneté: *nf.* (years of) service;
seniority; age
ancrage: *nm.* anchorage

ancre: *nf.* anchor
ancrer: *vt.* to anchor
âne: *nm.* ass, donkey
anéantir: *vt.* to annihilate
anéantissement: *nm.* annihilation
anecdote: *nf.* anecdote
anémie: *nf.* anemia
anémone: *nf.* anemone
anesthésie: *nf.* anaesthetic;
anaesthesia
anesthésique: *nm.* anaesthetic
ange: *nm.* angel
angélique: *adj.* angelic; *nf.* angelica
angine: *nf.* tonsillitis
anglais: *adj.* English; *nm.* (ling)
English
Anglais: *nmf.* Englishman;
Englishwoman
angle: *nm.* angle; corner
Angleterre: *nf.* England
anglophone: *adj.* English-speaking;
nmf. English speaker
angoissant: *adj.* agonising
angoisse: *nf.* anguish
angoisser: *vt.* to cause anguish
animal: *nm.* animal
animal domestique: *nm.* pet
animateur, -trice: *nmf.* host,
compère; leader
animation: *nf.* animation; hustle and
bustle
animé: *adj.* busy; lively
animer: *vt.* to lead; host; liven up; s'-
vr. = to liven up
animisme: *nm.* animism
animosité: *nf.* animosity
annales: *nfpl.* annals
anneau: *nm.* ring
année: *nf.* year
année bissextile: *nf.* leap year
annexe: *nf.* annexe; *adj.* subsidiary
annexer: *vt.* to annex; append
annihiler: *vt.* to annihilate
anniversaire: *nm.* birthday

annonce: *nf.* advertisement; announcement
annoncer: *vt.* to announce (à to)
annoter: *vt.* to annotate
annuaire: *nm.* telephone directory, phone book
annuel: *adj.* annual
annulation: *nf.* cancellation; nullification
annuler: *vt.* to cancel; nullify
annuler une commande: to cancel an order
anode: *nf.* anode
anodin: *adj.* insignificant
anomalie: *nf.* anomaly
anonyme: *adj.* anonymous; impersonal; -ment = *adv.* anonymously
anorexie: *nf.* anorexia
anorexique: *adj. nmf.* anorexic
anormal: *adj.* abnormal; -ement = *adv.* abnormally
anse: *nf.* handle
antagonisme: *nm.* antagonism
antagoniste: *adj.* antagonistic
antécédent: *nm.* antecedent
antenne: *nf.* (rad, TV) aerial; (zool) feeler
antérieur: *adj.* earlier, previous; -ement = *adv.* earlier, previously
anthologie: *nf.* anthology
anthracite: *nm.* anthracite
anthropologie: *nf.* anthropology
anthropologue: *nm.* anthropologist
antiaérien: *adj.* antiaircraft
anticancéreux: *adj.* cancer
antichambre: *nf.* antechamber
anticipation: *nf.* anticipation
anticonceptionnel: *adj.* contraceptive
anticonformiste: *adj. nmf.* nonconformist
anticorps: *nm.* antibody
anticyclone: *nm.* anticyclone
antidater: *vt.* to backdate

antidépresseur: *adj.* antidepressant
antidote: *nm.* antidote
antigel: *nm.* antifreeze
antimilitariste: *adj.* antimili-tarist
antinucléaire: *adj.* antinu-clear
antipathie: *nf.* antipathy
antipathique: *adj.* unpleasant
antipode: *nm.* antipodes
antiquaire: *nmf.* antique dealer
antique: *adj.* ancient
antiquité: *nf.* antiquity; antique
antirouille: *adj.* invar rustproof
antisémite: *nmf.* anti-semite; *adj.* anti-semitic
antiseptique: *adj.* antiseptic
antisocial: *adj.* antisocial
antitétanique: *adj.* anti-tetanus
antithèse: *nf.* antithesis
antitoxine: *nf.* antitoxin
antivol: *nm.* invar anti-theftou security device; lock; *adj.* invar anti-theft
antonyme: *nm.* antonym
antre: *nm.* den
anus: *nm.* anus
anxiété: *nf.* anxiety
anxieux: *adj.* anxious
aorte: *nf.* aorta
août: *nm.* August
apaisant: *adj.* soothing
apaisement: *nm.* calming down; relief
apaiser: *vt.* to calm (down); relieve
apathie: *nf.* apathy
apathique: *adj.* apathetic
apercevoir: *vt.* to see; catch a glimpse of
aperçu: *nm.* (overall ou general) idea
apéritif: *nm.* aperitif
apesanteur: *nf.* weightlessness
apeuré: *adj.* frightened
aphone: *adj.* voiceless, hoarse
aphrodisiaque: *adj.* aphrodisiac
apiculteur: *nm.* beekeeper

apitoyer: *vt.* to move to pity
aplanir: *vt.* to level (out); smooth away
aplati: *adj.* flat
aplatir: *vt.* to flatten (out)
apocalypse: *nf.* apocalypse
apocalyptique: *adj.* apocalyptic
apogée: *nm.* apogee, peak
apolitique: *adj.* apolitical; nonpolitical
apologie: *nf.* apology
apoplexie: *nf.* apoplexy
apostrophe: *nf.* apostrophe
apothéose: *nf.* apotheosis
apôtre: *nm.* apostle
apparaître: *vi.* to appear
appareil: *nm.* device; appliance
appareil de levage: hoisting device
appareil photo: camera
appareil photo numérique: digital camera
appareillage: *nm.* casting off; equipment
appareiller: *vi.* (mar) to cast off
apparemment: *adv.* apparently
apparence: *nf.* appearance
apparent: *adj.* apparent
apparition: *nf.* appearance; apparition
appartement: *nm.* flat, appartment
appartenir à: *vi.* to belong to
appât: *nm.* bait
appâter: *vt.* to lure; bait
appauvrir: *vt.* to impoverish
appauvrissement: *nm.* impoverishment
appel: *nm.* call; appeal
appel d'offres: notice of tender
appeler: *vt.* to call; call out
appellation: *nf.* appelation; name
appendicite: *nf.* appendicitis
appesantir: *vt.* to weigh down
appétissant: *adj.* appetizing
appétit: *nm.* appetite (de for)

applaudir: *vt.* and *vi.* to applaude
applaudissements: *nmpl.* applause
applicable: *adj.* applicable (à to)
application: *nf.* application; use
appliqué: *adj.* thorough, industrious
appliquer: *vt.* to apply (à to); s'- vr. = to apply
apport: *nm.* supply
apporter: *vt.* to bring
apposer: *vt.* to append; affix
appréciable: *adj.* appreciable
apprêciatif: *adj.* evaluative; appreciative
appréciation: *nf.* estimation, assessment
apprécier: *vt.* to appreciate; to assess
appréhender: *vt.* to apprehend; dread
appréhension: *nf.* apprehension
apprendre: *vt.* to learn; - à lire = to learn to read
apprenti: *nmf.* apprentice
apprentissage: *nm.* apprenticeship
apprêter: *vt.* to dress; to size
apprivoiser: *vt.* to tame
approbateur: *adj.* approving
approbation: *nf.* approval
approche: *nf.* approach
approcher: *vt.* to move near; approach; s'- vr. = to approach
approfondir: *vt.* to deepen
approfondissement: *nm.* deepening
approprier (s'): *vr.* to appropriate
approuver: *vt.* to approve of
approvisionnement: *nm.* supplying
approvisionner: *vt.* to supply
approximatif: *adj.* approximate
approximation: *nf.* approximation
approximativement: *adv.* approximately
appui: *nm.* support
appuie-tête: *nm.* invar headrest
appurtenance: *nf.* membership
appuyer: *vt.* to press; lean
âpre: *adj.* bitter, harsh;

-ment = *adv.* bitterly
après: *prép.* after
après-demain: *adv.* the day after tomorrow
après-midi: *nf.* invar afternoon
âpreté: *nf.* bitterness
apte: *adj.* capable (à of)
aptitude: *nf.* aptitude; ability
aquarium: *nm.* aquarium
aquatique: *adj.* aquatic
aqueduc: *nm.* aqueduct
aqueux: *adj.* aqueous, watery
Arabe: *adj.* Arab; Arabic
arabesque: *nf.* arabesque
arable: *adj.* arable
arachide: *nf.* peanut, groundnut
araignée: *nf.* spider
arbalète: *nf.* crossbow
arbitrage: *nm.* arbitration
arbitraire: *adj.* arbitrary;
-ment = *adv.* arbitrarily
arbitre: *nm.* arbiter; referee
arbitrer: *vt.* to arbitrate; referee
arborer: *vt.* to wear; bear
arborescence: *nf.* arborescence
arboriculture: *nf.* arboriculture, tree cultivation
arbre: *nm.* tree
arbrisseau: *nm.* shrub
arbuste: *nm.* bush
arc: *nm.* bow; arc; arch
arc- bouter (s'): *vr.* to lean
arcade: *nf.* arcade
arc-en-ciel: *nmpl.* arcs-en-ciel rainbow
archaïque: *adj.* archaic
archange: *nm.* archangel
arche: *nf.* arch
archéologie: *nf.* archaeology
archéologue: *nmf.* archaeologist
archétype: *nm.* archetype
archevêque: *nm.* archbishop
archipel: *nm.* archipelago
architecte: *nmf.* architect

architectonique: *adj.* architectonic
architectural: *adj.* architectural
architecture: *nf.* architecture
archiver: *vt.* to file, archive
archives: *nfpl.* archives, records
archiviste: *nmf.* archivist
ardemment: *adv.* ardently
ardent: *adj.* ardent, burning
ardeur: *nf.* ardour
ardoise: *nf.* slate
ardu: *adj.* difficult
are: *nf.* are, a hundred square meters
arène: *nf.* arena
arête: *nf.* (fish) bone
argent: *nm.* silver; money
argenté: *adj.* silver; silver-plated
argenterie: *nf.* silverware
argile: *nf.* clay
argot: *nm.* slang
argument: *nm.* argument
argumentation: *nf.* argumentation
argumenter: *vi.* to argue (sur about)
aride: *adj.* arid
aridité: *nf.* aridity
aristocrate: *nmf.* aristocrat
aristocratie: *nf.* aristocracy
aristocratique: *adj.* aristocratic
arithmetical: *adj.* aritmetical
arithmétique: *nf.* arithmetic
armature: *nf.* (frame) work
arme: *nf.* arm, weapon
armée: *nf.* army
armement: *nm.* arms, weapons; armaments
armer: *vt.* to arm
armistice: *nm.* armistice
armoire: *nf.* cupboard; wardrobe
armure: *nf.* armour
aromate: *nm.* herb; spice
aromatique: *adj.* aromatic
aromatiser: *vt.* to flavour
arôme: *nm.* aroma; flavour
arpenteur: *nm.* (land) surveyor
arqué: *adj.* curved, arched

arquebuse: *nf.* arquebus
arrachement: *nm.* wrench; pulling out tearing off
arracher: *vt.* to pull (out); tear off
arrangeant: *adj.* obliging
arrangement: *nm.* arrangement
arranger: *vt.* to arrange; fix
arrestation: *nf.* arrest
arrêt: *nm.* stopping; stop (button)
arrêté: *nm.* order
arrêter: *vt.* to stop; s'- vr. = to stop
arrhes: *nfpl.* deposit
arriéré: *adj.* backward
arrière: *nm.* invar back
arrière-goût: *nm.* aftertaste
arrière-grand-mère: *nf.* great-grandmother
arrière-grand-père: *nm.* great-grandfather
arrière-pays: *nm.* hinterland
arrière-pensée: *nf.* ulterior motive
arrière-petits-enfants: *nmpl.* great grandchildren
arrière-plan: *nm.* background
arrimer: *vt.* to stow
arrivage: *nm.* delivery
arrivant: *nmf.* newcomer
arrivée: *nf.* arrival, coming
arriver: *vi.* to arrive, come
arriver à échéance: to fall due
arriviste: *nmf.* careerist; social climber
arrogance: *nf.* arrogance
arrogant: *adj.* arrogant
arroger (s'): *vr.* to assume (without rights to)
arrondi: *adj.* rounded
arrondir: *vt.* to make round; round off
arrondissement: *nm.* district
arrosage: *nm.* watering
arroser: *vt.* to water
arsenal: *nm.* arsenal
arsenic: *nm.* arsenic

art: *nm.* art
artère: *nf.* artery; road
artériel: *adj.* arterial
arthrite: *nf.* arthritis
artichaut: *nm.* artichoke
article: *nm.* article, item
article défectueux: defective item
articulation: *nf.* joint; knuckle
articuler: *vt.* to articulate
artifice: *nm.* trick
artificiel: *adj.* artificial
artillerie: *nf.* artillery
artisan: *nm.* artisan, craftsman
artisanal: *adj.* craft
artisanat: *nm.* craft industry
artiste: *nmf.* artist
artistique: *adj.* artistic
as: *nm.* ace
ascendance: *nf.* ancestry
ascendant: *adj.* upward, rising
ascenseur: *nm.* lift, elevator
ascension: *nf.* ascent
ascète: *nmf.* ascetic
ascétique: *adj.* ascetic
aseptiser: *vt.* to sterilise; disinfect
asexué: *adj.* asexual
asiatique: *adj.* Asian
Asie: *nf.* Asia
asile: *nm.* refuge; asylum
aspect: *nm.* appearance, look
asperge: *nf.* asparagus
asperger: *vt.* to splash (de with)
aspérité: *nf.* bump
asphalte: *nm.* asphalt
asphyxie: *nf.* asphyxiation, suffocation
asphyxier: *vt.* to asphyxiate, suffocate
aspirateur: *nm.* vacuum cleaner
aspiration: *nf.* inhalation
aspirer: *vt.* to inhale
aspirine: *nf.* aspirin
assagir: *vt.* to quieten (down)
assaillant: *nm.* assailant

assaillir: *vt.* to assail
assainir: *vt.* to clean up; purify
assainissement: *nm.* cleaning up
assaisonnement: *nm.* seasoning
assaisonner: *vt.* to season
assassin: *nm.* murderer; assassin
assassinat: *nm.* murder; assassination
assassiner: *vt.* to assassinate
assaut: *nm.* assault, attack (de on)
assécher: *vt.* to drain
assemblage: *nm.* assembly; assembling
assemblée: *nf.* meeting
assemblée générale: general meeting
assembler: *vt.* to assemble; s'- vr. = to assemble
assentiment: *nm.* assent
asseoir (s'): *vr.* to sit down
assermenté: *adj.* on oath
assertion: *nf.* assertion
asservissement: *nm.* enslavement; slavery
assez: *adv.* enough; quite, rather
assidu: *adj.* assiduous; regular
assiduité: *nf.* assiduity; regularity
assiéger: *vt.* to besiege
assiette: *nf.* plate
assigner: *vt.* to assign
assimilation: *nf.* assimilation; comparison; classification
assimiler: *vt.* to assimilate
assis: *adj.* seated, sitting (down)
assistance: *nf.* audience; assistance
assistant: *nm.* assistant
assister: *vt.* to attend; assist
association: *nf.* association
associé: *nm.* associate, partner
associé gérant: general partner
associer: *vt.* to associate (à with); s'- vr. = to join together
assoiffé: *adj.* thirsty
assombrir: *vt.* to darken; s'- = to darken
assommer: *vt.* to stun

assomption: *nf.* assumption
assortiment: *nm.* assortment
assortir: *vt.* to match; s'- vr. = to go well together
assoupir (s'): *vr.* to doze off
assoupissement: *nm.* doze
assouplir: *vt.* to make supple; relax
assouplissement: *nm.* softening; relaxing
assourdir: *vt.* to deafen; muffle
assourdissant: *adj.* deafening
assouvir: *vt.* to satisfy
assouvissement: *nm.* satisfying, satisfaction
assujettir: *vt.* to subjugate
assumer: *vt.* to assume
assurance: *nf.* assurance; insurance (policy)
assurance maladie: sickness benefits
assurance vieillesse: old age insurance
assuré: *nm.* assured; *adj.* confident
assuré, un: an insured person
assurer: *vt.* to assure
assureur: *nm.* (insurance) agent; insurer(s), insurance company
astérisque: *nm.* asterisk
asthmatique: *adj.* asthmatic
asthme: *nm.* asthma
asticot: *nm.* maggot
astigmate: *adj.* astigmatic
astiquer: *vt.* to polish
astre: *nm.* star
astreignant: *adj.* demanding
astreindre: *vt.* to force, to compel
astrologie: *nf.* astrology
astrologique: *adj.* astrological
astrologue: *nm.* astrologer
astronaute: *nm.* astronaut
astronome: *nm.* astronomer
astronomie: *nf.* astronomy
astronomique: *adj.* astronomical
astuce: *nf.* shrewdness; (clever) trick; pun

astucieux: *adj.* astute
asymétrique: *adj.* asymmetric (al)
atelier: *nm.* workshop; studio
atermoyer: *vi.* to procrastinate
athée: *nmf.* atheist; *adj.* atheistic
athéisme: *nm.* atheism
athlète: *nmf.* athlete
athlétique: *adj.* athletic
athlétisme: *nm.* athletics
atlas: *nm.* atlas
atmosphère: *nf.* atmosphere
atmosphérique: *adj.* atmospheric
atome
atome: *nm.* atom
atomique: *adj.* atomic
atomiseur: *nm.* spray; atomiser
atout: *nm.* trump; advantage, asset
âtre: *nm.* hearth
atroce: *adj.* atrocious; dreadful;
-ment = *adv.* atrociously; dreadfully
atrocité: *nf.* atrocity
atrophié: *adj.* atrophied
attachant: *adj.* endearing
attache: *nf.* fastener
attachement: *nm.* attachment (à to)
attacher: *vt.* to tie together; tie up;
fasten; attach (a to)
attaque: *nf.* attack
attaquer: *vt.* to attack; tackle
attarder (s'): *vr.* to linger
atteindre: *vt.* to reach; affect; contact
atteinte: *nf.* attack (à on); hors d'-
beyond ou out of reach
attenant: *adj.* adjoining
attendre: *vt.* to wait
attendrir: *vt.* to fill with pity; move
attendrissant: *adj.* touching, moving
attendrissement: *nm.* emotion
attendu: *adj.* expected; long-awaited
attentat: *nm.* attack (contre on);
murder attempt
attente: *nf.* wait; expectation
attentif: *adj.* attentive; careful
attention: *nf.* attention; care

attentionné: *adj.* considerate,
attentivement: *adv.* attentively;
carefully
atténuation: *nf.* alleviation; easing
atténuer: *vt.* to alleviate; ease
atterrir: *vi.* to land, touch down
atterrissage: *nm.* landing, touch
down
attester: *vt.* to testify to
attirail: *nm.* gear
attirant: *adj.* attractive
attirer: *vt.* to attract;
- des ennuis à qn = to cause sb trouble
attiser: *vt.* to stir up
attitude: *nf.* attitude; bearing
attraction: *nf.* attraction
attrait: *nm.* attraction, appeal
attraper: *vt.* to catch
attrayant: *adj.* attractive
attribuer: *vt.* to attribute; award
attribut: *nm.* attribute
attribution: *nf.* attribution
attrister: *vt.* to sadden
attroupement: *nm.* crowd, gathering
aube: *nf.* dawn, daybreak
auberge: *nf.* inn; - de jeunesse youth
hostel
aubergine: *nf.* aubergine
aucun: *adj.* no; not any; any; sans -
doute = without (any) doubt;
-ement = *adv.* in no way; not **in the
least**: *pron.* none; not any; any (one)
audace: *nf.* audacity; daring
audacieux: *adj.* audacious, bold;
daring
audience: *nf.* audience; hearing
audiovisuel: *adj.* audio-visual
auditeur: *nm.* listener; auditor
auditoire: *nm.* audience
augmentation: *nf.* increase, rise (de
in); increasing, raising (de of)
augmenter: *vt.* to increase, raise
augure: *nf.* omen; oracle
aujourd'hui: *adv.* today

aumône: *nm.* calms
auparavant: *adv.* before, previously; before, first
auprès: *prép.* de next to; (compared) with
auquel: pron. à lequel
auréole: *nf.* halo, aureole; ring (mark)
auriculaire: *adj.* auricular; *nm.* little finger
aurore: *nf.* dawn, first light
ausculter: *vt.* to auscultate
aussi: *adv.* too, also; so
aussitôt: *adv.* immediately
austère: *adj.* austere; -ment = *adv.* austerely
austérité: *nf.* austerity
autant: *adv.* as much; as many; so much; such
autel: *nm.* altar
auteur: *nm.* author
authenticité: *nf.* authenticity
authentifier: *vt.* to authenticate
authentique: *adj.* authentic; -ment = *adv.* authentically
autobiographie: *nf.* autobiography
autobiographique: *adj.* autobiographical
autocar: *nm.* coach
autochtone: *nm.* native
autocollant: *adj.* self-adhesive
autocuiseur: *nm.* pressure cooker
autodéfense: *nf.* self-defence
autodestruction: *nf.* self-destruction
autodidacte: *nmf.* self-taught
auto-école: *nf.* driving school
auto-inflammation: self-ignition
auto-inhibition: self-inhibition
automate: *nm.* automaton
automatique: *adj.* automatic; -ment = *adv.* automatically
automatiser: *vt.* to automate
automatisme: *nm.* automatism
automne: *nm.* autumn
automobile: *nf.* (motor) car

automobiliste: *nmf.* motorist
autonome: *adj.* autonomous; self-governing
autonomie: *nf.* autonomy; self-government
autoportrait: *nm.* self-portrait
autopsie: *nf.* autopsy, post-mortem (examination)
autoradio: *nm.* car radio
autorisation: *nf.* authorisation, permission; permit
autoriser: *vt.* to authorise, give permission for; allow
autoritaire: *adj.* authoritarian
autorité: *nf.* authority
autoroute: *nf.* motorway
autosatisfaction: *nf.* self-satisfaction
auto-stop: *nm.* hitch-hiking
auto-stoppeur: *nmf.* hitch-hiker
autour: *prép.* around; *adv.* around
autre: *adj.* other
autrefois: *adv.* in the past, in days gone by
autrement: *adv.* differently; otherwise
autruche: *nf.* ostrich
autrui: pron. others
auxin: *adj.* auxiliary; *nm.* auxiliary; *nmf.* assistant
avalanche: *nf.* avalanche
avaler: *vt.* to swallow
avaliser une traite: to back a draft
avance: *nf.* advance; lead
avance (à l'): *adv.* ahead, in advance
avancement: *nm.* promotion; progress; forward movement
avancer: *vt.* to move forward; bring forward
avant: *prép.* before
avantage: *nm.* advantage
avantager: *vt.* to favour; flatter
avantageux: *adj.* profitable
avant-bras: *nm.* invar forearm
avant-coureur: *adj.* precursory

avant-dernier: *adj.* next to last, second last, last but one
avant-goût: *nm.* foretaste
avant-hier: *adv.* the day before yesterday
avant-première: *nf.* preview

avant-tarde: *nf.* avant-garde; vanguard
avare: *nmf.* miser; *adj.* miserly
avarice: *nf.* avarice, miserliness
avarie: *nf.* damage
avarié: *adj.* rotting; damaged
avarie, en cas de: in case of damage
avec: *prép.* with; to
avènement: *nm.* accession (à to); advent
avenir: *nm.* future
aventure: *nf.* adventure; venture; experience; affair
aventurer (s'): *vr.* to venture
aventurier: *nm.* adventurer
avenue: *nf.* avenue
avérer (s'): *vr.* to turn out, prove to be
averse: *nf.* shower (of rain)
aversion: *nf.* aversion (pour to); loathing (pour for)
avertir: *vt.* to warn; inform (de of)
avertissement: *nm.* warning
aveu: *nm.* admission, confession
aveuglant: *adj.* blinding
aveugle: *adj.* blind; *nmf.* blind person
aveuglement: *nm.* blindness
aveugler: *vt.* to blind
aviateur: *nm.* pilot, aviator
aviation: *nf.* flying; aviation
avide: *adj.* greedy; eager;
-ment = *adv.* greedily; eagerly
avidité: *nf.* greed; eagerness
avilir: *vt.* to degrade
avilissant: *adj.* degrading
avion: *nm.* airplane, aircraft
aviron: *nm.* oar; rowing

avis: *nm.* opinion
avis de virement: notice of transfer
avisé: *adj.* wise, sensible
aviser: *vt.* to advise, inform; notice
aviver: *vt.* to sharpen; deepen; arouse
avocat: *nm.* lawyer, advocate; *nm.* avocado (pear)
avoine: *nf.* oats
avoir: *vt.* to have
avoir besoin de: *v.* to need
avoir confiance: *v.* to trust
avoir les moyens (de): *v.* to afford
avoir mal au coeur: *v.* to feel sick
avoir un solde créditeur: to be in the black
avortement: *nm.* abortion
avorter: *vi.* to abort; fail
avoué: *nm.* solicitor
avouer: *vt.* to admit (to); confess (to)
avril: *nm.* April
axe: *nm.* axis; axle; main road
axial: *adj.* axial
azéotrope: azeotrope
azote: *nm.* nitrogen

B

babines: *nfpl.* chops
babiole: *nf.* trinket, trifle
bâbord: *nm.* (mar) port
babouin: *nm.* baboon
baby-sitter: *nf.* baby-sitter
bac: *nm.* ferry
bâche: *nf.* tarpaulin, cover
bâcler: *vt.* to botch
bactérie: *nf.* bacterium
badaud: *nm.* idle onlooker
badge: *nm.* badge
bafouer: *vt.* to scorn
bafouiller: *vi.* to stammer; babble
bagage: *nm.* luggage; stock of knowledge
bagarre: *nf.* fight, brawl
bagarrer (se): *vr.* fight; riot
bagatelle: *nf.* trinket; trifling sum
bagne: *nm.* penal servitude; (fig) grind
bague: *nf.* ring
baguette: *nf.* stick; loaf of French bread
baie: *nf.* (geog) bay
baigner: *vt.* to bathe;
se - *vr.* = to have a bath, swim
baignoire: *nf.* bath(tub)
bail: n f lease
bâiller: *vi.* to yawn
bâillon: *nm.* gag
bâillonner: *vt.* to gag
bain: *nm.* bath; bathe; swim
baiser: *nm.* kiss; *vt.* to kiss
baisse: *nf.* fall, drop
baisser: *vi.* to fall, drop; *vt.* to lower
bal: *nm.* dance
balade: *nf.* (fam) walk; drive
balader (se): *vr.* (fam) to go for a walk; to go for a drive
balai: *nm.* broom, brush. balai à franges; mop
balance: *nf.* scales; balance
balancement: *nm.* sway; rocking

balancer: *vt.* to swing; to balance
balançoire: *nf.* swing; seesaw
balayer: *vt.* to sweep, brush
balbutiement: *nm.* stammering, babbling
balbutier: *vt.* to stammer, babble
balbuzard: *nm.* osprey
balcon: *nm.* balcony
baleine: *nf.* whale
balistique: *nf.* ballistics
ballast: *nm.* ballast
balle: *nf.* bullet; ball
ballet: *nm.* ballet
ballon: *nm.* ball; balloon
ballotter: *vt.* jolt, shake about
balourd: *adj.* stupid; clumsy
balustrade: *nf.* balustrade; handrail
bambou: *nm.* bamboo
banal: *adj.* banal, trite; -ement = *adv.* tritely
banalisation: *nf.* vulgarising; standardisation
banalité: *nf.* banality, triteness
banane: *nf.* banana
banc: *nm.* bench
bancaire: *adj.* banking, bank
bancal, pl bancals: *adj.* lame; rickety
bandage: *nm.* bandage
bande: *nf.* band; tape; - dessinée strip cartoon
bande dessinée: strip cartoon
bandeau: *nm.* headband; blindfold
bander: *vt.* to bandage; stretch
banderole: *nf.* banner streamer
bandit: *nm.* bandit
banlieue: *nf.* suburbs
bannière: *nf.* banner
bannir: *vt.* to banish; prohibit
bannissement: *nm.* banishment
banque: *nf.* bank; banking
banque d'affaires: merchant bank
banque de dépôts: clearing bank
banque d'émission: issuing bank
banque d'outremer: overseas bank

banqueroute: *nf.* bankruptcy
banquet: *nm.* banquet
banquette: *nf.* seat, stool
banquier: *nm.* banker
banquise: *nf.* ice floe
baptême: *nm.* baptism
baptiser: *vt.* to baptise
bar: *nm.* bar; (zool) bass
barbare: *adj.* barbarian; barbaric
barbarie: *nf.* barbarism; barbarity
barbarisme: *nm.* (gr) barbarism
barbe: *nf.* beard
barbelé: *adj.* barbed
barbiturique: *adj.* barbituric; *nm.* barbiturate
barboter: *vi.* to dabble; splash
barbouillage: *nm.* scribble; daub
barbouiller: *vt.* to smear; scrawl
barbu: *adj.* bearded; *nm.* bearded man
barème: *nm.* list, schedule
baril: *nm.* barrel, cask
bariolé: *adj.* multicoloured, motley
baromètre: *nm.* barometer
baron: *nm.* baron
baroque: *adj.* baroque; *nm.* baroque
barque: *nf.* small boat
barrage: *nm.* barrage, barrier, dam
barre: *nf.* bar, rod
barré: *adj.* barred, blocked
barreau: *nm.* rung; bar (cage)
barrer: *vt.* to bar, block
barrer un chèque: to cross a cheque
barrette: *nf.* (hair) slide, brooch
barricader: *vt.* to barricade
barrière: *nf.* barrier; fence
barrière d'activation: activation energy
baryton: *nm.* baritone
bas: *adj.* low, base
basalte: *nm.* basalt
bas-côté: *nm.* verge; aisle
bascule: *nf.* weighing machine, scales
basculer: *vi.* to tip up, topple over

base: *nf.* base; basis
baser: *vt.* to base
bas-fond: *nm.* (naut) shallow, shoal
basilic: *nm.* (bot) basil
basilique: *nf.* basilica
basket: *nm.* basketball
basketteur: *nm.* basketball player
bas-relief: *nm.* bas-relief
basse: *nf.* (mus) bass
basse-cour: *nf.* poultry-yard
bassesse: *nf.* meanness; vulgarity
bassin: *nm.* pond, pool; dock
bassine: *nf.* bowl
basson: *nm.* bassoon
bastion: *nm.* bastion
bas-ventre: *nm.* lower abdomen
bataille: *nf.* battle
batailler: *vi.* (fig) to fight, battle
batailleur: *adj.* combative, aggressive
bataillon: *nm.* (mil) battalion
batard: *adj.* bastard, illegitimate
bateau: *nm.* boat, ship
batelier: *nm.* boatman
bâtiment: *nm.* building; ship
bâtir: *vt.* to build
batisse: *nf.* building, house
bâton: *nm.* stick, staff
batracien: *nm.* batrachian
battant: *nm.* clapper (bell); shutter
batte: *nf.* bat
battement: *nm.* banging; beating
batterie: *nf.* battery
batteur: *nm.* drummer; batsman
battre: *vt.* to beat, defeat
battu: *adj.* beaten
baudet: *nm.* donkey
baume: *nm.* balm, balsam
bauxite: *nf.* bauxite
bavard: *nm.* chatterbox; *adj.* talkative, loquacious
bavardage: *nm.* chatting, gossiping
bavarder: *vi.* to chat, gossip
bave: *nf.* dribble, slobber

baver: *vi.* to dribble, drool
bavoir: *nm.* bib
bavure: *nf.* smudge, blunder
bazar: *nm.* bazaar; general store
béant: *adj.* gaping, wide open
béat: *adj.* blissful; -ement = *adv.* rapturously
béatitude: *nf.* beatitude; bliss
beau, belle: *adj.* beautiful, lovely
beaucoup: *adv.* a lot, a great deal
beau-fils: *nm.* son-in-law; stepson
beau-frère: *nm.* brother-in-law
beau-père: *nm.* father-in-law; step-father
beauté: *nf.* beauty, loveliness
beaux-arts: *nmpl.* fine arts
beaux-parents: *nmpl.* parents-in-laws
bébé: *nm.* baby
bec: *nm.* beak, bill
béchamel: *nf.* béchamel (sauce)
bée: *adj.* open-mouthed, flabber-gasted
bégaiement: *nm.* stammering, faltering
bégayer: *vi.* to stammer, stutter
bégonia: *nm.* begonia
beige: *adj.* beige; *nm.* beige
beignet: *nm.* fritter; doughnut
bêlement: *nm.* bleating
bêler: *vi.* to bleat
belge: *adj.* Belgian
Belge: *nmf.* Belgian
Belgique: *nf.* Belgium
belle-fille: *nf.* daughter-in-law, stepdaugher
belle-mère: *nf.* mother-in-law, step-mother
belle-soeur: *nf.* sister-in-law
belligérant: *nm.* belligerent; *adj.* belligerent
belliqueux: *adj.* aggressive; warlike
bémol: *nm.* (mus) flat
bénédictin: *nmf.* Benedictine

bénédiction: *nf.* benediction, blessing
bénéfice: *nm.* profit; benefit
bénéficiaire: *nmf.* beneficiary
bénéficier: *vi.* to benefit; enjoy
bénévole: *adj.* voluntary; unpaid; -ment = *adv.* voluntarily
bénin: *nf.* bénigne; *adj.* benign; minor; harmless
bénir: *vt.* to bless
bénit: *adj.* consecrated, holy
benne: *nf.* skip; tipper
benzène: *nm.* benzene
béquille: *nf.* crutch; prop
berceau: *nm.* cradle
bercement: *nm.* rocking
bercer: *vt.* to rock, cradle
berceuse: *nf.* lullaby; rocking chair
béret: *nm.* beret
berge: *nf.* riverbank
berger: *nm.* shepherd, -ère
bergerie: *nf.* sheepbarn
berner: *vt.* to fool, hoax
besogne: *nf.* work; job
besoin: *nm.* need; want; avoir - de = to need
bestial: *adj.* bestial; -ement = *adv.* bestially
bestialité: *nf.* bestiality; brutish-ness
bétail: *nm.* livestock; cattle
bête: *adj.* stupid, silly; -ment adv. = stupidly, foolishly; *nf.* animal
bêtifier: *vt.* to play the fool; prattle stupidly
bêtise: *nf.* stupidity, foolishness
béton: *nm.* concrete
betterave: *nf.* beetroot, beet
beurre: *nm.* butter
beurrer: *vt.* to butter
bévue: *nf.* blunder
biais: *nm.* slant angle; bias
biathlon: *nm.* biathlon
bibelot: *nm.* curio
biberon: *nm.* baby's bottle
Bible: *nf.* Bible

bibliographie: *nf.* bibliography
bibliothécaire: *nmf.* librarian
bibliothèque: *nf.* library; bookcase
bicarbonate: *nm.* bicarbonate
bicentenaire: *nm.* bicentenary
biceps: *nm.* biceps
biche: *nf.* doe; darling, pet
bicolore: *adj.* bi-coloured, two-tone
bicyclette: *nf.* bicycle
bidon: *nm.* tin, can; flask
bidonville: *nm.* shanty town
bien: *adv.* well; properly; very
bien entendu: of course
bien sûr: *adv.* of course
bien-être: *nm.* well-being
bienfaisant: *adj.* beneficial, kind
bienfaiteur: *nm.* benefactor
bienheureux: *adj.* blessed; lucky;
happy
biens de consommation: consumer
goods
biens immobiliers: real estate
bientôt: *adv.* soon
bienveillant: *adj.* benevolent, kindly
bienvenu: *adj.* welcome
bienvenue: *nf.* welcome
bière: *nf.* beer; coffin
bifteck: *nm.* steak
bifurcation: *nf.* bifurcation, fork
bifurquer: *vi.* to fork, branch off
bigot: *adj.* bigoted
bihebdomadaire: *adj.* twice weekly
bijou: *nm.* jewel
bijouterie: *nf.* jewellery
bijoutier: *nm.* jeweller
bilan: balance sheet
bilan: *nm.* balance sheet; assessment
bilan de faillite: statement of affairs
bilan de santé: check up
bilatéral: *adj.* bilateral
bile: *nf.* bile
bilingue: *adj.* bilingual
billard: *nm.* billiards
bille: *nf.* marble; billiard ball

billet: *nm.* ticket; note
billet à ordre: promissory note (P/N)
billet de banque: n m bill (cash)
billetterie: *nf.* cash dispenser
billion: *nm.* billion
bimensuel: *adj.* fortnightly
bimestriel: *adj.* every two months
binaire: *adj.* binary
biochimie: *nf.* biochemistry
biochimiste: *nmf.* biochemist
biodégradable: *adj.* biodegradable
bioéthique: *nf.* bioethics
biographie: *nf.* biography
biologie: *nf.* biology
biologique: *adj.* biological
biologiste: *nmf.* biologist
biosphère: *nf.* biosphere
bioxyde: *nm.* dioxide
bipède: *nm.* biped
bipolaire: *adj.* bipolar
bisannuel: *adj.* biennial
biscornu: *adj.* crooked, misshapen;
odd, outlandish
biscuit: *nm.* cake; biscuit
bisexuel: *adj.* bisexual
bissextile: *adj.* bissextile, leap (year)
bistouri: *nm.* bistoury
bitume: *nm.* bitumen
bitumer: *vt.* to asphalt, tarmac
bizarre: *adj.* bizarre, strange;
-ment = *adv.* strangely, oddly
bizarrerie: *nf.* strangeness,
singularity
blafard: *adj.* pale, pallid
blague: *nf.* joke, trick
blaguer: *vi.* to joke
blagueur: *nm.* joker, wag
blaireau: *nm.* badger
blame: *adj.* pale, wan
blâme: *nm.* blame, rebuke
blâmer: *vt.* to blame, rebuke
blanc *adj.*: *nf.* blanche white
blancheur: *nf.* whiteness
blanchir: *vi.* to turn white; to become

lighter; *vt.* to whiten; to lighten
blanchissage: *nm.* laundering; refining
blanchisserie: *nf.* laundry
blasé: *adj.* blasé
blason: *nm.* blazon, coat of arms
blasphème: *nm.* blasphemy
blasphémer: *vi.* to blaspheme
blé: *nm.* wheat
blêmir: *vi.* to turn pale
blessant: *adj.* cutting, hurtful
blessé: *adj.* injured, wounded
blesser: *vt.* to injure, wound
blessure: *nf.* injury, wound
bleu: *adj.* blue; *nm.* blue; bruise
bleuet: *nm.* cornflower
bleuir: *vt.* to turn blue
bleuté: *adj.* bluish
blindage: *nm.* armour plating
blindé: *adj.* armoured, reinforced
bloc: *nm.* block, group, unit
blocage: *nm.* blocking, freezing
blocus: *nm.* blockade
blond: *adj.* blond, fair
blondir: *vi.* to turn blond, turn golden
bloquer: *vt.* to block, blockade
blottir (se): *vr.* to curl up, snuggle up
blouse: *nf.* blouse; overall
blouson: *nm.* windcheater, bomber jacket
bobine: *nf.* reel, bobbin
bocal: *nm.* jar; bowl
boeuf: *nm.* ox, bullock
bohémien: *nmf.* Bohemian
boire: *vt.* to drink; *vi.* to drink, tipple
bois: *nm.* wood
bois de construction: timber
boisé: *adj.* wooded
boisson: *nf.* drink
boîte: *nf.* box
boîte aux lettres: mailbox
boite de conserve: can
boîte de nuit: dance club
boiter: *vi.* to limp

boiteux: *adj.* lame
boîtier: *nm.* case, body
boitillant: *adj.* limping
boitiller: *vi.* to hobble slightly
bol: *nm.* bowl
bolet: *nm.* boletus
bombardement: *nm.* bombardment, bombing
bombarder: *vt.* to bombard, bomb
bombe: *nf.* bomb
bombé: *adj.* rounded, domed
bon: *adj.* good; *nm.* slip, coupon, bond
bon de commande: order form
bon de livraison: delivery note
bon d'état: bond
bon marché: *adj.* cheap
bon vivant: *nm.* bon vivant
bonbon: *nm.* sweet, candy
bond: *nm.* leap; bounce
bonde: *nf.* stopper, plug
bondé: *adj.* packed
bondir: *vi.* to jump, leap; to bounce
bonheur: *nm.* happiness; luck
bonhomme: chap, fellow
bonification: *nf.* improvement; bonus
bonifier: *vt.* to improve; se- *vr.* = to improve
bonjour: *nm.* hello, good morning
bonne: n maid
bonnet: *nm.* bonnet, hat
bonneterie: *nf.* hosiery
bonsoir: *nm.* good evening
bonté: *nf.* goodness, kindness
bord: *nm.* side, edge
bordé: *adj.* edged, bordered
bordée: *nf.* broadside, volley
border: *vt.* to edge, border
bordereau: *nm.* note; invoice
bordereau de remboursement: withdrawal slip
bordereau de versement: deposit slip
bordereau d'expédition:

consignment note
bordure: *nf.* frame, border
borgne: *adj.* one-eyed
borne: *nf.* boundary; milestone
borné: *adj.* narrow-minded
borner: *vt.* to restrict, limit
bosse: *nf.* hump, knob
bosseler: *vt.* to dent, emboss
bossu: *nm.* hunchback; *adj.*
hunchbacked
botanique: *nf.* botany; *adj.* botanical
botaniste: *nf.* botanist
botte: *nf.* boot
bottine: *nf.* ankle boot, bootee
bouche: *nf.* mouth
bouché: *adj.* cloudy, overcast
bouche-à-bouche: *nm.* kiss of life
bouchée: *nf.* mouthful
boucher: *vt.* to block, clog up
boucherie: *nf.* butchery
bouchon: *nm.* cork
boucle: *nf.* curl; buckle
boucle d'oreille: earring
boucler: *vt.* to buckle; to surround
bouclier: *nm.* shield
bouddhisme: *nm.* Buddhism
boudeur: *adj.* sullen, sulky
boudin: *nm.* (black) pudding
boue: *nf.* mud
bouée: *nf.* buoy
boueur: *nm.* dustman
bouffée: *nf.* whiff, puff
bouffi: *adj.* swollen, puffed up
bouffon: *nm.* buffoon, clown
bougeoir: *nm.* candlestick
bouger: *vi.* to move; *vt.* to move, shift
bougie: *nf.* candle
bouillir: *vi.* to boil
bouilloire: *nf.* kettle
bouillon: *nm.* broth
bouillonner: *vi.* to bubble, foam
bouillotte: *nf.* hot-water bottle
boulanger: *nm.* baker
boulangerie: *nf.* bakery

boule: *nf.* ball, bowl
boulet: *nm.* cannonball; (fig)
millstone
boulevard: *nm.* boulevard
bouleversant: *adj.* upsetting,
confusing
bouleversement: *nm.* confusion,
disruption
bouleverser: *vt.* to confuse, disrupt
boulimie: *nf.* bulimia
boulimique: *adj.* bulimic
boulon: *nm.* bolt
bouquet: *nm.* bouquet, posy
bouquin: *nm.* book
bouquiniste: *nmf.* second-hand
bookseller
bourbeux: *adj.* muddy
bourbier: *nm.* quagmire
bourdon: *nm.* bumblebee
bourdonnement: *nm.* buzz, buzzing
bourdonner: *vi.* to buzz, hum
bourg: *nm.* market-town
bourgeois: *nm.* bourgeois, middle-
class person
bourgeoisie: *nf.* bourgeoisie, middle
classes
bourgeon: *nm.* bud
bourgeonner: *vi.* to bud
bourrasque: *nf.* squall, gust
bourreau: *nm.* torturer, executioner
bourrelet: *nm.* pad, cushion
bourrer: *vt.* to stuff, cram
bourse: *nf.* purse; la Bourse stock
bourse des valeurs: Stock Exchange
boursier: *nm.* broker; speculator
boursouflé: *adj.* bloated, swollen
bousculade: *nf.* hustle, scramble
boussole: *nf.* compass
bout: *nm.* end; piece, scrap
boutade: *nf.* whim, caprice; jest
bouteille: *nf.* bottle
boutique: *nf.* shop, store
bouton: *nm.* button
boutonner: *vt.* to button

boutonnière: *nf.* buttonhole
bouture: *nf.* cutting
bovin: *nm.* bovine
boxe: *nf.* boxing
boxer: *vi.* to box
boxeur: *nm.* boxer
boyau: *nm.* guts, insides
boycottage: *nm.* boycotting
boycotter: *vt.* to boycott
bracelet: *nm.* bracelet
braconnier: *nm.* poacher
brader: *vt.* to sell at a discount
braderie: *nf.* discount sale
braguette: *nf.* fly (trousers)
braise: *nf.* embers
brancard: *nm.* shaft, stretcher
branche: *nf.* branch
branchement: *nm.* branching; connection
brancher: *vt.* to connect, link
branchies: *nfpl.* gills
brandir: *vt.* to brandish, flourish
branlant: *adj.* loose; shaky
bras: *nm.* arm
brasier: *nm.* brazier, furnace
brasse: *nf.* breaststroke
brassée: *nf.* armful
brasser: *vt.* to brew; to mix
brasserie: *nf.* bar; brewery
bravade: *nf.* bravado
brave: *adj.* brave, courageous; -ment = *adv.* bravely, courageously
braver: *vt.* to brave, defy
bravoure: *nf.* bravery, courage
brebis: *nf.* ewe
brèche: *nf.* breach, gap
bredouillant: *adj.* mumbling
bredouille: *adj.* empty-handed
bredouiller: *vi.* to mumble
bref: *adj.* brief, concis
bretelle: *nf.* strap, sling
brevet: *nm.* licence, patent
breveté: *adj.* patented
bribe: *nf.* bit, scrap

bric-à-brac: *nm.* bric-a-brac
bricolage: *nm.* odd jobs
bricole: *nf.* small job
bricoler: *vi.* to do odd jobs
bricoleur: *nm.* handyman, *nf.* handywoman
bride: *nf.* bridle
bridé: *adj.* restrained, restricted
brider: *vt.* to restrain, restrict
brièvement: *adv.* briefly, concisely
brièveté: *nf.* brevity
brigade: *nf.* brigade
brigadier: *nm.* corporal, sergeant (police)
brillamment: *adv.* brilliantly
brillant: *adj.* brilliant, shining
briller: *vi.* to shine
brin: *nm.* stalk, strand
brindille: *nf.* twig
brique: *nf.* brick, slab
briquet: *nm.* lighter
brise: *nf.* breeze
briser: *vt.* to smash, shatter
brocante: *nf.* second-hand dealing
brocanteur: *nm.* secondhand dealer
broche: *nf.* brooch
brochure: *nf.* brochure, booklet
broder: *vt.* to embroider; *vi.* to embellish, elaborate
broderie: *nf.* embroidery
bronche: *nf.* bronchus
bronchite: *nf.* bronchitis
bronzage: *nm.* tan
bronze: *nm.* bronze
bronzer: *vi.* to get a tan
brosse: *nf.* brush
brosse à dents: n f toothbrush
brosser: *vt.* to brush
brouette: *nf.* wheelbarrow
brouillard: *nm.* fog, mist
brouiller: *vt.* to blur, confuse
brouillon: *nm.* rough copy, draft
broussaille: *nf.* brushwood, undergrowth

broussailleux: *adj.* bushy, overgrown
brousse: *nf.* undergrowth, bush
brouter: *vt.* to graze
broyer: *vt.* to grind, pulverise
broyeur: *adj.* crushing, grinding
bruine: *nf.* drizzle
bruissement: *nm.* rustle
bruit: *nm.* noise, sound
bruitage: *nm.* sound-effects
brûlant: *adj.* burning, scorching
brûler: *vt.* to burn
brûlure: *nf.* burn
brume: *nf.* haze, mist
brumeux: *adj.* hazy, misty
brun: *nm.* dark-haired man
brune: *nf.* brunette; *adj.* brown
brusque: *adj.* brusque, abrupt;
-ment = *adv.* brusquely, abruptly
brusquer: *vt.* to offend; hasten
brut: *adj.* crude, raw
brut 1: *adj.* brutal, rough;
-ement = *adv.* brutally, roughly
brutaliser: *vt.* to brutalise; to bully
brutalité: *nf.* brutality
brute: *nf.* brute; beast
bruyamment: *adv.* noisily
bruyant: *adj.* noisy
bruyère: *nf.* heather
bûche: *nf.* log
bûcheron: *nm.* woodcutter, lumberjack
budget: *nm.* budget
budgétaire: *adj.* budgetary
buée: *nf.* condensation; steam
buffet: *nm.* sideboard, buffet
buisson: *nm.* bush
bulbe: *nm.* bulb
bulle: *nf.* bubble; blister
bulletin: *nm.* bulletin
buraliste: *nmf.* tobacconist
bureau: *nm.* office; desk
bureau de douane: Custom House
bureaucrate: *nmf.* bureaucrat
bureaucratie: *nf.* bureaucracy

bureaucratique: *adj.* bureaucratic
bureautique: office automation
burin: *nm.* chisel
bus: *nm.* bus
buste: *nm.* bust, chest
but: *nm.* objective, goal
butane: *nm.* butane
buté: *adj.* stubborn
butin: *nm.* booty, loot
butte: *nf.* knoll, mound
buvable: *adj.* drinkable
buvard: *nm.* blotting paper
buvette: *nf.* refreshment-room
buveur: *nm.* drinker

C

ça: that; it
cabale: *nf.* cabal, intrigue
cabane: *nf.* cabin, shed
cabanon: *nm.* cottage; chalet
cabaret: *nm.* cabaret; tavern
cabine: *nf.* cabin, cab; cockpit
cabinet: *nm.* surgery; office, study
cable: *nm.* cable
câbler: *vt.* to cable
câbles de démarrage: jumper cables
cabosser: *vt.* to dent
cabotage: *nm.* coastal navigation
cabriolet: *nm.* convertible
cacahuète: *nf.* peanut
cacao: *nm.* cocoa
cache: *nm.* cache; mask; hiding place
caché: *adj.* hidden, secluded
cache-col: *nm.* invar scarf
cache-nez: *nm.* invar scarf, muffler
cacher: *vt.* to hide, conceal;
se - *vr.* = to hide o. s
cacheter: *vt.* to seal
cachette: *nf.* hideout, hiding place
cachot: *nm.* dungeon, prison cell
cachottier: *nm.* secretive
cactus: *nm.* cactus
cadavre: *nm.* corpse
cadeau: *nm.* present
cadenas: *nm.* padlock
cadenasser: *vt.* to padlock
cadence: *nf.* rhythm, time, cadence
cadet: *nm.* youngest child
cadrage: *nm.* framing
cadran: *nm.* dial, face
cadre: *nm.* frame; context; scope
cadrer: *vt.* to centre, fit with
caduc: *adj.* null and void; obsolete
cafard: *nm.* hypocrite; cockroach
café: *nm.* coffee
cafétéria: *nf.* cafeteria
cafetière: *nf.* coffeepot
cage: *nf.* cage
cageot: *nm.* crate

cagoule: *nf.* cowl; balaclava
cahier: *nm.* notebook
cahier des charges: book of specifications
cahot: *nm.* jerk, jolt
caillot: *nm.* clot
caillou: *nm.* stone; pebble
câiner: *vt.* to cuddle
caisse: a case
caisse: *nf.* box; till; fund
caisse à claire-voie: a crate
caissier: *nm.* cashier
cajoler: *vt.* to cajole, coax; to pet
cajou: *nm.* cashew
calamité: *nf.* calamity
calcaire: *nm.* calcareous, chalky
calcination: *nf.* calcination
calciner: *vt.* to calcine; to char
calcium: *nm.* calcium
calcul: *nm.* sum, calculation
calculateur: *adj.* calculating
calculatrice, calculette: *nf.* calculator
calculer: *vt.* to calculate, reckon
cale: *nf.* wedge, hold
caleçon: *nm.* shorts, pants
calembour: *nm.* pun
calendrier: *nm.* calendar
calepin: *nm.* notebook
caler: *vi.* to stall; to give up; to wedge
calfeutrer: *vt.* to make airtight, draughtproof
calibre: *nm.* calibre, bore
calibrer: to grade
calibrer: *vt.* to calibrate
calice: *nm.* chalice
câlin: *nm.* cuddle; *adj.* cuddly
calligraphie: *nf.* calligraphy
callosité: *nf.* callosity
calmant: *nm.* tranquilliser, sedative; *adj.* tranquillising
calmar: *nm.* squid
calme: *nm.* calm, stillness
calmer: *vt.* calm, soothe, pacify
calomnie: *nf.* slander, calumny

calomnier: *vt.* to slander; libel
calomnieux: *adj.* slanderous, calumnious
caloporteur: coolant
calorie: *nf.* calorie
calorifique: *adj.* calorific
calque: *nm.* tracing; copy
calquer: *vt.* to trace; to copy
calvaire: *nm.* calvary; ordeal
calvitie: *nf.* baldness
camarade: *nmf.* companion, friend
camaraderie: *nf.* camaraderie, friendship
cambouis: *nm.* dirty grease
cambré: *adj.* arched
cambriolage: *nm.* burglary
cambrioler: *vt.* to burgle
cambrioleur: *nm.* burglar
caméléon: *nm.* chameleon
camélia: *nm.* camelia
camelote: junk (objects)
caméra: *nf.* camera
caméscope: *nm.* camcorder
camion: *nm.* lorry
camionnette: *nf.* van
camionneur: *nm.* lorry driver, trucker
camomille: *nf.* camomile
camouflage: *nm.* camouflage
camoufler: *vt.* to camouflage
camp: *nm.* camp
camp guard: *nm.* countryman
campagne: *nf.* country, countryside
campement: *nm.* camp, encampment
camper: *vi.* to camp
campeur: *nm.* camper
canal: *nm.* canal, channel
canalisation: *nf.* canalisation; mains
canaliser: *vt.* to channel, funnel
canapé: *nm.* sofa, settee
canapé-lit: n m sofa bed
canard: *nm.* duck
cancer: *nm.* cancer
cancéreux: *adj.* cancerous
candeur: *nf.* ingeniousness

candidat: *nm.* candidate
candidature: *nf.* candidature, candidacy
candide: *adj.* guileless, ingenuous
canevas: *nm.* canvas; framework
canicule: *nm.* heatwave
canif: *nm.* penknife
canine: *nf.* eye tooth
caniveau: *nm.* gutter
canne: *nf.* cane, rod
canne à pêche: fishing rod
cannelle: *nf.* cinnamon
canoë: *nm.* canoe
canon: *nm.* cannon, gun
canot: *nm.* boat, dinghy
cantate: *nf.* cantata
cantatrice: *nf.* opera singer
cantine: *nf.* canteen
cantique: *nm.* canticle, hymn
canton: *nm.* canton
caoutchouc: *nm.* rubber
cap: *nf.* cape; course
capable: *adj.* capable, competent
capacité: *nf.* capacity
capacité calorifique: heat capacity
cape: *nf.* cloak
capillaire: *adj.* capillary
capitaine: *nm.* captain
capital: *adj.* capital, cardinal, major; *nm.* capital, stock
capitale: *nf.* capital (letter, city)
capitalisme: *nm.* capitalism
capitaliste: *nmf.* capitalist
capiteux: *adj.* heady, strong
capitonner: *vt.* to pad
capitulation: *nf.* capitulation
capituler: *vt.* to capitulate
caporal: *nm.* corporal
capot: *nm.* bonnet, hood
capote: *nf.* great-coat, hood
capoter: *vt.* to capsize, overturn
câpre: *nm.* caper
caprice: *nm.* caprice, whim
capricieusement: *adv.* capriciously

capricieux: *adj.* capricious
capricorne: *nm.* capricorn
capsule: *nf.* capsule
capter: *vt.* to catch; to pick up
capteur: *nm.* captor; pick-up
captif: *nm.* captive; *adj.* captive
captivant: *adj.* enthralling, captivating
captiver: *vt.* to captivate, enthrall
captivité: *nf.* captivity
capture: *nf.* capture
capturer: *vt.* to capture
capuche: *nf.* hood
car: *conj.* for; because
carabine: *nf.* carbine, rifle
caractère: *nm.* character, disposition
caractérisé: *adj.* marked, blatant
caractériser: *vt.* to characterise
caractérisque: *nf.* characteristic, feature
carafe: *nf.* carafe
carambolage: *nm.* pile-up (car)
caramel: *nm.* caramel
caraméliser: *vt.* to caramelise
carapace: *nf.* carapace, shell
carat: *nm.* carat
caravane: *nf.* caravan
caravelle: *nf.* caravel
carbonate: *nm.* carbonate
carbone: *nm.* carbon
carbonique: *adj.* carbonic
carboniser: *vt.* to carbonise; to char
carburant: *nm.* motor-fuel
carburateur: *nm.* carburettor
carburation: *nf.* carburation
carbure: *nm.* carbide
carcasse: *nf.* carcass
carcéral: *adj.* prison
cardiaque: *adj.* cardiac
cardigan: *nm.* cardigan
cardinal: *nm.* cardinal; *adj.* cardinal
cardiologie: *nf.* cardiology
cardiologue: *nm.* cardiologist
cardio-vasculaire: *adj.*

cardiovascular
carême: *nm.* fast, fasting
carence: *nf.* deficiency; insolvency
caressant: *adj.* affectionate
caresse: *nf.* caress
caresser: *vt.* to caress, fondle
cargaison: *nf.* cargo, freight
cargo: *nm.* cargo-boat
caricatural: *adj.* caricatural; grotesque
caricature: *nf.* caricature
caricaturer: *vt.* to caricature
caricaturiste: *nm.* caricaturist
carie: *nf.* decay; caries
carié: *adj.* decayed
carillon: *nm.* carillon, chime, peal
caritatif: *adj.* charitable
carnage: *nm.* carnage
carnassier: *nm.* carnivore
carnaval: *nm.* carnival
carnet: *nm.* notebook
carnet de chèques: cheque book
carnivore: *nmf.* carnivore; *adj.* carnivorous
carotide: *nf.* carotid
carotte: *nf.* carrot
carpe: *nf.* carp
carpette: *nf.* rug, doormat
carré: *nm.* square; *adj.* square; straightforward
carreau: *nm.* tile; pane
carrefour: *nm.* crossroads
carrelage: *nm.* tiling
carrément: *adv.* bluntly, directly
carrosse in coach
carrosserie: *nf.* bodywork, coach-work
carrossier: *nm.* coachbuilder
carrure: *nf.* build, stature
carrure: *nf.* career
cartable: *nm.* satchel
carte: *nf.* card; map
carte d'abonnement: nf pass (season ticket)

carte de credit: credit card
carte de téléphone: calling card
carte d'embarquement: boarding pass
carte d'identité: identity card
carte postale: postcard
cartel: *nm.* cartel
cartésien: *adj.* Cartesian
cartilage: *nm.* cartilage
cartilagineux: *adj.* cartilaginous
cartomancien: *nm.* fortuneteller
carton: *nm.* cardboard
cartonner: *vt.* to bind (book)
cartouche: *nf.* cartridge
cas: *nm.* case; circumstance
casanier: *nm.* homebody
cascade: *nf.* waterfall; stunt
cascadeur: *nm.* acrobat, stuntman
case: *nf.* square; box
caser: *vt.* (fain) to set up (job, marriage)
caserne: *nf.* barracks
casier: *nm.* compartment; filing cabinet
casino: *nm.* casino
casque: *nm.* helmet
casquette: *nf.* peaked cap
cassant: *adj.* brittle
casse-croûte: *nm.* invar snack
casser: *vt.* to break; se - *vr.* = to break
casser les prix: to slash prices
casserole: *nf.* saucepan
casse-tête: *nm.* invar puzzle, conundrum
cassette: *nf.* cash-box
cassis: *nm.* blackcurrant
cassure: *nf.* break, crack
caste: *nf.* caste
castor: *nm.* beaver
castration: *nf.* castration
castrer: *vt.* to castrate
cat strophe: catastrophe
cataclysme: *nm.* cataclysm
catacombe: *nf.* catacomb

catalogue: *nm.* catalogue
cataloguer: *vt.* to catalogue
catalyse: *nf.* catalysis
catalyseur: *nm.* catalyst
catalytique: *adj.* catalytic
cataplasme: *nm.* cataplasm
catapulte: *nf.* catapult
cataracte: *nf.* cataract
catastrophique: *adj.* catastrophic
catéchisme: *nm.* catechism
catégorie: *nf.* category
catégorique: *adj.* categorical
cathédrale: *nf.* cathedral
cathode: *nf.* cathode
cathodique: *adj.* cathodic
catholicisme: *nm.* Catholicism
catholique: *adj.* Catholic
cauchemar: *nm.* nightmare
cause: *nf.* cause, reason
causer: *vt.* to cause; to chat; *vi.* to talk, chat
causette: *nf.* chat
caustique: *adj.* caustic
caution: *nf.* deposit; guarantee
caution pour un prêt: collateral
cautionner: *vt.* to guarantee
cavalerie: *nf.* cavalry
cavalier: *nm.* rider
cave: *nf.* cellar
caveau: *nm.* tomb; small cellar
caverne: *nf.* cave, cavern
caverneux: *adj.* cavernous
caviar: *nm.* caviar
cavité: *nf.* cavity
ce: *adj.* cet, cette
ceci: pron. this
cécité: *nf.* blindness
céder: *vi.* to give in; *vt.* to give up, transfer
ceindre: *vt.* to put round, encircle
ceinture: *nf.* belt, girdle
ceinture de sécurité: *nf.* seat belt
ceinturer: *vt.* to surround
ceinturon: *nm.* belt

cela: *pron.* that
célébration: *nf.* celebration
célèbre: *adj.* famous
célébrer: *vt.* to celebrate
célébrité: *nf.* fame, celebrity
célérité: *nf.* celerity, speed
céleste: *adj.* celestial
célibat: *nm.* celibacy
célibataire: *nmf.* single person; *adj.* single, unmarried
cellulaire: *adj.* cellular
cellule: *nf.* cell, unit
cellulite: *nf.* cellulite
celluloïd: *nm.* celluloid
cellulose: *nf.* cellulose
Celsius, échelle: Celcius scale
celui: *pron.* this one
cendre: *nf.* ash
cendrier: *nm.* ashtray
censé: *adj.* supposed; deemed
censure: *nf.* censorship
censurer: *vt.* to censor
cent: *adj.* a hundred
centaine: *nf.* about a hundred, a hundred or so
centenaire: *nm.* centenarian; *adj.* a hundred years old
centésimal: *adj.* centesimal
centième: *nmf.* hundredth; *adj.* hundredth
centigrade de: *nm.* centigrade
centigramme: *nm.* centigram
centime: *nm.* centime
centimètre: *nm.* centimetre
central: *adj.* central
centraliser: *vt.* to centralise
centre: *nm.* centre
centre commercial: mall
centre de masse: center of mass
centre médical: clinic
centrer: *vt.* to centre, focus
centrifuge: *adj.* centrifugal
centuple: *adj.* centuple, hundred-fold
cependant: *conj.* however

céramique: *nf.* ceramic
cerceau: *nm.* hoop
cercle: *nm.* circle, ring
cercueil: *nm.* coffin
céréale: *nf.* cereal
cérébral: *adj.* cerebral
cérémonial: *adj.* ceremonial
cérémonie: *nf.* ceremony
cérémonieux: *adj.* ceremonious
cerf-volant: *nm.* kite
cerise: *nf.* cherry
cerisier: *nm.* cherry tree
cerne: *nf.* ring
cerner: *vt.* to circle, encompass
certificat: *nm.* certificate
certifier: *vt.* to certify; to guarantee
certitude: *nf.* certainty, certitude
cerveau: *nm.* brain
cervelle: *nf.* brain
cervical: *adj.* cervical
césarienne: *nf.* Caesarean
cesser: *nf.* to cease, stop
cessez-le-feu: *nm.* cease-fire
cétacé: *nm.* cetacean
cette nuit: *adv.* tonight
chacun: *pron.* each one
chagrin: *nm.* sorrow, grief
chahut: *nm.* row, uproar
chahuter: *vi.* to make a row
chaîne: *nf.* chain
chaîne de magasins: a chain of stores
chaîne de montage: assembly line
chaînon: *nm.* link
chair: *nf.* flesh
chaise: *nf.* chair
châlet: *nm.* chalet
chaleur: *nf.* heat
chaleur latente: heat latent
chaleureusement: *adv.* warmly
chaleureux: *adj.* warm, cordial
chalumeau: *nm.* blowlamp
chalutier: *nm.* trawler
chambre: *nf.* room
chambre de compensation: clearing

house
chambre froide: cold-storage unit
chambre libre: vacancy
champ: *nm.* field
champêtre: *adj.* rural, country
champignon: *nm.* mushroom
champion: *nm.* champion
championnat: *nm.* championship
chance: *nf.* luck
chancel: *adj.* staggering, tottering
chanceler: *vi.* to stagger, totter
chancelier: *nm.* chancellor
chanceux: *adj.* lucky, fortunate
chandail: *nm.* sweater
chandeleur: *nf.* candlemas
chandelier: *nm.* candlestick
chandelle: *nf.* candle
changeant: *adj.* changeable, variable
changement: *nm.* change, changing
changer: *vi.* to change; *vt.* to change
chanson: *nf.* song
chant: *nm.* song; singing
chantage: *nm.* blackmail
chanter: *vt.* to sing
chanteur: *nm.* singer
chantier: *nm.* building site
chantonner: *vt.* to hum
chanvre: *nm.* hemp
chaos: *nm.* chaos
chaotique: *adj.* chaotic
chapeau: *nm.* hat
chapelet: *nm.* rosary; string
chapelle: *nf.* chapel
chapiteau: *nm.* camel
chapiteau: *nm.* capital (column)
chapitre: *nm.* chapter
chaque: *adj.* each
char: *nm.* tank; chariot
charabia: *nm.* gibberish
charbon: *nm.* coal
charcuterie: *nf.* pork meat trade
charcutier: *nf.* pork butcher
chardon: *nm.* thistle
charge: *nf.* load; responsibility

chargé: *adj.* loaded
charge électrique élémentaire:
proton charge, electronic charge
chargement: *nm.* loading; freight
charger: to load
charger: *vt.* to load; se - de = to take
responsibility for, attend to
chariot: *nm.* waggon; freight car
charisme: *nm.* charisma
charitable: *adj.* charitable, kind;
-ment = *adv.* charitably
charité: *nf.* charity
charlatan: *nm.* charlatan
charmant: *adj.* charming, delightful
charme: *nm.* charm
charmer at: *vt.* to charm, beguile
charmeur: *nm.* charmer; *adj.*
winning, enchanting
charnel: *adj.* carnal
charnière: *nf.* hinge, pivot
charnu: *adj.* fleshy
charogne: *nf.* carrion
charpente: *nf.* structure, framework
charpentier: *nm.* carpenter
charrette: *nf.* cart
charrier: *vt.* to cart, carry
charrue: *nf.* plough
charte partie: charter party (C/P)
chasse: *nf.* hunting; chase
chasse-neige: *nm.* invar snow-plough
chasser: *vt.* to hunt, chase
chasseur: *nm.* hunter
châssis: *nm.* chassis
chaste: *adj.* chaste;
-ment = *adv.* chastely
chasteté: *nf.* chastity
chat: *nm.* cat
châtaigne: *nf.* chestnut
châtain: *adj.* chestnut brown
château: *nm.* castle
châtiment: *nm.* chastisement,
punishment
chaton: *nm.* kitten
chatouiller: *vt.* to tickle

chatoyant: *adj.* shimmering
châtrer: *vt.* to castrate
chaud: *adj.* warm, hot; -ement = *adv.* warmly, hotly
chaudière: *nf.* boiler
chaudron: *nm.* cauldron
chauffage: *nm.* heating
chauffard: *nm.* road-hog
chauffe-eau: *nm.* invar water-heater
chauffer: *vi.* to heat; *vt.* to heat up
chauffeur: *nm.* driver
chaumière: *nf.* cottage
chausette: *nf.* sock
chaussée: *nf.* road, street
chausse-pied: *nm.* shoehorn
chausson: *nm.* slipper
chaussure: *nf.* shoe
chauve: *adj.* bald
chauve-souris: *nf.* bat
chauvin adj.: *nf.* chauvine chauvinistic
chauvinisme: *nm.* chauvinism
chaux: *nf.* lime
chavirer: *vi.* to capsize, overturn
chef: *nm.* head, boss; chef
chef d'orchestre: conductor
chef magasinier: head storekeeper
chef-d'oeuvre: *nm.* masterpiece
chemin: *nm.* way, road;
- de fer = railway
chemin réactionnel: reaction path
cheminée: *nf.* chimney
cheminement: *nm.* progress; course
chemise: *nf.* shirt
chemisier: *nm.* shirtmaker
chêne: *nm.* oak
chenil: *nm.* kennel
chenille: *nf.* caterpillar
chèque: *nm.* cheque
chèque au porteur: cheque to bearer
chèque barré: crossed cheque
chèque certifié: certified cheque
chèque de voyage: *nm.* traveler's check

chèque en bois: dud cheque
chèque sans provisions: cheque without cover
chéquier: *nm.* chequebook
cher: *adj.* dear; expensive
chercher: *vt.* to look for
chercheur: *nm.* researcher; seeker
chéri: *nm.* darling, dearest; *adj.* beloved, cherished
chétif: *adj.* puny, paltry
cheval: *nm.* horse
chevalet: *nm.* easel
chevalier: *nm.* knight
chevelu: *adj.* long-haired
chevelure: *nf.* hair, head of hair
chevet: *nm.* chevet; bedside
cheveu: *nm.* hair
cheville: *nf.* ankle
chèvre: *nf.* goat
chèvrefeuille: *nm.* honeysuckle
chevreuil: *nm.* roe deer
chez: *prép.* at home
chic: *nm.* style, stylishness
chicorée: *nf.* chicory
chien: *nm.* dog
chiffon: *nm.* rag, cloth
chiffonné: *adj.* crumpled, rumpled
chiffre: *nm.* figure
chiffre d'affaires: turnover
chignon: *nm.* chignon, bun
chile: *nm.* shawl
chimère: *nf.* chimera
chimérique: *adj.* chimerical, fanciful
chimie: *nf.* chemistry
chimiionisation: chemi-ionization
chimiluminescence: chemiluminescence
chimique: *adj.* chemical;
-ment = *adv.* chemically
chimiste: *nmf.* chemist
chimpanzé: *nm.* chimpanzee
chiot: *nm.* puppy
chipoteur: *nm.* haggler
chirurgical: *adj.* surgical

chirurgie: *nf.* surgery
chirurgien: *nm.* surgeon
chlore: *nm.* chlorine
chloroforme: *nm.* chloroform
chlorophyle: *nf.* chlorophyll
chlorure: *nm.* chloride
choc: *nm.* shock, crash
chocolat: *nm.* chocolate
choeur: *nm.* choir, chorus
choir: *vi.* to fall
choisir: *vt.* to choose
choix: *nm.* choice
choléra: *nm.* cholera
chômage: *nm.* unemployment
chômeur: *nm.* unemployed person
chope: *nf.* mug
choquant: *adj.* shocking, appalling
choquer: *vt.* to shock
chorale: *nf.* choral
chorégraphe: *nmf.* choreographer
chorégraphie: *nf.* choreography
choriste: *nmf.* chorister
chose: *nf.* thing, matter, object
chou: *nm.* cabbage
chouette: *nf.* owl
chou-fleur: *nm.* cauliflower
choyer: *vt.* to cherish
chrétien: *nm.* Christian; *adj.* christian
christianisme: *nm.* Christianity
chromatographie: chromatography
chrome: *nm.* chromium
chromosome: *nm.* chromosome
chronique: *adj.* chronic; *nf.* chronicle, column, page
chronologie: *nf.* chronology
chronologique: *adj.* chronological; -ment = *adv.* chronologically
chronomètre: *nm.* chronometer
chronométrer: *vt.* to time
chrysanthème: *nm.* chrysanthemum
chuchotement: *nm.* whisper, rustling
chuchoter: *vi.* to whisper
chuintement: *nm.* hissing
chuinter: *vi.* to hiss

chute: *nf.* fall, drop
chuter: *vi.* to fall
cible: *nf.* target
cibler: *vt.* to target
cicatrice: *nf.* scar
cicatrisation: *nf.* cicatrisation, healing
cicatriser: *vt.* to heal
cidre: *nm.* cider
ciel: *nm.* sky
cierge: *nm.* candle
cigale: *nf.* cicada
cigare: *nm.* cigar
cigarette: *nf.* cigarette
cil: *nm.* eyelash
ciller: *vi.* to blink
cime: *nf.* summit
ciment: *nm.* cement
cimenter: *vt.* to cement
cimetière: *nm.* cemetery
cinéaste: *nmf.* film-maker
cinéma: *nm.* cinema
cinémathèque: *nf.* film library
cinématographique: *adj.* film, cinema
cinéphile: *nmf.* film enthusiast
cinétique: *adj.* kinetic
cinglant: *adj.* bitter, lashing, cutting
cingler: *vt.* to lash, sting
cinq: *nm.* five
cinquantaine: *nf.* about fifty
cinquante: *nm.* fifty
cinquantenaire: *nm.* fiftieth anniversary
cinquantième: *nmf.* fiftieth; *adj.* fif-tieth
cinquième: *nmf.* fifth; *adj.* fifth; -ment = *adv.* in fifth place
cintre: *nm.* arch
cirage: *nm.* polish
circonférence: *nf.* circumference
circonscription: *nf.* division, constituency
circonspect: *adj.* circumspect

circonstance: *nf.* circumstance
circuit: *nm.* circuit, tour
circulaire: *adj.* circular;
-ment = *adv.* circularly
circulation: *nf.* circulation; traffic
circuler: *vi.* to circulate, move
cire: *nf.* wax
cirer: *vt.* to polish
cirque: *nm.* circus
cisaillement, force de: shear stress
ciseau: *nm.* chisel; pl scissors
citadelle: *nf.* citadel
citadin: *nm.* city dweller
citation: *nf.* citation, summons
cité: *nf.* city
citer: *vt.* to quote, cite
citerne: *nf.* water tank
citoyen: *nm.* citizen
citron: *nm.* lemon
citrouille: *nf.* pumpkin
civière: *nf.* stretcher
civil: *adj.* civil; -ement = *adv.* civilly
civilisation: *nf.* civilisation
civilisé: *adj.* civilised
civiliser: *vt.* to civilise
civique: *adj.* civic
clair: *adj.* clear, bright;
-ement = *adv.* clearly
clairière: *nf.* clearing, glade
clairsemé: *adj.* scattered
clairvoyance: *nf.* perspicacity;
clairvoyance
clairvoyant: *adj.* perceptive;
clairvoyant
clameur: *nf.* clamour
clan: *nm.* clan
clandestin: *adj.* clandestine;
-ement *adv.* = clandestinely
clandestinité: *nf.* secrecy
clapoter: *vi.* to lap (water)
clapotis: *nm.* lapping
claque: *nf.* slap, smack
claquement: *nm.* clapping, slamming
claquer: *vi.* to bang, slam

clarifier: *vt.* to clarify; se - *vr.* = to become clear
clarinette: *nf.* clarinet
clarté: *nf.* light, brightness
classe: *nf.* class, standing
classement: filing
classement: *nm.* filing; grading
classer: to file
classer: *vt.* to file, classify
classeur: *nm.* filing cabinet
classification: *nf.* classification
classique: *adj.* classical, standard;
-ment = *adv.* classically
clause: *nf.* clause
claustrer: *vt.* to confine
claustrophobie: *nf.* claustrophobia
clavecin: *nm.* harpsichord
clavicule: *nf.* collarbone
clavier: *nm.* keyboard
clé, clef: *nf.* key
clémence: *nf.* clemency, mildness
clergé: *nm.* clergy
cliché: *nm.* cliché; negative
client: *nm.* client
client éventuel: prospective customer
clientèle: *nf.* clientele; customers
cligner: *vi.* to blink
clignotant: *adj.* blinking, flickering
clignotement: *nm.* blinking, flickering
clignoter: *vi.* to blink, flicker
climat: *nm.* climate
climatique: *adj.* climatic
climatisation: *nf.* air conditioning
climatiser: *vt.* to air condition
clin d'oeil: *nm.* wink
clinique: *nf.* clinic
cliqueter: *vi.* to jingle, clink
clitoris: *nm.* clitoris
clochard: *nm.* tramp
cloche: *nf.* bell
clocher: *nm.* steeple, bell tower
clochette: *nf.* hand-bell
cloison: *nf.* partition

cloîtrer (se): *vr.* to enter the monastic life
cloque: *nf.* blister
clore: *vt.* to close, conclude
clos: *adj.* closed, enclosed
clôture: *nf.* fence, hedge
clou: *nm.* nail
clouer: *vt.* to nail
club: *nm.* club
coagulation: *nf.* coagulation
coaguler: *vi.* to coagulate
coaliser: *vt.* to form a coalition
coalition: *nf.* coalition
coat: *nm.* cost, charge
cobalt: *nm.* cobalt
cobaye: *nm.* guinea-pig
cobra: *nm.* cobra
cocaïne: *nf.* cocaine
coccinelle: *nf.* ladybird
coccyx: *nm.* coccyx
cocher: *vt.* to notch, tick off
cochon: *nm.* pig
code: *nm.* code
code postal: *nm.* zip code
coder: *vt.* to code
codifier: *vt.* to codify
coefficient: *nm.* coefficient
coefficient d'extinction: extinction coefficient
coefficient de diffusion: diffusion coefficien
coefficient de dilatation thermique: thermal expansion coefficient
coefficient isentropique: isentropic expansion factor ou adiabatic index
coéquipier: *nm.* -fibre, team mate
coeur: *nm.* heart
coexister: *vi.* to coexist
coffre fort: a safe
coffret: *nm.* casket
cognement: *nm.* knock
cogner: *vi.* to hammer, bang
cohabitation: *nf.* cohabitation
cohabiter: *vi.* to cohabit

cohérence: *nf.* coherence
cohérent: *adj.* coherent
cohésion: *nf.* cohesion
cohue: *nf.* crowd
coiffer: *vt.* to arrange so's hair; se - *vr.* = to do one's hair
coiffeur: *nm.* hairdresser
coiffure: *nf.* hairstyle
coil: *nm.* collar; neck
coils: *nm.* parcel
coin: *nm.* corner
coincer: *vt.* to wedge, jam
coïncidence: *nf.* coincidence
coït: *nm.* coitus
col: *nm.* collar
colère: *nf.* anger
colérique: *adj.* quick-tempered, irascible
colibri: *nm.* hummingbird
colique: *nf.* diarrhoea
collaborateur: *nm.* collaborator, colleague
collaboration: *nf.* collaboration
collaborer: *vi.* to collaborate
collant: *adj.* clinging, sticky; *nm.* leotard
colle: *nm.* glue
collecte: *nf.* collection
collectif: *adj.* collective
collection: *nf.* collection
collectionner: *vt.* to collect
collectionneur: *nm.* collector
collectivement: *adv.* collectively
collectivité: *nf.* community; collective ownership
collège: *nm.* secondary school
collègue: *nmf.* colleague
coller: *vt.* to stick, glue; *vi.* to stick, be sticky
collier: *nm.* necklace
colline: *nf.* hill
collision: *nf.* collision
colloque: *nm.* colloquium
colocataire: *nmf.* cotenant, roomate

colombe: *nf.* dove
colon: *nm.* colonist
colonel: *nm.* colonel
colonie: *nf.* colony
colonisation: *nf.* colonisation
coloniser: *vt.* to colonise
colonne: *nf.* column
colonne à plateaux: fractionating column
colonne vertébrale: n backbone, spine
colorant: *nm.* colouring
coloration: *nf.* colouring, staining
coloré: *adj.* coloured
colorier: *vt.* to colour in
coloris: *nm.* colouring, shade
colossal: *adj.* colossal
colporter: *vt.* to peddle
colza: *nm.* rape seed
coma: *nm.* coma
comateux: *adj.* comatose
comb t: *nm.* combat, fight
combatif: *adj.* combative
combativité: *nf.* combativeness
combattant: *adj.* fighting, combatant
combattre: *vt.* to fight, combat; *vi.* to fight
combien: *adv.* how much, how many
combinaison: *nf.* combination
combiner: *vt.* to combine
comble: *nm.* height, peak
combler: *vt.* to fill; to fulfil
combustible: *nm.* fuel; *adj.* combustible
combustion: *nf.* combustion
comédie: *nf.* comedy
comédien: *nm.* actor
comestible: *adj.* edible
comète: *nf.* comet
comique: *adj.* comic; -ment = *adv.* comically
comité: *nm.* committee
commandant: *nm.* commander
commande: *nf.* command, order

commande de l'étranger: shipping order
commande, passer une: to place an order
commandement: *nm.* command,
commander: to order
commander: *vt.* to order, command
commanditaire, bailleur de fonds: silent partner (sleeping partner)
commandité, associé gérant: active partner
commanditer: *vt.* to finance, sponsor
commando: *nm.* commando
comme: *conj.* as, like
commémoration: *nf.* commemoration
commémorer: *vt.* to commemorate
commencement: *nm.* beginning, start
commencer: *vt.* to begin, start
comment: *adv.* how
commentaire: *nm.* comment; commentary
commentateur: *nm.* commentator
commenter: *vt.* to comment
commérage: *nm.* piece of gossip
commerçant: indépendant sole trader
commerçant: *nm.* merchant, trader
commerçant: *nm.* shopkeeper, trader
commerce: *nm.* business, commerce
commerce de détail: retail trade
commerce de gros: wholesale trade
commerce extérieur: foreign trade
commerce intérieur: home trade
commercial: *adj.* commercial; -ement = *adv.* commercially
commercialiser: *vt.* to market
commère: *nf.* gossip
commettant: the principal
commettre: *vt.* to commit
commissaire: *nm.* representative; commissioner
commissaire aux comptes: auditor
commissaire priseur: auctioneer
commissariat: *nm.* police station;

commissionership; commissariat
commission: *nf.* commission,
committee
commissionnaire: *nm.* commission
agent
commissionnaire: *nm.* messenger;
agent
commode: *adj.* convenient,
comfortable
commodité: *nf.* convenience
commun: *adj.* common, joint
communal: *adj.* council; common,
communal
communautaire: *adj.* community
communauté: *nf.* community; joint
estate
commune: *nf.* town, district
communication: *nf.* communication
communier: *vi.* to receive
communion
communion: *nf.* communion
communiqué: *nm.* communiqué
communiquer: *vt.* to communicate,
transmit
communisme: *nm.* communism
communiste: *nmf.* communist
compact: *adj.* compact, dense
compagne: *nf.* companion
compagnie: *nf.* company
compagnie aérienne: airline
compagnie d'assurance: insurance
company
compagnie maritime: shipping
company
compagnon: *nm.* companion
comparable: *adj.* comparable
comparaison: *nf.* comparison
comparaître: *vi.* to appear
comparativement: *adv.*
comparatively
comparer: *vt.* to compare
compartiment: *nm.* compartment
compartimenter: *vt.* to compart,
partition

compas: *nm.* compass
compassion: *nf.* compassion
compatibilité: *nf.* compatibility
compatible: *adj.* compatible
compatir: *vi.* to sympathise
compatissant: *adj.* compassionate
compatriote: *nmf.* compatriot
compensation: *nf.* compensation
compenser: *vt.* to compensate
compétence: *nf.* competence
compétent: *adj.* competent, capable
compétitif: *adj.* competitive
compétition: *nf.* competition
compétitivité: *nf.* competitiveness
complaisance: *nf.* kindness;
complacency
complaisant: *adj.* kind; complacent
complément: *nm.* complement;
extension
complémentaire: *adj.*
complementary, supplementary
complet: *adj.* complete, full
complètement: *adv.* completely,
fully
compléter: *vt.* to complete
complexe: *adj.* complex,
complicanted
complexé: *adj.* mixed up
complexe activé, théorie: activated
complex theory
complication: *nf.* complication
complice: *nmf.* accomplice
complicité: *nf.* complicity, collusion
compliment: *nm.* compliment
complimenter: *vt.* to compliment,
congratulate
compliqué: *adj.* complicated,
intricate
compliquer: *vt.* to complicate
complot: *nm.* plot
comportement: *nm.* behaviour;
performance
comporter: *vt.* to consist of,
comprise

composant: *nm.* component, constituent
composante: *nf.* component
composer: *vt.* to compose, make up
compositeur: *nm.* composer; typesetter
composition: *nf.* composition, formation
composter: v to validate (train ticket)
compréhensible: *adj.* comprehensible
compréhensif: *adj.* comprehensive, understanding
compréhension: *nf.* comprehension, understanding
comprendre: *vt.* to understand; consist of
compresse: *nf.* compress
compresseur: *nm.* compressor
compression: *nf.* compression; reduction
comprimé: *adj.* compressed; restrained; *nm.* tablet
comprimer: *vt.* to compress; to restrain
compromettant: *adj.* compromising
compromettre: *vt.* to compromise
compromis: *nm.* compromise
comptabilité: *nm.* bookkeeping
comptabilité: *nf.* accountancy

comptabilité en partie double: double-entry bookkeeping
comptabilité en partie simple: single-entry bookkeeping
comptable: *adj.* accounting; *nmf.* accountant
comptable: *nm.* accountant
comptant d'usage: prompt cash
compte: *nm.* account
compte courant: current account
compte de dépôts: deposit account
compter: *vi.* to count
compteur: *nm.* meter

comptoir: *nm.* counter, bar
compton, effet: compton scattering
comte: *nm.* count
comtesse: *nf.* countess
concave: *adj.* concave
concéder: *vt.* to grant, concede
concentration: *nf.* concentration
concentré: *adj.* concentrated; reserved
concentrer: *vt.* to concentrate; se *vr.* to concentrate
concept: *nm.* concept
concepteur publicitaire: designer
conception: *nf.* conception, design
concerner: *vt.* to concern, regard
concert: *nm.* concert
concertation: *nf.* dialogue, consultation
concession: *nf.* concession; privilege
concessionnaire: *nmf.* concessionaire, grantee
concevoir: *vt.* to imagine, conceive
concierge: *nmf.* caretaker, concierge
conciliant: *adj.* conciliatory
conciliation: *nf.* conciliation; reconciliation
concilier: *vt.* to reconcile; to attract
concis: *adj.* concise
concision: *nf.* conciseness, brevity
concluant: *adj.* conclusive, decisive
conclure: *vt.* to conclude; to decide
conclusion: *nf.* conclusion
concombre: *nm.* cucumber
concordance: *nf.* agreement, accord
concorder: *vi.* to agree, coincide
concours: *nm.* competition; conjuncture
concret: *adj.* concrete, solid
concrètement: *adv.* concretely
concrétiser: *vt.* to put in concrete form
concubin: *nmf.* concubine; cohabitant
concubinage: *nm.* concubinage; cohabitation

concurrence: *nf.* competition
concurrent: *nmf.* concurrent;
competitor
condamnation: *nf.* condemnation;
sentencing
condamné: *nmf.* convict; sentenced
person
condamner: *vt.* to condemn; to
sentence
condensation: *nf.* condensation
condensé: *adj.* condensed,
evaporated
condenser: *vt.* to condense, compress
condescendant: *adj.* condescending
condiment: *nm.* condiment
condition: *nf.* condition, term
conditionné: *adj.* conditioned;
packaged
conditionnement: *nm.* conditioning;
packaging
conditionner: *vt.* to condition; to
package
conditions de vente: sales terms
condoléances: *nfpl.* condolences
conducteur: *nm.* driver; operator
conduire: *vi.* to lead; to drive
conduit: *nm.* conduit, pipe
conduite: *nf.* conduct; driving;
behaviour
cône: *nm.* cone
confédération: *nf.* confederation
conférence: *nf.* conference
conférencier: *nm.* speaker; lecturer
confesser: *vt.* to confess
confession: *nf.* confession
confiance: *nf.* confidence, trust
confidant: *adj.* confident; confiding
confidence: *nf.* confidence;
disclosure
confident: *nm.* confidant
confidentiel: *adj.* confidential
confier: *vt.* to confide, entrust; se *vr.*
to confide in
confiner: *vt.* to confine; se to be

confined
confirmation: *nf.* confirmation
confirmer: *vt.* to confirm
confiserie: *nf.* confectionery
confisquer: *vt.* to confiscate,
impound
confiture: *nf.* jam
conflictuel: *adj.* conflicting
conflit: *nm.* conflict, contention
confondre: *vt.* to confuse, mingle
conforme: *adj.* consistent; true
conforme à l'échantillon: up to
sample
conformément: *adv.* in accordance
with
conformer: *vt.* to model
conformiste: *nmf.* conformist
conformité: *nf.* conformity; likeness
confort: *nm.* comfort
confortable: *adj.* comfortable, cosy;
-ment = *adv.* comfortably
confrère: *nm.* colleague
confrontation: *nf.* confrontation;
comparison
confronter: *vt.* to confront
confus: *adj.* confused, indistinct
confusion: *nf.* confusion, disorder
congé: *nm.* leave; holiday
congé de maladie: sick leave
congédier: *vt.* to dismiss
congélateur: *nm.* freezer
congeler: *vt.* to freeze
congestion: *nf.* congestion; stroke
congratulation: *nf.* congratulation
congratuler: *vt.* to congratulate
congrégation: *nf.* congregation
congrès: *nm.* congress, conference
conifère: *nm.* conifer
conjoint: *nmf.* spouse; *adj.* joint;
linked
conjointement: *adv.* jointly
conjonctivite: *nf.* conjunctivitis
conjoncture: *nf.* conjuncture;
situation

conjugaison: *nf.* conjugation
conjugal: *adj.* conjugal
conjuguer: *vt.* to conjugate; to combine
conjuration: *nf.* conspiracy, plot
conjurer: *vt.* to conspire; to implore; to ward off
connaissance: *nf.* knowledge; consciousness
connaissement: bill of lading (B/L)
connaisseur: *nm.* connois-seur; expert
connaître: *vt.* to know, be acquainted with
connecter: *vt.* to connect
connecteur: *nm.* connective
connexion: *nf.* connection, link
connivence: *nf.* connivance
connotation: *nf.* connotation
connu: *adj.* known; famous
conquérant: *nm.* conqueror
conquérir: *vt.* to conquer
conquête: *nf.* conquest
conquis: *adj.* conquered, vanquished
consacrer: *vt.* to devote, dedicate
consciemment: *adv.* consciously, knowingly
conscience: *nf.* consciousness; conscience
consciencieusement: *adv.* conscientiously
consciencieux: *adv.* conscientious
conscient: *adj.* conscious, aware
consécration: *nf.* consecration
consécutif: *adj.* consecutive
consécutivement: *adv.* consecutively
conseil: *nm.* advice, counsel
conseil d'administration: board of directors
conseiller: *nm.* counsellor, adviser
conseiller, un: a consultant
consentant: *adj.* consenting, willing
consentement: *nm.* consent
consentir: *vi.* to consent, acquiesce

conséquence: *nf.* consequence, result
conséquent: *adj.* consequent; substantial
conservateur: *nm.* conservative; curator
conservation: *nf.* conservation
conservation, loi de: conservation laws
conservatoire: *nm.* conservatory; academy
conserve: *nf.* canned food
conserver: *vt.* to keep, preserve
considérable: *adj.* considerable
considérablement: *adv.* considerably
considération: *nf.* consideration, respect
considérer: *vt.* to consider, regard
consignataire, destinataire: the consignee
consigne: *nf.* orders, instructions
consistance: *nf.* consistency; strength
consister vi: to consist
console: *nf.* console
consoler: *vt.* to console, comfort
consolidation: *nf.* consolidation, reinforcement
consolider: *vt.* to consolidate, reinforce
consommateur: *nm.* consumer
consommation: consumption
consommation: *nf.* consumption; accomplishment
consommé: *adj.* consummate, accomplished
consommer: *vt.* to consume, use
consonne: *nf.* consonant
conspirateur: *nm.* conspirator
conspiration: *nf.* conspiracy, plot
conspirer: *vi.* to conspire, plot
constamment: *adv.* constantly, continually
constant: *adj.* constant, continuous
constante: *nf.* constancy
constante d'équilibre: equilibrium

constant
constante de dissociation: dissociation constant
constante de force: force constant
constante de rotation: rotational constant
constante de vitesse: rate constant
constante des gaz parfaits: gas constant per mole
constante diélectrique: dielectric constant
constat: *nm.* report; acknowledgement
constatation: *nf.* authentication, verification
constater: *vt.* to record; to verify
constellation: *nf.* constellation, galaxy
consternation: *nf.* consternation, dismay
consterner: *vt.* to dismay
constipation: *nf.* constipation
constituer: *vt.* to constitute, form
constitution: *nf.* constitution, formation
constitutionnel: *adj.* constitutional
constructeur: *nm.* builder, maker
constructif: *adj.* constructive
construction: *nf.* building, construction
construire: *vt.* to construct, build
consul: *nm.* consul
consulaire: *adj.* consular
consulat: *nm.* consulate
consultant: *nm.* consultant; *adj.* consulting
consultation: *nf.* consultation, advice
consulter: *vt.* to consult, take advice from
consumer: *vt.* to consume, spend
contact: *nm.* contact, touch
contacter: *vt.* to contact, approach
contagieux: *adj.* contagious, infectious

contamination: *nf.* contamination, pollution
contaminer: *vt.* to contaminate, pollute
conte: *nm.* story, tale
contemplation: *nf.* contemplation, meditation
contempler: *vt.* to contemplate, meditate
contemporain: *adj.* contemporary
contenance: *nf.* capacity, volume
conteneur hermétique: air-tight container
conteneurs étanches: waterproof containers
conteneurs, mise en: containerization
contenir: *vt.* to contain
content: *adj.* glad
contentement: *nm.* contentment, satisfaction
contenter: *vt.* to please, satisfy
contenu: *nm.* contents, enclosure
contestation: *nf.* dispute, controversy
contester: *vt.* to contest, dispute
contexte: *nm.* context
contigu: *adj.* contiguous, adjacent
continent: *nm.* continent
continental: *adj.* continental
contingent: *nm.* quota; draft
contingents d'importation: import quotas
continu: *adj.* continuous, incessant
continuation: *nf.* continuation
continuel: *adj.* continual, continuous
continuellement: *adv.* continuously, continually
continuer: *vt.* to continue, proceed with
contour: *nm.* contour, outline
contourner: *vt.* to bypass, skirt
contraceptif: *adj.* contraceptive
contraception: *nf.* contraception
contracter: *vt.* to contract, acquire

contraction: *nf.* contraction
contradiction: *nf.* contradiction, discrepancy
contradictoire: *adj.* contradictory, conflicting
contraindre: *vt.* to constrain, compel
contrainte: *nf.* constraint, compulsion
contraire: *nm.* opposite, contrary; *adj.* opposite, contrary; -ment = *adv.* contrarily
contrariant: *adj.* contrary; perverse
contrarier: *vt.* to annoy; to oppose
contrariété: *nf.* annoyance, disappointment
contraste: *nm.* contrast
contrat: *nm.* contract, agreement
contre: *prép.* against
contre-attaque: *nf.* counter-attack
contre-attaquer: *vi.* to counter-attack
contrebalancer: *vt.* to counterbalance
contrebande: *nf.* contraband, smuggling
contrebandier: *nm.* smuggler
contrebasse: *nf.* double bass
contrecarrer: *vt.* to thwart, oppose
contrecoeur (à): reluctantly
contrecoup: *nm.* rebound, repercussion
contredire: *vt.* to contradict, refute
contrefaçon: *nf.* counterfeit, forgery
contrefaire: *vt.* to counterfeit, forge
contre-indication: *nf.* contra-indication
contremaître: *nm.* foreman
contre-offensive: *nf.* counter-offensive
contrepartie: *nf.* compensation; consideration
contre-plaqué: *nm.* plywood
contrepoison: *nm.* antidote, counter-poison
contresens: *nm.* nonsense; misunderstanding; mistranslation.

contretemps: *nm.* mishap; contretemps, syncopation
contribuable: *nmf.* taxpayer
contribuer: *vt.* to contribute
contribution: *nf.* contribution; tax
contrôle: *nm.* control, check
contrôler: *vt.* to control, check
contrôleur: *nm.* inspector; auditor
controverse: *nf.* controversy
controversé: *adj.* disputed
contusion: *nf.* bruise, contusion
convaincant: *adj.* convincing
convaincre: *vt.* to convince, persuade
convaincu: *adj.* convinced, persuaded
convalescence: *nf.* convalescence
convenable: *adj.* fitting, suitable
convenablement: *adv.* suitably, fitly
convenir: *vi.* to agree, accord
convention: *nf.* convention, agreement
conventionnel: *adj.* conventional; contractual
conventionnellement: *adv.* conventionally
convenu: *adj.* agreed; stipulated
convergent: *adj.* convergent
converger: *vi.* to converge
conversation: *nf.* conversation, talk
conversion: *nf.* conversion
convertir: *vt.* to convert
convexe: *adj.* convex
conviction: *nf.* conviction
convier: *vt.* to invite; to urge
convivial: *adj.* convivial; user-friendly
convocation: *nf.* convocation, summoning
convoi: *nm.* convoy; train
convoiter: *vt.* to covet
convoquer: *vt.* to convoke, convene
convulsion: *nf.* convulsion
coopératif: *adj.* cooperative
coopération: *nf.* cooperation

coopérative: *nf.* cooperative
coopérer: *vi.* to cooperate, collaborate
coordinateur: *nm.* coordinator
coordination: *nf.* coordination; committee
coordonnées: *nfpl.* coordinates
coordonnées de réaction, diagramme des: reaction coordinate
coordonner: *vt.* to coordinate
copain: *nm.* friend, pal
copeau: *nm.* shaving, chip
copie: *nf.* copy, reproduction
copier: *vt.* to copy, reproduce
copieusement: *adv.* copiously, abundantly
copieux: *adj.* copious, abundant
copilote: *nm.* co-pilot
copine: *nf.* friend, mate
coproduction: *nf.* coproduction
copropriété: *nf.* co-ownership, joint ownership
coq: *nm.* cock, rooster
coque: *nf.* hull; shell
coquelicot: *nm.* poppy
coquet: *adj.* stylish, smart
coquettement: *adv.* stylishly, smartly
coquetterie: *nf.* smartness, stylishness
coquillage: *nm.* shellfish
coquille: *nf.* shell, scallop
coquin: *nm.* naughty, mischie-vous
cor: *nm.* horn; corn
corail: *nm.* coral
coran: *nm.* Koran
corbeau: *nm.* crow
corbeille: *nf.* basket
corbeille à classement: filing tray
corbillard: *nm.* hearse
cordage: *nm.* rope; rigging
corde: *nf.* rope; string
cordée: *nf.* roped mountaineering party
cordial: *adj.* cordial, warm

cordialité: *nf.* cordiality, warmth
cordiallement: *adv.* cordially, warmly
cordon: *nm.* cord, string; cordon
cordonnerie: *nf.* shoemending
cordonnier: *nm.* shoemender, cobbler
coriace: *adj.* tough; tight
coriandre: *nm.* coriander
corne: *nf.* horn, antler
cornée: *nf.* cornea
corneille: *nf.* crow
cornemuse: *nf.* bagpipes
cornet: *nm.* cone, cornet
corniche: *nf.* cornice; ledge
cornichon: *nm.* gherkin; greenhorn
corporatif: *adj.* corporative, corporate
corporation: *nf.* corporation, guild
corporatisme: *nm.* corporatism
corporel: *adj.* corporal, bodily
corps: *nm.* body, corpse
corps noir: blackbody
corpulence: *nf.* corpulence
corpulent: *adj.* corpulent
corpus: *nm.* corpus
correct: *adj.* correct, accurate
correctement: *adv.* correctly, accurately
correcteur: *nm.* examiner; proofreader
correction: *nf.* correction; proofreading
corrélation: *nf.* correlation
correspondance: *nf.* correspondence, communication
correspondant: *nm.* correspondent; *adj.* corresponding
correspondre: *vi.* to correspond, communicate
corridor: *nm.* corridor, passage
corrigé: *nm.* corrected version, fair copy
corriger: *vt.* to correct

corroborer: *vt.* to corroborate
corroder: *vt.* to corrode
corrompre: *vt.* to corrupt, debase
corrompu: *adj.* corrupt
corrosif: *adj.* corrosive
corrosion: *nf.* corrosion
corruption: *nf.* corruption, debasement
corsage: *nm.* blouse, bodice
corsaire: *nm.* corsair
corsé: *adj.* rich, full-bodied
corset: *nm.* corset
cortège: *nm.* cortège, procession
cortex: *nm.* cortex
cortical: *adj.* cortical
cortisone: *nf.* cortisone
corvée: *nf.* fatigue duty; forced
cosmétique: *nm.* cosmetic
cosmique: *adj.* cosmic
cosmonaute: *nmf.* cosmonaut
cosmopolite: *adj.* cosmopolitan
cosmos: *nm.* cosmos
costume: *nm.* costume, dress
cota tion: *nf.* quotation, valuation
côte: *nf.* coast; rib; slope
coteau: *nm.* hill
côtelé: *adj.* ribbed
côtelette: *nf.* cutlet
coter: *vt.* to quote; to classify
côtier: *adj.* coastal, inshore
coton: *nm.* cotton
cotonneux: *adj.* fleecy, fluffy
côtoyer: *vt.* to mix with, skirt
cou: *nm.* neck
couchant: *adj.* setting
couche: *nf.* layer, coat
coucher: *vt.* to put to bed
coucher de soleil: *nm.* sunset
coucou: *nm.* cuckoo
coude: *nm.* elbow
coudé: *adj.* angled, bent
coudoyer: *vt.* mix with, rub shoulders with
coudre: *vi.* to sew

couette: *nf.* duvet
coulant: *adj.* flowing; smooth
couler: *vi.* to flow, run
couleur: *nf.* colour, shade
couleuvre: *nf.* grass snake
coulis: *nm.* sauce, purée
coulissant: *adj.* sliding
coulisse: *nf.* groove; (thea) wings
coulisser: *vi.* to slide, run
couloir: *nm.* corridor, passage
coulomb, loi de: coulomb's law
coup: *nm.* blow; shot
coup de telephone: n m call
coupable: *nmf.* culprit; *adj.* guilty
coupant: *adj.* cutting, sharp
coupe: *nf.* cut; cutting bour
coupe de cheveux: haircut
coupe-papier: *nm.* Invar paper knife
couper: *vt.* to cut, slice
couple: *nm.* couple, pair
couplet: *nm.* couplet, verse
coupole: *nf.* dome
coupon: *nm.* coupon, voucher, ticket
coupure: *nf.* cut; break
cour: *nf.* court, yard, courtyard
courage: *nm.* courage, daring
courageusement: *adv.* courageously
courageux: *adj.* courageous
couramment: *adv.* fluently; commonly
courant: *adj.* current; present; *nm.* stream, current
courant d'air: *nm.* draft
courbature: *nf.* stiffness; ache
courbaturé: *adj.* aching
courbe: *nf.* curve; contour
courbé: *adj.* curved, stooped
courbe d'énergie potentielle: potential energy curve
courber: *vt.* to curve, bend
coureur: *nm.* runner
courgette: *nf.* courgette
courir: *vi.* to run, race
couronne: *nf.* crown, wreath

couronnement: *nm.* coronation
couronner: *vt.* to crown
courrier: *nm.* mail, post
courrier électronique: email
courroie: *nf.* strap, belt
cours: *nm.* course; flow; path
course: *nf.* running; race; flight; journey
courses: *nfpl.* shopping; horse racing
coursier: *nm.* courier, messenger
court: *adj.* short, brief
court d'argent, être à: to be out of cash
court-bouillon: *nm.* court-bouillon, wine sauce
court-circuit: *nm.* short-circuit
court-circuiter: *vt.* to short-circuit
courtier: *nm.* broker, agent
courtiser: *vt.* to court
courtois: *adj.* courteous;
courtoisement: *adv.* courteously
courtoisie: *nf.* courtesy, courteousness
cousin: *nm.* cousin
coussin: *nm.* cushion, pillow
coussinet: *nm.* pad; bearing
coût: *nm.* cost
couteau: *nm.* knife
coûter: *vt.* to cost
coûteusement: *adv.* expensively
coûteux: *adj.* costly, expensive
coûts de production: production costs
coûts d'exploitation: operating costs
coutume: *nf.* custom, habit
coutumier: *adj.* customary, usual
couture: *nf.* sewing, needlework
couturier: *nm.* couturier, fashion designer
couturière: *nf.* dressmaker
couvent: *nm.* convent
couver: *vt.* to hatch, incubate
couvercle: *nm.* lid, cap
couvert: *nm.* shelter; cover; pretext

couverture: *nf.* blanket; cover; roofing; wrapping
couvre-feu: *nm.* curfew
couvreur: *nm.* roofer
couvrir: *vt.* to cover
crabe: *nm.* crab
crachement: *nm.* spitting
cracher: *vt.* to spit
crachin: *nm.* drizzle
craie: *nf.* chalk
craindre: *vt.* to fear
crainte: *nf.* fear, dread
craintif: *adj.* timid, cowardly
crampe: *nf.* cramp
crampon: *nm.* stud, spike, crampon
cramponner: *vt.* to cramp, clamp
cran: *nm.* notch, cog
crâne: *nm.* cranium, skull
crânien: *adj.* cranial
crapaud: *nm.* toad
crapule: *nf.* villain
crapuleux: *adj.* villainous, vicious
craquellement: *nm.* cracking
craquement: *nm.* crack, creaking, snap
craquer: *vi.* to creak, squeak, crack
crasseux: *adj.* grimy, filthy
cratère: *nm.* crater
cravate: *nf.* tie
crayon: *nm.* pencil
créancier: *nm.* creditor
créateur: *nm.* creator, author
créatif: *adj.* creative
création: *nf.* creation
créativité: *nf.* creativity
créature: *nf.* creature
crèche: *nf.* crèche; crib
crédibilité: *nf.* credibility
crédible: *adj.* credible
crédit: *nm.* credit, trust
crédit-bail: *nm.* lease; leasing
crédule: *adj.* credulous, gullible
crédulité: *nf.* credulity, gullibility
créer: *vt.* to create, produce

crémaillère: *nf.* rack, chimney hook
crème: *nf.* cream
crème à raser: *nf.* shaving cream
crème solaire: *nf.* sunscreen
crémerie: *nf.* dairy
crémeux: *adj.* creamy
crémier: *nm.* dairyman
créneau: *nm.* battlement
crêpe: *nf.* pancake
crêperie: *nf.* pancake restaurant
crépitement: *nm.* crackling; rattling
crépiter: *vi.* to crackle; to rattle
crépu: *adj.* frizzy, woolly
crépuscule: *nm.* twilight, dusk
cresson: *nm.* watercress
crête: *nf.* crest, comb
crétin: *nm.* cretin, idiot
creuser: *vi.* to dig, burrow
creuset: *nm.* crucible
creux: *adj.* hollow, empty
crevaison: *nf.* puncture, flat
crevé: *adj.* burst, punctured
crever: *vt.* to burst; to gouge
crevette: *nf.* prawn
cri: *nm.* cry, howl, yell
criant: *adj.* crying; striking, glaring
criard: *adj.* yelling; scolding
cribler: *vt.* to sift, riddle
cric: *nm.* jack
crier: *vi.* to cry, shout
crime: *nm.* crime, offence
criminel: *nm.* criminal; *adj.* criminal
crin: *nm.* horsehair
crinière: *nf.* mane
criquet: *nm.* locust
crise: *nf.* crisis, attack
crisper: *vt.* to shrivel; to clench
cristal: *nm.* crystal, glassware
cristallin: *adj.* crystalline
cristallisation: *nf.* crystallisation
cristalliser: *vt.* to crystallise
critère: *nm.* criterion, standard
critiquable: *adj.* censurable, open to criticism

critique: *adj.* critical, censorious
critiquer: *vt.* to criticise, censure
croc: *nm.* fang; hook
croche: *nf.* quaver
crochet: *nm.* hook, clasp
crochu: *adj.* hooked, clawlike
crocodile: *nm.* crocodile
croire: *vt.* to believe, think
croisade: *nf.* crusade
croisement: *nm.* crossing, junction
croiser: *vt.* to cross; to fold
croisière: *nf.* cruise
croissance: *nf.* growth, increase
croissant: *adj.* growing, increasing; *nm.* croissant; crescent
croître: *vi.* to grow, rise
croix: *nf.* cross
croque-monsieur: *nm.* toasted
croquer: *vt.* to crunch
croquette: *nf.* croquette
croquis: *nm.* sketch, outline
crosse: *nf.* (rel) crozier; butt, grip
crotte: *nf.* manure, dung
croupir: *vi.* to stagnate, wallow
croustillant: *adj.* crusty, crisp
croustiller: *vi.* to be crusty, crispy
croûte: *nf.* crust
croûton: *nm.* crust, crouton
croyance: *nf.* belief
croyant: *adj.* believing
cru: *adj.* raw, uncooked; *nm.* vineyard; wine
cruauté: *nf.* cruelty, inhumanity
cruche: *nf.* pitcher
crucial: *adj.* crucial, decisive
crucifix: *nm.* crucifix
crucifixion: *nf.* crucifixion
crudité: *nf.* crudity, coarseness
crue: *nf.* flood
cruel: *adj.* cruel
cruellement: *adv.* cruelly
crustacé: *nm.* crustacean, shellfish
cryométrie, cryoscopie: cryoscopy
crypte: *nm.* crypt

crypter: *vt.* to encode, scramble
cube: *nm.* cube, block
cubique: *adj.* cubic
cubisme: *nm.* cubism
cueillette: *nf.* picking, gathering
cueillir: *vt.* to pick, gather
cuiller, cuillère: *nf.* spoon, spoonful
cuillère à café: *nf.* teaspoon
cuillère à soupe: *nm.* tablespoon
cuir: *nm.* leather, hide
cuirasse: *nf.* cuirass, breastplate
cuirassé: *adj.* armoured; *nm.* battleship
cuire: *vi.* to cook
cuisine: *nf.* kitchen; cookery
cuisiner: *vt.* to cook
cuisinier: *nm.* cook
cuisinière: *nf.* cooker, stove
cuisse: *nf.* thigh
cuisson: *nf.* cooking, baking
cuit: *adj.* cooked
cuivre: *nm.* copper
cul: *nm.* bottom, ass
culasse: *nf.* cylinder-head; breech
cul-de-jatte: *nmf.* legless cripple
cul-de-sac: *nm.* blind alley, cul-de-sac
culinaire: *adj.* culinary
culminer: *vi.* to culminate, tower
culot: *nm.* cheek, nerve
culotte: *nf.* knickers; underpants; shorts
culpabiliser: *vt.* to make someone feel guilty
culpabilité: *nf.* guilt, culpability
culte: *nm.* cult, veneration
cultivable: *adj.* cultivable
cultivateur: *nm.* farmer
cultivé: *adj.* cultured
cultiver: *vt.* to cultivate
culture: *nf.* culture; cultivation
culturel: *adj.* cultural
culturisme: *nm.* body-building
cumin: *nm.* cumin

cumul: *nm.* pluralism; accumulation
cumuler: *vt.* to accumulate; to hold concurrently
cupide: *adj.* greedy
cupidement: *adv.* greedily
cupidité: *nf.* greed, cupidity
cure: *nf.* cure; treatment
curé: *nm.* parish priest, parson
cure-dents: *nm.* toothpick
curie, température de: curie temperature
curieusement: *adv.* curiously
curieux: *nm.* inquisitive person; onlooker; *adj.* curious, inquisitive
curie-weiss, loi de: curie-weiss' law
curiosité: *nf.* curiosity, inquisitiveness
cursus: *nm.* degree course
cutané: *adj.* skin, cutaneous
cuve: *nf.* vat, tank
cuvette: *nf.* basin, bowl
cyanure: *nm.* cyanide
cybernétique: *nf.* cybernetics
cyclable: *adj.* cycle, for cycling
cyclamen: *nm.* cyclamen
cycle: *nm.* cycle; stage
cycle de carnot: carnot cycle
cyclique: *adj.* cyclical
cyclisme: *nm.* cycling
cycliste: *nmf.* cyclist; *adj.* cycle
cyclomoteur: *nm.* moped
cyclone: *nm.* cyclone
cyclope: *nm.* Cyclops
cygne: *nm.* swan
cylindre: *nm.* cylinder
cylindrée: *nf.* capacity (engine)
cylindrique: *adj.* cylindrical
cymbale: *nf.* cymbal
cynique: *adj.* cynical
cyniqueement: *adv.* cynically
cynisme: *nm.* cynicism
cytologie: *nf.* cytology
cytoplasme: *nm.* cytoplasm

𝒟

dactylographe: *nmf.* typist
dactylographie: *nf.* typing, typewriting
dactylographier: *vt.* to type
dada: *nm.* hobbyhorse; gee-gee
dahlia: *nm.* dahlia
daigner: *vt.* to deign, condescend
daim: *nm.* deer
dalle: *nf.* flagstone, slab
dalmatien: *nm.* Dalmatian
Dalton, loi de: Dalton's law
daltonien: *adj.* colour-blind
dame: *nf.* lady; dame
damier: *nm.* draughtboard
damn tion: *nf.* damnation
damné: *adj.* damned
damner: *vt.* to damn
danger: *nm.* danger, risk
dangereusement: *adv.* dangerously
dangereux: *adj.* dangerous, risky
dans: *prép.* in; into
dansant: *adj.* dancing
danse: *nf.* dance; dancing
danser: *vi.* to dance
danseur: *nm.* dancer
dard: *nm.* sting
datation: *nf.* dating
datation au 14c: 14c radioactive dating
date: *nf.* date
date d'échéance: date of maturity
dater: *vt.* to date
datif: *nm.* dative
datte: *nf.* (bot) date
dattier: *nm.* date palm
dauphin: *nm.* dolphin
davantage: *adv.* more
de: *prép.* of; from
dé: *nm.* dice; thimble
de nos jours: *adv.* nowadays
de nouveau: *adv.* again
de retour: *adv.* back, returned
déambuler: *vi.* to stroll

débâcle: *nf.* disaster; collapse
déballage: *nm.* unpacking; display
déballer: *vt.* to unpack; to display
débandade: *nf.* rout, stampede
débarbouiller: *vt.* to wash
débarcadère: *nm.* landing; wharf
débardeur: *nm.* docker, stevedore
débarquement: *nm.* landing, disembarkment
débarquer: *vt.* to land, unship; *vi.* to disembark, land
débarrasser: *vt.* to clear, rid
débat: *nm.* debate; dispute, contest
débattre: *vi.* to debate, discuss
débauche: *nf.* debauchery, dissoluteness
débaucher: *vt.* to debauch, corrupt
débile: *adj.* weak, feeble
débilitant: *adj.* debilitating, weakening
débit: *nm.* debit; turnover; flow
débiter: *vt.* to debit; to produce
débiteur: *nm.* debtor
débiteur: *nm.* debtor
déblayer: *vt.* to clear away, remove
déblocage: *nm.* unblocking; freeing, releasing
débloquer: *vt.* to release, unlock
déboisement: *nm.* deforestation
déboiser: *vt.* to deforest
déboîtement: *nm.* dislocation
débordant: *adj.* exuberant, overflowing
débordé: *adj.* overwhelmed
débordement: *nm.* overflowing; outflanking
déborder: *vi.* to overflow; to out-flank
débouché: *nm.* outlet; issue
debout: *adv.* upright, standing
déboutonner: *vt.* to unbutton
débraillé: *adj.* untidy, disordered
débrancher: *vt.* to disconnect
débrayer: *vi.* to declutch; to stop

work
débris: *nm.* debris, waste
débrouiller: *vt.* to disentangle, unravel
début: *nm.* beginning, outset
débutant: *adj.* novice
débuter: *vi.* to start, begin
décacifier: *vt.* to decalcify
décadence: *nf.* decadence, decline
decadent: *adj.* decadent
décaféiné: *adj.* decaffeinated
décagone: *nm.* decagon
décalage: *nm.* gap, interval; discrepancy
décaler: *vt.* to shift; to stagger
décalitre: *nm.* decalitre
décamètre: *nm.* decametre
décaper: *vt.* to clean, scour
décapotable: *adj.* convertible
décapsuler: *vt.* to take the lid off
décapsuleur: *nm.* bottle-opener
decathlon: *nm.* decathlon
décéder: *vi.* to die
décelable: *adj.* detectable
déceler: *vt.* to detect; to disclose
décembre: *nm.* December
décemment: *adv.* decently
décence: *nf.* decency
décennal: *adj.* decennial
décennie: *nf.* decade
décent: *adj.* decent, proper
décentralisation: *nf.* decentralisation
décentraliser: *vt.* to decentralise
déception: *nf.* disappointment; deceit
décerner: *vt.* to award, confer
décès: *nm.* death, decease
décevant: *adj.* disappointing; deceptive
décevoir: *vt.* to disappoint; to deceive
déchaîné: *adj.* wild, unbridled
déchaîner: *vt.* to unleash
décharge: *nf.* discharge; receipt
déchargement: *nm.* unloading
décharger: *vt.* to unload, discharge

décharné: *adj.* lean, emaciated
déchausser: *vt.* to take off foot
déchéance: *nf.* decay, decline
déchet: *nm.* loss, waste
déchiffrer: *vt.* to decipher, decode
déchiqueter: *vt.* to tear; to slash; to shred
déchirant: *adj.* harrowing, excruciating
déchirement: *nm.* tearing, ripping
déchirer: *vt.* to tear, rip
déchirure: *nf.* tear, rip
déchoir: *vi.* to decline; to sink
déchu: *adj.* fallen; declined; deposed
décibel: *nm.* decibel
décidé: *adj.* decided; determined
décigramme: *nm.* decigram
décilitre: *nm.* decilitre
décimal: *adj.* decimal
décimètre: *nm.* decimetre
décisif: *adj.* decisive, conclusive
décision: *nf.* decision
declamation: *nf.* declamation
déclamer: *vt.* to declaim
déclaration en douane: customs entry
déclaré: *adj.* professed, avowed
déclarer: *vt.* to declare, announce
déclenchement: *nm.* release, setting off
déclencher: *vt.* to release, set off
déclic: *nm.* click; trigger
déclin: *nm.* decline, deterioration
déclinaison: *nf.* declension; declination
déclinant: *adj.* declining
décliner: *vi.* to decline, refuse
déclivité: *nf.* declivity, slope
décloisonner: *vt.* to decompart-mentalise
décoder: *vt.* to decode, decipher
décodeur: *nm.* decoder, decipherer
décoiffer: *vt.* to disarrange so's hair
décoincer: *vt.* to loose, release

décollage: *nm.* take-off, lift-off
décoller: *vi.* to unpaste, steam off, to take off
décolleté: *adj.* low-necked, low-cut; *nm.* decolletage, low neckline
décolorant: *adj.* bleaching
décolorer: *vt.* to decolour, bleach
decolorising: *nm.* bleaching substance
décombres: *nmpl.* rubble, debris
décomposer: *vt.* to decompose; to break up; to dissect
décomposition: *nf.* decomposition, breaking up
décompression: *nf.* decompression
décomprimer: *vt.* to decompress
décompte: *nm.* discount; deduction
déconcentrer: *vt.* to devolve
déconcertant: *adj.* disconcerting
déconcerter: *vt.* to disconcert
décongeler: *vt.* to thaw, defrost
déconnecter: *vt.* to disconnect
déconnexion: *nf.* disconnection
décontenancé: *adj.* embarrassed; disconcerted
décontracté: *adj.* relaxed
décontracter: *vt.* to relax
décontraction: *nf.* relaxation
décor: *nm.* scenery; setting
décorateur: *nm.* decorator; set designer
décoratif: *adj.* decorative, ornamental
décoration: *nf.* decoration, embellishment
décorer: *vt.* to decorate, adorn
décortiquer: *vt.* to husk, shell
découler: *vi.* to flow; to ensue
découpage: *nm.* cutting up, carving
découper: *vt.* to carve, cut up
décourageant: *adj.* discouraging, disheartening
découragement: *nm.* discouragement
décourager: *vt.* to discourage, dishearten

décousu: *adj.* unsewn; loose; disconnected
découvert: *nm.* overdraft; *adj. adj.* uncovered; open
découverte: *nf.* discovery
découvrir: *vt.* to discover
décret: *nm.* decree, enactment
décréter: *vt.* to decree, enact
décrire: *vt.* to describe
décrocher: *vt.* to take down; to unhook
décroissant: *adj.* decreasing, lessening
décroître: *vi.* to decrease, diminish
déçu: *adj.* disappointed
décupler: *vi.* to increase tenfold
dédaigner: *vt.* to disdain, scorn
dédaigneusement: *adv.* disdainfully
dédaigneux: *adj.* disdainful, scornful
dédain: *nm.* disdain, scorn
dedans: *adv.* inside, indoors; *nm.* inside; au - = inside
dédicace: *nf.* dedication
dédier: *vt.* to consecrate, dedicate to
dédommagement: *nm.* compensation, damages
dédommager: *vt.* to compensate, indemnify
dédouanement: *nm.* customs clearance
dédouaner les marchandises: to clear goods
dédoubler: *vt.* to divide in two; to remove lining
déduction: *nf.* deduction
déduire: *vt.* to deduct; to deduce
déesse: *nf.* goddess
défaillance: *nf.* faintness; exhaustion; blackout
défaillant: *adj.* faint; weakening
défaillir: *vi.* to faint; to weaken
défaire: *vt.* to undo, dismantle
défaite: *nm.* defeat, overthrow
défaitiste: *adj.* defeatist

défaut: *nm.* defect, fault
défavorable: *adj.* unfavourable
défavorablement: *adv.* unfavourably
défavoriser: *vt.* to penalise, treat unfairly
défection: *nf.* defection
défectueux: *adj.* defective, faulty
défendeur: *nm.* defendant
défendre: *vt.* to defend, protect; to prohibit
défense: *nf.* defence; prohibition
défense du consommateur: consumerism
défenseur: *nm.* defender
défensif: *adj.* defensive
défi: *nm.* defiance; challenge
défiant: *adj.* mistrustful, distrustful
déficience: *nf.* deficiency
déficient: *adj.* deficient; weak
déficit: *nm.* deficit, shortfall
déficitaire: *adj.* deficient, in deficit
défier: *vt.* to challenge, defy
défilé: *nm.* procession, parade
défiler: *vi.* to parade, march
défini: *adj.* definite, precise
définir: *vt.* to define, specify
définitif: *adj.* definitive, final
définition: *nf.* definition
définitivement: *adv.* definitively, finally
déflagration: *nf.* deflagration, explosion
déflation: *nf.* deflation
défoncer: *vt.* to smash in; to dig deeply
déformation: *nf.* deformation, distortion
déformer: *vt.* to deform, distort
défoulement: *nm.* outlet; release
défouler: *vt.* to unwind, relax
défraîchi: *adj.* shop-soiled
défricher: *vt.* to clear; to reclaim
défunt: *nm.* deceased; *adj.* late, deceased

dégagé: *adj.* clear; open
dégagement: *nm.* freeing, clearance
dégager: *vt.* to free, clear
dégarnir: *vt.* to empty; to clear
dégât: *nm.* havoc, damage
dégâts: *nm.* damage
dégel: *nm.* thaw
dégeler: *vi.* to thaw, melt
dégénérer: *vi.* to degenerate, decline
dégivrer: *vt.* to de-ice, defrost
dégonfler: *vt.* to deflate, empty
dégourdir: *vt.* to warm up, revive
dégourdissement: *nm.* reviving, return of circulation
dégoût: *nm.* disgust, distaste
dégoutant: *adj.* filthy, disgusting
dégoûter: *vt.* to disgust
dégradant: *adj.* degrading
dégradation: *nf.* degradation, debasement
dégradé: *nm.* shading off; gradation
dégrader: *vt.* to degrade, debase
dégrafer: *vt.* to unfasten, unhook
dégraisser: *vt.* to remove grease
degré: *nm.* degree; grade
dégrèvement: *nm.* reduction; redemption
dégripper: *vt.* to unblock; to unchoke
déguisement: *nm.* disguise
déguiser: *vt.* to disguise
dégustation: *nf.* tasting, sampling
dehors: *adv.* outside, outdoors
déjà: *adv.* already
déjeuner: *vi.* to lunch; *nm.* lunch
déjouer: *vt.* to elude; to thwart
delà: *adv.* au - de beyond; par beyond
délabré: *adj.* dilapidated, ramshackle
délacer: *vt.* to unlace, undo
délai: *nm.* delay; respite; time limit
délais de livraison: delivery dates
délaisser: *vt.* to abandon, quit
délassant: *adj.* relaxing, refreshing
délasser: *vt.* to refresh, relax

délateur: *nm.* informer
délation: *nf.* denouncement; informing
délavé: *adj.* diluted; faded
délayage: *nm.* dragging-out, spinning-out
délayer: *vt.* to thin; to drag out
delectation: *nf.* delectation, delight
délecter (se): *vr.* to delight, revel
délégation: *nf.* delegation
délégué: *nm.* delegate, representative; *adj.* delegate, delegated
déléguer: *vt.* to delegate
délibération: *nf.* deliberation; resolution
délibéré: *adj.* deliberate; resolute
délicat: *adj.* delicate, dainty
délicatement: *adv.* delicately
délicatesse: *nf.* delicacy, daintiness
délice: *nm.* delight, pleasure
délicieux: *adj.* delicious, delightful
délier: *vt.* to unbind, untie
délimitation: *nf.* delimitation
délimiter: *vt.* to delimit, demarcate
délinquance: *nf.* delinquency
délinquant: *nm.* delinquent
délirant: *adj.* delirious, frenzied
délire: *nm.* delirium, frenzy
délirer: *vi.* to be delirious
délit: *nm.* offence, misdemeanour
délivrance: *nf.* deliverance; release; delivery
délivrer: *vt.* to deliver; to release
déloger: *vt.* to evict, dislodge
déloyal: *adj.* disloyal, unfaithful
déloyauté: *nf.* disloyalty, treachery
delta: *nm.* delta
delta plane: *nm.* hang-glider
démagnétisation adiabatique: adiabatic demagnetization
démagogie: *nf.* demagogy
démagogique: *adj.* demagogic
démagogue: *nm.* demagogue
demain: *adv.* tomorrow

demande: *nf.* request, petition; question
demande de renseignements: inquiry/enquiry
demander: *vt.* to ask, request; se - *vr.* = to wonder
démangeaison: *nf.* itch; longing
démaquillant: *nm.* make-up remover; *adj.* make-up removing
démaquiller: *vt.* to remove make-up; se - *vr.* = to take one's make-up off
démarche: *nf.* gait, walk, step
démarrage: *nm.* moving off, casting off
démarrer: *vi.* to start up, move off; *vt.* to start, get started
démarreur: *nm.* starter
démasquer: *vt.* to unmask, uncover
démêlage: *nm.* disentangling; combing
démêler: *vt.* to disentangle, unravel; comb
déménagement: *nm.* removal; moving (house)
déménager: *vi.* to move house
déménageur: *nm.* removal man
démener (se): *vr.* to struggle, strive
dément: *adj.* mad, insane, crazy
démenti: *nm.* denial, refutation
démentir: *vt.* to deny, refute
démesuré: *adj.* excessive, inordinate
démesurément: *adv.* excessively, inordinately
démettre: *vt.* to dislocate; to dismiss
demeure: *nf.* residence, dwelling place
demeurer: *vi.* to live at, reside, stay
demi: *adj.* half; *nm.* half
demi-cercle: *nm.* semicircle
demi-douzaine: *nf.* half-dozen
demi-droite: *nf.* half-line
demi-finale: *nf.* semi-final
demi-frère: *nm.* half-brother
demi-heure: *nf.* half-hour

demi-jour: *nm.* half-light
démilitariser: *vt.* to demilitarise
demi-litre: *nm.* half-litre
demi-lune: *nf.* half-moon
demi-mesure: *nf.* half measure
demi-mot m: without spelling out
demi-pension: *nf.* half-board
demi-soeur: *nf.* half-sister
démission: *nf.* resignation
démissionner: *vi.* to resign
demi-tarif: *nm.* half-fare
demi-tour: *nm.* half-turn, U-turn
démocrate: *nmf.* democrat
démocratie: *nf.* democracy
démocratique: *adj.* democratic
démocratiquement: *adv.* democratically
démocratiser: *vt.* to democratise
démodé: *adj.* old-fashioned, out-of-date
démographie: *nf.* demography
démographique: *adj.* demographic
demoiselle: *nf.* young lady; spinster; damsel
démolir: *vt.* to demolish, knock down
démolition: *nf.* demolition
démon: *nm.* demon, fiend
démoniaque: *adj.* demoniac, fiendish
démonstrateur: *nm.* demonstrator
démonstratif: *adj.* demonstrative
démonstration: *nf.* demonstration; proof
démontable: *adj.* collapsible, that can be dismantled
démonte-pneu: *nm.* tyre lever
démonter: *vt.* to dismantle, take down, dismount
démontrer: *vt.* demonstrate; to prove
démoralisant: *adj.* demoralising
démoraliser: *vt.* to demoralise
démouler: *vt.* to take out of a mould
démunir: *vt.* to deprive; to divest
démystifier: *vt.* to demystify, disabuse

dénaturé: *adj.* denatured, disfigured
dénégation: *nf.* denial
déneiger: *vt.* to clear snow from
déni: *nm.* denial, refusal
dénicher: *vt.* to dislodge; to unearth
dénier: *vt.* to deny, disclaim
dénigrer: *vt.* to denigrate, disparage
dénivellation: *nf.* difference in level, unevenness
dénombrer: *vt.* to number, enumerate
dénomination: *nf.* denomination, designation
dénoncer: *vt.* to denounce; to inform against
dénonciation: *nf.* denunciation
dénouement: *nm.* dénouement; unravelling; outcome
dénouer: *vt.* to unravel, untie, undo
dénoyauter: *vt.* to stone (fruit)
denrée: *nf.* commodity, provisions, foodstuff
dense: *adj.* dense, thick
densité: *nf.* density, denseness, specific gravity
densité relative: relative density
dent: *nf.* tooth
dentaire: *adj.* dental
dentelé: *adj.* jagged, perforated
dentelle: *nf.* lace
dentier: *nm.* denture, dental plate
dentifrice: *nm.* toothpaste
dentiste: *nmf.* dentist
dentition: *nf.* dentition, teething
dénuder: *vt.* to bare, denude
dénué: *adj.* devoid, bereft
dénuement: *nm.* destitution; deprivation
déodorant: *nm.* deodorant
déontologie: *nf.* deontology
dépannage: *nm.* repairing, fixing
dépanner: *vt.* to repair, fix
dépanneur: *nm.* breakdown mechanic
dépanneuse: *nf.* breakdown lorry

dépareillé: *adj.* unmatched; odd
déparer: *vt.* to spoil; to disfigure
départ: *nm.* departure; start
département: *nm.* department
dépasser: *vt.* to exceed; to go past
dépaysé: *adj.* disoriented, out of one's element
dépaysement: *nm.* disorientation
dépêcher: *vt.* to dispatch, send
dépendance: *nf.* dependence; dependency
dépendant: *adj.* dependent
dépendre: *vi.* to depend on, be dependent on
dépens: *nmpl.* aux - de at the expense of
dépense: *nf.* expenditure, outlay
dépenser: *vt.* to expend, spend
dépérir: *vi.* to decline, waste away
dépeupler: *vt.* to depopulate; to clear
dépistage: *nm.* tracking; detection
dépister: *vt.* to track
dépit: *nm.* spite; grudge
dépité: *adj.* vexed; frustrated
déplacé: *adj.* misplaced; illtimed
déplacement: *nm.* displacement; removal
déplacer: *vt.* to displace; to move
déplaire: *vi.* to displease; to offend
déplaisant: *adj.* disagreeable, unpleasant
dépliant: *nm.* prospectus, leaflet; *adj.* extendible; folding
dépliant, un: a leaflet
déplier: *vt.* to unfold; to open out
déploiement: *nm.* deployment; display
déplorable: *adj.* deplorable, disgraceful
déplorer: *vt.* to deplore, bewail
déployer: *vt.* to deploy; to display
dépopulation: *nf.* depopulation
déportation: *nf.* deportation, transportation

déporté: *nm.* deportee
déporter: *vt.* to deport, transport
déposer: *vt.* to lodge, deposit
déposer le bilan: to file a petition in bankruptcy
dépositaire: *nmf.* depository; trustee
déposition: *nf.* deposition; evidence
dépôt: *nm.* deposit; warehouse
dépouillement: *nm.* scrutiny, perusal; despoiling
dépouiller: *vt.* to strip; to despoil; to peruse
dépourvu: *adj.* lacking, wanting; au - = off guard
dépoussiérer: *vt.* to dust
dépravation: *nf.* depravity, corruption
dépravé: *adj.* depraved, corrupt
dépréciation: *nf.* depreciation
déprécier: *vt.* to depreciate; to disparage
dépressif: *adj.* depressive
dépression: *nf.* depression, slump; dejection
déprimant: *adj.* depressing
déprimer: *vt.* to depress; to discourage
depuis: *prép.* since, from; after
député: *nm.* deputy, delegate
déracinement: *nm.* uprooting
déraciner: *vt.* to uproot
déraillement: *nm.* derailment
dérailler: *vi.* to be derailed, run off the rails
dérailleur: *nm.* derailleur, derailer (rail)
déraisonner: *vi.* to talk irrationally, rave
dérangement: *nm.* derangement; inconvenience
déranger: *vt.* to upset, unsettle; se *vr.* to move
dérapage: *nm.* skid
déraper: *vi.* to skid, slip

déréglé: *adj.* out of order; irregular; unruly

dérèglement: *nm.* disturbance; irregularity; dissoluteness

dérégler: *vt.* to disturb; to put out of order; to upset

dérision: *nf.* derision, mockery

dérisoire: *adj.* derisory; pathetic

dérivation: *nf.* derivation; diversion

dérive: *nf.* drift; aller à la - to drift away

dériver: *vi.* to drift

dermatologie: *nf.* dermatology

dermatologue: *nmf.* dermatologist

derme: *nm.* dermis

dernier: *adj.* last; latest; back; in -ière; *nf.* last one; latter

dernièrement: *adv.* recently; lately

dérobade: *nf.* sidestepping; evasion

dérober: *vt.* to steal; to hide; se *vr.* to steal away, escape

dérogation: *nf.* derogation; dispensation

déroger: *vi.* to derogate; to detract

déroulement: *nm.* unfolding; progress, development

dérouler: *vt.* to unwind, uncoil; se *vr.* to develop; to unfold

déroutant: *adj.* disconcerting

déroute: *nf.* rout, overthrow

dérouter: *vt.* to rout, overthrow

derrière: *prép.* behind; adv; at the back; *nm.* bottom; back

dertification: *nf.* desertification

dès: *prép.* from, since

désabusé: *adj.* disenchanted; disabused

désaccord: *nm.* disagreement, discord

désaffecté: *adj.* disused

désagréable: *adj.* disagreeable, unpleasant

désagréger: *vt.* to break up, disintegrate

désagrément: *nm.* displeasure, annoyance

désaltérant: *adj.* thirst-quenching

desaltérer: *vt.* to refresh

désamorcer: *vt.* to unprime, defuse

désapprobateur: *adj.* disapproving

désapprobation: *nf.* disapproval

désapprouver: *vt.* to disapprove, object

désarçonner: *vt.* to unsaddle; to nonplus, baffle

désarmant: *adj.* disarming

désarmement: *nm.* disarmament

désarmer: *vt.* to disarm; to unload

désarroi: *nm.* disarray, confusion

désarticuler: *vt.* to dislocate; to upset

désastre: *nm.* disaster

désastreux: *adj.* disastrous, unfortunate

désavantage: *nm.* disadvantage; prejudice

désavantager: *vt.* to disadvantage, handicap

désaveu: *nm.* disavowal, retraction

désavouer: *vt.* to disavow, retract

descendance: *nf.* descent, lineage

descendant: *nm.* descendant; *adj.* falling, descending

descendre: *vi.* to descend, go down; *vt.* to take down, bring down

descente: *nf.* descent, way down

descriptif: *adj.* descriptive, explanatory

description: *nf.* description

désemparé: *adj.* helpless; distraught

désenchantement: *nm.* disenchantment; disillusion

désenfler: *vi.* to become less swollen

désensibiliser: *vt.* to desensitise

déséquilibre: *nm.* imbalance, unbalance

déséquilibré: *adj.* unbalanced, unhinged

déséquilibrer: *vt.* to unbalance,

throw off balance

désert: *nm.* desert, wilderness; *adj.* deserted

déserter: *vt.* to desert

déserteur: *nm.* deserter

désertion: *nf.* desertion

désertique: *adj.* desert; barren

désespérant: *adj.* desperate, hopeless; discouraging

désespéré: *adj.* desperate, hopeless

désespérer: *vi.* to despair, give up hope

désespoir: *nm.* despair, despondency

déshabiller: *vt.* to undress; se - *vr.* to undress

désherbage: *nm.* weeding

désherbant: *nm.* weed killer

désherber: *vt.* to weed

déshériter: *vt.* to disinherit

déshonorant: *adj.* dishonourable, disgraceful

déshonorer: *vt.* to dishonour, disgrace

déshydratation: n f dehydration

déshydraté: *adj.* dehydrated

déshydrater: *vt.* to dehydrate; se *vr.* to become dehydrated

désignation: *nf.* designation, nomination; name

désigner: *vt.* to designate, indicate

désillusion: *nf.* disillusion; disappointment

désillusionner: *vt.* to disillusion; to disappoint

désincarné: *adj.* disincarnate, disembodied

désinfectant: *nm.* disinfectant; *adj.* disinfectant

désinfecter: *vt.* to disinfect

désinfection: *nf.* disinfection

désinformation: *nf.* disinformation

désintégration: *nf.* disintegration

désintégrer: *vt.* to split, break up

désintéressé: *adj.* disinterested, unselfish

désintéressement: *nm.* disinterestedness, unselfishness

désintéresser (se): *vr.* to lose interest in

désintoxiquer: *vt.* to detoxify; to dry out

désinvolte: *adj.* easy, offhand, casual

désinvolture: *nf.* casualness, off-handedness

désir: *nm.* desire, wish, longing

désirable: *adj.* desirable

désirer: *vt.* to desire, wish, long

désobéir: *vi.* to disobey

désobéissance: *nf.* disobedience

désobéissant: *adj.* disobedient

désobligeant: *adj.* disobliging; uncivil

désodorisant: *nm.* deodorant; *adj.* deodorising, deodorant

désodoriser: *vt.* to deodorise

désoeuvré: *adj.* unoccupied, idle

désoeuvrement: *nm.* idleness

désolation: *nf.* desolation; ruin; grief

désolé: *adj.* desolate; disconsolate, grieved

désordonné: *adj.* untidy; inordinate; reckless

désordre: *nm.* disorder, confusion, disturbance

désorganisation: *nf.* disorganisation

désorienté: *adj.* disorientated

désormais: *adv.* from now on, henceforth

désossé: *adj.* boned

despote: *nm.* despot

despotique: *adj.* despotic

despotiquement: *adv.* despotically

dessèchement: *nm.* dryness, drying up, withering

dessécher: *vt.* to dry, parch, wither

dessein: *nm.* design, plan, scheme

desserrer: *vt.* to loosen; to unscrew; to slacken; se - *vr.* = to work loose,

come undone
dessert: *nm.* dessert, sweet
desservir: *vt.* to clear (table); to do a disservice to
dessin: *nm.* drawing, sketch; draft
dessinateur: *nm.* drawer, draughtsman
dessinateur industriel: draughtsman
dessiner: *vt.* to draw, sketch; to design
dessous: *adv.* under, beneath; *nm.* underside, bottom
dessus: *adv.* over, above; m; prendre le - = to gain the upper hand
destabiliser: *vt.* to destabilise
destin: *nm.* destiny, fate, doom
destinataire: *nmf.* addressee, consignee
destination: *nf.* destination; purpose
destinée: *nf.* destiny, fate
destiner: *vt.* to determine; to intend, destine, aim
destituer: *vt.* to dismiss, depose
destructeur: *adj.* destructive, ruinous
destruction: *nf.* destruction
désuétude: *nf.* disuse tomber en - = to fall into disuse
détachable: *adj.* detachable
détachant: *nm.* cleaner, stain remover
détaché: *nm.* detached
détachement: *nm.* detachment, indifference
détacher: *vt.* to detach; to unfasten; se - *vr.* = to become detached
détail: *nm.* detail, particular
détaillant: *nm.* retailer
détailler: *vt.* to detail; to sell retail
détartrage: *nm.* descaling
détartrant: *nm.* descaling substance; *adj.* descaling
détartrer: *vt.* to descale
détaxe: *nf.* reduction in tax
détecter: *vt.* to detect

détecteur: *nm.* detector
détection: *nf.* detection
détective: *nm.* detective
déteindre: *vi.* to lose colour, fade
détendre: *vt.* to release, loosen; se - = to relax, calm down
détendu: *adj.* slack; relaxed
détenir: *vt.* to detain; to hold
détente: *nf.* relaxation, easing
détenteur: *nm.* holder, possessor
détergent: *nm.* detergent
détérioration: *nf.* deterioration
détériorer: *vt.* to damage, impair; se - *vr.* = to deteriorate, worsen
déterminant: *adj.* determining, deciding
détermination: *nf.* determination; resolution
déterminé: *adj.* determined, resolute
déterminer: *vt.* to determine, decide
déterrer: *vt.* to dig up, disinter
détestable: *adj.* detestable, odious; -ment *adv.* = detestably
détester: *vt.* to detest, hate
détonateur: *nm.* detonator
détonation: *nf.* detonation, explosion
détonner: *vi.* to clash; to go out of tune
détour: *nm.* detour; curve; evasion
détourné: *adj.* indirect, oblique
détournement: *nm.* diversion, rerouting
détourner: *vt.* to divert, reroute
détracteur: *nm.* detractor, disparager
détraquer: *vt.* to upset; to disorder; se - r = to become upset; to go wrong
détresse: *nf.* distress, trouble
détriment: *nm.* au - de = to the detriment of
détritus: *nm.* refuse, rubbish
détroit: *nm.* strait
détrôner: *vt.* to dethrone, depose
détruire: *vt.* to destroy, demolish
dette: *nf.* debt

deuil: *nm.* mourning, bereavement, grief

deux: *adj.* two; *nm.* two

deuxième: *adj.* second

deuxièmement: *adv.* secondly

deux-points: *nm.* colon

deux-roues: *nm.* two-wheeled vehicle

dévaler: *vt.* to hurry down, tear down

dévaliser: *vt.* to burgle; to rifle

dévalorisation: *nf.* depreciation

dévaloriser: *vt.* to depreciate, reduce the value of

dévaluation: *nf.* devaluation

devancer: *vt.* to outstrip, outrun; to precede

devant: *prép.* in front of, before; *adv.* in front; *nm.* front

développement: *nm.* development; growth; progress

développer: *vt.* to develop, expand; se - *vr.* = to develop, grow

devenir: *vi.* to become, grow

déverrouiller: *vt.* to unbolt, unlock

déverser: *vt.* to pour; to dump

dévêtir: *vt.* to undress; se – *vr.* = to get undressed

déviation: *nf.* deviation; diversion

dévier: *vi.* to deviate; to turn aside; to swerve

devin: *nm.* seer, sooth-sayer

deviner: *vt.* to guess; to solve; to foretell

devinette: *nf.* riddle

devis: *nm.* estimate, quotation

dévisager: *vt.* to stare at

devise: *nf.* currency

dévisser: *vt.* to unscrew, undo

dévoiler: *vt.* to unveil, disclose

devoir: *nm.* duty; homework; *vt.* to owe; to have to

dévorer: *vt.* to devour, consume

dévot: *adj.* devout, pious

dévotion: *nf.* devotion, piety

dévoué: *adj.* devoted, dedicated

dévouement: *nm.* devotion, dedication

dévouer (se): *vr.* to devote

dextérité: *nf.* dexterity, adroitness

diabète: *nm.* diabetes

diabétique: *adj.* diabetic

diable: *nm.* devil

diablotin: *nm.* imp; cracker

diabolique: *adj.* diabolical

diagnostic: *nm.* diagnosis

diagnostiquer: *vt.* to diagnose

diagonale: *nf.* diagonal

diagramme: *nm.* diagram; graph

diagramme des niveaux d'énergie: energy level diagram

dialecte: *nm.* dialect

dialectique: *nf.* dialectic; *adj.* dialectic

dialogue: *nm.* dialogue, conversation

dialoguer: *vt.* to write in dialogue form; *vi.* to have talks (with)

dialyse: *nf.* dialysis

diamagnétisme: diamagnetism

diamant: *nm.* diamond

diamètre: *nm.* diameter

diaphragme: *nm.* diaphragm

diarrhée: *nf.* diarrhoea

dictaphone: *nm.* dictaphone

dictateur: *nm.* dictator

dictatorial: *adj.* dictatorial

dictature: *nf.* dictatorship

dictée: *nf.* dictating; dictation

dicter: *vt.* to dictate, impose

dictionnaire: *nm.* dictionary

dicton: *nm.* saying, dictum

didactique: *adj.* didactic

diélectrique: dielectric

dièse: *nf.* sharp (mus)

diesel: *nm.* diesel

diète: *nf.* light diet

diététicien: *nm.* dietician

diététique: *adj.* dietary

Dieu: *nm.* God

diffamation: *nf.* defamation,

slandering
diffamer: *vt.* to defame, slander
différé: *adj.* postponed; pre-recorded
différemment: *adv.* differently
différence: *nf.* difference
différenciation: *nf.* differentiation
différencier: *vt.* to differentiate
différend: *nm.* disagreement, difference of opinion
différent: *adj.* different; various
différer: *vt.* to differ; to vary
difficile: *adj.* difficult; awkward, tricky
difficilement: *adv.* with difficulty
difficulté: *nf.* difficulty; problem
difforme: *adj.* deformed, misshapen
difformité: *nf.* deformity
diffraction: *nf.* diffraction
diffuser: *vt.* to diffuse, circulate, broadcast
diffusion: *nf.* diffusion, circulation, broadcasting
digérer: *vt.* to digest
digeste: *adj.* easily digestible
digestif: *adj.* digestive
digestion: *nf.* digestion
digital: *adj.* digital
digne: *adj.* worthy; dignified;
dignement: *adv.* worthily, deservedly
dignité: *nf.* dignity
digression: *nf.* digression
digue: *nf.* dyke; sea wall
dilapider: *vt.* to squander; to embezzle
dilatation: *nf.* dilation, distension
dilater: *vt.* to dilate, distend; se *vr.* to dilate, distend
dilemme: *nm.* dilemma
dilettante: *nm.* dilettante
diluer: *vt.* to dilute
dilution: *nf.* dilution
dimanche: *nm.* Sunday
dimension: *nf.* dimension, size
diminuer: *vt.* to diminish, reduce; *vi.*

to diminish, lessen
diminutif: *nm.* diminutive
diminution: *nf.* reduction, lessening
dinde: *nf.* turkey hen
dindon: *nm.* turkey cock
dindonneau: *nm.* young turkey
diner: *vi.* to dine
dinosaure: *nm.* dinosaur
diocèse: *nm.* diocese
diode: *nf.* diode
dioxyde: *nm.* dioxide
diphtérie: *nf.* diphtheria
diphtongue: *nf.* diphthong
diplomate: *nmf.* diplomat
diplomatie: *nf.* diplomacy
diplomatique: *adj.* diplomatic
diplomatiquement: *adv.* diplomatically
diplôme: *nm.* diploma, certificate
diplômé: *nm.* graduate; *adj.* qualified
dire: *vt.* to say; to tell
direct: *adj.* direct
directeur: *nm.* director
direction: *nf.* direction, management
directive: *nf.* directive, order
directly: *nm.* (rail) express
dirigeant: *nm.* leader, ruler; *adj.* ruling, executive
diriger: *vt.* to run, direct
discernement: *nm.* discernment, judgment
discerner: *vt.* to discern, distinguish
disciple: *nm.* disciple
disciplinaire: *adj.* disciplinary
discipline: *nf.* discipline
discipliné: *adj.* disciplined
discontinu: *adj.* discontinuous
discordant: *adj.* discordant, conflicting
discorde: *nf.* discord, dissension
discothèque: *nf.* discotheque
discours: *nm.* speech, talking
discourtois: *adj.* discourteous
discréditer: *vt.* to discredit

discret: *adj.* discreet
discrétion: *nf.* discretion, prudence
discrétionnaire: *adj.* discretionary
discrimination: *nf.* discrimination
discriminer: *vt.* to distinguish; to discriminate
disculper: *vt.* to excuse, exonerate
discussion: *nf.* discussion, debate
discutable: *adj.* debatable, questionable
discuter: *vt.* to discuss, debate
disgrâce: *nf.* disgrace
disgracieux: *adj.* awkward, ungraceful
disjoncter: *vi.* to cut off, disconnect
disjoncteur: *nm.* cutout, circuit breaker
disparaître: *vi.* to disappear, van-ish
disparate: *adj.* disparate, incongruous
disparité: *nf.* disparity, incongruity
disparition: *nf.* disappearance; death; extinction
disparu: *adj.* vanished; bygone; missing
dispensaire: *nm.* dispensary
dispense: *nf.* dispensation, exemption
dispenser: *vt.* to dispense, exempt
disperser: *vt.* to spread, scatter
dispersion: *nf.* dispersal, scattering
disponibilité: *nf.* availability
disponible: *adj.* available; transferable
dispos: *adj.* refreshed; alert; in form
disposer: *vt.* to arrange, dispose
dispositif: *nm.* device, mechanism
disposition: *nf.* arrangement, layout
dispositions: provisions (of a contract)
disproportionné: *adj.* disproportionate
dispute: *nf.* dispute, argument
disputer: *vt.* to dispute, rival; se - *vr.* = to quarrel, argue

disquaire: *nmf.* record-dealer
disqualifier: *vt.* to disqualify
disque: *nm.* disk; record
disquette: *nf.* diskette
dissection: *nf.* dissection
dissemblable: *adj.* dissimilar; different
disséminer: *vt.* to disseminate, scatter
dissentiment: *nm.* disagreement, dissent
disséquer: *vt.* to dissect
dissertation: *nf.* dissertation
dissidence: *nf.* dissidence, dissent
dissident: *adj.* dissident
dissimulation: *nf.* dissimulation, double-dealing
dissimulé: *adj.* double-faced, dissembling
dissimuler: *vt.* to dissemble, conceal
dissipation: *nf.* dissipation, waste
dissipé: *adj.* dissipated, undisciplined
dissiper: *vt.* to dispel; to dissipate
dissociation: *nf.* dissociation
dissocier: *vt.* to dissociate
dissolution: *nf.* dissolution
dissolvant: *nm.* solvent, dissolvent
dissonant: *adj.* dissonant; discordant
dissoudre: *vt.* to dissolve
dissoudre une société: to wind up a company
dissuader: *vt.* to dissuade
dissuasif: *adj.* dissuasive, deterrent
dissuasion: *nf.* dissuasion
distance: *nf.* distance, interval
distancier (se): *vr.* to distance o. s. from
distant: *adj.* distant
distendre: *vt.* to distend, strain; se *vr.* to slacken
distillation: *nf.* distillation
distiller: *vt.* to distil
distillerie: *nf.* distillery
distinct: *adj.* distinct, different
distinctif: *adj.* distinctive

distinction: *nf.* distinction
distingué: *adj.* distinguished
distinguer: *vt.* to distinguish; to
discern
distorsion: *nf.* distortion
distraction: *nf.* inattention;
absentmindedness; abstraction
distraire: *vt.* to distract; to amuse
distrait: *adj.* inattentive, absent-
minded
distrayant: *adj.* entertaining,
diverting
distribuer: *vt.* to distribute
distribuer un produit: to market a
product
distributeur: *nm.* distributor
distribution: *nf.* distribution
district: *nm.* district
diurétique: *adj.* diuretic; in diuretic
divagation: *nf.* wandering, rambling
divaguer: *vi.* to ramble, rave
divan: *nm.* divan
divergence: *nf.* divergence
divergent: *adj.* divergent
diverger: *vi.* to diverge, differ
divers: *adj.* diverse, varied
diversification: *nf.* diversification
diversifier: *vt.* to vary, diversify
diversion: *nf.* diversion
diversité: *nf.* diversity, variety
divertir: *vt.* to amuse, entertain
divertissant: *adj.* amusing,
entertaining
divertissement: *nm.* entertainment,
recreation
dividende: *nm.* dividend
divin: *adj.* divine, exquisite
divination: *nf.* divination
divinité: *nf.* divinity
diviser: *vt.* to divide, split
division: *nf.* division
divorce: *nm.* divorce
divorcé: *nm.* divorcee; *adj.* divorced
divorcer: *vi.* to divorce

divulgation: *nf.* disclosure,
divulgence
divulguer: *vt.* to divulge, disclose
dix: *adj.* ten
dix-huit: *adj.* eighteen
dix-huitième: *adj.* eighteenth
dixième: *adj.* tenth
dix-neuf: *adj.* nineteen
dix-neuvième: *adj.* nine-teenth
dix-sept: *adj.* seventeen
dix-septième: *adj.* seven-teenth
dizaine: *nf.* ten, ten or so
docile: *adj.* docile, submissive
docilement: *adv.* docilely
docilité: *nf.* docility, submissiveness
dock: *nm.* dock, dockyard
docteur: *nm.* doctor
doctorat: *nm.* doctorate
doctrine: *nf.* doctrine
document: *nm.* document
documentaire: *adj.* documentary
documentaliste: *nmf.* researcher
documentation: *nf.* documentation;
information
documenter: *vt.* to document
documents d'expédition: shipping
documents
dogmatique: *adj.* dogmatic
dogme: *nm.* dogma
doigt: *nm.* finger
doigté: *nm.* touch; fingering
technique
dollar: *nm.* dollar
domaine: *nm.* domain, estate;
to sphere
domanial: *adj.* state-owned
dôme: *nm.* dome, vault
domestique: *adj.* domestic,
household
domestiquer: *vt.* to domesticate,
tame
domicile: *nm.* domicile, address
domicilié: *adj.* domiciled
dominant: *adj.* dominant, prevailing

dominante: *nf.* dominant characteristic
dominateur: *adj.* governing; domineering
domination: *nf.* domination
dominer: *vt.* to dominate
dominical: *adj.* Sunday
dommage: *nm.* damage; harm
dompter: *vt.* to tame, train
dompteur: *nm.* trainer, tamer
don: *nm.* gift; talent
donateur: *nm.* donor
donation: *nf.* donation
donc: *conj.* so, therefore, thus; pourquoi
donné: *adj.* given; fixed
donnée: *nf.* datum
donner: *vt.* to give
donneur: *nm.* giver, donor; dealer
dont: *pron.* whose, of which
dopage: *nm.* doping
doper: *vt.* to dope
doré: *adj.* gilded; tanned
dorénavant: *adv.* from now on, henceforth
dorer: *vt.* to gild; to tan
dorloter: *vt.* to pamper, pet
dormir: *vi.* to sleep, be asleep; to be still
dortoir: *nm.* dormitory
dos: *nm.* back; top; ridge
dosage: *nm.* mixture; balance; proportioning
dose: *nf.* dose; amount; quantity
doser: *vt.* to measure out, proportion; to strike a balance
dossier: *nm.* dossier, file; case
dot: *nf.* dowry
doter: *vt.* to provide with a dowry; to endow
douane: *nf.* customs
douanier: *nm.* customs officer
double: *adj.* double, duplicate, dual
double exemplaire, en: in duplicate

doublement: *adv.* doubly
doubler: *vi.* to double, duplicate
doublure: *nf.* lining; (thea) under-study
doucement: *adv.* softly, gently
doucereux: *adj.* sugary; mawkish; suave
douceur: *nf.* softness, gentleness
douche: *nf.* shower
doucher: *vt.* to give a shower to; se - *vr.* = to take a shower
doué: *adj.* gifted, endowed with
douille: *nf.* case; cartridge
douillet: *adj.* delicate, tender; soft
douleur: *nf.* pain, ache; anguish
douloureusement: *adv.* painfully, grievously
douloureux: *adj.* painful, grievous
doute: *nm.* doubt; sans - = without doubt
douter: *vi.* to doubt, question
douteux: *adj.* doubtful, dubious
doux: *adj.* douce soft; sweet; mild
douzaine: *nf.* dozen
douze adj.: *nm.* twelve
douzième: *adj.* twelfth
doyen: *nm.* dean; doyen
draconien: *adj.* draconian, drastic
dragée: *nf.* bonbon, sugared almond
dragon: *nm.* dragon
dramatique: *adj.* dramatic, tragic
dramatiquement: *adv.* dramatically
dramatiser: *vt.* to dramatise
dramaturge: *nmf.* playwright
drame: *nm.* drama
drap: *nm.* sheet
drapeau: *nm.* flag
draper: *vt.* to drape
drawback: drawback
dressage: *nm.* taming; pitching
dresser: *vt.* to draw up; to put up
dresseur: *nm.* trainer, tamer
dribbler: *vi.* to dribble
drogue: *nf.* drug

drogué: *nm.* drug addict; *adj.* drugged
droguer: *vt.* to drug, administer drugs
droguerie: *nf.* hardware trade
droguiste: *nmf.* hardware store-keeper
droit: *adj.* right; straight; sound; honest; *nm.* right; law; tax
droit de courtage: brokerage fee
droit de régie, accises: excise duty
droite: *nf.* right side; right (wing); straight line
droitier: *adj.* right-handed
droits de douane: customs duties
droits de douane, être soumis aux: to be dutiable
droits spécifiques: specific duties
droiture: *nf.* uprightness, honesty
drôle: *adj.* funny, amusing; peculiar
drôlement: *adv.* funnily, peculiarly
dromadaire: *nm.* dromedary
dru: *adj.* thick, dense; sturdy
dû: *adj.* owed; due
dualité: *nf.* duality
dubitatif: *adj.* doubtful, dubious
dubitativement: *adv.* doubtfully, dubiously
duc: *nm.* duke
duché: *nm.* duchy
duchesse: *nf.* duchess
duel: *nm.* duel; dual
duettiste: *nmf.* duettist
dûment: *adv.* duly
dune: *nf.* dune
duo: *nm.* duo; duet
duodénum: *nm.* duodenum
dupe: *adj.* easily duped; *nf.* dupe
duper: *vt.* to dupe, take in
duplex: *nm.* duplex, two-way
dupliquer: *vt.* to duplicate
dur: *adj.* hard, tough; difficult
durable: *adj.* durable, lasting
durablement: *adv.* durably
duralumin: *nm.* duralumin

durant: *prép.* during, for
durcir: *vi.* to harden
durcissement: *nm.* hardening
durée: *nf.* duration, length
durée de vie: lifetime
durement: *adv.* harshly, severely
durer: *vi.* to last
dureté: *nf.* hardness; austerity, harshness
durillon: *nm.* callus, corn
duvet: *nm.* down
duveté: *adj.* downy
dynamique: *nf.* dynamic; dynamics; *adj.* dynamic
dynamiquement: *adv.* dy-namically
dynamiser: *vt.* to energise; to potentiate
dynamisme: *nm.* dynamism
dynamitage: *nm.* dynamiting
dynamite: *nf.* dynamite
dynamiter: *vt.* to dynamite
dynamo: *nf.* dynamo
dynastie: *nf.* dynasty
dynastique: *adj.* dynastic
dysenterie: *nf.* dysentery
dyslexie: *nf.* dyslexia
dyslexique: *adj.* dyslexic

ϛ

eau: *nf.* water; rain
eau de Javel: bleach
eau du robinet: tap water
eau-de-vie: *nf.* brandy
ébahir: *vt.* to astonish, stupefy, dumbfound
ébahissement: *nm.* astonishment, amazement
ébauche: *nf.* rough draft, rough outline
ébauche, traite: draft
ébaucher: *vt.* to sketch; to roughcast
ébène: *nf.* ebony
ébéniste: *nm.* cabinetmaker
éblouir: *vt.* to dazzle; to fascinate
éblouissant: *adj.* dazzling; amazing
éblouissement: *nm.* dazzle; bedazzlement
ébouillanter: *vt.* to scald; to blanch
éboulement: *nm.* collapse, caving in; fall
ébouriffé: *adj.* tousled, ruffled
ébranler: *vt.* to shake; to unsettle, disturb
ébrécher: *vt.* to chip, indent; to break into (fortune)
ébriété: *nf.* intoxication
ébrouerr (s'): *vr.* to shake oneself
ébruiter: *vt.* to disclose, divulge
ébulliométrie: *nf.* ebullioscopy
ébullition: *nf.* boiling; effervescence; turmoil
écailler: *vt.* to scale; to chip
écaillle: *nf.* scale; shell
écarlate: *adj.* scarlet
écart: *nm.* distance; interval; discrepancy; rester to steer clear of
écarteler: *vt.* to tear apart; to quarter
écarter: *vt.* to separate; to avert; to dismiss
ecchymose: *nf.* bruise, ecchymosis
ecclésiastique: *adj.* ecclesiastical; *nm.* ecclesiastic, clergyman

échafaud: *nm.* scaffold
échafaudage: *nm.* scaffolding
échange: *nm.* exchange, barter, trade
échanger: *vt.* to exchange
échantillon: *nm.* sample
échappée: *nf.* breakaway; glimpse
échappement: *nm.* exhaust; release
échapper: *vi.* to escape, avoid, elude
écharde: *nf.* splinter, sliver
écharpe: *nf.* scarf; armsling
échassier: *nm.* wader
échauffement: *nm.* heating; warm-up; constipation
échauffer: *vt.* to heat, overheat; to excite
échéance: *nf.* expiry; maturity date
échéance, venir à: to come to maturity
échec: *nm.* failure, defeat; chess
échelle: *nf.* ladder; scale
échelon: *nm.* rung; grade
échelonner: *vt.* to grade; to stagger, set at intervals
échine: *nf.* backbone, spine
échiquier: *nm.* chessboard
écho: *nm.* echo; rumour
échographie: *nf.* ultrasound scan
échoir: *vi.* to fall due; to befall, fall to so 's lot
échouer: *vi.* to fail; to end up; to run aground
éclabousser: *vt.* to splash, spatter
éclair: *nm.* flash; lightning flash; spark
éclairage: *nm.* lighting, light
éclairagiste: *nm.* electrician; light-ing engineer
éclaircie: *nf.* clear interval, bright spot; glade
éclaircir: *vt.* to lighten; to thin; to brighten up
éclaircissement: *nm.* clearing up, explanation, elucidation
éclairer: *vt.* to light, illuminate;

clarify, explain
éclat: *nm.* brightness, glare; splinter; splendour
éclatant: *adj.* bright, blazing; resounding; blatant
éclatement: *nm.* explosion, bursting, rupture
éclater: *vi.* to explode; to break out; to exclaim
éclectique: *adj.* eclectic
éclipse: *nf.* eclipse
éclipser: *vt.* to eclipse, overshadow
éclore: *vi.* to hatch out; to blossom
éclosion: *nf.* hatching; blooming; birth
écluse: *nf.* lock
écœurant: *adj.* disgusting, nauseating
écœurement: *nm.* nausea, disgust; discouragement
écoeurer: *vt.* to nauseate, disgust
école: *nf.* school, schooling; sect, doctrine
écolier: *nm.* schoolgirl, -ière
écologie: *nf.* ecology
écologique: *adj.* ecological
écologiste: *nmf.* ecologist
économe: *adj.* thrifty; *nmf.* steward, treasurer; (mar) bursar
économe: *nm.* thrifty
économie: *nf.* economy, thrift; economics
économique: *adj.* economic
économiquement: *adv.* economically
économiser: *vt.* to economise, save
économiser de l'argent: to save money
écorce: *nf.* bark, peel, skin
écorchure: *nf.* scratch; graze
écossais: *adj.* Scottish
Écossais: *nm.* Scotsman
Écosse: *nf.* Scotland
écoulement: *nm.* flow, discharge, outlet; disposal, selling
écouler: *vt.* to flow, discharge; to sell

écoute: *nf.* listening, audience
écouter: *vt.* to listen to
écran: *nm.* screen
écrasant: *adj.* crushing; overwhelming
écraser: *vt.* to crush; to overwhelm
écrémer: *vt.* to skim, cream
écrevisse: *nf.* crayfish
écrin: *nm.* box, casket
écrire: *vt.* to write; to spell
écrit: *adj.* written; *nm.* document; piece of writing
écrit, par: in writing
écriteau: *nm.* notice, sign
écriture: *nf.* writing; handwriting; script
écritures comptables: bookkeeping entries
écritures, passer les: to enter in the book
écrivain: *nm.* writer
écrou: *nm.* nut
écroulement: *nm.* collapse, caving in
écrouler (s'): *vr.* to collapse, crumble
écru: *adj.* raw; unbleached; untreated
ectoplasme: *nm.* ectoplasm
écueil: *nm.* reef, shelf; peril
écume: *nf.* foam, froth
écureuil: *nm.* squirrel
écurie: *nf.* stable
écusson: *nm.* badge, shield
eczéma: *nm.* eczema
édedron: *nm.* comforter, quilt
édification: *nf.* erection, construction
édifice: *nm.* edifice, building
édifier: *vt.* to build, construct; to edify
éditer: *vt.* to publish, produce; to edit
éditeur: *nm.* publisher; edi-tor
édition: *nf.* publishing; edition; editing
éditorial: *nm.* leading article, editorial
éducatif: *adj.* educational

éducation: *nf.* education; upbringing
édulcorant: *nm.* sweetener; *adj.* sweetening
éduquer: *vt.* to educate; to bring up, raise
effacer: *vt.* to delete, erase, wipe off
effaré: *adj.* alarmed, bewildered
effaroucher: *vt.* to frighten off; to arm
effectif: *nm.* staff; size, complement; *adj.* effective, positive
effectivement: *adv.* effectively, positively
effectuer: *vt.* to effect, execute, carry out
effervescence: *nf.* effervescence; excitement, ferment
effervescent: *adj.* effervescent; excited
effet: *nm.* effect, impression; spi bill, note
effet compton: compton effect
effet de cage: cage effect
effet de commerce: instrument of trade
effet de paroi: wall effect
effet photoélectrique: photoelectric effect
effet tunnel: tunnel effect
effet tyndall: tyndall effect
effet Zeeman: Zeeman effect
efficace: *adj.* effective; efficient
efficacement: *adv.* effectively, efficiently
efficacité: *nf.* effectiveness, efficiency
effleurer: *vt.* to touch lightly, skim across
effondrement: *nm.* collapse, caving in
efforcer (s'): *vr.* to endeavour, do one's best
effraction: *nf.* breaking and entering
effrayant: *adj.* frightening, fearsome

effrayé: *adj.* afraid
effrayer: *vt.* to frighten, scare
effriter: *vt.* to crumble; to exhaust (land)
effroi: *nm.* terror, dismay
effronté: *adj.* shameless, impudent, cheeky
effroyable: *adj.* horrifying, appalling
effroyablement: *adv.* horrifyingly, appallingly
égal: *adj.* equal; even, level; equable
également: *adv.* evenly; equally; so, as well
egaler: *vt.* to equal, match
egalisation: *nf.* equalisation; levelling
égaliser: *vt.* to equelise; to level out
égalité: *nf.* equality; equableness; evenness
égard: *nm.* consideration, respect
égarer: *vt.* to misled
égayer: *vt.* to enliven, cheer up
églantine: *nf.* dog-rose, wild rose
église: *nf.* church
égocentrique: *adj.* egocentric, self-centre
égoïsme: *nm.* selfishness, egoism
égoïste: *nmf.* egotist; *adj.* egotistic
égout: *nm.* sewer
égratignure: *nf.* scratch, scrape
éjecter: *vt.* to eject, throw out
élaboration: *nf.* elaboration, development
élaborer: *vt.* to elaborate, develop
élan: *nm.* surge, momentum, speed; spirit, elan
élancer (s'): *vr.* to rush, spring, hurl oneself
élargir: *vt.* to widen, stretch
élargissement: *nm.* widening, stretching, enlarging
élastique: *adj.* elastic; flexible; *nm.* elastic, elastic band
électeur: *nm.* voter, elector
élection: *nf.* election; choice

électorat: *nm.* electorate; constituency; franchise
électricien: *nm.* electrician
électricité: *nf.* electricity
électrique: *adj.* electric
électrocardiogramme: *nm.* electrocardiogram
électrode: *nf.* electrode
électrolyse: *nf.* electrolysis
électroménager: *nm.* household appliance; *adj.* electrical (household)
électron: *nm.* electron
électronégativité: *nf.* electronegativity
électronicien: *nm.* electronics engineer
électron-volt: electron volt
électrronique: *nf.* electronics; *adj.* electronic
élégance: *nf.* elegance, stylishness
élégant: *adj.* smart, elegant, stylish
élément: *nm.* element, component; cell; fact
élémentaire: *adj.* elementary; basic
éléphant: *nm.* elephant
élevage: *nm.* rearing, breeding
élevé: *adj.* high; heavy; lofty, exalted
élève: *nmf.* pupil, student
éleveur: *nm.* stockbreeder
éligible: *adj.* eligible
élimination: *nf.* elimination
éliminatoire: *adj.* eliminatory
éliminer: *vt.* to eliminate, discard
élire: *vt.* to elect
élite: *nf.* elite
élitisme: *nm.* elitism
elle: *pron.* she; it; her
elles: *pron.* they
elliptique: *adj.* elliptic
elliptiquement: *adv.* elliptically
élocution: *nf.* elocution, diction
éloge: *nm.* praise; eulogy
élogieux: *adj.* laudatory, eulogistic
éloigné: *adj.* distant, remote

éloigner: *vt.* to ove away
éloquence: *nf.* eloquence
éloquent: *adj.* eloquent
élu: *adj.* chosen, elected
élucider: *vt.* to elucidate, clear up
émacié: *adj.* emaciated, wasted
émail: *nm.* enamel
émailler: *vt.* to enamel
émancipation: *nf.* emancipation, liberation
émanciper: *vt.* to emancipate, liberate
émaner: *vi.* to emanate, issue
emballage: *nm.* packing paper, wrapping paper
emballer: *vt.* to pack up, wrap up
emballer (protection): to pack
emballer, conditionner: to package
embarcadère: *nm.* landing stage, pier
embarcation: *nf.* boat, craft
embargo: *nm.* embargo
embarquement: *nm.* loading; embarkation
embarquer: *vt.* to embark; to load; *vi.* to embark, go aboard
embarras: *nm.* embarrassment, confusion; trouble
embarrassant: *adj.* embarrassing, uncomfortable
embarrassé: *adj.* embarrassed, self-conscious
embarrasser: *vt.* to embarrass; to hinder, hamper
embaucher: *vt.* to take on, hire
embellir: *vt.* to beautify, make more attractive
embellissement: *nm.* embellishment, improvement
embêter: *vt.* to bore; to get on one's nerves
emblème: *nm.* symbol, emblem
emboîter: *vt.* to fit together
embonpoint: *nm.* stoutness, plumpness

embouchure: *nf.* mouth (river); mouthpiece

embouteillage: *nm.* traffic jam; bottling

embranchement: *nm.* junction; side road

embrasser: *vt.* to kiss, embrace

embrayage: *nm.* clutch

embrayer: *vi.* to engage the clutch

embrouiller: *vt.* to tangle up, mix up

embryon: *nm.* embryo

embryonnaire: *adj.* embryonic

embuscade: *nf.* ambush

émeraude: *nf.* emerald

émerger: *vi.* to emerge; to stand out

émeri: *nm.* emery

émerveiller: *vt.* to astonish

émetteur: *nm.* transmitter

émettre: *vt.* to send out, emit, transmit

émietter: *vt.* to crumble; to disperse, break up

émigration: *nf.* emigration

émigré: *nm.* émigré, expatriate

émigrer: *vi.* to emigrate

éminence: *nf.* hill, elevation; eminence, distinction

éminent: *adj.* eminent, distinguished

émir: *nm.* emir

émission: *nf.* sending out; transmission; broadcast; emission

emmêler: *vt.* to entangle; confuse

emménager: *vi.* to move in

emmener: *vt.* to take away; to lead

émmeute: *nf.* riot

émoi: *nm.* agitation, emotion

émotif: *adj.* emotional; emotive

émotion: *nf.* emotion; commotion

émotivité: *nf.* emotionalism

émouvant: *adj.* moving, touching

émouvoir: *vt.* to move, disturb, upset

empailler: *vt.* to stuff

empaqueter: *vt.* to parcel up, pack

emparer (s'): *vr.* to seize, grab; to

take possession of

empêchement: *nm.* obstacle, hitch; impediment

empêcher: *vt.* to prevent, stop

empereur: *nm.* emperor

empester: *vt.* to stink out; to poison, infect

empêtrer: *vt.* to entangle

emphase: *nf.* pomposity; emphasis, stress

empiéter: *vi.* to encroach, overlap

empiler: *vt.* to pile up, stack

empire: *nm.* empire; influence, ascendancy

empirer: *vi.* to get worse, deteriorate

empirique: *adj.* empirical

empiriquement: *adv.* empirically

emplacement: *nm.* site, location

emploi: *nm.* use; job, employment

employé: *nm.* employee

employer: *vt.* to use, spend; to employ

employeur: *nm.* employer

empoisonner: *vt.* to poison; to annoy

emporter: *vt.* to take; to carry off

empreinte: *nf.* imprint, impression, stamp

empresser (s'): *vi.* to rush to; to press around, fuss around

emprise: *nf.* hold, ascendancy

emprisonner: *vt.* to imprison, trap

emprunt: *nm.* borrowing, loan

emprunter: *vt.* to borrow; to assume; to derive

emprunteur: a borrower

ému: *adj.* moved, touched, excited

émulsion: *nf.* emulsion

en: *prep.* in; to; by; on

en arrière: *adv.* backwards; back

en avant: *adj. adv.* forward

en bas de: *prep.* down

en bonne santé: *adj.* healthy

en face: *adj.* opposite (across)

en forme: *adj.* fit

en haut: *adv.* up; upstairs
en outre: *adv.* besides
en plein air: *adj.* outdoor
en plus: *prep.* besides
en public: *adj.* live
en recommandé: *adj.* certified mail
en retard: *adj.* late
en vrac: in bulk
encadré: *nm.* box; framed text
encadrement: *nm.* framing; training; managerial staff
encadrer: *vt.* to frame; to train; to surround
encaissement: *nm.* collection; receipt; cashing
encaisser: *vt.* to collect, receive; to cash
encaisser un chèque: to cash a cheque
encastrer: *vt.* to embed, fit in, encase
enceinte: *nf.* pregnant
encens: *nm.* incense
encenser: *vt.* to cense to shower praise on
encercler: *vt.* to encircle, surround
enchaînement: *nm.* linking; link; sequence
enchaîner: *vt.* to chain
enchanté: *adj.* enchanted, delighted
enchantement: *nm.* enchantment, delight
enchanter: *vt.* to enchant, delight
enchâsser: *vt.* to set, imbed
enchère: *nf.* bid, offer
enchères, vente aux: auction sale
enchevêtrement: *nm.* entanglement, confusion
enclave: *nf.* enclave
enclencher: *vt.* to engage; to set in motion
enclin: *adj.* inclined, prone
enclore: *vt.* to enclose, shut in
enclume: *nf.* anvil; engine block
encoder: *vt.* to encode

encolure: *nf.* neck; collar size
encombrant: *adj.* unwieldy, cumbersome
encombrement: *nm.* congestion; jumble; obstruction
encombrer: *vt.* to clutter, obstruct
encore: *adv.* still; only; again; more
encourageant: *adj.* encouraging, heartening
encouragement: *nm.* encouragement
encourager: *vt.* to encourage; to incite
encre: *nf.* ink
encyclopédie: *nf.* encyclopaedia
endettement: *nm.* indebtedness; debt
endetter: *vt.* to get so into debt
endive: *nf.* chicory
endoctrinement: *nm.* indoctrination
endoctriner: *vt.* to indoctrinate
endommager: *vt.* to damage
endormir: *vt.* to put to sleep
endossement: *nm.* endorse
endosser: *vt.* to put on; to shoulder; to endorse
endosseur: *nm.* endorser
endroit: *nm.* place; side part
enduire: *vt.* to coat, smear
enduit: *nm.* coating
endurance: *nf.* endurance, stamina
endurci: *adj.* hardened; hard-hearted
endurcir: *vt.* to harden
endurer: *vt.* to endure, bear
énergétique: *adj.* energy; energising
énergie: *nf.* energy; spirit, vigour
énergie d'activation: activation energy
énergie de dissociation: dissociation energy
énergie de liaison: bond energy
énergie libre: free energy
énergie potentielle: potential energy
énergique: *adj.* energetic, vigorous
énergiquement: *adv.* energetically
énervant: *adj.* enervating; irritating

énervement: *nm.* irritation; nervousness

énerver: *vt.* to irritate, annoy; to get on one's nerves

enfance: *nf.* childhood; infancy

enfant: *nmf.* child; native

enfanter: *vt.* to give birth to

enfantillage: *nm.* childishness

enfantin: *adj.* childish, infantile

enfer: *nm.* hell

enfermer: *vt.* to lock up; to confine; to box in

enfiévrer: *vt.* to stir up, inflame

enfiler: *vt.* to string, thread; to put on

enfin: *adv.* at last; in short; after all

enflammer: *vt.* to set on fire; to inflame, kindle

enflé: *adj.* swollen; bombastic, turgid

enfler: *vi.* to swell up, inflate

enfoncer: *vt.* to stick in, thrust; to break open

enfouir: *vt.* to bury

enfuir (s'): *vr.* to run away, flee

engagement: *nm.* agreement, commitment, undertaking

engager: *vt.* to bind; to involve; to insert; to open

engelure: *nf.* chilblain

engendrer: *vt.* to create, engender; to father

engin: *nm.* machine; instrument; contraption

englober: *vt.* to include, encompass

engloutir: *vt.* to wolf down; to engulf

engorgement: *nm.* obstruction, clogging; glut

engouement: *nm.* infatuation; fad, craze

engouffrer: *vt.* to devour, swallow up, engulf

engourdi: *adj.* numb; dull

engourdir: *vt.* to numb; to dull, blunt

engourdissement: *nm.* numbness; sleepiness

engrais: *nm.* fertiliser; manure

engraisser: *vi.* to get fatter; *vt.* to fatten; to fertilise

engrenage: *nm.* gears, gearing

énigmatique: *adj.* enigmatic; *nf.* enigma, riddle

énigmatiquement: *adv.* enigmatically

enivrer: *vt.* to intoxicate, make drunk

enjoliver: *vt.* to ornament; to embroider (truth)

enlacer: *vt.* to embrace, intertwine

enlaidir: *vt.* to make ugly

enlèvement: *nm.* abduction, kidnapping; removal

enlever: *vt.* to remove; to take off; to deprive; to abduct

enliser: *vt.* to get stuck (car)

enneigé: *adj.* snowy, snowbound

enneigement: *nm.* snow coverage

ennemi: *nm.* enemy

ennui: *nm.* boredom, tedium, weariness

ennuyer: *vt.* to bore, bother

ennuyeux: *adj.* boring, tedious

énorme: *adj.* enormous, huge

énormément: *adv.* enormously

énorrmité: *nf.* enormity, hugeness; howler

enquête: *nf.* inquiry, investigation; survey

enquêter: *vi.* to hold an inquiry; to investigate

enraciner: *vt.* to implant, root

enragé: *adj.* furious; keen

enregistrement: *nm.* recording; registration

enregistrer: *vt.* to record; to register

enregistrer une commande: to book an order

enrichi: *adj.* improved, enriched; nouveau riche

enrichir: *vt.* to enrich, expand

enrichissant: *adj.* enriching

enrichissement: *nm.* enrichment
enrober: *vt.* to wrap, cover, coat
enrôler: *vt.* to enlist, enrol
enrouement: *nm.* hoarseness
enrouer: *vt.* to make hoarse
enrouler: *vt.* to roll up, wind up
enseignant: *nm.* teacher
enseigne: *nf.* sign; (mil) ensign
enseignement: *nm.* education, training, instruction
enseigner: *vt.* to teach
ensemble: *adv.* together, at the same time
ensoleillé: *adj.* sunny
ensorceler: *vt.* to bewitch, enchant
ensuite: *adv.* then, next, afterwards
entaille: *nf.* cut, gash
entamer: *vt.* to start, open, make a hole in
entassement: *nm.* piling up, heaping up
entasser: *vt.* to pile up, heap up
entendement: *nm.* understanding, comprehension
entendre: *vt.* to hear; to intend, mean; to understand
entendu: *adj.* agreed
entente: *nf.* harmony, understanding; accord
enterrement: *nm.* burial; funeral
enterrer: *vt.* to bury, inter
en-tête: *nm.* heading, header
entêté: *adj.* stubborn, obstinate
entêtement: *nm.* stubbornness, obstinacy
entêter: *vt.* to go to the head of
enthalpie: *nf.* enthalpy
enthousiasme: *nm.* enthusiasm
enthousiasmer: *vt.* to fill with enthusiasm
enthousiaste: *adj.* enthusiastic; *nmf.* enthusiast
entier: *adj.* entire, whole; intact
entièrement: *adv.* entirely, wholly, completely
entité: *nf.* entity
entonnoir: *nm.* funnel; swallow hole; shell-hole
entorse: *nf.* sprain
entortiller: *vt.* to twist, twine; to hoodwink, wheedle
entourage: *nm.* set, circle; entourage
entourer: *vt.* to surround, frame, encircle
entracte: *nm.* interval, intermission
entraide: *nf.* mutual aid
entraider (s'): *vr.* to help one another
entrailles: *nfpl.* entrails, guts; womb
entrain: *nm.* spirit, liveliness
entraînement: *nm.* training, coaching; force, impetus
entraînement à la vapeur: steam distillation
entraîner: *vt.* to drag; to lead; to train
entraîneur: *nm.* trainer, coach
entrave: *nf.* hindrance, obstacle; shackle
entraver: *vt.* to hold up; to shackle
entre: *prép.* between, among, into
entrebâiller: *vt.* to half-open
entrecôte: *nf.* rib steak
entrecouper: *vt.* to intersperse, interrupt with
entrée: *nf.* entry, entrance; admission; insertion
entrejambes: *nm.* crotch
entrelacer: *vt.* to intertwine, interlace
entremêler: *vt.* to intermingle, intermix
entremets: *nm.* sweet, dessert
entreposage: *nm.* warehousing
entreposer: *vt.* to store, put into storage
entrepôt: *nm.* warehouse, bonded warehouse
entreprenant: *adj.* enterprising
entreprendre: *vt.* to embark upon, undertake

entrepreneur: *nm.* contractor; entrepreneur
entreprise: *nf.* company; venture, business
entreprise adjudicataire ou soumissionnaire: bidder, bidding company
entreprise individuelle: one-man concern
entrer: *vi.* to enter, go in
entresol: *nm.* entresol, mezzanine
entretemps: *adv.* meanwhile
entretenir: *vt.* to maintain, look after; to speak with
entretien: *nm.* upkeep, maintenance; conversation
entrevoir: *vt.* to make out; to glimpse; to anticipate
entrevue: *nf.* meeting, interview
entropie: *nf.* entropy
entrouvert: *adj.* half open
entrouvrir: *vt.* to half-open
énumération: *nf.* enumeration, listing
énumérer: *vt.* to enumerate, list
envahir: *vt.* to invade, overrun
envahisant: *adj.* invasive; intrusive; pervasive
enveloppe: *nf.* envelope; covering; exterior
envelopper: *vt.* to envelop; to wrap up; to veil
envergure: *nf.* breadth, scope, scale
envers: *prép.* towards, to
envers (à l'): upside-down
envie: *nf.* desire, longing, inclination; envy
envier: *vt.* to envy
envieux: *adj.* envious
environ: *adv.* about, around
environnant: *adj.* surrounding
environnement: *nm.* environment
environnemental: *adj.* environmental
environner: *vt.* to surround, encircle

envisager: *vt.* to view, envisage
envoi: *nm.* dispatch, remittance; kick-off
envoi: *nm.* takeoff, flight
envoi, expédition: a shipment
envoler (a'): *vr.* to fly away; to disappear
envoûtant: *adj.* bewitching, entrancing
envoûter: *vt.* to bewitch
envoyé: *nm.* messenger, envoy
envoyer: *vt.* to send, dispatch; hurl, fire
enzyme: *nm.* enzyme
épais: *adj.* thick; deep
épaisseur: *nf.* thickness; depth
épaissir: *vi.* to thicken; to deepen
épanoui: *adj.* radiant, beaming
épanouir: *vt.* to brighten, light up; open out
épanouissement: *nm.* blooming; lighting up; opening out
épargne: *nf.* saving, savings
épargner: *vt.* to save; to spare
éparpiller: *vt.* to scatter, distribute
épaule: *nf.* shoulder
épauler: *vt.* to support, back up
épave: *nf.* wreck; derelict; ruin
épée: *nf.* sword
épeler: *vt.* to spell
éperdu: *adj.* distraught, overcome
éperdument: *adv.* frantically, desperately
éperon: *nm.* spur; (mar) ram
épervier: *nm.* sparrowhawk
éphémère: *adj.* ephemeral, fleeting
épi: *nm.* ear; tuft
épice: *nm.* spice
épicé: *adj.* spicy; juicy
épicerie: *nf.* grocery trade; grocer's shop
épicier: *nm.* grocer; green-grocer
épidémie: *nf.* epidemic
épidémique: *adj.* epidemic;

contagious
épiderme: *nm.* epidermis; skin
épier: *vt.* to spy on
épiglotte: *nf.* epiglottis
épilation: *nf.* removal of hair
épilepsie: *nf.* epilepsy
épileptique: *adj.* epileptic
épiler: *vt.* to remove hair, pluck
épilogue: *nm.* epilogue; conclusion
épinard: *nm.* spinach
épine: *nf.* spine; thorn
épineux: *adj.* thorny, prickly; tricky
épingle: *nf.* pin
Epiphanie: *nf.* Epiphany
épique: *adj.* epic
episcopal: *adj.* episcopal
épiscopat: *nm.* episcopate
épisode: *nm.* episode
épisodique: *adj.* occasional; transitory
épitaphe: *nf.* epitaph
épithète: *nf.* epithet
éplucher: *vt.* to clean; to peel; to sift
épluchure: *nf.* peeling, paring
éponge: *nf.* sponge
éponger: *vt.* to sponge, mop
épopée: *nf.* epic
époque: *nf.* time, epoch, age, period
épouser: *vt.* to marry, wed; espouse
épousseter: *vt.* to dust
épouvantable: *adj.* terrible, appalling
épouvantail: *nm.* scarecrow
épouvante: *nf.* terror, dread
épouvanter: *vt.* to terrify, appall
époux: *nm.* spouse
épreuve: *nf.* test; ordeal, trial
éprouver: *vt.* to feel, experience
éprouvette: *nf.* test tube
épuisé: *adj.* exhausted; sold out
épuisement: *nm.* exhaustion
épuiser: *vt.* to exhaust, wear out
épuisette: *nf.* landing net
épurer: *vt.* to purify, refine
équateur: *nm.* equator

équation: *nf.* equation
équation d'arrhenius: arrhenius' equation
équation d'onde de schrödinger: schrödinger equation
équatorial: *adj.* equatorial
équerre: *nf.* square; bracket
équestre: *adj.* equestrian
équilibre: *nm.* balance, equilibrium; harmony
équilibre de phase: phase equilibrium
équilibrer: *vt.* to balance
équipage: *nm.* crew; gear, equipment
équipe: *nf.* team, crew, gang, staff
équipement: *nm.* equipment; fitting out, fittings
équipement informatique: hardware
équiper: *vt.* to equip, fit out
équipier: *nm.* team member
équitable: *adj.* equitable, fair
équitation: *nf.* equitation, riding
équivalence: *nf.* equivalence
équivalent: *adj.* equivalent, same; *nm.* equivalent
équivoque: *adj.* equivocal, questionable
érable: *nm.* maple
érafler: *vt.* to scratch, scrape
ère: *nf.* era
érection: *nf.* erection; establishment
éreintant: *adj.* exhausting, backbreaking
ergot: *nm.* spur; (tec) lug
ériger: *vt.* to erect; to establish
ermite: *nm.* hermit
éroder: *vt.* to erode
érosion: *nf.* erosion
érotique: *adj.* erotic
érotisme: *nm.* eroticism
errant: *adj.* wandering, stray
errer: *vi.* to wander, roam
erreur: *nf.* error, mistake, fault
erroné: *adj.* erroneous

éructation: *nf.* eructation
érudit: *adj.* erudite, learned;
nm. scholar
érudition: *nf.* erudition, learning
éruptif: *adj.* eruptive
éruption: *nf.* eruption
escabeau: *nm.* stool; stepladder
escadron: *nm.* squadron, platoon
escalade: *nf.* climbing; escalation
escalader: *vt.* to climb, scale
escale: *nf.* port of call, touchdown
escalier: *nm.* stairs, steps
escalier roulant: *nm.* escalator
escalope: *nf.* escalope
escamoter: *vt.* to dodge, evade; to pilfer
escapade: *nf.* escapade; prank, jaunt
escargot: *nm.* snail
escarpement: *nm.* escarpment; steepness
esclavage: *nm.* slavery, bondage
esclavagisme: *nm.* proslavery
esclave: *nmf.* slave
escompte: *nm.* discount
escompte d'usage: trade discount
escompter: *vt.* to discount
escompter une traite: to discount a bill
escorte: *nf.* escort; retinue
escorter: *vt.* to escort
escrime: *nf.* fencing
escrimeur: *nm.* fencer
escroc: *nm.* crook, con man
escroquer: *vt.* to swindle, con
ésotérique: *adj.* esoteric
espace: *nm.* space, interval
espacement: *nm.* spacing, interval
espacer: *vt.* to space out
espadon: *nm.* swordfish
espadrille: *nf.* espadrille, ropesoled sandal
Espagne: *nf.* Spain
espèce: *nf.* sort, kind; species
espérance: *nf.* hope, expectation

espérer: *vt.* to hope
espion: *nm.* spy
espionnage: *nm.* espionage, spying
espionner: *vt.* to spy
esplanade: *nf.* esplanade
espoir: *nm.* hope
esprit: *nm.* mind, intellect; spirit; wit
esquimau: *nm.* Eskimo
esquisse: *nf.* sketch, outline
esquisser: *vt.* to sketch, outline
esquiver: *vt.* to dodge; to shirk
essai: *nm.* test, trial; attempt; essay
essaim: *nm.* swarm
essayage: *nm.* fitting, trying on
essayer: *vt.* to test, try, try on
essence: *nf.* petrol; essential oil
essentiel: *adj.* essential, basic
essentiellement: *adv.* essentially, basically
essieu: *nm.* axle
essorage: *nm.* wringing, mangling
essorer: *vt.* to wring, mangle
essouffler: *vt.* to wind
essuyer: *vt.* to wipe, mop
est: *nm.* east
esthète: *nmf.* aesthete
esthéticien: *nm.* beautician
esthétique: *adj.* aesthetic;
nf. aesthetics
esthétiquement: *adv.* aesthetically
estimation: *nf.* valuation; estimation, reckoning
estimation: *nm.* estimate
estime: *nf.* esteem, respect, regard
estimer: *vt.* to value, assess, estimate
estival: *adj.* summer; summery
estivant: *nm.* holidaymaker, summer visitor
estomac: *nm.* stomach
estomper: *vt.* to blur, dim
estrade: *nf.* platform, rostrum
estragon: *nm.* tarragon
et: *conj.* and
étable: *nf.* cowshed

établi: *adj.* established;
nm. workbench
établir: *vt.* to establish, set up
établir un document: to issue a
document
établir une facture: to make out an
invoice
établissement: *nm.* establishing,
building; establishment
étage: *nm.* display, display window;
stall
étage: *nm.* floor, storey; stage, level
étagère: *nf.* shelf
étalagiste: *nmf.* window dresser
étaler: *vt.* to spread, strew; to stagger;
to display
étalon: *nm.* stallion
étanche: *adj.* waterproof
étanchéité: *nf.* waterproofness
étang: *nm.* pond
étape: *nf.* stage, leg; staging point
étape déterminante: determining
step
état: *nm.* state, condition; statement
état quasistationnaire: steady-state
étatique: *adj.* under state control
étatiser: *vt.* to bring under state
control, nationalise
état-major: *nm.* (mil) staff;
staff headquarters
États-Unis: *npl.* United States
étau: *nm.* vice
étayer: *vt.* to prop up, support
été: *nm.* summer
éteindre: *vt.* to put out, extinguish
éteint: *adj.* faded; extinct
étendard: *nm.* standard, flag
étendre: *vt.* to spread, extend; to floor
étendu: *adj.* extensive, sprawling,
wide
étendue: *nf.* expanse, area; duration
éternel: *adj.* eternal, everlasting
éternellement: *adv.* eternally
éterniser: *vt.* to draw out; to

immortalise
éternité: *nf.* eternity; ages
éternuer: *vi.* to sneeze
éthane: *nm.* ethane
éther: *nm.* ether
ethnie: *nf.* ethnic unit
ethnique: *adj.* ethnic
ethnologie: *nf.* ethnology
ethnologue: *nmf.* ethnologist
étincelant: *adj.* sparkling; gleaming
étinceler: *vi.* to sparkle, gleam
étincelle: *nf.* spark; gleam, glimmer
étiqueter: *vt.* to label, mark
étiquette: *nf.* label, tag; etiquette
étirement: *nm.* stretching
étirer: *vt.* to stretch, draw out
étoffe: *nf.* material, fabric; stuff
étoile: *nf.* star
étoilé: *adj.* starry
étonnant: *adj.* astonishing, surprising
étonné: *adj.* astonished, surprised
étonnement: *nm.* surprise,
astonishment
étonner: *vt.* to astonish, surprise
étouffant: *adj.* stifling
étouffer: *vt.* to suffocate; to muffle
étourderie: *nf.* absentmindedness
étourdi: *adj.* absentminded
étourdir: *vt.* to stun, daze; to deafen
étourdissant: *adj.* deafening;
stunning
étourdissement: *nm.* blackout, dizzy
spell; surprise
étourneau: *nm.* starling
étrange: *adj.* strange, funny
étrangement: *adv.* strangely, oddly
étranger: *nm.* foreigner, stranger,
alien; *adj.* foreign, strange, unknown
étranger (à l'): *adv.* abroad
étrangeté: *nf.* strangeness, oddness
étranglement: *nm.* strangulation;
bottleneck
étrangler: *vt.* to strangle, stifle
être: *vi.* to be

être d'accord: *v.* to agree
étreindre: *vt.* to embrace, hug; to seize
étreinte: *nf.* embrace; stranglehold
étrier: *nm.* stirrup
étroit: *adj.* narrow; strict
étroitement: *adv.* closely; strictly
étude: *nf.* study; survey; office
étudiant, e: *nmf.* student
étudier: *vt.* to study, examine
étui: *nm.* case; holster
étymologie: *nf.* etymology
étymologique: *adj.* etymological
eucalyptus: *nm.* eucalyptus
eucharistie: *nf.* eucharist
euphémisme: *nm.* euphemism
euphorie: *nf.* euphoria
euphorique: *adj.* euphoric
euro: *nm.* euro
Europe: *nf.* Europe
européen: *nm.* European; *adj.* European
euthanasie: *nf.* euthanasia
eux: pron. they, them
évacuation: *nf.* evacuation; emptying
évacuer: *vt.* to evacuate, clear
évader (s'): *vr.* to escape
évaluation: *nf.* evaluation, appraisal
évaluer: *vt.* to evaluate, appraise
évangélique: *adj.* evangelical
évangéliser: *vt.* to evangelise
évangile: *nm.* gospel
évanouir (s'): *vr.* to faint, pass out
évanouissement: *nm.* faint, blackout
évaporation: *nf.* evaporation
évaporer (s'): *vr.* to evaporate
évasif: *adj.* evasive
évasion: *nf.* escape; escapism
évasivement: *adv.* evasively
évêché: *nm.* bishopric
éveil: *nm.* awakening; dawning
éveiller: *vt.* to waken, arouse
événement: *nm.* event, incident
éventail: *nm.* fan; range

éventaire: *nm.* tray; stall
éventualité: *nf.* eventuality, possibility
éventuel: *adj.* possible
éventuellement: *adv.* possibly
évêque: *nm.* bishop
évertuer (s'): *vr.* to strive to
évidemment: *adv.* obviously, evidently
évidence: *nf.* evidence, proof
évident: *adj.* obvious, evident
évier: *nm.* sink
évincer: *vt.* to oust; to evict
éviter: *vt.* to avoid; to spare
évocation: *nf.* evocation, recall
évolué: *adj.* developed, advanced; enlightened
évoluer: *vi.* to evolve, develop
évolution: *nf.* evolution, development
évoquer: *vt.* to evoke, recall
exacerber: *vt.* to exacerbate, aggravate
exact: *adj.* exact, accurate
exactement: *adv.* exactly
exactitude: *nf.* exactness, accuracy
exagération: *nf.* exaggeration
exagéré: *adj.* exaggerated, excessive
exagérément: *adv.* exaggeratedly
exagérer: *vt.* to exaggerate
exaltation: *nf.* elation; extolling, praising
exalter: *vt.* to exalt, glorify; to elate
examen: *nm.* examination, survey, investigation
examinateur, trice: *nmf.* examiner
examiner: *vt.* to examine, survey
exaspération: *nf.* exasperation
exaspérer: *vt.* to exasperate
exaucer: *vt.* to fulfil, grant
excédent: *nm.* surplus, excess
excédentaire: *adj.* surplus, excess
excellent: *adj.* excellent
exceller: *vi.* to excel
excentricité: *nf.* eccentricity

excentrique: *adj.* eccentric
excentriquement: *adv.* eccentrically
excepté: *adj.* apart, aside
exception: *nf.* exception
exceptionnel: *adj.* exceptional
exceptionnellement:
adv. exceptionally
excès: *nm.* excess, surplus
excessivement: *adv.* excessively
excitant: *nm.* stimulant; *adj.* exciting,
stimulating
excitation: *nf.* excitation, stimulation;
incitement
exciter: *vt.* to excite, stimulate
exclamation: *nf.* exclamation
exclamer (s'): *vr.* to exclaim
exclu: *adj.* excluded, outcast
exclure: *vt.* to exclude, oust, expel
exclusif: *adj.* exclusive
exclusion: *nf.* exclusion, suspension
exclusivement: *adv.* exclusively
exclusivité: *nf.* exclusive rights
excrément: *nm.* excrement
excroissance: *nf.* excrescence,
outgrowth
excursion: *nf.* excursion, trip
excursionniste: *nmf.* tripper; walker
excuse: *nf.* excuse, pretext
excuser: *vt.* to excuse, forgive
exécrable: *adj.* execrable, atrocious
exécrablement: *adv.* atrociously,
execrably
exécration: *nf.* execration, loathing
exécrer: *vt.* to execrate, loathe
exécuter: *vt.* to execute, carry out,
perform; to produce
exécuter une commande: to meet an
order
exécution: *nf.* execution, carrying
out, performance
exemplaire: *nm.* copy, archetype;
adj. model, exemplary
exemple: *nm.* example, model,
instance

exempt: *adj.* exempt, free from
exercer: *vt.* to exercise, perform,
fulfil
exercice: *nm.* exercise, practice, use;
financial year
exercice financier: financial year
exhaustif: *adj.* exhaustive
exhaustivement: *adv.* exhaustively
exhiber: *vt.* to exhibit, show; to
produce
exhibition: *nf.* exhibition, show;
display
exhibitionniste: *nmf.* exhibitionist
exhortation: *nf.* exhortation
exhorter: *vt.* to exhort, urge
exigeant: *adj.* demanding, exacting
exigence: *nf.* demand, requirement;
exigency
exiger: *vt.* to demand, require
exigu: *adj.* exiguë scanty, exiguous
exiguïté: *nf.* exiguity, scantiness
exil: *nm.* exile
exilé: *nm.* exile; *adj.* exiled
exiler: *vt.* to exile, banish
existant: *adj.* existing
existence: *nf.* existence, life
exister: *vi.* to exist; to be
exode: *nm.* exodus; drift, loss
exonération: *nf.* exemption
exonérer: *vt.* to exempt
exorbitant: *adj.* exorbitant,
outrageous
exorciser: *vt.* to exorcise
exotique: *adj.* exotic
exotisme: *nm.* exoticism
expansif: *adj.* expansive, outgoing
expansion: *nf.* expansion,
development
expatrié: *nm.* expatriate; *adj.*
expatriate
expatrier: *vt.* to expatriate
expectative: *nf.* expectation, hope;
expédier: *vt.* to send, dispatch; to
dispose of

expédier (des marchandises): to ship, consign, dispatch, send (goods)
expéditeur: *nm.* sender; shipper, consignor
expéditeur, agent d'expédition: shipper, consignor
expéditif: *adj.* quick, expeditious
expédition: *nf.* dispatch; consignment
expérience: *nf.* experience; experiment
expérimental: *adj.* experimental
expérimentateur: *nm.* experimenter
expérimentation: *nf.* experimentation
expérimenté: *adj.* experienced
expérimenter: *vt.* to test; to experiment with
expert: *adj.* expert, skilled in
expert: *nm.* connoisseur; assessor
expertise: *nf.* expertise; expert appraisal
expiation: *nf.* expiation, atonement
expier: *vi.* to expiate, atone for
expiration: *nf.* expiry; expiration, exhalation
expirer: *vi.* to breathe out, expire
explicatif: *adj.* explanatory
explication: *nf.* explanation, analysis
explicite: *adj.* explicite
explicitement: *adv.* explicitly
expliquer: *vt.* to explain, account for; to analyse
exploitant: *nm.* farmer, small-holder
exploitation: *nf.* working; exploitation; operating; concern; small-holding
exploiter: *vt.* to work, exploit; run, operate
explorateur: *nm.* explorer
exploration: *nf.* exploration
explorer: *vt.* to explore
exploser: *vi.* to explode
explosif: *adj.* explosive; *nm.* explosive

explosion: *nf.* explosion
exportateur: *nm.* exporter
exportation: *nf.* export, exportation
exporter: *vt.* to export
exposé: *nm.* exposition, overview, statement
exposer: *vt.* to display; to explain, state; to expose
exposition: *nf.* display; exposition; exposure
exprès: *adj.* express
express: *adj.* fast
expressif: *adj.* expressive
expression: *nf.* expression
expressionnisme: *nm.* expressionism
expressionniste: *nmf.* expressionist
exprimer: *vt.* to express, voice
expropriation: *nf.* expropriation
expulser: *vt.* to expel; to evict
expulsion: *nf.* expulsion; eviction
exquis: *adj.* exquisite
extase: *nf.* ecstasy; rapture
extasier (s'): *vr.* to go into ecstasies
extensible: *adj.* extensible, extendable
extension: *nf.* extension; stretching; expansion
exténuant: *adj.* exhausting
exténuer: *vt.* to exhaust
extérieur: *nm.* exterior, outside
extérioriser: *vt.* to show, express; to exteriorise
extermination: *nf.* extermination
exterminer: *vt.* exterminate
externe: *adj.* external, outer
extincteur: *nm.* extinguisher
extinction: *nf.* extinction, extinguishing
extraction: *nf.* extraction; mining
extradition: *nf.* extradition
extraire: *vt.* to extract; to mine
extrait: *nm.* extract; (jar) abstract
extraordinaire: *adj.* extraordinary
extraordinairement:

adv. extraordinarily
extraterrestre: *nmf.* extraterrestrial; *adj.* extraterrestrial
extravagant: *adj.* extravagant, wild
extraverti: *nm.* extrovert; *adj.* extrovert
extrême: *adj.* extreme
extrêmement: *adv.* extremely
extrémiste: *nmf.* extremist; *adj.* extremist
extrémité: *nf.* end, extremity, limit
exubérance: *nf.* exuberance
exubérant: *adj.* exuberant
exulter: *vi.* to exult

F

fable: *nf.* fable, story, tale
fabricant: *nm.* manufacturer, maker
fabrication: *nf.* manufacture, production
fabrique: *nf.* factory
fabriquer: *vt.* to manufacture; to forge; to fabricate
fabuleux: *adj.* fabulous, mythical, legendary
façade: *nf.* façade, front
face: *nf.* face, side, surface, aspect
face it face: *nm.* encounter, interview
facette: *nf.* facet
fâché: *adj.* angry; sorry
fâcher: *vt.* to anger, make angry; to grieve
fâcheux: *adj.* deplorable, regrettable
facile: *adj.* easy; facile
facilement: *adv.* easily
facilité: *nf.* easiness, ease; ability; facility
faciliter: *vt.* to make easier, facilitate
façon: *nf.* way, fashion; make; imitation
façonner: *vt.* to shape, fashion, model; to till
facsimilé: *nm.* facsimile
facteur: *nm.* postman
facteur de fréquence: frequency factor
facteur préexponentiel: a factor
facteur stérique: steric factor
factice: *adj.* artificial, imitation
faction: *nf.* faction; sentry-duty
facturation: *nf.* invoicing
facture: *nf.* bill, invoice; construction, technique
facture: invoice
facture consulaire: consular invoice
facture des services publics (gaz, électricité): utility bill
facture pro-forma: pro-forma invoice

facturer: *vt.* to invoice, charge for
facultatif: *adj.* optional
faculté: *nf.* faculty; power, ability; right
fade: *adj.* insipid, bland, dull
fagot: *nm.* faggot, bundle of firewood
faible: *adj.* weak, feeble; slight, poor
faiblement: *adv.* weakly, faintly, feebly
faiblesse: *nf.* weakness, feebleness, faintness
faiblir: *vi.* to fail, flag, weaken; to wane
faïence: *nf.* earthenware, crockery
faille: *nf.* fault; flaw; weakness
failli, un: a bankrupt
faillir vi: to come close to; to fail j'ai failli tomber l almost fell
faillite: *nf.* bankruptcy; collapse
faillite, une: a bankruptcy (faire faillite to go bankrupt)
faim: *nf.* hunger; appetite; famine
fainéant: *nm.* idler, loafer
faire: *vt.* to do; to make
faire des achats: *v.* to shop
faire du jogging: *v.* to jog
faire la course: *v.* to race
faire la cuisine: *v.* to cook
faire les bagages: *v.* to pack (suitcase)
faire mal: *v.* to hurt
faire payer: *v.* to charge (price)
faire peur: *v.* to frighten; to scare
faire un somme: *v.* to nap
faire-part: *nm.* announcement (birth, marriage, death)
faisable: *adj.* feasible
faisan: *nm.* pheasant
faisceau: *nm.* bundle, stack; beam
faisceau moléculaire: molecular beam
fait: *nm.* event; fact; act
faîte: *nm.* summit; rooftop
falaise: *nf.* cliff

falloir vi: to be necessary; il faut, que tu partes you must leave
falsifier: *vt.* to falsify, alter
famélique: *adj.* starving, scrawny
fameux: *adj.* famous; excellent
famiariser: *vt.* to familiarise; se *vr.* to familiarise
familial: *adj.* fa family, domestic
familiarité: *nf.* familiarity
familier: *adj.* familiar; colloquial; informal
familièrement: *adv.* familiarly, informally
famille: *nf.* family
famine: *nf.* famine
fanatique: *adj.* fanatic; *nmf.* fanatic; zealot
fané: *adj.* faded, withered
faner: *vt.* to turn (hay); to fade; se *vr.* to wither, fade
fanfare: *nf.* fanfare, flourish; brass band
fantaisie: *nf.* whim, extravagance; imagination
fantasme: *nm.* fantasy
fantasmer: *vi.* to fantasise
fantastique: *adj.* fantastic;
fantastiquement: *adv.* fantastically; eerily
fantôme: *nm.* ghost, phantom
faon: *nm.* fawn
farce: *nf.* joke, prank; farce
farceur: *nm.* joker; clown
farci: *adj.* stuffed, crammed, packed
farcir: *vt.* to stuff, cram
fard: *nm.* make-up
fardeau: *nm.* load, burden
farder: *vt.* to make up; to disguise
farine: *nf.* flour
farineux: *adj.* floury, powdery; *nm.* starchy food
farouche: *adj.* shy, timid; unsociable; fierce
farouchement: *adv.* fiercely

fascicule: *nm.* booklet, fascicule, part, instalment
fascinant: *adj.* fascinating
fascination: *nf.* fascination
fasciner: *vt.* to fascinate, bewitch
fascisme: *nm.* fascism
fasciste: *nmf.* fascist; *adj.* fascist
faste: *nm.* pomp, ostentation
fastidieux: *adj.* tedious, boring
fastueux: *adj.* sumptuous, luxurious
fatal: *adj.* fatal, deadly; fateful
fataliste: *nmf.* fatalist; *adj.* fatalistic
fatalité: *nf.* fatality; inevitability
fatidique: *adj.* fateful; fatal
fatigant: *adj.* tiring, fatiguing
fatigue: *nf.* fatigue, tiredness
fatigué: *adj.* tired, weary; overworked, strained
fatiguer: *vt.* to tire; to overwork, strain
fatisme: *nm.* fanaticism
faubourg: *nm.* suburb
fauché, être: to be broke
faucher: *vt.* to reap; to flatten, knock down
faucille: *nf.* sickle
faucon: *nm.* falcon, hawk
faufiler: *vt.* to tack; to insinuate, introduce
faune: *nf.* wildlife, fauna
faussaire: *nmf.* forger
faussement: *adv.* wrongly; falsely
fausser: *vt.* to distort, alter; to warp
fausseté: *nf.* falseness; deceitfulness
faute: *nf.* mistake, foul, fault
fauteuil: *nm.* armchair
fautif: *nm.* culprit, guilty party; *adj.* at fault, guilty; faulty, incorrect
fauve: *nm.* wild animal; fawn (colour)
faux: *adj.* false, forged, fake; wrong; bogus
faux-filet: *nm.* sirloin
faux-fuyant: *nm.* evasion, equivocation
faux-semblant: *nm.* sham, pretence
faveur: *nf.* favour
favorable: *adj.* favourable, sympathetic
favorablement: *adv.* favourably
favori: *nm.* favourite; *adj.* favourite
favoriser: *vt.* to favour, further
fébrile: *adj.* feverish, febrile; -ment = *adv.* feverishly
fébrilité: *nf.* feverishness
fécond: *adj.* fertile; prolific, fruitful; creative
fécondation: *nf.* impregnation,
féconder: *vt.* to impregnate; to fertilise, pollinate
fécondité: *nf.* fertility, fecundity
fécule: *nf.* starch
féculent: *adj.* starchy; *nm.* starchy food
fédéral: *adj.* federal
fédération: *nf.* federation
fée: *nf.* fairy
féerique: *adj.* magical, fairy
feindre: *vt.* to feign, pretend
feinte: *nf.* dummy, feint
fêlé: *adj.* cracked, hare-brained
félicitation: *nf.* congratulation
féliciter: *vt.* to congratulate
félin: *adj.* feline; *nm.* feline
femelle: *nf.* female
féminin: *adj.* feminine, female
féminisme: *nm.* feminism
féministe: *nmf.* feminist; *adj.* feminist
féminité: *nf.* femininity
femme: *nf.* woman; wife
fémur: *nm.* femur
fendiller: *vt.* to chink, crack, craze; se - *vr.* = to be covered in small cracks
fendre: *vt.* to split, cleave, crack; se - *vr.* = to crack
fenêtre: *nf.* window
fenouil: *nm.* fennel
fente: *nf.* crack, fissure; slot

féodal: *adj.* feudal
fer: *nm.* iron, point, blade;
- à cheval = horseshoe
férié: *adj.* public holiday
ferme: *adj.* firm, steady; definite;
nf. farm
fermé: *adj.* closed; exclusive;
inscrutable
fermement: *adv.* firmly
ferment: *nm.* ferment, leaven
fermentation: *nf.* fermentation,
fermenting
fermenter: *vi.* to ferment, work
fermer: *vt.* to close; block; turn off
fermeté: *nf.* firmness, steadiness
fermeture: *nf.* closing, shutting;
latch; fastener
fermier: *nm.* farmer
féroce: *adj.* ferocious, savage
férocement: *adv.* ferociously,
savagely
férocité: *nf.* ferocity, fierceness
fête: *nf.* party
fêter: *v.* to celebrate
feu: *nm.* fire
feu d'artifice: fireworks
feuille: sheet (paper); leaf (tree)
feuille de route, lettre de voiture:
waybill
feuilleter: *v.* to browse
février: *nm.* February
fiable: *adj.* reliable
fiançailles: *nm.* engagement
fibreux: *adj.* fibrous, stringy
fibrome: *nm.* fibroid, fibroma
ficeler: *vt.* to tie up
ficelle: *nf.* string; stick (bread)
fiche: *nf.* card; sheet; certificate
fiche de stock: stock control card
ficher: *vt.* to file, put on file
fichier: *nm.* catalogue; file
fictif: *adj.* fictitious; imaginary
fiction: *nf.* imagination, fiction
fidèle: *adj.* faithful, loyal; *nmf.*

believer
fidèlement: *adv.* faithfully
fidélité: *nf.* fidelity, loyalty
fief: *nm.* fief; stronghold, preserve
fier: *adj.* proud, haughty; noble
fier (se): *vr.* to trust, rely on
fièrement: *adv.* proudly
fierté: *nf.* pride; arrogance
fièvre: *nf.* fever, temperature;
excitement
fiévreux: *adj.* feverish
figer: *vt.* to congeal, freeze; to clot
figue: *nf.* fig
figuier: *nm.* fig tree
figurant: *nm.* extra, walk-on; stooge
figuratif: *adj.* figurative,
representational
figure: *nf.* face; figure; illustration,
diagram
figuré: *adj.* figurative, metaphorical,
diagrammatic
figurer: *vt.* to represent; *vi.* to appear,
feature
figurine: *nf.* figurine
fil: *nm.* thread; wire; cord
filament: *nm.* filament, strand, thread
filature: *nf.* spinning; mill; tailing
filer: *vt.* to spin; to tail; to draw out;
vi. to run, trickle; to fly by; to make
off
filet: *nm.* dribble, trickle; fillet; net
filiale: a subsidiary
filiation: *nf.* filiation; relation
filière: *nf.* path; procedures; network
fille: *nf.* daughter, girl
fillette: *nf.* (small) girl
filleul, e: *nmf.* godson, godchild
film: *nm.* film, picture
filmer: *vt.* to film
filon: *nm.* vein, seam
filou: *adj.* blurred, hazy
fils: *nm.* son
filtre: *nm.* filter
filtrer: *vt.* to filter; to screen

fin: *nf.* end, finish; prendre
final: *adj.* final
finale: *nf.* finale
finalement: *adv.* finally
finance: *nf.* finance
financement: *nm.* financing
financer: *vt.* to finance
financier: *nm.* financier
financièrement: *adv.* financially
fine: *nf.* daughter, girl
finesse: *nf.* fineness; sharpness;
neatness; delicacy
fini: *adj.* finished, over, complete
finir: *vt.* to finish, complete
finition: *nf.* finish, finishing
fisc: *nm.* tax department
fiscal: *adj.* fiscal, tax
fission nucléaire: nuclear fission
fissure: *nf.* crack, fissure
fixation: *nf.* fixation; fixing, fastening
fixe: *adj.* fixed, permanent, set
fixer: *vt.* to fix, fasten; to arrange
flacon: *nm.* bottle, flask
flageolant: *adj.* shaky
flageolet: *nm.* flageolet
flagrant: *adj.* flagrant, blatant
flair: *nm.* sense of smell, nose;
intuition
flairer: *vt.* to smell, sniff; to scent
flambeau: *nm.* torch; candlestick
flamboyant: *adj.* flamboyant
flamme: *nf.* flame; fervour; ardour
flan: *nm.* custard tart; mould
flanc: *nm.* flank, side
flanelle: *nf.* flannel
flâner: *vi.* to stroll; to lounge about
flash: *nm.* flash
flasque: *adj.* flaccid; spineless
flatter: *vt.* to flatter, gratify; to
pander; to delight
flatterie: *nf.* flattery
flatteur: *nm.* flatterer
fléau: *nm.* scourge; plague
flèche: *nf.* arrow

fléchir: *vi.* to bend, yield, weaken
fléchissement: *nm.* bending; flexing;
bowing
flegmatique: *adj.* phlegmatic
flegme: *nm.* composure, phlegm
flétrir: *vt.* to wither, fade; to
stigmatise
fleur: *nf.* flower
fleuri: *adj.* in bloom; flowery
fleurir: *vi.* to blossom, flower; *vt.* to
decorate with flowers
fleuriste: *nmf.* florist
fleuve: *nm.* river
flexibilité: *nf.* flexibility
flexible: *adj.* flexible, pliant
flic: *nm.* (fam) cop, policeman
flocon: *nm.* fleck, flake
floraison: *nf.* flowering, blossoming
floral: *adj.* floral, flower
flore: *nf.* flora
florissant: *adj.* flourishing, blooming
flot: *nm.* stream, flood; floodtide;
wave
flotte: *nf.* fleet; (col) rain
flottement: *nm.* wavering; vagueness,
imprecision
flotter: *vi.* to float; to drift; to
wander; to waver
flotteur: *nm.* float
fluctuant: *adj.* fluctuating
fluctuation: *nf.* fluctuation
fluide: *adj.* fluid, flowing
fluidité: *nf.* fluidity
fluor: *nm.* fluorine
fluorescent: *adj.* fluorescent
fluorure: *nm.* fluoride
flûte: *nf.* flute; French stick (bread)
flûtiste: *nmf.* flautist
flux: *nm.* flood; flow; flux
focaliser: *vt.* to focus
foetus: *nm.* foetus
foi: *nf.* faith, trust
foie: *nm.* liver
foin: *nm.* hay

foire: *nf.* fair, trade fair
fois: *nf.* time, occasion
folie: *nf.* madness, insanity; extravagance
folklore: *nm.* folklore
folklorique: *adj.* folk
follement: *adv.* madly, wildly
foncé: *adj.* dark, deep (colours)
foncer: *vi.* to hammer along, rush at
foncier: *adj.* land, landed, property
foncièrement: *adv.* fundamentally, basically
fonction: *nf.* post, duty; function
fonctionnaire: *nmf.* civil servant
fonctionnement: *nm.* working
fonctionner: *vi.* to work, function, operate
fond: *nm.* bottom, back
fondamental: *adj.* fundamental, basic
fondamentalement: *adv.* fundamentally
fondamentalisme: *nm.* fundamentalism
fondamentaliste: *nmf.* fundamentalist; *adj.* fundamentalist
fondant: *adj.* thawing, melting
fondateur, trice: *nmf.* founder
fondation: *nf.* foundation
fondement: *nm.* foundation; ground
fonder: *vt.* to found; to base
fondre: *vi.* to melt; to vanish; to slim
fonds: *nm.* business; fund; money; stock
fonds, être en: to be in cash
fondu: *adj.* melted; molten; cast
fontaine: *nf.* fountain, spring
fonte: *nf.* melting; casting; smelting
football: *nm.* football, soccer
forage: *nm.* drilling, boring
forain, e: *nmf.* stallholder; fairground entertainer; *adj.* fair-ground
force: *nf.* strength, force, violence, energy
forcé: *adj.* forced; emergency

forcément: *adv.* inevitably
forcené: *adj.* deranged, frenzied
forcer: *vt.* to force, compel; track down
forestier: *adj.* forest; forestry
forêt: *nf.* forest
forfait: *nm.* set price, package; (sport) withdrawal
forfaitaire: *adj.* fixed, set, inclusive
forge: *nf.* forge, smithy
forger: *vt.* to forge, form, mould
forgeron: *nm.* blacksmith, smith
formalaire: *nm.* form
formaliser (se): *vr.* to take offence at
formalité: *nf.* formality
format: *nm.* format, size
formation: *nf.* formation; training
forme: *nf.* form, shape; mould, fitness
formel: *adj.* definite, positive
formellement: *adv.* positively, definitely; formally
former: *vt.* to form, make up; to train
former une société en nom collectif: to enter into partnership
formidable: *adj.* tremendous; fantastic
formidablement: *adv.* tremendously, fantastically
formulaire: *nm.* form
formule: *nf.* formula; phrase; system
formuler: *vt.* to formulate; express
fort: *adj.* strong; high; loud; pronounced; *nm.* fort; strong point
fortement: *adv.* strongly; highly; very much
forteresse: *nf.* fortress
fortication: *nf.* fortification
fortifiant: *nm.* tonic; *adj.* fortifying; invigorating
fortifier: *vt.* to fortify, strengthen
fortrat, parabole de: fortrat parabola
fortuit: *adj.* fortuitous, chance
fortuitement: *adv.* fortuitously
fortune: *nf.* fortune, luck

fortuné: *adj.* wealthy; fortunate
fosse: *nf.* pit; grave
fossé: *nm.* ditch; gulf
fossette: *nf.* dimple
fossile: *nm.* fossil
fou: *adj.* mad, wild; tremendous; erratic
foudre: *nf.* lightning, thunderbolt
foudroyant: *adj.* lightning; thundering; violent
foudroyer: *vt.* to strike (lightning)
fouet: *nm.* whip; whisk
fouetter: *vt.* to whip, flog
fougère: *nf.* fern
fougue: *nf.* ardour, spirit
fougueux: *adj.* fiery, ardent
fouille: *nf.* frisking; excavations
fouiller: *vt.* to search, scour
foulard: *nm.* scarf
foule: *nf.* crowd; masses, heaps
four: *nm.* oven; furnace; fiasco
fourbe: *adj.* deceitful, two-faced
fourbu: *adj.* exhausted
fourche: *nf.* pitchfork; crotch
fourchette: *nf.* fork
fourchu: *adj.* forked; cloven
fourgon: *nm.* coach, wagon, van
fourier, série de (transformée de): fouriertransform series
fourmi: *nf.* ant
fourmilière: *nf.* anthill
fourmillement: *nm.* swarming, milling
fourmiller: *vi.* to swarm, teem
fourneau: *nm.* stove
fournir: *vt.* to supply, provide
fournir quelque chose à quelqu'un: to supply someone with something
fournir un prix: to quote a price
fournisseur: *nm.* supplier
fournisseur: *nm.* purveyor, supplier
fourniture: *nf.* supplying, provision
fourrage: *nm.* fodder, forage
fourré: *adj.* filled; furlined; *nm.*

thicket
fourrer: *vt.* to stuff; to line
fourrière: *nf.* pound (car)
fourrure: *nf.* coat, fur
foutu: *adj.* bloody, damned; lousy
foyer: *nm.* home; fireplace; club; focus
fracas: *nm.* crash; roar, din
fraction: *nf.* fraction, part
fractionnement: *nm.* splitting up, division
fracture: *nf.* fracture
fracturer: *vt.* to fracture, break open
fragile: *adj.* fragile, delicate
fragilité: *nf.* fragility, flimsiness
fragment: *nm.* fragment
fragmentation: *nf.* fragmentation; splitting up
fragmenter: *vt.* to break up, fragment; se - *vr.* = to fragment, break up
fraîche: *adj.* fresh, cool
fraîcheur: *nf.* freshness, coolness
frais: *nmpl.* expenses
frais de scolarité: *nmpl.* tuition
frais généraux: overheads
fraise: *nf.* strawberry
framboise: *nf.* raspberry
franc: *adj.* rank, open; clear; absolute
français: *adj.* French; *nm.* French
France: *nf.* France
franchement: *adv.* frankly, openly; boldly; clearly
franchir: *vt.* to clear, get over, cross
franchise: *nf.* frankness, openness; exemption; franchise
franco: free of charge
franco transporteur: free carrier
francophone: *nmf.* French-speaker; *adj.* French-speaking
francophonie: *nf.* French-speaking communities
frange: *nf.* fringe; threshold
frappant: *adj.* striking

frapper: *vt.* to hit; to strike down; to infringe
fraternel: *adj.* fraternal
fraternellement: *adv.* fraternally
fraterniser: *vi.* to fraternise
fraternité: *nf.* fraternity
fraude: *nf.* fraud, cheating
frauduleux: *adj.* fraudulent
frayeur: *nf.* fright
frein: *nm.* brake; check
freinage: *nm.* braking; slowing down
freiner: *vi.* to brake, slow down
frêle: *adj.* flimsy, fragile
frelon: *nm.* hornet
frémir: *vi.* to quiver, tremble
frémissant: *adj.* quivering, trembling
frémissement: *nm.* shudder, quiver
frénétique: *adj.* frenetic
frénétiquement: *adv.* frenetically
fréquemment: *adv.* frequently
fréquence: *nf.* frequency
fréquent: *adj.* frequent
frère: *nm.* brother
fresque: *nf.* fresco
fret aérien: airborne freight
fret maritime: seaborne freight
friand: *adj.* partial to, fond of
friandise: *nf.* delicacy, sweetmeat
fric: *nm.* (lam) cash, lolly
friction: *nf.* friction
frigidaire: *nm.* refrigerator
frigide: *adj.* frigid
frileux: *adj.* susceptible to cold; chilly
frire: *vt.* to fry
frisé: *adj.* curly, curly-haired
friser: *vi.* to curl, be curly; *vt.* to curl; to graze, skim
frisson: *nm.* shiver, shudder
frissonnant: *adj.* shivering, shud-dering
frissonnement: *nm.* shuddering, shivering
frissonner: *vi.* to shudder, tremble, shiver
frite: *nf.* chip
friteuse: *nf.* chip pan
friture: *nf.* frying; frying fat
frivole: *adj.* frivolous, shallow
frivolité: *nf.* frivolity
froid: *adj.* cold, cool; *nm.* cold; coolness; refrigeration
froidement: *adv.* coldly, coolly
froideur: *nf.* coldness, chilliness
froissement: *nm.* creasing; rustling, rustle
froisser: *vt.* to crease; to offend; se *vr.* to crease; to take offence
frôler: *vt.* to brush against; to verge on
fromage: *nm.* cheese
front: *nm.* forehead; face; front
frontal: *adj.* frontal
frontalier: *adj.* border, frontier
frontière: *nf.* border, frontier
frottement: *nm.* rubbing, scraping
frotter: *vt.* to rub, scrape
fructifier: *vi.* to bear fruit
fructueux: adj fruitful, profitable
frugalité: *nf.* frugality
frugal: *adj.* frugal
fruit: *nm.* fruit, result
fruité: *adj.* fruity
frustration: *nf.* frustration
frustrer: *vt.* to frustrate, deprive
fugace: *adj.* fleeting, transient
fugitif: *nm.* fugitive
fugue: *nf.* running away
fuir: *vi.* to avoid; to flee; to leak
fuite: *nf.* flight, escape; leak
fulgurant: *adj.* lightning; dazzling
fumant: *adj.* smoking, fuming
fumé: *adj.* smoked
fumée: *nf.* smoke; vapour
fumer: *vi.* to smoke, to steam
fumet: *nm.* aroma
fumeur: *nm.* smoker
fumier: *nm.* dung, manure

funèbre: *adj.* funeral; funerary
funérailles: *nfpl.* funeral
funéraire: *adj.* funeral, funerary
funeste: *adj.* disastrous; harmful
fureur: *nf.* fury; violence
furie: *nf.* fury, rage
furieusement: *adv.* furiously
furieux: *adj.* furious, violent
furtif: *adj.* furtive; stealthy
furtivement: *adj.* furtively
fusée: *nf.* rocket, missile
fusible: *nm.* fuse
fusil: *nm.* rifle, gun
fusillade: *nf.* fusillade; gunfire; shoot-out
fusiller: *vt.* to shoot
fusion: *nf.* fusion; melting; merger; blending
fusion nucléaire: nuclear fusion
fusionner: *vt.* to merge, combine
fût: *nm.* trunk; shaft; barrel
futé: *adj.* crafty, cunning
futile: *adj.* futile
futilement: *adv.* futilely
futilité: *nf.* futility
futur: *adj.* future; *nm.* intended, fiancé; future
fuyant: *adj.* fleeting; evasive
fuyard: *nm.* runaway

G

gabarit: *nm.* size, build; calibre
gâcher: *vt.* to mix; to waste
gachette: *nf.* trigger
gâchis: *nm.* mess
gadget: *nm.* gadget; gimmick
gadspillage: *nm.* waste; squandering
gaffe: *nf.* blunder; boat hook
gage: *nm.* security; pledge; proof
gagnant: *nm.* winner; *adj.* winning
gagner: *vt.* to earn, to win, beat; to gain; *vi.* to win; to spread
gai: *adj.* cheerful, happy, gay
gaieté: *nf.* cheerfulness, gaiety
gain: *nm.* earnings; gain, profit, benefit; saving
gait: *nm.* taste; liking; style
gaiter: *vt.* to taste; to appreciate; *vi.* to have a snack; to taste
gala: *nm.* official reception; gala
galamment: *adv.* courteously, gallantly
galant: *adj.* gallant, courteous
galanterie: *nf.* gallantry
galaxie: *nf.* galaxy
galère: *nf.* galley
galerie: *nf.* gallery; tunnel
galet: *nm.* pebble
galette: *nf.* paned
gallois: *adj.* Welsh
gallon: *nm.* gallon
galloper: *vi.* to gallop; to run wild
galon: *nm.* braid; stripe
galop: *nm.* gallop; canter
galvaniser: *vt.* to galvanise
gamba: *nf.* large prawn
gamin: *nm.* kid, street urchin
gaminerie: *nf.* playfulness; childishness
gamme: *nf.* range; scale
ganglion: *nm.* ganglion
gangrène: *nf.* gangrene
gant: *nm.* glove
garage: *nm.* garage

garagiste: *nmf.* garage owner
garant: *nm.* guarantor
garantie: *nf.* guarantee, surety
garantir: *vt.* to guarantee, secure
garçon: *nm.* boy; assistant; waiter
garde: *nf.* custody; guard; surveillance, warder
garde-à-vous: *nm.* standing to attention
garde-bone: *nm.* mudguard
garde-chasse: *nm.* gamekeeper
garde-fou: *nm.* railing, parapet; safeguard
garder: *vt.* t look after; to stay in; to keep on
garder les enfants: *v.* to baby-sit
garderie: *nf.* day nursery
garde-robe: *nf.* wardrobe
gardien: *nm.* guard, guardian, warden; protector
gare: *nf.* rail station; basin; depot
gare d'arrivée: receiving station
garer: *vt.* to park; to dock
gargarisme: *nm.* gargle
gargouillement: *nm.* gurgling; rumbling
gargouiller: *vi.* to gurgle; to rumble
garni on: *nf.* (mil) garrison
garnir: *vt.* to fit with; to trim, decorate
garniture: *nf.* trimming, lining; garnish
garrot: *nm.* garrotte; (med) tourniquet
gars: *nm.* lad; bloke
gaspiller: *vt.* to waste, squander
gastrique: *adj.* gastric
gastronome: *nm.* gourmet, gastronome
gastronomie: *nf.* gastronomy
gâté: *adj.* ruined; spoiled
gâteau: *nm.* cake
gâter: *vt.* to ruin; to spoil
gâteux: *adj.* senile

gauche: *adj.* left; awkward, clumsy
gaucher: *adj.* left-handed
gauchisant: *nm.* leftist; *adj.* of leftist tendencies
gauchiste: *nmf.* leftist
gaufre: *nf.* waffle
gaver: *vt.* to force-feed, fill up
gaz: *nm. invar* gas; fizz; wind
gaz idéal: ideal gas law
gaz parfait: ideal gas
gaze: *nf.* gauze
gazelle: *nf.* gazelle
gazeux: *adj* gaseous; fizzy
gazon: *nm.* lawn; turf
gazouiller: *vi.* to chirp, warble
géant: *nm.* giant
geindre: *vi.* to groan; to whine
gel: *nm.* frost; gel
gélatine: *nf.* gelatine
gelé: *adj.* frozen; cold, unresponsive
gelée: *nf.* frost; jelly
geler: *vi.* to freeze, be frozen
gélule: *nf.* capsule
gémir: *vi.* to groan, moan
gémissement: *nm.* groan, moan; groaning
gênant: *adj.* annoying; awkward
gencive: *nf.* gum
gendarme: *nm.* policeman; gendarme
gendarmerie: *nf.* police force, constabulary
gendre: *nm.* son-in-law
gêne: *nf.* discomfort; trouble; embarrassment; être sans
généalogie: *nf.* genealogy
généalogique: *adj.* genealogical
gêner: *vt.* to bother; to hinder; to make uneasy
général: *adj.* general, broad; common; *nm.* general
généralisation: *nf.* generalisation
généraliser: *vt.* to generalise
généraliste: *nm.* general practitioner; *adj.* general-interest; non-specialised

généralité: *nf.* majority; general points
générateur: *nm.* generator
génération: *nf.* generation
générer: *vt.* to generate
généreusement: *adv.* generously; nobly
généreux: *adj.* generous; noble; magnanimous
générosité: *nf.* generosity; nobility; magnanimity
génétique: *adj.* genetic
génétiquement: *adv.* genetically
génial: *adj.* inspired, of genius
génie: *nm.* genius; spirit; genie
génital: *adj.* genital
génocide: *nm.* genocide
genou: *nm.* knee
genre: *nm.* kind, type; gender; genre
gens: *nmpl.* people, folk
gentil: *adj.* kind; good; pleasant
gentillesse: *nf.* kindness; favour
gentiment: *adv.* kindly; nicely
géographe: *nmf.* geographer
géographie: *nf.* geography
géographique: *adj.* geographic
géologie: *nf.* geology
géologue: *nmf.* geologist
géomètre: *nm.* land surveyor
géométrie: *nf.* geometry
géométrique: *adj.* geometric
géométriquement: *adv.* geometrically
géranium: *nm.* geranium
gérant: *nm.* manager
gerbe: *nf.* sheaf, bundle; collection
gercer: *vt.* to chap, crack
gerçure: *nf.* (small) crack
gérer: *vt.* to manage, administer
germe: *nm.* germ; seed
germer: *vi.* to sprout, germinate
gérondif: *nm.* gerundive; gerund
gésier: *nm.* gizzard
gestation: *nf.* gestation

geste: *nm.* gesture; act, deed
gesticuler: *vi.* to gesticulate
gestion: *nf.* management, administration
gestion de stock zéro: just-in-time stock control
gestionnaire: *adj.* administrative, management
ghetto: *nm.* ghetto
gibier: *nm.* game; prey
gicler: *vi.* to spurt, squirt
gicleur: *nm.* jet
giffler: *vt.* to slap, smack
gifle: *nf.* slap, smack
gigantesque: *adj.* gigantic, immense
gigot: *nm.* leg (mutton/lamb), haunch
gilet: *nm.* waistcoat
gilet de sauvetage: life jacket
gingembre: *nm.* ginger
girafe: *nf.* giraffe
giratoire: *adj.* gyrating, gyratory
girouette: *nf.* weather vane
gisement: *nm.* deposit; mine; pool
gitan: *nm.* gipsy
gite: *nm.* shelter; home
givre: *nm.* frost, rime
givré: *adj.* covered in frost
glace: *nf.* ice; ice cream; mirror
glacé: *adj.* icy; frozen; glazed; chilly
glacer: *vt.* to freeze; to chill; to glaze
glacial: *adj.* icy; freezing
glacier: *nm.* glacier; ice cream maker
glacière: *nf.* icebox
glaçon: *nm.* icicle; ice cube
glaïeul: *nm.* gladiola
glaise: *nf.* clay
gland: *nm.* acorn
glande: *nf.* gland
glaner: *vt.* to glean
glauque: *adj.* murky; shabby, rundown
glissade: *nf.* slide, skid
glissant: *adj.* slippery
glissement: *nm.* sliding; gliding;

downturn, downswing
glisser: *vi.* to slide, slip, skid
glissière: *nf.* slide; runner
global: *adj.* global, overall
globalement: *adv.* globally
globe: *nm.* globe, sphere; earth
globulaire: *adj.* global, corpuscular
globule: *nm.* globule; corpuscle
globuleux: *adj.* globular; protruding
gloire: *nf.* glory; distinction; celebrity
glorieux: *adj.* glorious
glorifier: *vt.* to glory, honour
glossaire: *nm.* glossary
glouton: *nm.* glutton; *adj.* gluttonous, ravenous
gluant: *adj.* sticky, slimy
glucide: *nm.* glucide
glucose: *nm.* glucose
glycérine: *nf.* glycerine
gobelet: *nm.* beaker, tumbler
gober: *vt.* to swallow; to fall for
goéland: *nm.* gull
goinfre: *nm.* pig; *adj.* piggish
golf: *nm.* golf
golfeur: *nm.* golfer
gomme: *nf.* gum; rubber, eraser
gommer: *vt.* to rub out; to gum
gond: *nm.* hinge
gondole: *nf.* gondola
gondoler: *vi.* to crinkle, warp, buckle
gonflable: *adj.* inflatable
gonflement: *nm.* inflation, swelling
gonfler: *vt.* to pump up, inflate
gong: *nm.* gong; bell
gore: *nm.* gulf, chasm, abyss
gorge: *nf.* throat
gorgée: *nf.* sip, gulp
gorille: *nm.* gorilla
gosier: *nm.* throat, gullet
gosse: *nmf.* kid
gothique: *adj.* Gothic
goudron: *nm.* tar
goudronner: *vt.* to tar
goulu: *adj.* greedy, gluttonous

goulûment: *adv.* greedily, gluttonously
goupille: *nf.* pin
gourd: *adj.* numb (with cold)
gourde: *nf.* gourd; flask
gourdin: *nm.* club, cudgel
gourmand: *adj.* greedy
gourmandise: *nf.* greed, greediness
gourmet: *nm.* gourmet
gourmette: *nf.* chain bracelet
gousse: *nf.* pod
goût: *nm.* flavor, taste
goutte: *nf.* drop; dram; gout
goutter: *v.* to taste, to sample
gouttière: *nf.* gutter; drainpipe
gouvernail: *nm.* rudder; helm
gouvernement: *nm.* government
gouvernemental: *adj.* government, governmental
gouverner: *vt.* to govern, rule; to control; to steer
gouverneur: *nm.* governor
goyave: *nf.* guava
grâce: *nf.* grace; favour; mercy; pardon
gracier: *vt.* to pardon
gracieusement: *adv.* gracefully; kindly
gracieux: *adj.* gracious
grade: *nm.* rank; grade; degree
gradé: *nm.* car; *adj.* promoted
gradin: *nm.* tier; step; terrace
graduel: *adj.* gradual; progressive
graduellement: *adv.* gradually
graduer: *vt.* to step up; to graduate
graffiti: *nmpl.* graffiti
graham, loi de: graham's law
grain: *nm.* grain, seed; bead
graine: *nf.* seed
graissage: *nm.* greasing, lubricating
graisse: *nf.* grease, fat
graisser: *vt.* to grease, lubricate
grammaire: *nf.* grammar
grammairien: *nm.* grammarian

grammatical: *adj.* grammatical
grammaticalement: *adv.*
grammatically
gramme: *nm.* gram
gramme: gram
grand: *adj.* big; tall; great; leading
grand livre: the Ledger
grand magasin: department store
Grande-Bretagne: Great Britain
grandeur: *nf.* size; greatness;
magnitude
grandiose: *adj.* imposing, grandiose
grandir: *vi.* to grow bigger, increase;
to magnify; exaggerate
grandissement: *nm.* enlargement
grand-mère: *nf.* grandmother
grand-parents: *nmpl.* grandparents
grand-père: *nm.* grandfather
grange: *nf.* barn
granite: *nm.* granite
granulé: *nm.* granule; *adj.* granular
granuleux: *adj.* granular; grainy
graphique: *nm.* graph; *adj.* graphique
graphiquement: *adv.* graphically
graphite: *nm.* graphite
grappe: *nf.* cluster, bunch
gras: *adj.* fatty; fat; greasy; crude
grate: *nf.* crane
gratification: *nf.* gratuity; bonus
gratin: *nm.* cheese dish, gratin
gratis: *adv.* free, gratis
gratitude: *nf.* gratitude, gratefulness
gratter: *vt.* to scratch, scrape
gratuit: *adj.* free, gratuitous
grave: *adj.* grave, sole
graver: *vt.* to engrave, imprint
graveur: *nm.* engraver, woodcutter
gravier: *nm.* gravel
gravir: *vt.* to climb
gravitation: *nf.* gravitation
gravité: *nf.* gravity
gravure: *nf.* engraving, carving
gré m: liking, taste
greffe: *nf.* transplant, graft

greffer: *vt.* to transplant, graft
grégaire: *adj.* gregarious
grêle: *nf.* hail
grellotter: *vi.* to shiver
grêlon: *nm.* hailstone
grenade: *nf.* pomegranate; grenade
grenat: *nm.* garnet
grenier: *nm.* attic, garret
grenouille: *nf.* frog
grès: *nm.* sandstone; stoneware
grésiller: *vi.* to sizzle; splutter
grève: *nf.* strike; shore
gribouillage: *nm.* scrawl, scribble
gribouiller: *vi.* to doodle; *vt.* to
scribble, scrawl
grièvement: *adv.* seriously
griffe: *nf.* claw
griffer: *vt.* to scratch
griffonner: *vt.* to scribble, jot down
grignoter: *vi.* to nibble at, pick at; *vt.*
to nibble at; to eat away
gril: *nm.* grill pan; rack
grillade: *nf.* grilled meat
grillage: *nm.* toasting; grilling
grille: *nf.* railings; gate; grill
grille-pain: *nm.* invar toaster
griller: *vt.* to toast, scorch; to put bars
on; *vi.* to toast, grill
grillon: *nm.* cricket
grimace: *nf.* grimace; funny face
grimper: *vi.* to climb up
grincement: *nm.* grating, creaking
grincer: *vi.* to grate, creak
grincheux: *adj.* grumpy
grippe: *nf.* flu, influenza
grippé: *adj.* suffering from flu
gris: *adj.* grey
grisant: *adj.* exhilarating;
intoxicating
griser: *vt.* to intoxicate
grisonnant: *adj.* greying
grive: *nf.* thrush
grog: *nm.* grog
grognement: *nm.* grunt, grunting

grognner: *vi.* to grumble, moan
grognon: *nm.* grumbler, moaner; *adj.* grumpy, surly
grommeler: *vi.* to mutter; to grumble; *vt.* to mutter
grondement: *nm.* rumbling, growling
gronder: *vt.* to scold
gros: *adj.* big; fat; thick
groseille: *nf.* currant
grossesse: *nf.* pregnancy
grosseur: *nf.* thickness; lump; fatness
grossier: *adj.* coarse; unrefined; base
grossièrement: *adv.* roughly; coarsely
grossièreté: *nf.* rudeness; coarseness
grossir: *vi.* to get fatter; to swell, grow; *vt.* to magnify; to exaggerate
grossiste: *nmf.* wholesaler
grotesque: *adj.* grotesque, ludicrous
grotte: *nf.* cave; grotto
grouiller: *vi.* to mill about; to swarm
groupe: *nm.* group; party; cluster
groupement: *nm.* grouping; group
grouper: *vt.* to group together; to bulk
grumeau: *nm.* lump
gruyère: *nm.* gruyère (cheese)
guenon: *nf.* female monkey; hag
guépard: *nm.* cheetah
guêpe: *nf.* wasp
guêpier: *nm.* trap; wasp's nest
guère: *adv.* hardly, scarcely
guéri: *adj.* cured
guéridon: *nm.* pedestal table
guérir: *vi.* to get better; to heal; ut to cure, heal
guérison: *nf.* recovery; curing
guérisseur: *nm.* healer
guerre: *nf.* war; warfare
guerrier: *nm.* warrior
guet: *nm.* watch
guetter: *vt.* to watch; to lie in wait for
gueule: *nf.* mouth; face; muzzle
gueule de boir: *nf.* hangover

gueuler: *vi.* to bawl; bellow
guichet: *nm.* counter; ticket office, booking office
guichet automatique: automatic teller machine (ATM)
guichetier: *nm.* counter clerk
guidage: *nm.* guides; guidance
guide: *nm.* guide
guider: *vt.* to guide
guidon: *nm.* handlebars
guignol: *nm.* puppet; puppet show
guillemet: *nm.* inverted comma; quotation mark
guillotine: *nf.* guillotine
guimauve: *nf.* marshmallow
guindé: *adj.* stiff, uptight
guirlande: *nf.* garland
guise: *nf.* manner, way
guitare: *nf.* guitar
guitariste: *nmf.* guitarist
guttural: *adj.* guttural
gymnase: *nm.* gymnasium
gymnastique: *nf.* gymnastics
gynécologie: *nf.* gynaecology
gynécologue, gynécologiste: *nmf.* gynaecologist
gyrophare: *nm.* revolving light

H

habile: *adj.* skilful, skilled; clever
habileté: *nf.* skill, skilfulness; clever move
habiliter: *vt.* to qualify; to authorise
habillement: *nm.* clothing, dress, outfit
habiller: *vt.* to dress, clothe
habit: *nm.* clothes; apparel; dresscoat; outfit
habitable: *adj.* inhabitable
habitant: *nm.* inhabitant; occupant; dweller
habitat: *nm.* habitat; housing conditions
habitation: *nf.* dwelling; residence; house
habité: *adj.* manned
habiter: *vi.* to live; *vt.* to live in; occupy
habitude: *nf.* habit, custom, routine
habituel: *adj.* usual, customary
habituellement: *adv.* usually, generally
habituer: *vt.* to accustom; to teach
hache: *nf.* axe, hatchet
hacher: *vt.* to chop, mince
hachoir: *nm.* chopper, cleaver
hachure: *nf.* hatching
hagard: *adj.* wild; haggard; distraught
haie: *nf.* hedge
haine: *nf.* hatred
haineux: *adj.* full of hatred; malevolent
haïr: *vt.* to hate, detest
hâle: *nm.* tan, sunburn
hâlé: *adj.* tanned, sunburnt
haleine: *nf.* breath, breathing
haletant: *adj.* panting, gasping
haleter: *vi.* to pant, gasp for breath
hall: *nm.* hall, foyer
halle: *nf.* covered market; hall
hallucinationation: *nf.* hallucination

halo: *nm.* halo
halte: *nf.* stop, break; stopping place
haltère: *nf.* dumbbell
hamac: *nm.* hammock
hameçon: *nm.* fish-hook
hamster: *nm.* hamster
hanche: *nf.* hip
handball: *nm.* handball
handballeur: *nm.* handball player
handicap: *nm.* handicap
handicaper: *vt.* to handicap
handle: *nf.* hip; haunch
hangar: *nm.* shed, barn; hangar
hanneton: *nm.* maybug
hanter: *vt.* to haunt
happer: *vt.* to snap up, snatch
harassant: *adj.* exhausting, wearing
harcèlement: *nm.* harassment; pestering
harceler: *vt.* to harass; to pester; to plague
hardi: *adj.* bold, daring; brazen
hardiment: *adv.* boldly, daringly; brazenly
hareng: *nm.* herring
hargne: *nf.* spite
hargneux: *adj.* aggressive, belligerent
haricot: *nm.* bean
harmonica: *nm.* harmonica
harmonie: *nf.* harmony; wind section
harmonieusement: *adv.* harmoniously
harmonieux: *adj.* harmonious; well-matched
harmoniser: *vt.* to harmonise
harnacher: *nm.* to harness
harnais: *nm.* harness; equipment
harpe: *nf.* harp
harpiste: *nmf.* harpist
harpon: *nm.* harpoon
hasard: *nm.* chance; accident; hazard; risk
hasarrdeux: *adj.* hazardous, risky

hate: *nf.* haste; impatience
hâter: *vt.* to hasten; to quicken
hâtif: *adj.* precocious; early; hasty
hâtivement: *adv.* hastily
hausse: *nf.* rise, increase
hausser: *vt.* to raise; to heighten
haut: *adj.* high, tall; upper; superior
hautain: *adj.* haughty, lofty
hautbois: *nm.* oboe
haute voix (à): *adv.* aloud
hautement: *adv.* highly
hauteur: *nf.* height; elevation; haughtiness; bearing
haut-parleur: *nm.* loudspeaker
hebdomadaire adj.: *nm.* weekly
hébergement: *nm.* accommodation; lodging
héberger: *vt.* to accommodate, lodge
hectare: *nm.* hectare
hectogramme: *nm.* hectogram
hectolitre: *nm.* hectolitre
hectomètre: *nm.* hectometre
hélice: *nf.* propeller; helix
hélicoptère: *nm.* helicopter
hélium: *nm.* helium
helmholtz: helmhotz free energy
hématome: *nm.* severe bruise, haematoma
hémicycle: *nm.* semicircle, hemicycle; amphitheatre
hémiplégique: *nmf.* person paralysed on one side, hemiplegic; *adj.* hemiplegic
hémisphère: *nm.* hemisphere
hémoglobine: *nf.* haemoglobin
hémophile: *adj.* haemophiliac
hémophilie: *nf.* haemophilia
hémorragie: *nf.* bleeding, haemorrhage
hémorroïde: *nf.* haemorrhoid, pile
henné: *nm.* henna
hépatique: *adj.* hepatic
hépatite: *nf.* hepatitis
herbe: *nf.* grass; en - in = the blade

herbivore: *nm.* herbivore; *adj.* herbivorous
herboriste: *nmf.* herbalist
héréditaire: *adj.* hereditary
hérédité: *nf.* heredity; heritage; right of inheritance
hérésie: *nf.* heresy
hérétique: *adj.* heretical
hérissé: *adj.* bristling; spiked
hérisser: *vt.* to bristle; to spikee
hérisson: *nm.* hedgehog
héritage: *nm.* inheritance; heritage, legacy
hériter: *vi.* to inherit
héritier: *nm.* heir
héritière: *nf.* heiress
hermaphrodite: *nm.* hermaphrodite; *adj.* hermaphrodite
hermétique: *adj.* airtight, watertight, hermetic
hermétiquement: *adv.* hermetically
hermine: *nf.* ermine; stoat
hernie: *nf.* hernia, rupture
héroïne: *nf.* heroine; heroin
héroïsme: *nm.* heroism
hérolque: *adj.* heroic
héron: *nm.* heron
héros: *nm.* hero
herpès: *nm.* herpes; cold sore
hésitant: *adj.* hesitant
hésitation: *nf.* hesitation
hésiter: *vi.* to hesitate
hétéroclite: *adj.* heterogeneous; sundry; eccentric
hétérogène: *adj.* heterogeneous
hétérosexuel: *adj.* heterosexual
hêtre: *nm.* beech
heure: *nf.* hour; time of day
heure supplémentaire: *adv.* overtime
heureusement: *adv.* luckily; happily
heureux: *adv.* lucky; happy
heurter: *vt.* to strike, hit; to jostle
hexagone: *nm.* hexagon

hibernation: *nf.* hibernation
hibou: *nm.* owl
hideux: *adj.* hideous
hier: *adv.* yesterday
hiérarchie: *nf.* hierarchy
hiérarchique: *adj.* hierarchical
hiérarchiquement: *adv.*
hierarchically
hilarant: *adj.* hilarious, sidesplitting
hilarité: *nf.* hilarity, laughter
hindouisme: *nm.* Hinduism
hippisme: *nm.* riding, equestrianis
hippocampe: *nm.* sea horse
hippodrome: *nm.* racecourse
hippopotame: *nm.* hippopotamus
hirondelle: *nf.* swallow
hirsute: *adj.* dishevelled, tousled
hisser: *vt.* to hoist, haul up
histoire: *nf.* history; story
historien: *nm.* historian
historique: *adj.* historic; historical
historiquement: *adv.* historically
hiver: *nm.* winter
hivernai: *adj.* winter; wintry
hocher: *vt.* to nod; to shake one's
head
hochet: *nm.* rattle; toy
hockey sur glace: *nm.* ice hockey
holocauste: *nm.* holocaust
homard: *nm.* lobster
homéopathe: *nm.* homeopath
homéopathie: *nf.* homeopathy
homicide: *nm.* homicide
hommage: *nm.* homage, tribute;
rendre - à = to pay homage to
homme: *nm.* man
homme-grenouille: *nm.* frogman
homogène: *adj.* homogeneous
homogénéiser: *vt.* to homogenise
homogénéité: *nf.* homogeneity
homologue: *adj.* homologous;
equivalent
homologuer: *vt.* to ratify; to approve
homonyme: *nm.* homonym; *adj.*

homonymous
homosexualité: *nf.* homosexuality
homosexuel: *nm.* homosexual
honnête: *adj.* honest; decent;
honourable
honnêtement: *adv.* honestly,
decently
honnêteté: *nf.* honesty, decency
honneur: *nm.* honour; integrity;
credit
honorable: *adj.* honourable;
reputable
honorablement: *adv.* honourably
honoraire: *adj.* honorary
honoraires: *nmpl.* fees
honorer: *vt.* to honour; to esteem; to
do credit to
honte: *nf.* shame, disgrace
honteusement: *adv.* shamefully;
disgracefully
honteux: *adj.* shameful; disgraceful
hôpital: *nm.* hospital
hoquet: *nm.* hiccough, hiccup
horaire: *nm.* timetable; *adj.* hourly
horizon: *nm.* horizon
horizontal: *adj.* horizontal
horizontalement: *adv.* horizontally
horloge: *nf.* clock
horloger: *nm.* watchmaker,
clockmaker
hormone: *nf.* hormone
horoscope: *nm.* horoscope
horreur: *nf.* horror
horrible: *adj.* horrible; dreadful
horriblement: *adv.* horribly
horrifier: *vt.* to horrify
hors: *prép.* outside; beyond; save;
except
hors-bord: *nm.* invar speedboat
hors-d'oeuvre: *nm.* inuar hors
d'oeuvre, starter
hors-jeu: *nm.* inuar offside
hors-piste: *nm.* inuar off-piste
hortensia: *nm.* hydrangea

horticulteur: *nm.* horticulturist
horticulture: *nf.* horticulture
hospice: *nm.* home, asylum; hospice
hospitalier: *adj.* hospital; hospitable
hospitalisation: *nf.* hospitalisation
hospitaliser: *vt.* to hospitalise
hospitalité: *nf.* hospitality
hostie: *nf.* host
hostile: *adj.* hostile
hostilement: *adv.* hostilely
hostilité: *nf.* hostility
hôte: *nm.* host; landlord, hostess
hôtel: *nm.* hotel
hôtelier: *nm.* hotelier
hôtellerie: *nf.* hotel business
hôtesse se l'air: *nf.* flight attendant
hotte: *nf.* basket
houblon: *nm.* hop
houille: *nf.* coal
houle: *nf.* swell
houleux: *adj.* stormy; turbulent
houppe: *nf.* tuft; tassel
housse: *nf.* cover, dustsheet
houx: *nm.* holly
hublot: *nm.* porthole
huer: *vt.* to boo
huile: *nf.* oil; petroleum
huileux: *adj.* oily
huissier: *nm.* bailiff; usher
huit: *adj.* eight
huitaine: *nf.* eight or so
huitième: *adj.* eighth
huitièmement: *adv.* eighthly
huître: *nf.* oyster
humain: *adj.* human; humane
humanisme: *nm.* humanism
humaniste: *nm.* humanist; *adj.* humanist
humanitaire: *adj.* humanitarian
humanité: *nf.* humanity
humble: *adj.* humble; modest
humblement: *adv.* humbly
humecter: *vt.* to dampen, moisten
humeur: *nf.* mood, humour; temper

humide: *adj.* humid
humidité: *nf.* humidity
humiliant: *adj.* humiliating
humiliation: *nf.* humiliation
humilier: *vt.* to humiliate
humilité: *nf.* humility
humoristique: *adj.* humorous
humour: *nm.* humour
hurlement: *nm.* roar, yell; howl
hurler: *vt.* to roar, yell
hutte: *nf.* hut
hybride: *adj.* hybrid; *nm.* hybrid
hydratant: *adj.* moisturising
hydratation: *nf.* hydration; moisturising
hydrates: *vt.* to hydrate; to moisturise
hydraulique: *adj.* hydraulic
hydravion: *nm.* seaplane
hydrocarbure: *nm.* hydrocarbon
hydrogène: *nm.* hydrogen
hydrolyse: *nf.* hydrolysis
hydrophile: *adj.* absorbent
hydroxyde: *nm.* hydroxide
hyène: *nf.* hyena
hygiène: *nf.* hygienics; hygiene
hygiénique: *adj.* hygienic
hygiéniquement: *adv.* hygienically
hymne: *nm.* hymn
hyperbole: *nf.* hyperbole; hyperbola
hypermarché: *nm.* hypermarket
hypermétrope: *adj.* long-sighted
hypertension: *nf.* hypertension
hypertrophié: *adj.* (med) enlarged; overdeveloped
hypnose: *nf.* hypnosis
hypnotique: *adj.* hypnotic
hypnotiser: *vt.* to hypnotise
hypocondriaque: *nmf.* hypochondriac; *adj.* hypochondriac
hypocrisie: *nf.* hypocrisy
hypocrite: *nmf.* hypocrite
hypophyse: *nf.* pituitary gland, hypophysis
hypothalamus: *nm.* hypothalamus

hypothèque: *nf.* mortgage
hypothéquer: *vt.* to mortgage
hypothèse: *nf.* hypothesis; assumption
hypothétique: *adj.* hypothetical
hypothétiquement: *adv.* hypothetically
hystérie: *nf.* hysteria
hystérique: *nmf.* hysterical; *adj.* hysteric

I

ibis: *nm.* ibis
iceberg: *nm.* iceberg
ici: *adv.* here
idéaliste: *adj.* idealistic; *nmf.* idealist
idéal adj.: *nm.* ideal
idéaliser: *vt.* to idealize
idée: *nf.* idea
identifier: *vt.* to identify
identique: *adj.* identical
identiquement: *adv.* identically
identité: *nf.* identity; similarity
idéologie: *nf.* ideology
idiot: *nm.* idiot, fool; *adj.* idiotic, stupid
idole: *nf.* idol
igloo: *nm.* igloo
ignoble: *adj.* ignoble, mean, base
ignorance: *nf.* ignorance
ignorant: *adj.* ignorant; unacquainted; uninformed
ignorer: *vt.* to be ignorant of; to be unaware of; to ignore
iguane: *nm.* iguana
île: *nf.* island, isle
illégal: *adj.* illegal; unlawful
illégalement: *adv.* illegally
illégalité: *nf.* illegality
illégitime: *adj.* illegitimate; unwarranted
illettré: *adj.* illiterate
illicite: *adj.* illicit
illicitement: *adv.* illicitly
illimité: *adj.* unlimited; limitless
illisible: *adj.* illegible, unreadable
illogique: *adj.* illogical
illumination: *nf.* illumination, lighting
illuminer: *vt.* to light up, illuminate; to enlighten
illusion: *nf.* illusion
illusoire: *adj.* illusory; illusive
illustration: *nf.* illustration
illustre: *adj.* illustrious, renowned

illustrer: *vt.* to illustrate
ilot: *nm.* islet; block (flats)
image: *nf.* image, picture; reflection
imagé: *adj.* colourful; full of imagery
imaginaire: *adj.* imaginary
imagination: *nf.* imagination
imaginer: *vt.* to imagine; to suppose; to devise; to imagine; to think
imbattable: *adj.* unbeatable
imbécile: *nmf.* idiot, imbecile; *adj.* stupid, idiotic
imbiber: *vt.* to soak, moisten
imbriquer: *vt.* to fit into; to overlap
imbuvable: *adj.* undrinkable; unbearable
inﾉtation: *nf.* imitation; mimicry; forgery
immaculé: *adj.* spotless, immaculate
immangeable: *adj.* inedible
immatriculation: *nf.* registration
immatriculer: *vt.* to register
immédiat: *adj.* immediate; instant
immédiatement: *adv.* immediately, instantly
immense: *adj.* immense, boundless
immensément: *adv.* immensely; hugely
immensité: *nf.* immensity; immenseness
immergé: *adj.* submerged
immersion: *nf.* immersion; submersion
immeuble: *nm.* building; block of flats; real estate
immigrant: *nm.* immigrant
immigration: *nf.* immigration
immigré, e: *nmf.* immigrant
imminent: *adj.* imminent, impending
immobile: *adj.* motionless, still
immobilier: *adj.* property; *nm.* property business
immobilisations: fixed assets
immobiliser: *vt.* to immobilise; to bring to a standstill

immobilité: *nf.* stillness; immobility; permanence
immonde: *adj.* squalid; base, vile
immoral: *adj.* immoral
immoralité: *nf.* immorality
immortaliser: *vt.* to immortalise
immortel: *adj.* immortal
immuable: *adj.* unchanging, immutable
immuniser: *vt.* to immunise
immunité: *nf.* immunity
impact: *nm.* impact
impair: *adj.* odd, uneven
impalpable: *adj.* impalpable
impardonnable: *adj.* unforgivable, unpardonable
imparfait: *adj.* imperfect
impartial: *adj.* impartial
impartialité: *nf.* impartiality
impasse: *nf.* dead end, cul-de-sac; impasse
impassible: *adj.* impassive
impatiemment: *adv.* impatiently
impatience: *nf.* impatience
impatient: *adj.* impatient
impatienter: *vt.* to irritate, annoy
impeccablement: *adv.* perfectly, impeccably
impénétrable: *adj.* impenetrable; inscrutable
impensable: *adj.* unthinkable
impératif: *adj.* imperative; mandatory; *nm.* requirement; demand; constraint
impératrice: *nf.* empress
imperceptible: *adj.* imperceptible
imperceptiblement: *adv.* imperceptibly
imperfection: *nf.* imperfection
impérial: *adj.* imperial
impérialisme: *nm.* imperialism
imperméable: *adj.* impermeable, waterproof
impersonnel: *adj.* impersonal

impertinence: *nf.* impertinence
impertinent: *adj.* impertinent
imperturbable: *adj.* unshakeable
impétueux: *adj.* impetuous
impitoyable: *adj.* merciless, pitiless
implacable: *adj.* implacable
implantation: *nf.* implantation; establishment; introduction
implanter: *vt.* to introduce; to establish; to implant
implication: *nf.* implication; involvement
implicite: *adj.* implicit
implicitement: *adv.* implicitly
impliquer: *vt.* to imply; to necessitate; to implicate
impoli: *adj.* impolite, rude
impolitese: *nf.* impoliteness, rudeness
impopulaire: *adj.* unpopular
importance: *nf.* importance, significance; size
important: *adj.* important, significant; sizeable
importateur: *nm.* importer; *adj.* importing
importation: *nf.* import, importation
importer: *vt.* to import
importuner: *vt.* to importune, to bother
imposant: *adj.* imposing; stately
imposer: *vt.* to impose, lay down
impossibilité: *nf.* impossibility
impossible: *adj.* impossible
imposteur: *nm.* impostor
impôt: *nm.* tax, duty
impotent: *adj.* disabled, crippled
imprégner: *vt.* impregnate; to permeate; to imbue
impresario: *nm.* manager, impresario
impression: *nf.* feeling, impression
impressionisme: *nm.* impressionism
impressioniste: *nm.* impressionist
impressionnant: *adj.* impressive; upsetting

impressionner: *vt.* to impress; to upset
imprévisible: *adj.* unforeseeable; unpredictable
imprévoyant: *adj.* improvident
imprévu: *adj.* unforeseen, unexpected
imprimante: *nf.* printer
imprimé: *adj.* printed; *nm.* printed form; printed material
imprimer: *vt.* to print
imprimerie: *nf.* printing works; printing house
imprimeur: *nm.* printer
improbable: *adj.* improbable, unlikely
improductif: *adj.* unproductive
improvisation: *nf.* improvisation
improviser: *vt.* to improvise
improviste (à l'): unexpectedly
imprudence: *nf.* carelessness, imprudence
imprudent: *adj.* careless, imprudent
impudence: *nf.* impudence; shame-lessness
impudique: *adj.* immodest, shameless
impuissance: *nf.* powerlessness, helplessness
impuissant: *adj.* powerless, helpless
impulsif: *adj.* impulsive
impulsion: *nf.* impulse; impetus
impulsivement: *adv.* impulsively
impunément: *adv.* with impunity
impur: *adj.* impure; mixed
impureté: *nf.* impurity
imputer à un compte: to charge to an account
inacceptable: *adj.* unacceptable
inaccessible: *adj.* inaccessible
inaccoutumé: *adj.* unusual
inachevé: *adj.* unfinished, uncompleted
inactif: *adj.* inactive, idle

inactivité: *nf.* inactivity
inadapté: *adj.* unsuitable; aladjusted
inadéquat: *adj.* inadequate
inadmissible: *adj.* inadmissible
inaltérable: *adj.* stable; unchanging, permanent
inamovible: *adj.* irremovable; fixed
inanimé: *adj.* inanimate; unconscious
inaperçu: *adj.* unnoticed to go unnoticed
inappréciable: *adj.* invaluable, inestimable
inapte: *adj.* unfit
inattaquable: *adj.* unassailable; irrefutable
inattendu: *adj.* unexpected, unforeseen
inattention: *nf.* inattention, lack of attention
inauguration: *nf.* inauguration, opening
inaugurer: *vt.* to inaugurate, open
inavouable: *adj.* shameful; undisclosable
incapable: *adj.* unable
incapable: *adj.* incapable; incompetent
incapacité: *nf.* incompetence; disability
incarcérer: *vt.* to incarcerate
incarnation: *nf.* incarnation
incarner: *vt.* to incarnate, embody
incendiaire: *adj.* incendiary; inflammatory; *nmf.* arsonist
incendie: *nm.* fire, blaze
incendier: *vt.* to set alight; to kindle
incertain: *adj.* uncertain, unsure
incertitude: *nf.* uncertainty
incessant: *adj.* incessant, ceaseless
inceste: *nm.* incest
incident: *nm.* incident, point of law
incinération: *nf.* incineration; cremation
inciser: *vt.* to incise; (med) to lance

incisive: *nf.* incisive; piercing
incitation: *nf.* incitement; incentive
inciter: *vt.* to incite, urge
inclinaison: *nf.* incline; gradient
incliner: *vt.* to bend; to slope; to bow
inclure: *vt.* to include; to insert
inclus: *adj.* enclosed; included; ci-herein enclosed
incohérence: *nf.* incoherence; inconsistency
incohérent: *adj.* incoherent; inconsistent
incolore: *adj.* colourless; clear
incommode: *adj.* inconvenient; awkward
incommoder: *vt.* to disturb, bother
incomparable: *adj.* incomparable; -ment = *adv.* incomparably
incompatibilité: *nf.* incompatibility
incompatible: *adj.* incompatible
incompétence: *nf.* incompetence
incompétent: *adj.* incompetent; inexpert
incomplet: *adj.* incomplete
incompréhensible: *adj.* obscure; incomprehensible
incompréhensible: *adj.* incomprehensible
incompréhension: *nf.* lack of understanding
inconcevable: *adj.* inconceivable
inconciliable: *adj.* irreconcilable
inconditionnel: *adj.* unconditional; unreserved; unquestioning
inconfortable: *adj.* uncomfortable; awkward
incongru: *adj.* unseemly; incongruous
inconnu: *nm.* stranger, unknown person; *nm.* unknown; *adj.* unknown
inconsciemment: *adv.* unconsciously; thoughtlessly
inconscience: *nf.* unconsciousness; thoughtlessness

inconscient: *adj.* unconscious; thoughtless, reckless; *nm.* subconscious, unconscious
inconsidéré: *adj.* inconsiderate; thoughtless; -ment = *adv.* inconsiderately
inconsistant: *adj.* flimsy; colourless; watery
inconsolable: *adj.* disconsolate; inconsolable
inconstant: *adj.* fickle; variable, inconstant
incontestable: *adj.* incontestable, unquestionable
incontestablement: *adv.* incontestably, unquestionably
inconvénient: *nm.* drawback, inconvenience
incorporation: *nf.* incorporation
incorporer: *vt.* to incorporate, integrate
incorrect: *adj.* faulty, incorrect
incorrectement: *adv.* incorrectly
incorrigible: *adj.* incorrigible
incorruptible: *adj.* incorruptible
incrédule: *adj.* incredulous; *nmf.* unbeliever, non-believer
incrédulité: *nf.* incredulity, lack of belief
incroyable: *adj.* incredible; unbelievable; -ment = *adv.* incredibly, unbelievably
incruster: *vt.* to inlay; to superimpose
inculpation: *nf.* inculcation, instilling
inculpé, e: *nmf.* accused; *adj.* accused
inculper: *v.* to charge (law)
incurable: *adj.* incurable
indécent: *adj.* indecent, improper
indéchiffrable: *adj.* indecipherable; incomprehensible
indécis: *adj.* indecisive; unsettled; undefined
indéffinissable: *adj.* indefinable
indéfini: *adj.* undefined; indefinite; -ment = *adv.* indefinitely
indéfinissable: *adj.* indefinable
indemne: *adj.* unharmed, unhurt
indemniser: *vt.* to indemnify; to compensate
indemnité: *nf.* compensation; indemnity
indéniable: *adj.* undeniable, indisputable; -ment = *adv.* undeniably
indépendance: *nf.* independence
indépendant: *adj.* independent
indestructible: *adj.* indestructible
indéterminé: *adj.* undetermined; unspecified; undecided
index: *nm.* index; index finger
indexer: *vt.* to index
indicatif: *nm.* signature tune; dialling code; *adj.* indicative
indication: *nf.* indication; piece of information; instruction
indice: *nm.* indication; clue; sign
indice d'octane: octane number
indifferemment: *adv.* indifferently; poorly
indifféremment: *adv.* indiscriminately, equally
indifférence: *nf.* indifference
indifférent: *adj.* indifferent; immaterial
indigène: *nmf.* native; local; *adj.* indigenous, native
indigeste: *adj.* indigestible
indigestion: *nf.* indigestion
indigne: *adj.* unworthy; undeserving
indigner: *vt.* to annoy, make indignant
indiquer: *vt.* to indicate, point out; to tell
indirect: *adj.* indirect; circumstantial; collateral; -ement = *adv.* indirectly
indiscipliné: *adj.* undisciplined
indiscret: *adj.* indiscreet; inquisitive
indiscrétion: *nf.* indiscretion;

inquisitiveness
indiscutable: *adj.* indisputable;
unquestionable;
-ment = *adv.* indisputably
indispensable: *adj.* indispensable;
essential
indisponible: *adj.* unavailable
indistinct: *adj.* indistinct, vague; -
ement = *adv.* indistinctly individu:
nm. individual
individuel: *adj.* individual
indolore: *adj.* painless
indubitable: *adj.* indubitable; certain
indulgence: *nf.* indulgence
indulgent: *adj.* indulgent
industrialisation: *nf.* industrialisation
industrie: *nf.* industry; dexterity,
ingenuity
industriel: *nm.* industrialist,
manufacturer; *adj.* industrial
inébranlable: *adj.* steadfast,
unwavering
inédit: *adj.* unpublished; original
inefficace: *adj.* ineffective; inefficient
inefficacité: *nf.* ineffectiveness;
inefficiency
inégal: *adj.* unequal; uneven;
irregular
inégalité: *nf.* inequality; difference,
disparity
inéluctable: *adj.* ineluctable,
unavoidable; -ment = *adv.*
ineluctably
inépuisable: *adj.* inexhaustible
inerte: *adj.* inert; lifeless
inertie: *nf.* inertia, apathy
inespéré: *adj.* unexpected
inestimable: *adj.* inestimable,
invaluable
inévitable: *adj.* inevitable,
unavoidable
inexact: *adj.* inexact, inaccurate
inexactitude: *nf.* inaccuracy
inexistant: *adj.* nonexistent

inexorable: *adj.* inexorable;
-ment = *adv.* inexorably
inexpérimenté: *adj.* inexperienced;
inexpert
inexplicable: *adj.* inexplicable;
-ment = *adv.* inexplicably
inexprimable: *adj.* inexpressible
infaillible: *adj.* infallible
infâme: *adj.* infamous; base, vile
infantile: *adj.* infantile, childish
infatigable: *adj.* indefatigable,
tireless; -ment = *adv.* indefatigably
infect: *adj.* vile; revolting; filthy
infecter: *vt.* to infect; to contaminate
infection: *nf.* infection
inférieur: *adj.* inferior; lower
infériorité: *nf.* inferiority
infernal: *adj.* infernal, diabolical
infester: *vt.* to infest, overrun
infidèle: *adj.* unfaithful, disloyal
infidélité: *nf.* infidelity
infiltration: *nf.* infiltration
infini: *adj.* infinite; interminable; -
ment = *adv.* infinitely
infinitif: *nm.* infinitive
infirme: *adj.* feeble; crippled,
disabled
infirmerie: *nf.* infirmary; sick bay
infirmier, ière: *nmf.* nurse
infirmité: *nf.* disability; infirmity
inflammation: *nf.* inflammation
inflation: *nf.* inflation
inflexible: *adj.* inflexible, rigid
infliger: *vt.* to inflict; to impose
influence: *nf.* influence
influencer: *vt.* to influence, sway
informaticien: *nm.* computer
scientist
information: *nf.* piece of
information; information; inquiry
informatique: *nf.* computing; data
processing; *adj.* computer
**informatiser, mettre sur
ordinateur**: to computerize

informer: *vt.* to inform, tell;
s'- *vr.* = to find out, inquire
infraction: *nf.* infraction,
infringement; offence
infranchissable: *adj.* impassable;
insuperable
infrarouge: *adj.* infrared
infrastructure: *nf.* infrastructure;
substructure
infructueux: *adj.* fruitless,
unsuccessful
infusion: *nf.* infusion, herb tea
ingénieur: *nm.* engineer
ingénieux: *adj.* ingenious, clever
ingénu: *adj.* ingenuous, naive
ingrat: *adj.* ungrateful; unprofitable
ingratitude: *nf.* ingratitude
ingrédient: *nm.* ingredient;
component
inhabité: *adj.* uninhabited,
unoccupied
inhabituel: *adj.* unusual,
unaccustomed
inhibiteur: *nm.* inhibitor
inhumain: *adj.* inhuman
inimaginable: *adj.* unimaginable
inimitable: *adj.* inimitable
ininterrompu: *adj.* uninterrupted;
unbroken
initial: *adj.* initial; -ement = *adv.*
initially
initiation: *nf.* initiation
initiative: *nf.* initiative; enterprise
initier: *vt.* to initiate
injecter: *vt.* to inject
injection: *nf.* injection
injure: *nf.* injury; insult
injurier: *vt.* to abuse; insult
injuste: *adj.* unjust, unfair;
-ment = *adv.* unjustly
injustice: *nf.* injustice
injustifié: *adj.* unjustified
inné: *adj.* innate, inborn
innocence: *nf.* innocence

innocent: *nm.* innocent person;
simpleton; *adj.* innocent
innocenter: *vt.* to clear, prove
innocent
innovation: *nf.* innovation
innover: *vi.* to innovate, make
innovations
inodore: *adj.* odourless, scentless
inoffensif: *adj.* inoffensive, harmless
inondation: *nf.* flood
inonder: *vt.* to flood, inundate
inopportun: *adj.* ill-timed,
inopportune
inoubliable: *adj.* unforgettable
inouï: *adj.* unprecedented, unheard of
inox: *nm.* stainless steel
inqualifiable: *adj.* unspeakable
inquiet: *adj.* worried, anxious,
uneasy
inquiéter: *vt.* to worry, disturb
inquiétude: *nf.* restlessness,
uneasiness
insaisissable: *adj.* elusive;
imperceptible
insalubre: *adj.* insalubrious;
unhealthy
insatiable: *adj.* insatiable
insatisfaction: *nf.* dissatisfaction
inscription: *nf.* inscription;
registration; matriculation
inscrire: *vt.* to inscribe; to enter; to
set down; to register
inscrit, être: to be registered
insecte: *nm.* insect
insecticide: *nm.* insecticide
insectifuge: *nm.* repellent
insémination: *nf.* insemination
insensé: *adj.* insane, demented
insensible: *adj.* insensible, unfeeling,
insensitive; imperceptible
inséparable: *adj.* inseparable
insérer: *vt.* to insert
insertion: *nf.* insertion, inserting
insidieux: *adj.* insidious

insignifiant: *adj.* insignificant, trifling
insinuation: *nf.* insinuation
insinuer: *vt.* to insinuate, imply
insipide: *adj.* insipid, tasteless
insister: *vi.* to insist, be insistent; to stress
insolation: *nf.* sunstroke
insolence: *nf.* insolence
insolent: *adj.* insolent; brazen
insolite: *adj.* unusual; strange
insolvabilité: *nf.* insolvency
insomnie: *nf.* insomnia
insouciance: *nf.* unconcern, carelessness
insouciant: *adj.* carefree; careless
insoutenable: *adj.* unbearable; untenable
inspecter: *vt.* to inspect, examine
inspecteur: *nm.* inspector
inspection: *nf.* inspection
inspiration: *nf.* inspiration; suggestion
inspirer: *vt.* to inspire; to breathe in
instable: *adj.* unstable; unsettled
installation: *nf.* installation; installing
installer: *vt.* to install; to fit out
instant: *nm.* moment
instantatané: *adj.* instantaneous
instaurer: *vt.* to institute
instinct: *nm.* instinct
instinctif: *adj.* instinctive
instinctivement: *adv.* instinctively
institut: *nm.* institute; school
instituteur: *nm.* teacher
institution: *nf.* institution; establishment
instructif: *adj.* instructive
instruction: *nf.* instruction; education; inquiry
instruire: *vt.* to instruct; to teach; to conduct an inquiry
instrument: *nm.* instrument, implement

insuffisance: *nf.* insufficiency, inadequacy
insuffisant: *adj.* insufficient, inadequate
insuline: *nf.* insulin
insulte: *nf.* insult
insulter: *vt.* to insult, affront
insupportable: *adj.* unbearable
insurrection: *nf.* insurrection, revolt
intact: *adj.* intact
intégral: *adj.* integral; uncut; complete; -ement = *adv.* integrally; in full
intégralité: *nf.* whole; entirety
intégrer: *vt.* to integrate
intégrité: *nf.* integrity
intellectuel: *nm.* intellectual; *adj.* intellectual, mental
intelligence: *nf.* intelligence; understanding
intelligent: *adj.* intelligent, shrewd, bright
intelligible: *adj.* intelligible
intempéries: *nfpl.* bad weather
intendant: *nm.* bursar; steward, stewardess
intense: *adj.* intense; severe
intensément: *adv.* intensely
intensif: *adj.* intensive
intensifier: *vt.* to intensify
intensité: *nf.* intensity; severity
intention: *nf.* intention; purpose, intent
interaction: *nf.* interaction
intercaler: *vt.* to intercalate; to interpolate
intercepter: *vt.* to intercept
intercepteur ionique: ionic scavenger
intercepteur radicalaire: radical scavenger
interchangeable: *adj.* interchangeable
interdiction: *nf.* interdiction,

prohibition, ban
interdire: *vt.* to ban
interdire: *vt.* to forbid, ban, prohibit
interdit: *adj.* forbidden, prohibited; dumbfounded
intéressant: *adj.* interesting; attractive, worthwhile
intéresser: *vt.* to interest; to concern
intérêt: *nm.* interest; significance, importance
interférence: *nf.* interference; conjunction
intérieur: *adj.* interior, internal
intérimaire: *adj.* interim; acting; temporary
interligne: *nm.* line space; interlining; lead
interlocuteur: *nm.* interlocutor, speaker
intermède: *nm.* interlude
intermédiaire: *adj.* intermediate; intermediary
interminable: *adj.* interminable; endless
intermittent: *adj.* intermittent, sporadic
international: *adj.* international
interne: *adj.* internal
Internet: *nm.* Internet
interpeller: *vt.* to call out to
interphone: *nm.* intercom, entryphone
interposer: *vt.* to interpose
interprétation: *nf.* interpretation, rendering
interprète: *nmf.* interpreter
interpréter: *vt.* to interpret; to perform
interrogation: *nf.* interrogation, questioning; question
interrogatoire: *nm.* questioning; cross-examination
interroger: *vt.* to question; to interrogate

interrompre: *vt.* to interrupt, break
interrupteur: *nm.* switch
interruption: *nf.* interruption, break
intervalle: *nm.* interval; space, distance
intervenir: *vi.* to intervene; to take part in
intervention: *nf.* intervention; operation
intestin: *nm.* intestine
intestinal: *adj.* intestinal
intime: *adj.* intimate; private
intimement: *adv.* intimately
intimider: *vt.* to intimidate
intimité: *nf.* intimacy; privacy
intituler: *vt.* to call, entitle
intolérable: *adj.* intolerable
intolerablement: *adv.* unbearably, intolerably
intolérance: *nf.* intolerance
intolérant: *adj.* intolerant
intonation: *nf.* intonation
intoxication: *nf.* poisoning; indoctrination
intransigeant: *adj.* intransigent, uncompromising
intransitif: *adj.* intransitive
intrépide: *adj.* intrepid, fearless
intrigant: *adj.* scheming
introduction: *nf.* introduction
introduire: *vt.* to introduce, insert; to present
introuvable: *adj.* undiscoverable
introverti: *nm.* introvert; *adj.* introverted
intrus: *nm.* intruder; *adj.* intruding, intrusive
intuitif: *adj.* intuitive
intuition: *nf.* intuition
inutile: *adj.* useless; unavailing; pointless
inutilisable: *adj.* unusable
invalide: *adj.* disabled; invalid
invariable: *adj.* invariable;

unvarying; -ment = *adv.* invariably
invasion: *nf.* invasion
inventaire: *nm.* inventory; stocklist
inventaire, faire le: to take stock
inventer: *vt.* to invent; to devise; to make up
inventeur: *nm.* inventor
invention: *nf.* invention; inventiveness
inverse: *adj.* opposite; *nm.* opposite, reverse
inverser: *vt.* to reverse, invert
inversion: *nf.* inversion; reversal
investir: *vt.* to invest; to surround
investissement: *nm.* investment; investing
invincible: *adj.* invincible, indomitable
invisible: *adj.* invisible; unseen
invitation: *nf.* invitation
invité: *nm.* guest
inviter: *vt.* to imitate
inviter: *vt.* to invite
involontaire: *adj.* involuntary; unintentional
invoquer: *vt.* to invoke; to call up; to plead
invraisemblable: *adj.* unlikely, improbable
invulnérable: *adj.* invulnerable
iode: *nm.* iodine
ion: *nm.* ion
ionisation: ionization
iris: *nm.* iris
irlandais: *adj.* Irish
Irlandais: *nm.* Irishman
Irlande: *nf.* Ireland
ironie: *nf.* irony
ironique: *adj.* ironic
ironiquement: *adv.* ironically
irradiation: *nf.* irradiation; radiation
irrationnel: *adj.* irrational
irrécupérable: *adj.* irretrievable
irréel: *adj.* unreal

irréfléchi: *adj.* unconsidered; hasty
irrégularité: *nf.* irregularity; variation; unevenness
irrégulier: *adj.* irregular; varying; uneven
irrégulièrement: *adv.* irregularly; unevenly
irrémédiable: *adj.* irreparable; incurable
irremplaçable: *adj.* irreplaceable
irréparable: *adj.* irreparable; irretrievable
irresponsable: *adj.* irresponsible
irrigation: *nf.* irrigation
irriguer: *vt.* to irrigate
irriter: *vt.* to irritate; to provoke
irruption: *nf.* irruption
Islam: *nm.* Islam
isolation: *nf.* insulation
isolement: *nm.* loneliness
isoler: *vt.* to isolate; to insulate
issu: *adj.* descended from; stemming from
issue: *nf.* outlet; solution; outcome
Italie: *nf.* Italy
itinéraire: *nm.* route
ivoire: *nm.* ivory
ivre: *adj.* drunk, inebriated
ivresse: *nf.* drunkenness
ivrogne: *nmf.* dru card

J

jachère: *nf.* fallow; leaving land lying fallow
jade: *nm.* jade
jadis: *adv.* formerly, long ago
jaillir: *vi.* to spout, gush; to spring
jallonner: *vt.* to mark out
jalon: *nm.* staff; landmark, milestone
jalousie: *nf.* jealousy, envy
jaloux: *adj.* jealous, envious
jamais: *adv.* never, not ever
jambe: *nf.* leg
jambon: *nm.* ham
janvier: *nm.* January
jardin: *nm.* garden
jardin d'enfants: *nm.* kindergaten
jardinage: *nm.* gardening
jardiner: *vi.* to garden
jardinier: *nm.* gardener
jargon: *nm.* jargon, slang; gibberish
jarguar: *nm.* jaguar
jarret: *nm.* hock; hollow of the knee
jaser: *vi.* to chatter; to twitter; to babble
jasmin: *nm.* jasmine
jaugé: *nf.* gauge; capacity; tonnage
jauger: *vt.* to gauge the capacity of, to size up
jaunâtre: *adj.* yellowish
jaune: *adj.* yellow; *nm.* yellow
jaunir: *vi.* to yellow, turn yellow; *vt.* to make yellow
jaunisse: *nf.* jaundice
jazz: *nm.* jazz
jésuite: *nm.* Jesuit
jet: *nm.* jet, spurt; throwing
jetable: *adj.* disposable
jetée: *nf.* pier
jeter: *vt.* to throw; to discard; to give out
jeton: *nm.* token; counter
jeu: *nm.* play; game; gambling
jeu de carte: *nm.* deck of cards
jeudi: *nm.* Thursday

jeune: *adj.* young; junior; new; youthful; *nm.* youth, young man; *nf.* young girl
jeûne: *nm.* fast
jeûner: *vi.* to fast
jeunesse: *nf.* youth, youthfulness
joaillerie: *nf.* jewellery
joaillier: *nm.* jeweller
joie: *nf.* joy, happiness; pleasure
joindre: *vt.* to join, link; to attach
joint: *nm.* joint; join
jointure: *nf.* joint
joncher: *vt.* to strew with
jonction: *nf.* junction
jongler: *vi.* to juggle
jongleur: *nm.* juggler
jonquille: *nf.* daffodil, jonquil
joue: *nf.* cheek
jouer: *vi.* to play; to gamble; to act
jouet: *nm.* toy
joueur: *nm.* player; gambler
joufflu: *adj.* chubby; round-faced
joug: *nm.* yoke
joui: *adj.* pretty; good, handsome
jouir: *vi.* to enjoy; to delight in
jouissance: *nf.* enjoyment; use
jour: *nm.* day; daylight
jour de semaine: *nm.* weekday
jour férié: *nm.* holiday
journal: *nm.* newspaper; bulletin, journal
journal intime: *nm.* diary
journalisme: *nm.* journalism
journalist: *nmf.* journalist
journée: *nf.* day
jovial: *adj.* jovial, jolly
jovialité: *nf.* joviality
joyau: *nm.* jewel, gem
joyeusement: *adv.* joyfully, cheerfully
joyeux: *adj.* joyful, cheerful
jubiler: *vi.* to be jubilant, exult
judaïsme: *nm.* Judaism
judiciaire: *adj.* judicial, legal

judicieusement: *adv.* judiciously
judicieux: *adj.* judicious
judo: *nm.* judo
judoka: *nmf.* judoka
juge: *nm.* judge
jugement: *nm.* judgment; sentence; opinion
juger: *vt.* to judge; to decide; to consider
juif: *nm.* Jew; Jewish
juillet: *nm.* July
juin: *nm.* June
jumeau: *nm.* twin; *adj.* twin; double
jumelage: *nm.* twinning
jumelé: *adj.* twinned, twin
jumelle(s): nfp. binoculars
jument: *nf.* mare
jungle: *nf.* jungle
jupe: *nf.* skirt
jurer: *vt.* to swear, pledge
juridiction: *nf.* jurisdiction; court of law
juridique: *adj.* legal, juridical; -ment = *adv.* juridically, legally
jurisprudence: *nf.* case law, jurisprudence
juriste: *nm.* lawyer; jurist
juron: *nm.* oath, curse
jury: *nm.* jury; board of examiners
jus: *nm.* juice
justaucorps: *nm.* jerkin; leotard
juste: *adj.* just, fair; exact; sound; -ment = *adv.* exactly, precisely.
justesse: *nf.* accuracy; aptness; soundness
justice: *nf.* justice, fairness
justicier: *nm.* justiciary; dispenser of justice
justificatif: *adj.* supporting, justificatory
justification: *nf.* justification; proof
justifier: *vt.* to justify, prove
jute: *nm.* jute
juteux: *adj.* juicy; lucrative

juvénile: *adj.* young, youthful
juxtaposer: *vt.* to juxtapose
juxtaposition: *nf.* juxtaposition

K

kaki: *adj.* khaki
kaléidoscope: *nm.* kaleidoscope
kangourou: *nm.* kangaroo
karaté: *nm.* karate
kascher: *adj.* kosher
kayac, kayak: *nm.* kayak
képi: *nm.* kepi
kermesse: *nf.* fair; bazaar
kérosène: *nm.* kerosene, aviation fuel
kidnapper: *vt.* to kidnap, abduct
kidnappeur: *nm.* kidnapper
kilo: *nm.* kilo
kilogramme: *nm.* kilogram
kilohertz: *nm.* kilohertz
kilomètrage: *nm.* total kilometres travelled (mileage)
kilomètre: *nm.* kilometre
kimono: *nm.* kimono
kinésithérapeute: *nmf.* physiotherapist
kiosque: *nm.* kiosk, stall
kiosque à journaux: *nm.* newstand
kiwi: *nm.* kiwi, Chinese gooseberry
klaxon: *nm.* horn
klaxonner: *vi.* to sound one's horn
kleptomane: *nmf.* kleptomaniac
kleptomanie: *nf.* kleptomania
koala: *nm.* koala
kyste: *nm.* cyst

L

là: *adv.* there
label: *nm.* label; seal
labeur: *nm.* labour, toil
laboratoire: *nm.* laboratory
laborieux: *adj.* laborious, toilsome
labourer: *vt.* to plough; to dig over; to rip open
labyrinthe: *nm.* labyrinth
lac: *nm.* lake
lacer: *vt.* to lace up; to tie up
lacérer: *vt.* to lacerate; to tear
lacet: *nm.* lace
lâche: *adj.* slack; loose; lax; cowardly
lâcher: *vt.* to loosen; to release
lâcheté: *nf.* cowardice; meanness
laconique: *adj.* laconic
lacté: *adj.* milky, lacteal
lactique: *adj.* lactic
lacune: *nf.* lacuna; gap
lagon: *nm.* lagoon
lagune: *nf.* lagoon
laïc: *nm.* layman, laïque
laid: *adj.* ugly, unsightly
laideur: *nf.* ugliness, unsightliness
lainage: *nm.* woollen article
laine: *nf.* wool
laisse: *nf.* leash, string, lead
laisser: *vt.* to leave; to let
lait: *nm.* milk
laitage: *nm.* milk; milk products
laiterie: *nf.* dairy
laiton: *nm.* brass
laitue: *nf.* lettuce
lama: *nm.* llama; lama
lambeau: *nm.* shred; tatter
lambris: *nm.* plastering; panelling
lame: *nf.* blade; strip; metal plate
lamelle: *nf.* slide; small strip
lamentable: *adj.* lamentable, distressing; mentadv lamentably
lamentation: *nf.* lamentation; wailing
laminer: *vt.* to laminate
lampadaire: *nm.* standard-lamp;

street lamp
lampe: *nf.* lamp, light; bulb
lampe de poche: *nf.* flashlight
lance: *nf.* lance, spear
lance-flammes: *nm.* invar flamethrower
lancement: *nm.* launching; starting up; throwing
lance-pierres: *nm.* invar catapult
lancer: *vt.* to throw; to launch
lancinant: *adj.* nagging; haunting
lande: *nf.* moor
langage: *nm.* language, speech
langage des signes: *nm.* sign language
langoureux: *adj.* languid, languorous
langouste: *nf.* spiny lobster
langue: *nf.* tongue; language
languette: *nf.* tongue; tongue-like strip
langueur: *nf.* languor
languir: *vi.* to languish; to linger
lanière: *nf.* thong; lash
lanoline: *nf.* lanolin
lanterne: *nf.* lantern; lamp
lapin: *nm.* rabbit
lapsus: *nm.* slip, mistake
laque: *nf.* hairspray; lacquer; *nm.* lacquer wax
lard: *nm.* fat; bacon
lardon: *nm.* bacon cube
large: *adj.* wide; generous
largeur: *nf.* width, breadth
larguer: *vt.* to loose, release; cast off
larme: *nf.* tear
larmoyant: *adj.* tearful, weeping
larve: *nf.* larva, grub
laryngite: *nf.* laryngitis
larynx: *nm.* larynx
las: *adj.* weary, tired
lasagne: *nf.* lasagne
laser: *nm.* laser
lasser: *vt.* to tire
lassitude: *nf.* tiredness, weariness

latent: *adj.* latent
latéral: *adj.* lateral, side
latest: *nm.* latex
latin: *adj.* Latin; *nm.* Latin
latitude: *nf.* latitude; margin
latte: *nf.* lath
lauréat: *nm.* prize winner
laurier: *nm.* bay-tree, laurel
lavabo: *nm.* washbasin
lavage: *nm.* washing; bathing
lavande: *nf.* lavender
lave: *nf.* lava
lavement: *nm.* enema
laver: *vt.* to wash; to cleanse
laverie: *nf.* laundry
lave-vaisselle: invar. dishwasher
laxatif: *adj.* laxative
laxisme: *nm.* laxness
layette: *nf.* baby clothes
lécher: *vt.* to lick
leçon: *nf.* lesson; reading; class
lecteur: *nm.* reader
lecteur de CD: CD player
lecture: *nf.* reading; perusal
légal: *adj.* legal, lawful; -ement = *adv.* legally
légaliser: *vt.* to legalise
legalité: *nf.* legality, lawfulness
légendaire: *adj.* legendary
légende: *nf.* legend; inscription
léger: *adj.* light; slight; faint; inconsiderate
légèrement: *adv.* lightly; thought-lessly
légèreté: *nf.* lightness; nimbleness; thoughtlessness
légion: *nf.* legion
législatif: *adj.* legislative; *nm.* legislature
législation: *nf.* legislation, laws
légitime: *adj.* legitimate, lawful; -ment = *adv.* legitimately
légitimité: *nf.* legitimacy
legs: *nm.* legacy, bequest

léguer: *vt.* to bequeath; (jar) to devise
legume: *nm.* végétable
lendemain: *nm.* next day, day after
lent: *adj.* slow; tardy; sluggish
lente: *nf.* nit
lenteur: *nf.* slowness
lentille: *nf.* lentil; lens
léopard: *nm.* leopard
lépre: *nf.* leprosy
lépreux: *adj.* leprous
les deux: *adj.* both
lesbienne: *nf.* lesbian
léser: *vt.* to wrong; to damage
lésion: *nf.* wrong; lesion, wound
lessive: *nf.* washing powder
leste: *adj.* nimble, agile
lester: *vt.* to fill; to ballast
léthargic: *adj.* lethargic
léthargie: *nf.* lethargy
lettre: *nf.* letter, note; literature
lettre de change: bill of exchange (B/E)
lettre de crédit: letter of credit (L/C)
lettre de recouvrement: collection letter
lettre de transport aérien: (LTA) air waybill
leucémie: *nf.* leukaemia
leucocyte: *nm.* leucocyte
leur: pron. them
leurrer: *vt.* to deceive
levain: *nm.* leaven
lever: *vt.* to lift, raise; to levy
lever de soleil: sunrise
levier: *nm.* lever
lévre: *nf.* lip
lévrier: *nm.* greyhound
levure: *nf.* yeast
lexique: *nm.* vocabulary, lexis
lézard: *nm.* lizard
lézarde: *nf.* crack
liaison: *nf.* affair; connection; liaison, link
liasse: *nf.* bundle

libellule: *nf.* dragonfly
libéral: *adj.* liberal
libéraliser: *vt.* to liberalise
libéralisme: *nm.* liberalism
libéralité: *nf.* liberality, generosity
libération: *nf.* release, liberation
libérer: *vt.* to release; to liberate
liberté: *nf.* liberty, freedom
libido: *nf.* libido
libraire: *nmf.* bookseller
librairie: *nf.* bookshop; bookselling
libre: *adj.* free; independent
libre parcours moyen: mean free path
licence: *nf.* degree
licenciement: *nm.* redundancy; dismissal
licencier: *vt.* to make redundant; to dismiss
lichen: *nm.* lichen
licorne: *nf.* unicorn
lie: *nf.* dregs, sediment
liège: *nm.* cork
lien: *nm.* bond; link, connection; tie
lier: *vt.* to bind; to link
lierre: *nm.* ivy
lieu: *nm.* place, position; cause; occasion
lieu d'émission: place of issue
lieutenant: *nm.* lieutenant
lièvre: *nm.* hare
ligament: *nm.* ligament
ligature: *nf.* ligature; tying up
ligne: *nf.* line; row; range
lignée: *nf.* lineage
lignite: *nm.* lignite
ligoter: *vt.* to bind hand and foot
ligue: *nf.* league
lilas: *nm.* lilac; *adj.* lilac
limace: *nf.* slug
limande: *nf.* dab
lime: *nf.* file
limer: *vt.* to file down
limitation: *nf.* limitation, restriction

limite: *nf.* boundary, limit
limiter: *vt.* to limit, restrict
limitrophe: *adj.* border
limon: *nm.* silt
limonade: *nf.* lemon
limpide: *adj.* limpid, clear
limpidité: *nf.* limpidity, clearness
lin: *nm.* flax; linen
linceul: *nm.* shroud
linde, machine de: linde process
linéaire: *adj.* linear
linge: *nm.* linen; washing
lingerie: *nf.* linen room; underwear, lingerie
lingot: *nm.* ingot
linguiste: *nmf.* linguist
linguistique: *nf.* linguistics; *adj.* linguistic
lion: *nm.* lion
lionceau: *nm.* lion cub
lipide: *nm.* lipid
liquéfier: *vt.* to liquefy
liqueur: *nf.* liqueur; liquid
liquidation: *nf.* liquidation; winding up; elimination
liquide: *nm.* liquid
liquider: *vt.* to settle; to wind up; to eliminate
lire: *vt.* to read
lisible: *adj.* legible; readable; -ment = *adv.* legibly
lisière: *nf.* edge; border; outskirts
lisse: *adj.* smooth, glossy
lisser: *vt.* to smooth, gloss
liste: *nf.* list; schedule
liste de colisage: packing list
liste de tarifs: pricelist
lit: *adv.* there; over there; then
lit: *nm.* bed; layer
litanie: *nf.* litany
literie: *nf.* bedding
lithographie: *nf.* lithography
litière: *nf.* litter
litige: *nm.* lawsuit; dispute

litige legal: dispute; litigation, lawsuit
litigieux: *adj.* litigious
litre: *nm.* litre
littéraire: *adj.* literary
littéral: *adj.* literal; -ement = *adv.* literally
littérature: *nf.* literature; writing
littoral: *nm.* coast; *adj.* coastal, littoral
liturgie: *nf.* liturgy
livide: *adj.* livid, pale
livraison: *nf.* delivery; number, issue
livraison retardée: overdue delivery
livre: *nm.* book; *nf.* pound (weight, currency)
livre de caisse: cash book
livre de comptes: a ledger
livre des effets à payer: accounts payable book
livre des effets à recevoir: accounts receivable book
livre des salaires, les salaires: the payroll
livré droits acquittés: delivered duty paid (DDP)
livré droits non acquittés: delivered duty unpaid (DDU)
livrer: *vt.* to deliver, hand over; to give away
livret: *nm.* libretto; booldet
livret d'épargne: passbook
livreur: *nm.* delivery man
lobe: *nm.* lobe
lobotomie: *nf.* lobotomy
local: *adj.* local; -ement = *adv.* locally
localisation: *nf.* localisation
localiser: *vt.* to localise
localité: *nf.* locality; town
locataire: *nmf.* tenant; lodger
location: *nf.* renting; lease, leasing
location: *nf.* rental
locaux: *nmpl.* premises

locomotion: *nf.* locomotion
locomotive: *nf.* locomotive, engine; dynamo
locution: *nf.* locution, idiom
logarithme: *nm.* logarithm
loge: *nf.* lodge; dressing room; box
logement: *nm.* housing; accommodation
loger: *vt.* to accommodate; to billet; *vi.* to live in
logiciel: *nm.* software
logique: *nf.* logic; *adj.* logical; -ment = *adv.* logically
logistique: *nf.* logistics
logo: *nm.* logo
loi: *nf.* law; act, statute; rule
loin: *adv.* far, a long way
lointain: *adj.* distant, remote; *nm.* distance; background
loir: *nm.* dormouse
loisir: *nm.* leisure, spare time
lombaire: *adj.* lumbar
lombric: *nm.* earthworm
long: *adj.* long, lengthy
longer: *vt.* to border; to walk along
longévité: *nf.* longevity
longitude: *nf.* longitude
longtemps: *adv.* for a long time
longueur: *nf.* length
longue-vue: *nf.* telescope
loquace: *adj.* loquacious, talkative
loque: *nf.* rag
loquet: *nm.* latch; clasp
lorgner: *vt.* to leer, ogle
lors: *adv.* then
lorsque: *conj.* when
losange: *nm.* lozenge, diamond
lot: *nm.* prize; lot; portion
loterie: *nf.* lottery; raffle
lotion: *nf.* lotion
lotissement: *nm.* allotment; site, housing development
lotus: *nm.* lotus
louange: *nf.* praise, commendation

louche: *adj.* dubious; suspicious, shady
loucher: *vi.* to squint; to ogle
louer: *vt.* to rent, lease; to book
loup: *nm.* wolf
loupe: *nf.* magnifying glass
louper: *vt.* to botch, bungle; to flunk
lourd: *adj.* heavy; sultry; unwieldy
lourdeur: *nf.* heaviness
loutre: *nf.* otter
louve: *nf.* she-wolf
louvete u: *nm.* wolf-cub
loyal: *adj.* loyal, faithful
loyauté: *nf.* loyalty
loyer: *nm.* rent
lubrifiant: *nm.* lubricant; *adj.* lubricating
lubrifier: *vt.* to lubricate
lubrique: *adj.* lustful, lecherous; -ment = *adv.* lustfully
lucarne: *nf.* skylight
lucide: *adj.* lucid, clear; -ment = *adv.* lucidly
lucidité: *nf.* lucidity, clearness
lucratif: *adj.* lucrative
ludique: *adj.* play
lueur: *nf.* glimmer, gleam; glimpse
luge: *nf.* sledge, toboggan
lugubre: *adj.* lugubrious, gloomy; -ment = *adv.* lugubriously
lui: *pron.* him, her, it
luire: *vt.* to shine, gleam
luisant: *adj.* gleaming, shining
lumbago: *nm.* lumbago
lumière: *nf.* light; daylight; lamp; insight
lumineux: *adj.* luminous; illuminated
lunaire: *adj.* lunar, moon
lunatique: *adj.* fantastical, whimsical, quirky
lundi: *nm.* Monday
lune: *nf.* moon
lunette: *nf.* telescope
lunettes de soleil: sunglasses

lustré: *adj.* glossy; shiny
luth: *nm.* lute
luthérien: *adj.* Lutheran
luthiste: *nmf.* lutanist
lutte: *nf.* struggle; contest; strife
lutter: *vi.* to struggle, fight
lutteur: *nm.* wrestler, fighter
luxation: *nf.* dislocation, luxation
luxe: *nm.* luxury, excess
luxueusement: *adv.* luxuriously
luxueux: *adj.* luxurious
luxure: *nf.* lust
luxuriance: *nf.* luxuriance
luxuriant: *adj.* luxuriant
luzerne: *nf.* lucerne, alfalfa
lycée: *nm.* secondary school
lycéen: *nm.* secondary school boy
lymphatique: *adj.* lymphatic
lymphe: *nf.* lymph
lymphocyte: *nm.* lymphocyte
lyncher: *vt.* to lynch
lynx: *nm.* lynx
lyre: *nf.* lyre
lyrique: *adj.* lyric
lyrisme: *nm.* lyricism
lys: *nm.* lily

M

macabre: *adj.* macabre
macadam: *nm.* tarmac
macaque: *nm.* macaque
macédoine: *nf.* medley, hotchpotch; macedoine
macérer: *vt.* to macerate; to mortify
mâche: *nf.* corn-salad
mâcher: *vt.* to chew
machiavélique: *adj.* Machiavellian
machin: *nm.* gadget; thingamajig
machinal: *adj.* mechanical, automatic
machination: *nf.* machination, plot
machine: *nf.* machine; engine; apparatus
machine à adresser: addressing machine
machinerie: *nf.* machinery, plant
machines de bureau: office equipment
machiniste: *nm.* machinist; driver; stagehand
machite: *nf.* malachite
mâchoire: *nf.* jaw
maçon: *nm.* builder, mason
maçonnerie: *nf.* masonry; building
macoquinerie: *nf.* tannery; fine leather craft
macrobiotique: *adj.* macrobiotic; *nf.* macrobiotics
madame: *nf.* Madam; Mrs; lady madeleine
mademoiselle: *nf.* Miss; young lady
magasin: *nm.* shop, store; warehouse
magasin de vente directe d'usine: factory outlet
magasin général de douane: bonded warehouse
magasin store: warehouse
magasinier: storekeeper, warehouseman
magazine: *nm.* magazine
mage: *nm.* magus; seer
magicien: *nm.* magician

magie: *nf.* magic
magique: *adj.* magic; magical; -ment = *adv.* magically
magistrat: *nm.* magistrate
magistrature: *nf.* magistracy; magistrature
magitral: *adj.* masterly
magnanime: *adj.* magnanimous
magnat: *nm.* magnate
magnesium: *nm.* magnesium
magnétique: *adj.* magnetic
magnétiser: *vt.* to magnetise; to hypnotise
magnétisme: *nm.* magnetism; hypnotism
magnétophone: *nm.* tape recorder
magnifique: *adj.* magnificent; sumptuous; -ment = *adv.* magnificently
magnolia: *nm.* magnolia
magot: *nm.* savings, hoard, nest egg
magouille: *nf.* fiddle, scam; scheming
mai: *nm.* May
maigre: *adj.* thin; meagre, scarce; -ment = *adv.* meagrely
maigreur: *nf.* thinness; meagreness; sparseness
maigrir: *vi.* to get thinner; to waste away
maille: *nf.* stitch; mesh; link
maillet: *nm.* mallet
maillon: *nm.* link; shackle.
maillot: *nm.* jersey; leotard
maillot de bain: swimsuit
main: *nf.* hand; avoir la a to have the lead
main-d'oeuvre: *nf.* workforce
maintenance: *nf.* maintenance, servicing
maintenant: *adv.* now
maintenir: *vt.* to keep, maintain; preserve
maintien: *nm.* maintenance; preservation; keeping up

maire: *nm.* mayor; *nf.* mayoress
mairie: *nf.* mayoralty; town hall
mais: *conj.* but
maïs: *nm.* maize; corn
maison: *nf.* house; home; building; premises
maître: *nm.* master; ruler; lord; proprietor
maîtresse: *nf.* mistress; teacher
maîtrise: *nf.* mastery; control; expertise
maîtriser: *vt.* to control; to master
majesté: *nf.* majesty, grandeur
majestueusement: *adv.* majestically
majestueux: *adj.* majestic
majeur: *adj.* major; main; chief; superior; *nm.* major: *nmf.* adult.
majoration: *nf.* increased charge; overestimation
majordome: *nm.* majordomo, butler
majorer: *vt.* to increase, raise
majorette: *nf.* majorette
majoritaire: *adj.* majority
majorité: *nf.* majority
majuscule: *nf.* capital letter
mal: *adv.* wrong, badly; *nm.* evil, wrong; harm; pain
mal à l'aise: *adj.* uneasy
mal de dent: *nm.* toothache
mal de mer: *nm.* seasickness
mal de tête: *nm.* headache
mal du pays: *nm.* homesickness
malade: *adj.* sick, ill; diseased; *nmf.* invalid, sick person
maladie: *nf.* illness; malady, complaint; disorder
maladie vénérienne: *nf.* veneral disease
maladresse: *nf.* clumsiness; awkwardness
maladroit: *adj.* clumsy, awkward
malaise: *nm.* uneasiness, discomfort; indisposition
malchance: *nf.* ill luck; misfortune;

mishap

malchanceux: *adj.* unlucky, unfortunate

mâle: *nm.* male; *adj.* male; manly, virile

malédiction: *nf.* malediction, curse

maléfique: *adj.* hurtful; malignant; baleful

malencontreux: *adj.* unfortunate, untoward

malentendu: *nm.* misunderstanding

malfaisant: *adj.* malevolent; harmful; wicked

malfaiteur: *nm.* criminal; malefactor

malgré: *prép.* in spite of; despite

malheur: *nm.* misfortune; calamity

malheureusement: *adv.* unfortunately

malheureux: *adj.* unfortunate; unlucky; unhappy

malhonnêteté: *nf.* dishonesty; incivility

malice: *nf.* malice, spite; mischievousness

malicieux: *adj.* malicious, spiteful; mischievous

malin: *adj.* shrewd, cunning, crafty; malignant

malintentionné: *adj.* ill-disposed, spiteful

malle: *nf.* trunk

malléable: *adj.* malleable

mallhonnête: *adj.* dishonest, crooked; uncivil; -ment = *adv.* dishonestly

malmener: *vt.* to illtreat, to maltreat, to mishandle

malnutrition: *nf.* malnutrition

malsain: *adj.* unhealthy, unwholesome; immoral

malt: *nm.* malt

maltraiter: *vt.* to abuse; to handle roughly

malveillance: *nf.* malevolence, spite

malveillant: *adj.* malevolent, spiteful

maman: *nf.* mother, mummy, mum

mamelle: *nf.* breast; udder

mamelon: *nm.* nipple, teat

mammifère: *nm.* ma mal

manche: *nf.* sleeve; game, round; *nm.* handle, shaft

manchot: *nm.* one-armed person; *adj.* one-armed; *nm.* penguin

mandarin: *nm.* mandarin; Mandarin

mandarine: *nf.* tangerine

mandat: *nm.* mandate; money order; proxy

mandat postal: money order

mandataire: *nmf.* proxy; representative

mandibule: *nf.* mandible, jaw

mandoline: *nf.* mandolin

manège: *nm.* roundabout, merry-go-round

manette: *nf.* lever, tap

manganèse: *nm.* manganese

mangeable: *adj.* edible

manger: *vt.* to eat; to consume

mangeur: *nm.* eater

mangouste: *nf.* mongoose

mangue: *nf.* mango

maniable: *adj.* handy, workable, tractable; amenable

maniaque: *adj.* eccentric; fussy; *nmf.* maniac; fusspot; fanatic

manie: *nf.* mania

maniement: *nm.* handling; management, use

manier: *vt.* to handle; to manipulate

manier avec soin: handle with care

maniéré: *adj.* affected

manière: *nf.* manner, way, style

manifestation: *nf.* demonstration; expression, manifestation

manifeste: *adj.* manifest, evident, obvious

manifester: *vt.* to display, make known; to demonstrate

manigancer: *vt.* to contrive; to scheme

manipulation: *nf.* handling; manipulation

manipuler: *vt.* to handle; to manipulate

manivelle: *nf.* crank

mannequin: *nm.* model; dum

manoeuvre: *nf.* manoeuvre, operation; scheme; *nm.* labourer

manoeuvrer: *vt.* to manoeuvre; to operate; *vi.* to manoeuvre, move

manoir: *nm.* manor

manomètre: *nm.* manometer

manquant: *adj.* missing

manque: *nm.* lack, shortage; short-coming, deficiency

manquer: *vt.* to miss; to fail; to be absent

mansarde: *nf.* attic, garret

manteau: *nm.* coat; mantle, blanket; cloak

manuel: *nm.* manual, handbook; *adj.* manual; -lement = *adv.* manually

manufacture: *nf.* factory; manufacture

manufacturier: *nm.* factory owner; manufacturer; *adj.* manufacturing

manuscrit: *nm.* manuscript; typescript; *adj.* handwritten

manutention: *nf.* handling

manutention, opérations de: handling operations

manutentionnaire: *nm.* packer

mappemonde: *nf.* map of the world

maquereau: *nm.* mackerel

maquette: *nf.* model; mock-up; dummy; sketch

maquillage: *nm.* make-up

maquiller: *vt.* to make up; to fake; to fiddle; se – vr. = to put make-up on

marais: *nm.* marsh, swamp

marasme: *nm.* stagnation; depression, slump

marathon: *nm.* marathon

marbre: *nm.* marble; marble statue

marbré: *adj.* marbled; mottled, blotchy

marbrier: *nm.* marble-cutter; monumental mason

marchand: *nm.* shopkeeper; dealer; merchant; *adj.* market, trade

marchander: *vi.* to bargain over, haggle

marchandise: *nf.* merchandise, commodity; goods

marchandises présentant un défaut: flawed goods

marche: *nf.* walk; journey; progress; movement

marché: *nm.* market; transaction, contract

marcher: *vi.* to walk, march; to progress; to work

marcheur: *nm.* walker, pedestrian

mardi: *nm.* Tuesday

mare: *nf.* pool, pond

marécage: *nm.* marsh, swamp

maréchal: *nm.* marshal

marée: *nf.* tide

margarine: *nf.* margarine

marge: *nf.* margin; latitude, freedom; mark-up

marges bénéficiaires: profit margins

marginal: *adj.* marginal

marginaliser: *vt.* to marginalise

marguerite: *nf.* daisy

mari: *nm.* husband

mariage: *nm.* marriage

marié: *nm.* bride groom; *adj.* married

marier: *vt.* to marry; blend, harmonise

marin: *nm.* sailor

marine: *nf.* navy; seascape; marine

mariner: *vi.* to marinate; to hang about; at to marinate

marionnette: *nf.* puppet; puppet

show
maritime: *adj.* maritime; sea-board
marjolaine: *nf.* marjoram
marmelade: *nf.* stewed fruit; marmalade
marmite: *nf.* pot
marmonner: *vt.* to mumble, mutter
marmotte: *nf.* marmot
maroquinier: *nm.* leather craftsman; dealer in fine leather
marquant: *adj.* outstanding, vivid
marque: *nf.* mark, sign; brand; make
marquer: *vt.* to mark; to note down; to score
marquis: *nm.* marquis
marraine: *nf.* godmother; sponsor
marron: *nm.* chestnut; brown
marronnier: *nm.* chestnut tree
mars: *nm.* March
marshandage: *nm.* bargaining, haggling
marsouin: *nm.* porpoise
marteau: *nm.* hammer; knocker
marteler: *vt.* to hammer; to beat
martial: *adj.* martial, warlike
martin-pêcheur: *nm.* kingfisher
martyr: *nm.* martyr; *adj.* martyred
martyre: *nm.* martyrdom
martyriser: *vt.* to torture, martyrise
mascarade: *nf.* farce, mascarade
masculin: *adj.* masculine
masochisme: *nm.* masochism
masochiste: *nmf.* masochist; *adj.* masochistic
masque: *nm.* mask; facade, front
masquer: *vt.* to mask, conceal; to disguise
massacre: *nm.* massacre; slaughter
massacrer: *vt.* to massacre, slaughter
massage: *nm.* massage
masse: *nf.* mass, heap; bulk; mob
masse moléculaire moyenne: number average molecular weight
masse monétaire: money supply

masse réduite: reduced mass
masser: *vt.* to mass, assemble; to massage
masseur: *nm.* masseur, -euse
massif: *adj.* massive, solid, heavy; *nm.* massif; clump
massivement: *adv.* en masse
massue: *nf.* club
mastic: *nm.* mastic
mastiquer: *vt.* to chew, masticate
masturbation: *nf.* masturbation
masturber: *vi.* to masturbate
mat: *adj.* matt, dull; dead, dull-sounding
mat: *nm.* mast; pole
match: *nm.* match; game
matelas: *nm.* mattress
matelassé: *adj.* stuffed; padded, cushioned
matelot: *nm.* sailor; seaman
mater: *vt.* to subdue; to control, curb; to spy on; to ogle
matérialiser: *vt.* to embody
matériaux: *nmpl.* material, materials
matériel: *adj.* material, physical; practical
maternel: *adj.* maternal, motherly
maternité: *nf.* motherhood; pregnancy; maternity hospital
mathématicien: *nm.* mathematician
mathématique: *adj.* mathematical
matière: *nf.* material, matter; subject
matin: *nm.* morning; dawn
matinal: *adj.* morning
matinée: *nf.* morning; matinée
matraque: *nf.* truncheon; cosh
matrice: *nf.* womb; mould; matrix
matricule: *nm.* reference number
matrimonial: *adj.* matrimonial, marriage
maturation: *nf.* maturing; maturation
maturité: *nf.* maturity; prime
maudire: *vt.* to curse
maudit: *adj.* cursed; blasted, damned

maussade: *adj.* sulky, sullen;
-ment = *adv.* sulkily, sullenly
mauvais: *adj.* bad; wicked; faulty;
hurtful; poor
mauve: *adj.* mauve; *nf.* mallow
maximal: *adj.* maximal
maxime: *nf.* maxim
maximum: *nm.* maximum
mayonnaise: *nf.* mayonnaise
mécanicien: *nm.* mechanic; engineer
mécanique: *nf.* mechanics;
mechanical engineering
mécanisme: *nm.* mechanism,
working
mécanisme réactionnel: reaction
mechanism
mécène: *nm.* patron
méchanceté: *nf.* spitefulness
méchant: *adj.* spiteful; wicked
mèche: *nf.* wick, fuse; tuft
méconnaissable: *adj.* unrecognisable
méconnu: *adj.* unrecognised;
misunderstood
mécontent: *adj.* discontent,
displeased
mécontentement: *nm.* discontent;
displeasure
médaille: *nf.* medal; stain, mark
médaillon: *nm.* medallion; locket
médecin: *nm.* doctor, physician
médecine: *nf.* medicine
médiateur: *nm.* mediator; arbitrator
médiatique: *adj.* media
médical: *adj.* medical
médicament: *nm.* medicine, drug
médicinal: *adj.* medicinal
médiéval: *adj.* medieval
médiocre: *adj.* mediocre; passable
médisent: *adj.* slanderous
méditation: *nf.* meditation
méditer: *vi.* to meditate; *vt.* to
contemplate, have in mind
Méditerranée: *nf.* Mediterranean Sea
médium: *nm.* medium

méduse: *nf.* jellyfish
méfiance: *nf.* distrust, mistrust
méfiant: *adj.* distrustful, mistrustful
méfier (se): *vr.* to mistrust, distrust;
to be suspicious
mégalomane: *adj.* megalomaniac;
nmf. megalomaniac
mégaphone: *nm.* megaphone
mégot: *nm.* cigarette-end, stub
meilleur: *adj.* better, preferable
melancholiquement: *adv.*
melancholically
mélancolie: *nf.* melancholy, gloom
mélancolique: *adj.* melancholy
mélange: *nm.* mixing, blending;
mixture
mélanger: *vt.* to mix, blend; to
muddle
mêlée: *nf.* melée, fray; scrum
mêler: *vt.* to mix; to combine; se *vr.*
to mix, mingle
mélisse: *nf.* lemon balm
mélodie: *nf.* melody, tune
mélodieusement: *adv.* melodiously,
tunefully
mélodieux: *adj.* melodious, tuneful
mélomane: *nmf.* music lover
melon: *nm.* melon
membrane: *nf.* membrane
membre: *nm.* member; limb
même: *adv.* even; tout de - =
nevertheless, all the same, the same
ones
mémoire: *nf.* memory
mémorable: *adj.* memorable
mémoriser: *vt.* to memorise
menaçant: *adj.* menacing,
threatening
menace: *nf.* threat; intimidation;
danger
menacer: *vt.* to threaten, to menace
ménage: *nm.* housework, housekeeping; household
ménager: *vt.* to treat with caution; to

manage; to arrange
ménagère: *nf.* housewife
ménagerie: *nf.* menagerie
mendiant: *nm.* beggar
mendier: *vt.* to beg; to implore
mener: *vt.* to lead, guide; to steer; to manage
meneur: *nm.* leader; agitator
menhir: *nm.* menhir, standing stone
méningite: *nf.* meningitis
ménopause: *nf.* menopause
menotte: *nf.* handcuff
mensonge: *nm.* lie, falsehood, error, illusion
menstruation: *nf.* menstruation
mensuel: *adj.* monthly
mental: *adj.* mental;
-ement = *adv.* mentally
mentalité: *nf.* mentality
menteur: *nm.* liar; *adj.* lying, deceitful
menthe: *nf.* mint
menthol: *nm.* menthol
mention: *nf.* mention; comment; grade
mentionner: *vt.* to mention
mentir: *vi.* to lie; to be deceptive
menton: *nm.* chin
menu: *nm.* menu; meal; *adj.* slender, thin; petty, minor
menuiserie: *nf.* joinery, carpentry
menuisier: *nm.* joiner, carpenter
mépris: *nm.* contempt, scorn
méprisant: *adj.* contemptuous, scornful
mépriser: *vt.* to scorn, despise
mer: *nf.* sea; tide
mercenaire: *nm.* mercenary
mercerie: *nf.* haberdashery
merci: *nm.* thank you
mercredi: *nm.* Wednesday
mercure: *nm.* mercury
mère: *nf.* mother
méridien: *nm.* meridian

meringue: *nf.* meringue
merisier: *nm.* wild cherry
mériter: *vt.* to deserve, merit
merlan: *nm.* whiting
merle: *nm.* blackbird
merveille: *nf.* marvel, wonder
merveilleusement: *adv.* marvellously, wonderfully
merveilleux: *adj.* marvellous, wonderful
mésange: *nf.* tit
mésentente: *nf.* misunderstanding
mesquin: *adj.* mean, niggardly; petty
message: *nm.* message
messager: *nm.* messenger
messagerie: *nf.* parcels office, parcels service
messe: *nf.* mass
messie: *nm.* messiah
mesure: *nf.* measure; gauge; measurement; moderation; step
mesurer: *vt.* to measure; to assess; to limit
mesures non tarifaires: non-tariff measures
métabolisme: *nm.* metabolism
métal`: *nm.* metal
métallique: *adj.* metallic
métallisé: *adj.* metallic, metallised
métallurgie: *nf.* metallurgy
métamorphoser: *vt.* to transform, metamorphose
métaphore: *nf.* metaphor
métaphorique: *adj.* metaphorical; -ment = *adv.* metaphorically
métaphysique: *adj.* metaphysical; *nf.* metaphysics
métarmorphose: *nf.* metamorphosis
météo: *nf.* weather, forecast
météore: *nm.* meteor
météorite: mn. meteorite
météorologue, météorologiste: *nmf.* meteorologist
méthane: *nm.* methane

méthode: *nf.* method
méthylène: *nm.* methyl alcohol; methylene
méticuleusement: *adv.* meticulously
méticuleux: *adj.* meticulous métier
métier: *nm.* job; occupation
métier artisanal: *nm.* craft
métis: *nm.* half-caste; hybrid; mongrel
métllurgiste: *nm.* steelworker, metalworker
mètre: *nm.* metre
métro: *nm.* underground, metro
métronome: *nm.* metronome
métropole: *nf.* metropolis
métropolitain: *adj.* metropolitan; underground
mets: *nm.* dish
metteur en scène: *nm.* director
mettre: *vt.* to put, place; to put on
meuble: *nm.* piece of furniture
meuble de classement: filing cabinet
meubler: *vt.* to furnish
meule: *nf.* millstone; grindstone
meurtre: *nm.* murder
meurtrier: *nm.* murderer
meurtrir: *vt.* to bruise
meute: *nf.* pack
mezzanine: *nf.* mezzanine
mi taller: *vi.* to mew
miche: *nf.* round loaf
microbe: *nm.* germ, microbe
microbien: *adj.* microbial, microbic
midi: *nm.* noon
miel: *nm.* honey
miette: *nf.* crumb
milieu: *nm.* middle
militaire: *adj.* military
mille: *adj.* thousand
miller, indices de: miller indices
milliard: *adj.* billion
million: *adj.* million
mince: *adj.* thin
minimum: adj minimum

minorité: *nf.* minority
minuit: *nm.* midnight
minute: *nf.* minute
miroir: *nm.* mirror
mode: *nf.* fashion
modem: *nm.* modem
moderne: *adj.* modern; up-to-date
moine: *nm.* monk
moins: *adv.* ; *pron.* ; *prep.* less; minus
mois: *nm.* month
moisissure: *nf.* mold
moisson: *nm.* harvest
moitié: *nf.* half
moment: *nm.* moment
moment angulaire: angular momentum
moment d'inertie: moment of inertia
moment dipolaire: dipole moment
monastère: *nm.* monastery
monde: *nm.* world
monnaie: *nf.* change (coins); currency
monomoléculaire, réaction: monomolecular reaction
monsieur: *nm.* (pl. messieurs); sir
mont: *nm.* mount
montagne: *nf.* mountain
montant de tente: *nm.* tent pole
monter: *v.* to rise
monter à bord: *v.* to board (ship; plane)
monter dans: *v.* to board (train)
montre: *nf.* watch
montrer: *v.* to show
monture: *nf.* frame (glasses)
monument: *nm.* monument
morceau: *nm.* piece; bit
mordre: *v.* to bite
morsure: *nf.* bite
mort: *nf.* death; *adj.* dead
mortel: *adj.* deadly
mosquée: *nf.* mosque
mot: *nm.* word
moteur: *nm.* engine

moto: *nf.* motorbike
mots croisés: *nmpl.* crossword
mouche: *nf.* fly
mouchoir: *nm.* tissue
moudre: *v.* to grind
mouillé: *adj.* wet
moulin: *nm.* mill
moulu: *adj.* ground (coffee)
mourir: *v.* to die
moustache: *nf.* mustache
moustiquaire: *nf.* mosquito net
moustique: *nm.* mosquito
moutarde: *nf.* mustard
mouvement: *nm.* move; motion
moyen: *adj.* average
moyens de transport: means of conveyance
muet: *adj.* mute
multiplier: *v.* to multiply
mur: *nm.* wall
mûr: *adj* ripe; mature
muscle: *nm.* muscle
musée: *nm.* museum
musicien: *nm.* musician
musique: *nf.* music

N

nager: *v.* to swim
nain: *nm.* dwarf
naissance: *nf.* birth
nappe: *nm.* tablecloth
narine: *nf.* nostril
natal: *adj.* native (country)
nation: *nf.* nation
nationalité: *nf.* nationality
nature: *nf.* nature
naturel: *adj.* natural
nausée: *nf.* nausea
navette: *nf.* shuttle
naviguer: *v.* navigate
né: *adj.* born
ne pas être d'accord: *v.* to disagree
nécessaire: *adj.* necessary
négatif: *adj.* negative
neige: *nf.* snow
neiger: *v.* to snow
nerf: *nm.* nerve
nerveux: *adj.* nervous
nettoyer: *v.* to clean
neuf: *adj.* nine; *adj.* new
neutre: *adj.* neutral
neveu: *nm.* nephew
nez: *nm.* nose
nid: *nm.* nest
nièce: *nm.* niece
noblesse: *nf.* nobility
Noël: *nm.* Christmas
noeud: *nm.* bow; knot
noir: *adj.* black
noir de carbone: carbon black
nom: *nm.* name; noun
nom de jeune fille: *nm.* maiden name
nombre: *nm.* number
nombre d'ondes: wave number
nombre quantique: quantum number
nombreux: *adj.* numerous
nombril: *nm.* navel
nomination: *nf.* appointment
nommer: *v.* to name
non: *adv.* no

non autorisé: unauthorized
non comestible: toxic
nord: *nm.* north
normal: *adj.* normal
note: *nf.* note
note de débit: debit note
noter: *v.* to write down
nouer: *v.* to tie a knot
nourrir: *v.* to feed
nourrissant: adj nourishing
nourriture: *nf.* food
nous: pron. we
nouveau: *adj.* new
nouvelles: *nfpl.* news
novembre: *nm.* November
noyau: *nm.* core
noyer: *v.* to drown
nuage: *nm.* cloud
nul: *adj.* void
numéro: *nm.* number; issue (magazine)
numéro de téléphone: telephone number
nu-pieds: *adj.* barefoot
nuque: *nf.* neck

O

obèse: *adj.* obese
objectif: *nm.* lens (camera)
objection: *nf.* objection
objet: *nm.* object
objet de valeur: *nm.* valuables
objets de valeur: valuables
obligation: *nf.* debenture
obligatoire: *adj.* mandatory; compulsory
obscène: *adj.* obscene
obscurité: *nf.* darkness
observer: *v.* to observe
obstacle: *nm.* obstacle
obtenir: *v.* to get; to obtain
occasion: *nf.* opportunity
occupation: *nf.* occupation
occupé: *adj.* busy
occuper: *v.* to occupy
océan: *nm.* ocean
octobre: *nm.* October
odeur: *nf.* scent; smell; odor
oeil: *nm.* eye
oeuf: *nm.* egg
offender: *nm.* delinquent
officiel: *adj.* official
officier: *nm.* officer
offre: *nm.* offer
oignon: *nm.* onion
oiseau: *nm.* bird
ombre: *nf.* shade
once: *nf.* ounce
oncle: *nf.* uncle
ongle: *nm.* nail (finger)
onze: *adj.* eleven
opération: *nf.* operation
opinion: *nf.* opinion
opposé: *adj.* opposite
opposition à un cheque, faire: to stop a cheque
opticien: *nm.* optician
option: *nf.* option
or: *nm.* gold
orage: *nm.* thunderstorm; storm

oral: *adj.* oral
orange: *nf.* orange
orchestre: *nm.* orchestra
ordinaire: *adj.* ordinary
ordinateur: *nm.* computer
ordinateur: a computer
ordonnance: *nf.* prescription
ordre: *nm.* order
ordre d'une réaction: reaction order
ordre du jour: agenda
ordures: *nfpl.* trash; garbage
oreille: *nf.* ear
oreiller: *nm.* pillow
organigramme: *nm.* flow chart
organisation: *nf.* organization
organiser: *v.* to organize
origine: *nf.* origin
orteil: *nm.* toe
os: *nm.* bone
oscillateur harmonique: harmonic oscillator
osmométrie: *nf.* osmometry
ou: *conj.* or
où: *adv.* where
oublier: *v.* to forget
ouest: *nm.* west
oui: *adv.* yes
ouragan: *nm.* hurricane
outil: *nm.* tool
ouvert: *adj.* open
ouvrier qualifié: skilled worker
ouvrir: *v.* to open
oxygène: *nm.* oxygen

$\mathcal{P}$

page: *nf.* page
paie: *nf.* pay; wage
paiement: *nm.* payment
paiement à vue: payment at sight
paiement comptant à la commande: cash with order (CWO)
paiement comptant à la livraison cash: on delivery (COD)
paille: *nf.* straw
pain: *nm.* bread
paix: *nf.* peace
palais: *nm.* palate
pâle: *adj.* pale
panier: *nm.* basket
panne: *nf.* breakdown
panneau: *nm.* sign (road)
pansement: *nm.* bandage
pantalon: *nm.* pants
pantoufle: *nf.* slipper
papa: *nm.* dad
pape: *nm.* pope
papeterie: *nf.* stationery
papier: *nm.* paper
papier hygiénique: toilet paper
par avion: airmail
paradis: *nm.* heaven
paralyser: *v.* to paralyze
paramagnétisme: *nm.* paramagnetism
parapluie: *nm.* umbrella (rain)
parasol: *nm.* umbrella (sun)
parc: *nm.* park
pare-brise: *nm.* windshield
pareil: *adj.* alike; same
parent: *nm.* relative
parents: *nmpl.* parents
paresse: *nf.* laziness; sluggishness
paresseux: *adj.* lazy

parfaire: *vt.* to perfect, bring to perfection
parfait: *adj.* perfect, flawless
parfois: *adv.* sometimes, occasionally
parfum: *nm.* flavor, perfume, scent
parfumer: *vt.* to perfume, scent
parfumerie: *nf.* perfumery
parfumeur: *nm.* perfumer
pari: *nm.* bet, wager
parier: *vt.* to bet, wager
parking: *nm.* car park; parking
parlement: *nm.* Parliament
parlementaire: *adj.* parliamentary
parler: *vi.* to talk, speak; vt to speak
parmesan: *nm.* parmesan
parmi: *prép.* among
parodie: *nf.* parody
paroi: *nf.* wall; surface
paroisse: *nf.* parish
parole: *nf.* word; speech; voice; lyrics
paroxysme: *nm.* paroxysm; crisis
parquer: *vt.* to park; to enclose, pen
parquet: *nm.* floor, floorboards
parrain: *nm.* godfather; patron; pro-moter
parrainage: *nm.* sponsorship; promoting; patronage
parrainer: *vt.* to sponsor; propose
parsemer: *vt.* to sprinkle, strew
part: *nf.* part; share; portion
part (à): *adv.* apart (to one side)
partage: *nm.* sharing, distribution; portion
partager: *vt.* to divide up, share out
partenaire: *nmf.* partner
parti: *nm.* party; option; match
partial: *adj.* partial, biased
participant: *nm.* participant
participation: *nf.* participation; involvement
participe: *nm.* participle
participer: *vi.* to take part in, participate
particularité: *nf.* particularity, characteristic
particule: *nf.* particle
particulier: *adj.* particular, specific; peculiar, characteristic; character
particulièrement: *adv.* particularly, especially
partie: *nf.* part; subject; game; party
partiel: *adj.* part, partial
partir: *vi.* to leave, set off; to start up
partir de (à): *prep.* from
partisan: *nm.* partisan, supporter, proponent
partition: *nf.* partition; score
partout: *adv.* everywhere
parvenir: *vi.* to reach; to achieve
pas: *nm.* step; pace; footprint; gait
passable: *adj.* passable, tolerable
passage: *nm.* passage, passing by; transit
passager: *nm.* passenger
passant: *nm.* passer-by, way-farer; *adj.* much-frequented, busy
passe: *nf.* pass; permit; channel
passé: *nm.* past
passeport: *nm.* passport
passer: *vi.* to pass; to elapse; to disappear, fade
passerelle: *nf.* footbridge; bridge; gangway
passe-temps: *nm.* invar pastime
passible de droits, être: to be liable to duty
passif: *nm.* liabilities
passif: *adj.* passive; m passive
passion: *nf.* passion; fondness
passionnant: *adj.* fascinating; exciting
passionné: *adj.* passionate, impassioned; -ment adv. = passionately
passionner: *vt.* to fascinate; to interest deeply, impassion
passivement: *adv.* passively
passivité: *nf.* passivity, passiveness

pastel: *nm.* pastel
pastèque: *nf.* watermelon
pasteur: *nm.* minister, pastor
pasteuriser: *vt.* to pasteurise
pastiche: *nm.* pastiche
pastille: *nf.* pastille, lozenge
patate: *nf.* spud; sweet potato
patauger: *vi.* to wade about, splash about
pâte: *nf.* pastry, pasta, dough, batter
pâté: *nm.* pâté
paternel: *adj.* paternal, fatherly
paternité: *nf.* paternity; fatherhood
pathétique: *adj.* pathetic
patiemment: *adv.* patiently
patience: *nf.* patience, endurance
patient: *adj.* patient, enduring
patienter: *vi.* to wait
patin: *nm.* skate; - à glace = iceskate; - à roulettes = roller skate
patinage: *nm.* skating; slipping; spinning
patiner: *vi.* to skate; to slip; to spin
patineur: *nm.* skater
patinoire: *nf.* ice rink
pâtisserie: *nf.* cake shop, confectioner
pâtissier: *nm.* pastry cook, confectioner
patois: *nm.* patois, provincial dialect
patrie: *nf.* homeland, country
patrimoine: *nm.* inheritance, patrimony
patriote: *nm.* patriot
patriotisme: *nm.* patriotism
patron: *nm.* owner, boss, proprietor
patron: *adj.* protective; patronising
patronat: *nm.* employers
patronner: *vt.* to patronise, to sponsor
patrouille: *nf.* patrol
patte: *nf.* leg, paw, foot
pâturage: *nm.* pasture, pasturage, grazing

pâture: *nf.* pasture; food
paume: *nf.* palm
paumer: *vt.* to lose
paupière: *nf.* eyelid
paupiette: *nf.* stuffed slice of meat
pause: *nf.* pause; half-time
pauvre: *adj.* poor; indigent; scanty; weak
pavé: *nm.* cobblestone, paving stone
pavillon: *nm.* house; pavilion; flag
pavot: *nm.* poppy
paye: *nf.* pay, wages
payer: *vt.* to pay, settle; to reward
pays: *nm.* country; region; village; land
paysage: *nm.* landscape; scenery
paysan: *nm.* countryman, farmer
péage: *nm.* toll; tollgate
peau: *nf.* skin; hide, pelt
pêche: *nf.* peach; fishing
pécher: *vi.* to sin
pêcher: *vt.* to fish; to catch
pécheur: *nm.* sinner
pêcheur: *nm.* fisherman
pectoral: *adj.* pectoral; cough
pectoraux: *nmpl.* pectorals
pédagogie: *nf.* education; educational methods
pedagogue: *nmf.* teacher; educationalist; *adj.* pedagogic
pédale: *nf.* pedal; treadle
pédaler: *vi.* to pedal
pédalier: *nm.* pedalboard, crankgear
pédestre: *adj.* pedestrian
pédiatre: *nmf.* paediatrician
pedicure: *nmf.* chiropodist
peigne: *nm.* comb
peigner: *vt.* to comb; to card; se *vr.* to comb one's hair
peignoir: *nm.* dressing gown
peindre: *vt.* to paint; to depict, to portray
peine: *nf.* effort; sadness; pain; punishment; difficulty

peiner: *vi.* to toil; to struggle
peintre: *nm.* painter; portrayer
peinture: *nf.* painting, picture; paintwork
péjoratif: *adj.* pejorative
pelage: *nm.* coat, fur
peler: *vi.* to peel
pèlerin: *nm.* pilgrim; peregrine falcon
pèlerinage: *nm.* pilgrimage
pélican: *nm.* pelican
pelle: *nf.* shovel; spade
pellicule: *nf.* film; thin layer
pelote: *nf.* ball; pelota ball
peloton: *nm.* pack; squad; platoon
pelouse: *nf.* lawn, field; ground
pelure: *nf.* peeling, piece of peel
pénal: *adj.* penal; criminal
pénaliser: *vt.* to penalise
pénalité: *nf.* penalty
penalty: *nm.* penalty (kick)
pencher: *vi.* to lean; to tilt
pendant: *prép.* during; for
pendentif: *nm.* pendant; pendentive
pendre: *vi.* to hang, dangle; *vt.* to perception hang
pendule: *nf.* clock; m pendulum
pénétrant: *adj.* penetrating, piercing; searching; acute
pénétration: *nf.* penetration; perception
pénétrer: *vi.* to enter, penetrate; vt to penetrate, pierce; to pervade
pénible: *adj.* hard, tiresome; difficult; laborious
péniche: *nf.* barge
péniciline: *nf.* penicillin
péninsule: *nf.* peninsula
pénis: *nm.* penis
pénitence: *nf.* penitence, penance; punishment
pénitencier: *nm.* prison, penitentiary
pénitent: *nm.* penitent; *adj.* penitent
pénombre: *nf.* half-light; penumbra (astronomy)

pensée: *nf.* thought; thinking; mind
penser: *vt.* to think, suppose, believe; *vi.* to think
pensif: *adj.* pensive, thoughtful
pension: *nf.* pension; boarding house
pensionnaire: *nmf.* boarder; lodger
pensionnat: *nm.* boarding school
pensivement: *adv.* pensively, thoughtfully
pentagone: *nm.* pentagon
pentathlon: *nm.* pentathlon
pente: *nf.* slope; gradient
Pentecôte: *nf.* Pentecost, Whitsun
pénurie: *nf.* shortage, scarcity; penury
pépère: *nm.* granddad, grandpa
pépin: *nm.* pip; snag, hitch
pépinière: *nf.* tree nursery; breeding-ground
pépite: *nf.* nugget
perçant: *adj.* piercing, shrill
percée: *nf.* opening, clearing; breach; breakthrough
perce-oreille: earwig
perception: *nf.* perception; collection
percer: *vt.* to pierce; to drill; to see through
percevoir: *vt.* to perceive, detect; to collect
percevoir des intérêts: to charge interest
percher: *vt.* to stick; to place on
percussion: *nf.* percussion
percussionniste: *nmf.* percussionist
percuter: *vt.* to strike; to crash into
perdant: *nm.* loser; *adj.* losing
perdre: *vt.* to lose; to waste; to miss
perdrix: *nf.* partridge
perdu: *adj.* lost; wasted; missed
père: *nm.* father; sire
péremptoire: *adj.* peremptory
perfection: *nf.* perfection
perfectionnement: *nm.* perfection, perfecting; improvement

perfectionner: *vt.* to improve, to perfect
perfectionniste: *nmf.* perfectionist; *adj.* perfectionist
perfide: *adj.* perfidious, treacherous
perforation: *nf.* perforation
perforer: *vt.* to perforate; to pierce
performance: *nf.* result, performance
performant: *adj.* outstanding; high-performance, high-return
péricliter: *vi.* to collapse; to be in jeopardy
péril: *nm.* peril, danger
périlleux: *adj.* perilous
périmé: *adj.* out-of-date; expired
périmètre: *nm.* perimeter
période: *nf.* period; epoch, era; wave, spell
périodique: *adj.* periodic
périphérie: *nf.* periphery
périphérique: *adj.* peripheral, outlying; m ring road; peripheral
périple: *nm.* voyage; journey
périr: *vi.* to perish, die
périscope: *nm.* periscope
périssable: *adj.* perishable
perle: *nf.* pearl; bead; gem
permanence: *nf.* permanence; permanency
permanent: *adj.* permanent, continuous
permanente: *nf.* perm
permanenter: *vt.* to perm
perméabilité: *nf.* permeability
perméable: *adj.* permeable; pervious
permettre: *vt.* to allow, permit
permis: *adj.* permitted; *m.* permit, licence
permission: *nf.* permission; leave
permittivité: *nf.* permitivity
permutation: *nf.* permutation
permuter: *vt.* to change, switch round; to permutate
pernicieux: *adj.* pernicious

perpendiculaire: *adj.* perpendicular
perpétuel: *adj.* perpetual; permanent
perpétuer: *vt.* to perpetuate, carry on
perpétuité: *nf.* perpetuity
perplexe: *adj.* perplexed, confused
perplexité: *nf.* perplexity, confusion
perquisition: *nf.* search
perquisitionner: *vt.* to make a search
pérripétie: *nf.* event, episode
perron: *nm.* flight of steps
perroquet: *nm.* parrot
perruche: *nf.* budgerigar; chatterbox
perruque: *nf.* wig
persécuter: *vt.* to persecute; to harass
persécution: *nf.* persecution
persévérance: *nf.* perseverance
persévérant: *adj.* persevering
persévérer: *vi.* to persevere; to persist in
persil: *nm.* parsley
persistance: *nf.* persistence
persistant: *adj.* persistent; evergreen
persister: *vi.* to persist, keep up
personnage: *nm.* character, individual
personnaliser: *vt.* to personalise
personnalité: *nf.* personality
personne: *nf.* person; self; appearance
personnel: *adj.* personal; selfish
personnifier: *vt.* to personify
perspective: *nf.* perspective; view; angle
perspicace: *adj.* shrewd, perspicacious
perspicacité: *nf.* insight, perspicacity
persuader: *vt.* to persuade; to convince
persuasif: *adj.* persuasive; convincing
persuasion: *nf.* persuasion; conviction
perte: *nf.* loss, losing; ruin
pertinent: *adj.* pertinent

perturbation: *nf.* disruption; perturbation
perturber: *vt.* to disrupt, disturb
pervenche: *nf.* periwinkle
pervers: *adj.* perverse; perverted
perversité: *nf.* perversity
pesant: *adj.* heavy, weighty
pesanteur: *nf.* gravity; heaviness
pèse-personne: *nm.* scales
peser: *vt.* to weigh; to press; to evaluate
pessimiste: *nmf.* pessimist; *adj.* pessimistic
peste: *nf.* pest, nuisance; plague
pesticide: *nm.* pesticide
pétale: *nf.* petal
pétanque: *nf.* petanque
pétard: *nm.* firecracker; detonator; charge; racket, row
pétillant: *adj.* bubbly, fizzy
pétiller: *vi.* to crackle; to bubble; to sparkle
petit: *adj.* small, tiny; slim; young
petite-fille: *nf.* granddaughter
petitesse: *nf.* smallness, modesty; meanness
petit-fils: *nm.* grandson
pétition: *nf.* petition
petits-enfants: *nmpl.* grandchildren
pétrifié: *adj.* petrified; transfixed; fossilised
pétrin: *nm.* kneading trough; scrape, mess, tight spot
pétrir: *vt.* to knead; to mould, shape
pétrole: *nm.* oil, petroleum
pétrolier: *nm.* oil tanker; *adj.* petroleum, oil, oil-producing
pétrolifère: *adj.* oil-bearing
pétuni: *nm.* petunia
peu: *adv.* little, not much, few
peu près (à): *adv.* about
peuplade: *nf.* tribe, people
peuple: *nm.* people, nation; crowd
peuplement: *nm.* populating; stocking
peupler: *vt.* to populate, stock; to plant
peuplier: *nm.* poplar
peur: *nf.* fear, terror, apprehension
peureux: *adj.* fearful, timorous
peut-être: *adv.* perhaps
phalange: *nf.* phalanx
phallocrate: *nm.* male chauvinist
pharaon: *nm.* pharaoh
phare: *nm.* lighthouse; headlight
pharmaceutique: *adj.* pharmaceutical
pharmacie: *nf.* pharmacy; pharmacology
pharmacien: *nm.* pharmacist; chemist
pharynx: *nm.* pharynx
phase: *nf.* phase, stage
phases, règle des: phase rule
phénoménal: *adj.* phenomenal
phénomène: *nm.* phenomenon; freak; character
philanthrope: *nmf.* philanthropist
philatélie: *nf.* philately, stamp collecting
philologie: *nf.* philology
philosophe: *nmf.* philosopher; *adj.* philosophical
philosopher: *vi.* to philosophise
philosophie: *nf.* philosophy
philosophique: *adj.* philosophical
phobie: *nf.* phobia
phonétique: *nf.* phonetics; *adj.* phonetic
phoque: *nm.* seal; sealskin
phosphate: *nm.* phosphate
phosphore: *nm.* phosphorus
phosphorescent: *adj.* luminous
photo: *nf.* photo
photochimie: *nf.* photochemistry
photocopie: *nf.* photocopy
photocopier: *vt.* to photocopy
photocopieue: *nf.* photocopier

photogénique: *adj.* photogenic
photographe: *nmf.* photograph
photographie: *nf.* photography
photographier: *vt.* to photograph
photographique: *adj.* photographic
photolyse éclair: flash photolysis
photosensibilisation: *nf.*
photosensitization
phrase: *nf.* sentence; phrase
physicien: *nm.* physicist
physiologie: *nf.* physiology
physiologique: *adj.* physiological
physionomie: *nf.* countenance,
physiognomy
physionomiste: *adj.* good at
remembering faces
physiothérapie: *nf.* physiotherapy
physique: *nf.* physics
pianiste: *nmf.* pianist
piano: *nm.* piano
pic: *nm.* peak
pichet: *nm.* pitcher, jug
picorer: *vt.* to peck; to nibble
picot: *nm.* picot; (bot) burr; (tec)
tooth
picotement: *nm.* tickle; prickling
picoter: *vt.* to tickle; to prickle; to
pinte smart, sting
pictural: *adj.* pictorial
pie: *nf.* magpie; chatterbox
pièce: *nf.* piece; object; component;
room; paper, document, coin
pièce de monnaie: *nf.* coin
pièce de rechange: spare part
pièce de théâtre: drama
pied: *nm.* foot; track; hoof; bottom
pied-à-terre: pied-à-terre
piédestal: *nm.* pedestal
piège: *nm.* trap; pit; snare
piéger: *vt.* to trap, set a trap
pierre: *nf.* stone
piété: *nf.* piety
piétiner: *vi.* to stamp
piéton: *nm.* pedestrian; *adj.*
pedestrian
pieu: *nm.* post, stake, pile
pieusement: *adv.* piously, devoutly
pieux: *adj.* pious, devout
pigeon: *nm.* pigeon; dupe, mug
pigment: *nm.* pigment
pigmentation: *nf.* pigmentation
pignon: *nm.* gable; cogwheel
pile: *nf.* pile; pier; battery; adv dead;
just, right, exactly
pilier: *nm.* pillar
pilier: *vt.* to crush, pound
pillage: *nm.* pillaging, looting
piller: *vt.* to pillage, loot
pilon: *nm.* pestle; wooden leg
pilote: *nm.* pilot; driver
piloter: *vt.* to pilot, fly; to drive
pilotis: *nm.* stilts; pilotis
pilule: *nf.* pill
piment: *nm.* hot pepper, capsicum
pimenter: *vt.* to add spice
pin: *nm.* pine
pince: *nf.* pliers, crowbar; pincer; dart
pince à épiler: n tweezers
pinceau: *nm.* brush, paintbrush
pincée: *nf.* pinch
pincer: *vt.* to pinch, nip; to grip
pinède: *nf.* pine forest
pingouin: *nm.* penguin
ping-pong: *nm.* table tennis
pintade: *nf.* guinea-fowl
pinte: *nf.* pint
pioche: *nf.* pick, pickaxe
piocher: *vt.* to use a pick; to swot
piolet: *nm.* ice axe
pion: *nm.* pawn; draught
pionnier: *nm.* pioneer
pipe: *nf.* pipe
pipette: *nf.* pipette
piquant: *adj.* prickly; pungent;
piquant; m quill, spine; prickle
pique: *nf.* pike, lance
pique-nique: *nm.* picnic
pique-niquer: *vi.* to picnic

piquer: *vt.* to sting, bite; to goad; to puncture

piquet: *nm.* post, picket

piqûre: *nf.* prick; sting; bite

pirate: *nm.* pirate

pire: *adj.* worse

pirogue: *nf.* pirogue, dugout canoe

pirouette: *nf.* pirouette; bout-turn

pis: *nm.* udder

pis-aller: *nm.* invar last resort, stop-gap

piscine: *nf.* swimming pool

pissenlit: *nm.* dandelion

pistache: *nf.* pistachio

piste: *nf.* track, trail; course; run-way; lead, clue

pistolet: *nm.* pistol, gun

piston: *nm.* piston

pistonner: *vt.* to pull strings for, recommend

piteux: *adj.* pitiful, pathetic

pitié: *nf.* pity, mercy

pitoyable: *adj.* pitiful, pitiable

pittoresque: *adj.* picturesque

pivoine: *nf.* peony

pivot: *nm.* pivot; mainspring

pivoter: *vi.* to revolve, pivot

placard: *nm.* cupboard; poster, notice

place: *nf.* place; square; seat; space

placebo: *nm.* placebo

placement: *nm.* placing; investment

placenta: *nm.* placenta; afterbirth

placer: *vt.* to place, put; to fit; to plante seat; to sell; to invest

placide: *adj.* placid, calm

placidity: *nf.* placidity, cal ness

plafond: *nm.* ceiling; roof

plafonner: *vi.* to reach a ceiling maximum

plage: *nf.* beach

plagiat: *nm.* plagiarism, plagiary

plagier: *vt.* to plagiarise

plaider: *vt.* to plead; to defend; *vi.* to plead for, go to court

plaidoirie: *nf.* defence speech; plea

plaidoyer: *nm.* defence speech; plea

plaie: *nf.* wound, cut; scourge

plaignant: *nm.* plaintiff

plain: *nf.* plain

plaindre: *vt.* to pity; to begrudge

plainte: *nf.* complaint; moan,

plaire: *vi.* to please, be pleasant

plaisant: *adj.* pleasant, agreeable

plaisanter: *vi.* to joke, jest

plaisanterie: *nf.* joking; pleasantry; humour

plaisir: *nm.* pleasure; delight; entertainment

plan: plan, scheme, project; plane, level

plan comptable: accounting system

planche: *nf.* plank, board; plate; shelf

plancher: *nm.* floor

planchette: *nf.* small board, small shelf

plancton: *nm.* plankton

planer: *vi.* to glide, soar; to hover over

planétaire: *adj.* planetary

planète: *nf.* planet

planeur: *nm.* glider

planification: *nf.* planning

planifier: *vt.* to plan

planisphère: *nm.* planisphere

planning: *nm.* programme, schedule

plantation: *nf.* plantation; planting

plante: *nf.* plant

planter: *vt.* to plant; to hammer in; to stick, dump

plantureux: *adj.* copious, ample

plaque: *nf.* sheet, plate; plaque; slab

plaqué: *nm.* plated

plaquer: *vt.* to plate, veneer; to jilt; to tackle

plaquette: *nf.* plaque; tablet; slab

plasma: *nm.* plasma

plastifier: *vt.* to coat with plastic

plastique: *nm.* plastic; *adj.* plastic
plat: *adj.* flat; straight; dull, insipid
platane: *nm.* plane tree
plateau: *nm.* tray; turntable; plateau; stage
plate-bande: *nf.* border, flower-bed
plate-forme: *nf.* platform
platine: *nf.* platinum
platitude: *nf.* platitude; flatness, dullness
platonique: *adj.* platonic
plâtre: *nm.* plaster
plâtrer: *vt.* to plaster; to set in plaster
plâtrier: *nm.* plasterer
plausible: *adj.* plausible
plébiscite: *nm.* plebiscite
plébisciter: *vt.* to elect by plebiscite
plein: *adj.* full; entire, whole; busy
plein temps (à): full time
plénitude: *nf.* plenitude, fullness
pléonasme: *nm.* pleonasm
pleur: *nm.* tear, sob
pleurer: *vi.* to cry, weep
pleurésie: *nf.* pleurisy
pleuvoir: *vi.* to rain; to shower down, rain down
plexus: *nm.* plexus
pli: *nm.* fold; crease; wrinkle; envelope
pliant: *adj.* collapsible, folding
plier: *vt.* to fold; to bend; *vi.* to bend; to yield
plinthe: *nf.* plinth; skirting board
plissement: *nm.* creasing, folding; puckering
plisser: *vt.* to pleat, fold; to pucker; *vi.* to become creased
pliure: *nf.* fold; bend
plomb: *nm.* lead; sinker; fuse
plombage: *nm.* weighting; leading; filling
plomber: *vt.* to weight; to fill
plomberie: *nf.* plumbing
plombier: *nm.* plumber

plongée: *nf.* diving, dive
plongeoir: *nm.* diving board
plongeon: *nm.* dive
plonger: *vi.* to dive; to plunge, dip sharply
plongeur: *nm.* diver; washer-up
ployer: *vi.* to bend, to sag
pluie: *nf.* rain; shower
plumage: *nm.* plumage, feathers
plume: *nf.* feather
plumeau: *nm.* feather duster
plumer: *vt.* to pluck
plupart: *nf.* most, most part, majority
pluriel: *nm.* plural; *adj.* plural
plus: *adv.* more, most
plusieurs: *adj.* several
plus-que-parfait: *nm.* pluperfect
plus-value: *nf.* appreciation; increase in value
plutonium: *nm.* plutonium
plutôt: *adv.* rather, quite, fairly; sooner
pluvieux: *adj.* rainy, wet
pneu: *nm.* tyre
pneumatique: *adj.* pneumatic
pneumonie: *nf.* pneumonia
poche: *nf.* pocket; pouch; bag
pocher: *vt.* to poach
pochette: *nf.* pocket handkerchief
pochoir: *nm.* stencil
podium: *nm.* podium
poêle: *nm.* stove; *f.* frying pan
poème: *nm.* poem
poésie: *nf.* poetry
poète: *nm.* poet
poétique: *adj.* poetic
poids: *nm.* weight, influence
poignant: *adj.* poignant
poignard: *nm.* dagger
poignarder: *vt.* to stab
poigne: *nf.* grip; hand
poignée: *nf.* handful;
- de mains = handshake
poignet: *nm.* wrist; cuff

poil: *nm.* hair; coat; bristle
poilu: *adj.* hairy
poinçon: *nm.* hallmark, style; awl
poinçonner: *vt.* to stamp; to hallmark
poindre: *vi.* to break, dawn
poing: *nm.* fist; coup de - = punch
point: *nm.* point, spot; stage; full stop
point d'énergie zéro: zero-point
energy
point de vente: retail outlet
pointillé: *nm.* stipple engraving;
dotted line
pointilleux: *adj.* particular, fastidious
pointu: *adj.* pointed, sharp; subtle
pointure: *nf.* size, number
poire: *nf.* pear
poireau: *nm.* leek
poirier: *nm.* pear tree
pois: *nm.* pea
poison: *nm.* poison
poisseux: *adj.* sticky
poisson: *nm.* fish
poissonnerie: *nf.* fish shop
poitrail: *nm.* breast, chest
poitrine: *nf.* chest, breast; bosom
poivre: *nm.* pepper
poivrer: *vt.* to pepper, put pepper in
poivrière: *nf.* pepperpot
poivron: *nm.* green pepper, capsicum
polaire: *adj.* polar
polarisabilité: *nf.* polarisability
polariser: *vt.* to polarise; to attract
polarité: *nf.* polarity
pole: *nm.* pole; centre
polémique: *nf.* controversy, polemic;
adj. controversial, polemic
poli: *adj.* polite; polished, smooth
police: *nf.* police; policing;
regulations
police d'assurance: insurance policy
polichinelle: *nm.* buffoon
policier: *nm.* policeman
poliomyélite: *nf.* poliomyelitis
polir: *vt.* to polish; to refine

politesse: *nf.* politeness, courtesy
politicien: *nm.* politician
politique: *nf.* politics; policy
politique de vente: sales policy
politiser: *vt.* to politicise; to make a
political issue of
pollaroïd: *nm.* polaroid; *adj.* polaroid
pollen: *nm.* pollen
polluant: *adj.* polluting; *nm.* pollutant
polluer: *vt.* to pollute
pollution: *nf.* pollution
polo: *nm.* polo
poltron: *nm.* coward; adj cowardly,
craven
polyamide: *nm.* polyamide
polycopier: *vt.* to duplicate, stencil
polyester: *nm.* polyester
polygame: *nm.* polygamist
polygamie: *nf.* polygamy
polyglotte: *adj.* polyglot; *nmf.*
polyglot
polygone: *nm.* polygon
polymère: *nm.* polymer
polymérisation ionique: ionic
polymerization
polymorphisme: *nm.* polymorphism
polyvalent: *adj.* polyvalent; varied;
versatile
pommade: *nf.* ointment
pomme: *nf.* apple
pomme de terre: *nf.* potato
pommette: *nf.* cheekbone
pommier: *nm.* apple tree
pompe: *nf.* pump
pomper: *vt.* to pump
pompeux: *adj.* pompous; pretentious
pompier: *nm.* fireman
pompiste: *nmf.* pump attendant
poncer: *vt.* to sand down, rub down
ponction: *nf.* puncture
ponctualité: *nf.* punctuality
ponctuation: *nf.* punctuation
ponctuel: *adj.* punctual
ponctuer: *vt.* to punctuate; to phrase

pondéré: *adj.* weighted; levelheaded
pondre: *vt.* to lay; to produce
poney: *nm.* pony
pont: *nm.* bridge; deck; axle
ponte: *nf.* laying; clutch
pontifical: *adj.* pontifical
ponton: *nm.* pontoon; landing stage
populaire: *adj.* popular; working class; vernacular
populariser: *vt.* to popularise
popularité: *nf.* popularity
population: *nf.* population
porc: *nm.* pig; pork
porcelaine: *nf.* porcelain, china
porc-épic: *nm.* porcupine
porche: *nm.* porch
porcherie: *nf.* pigsty
pore: *nm.* pore
poreux: *adj.* porous
pornographique: *adj.* pornographic
port: *nm.* port, harbour; carrying, wearing
port d'embarquement: port of loading
portail: *nm.* portal, gate
portatif: *adj.* portable
porte: *nf.* door; gate; threshold
porte-avions: *nm.* invar aircraft carrier
porte-bonheur: *nm.* invar lucky charm
porte-documents: *nm.* invar brief-case
portée: *nf.* reach, range; capacity; impact, significance
portefeuille: *nm.* wallet; portfolio
porte-jarretelles: *nm.* invar suspender belt
portemanteau: *nm.* coat hanger; hat stand
porte-parole: *nm.* invar spokesperson
porte-plume: *nm.* invar penholder
porter: *vt.* to carry; to take; to wear; to hold, keep

porteur: *nm.* porter; carrier; adj booster; strong, buoyant
porteur de chaîne: chain carrier
portier: *nm.* commissionaire
portière: *nf.* door
portillon: *nm.* gate, barrier
portion: *nf.* portion, share
portique: *nm.* portico
portrait: *nm.* portrait
portraitiste: *nmf.* portraitist
pose: *nf.* pose, posture; laying, fitting, setting
poser: *vt.* to put; to install; to set out; to ask
positif: *adj.* positive, definite
position: *nf.* position; situation; state; stance
positionner: *vt.* to position, locate
positivement: *adv.* positively
posologie: *nf.* posology
posséder: *vt.* to possess, have; to know inside out
possesseur: *nm.* possessor, owner
possessif: *adj.* possessive
possession: *nf.* possession, ownership
possibilité: *nf.* possibility; potential
possible: *adj.* possible, feasible
post: *adj.* postal, mail
poste: *nf.* post office, post; m post, position; station; job
poster: *vt.* to post, mail; to station
postérieur: *adj.* later, subsequent; back, posterior
postérité: *nf.* posterity; descendants
posthume: *adj.* posthumous
postiche: *adj.* false; postiche; pretended
postier: *nm.* post office worker
postillon: *nm.* postilion
postulant: *nm.* applicant
postuler: *vt.* to apply for; to postulate
posture: *nf.* posture, position
pot: *nm.* jar; pot; can
potable: *adj.* drinkable; passable

potage: *nm.* soup
potager: *nm.* kitchen garden; *adj.* vegetable, edible
potassium: *nm.* potassium
pot-au-feu: *nm.* invar stew
pot-de-vin: *nm.* bribe
poteau: *nm.* post, stake
potée: *nf.* hotpot
potelé: *adj.* plump, chubby
potentiel: *adj.* potential
potentiel d'ionisation: ionization potential
poterie: *nf.* pottery, piece of pottery
potiche: *nf.* vase, mere, puppet
potier: *nm.* potter
potion: *nf.* potion
potiron: *nm.* pumpkin
pou: *nm.* louse
poubelle: *nf.* dustbin
pouce: *nm.* thumb; big toe; inch
poudre: *nf.* powder, dust
poudrer: *vt.* to powder
poudrière: *nf.* powder magazine
poulailler: *nm.* henhouse
poulain: *nm.* foal
poule: *nf.* hen, fowl
poulet: *nm.* chicken
poulie: *nf.* pulley
poulpe: *nm.* octopus
pouls: *nm.* pulse
poumon: *nm.* lung
pounceau: *nm.* pig, swine
poupe: *nf.* stern
poupée: *nf.* doll
poupon: *nm.* baby
pouponnière: *nf.* day nursery, crèche
pour: *prép.* for; to; in favour of; on account of; in order
pourboire: *nm.* tip
pourcentage: *nm.* percentage
pourchasser: *vt.* to pursue; to harry
pourparlers: *nmpl.* talks, negotiations
pourpre: *adj.* crimson; *nm.* crimson

pourquoi: *adv.* why; - pas? = why not?
pourri: *adj.* rotten, decayed; corrupt
pourrir: *vi.* to rot, go rotten; to deteriorate
pourriture: *nf.* rot, rottenness
poursuite: *nf.* pursuit; prosecution
poursuivant: *nm.* pursuer
poursuivi, être: to be prosecuted
poursuivre: *vt.* to pursue; to seek; to prosecute
pourtant: *adv.* however, yet, nevertheless
pourtour: *nm.* circumference, perimeter
pourvoir: *vt.* to provide, equip
pourvu: *conj.* que provided that
pousse: *nf.* shoot; sprouting
poussée: *nf.* pressure, pushing; thrust; upsurge
pousser: *vt.* to push; to drive; to incite; *vi.* to push; to grow, expand
poussette: *nf.* pushchair
poussière: *nf.* dust
poussiéreux: *adj.* dusty
poussin: *nm.* chick; junior
poutre: *nf.* beam
pouvoir: *vi.* can, be able; may, be allowed
pouvoir: *nm.* power, ability; authority; proxy
pragmatique: *adj.* pragmatic
prairie: *nf.* meadow, prairie
praline: *nf.* sugared almond
praticable: *adj.* practicable; passable
pratiquant: *nm.* churchgoer; adj practising
pratique: *nf.* practice; exercise; observance; *adj.* practical
pratiquer: *vt.* to practise, exercise; to carry out
pré: *nm.* meadow
préalable: *adj.* preliminary; previous
préambule: *nm.* preamble, prelude

préau: *nm.* covered playground; inner yard

préavis: *nm.* notice, advance warning

précaire: *adj.* precarious

précarité: *nf.* precariousness

précaution: *nf.* precaution; care

précautionneux: *adj.* cautious, careful

précédent: *adj.* previous, preceding

précéder: *vt.* to precede, go before

précepte: *nm.* precept

prêcher: *vt.* to preach; *vi.* to preach, sermonise

prêcheur: *nm.* preacher

précieux: *adj.* precious; invaluable

précipice: *nm.* precipice; abyss

précipitamment: *adv.* hurriedly, hastily

précipitation: *nf.* haste, violent hurry

précipiter: *vt.* to throw, push down; to hasten, precipitate

précis: *adj.* precise, exact

préciser: *vt.* to specify; to clarify

précision: *nf.* precision, preciseness

précoce: *adj.* precocious, premature

préconçu: *adj.* preconceived

préconiser: *vt.* to recommend; to advocate

précurseur: *nm.* forerunner, precursor; *adj.* precursory, preceding

prédateur: *nm.* predator

prédécesseur: *nm.* predecessor

prédestiné: *adj.* predestined, fated

prédiction: *nf.* prediction

prédire: *vt.* to predict, foretell

prédisposition: *nf.* predisposition

prédominance: *nf.* predominance

prédominant: *adj.* predominant

prédominer: *vi.* to predominate

préfabriqué: *adj.* prefabricated

préface: *nf.* preface, prelude

préfecture: *nf.* prefecture

préférable: *adj.* preferable; better

préféré: *nm.* favourite; adj favourite, preferred

préférence: *nf.* preference

préférer: *vt.* to prefer

préfet: *nm.* prefect

préfigurer: *vt.* to prefigure

préhistoire: *nf.* prehistory

préhistorique: *adj.* prehistoric

préjudice: *nm.* loss; harm; wrong; damage

préjudiciable: *adj.* prejudicial, detrimental

préjudicier: *vt.* to be prejudicial

préjugé: *nm.* prejudice

prélasser (se): *vr.* to sprawl, lounge

prélèvement: *nm.* taking; levying; imposition

prélèvement automatique: automatic debiting

prélever: *vt.* to take; to levy; to deduct

prélever des taxes: to levy taxes

préliminaire: *nm.* preliminary; adj preliminary

prélude: *nm.* prelude; warm-up

prématuré: *adj.* premature; untimely

préméditation: *nf.* premeditation

prémédité: *adj.* premeditated

premier: *nm.* first, first floor

première: *nf.* première

premièrement: *adv.* firstly, in first place

prémonition: *nf.* premonition

prémonitoire: *adj.* premonitory

prénatal: *adj.* prenatal

prendre: *vt.* to take; to pick up; to catch

prendre sa retraite: to retire

prendre une décision: to make a decision

prénom: *nm.* first name, forename

préoccuper: *vt.* to worry; to preoccupy

préparatif: *nm.* preparation

préparation: *nf.* preparation; making

up; training
préparatoire: *adj.* preparatory
préparer: *vt.* to prepare, get ready; to train
prépondérant: *adj.* preponderant, dominating
préposition: *nf.* preposition
prérogative: *nf.* prerogative
près: *adv.* near, close; nearly, almost
présage: *nm.* omen; harbinger
presbytère: *nm.* presbytery
presbytie: *nf.* long-sightedness, presbyopia
prescrire: *vt.* to prescribe; to stipulate
prese-citron: *nm.* lemon squeezer
présélection: *nf.* preselection
présence: *nf.* presence
présent: *nm.* present, gift
présentable: *adj.* presentable
présentateur: *nm.* host, compère; presenter
présentation: *nf.* presentation; introduction
présenter: *vt.* to introduce; to present; to explain
présenter, exposer (un produit): to display
présentoir: *nm.* display shelf
préservatif: *nm.* condom
préserver: *vt.* to preserve; to protect
présidence: *nf.* presidency; chairmanship
président: *nm.* president
présidentiel: *adj.* presidential
présider: *vt.* to preside, chair; to direct
présider une réunion: to chair a meeting
présomption: *nf.* presumption, assumption
présomptueux: *adj.* presumptuous
presque: ado almost, nearly; hardly, scarcely
presqu'île: *nf.* peninsula

pressant: *adj.* urgent, pressing
presse: *nf.* press, newspapers; throng
pressé: *adj.* hurried, urgent
pressentiment: *nm.* presentiment, foreboding, premonition
pressentir: *vt.* to have a presentiment of
presse-papiers: *nm.* invar paperweight
presser: *vt.* to press; to squeeze; to hurry up
pression: *nf.* pressure
pression atmosphérique: atmospheric pressure
pression osmotique: osmotic pressure
pressoir: *nm.* press (wine, cider)
prestation: *nf.* benefit; service; payment; allowance
prestidigitateur: *nm.* conjurer; magician
prestigieux: *adj.* prestigious
présumer: *vt.* to presume, assume
prêt: *nm.* loan; *adj.* ready; prepared
prêt sans garantie: an unsecured loan
prêt sur titres: a secured loan
prétendant: *nm.* candidate
prétendre: *vt.* to claim, maintain; to want; to intend, mean
prétendu: *adj.* so-called, supposed
prétentieux: *adj.* pretentious
prétention: *nf.* pretension, claim; pretentiousness
prêter: *vt.* to lend; to attribute; to give
prêter de l'argent: to lend money
prêtre: *nm.* priest
preuve: *nf.* proof, evidence
prévaloir: *vi.* to prevail
prévenant: *adj.* considerate, thoughtful
prévenir: *vt.* to prevent; to warn, inform; to anticipate

préventif: *adj.* preventive
prévention: *nf.* prevention
prévisible: *adj.* foreseeable
prévision: *nf.* prediction; forecast
prévoir: *vt.* to anticipate; to plan; to provide for
prévoyance: *nf.* foresight, forethought
prévoyant: *adj.* provident
prévu: *adj.* provided for
prier: *vi.* to pray
prière: *nf.* prayer; entreaty
primaire: *adj.* primary; elementary
primauté: *nf.* primacy
prime: *nf.* (insurance) premium; bonus; subsidy; free gift
primer: *vi.* to dominate; to take first place; vt to outdo, prevail
primevère: *nf.* primrose
primitif: *adj.* primitive
primordial: *adj.* primordial, essential
prince: *nm.* prince
princesse: *nf.* princess
principe: *nm.* principle
principe d'action de masse: mass action law
printanier: *adj.* spring
printemps: *nm.* spring
prioritaire: *adj.* having priority, priority
priorité: *nf.* priority
pris: *adj.* taken; busy, engaged
prise: *nf.* hold, grip; catch; plug; dose
prisme: *nm.* prism
prison: *nf.* prison; jail
prisonnier: *nm.* prisoner
privation: *nf.* deprivation; forfeiture
privatiser: *vt.* to privatise
privé: *adj.* private; unofficial; independent
priver: *vt.* to deprive
privilege: *nf.* privilege
privilégier: *vt.* to favour
prix: *nm.* price, cost; prize

prix de revient: cost price
prix de soldes: bargain prices
prix imbattables: unbeatable prices
probabilité: *nf.* probability, likelihood
probable: *adj.* probable, likely; -ment adv. = probably
problématique: *adj.* problematical
problème: *nm.* problem, issue
procédé: *nm.* process; behaviour
procéder: *vi.* to proceed
procédure: *nf.* procedure; proceedings
procès: *nm.* proceedings; lawsuit, trial
procession: *nf.* procession
processus: *nm.* process; progress
procès-verbal: *nm.* minutes; report
prochain: *adj.* next; imminent
proche: *adj.* nearby; close, imminent
proclamation: *nf.* proclamation
proclamer: *vt.* to proclaim, declare
procuration: *nf.* proxy, power of attorney
procurer: *vt.* to procure, provide
procureur: *nm.* prosecutor
prodige: *nm.* marvel, wonder
prodigieusement: *adv.* prodigiously, incredibly
prodigieux: *adj.* prodigious
prodiguer: *vt.* to be lavish
producteur: *nm.* producer
productif: *adj.* productive
production: *nf.* production; generation; output
production en série: mass production
productivité: *nf.* productivity
produire: *vt.* to produce; to grow; to generate
produit: *nm.* product; goods; yield, profit
produits alimentaires: foodstuffs
proéminent: *adj.* prominent

profane: *adj.* secular, profane
profaner: *vt.* to profane; to defile
proférer: *vt.* to utter, pronounce
professeur: *nm.* teacher, professor
profession: *nf.* profession; occupation, trade
professionnel: *nm.* professional; skilled worker
profil: *nm.* profile, outline
profiler: *vt.* to profile; to streamline
profit: *nm.* profit; advantage, benefit
profitable: *adj.* profitable
profiter: *vi.* to profit; to thrive
profiteur: *nm.* profiteer
profond: *adj.* deep, profound; heavy
profondeur: *nf.* depth; profundity
profusion: *nf.* profusion, wealth
programme: *nm.* program; syllabus; schedule
programmer: *vt.* to program; to schedule
progrès: *nm.* progress; improvement; advance
progresser: *vi.* to progress; to advance
progression: *nf.* progress; progression, spread
progressivement: *adv.* progressively
prohiber: *vt.* to prohibit, ban
proie: *nf.* prey, victim
projecteur: *nm.* projector; spotlight, floodlight
projectile: *nm.* projectile; missile
projection: *nf.* projection, casting; showing
projet: *nm.* plan; draft
projeter: *vt.* to plan; to throw out; to cast, project
prolétaire: *nmf.* proletarian
prolétariat: *nm.* proletariat
prolifération: *nf.* proliferation
proliférer: *vi.* to proliferate
prologue: *nm.* prologue
prolongation: *nf.* prolongation, extension
prolongement: *nm.* continuation, extension
prolonger: *vt.* to prolong, extend
promenade: *nf.* walk, stroll; drive, spin
promener: *vt.* to take out for a walk
promeneur: *nm.* walker
promesse: *nf.* promise
prometteur: *adj.* promising
promettre: *vt.* to promise
promontoire: *nm.* promontory, headland
promoteur: *nm.* promoter, instigator
promotion: *nf.* promotion; advancement
promouvoir: *vt.* to promote, up-grade
prompt: *adj.* prompt; swift; ready; -ement *adv.* = promptly; swiftly
promptitude: *nf.* promptness; swiftness
promulgation: *nf.* promulgation
promulguer: *vt.* to promulgate
prôner: *vt.* to advocate
pronom: *nm.* pronoun
prononcer: *vt.* to pronounce, utter
prononciation: *nf.* pronunciation
pronostiquer: *vt.* to forecast, prognosticate
propagande: *nf.* propaganda
propagation: *nf.* propagation; spreading
propager: *vt.* to propagate, spread
propane: *nm.* propane
prophète: *nm.* prophet
prophétie: *nf.* prophecy
prophétique: *adj.* prophetic
prophétiser: *vt.* to prophesy
propice: *adj.* propitious, favourable
proportion: *nf.* proportion, ratio
proportionné: *adj.* proportional; proportionate
proportionnel: *adj.* proportional
propos: *nm.* talk, remarks; intention

proposer: *vt.* to propose, suggest
proposition: *nf.* proposition, suggestion
propre: *adj.* clean, neat; honest; own; peculiar; suitable
propreté: *nf.* cleanliness; tidiness
propriétaire: *nmf.* owner; landlord
propriété: *nf.* ownership, property; appropriateness, suitability
propulser: *vt.* to propel, power
propulsion: *nf.* propulsion
prorogation: *nf.* prorogation; deferment; extension
proroger: *vt.* to prorogue; to defer; to extend
prosaïque: *adj.* mundane, prosaic
proscrire: *vt.* to proscribe; to prohibit
prose: *nf.* prose
prospecter: *vt.* to prospect; to canvass
prospecteur: *nm.* prospector
prospection: *nf.* prospecting; canvassing
prospectus: *nm.* leaflet; prospectus
prospère: *adj.* prosperous, flourishing
prospérer: *vi.* to prosper, flourish
prospérité: *nf.* prosperity
prostate: *nf.* prostate
prosterner (se): *vr.* to prostrate
prostituée: *nf.* prostitute
prostitution: *nf.* prostitution
prostré: *adj.* prostrate, prostrated
protagoniste: *nm.* protagonist
protecteur: *nm.* protector
protection: *nf.* protection; patronage
protectionnisme: *nm.* protectionism
protégé: *nm.* favourite, protegé; *adj.* protected, sheltered
protéger: *vt.* to protect; to patronise
protéine: *nf.* protein
protestant: *nm.* Protestant; *adj.* Protestant
protestantisme: *nm.* Protestant

protestation: *nf.* protest, protestation
protester: *vi.* to protest; to affirm
protêt: *nm.* protest
prothèse: *nf.* prosthesis; prosthetics
protocole: *nm.* protocol; etiquette
prototype: *nm.* prototype
protubérance: *nf.* protuberance, bulge
proue: *nf.* prow; bows
prouesse: *nf.* prowess
prouver: *vt.* to prove; to demonstrate
provenir: *vi.* to come from; to be due to
proverbe: *nm.* proverb
proverbial: *adj.* proverbial
providence: *nf.* providence
providentiel: *adj.* providential
province: *nf.* province
provincial: *nm.* provincial; *adj.* provincial
provision: *nf.* provision; supply, stock
provisoire: *adj.* provisional, temporary
provocant: *adj.* provocative
provocation: *nf.* provocation
provoquer: *vt.* to provoke; to cause
proximité: *nf.* proximity, closeness; imminence
prudemment: *adv.* prudently, carefully
prudence: *nf.* prudence, care
prudent: *adj.* prudent, careful
prune: *nf.* plum
prune au: *nm.* prune
prunelle: *nf.* sloe; pupil, eye
prunier: *nm.* plum tree
psaume: *nm.* psalm
pseudonyme: *nm.* pseudonym; pen name; alias
psoriasis: *nm.* psoriasis
psychanalyse: *nf.* psychoanalysis
psychanalyste: mf psychoanalyst
psychanlyser: *vt.* to psychoanalyse

psychédélique: *adj.* psychedelic
psychiâtre: mf psychiatrist
psychiatrie: *nf.* psychiatry
psychiatrique: *adj.* psychiatric
psychique: *adj.* psychic, mental
psychisme: *nm.* psyche, mind
psychologie: *nf.* psychology
psychologique: *adj.* psychological
psychologue: mf psychologist; adj
psychological
psychopathe: *nmf.* psychopath;
mentally ill person
psychose: *nf.* psychosis; obsessive
fear
psychosomatique: *adj.*
psychosomatic
psychothérapie: *nf.* psychotherapy
pub: *nm.* pub
puberté: *nf.* puberty
pubis: *nm.* pubis
public: *adj.* public; *nm.* public,
audience; public sector
publication: *nf.* publication,
publishing
publicité: *nf.* publicity
publicité mensongère: deceptive
advertising
publier: *vt.* to publish; to make
public
publiquement: *adv.* publicly
puce: *nf.* flea
puceron: *nm.* aphid, greenfly
pudeur: *nf.* modesty, decency
pudique: *adj.* modest; chaste
puer: *vi.* to stink
puéricultrice: *nf.* paediatric nurse
puéril: *adj.* puerile, childish
puérilité: *nf.* puerility, childishness
puis: *adv.* then, next
puiser: *vt.* to draw from, extract
puisque: *conj.* since; as, seeing that
puissance: *nf.* power, strength;
output; force
puissant: *adj.* powerful; potent

puits: *nm.* well; shaft
pull: *nm.* sweater
pull-over: *nm.* pullover, sweater
pulluler: *vi.* to swarm, pullulate
pulmonaire: *adj.* pulmonary, lung
pulpe: *nf.* pulp
pulsation: *nf.* beat; beating; pulsation
pulsion: *nf.* drive, urge
pulvériser: *vt.* to pulverise; to
powder
puma: *nm.* puma
punaise: *nf.* bug; drawing pin
punir: *vt.* to punish
punition: *nf.* punishment
pupille: *nf.* pupil; ward
pupitre: *nm.* desk; console; lectern
pur: *adj.* pure; neat; clear
purée: *nf.* mashed potatoes; purée
pureté: *nf.* purity, pureness
purge: *nf.* purge; purgative; draining
purger: *vt.* to purge; to drain
purifier: *vt.* to purify, cleanse
purin: *nm.* liquid manure, slurry
puritain: *nf.* puritan; *adj.* puritan
puritanisme: *nm.* puritanism
purulent: *adj.* purulent
pus: *nm.* pus
putréfaction: *nf.* putrefaction
putréfier: *vt.* to putrefy, rot
pyramide: *nf.* pyramid
pyrolyse: pyrolysis
pyromane: *nmf.* pyromaniac; arsonist
python: *nm.* python

Q

quadragénaire: *adj.* mf forty-year-old
quadrangle: *nm.* quadrangle
quadrature: *nf.* quadrature
quadriceps: *nmpl.* quadriceps
quadrilatère: *nm.* quadrilateral
quadrillage: *nm.* covering, control; check pattern
quadriller: *vt.* to mark out in squares; to cover, to control
quadrupède: *nm.* quadruped
quadruple: *adj.* quadruple
quai: *nm.* quay, wharf; platform
qualificatif: *adj.* qualifying
qualification: *nf.* qualification
qualifier: *vt.* to describe; to qualify
qualitatif: *adj.* qualitative
qualitativement: *adv.* qualitatively
qualité: *nf.* quality; skill; position
quand: *conj.* when, whenever, while
quantifier: *vt.* to quantify
quantitatif: *adj.* quantitative
quantitativement: *adv.* quantitatively
quantité: *nf.* quantity, amount
quantum pluriel: quantum
quarantaine: *nf.* about forty
quarante: *adj.* forty
quarantième: *adj.* fortieth
quart: *nm.* quarter; beaker; watch
quartette: *nm.* quartet
quartier: *nm.* district, neighbourhood; quarters; quarter
quartz: *nm.* quartz
quasi: *adv.* almost, nearly
quasiment: *adv.* almost, nearly
quaternaire: *adj.* quaternary; *nm.* Quaternary
quatorze: *adj.* fourteen
quatorzième: *adj.* fourteenth
quatre: *adj.* four
quatre-vingt-dix: *adj.* ninety
quatre-vingtième: *adj.* eightieth
quatre-vingts: *adj.* eighty
quatrième: *adj.* fourth
que: *conj.* that; than; *pron.* that; whom; what; which
quel, quelle: *adj.* who, what, which
quelconque: *adj.* some, any; least, slight; poor, indifferent
quelque chose: something
quelquefois: *adv.* sometimes
quémander: *vt.* to beg for
querelle: *nf.* quarrel; row; debate
quereller: *vr.* to quarrel, squabble
question: *nf.* question; matter
questionnaire: *nm.* questionnaire
questionner: *vt.* to question
quête: *nm.* quest, search; collection
quêter: *vi.* to seek; to collect money
queue: *nf.* tail; stalk; queue
qui: *pron.* who, whom; which
quiche: *nf.* quiche
quiconque: *pron.* whoever, whosoever
quiétude: *nf.* quiet; peace; tranquillity
quille: *nf.* skittle; keel
quincaillerie: *nf.* hardware, ironmongery
quinine: *nf.* quinine
quinquagénaire: *adj.* fifty-year-old
quinquennal: *adj.* five-year, quinquennial
quinte: *nf.* fifth; coughing fit
quintette: *nm.* quintet
quintuple: *adj.* quintuple; *nm.* quintuple
quintupler: *vt.* to multiply by five
quintuplés: *nmpl.* quintuplets
quinzaine: *nf.* about fifteen; fortnight
quinze: *adj.* fifteen
quinzième: *adj.* fifteenth
quiproquo: *nm.* mistake; misunderstanding
quittance: *nf.* receipt; bill

quitte: *adj.* even, quits; être envers to be quits, all square with
quitter: *vt.* to leave; to give up; se *vr.* to part company, separate
quoi: pron. what; - que = whatever
quoique: *conj.* although, though
quolibet: *nm.* gibe, jeer
quote-part: *nf.* share
quotidien: *adj.* daily, everyday
quotient: *nm.* quotient; quota

R

rabâcher: *vi.* to harp on, keep on; *vt.* to rehearse, harp on
rabais: *nm.* reduction, discount
rabais: *nm.* rebate
rabaisser: *vt.* to humble, disparage; to reduce
rabattre: *vt.* to close; to pull down; to reduce
rabbin: *nm.* rabbi
rabot: *nm.* plane
raboter: *vt.* to plane; to scrape
rabougri: *adj.* stunted, puny
racaille: *nf.* rabble, scum
raccommodage: *nm.* mending, repairing
raccommoder: *vt.* to mend, to repair
raccompagner: *vt.* to see back to; to accompany home
raccord: *nm.* join; link; pointing
raccordement: *nm.* linking; joining; connecting
raccorder: *vt.* to link up, join up
raccourci: *nm.* shortcut
raccourcir: *vt.* to shorten, curtail
raccrocher: *vt.* to ring off; to hang up; to grab
race: *nf.* race; stock; breed
rachat: *nm.* repurchase, purchase
racheter: *vt.* to repurchase; to redeem; to ransom
rachitique: *adj.* rachitic; scrawny
racial: *adj.* racial
racine: *nf.* root
racisme: *nm.* racism
raciste: *nmf.* racist; *adj.* racist
racler: *vt.* to scrape; to rake
racoler: *vt.* to accost; to solicit
raconter: *vt.* to tell, recount
radar: *nm.* radar
rade: *nf.* harbour, roads
radiateur: *nm.* radiator; heater
radiation: *nf.* radiation
radical: *adj.* radical

radical libre: free radical
radieux: *adj.* radiant, dazzling
radin: *nm.* skinflint; *adj.* mean, stingy
radio: *nf.* radio; X-ray
radioactif: *adj.* radioactive
radioactivité: *nf.* radioactivity
radiodiffuser: *vt.* to broadcast
radiodiffusion: *nf.* broadcasting
radiographie: *nf.* radiography
radiologie: *nf.* radiology
radiologue: *nmf.* radiologist
radiolyse: *nf.* radiolysis
radiophonique: *adj.* radio
radioscopie: *nf.* radioscopy
radio-taxi: *nm.* radio taxi
radis: *nm.* radish
radium: *nm.* radium
radoter: *vi.* to ramble; to dote
radoucir: *vt.* to soften
rafale: *nf.* gust, blast; flurry
raffermir: *vt.* to harden; to strengthen
raffinage: *nm.* refining
raffiné: *adj.* refined, sophisticated
raffinement: *nm.* refinement, sophistication
raffiner: *vt.* to refine
raffoler: *vi.* to be crazy about
rafle: *nf.* raid, round-up
rafraîchir: *vt.* to cool, freshen, chill
rafraîchissant: *adj.* refreshing, cooling
rafraîchissement: *nm.* cooling; cold drink
rage: *nf.* rage, fury; mania; rabies
rageur: *adj.* quick-tempered; bad-tempered
ragot: *nm.* malicious gossip
ragoût: *nm.* ragout; stew
raid: *nm.* raid; trek
raide: *adj.* stiff; steep; rough
raideur: *nf.* stiffness; steepness; roughness
raidir: *vt.* to stiffen; to tighten; to harden

raie: *nf.* line; furrow; scratch
raifort: *nm.* horseradish
rail: *nm.* rail; railway
railler: *vt.* to scoff at, mock
raillerie: *nf.* mockery, scoffing
railleur: *adj.* mocking, scoffing
rainette: *nf.* tree frog
raisin: *nm.* grape
raison: *nf.* reason; motive; sense; ground; ratio
raisonnable: *adj.* reasonable, sensible
raisonnement: *nm.* reasoning; argument
raisonner: *vi.* to reason; to argue
rajeunir: *vi.* to feel younger; to be modernised; *vt.* to rejuvenate
rajouter: *vt.* to put in; to add; to exaggerate
rajuster: *vt.* to readjust, rearrange; to tidy up
râle: *nm.* groan; death rattle
ralenti: *adj.* slow; slackened
ralentir: *vi.* to slow down, let up; *vt.* to slow down, check
ralentissement: *nm.* slowing down; slowing up
râler: *vi.* to groan, moan
ralliement: *nm.* rallying, winning over; uniting
rallier: *vt.* to rally; to win over
rallonge: *nf.* extension, lengthening; extension lead
rallumer: *vt.* to relight; to switch on again; to revive
ramadan: *nm.* Ramadan
ramage: *nm.* song; foliage
ramassage: *nm.* collection; gathering
ramasser: *vt.* to pick up; to collect, gather
rambarde: *nf.* guardrail
rame: *nf.* oar; underground train; stake

rameau: *nm.* branch; ramification
ramener: *vt.* to bring back, restore
ramer: *vi.* to row
rameur: *nm.* rower
ramification: *nf.* ramification, branching
ramifier: *vr.* to ramify; to branch out
ramollir: *vt.* to soften; to weaken
ramoner: *vt.* to sweep
ramoneur: *nm.* chimney sweep
rampant: *adj.* crawling, creeping
rampe: *nf.* ramp, slope; gradient
ramper: *vi.* to crawl, slither
rance: *adj.* rancid, rank
rancoeur: *nf.* rancour, resentment
rançon: *nf.* ransom
rancune: *nf.* grudge, resentment
rancunier: *adj.* rancorous, spiteful
randonnée: *nf.* drive; ride; ramble
randonneur: *nm.* hiker, rambler
rang: *nm.* row, line; rank; class
rangée: *nf.* row, range, tier
rangement: *nm.* arranging, putting in order
ranger: *vt.* to arrange, array; to put in order
ranimer: *vt.* to reanimate, revive; to rekindle
rapace: *nm.* bird of prey
rapatrié, e: *nmf.* repatriate; *adj.* repatriated
rapatriement: *nm.* repatriation
rapatrier: *vt.* to repatriate
râpe: *nf.* rasp, rough file
râper: *vt.* to grate; to rasp
râpeux: *adj.* rough
rapide: *adj.* rapid, quick; steep
rapidité: *nf.* rapidity, quickness
rapiécer: *vt.* to patch up
rappel: *nm.* recall; reminder
rappeler: *vt.* to recall; to remind
rapport: *nm.* report; relation; reference; profit
rapporter: *vt.* to report; to bring

back; to yield
rapporteur: *nm.* reporter; tell-tale; (math) protractor
rapprochement: *nm.* drawing closer; reconciliation
rapprocher: *vt.* to bring nearer; to reconcile
rapt: *nm.* abduction
raquette: *nf.* racket
rare: *adj.* rare; few, odd; exceptional
raréfier (se): *vr.* to rarefy; become scarce
rareté: *nf.* rarity; scarcity; infrequency
rarissime: *adj.* extremely rare
ras: *adj.* close-shaven, shorn
rasage: *nm.* shaving; shearing
raser: *vt.* to shave off; to scrape; to raze
rasoir: *nm.* razor
rassasier: *vt.* to fill sb up
rassemblement: *nm.* assembling, mustering; crowd; political group
rassembler: *vt.* to rally, gather together
rasseoir (se): *vr.* to sit down again
rasséréner: *vt.* to clear up, restore serenity to
rassis: *adj.* settled; calm; stale
rassurant: *adj.* reassuring, comforting
rassurer: *vt.* to reassure; to comfort
rat: *nm.* rat
ratatiner: *vt.* to shrivel; to wrinkle
ratatouille: *nf.* ratatouille
rate: *nf.* spleen
raté: *nm.* failure
râteau: *nm.* rake
râtelier: *nm.* rack; denture
rater: *vt.* to miss; to spoil; to fail; *vi.* to misfire; to miss
ratification: *nf.* ratification
ratifier: *vt.* to ratify, confirm
ration: *nf.* ration, allowance

rationnel: *adj.* rational
rationnement: *nm.* rationing
rationner: *vt.* to ration, put on rations
ratisser: *vt.* to rake; to comb
rattacher: *vt.* to refasten; to attach; to link
rattraper: *vt.* to catch again, retake; to recover
rature: *nf.* crossing-out
raturer: *vt.* to cross out
rauque: *adj.* hoarse, raucous
ravage: *nm.* havoc; ravaging, laying waste
ravager: *vt.* to ravage; devastate
ravaler: *vt.* to swallow again; to restore
ravi: *adj.* delighted
ravin: *nm.* ravine, gully
ravir: *vt.* to delight
raviser: *vr.* to think better of it, change one's mind
ravissant: *adj.* ravishing, delightful
ravitailler: *vt.* to resupply
ravitaillement: *nm.* supplies; refuelling
raviver: *vt.* to revive, reanimate
rayer: *vt.* to scratch; to cross out
rayon: *nm.* ray, beam; spoke; shelf
rayonnage, étagère: shelf
rayonnant: *adj.* radiant, beaming
rayonnement: *nm.* radiance, effulgence; influence
rayonner: *vi.* to radiate, shine; to be influential
rayons x: x rays
rayure: *nf.* stripe; streak; groove
réaccoutumer: *vt.* to reaccustom
réacteur: *nm.* reactor; jet-engine
réactif: *nm.* reactant
réaction: *nf.* reaction
réaction bimoléculaire: bimolecular reaction
réaction chimique: chemical reaction

réaction de capture: electron scavenger reaction
réaction de combinaison: combination reaction
réaction de dismutation: disproportionation reaction
réaction de stabilisation: quenching reaction
réaction déterminante: determining step
réaction directe: direct reaction
réaction élémentaire: elementary reaction
réaction en chaîne: chain reactions
réaction en chaînes ramifiées: branching chain reaction
réaction globale: overall reaction
réaction inverse: reverse reaction
réaction ion/molécule: ion/molecule reaction
réaction monomoléculaire: unimolecular reaction
réaction trimoléculaire: trimolecular reaction
réaction unimoléculaire: unimolecular reaction
réactionnaire: *adj.* reactionary; mf reactionary
réactions parallèles: parallel reactions
réactions radicalaires: radical reactions
réactions thermoléculaires: termolecular reactions
réactiver: *vt.* to reactivate
réadaptation: *nf.* rehabilitation; readjustment
réadapter: *vt.* to readjust; to rehabilitate
réagir: *vi.* to react
réalisateur: *nm.* director, filmmaker
réalisation: *nf.* realisation; carrying out; achievement
réaliser: *vt.* to realise; to carry out; to

achieve

réalisme: *nm.* realism

réaliste: *adj.* realistic

réalité: *nf.* reality

réanimation: *nf.* resuscitation

réanimer: *vt.* to reanimate; to resuscitate

réapparaître: *vi.* to reappear

rébarbatif: *adj.* stern, grim, forbidding

rebattu: *adj.* hackneyed

rebel: *adj.* rebel, rebellious

rebeller (se): *vr.* to rebel

rébellion: *nf.* rebellion

reboisement: *nm.* reafforestation

reboiser: *vt.* to reafforest

rebondir: *vi.* to bounce; to rebound

rebondissement: *nm.* rebound; bouncing

rebord: *nm.* rim, edge; hem

rebrousser: *vt.* to brush back; chemin to turn back

rébus: *nm.* rebus, puzzle

rebut: *nm.* scrap; repulse, rebuff

recalcitrant: *adj.* recalcitrant, stubborn

rêcapituler: *vt.* to recapitulate, sum up

receler: *vt.* to receive; to harbour

récemment: *adv.* recently

recensement: *nm.* census, inventory

recenser: *vt.* to make a census of; to record

récent: *adj.* recent; new

récépissé: *nm.* receipt; acknowledgement

récepteur: *nm.* receiver

réceptif: *adj.* receptive

reception: *nf.* reception, welcome; receipt

réceptionniste: *nmf.* receptionist

récession: *nf.* recession

recette: *nf.* recipe; formula; receipt

receveur: *nm.* recipient; collector

recevoir: *vt.* to receive, welcome; to take, collect

rechange m: change; spare; de spare

recharge: *nf.* recharging; reloading

rechargeable: *adj.* rechargeable

recharger: *vt.* to recharge; to reload; to refill

réchaud: *nm.* stove; dishwarmer

réchauffer: *vt.* to reheat; to warm up

rêche: *adj.* rough, harsh

recherche: *nf.* search; inquiry; investigation; research

recherché: *adj.* sought after

rechercher: *vt.* to seek; to investigate

rechigner: *vt.* to balk; to grumble

rechute: *nf.* relapse; lapse

récidive: *nf.* second offence, relapse into crime

récidiver: *vi.* to reoffend; to recur

récidiviste: *nmf.* recidivist, habitual criminal

récif: *nm.* reef

récipient: *nm.* container, receptacle

réciproque: *adj.* reciprocal, mutual

récit: *nm.* account, story

recitation: *nf.* recitation; recital

reciter: *vt.* to recite

réclamation: *nf.* complaint; demand; claim

réclame: *nf.* advertisement; publicity

réclamer: *vt.* to claim, demand, ask for

reclus: *adj.* shut up, secluded

réclusion: *nf.* reclusion; confinement

recoiffer: *vt.* to do sb's hair

recoin: *nm.* corner, nook

recoller: *vt.* to restick

récolte: *nf.* harvest; collection; result

récolter: *vt.* to harvest; to collect

recommandation: *nf.* recommendation, reference

recommander: *vt.* to recommend; to commend; to register

recommencement: *nm.* renewal;

fresh beginning
recommencer: *vi.* to begin again; *vt.* to begin again, resume
récompense: *nf.* reward; award
récompenser: v to reward
réconciliation: *nf.* reconciliation
réconcilier: *vt.* to reconcile
reconduire: *vt.* to bring back; to see home, to escort
réconfort: *nm.* comfort
réconfortant: *adj.* comforting; tonic
réconforter: *vt.* to comfort; to fortify
reconnaissance: *nf.* recognition; acknowledgement; gratitude
reconnaissant: *adj.* grateful
reconnaître: *vt.* to recognise; to acknowledge; to be grateful
reconnu: *adj.* recognised, accepted
reconquérir: *vt.* to reconquer; to recover
reconsidérer: *vt.* to reconsider
reconstituer: *vt.* to reconstitute; rebuild, restore
reconstitution: *nf.* reconstitution; rebuilding, restoration
reconstruire: *vt.* to reconstruct, rebuild
reconversion: *nf.* reconversion, redeployment
recopier: *vt.* to copy out
record: *nm.* record
recoudre: *vt.* to sew up
recoupement: *nm.* crosscheck
recourbé: *adj.* curved, hooked
recourir: *vi.* to run again
recours: *nm.* recourse; redress
recouvrir: *vt.* to cover again; to cover up
récréatif: *adj.* recreative; entertaining
récréation: *nf.* recreation; break
récrimination: *nf.* recrimination, remonstration
récriminer: *vi.* to recriminate, remonstrate

recroqueviller (se): *vr.* to shrivel up
recrudescence: *nf.* recrudescence; upsurge; further outbreak
recrue: *nf.* recruit
recrutement: *nm.* recruiting, recruitment
recruter: *vt.* to recruit
rectal: *adj.* rectal
rectangle: *nm.* rectangle
rectangulaire: *adj.* rectangular
recteur: *nm.* priest, rector
rectificatif: *nm.* correction; *adj.* corrected, rectified
rectification: *nf.* rectification; correction
rectifier: *vt.* to rectify, correct; to adjust
recto: *nm.* recto, first side; front
rectum: *nm.* rectum
reçu (de paiement): *nm.* receipt
recueil: *nm.* collection, miscellany
recueillement: *nm.* meditation
recueillir: *vt.* to gather, collect; to record
recul: *nm.* retreat; recession; decline
reculer: *vi.* to fall back, retreat; *vt.* to move back; to defer
récupération: *nf.* recovery; retrieval
récupérer: *vt.* to recover, retrieve; to recuperate; *vi.* to recover
récurer: *vt.* to scour
recycler: *vt.* to recycle
rédacteur: *nm.* editor, compiler; drafter; writer; subeditor
rédacteur publicitaire: copywriter
rédaction: *nf.* drafting, drawing up
rédemption: *nf.* redemption
redescendre: *vi.* to go down again; *vt.* to bring down again
redevable: *adj.* indebted, owing; liable
redevance: *nf.* rent; tax; fees
rediffusion: *nf.* repeat, reshowing
rédiger: *vt.* to write; to compile;

to draft

redire: *vt.* to repeat, say again;

redoubler: *vt.* to increase, intensify; *vi.* to increase, intensify; de to redouble

redoutable: *adj.* redoubtable, formidable

redouter: *vt.* to dread, fear

redresser: *vt.* to rectify; to true; to set up again

réduction: *nf.* reduction; discount; mitigation

réduire: *vt.* to reduce, diminish

réduit: *adj.* reduced, limited; miniature; *nm.* retreat; recess; small room

rééducation: *nf.* re-education; rehabilitation

rééduquer: *vt.* to re-educate; to rehabilitate

réel: *adj.* real, genuine

réélire: *vt.* to re-elect

rééquilibrer: *vt.* to restabilise

réévaluer: *vt.* to revalue

refaire: *vt.* to redo; to remake; to renew

réfectoire: *nm.* canteen, refectory

référence: *nf.* reference

refermer: *vt.* to close again

réfférendum: *nm.* referendum

réfléchi: *adj.* well-considered; reflective, thoughtful

réfléchir: *vi.* to think, reflect; *vt.* to realise; to mirror

reflet: *nm.* reflection; reflex

refléter: *vt.* to reflect, mirror

réflexe: *nm.* reflex

réflexion: *nf.* thought, reflection

reflux: *nm.* reflux, ebb

réforme: *nf.* reform, amendment; discharge

réformer: *vt.* to reform, correct; to invalid out; to scrap

refouler: *vt.* to drive back, repel

réfraction: *nf.* refraction

refrain: *nm.* refrain, chorus

réfréner: *vt.* to curb, hold in check

réfrigérateur: *nm.* refrigerator

réfrigérer: *vt.* to refrigerate

refroidir: *vt.* to cool; *vi.* to cool down, get cold

refroidissement: *nm.* cooling; chill

refuge: *nm.* refuge, shelter; lay-by

réfugié: *nm.* refugee; *adj.* refugee

réfugier (se): *vr.* to take refuge

refus: *nm.* refusal

refuser: *vt.* to refuse; to reject; to deny

réfuter: *vt.* to refute

regagner: *vt.* to regain, win back

regain: *nm.* renewal; revival

régal: *nm.* delight, treat

régaler: *vt.* to regale; to treat

regard: *nm.* look; glance; expression; peephole

regardant: *adj.* particular, meticulous; stingy

regarder: *vt.* to look at; to glance; to be opposite; to concern

régates: *nfpl.* regattas

régénération: *nf.* regeneration

régénérer: *vt.* to regenerate, revive

régent: *nm.* regent

régenter: *vt.* to rule over, domineer

régi, être: to be regulated

régie: *nf.* administration; state control

régime: *nm.* system, régime; scheme; diet; rate, speed

régiment: *nm.* regiment

région: *nf.* region, area

régional: *adj.* regional

régir: *vt.* to govern, rule

régisseur: *nm.* manager; steward; bailiff

registre: *nm.* register, record; style; compass

registre des sociétés: Registrar of Companies

réglable: *adj.* adjustable
réglage: *nm.* regulation, adjustment; tuning
règle: *nf.* rule; order; regularity; period
règle des phases: phase rule
règlement: *nm.* regulation, rules; settlement
réglementaire: *adj.* regulation; statutory
réglementation: *nf.* regulations; control
réglementer: *vt.* to regulate, control
régler: *vt.* to settle, pay; to regulate
régler en numéraire (en espèces): to settle in cash
régler un différend: to settle a dispute
régler une dette: to settle a debt
réglisse: *nf.* liquorice
règne: *nm.* reign
régner: *vi.* to reign; to prevail
regorger: *vi.* de to overflow with, abound in
régresser: *vi.* to regress; to recede
régression: *nf.* regression
regret: *nm.* regret, yearning
regrettable: *adj.* regrettable
regretter: *vt.* to regret, be sorry; to miss
regroupement: *nm.* gathering together; merger
regrouper: *vt.* to group together; to reassemble
régulariser: *vt.* to regularise; straighten out
régularité: *nf.* regularity; consistency
régulier: *adj.* regular; consistent; steady; even; legitimate
régulièrement: *adv.* regularly; consistently; lawfully
réhabilitation: *nf.* rehabilitation; discharge; reinstatement
réhabiliter: *vt.* to rehabilitate; to

discharge; to reinstate
réhabituer: *vt.* to reaccustom sb to
rehausser: *vt.* to heighten, raise
rein: *nm.* kidney
réincarnation: *nf.* reincarnation
reine: *nf.* queen
reine-claude: *nf.* greengage
réinsertion: *nf.* reinsertion, reintegration
réintégrer: *vt.* to reinstate; to return to
réitérer: *vt.* to reiterate, repeat
rejaillir: *vi.* to gush out; to rebound on
rejet: *nm.* rejection, dismissal; throwing up
rejeter: *vt.* to reject, dismiss; throw up
rejoindre: *vt.* to rejoin; to catch up with
rejouer: *vt.* to replay; to perform again
réjouir: *vt.* to delight; to entertain
réjouissance: *nf.* rejoicing, merry-making
relâche: *nf.* intermission, respite
relâchement: *nm.* relaxation, loosening; laxity
relâcher: *vt.* to relax, slacken
relais: *nm.* relay; shift; staging post
relatif: *adj.* relative; relating to
relation: *nf.* relation, relationship
relations d'affaires: business connections
relativement: *adv.* relatively
relativisme: *nm.* relativism
relativité: *nf.* relativity
relax tion: *nf.* relaxation
relaxant: *adj.* relaxing
relaxer: *vt.* to relax; to acquit
relayer: *vt.* to relieve, take the place of; to relay
release (se): *vr.* to relax
relecture: *nf.* rereading

reléguer: *vt.* to relegate; to banish
relevé: *nm.* statement; list; bill;adj turned up, rolled up; elevated
relève: *nf.* relief; relief party
relevé de factures: statement of invoices
relever: *vt.* to set up again, raise again; to rebuild
relier: *vt.* to link up, connect; to bind
religieux: *nm.* monk
religion: *nf.* religion
relique: *nf.* relic
relire: *vt.* to reread
reliure: *nf.* binding; bookbinding
reluire: *vi.* to gleam, shine
remaniement: *nm.* recasting; altering; revision; amendment
remanier: *vt.* to recast, revise; to amend
remarquable: *adj.* remarkable, notable
remarque: *nf.* remark, comment
remarquer: *vt.* to remark; to notice
rembourrer: *vt.* to stuff; to pad
remboursement: *nm.* reimbursement, repayment
rembourser: to refund
rembourser: *vt.* to reimburse, pay back
remède: *nm.* remedy, cure
remédier vi: to remedy, cure
remerciement: *nm.* thanks; thanking
remercier: *vt.* to thank
remettre: *vt.* to put back; to replace; to restart; to revive
réminiscence: *nf.* reminiscence
remise: *nf.* delivery; remittance; discount; deferment
remmener: *vt.* to take back
remontant: *nm.* tonic; *adj.* invigorating, fortifying
remonte-pente: *nm.* ski tow
remonter: *vi.* to go up again; to rise, increase; to return; *vt.* to go up; to

take up
remontrance: *nf.* remonstrance
remords: *nm.* remorse
remorque: *nf.* trailer; towrope
remorquer: *vt.* to tow
remorqueur: *nm.* tug
rémouleur: *nm.* knife-grinder
remous: *nm.* back-wash; eddy, swirl
rempailler: *vt.* to reseat (chair)
rempart: *nm.* rampart; defence
remplaçant: *nm.* substitute
remplacement: *nm.* replacing; substitution
remplacer: *vt.* to replace, stand in for
remplir: *vt.* to fill; to fill in; to fulfil
remplir un document: to fill in a document
remplissage: *nm.* filling up; padding
remporter: *vt.* to take away
remuant: *adj.* restless, fidgety
remuer: *vi.* to move; to fidget; *vt.* to move, shift; to stir
rémunération: *nf.* remuneration, payment
rémunérer: *vt.* to remunerate, pay
renaissance: *nf.* rebirth, Renaissance
renaître: *vi.* to be reborn; to be revived; to reappear
renard: *nm.* fox
renchérir: *vi.* to go further, go one better; to bid higher
renchérissement: *nm.* increase in price
rencontre: *nf.* meeting, encounter; conjuncture; collision
rencontrer: *vt.* to meet; to find; to strike; se - *vr.* = to meet each other
rendement: *nm.* yield; output
rendement quantique: quantum yield
rendez-vous: *nm.* appointment; date; meeting place
rendormir: *vt.* to put to sleep again
rendre: *vt.* to render; to give back,

return; to yield
rendu à la frontière: delivered at frontier (DAF)
rêne: *nf.* rein
renfermé: *adj.* withdrawn, close
renfermer: *vt.* to contain, to hold
renflement: *nm.* bulge
renflouer: *vt.* to refloat; to bail out
renfoncement: *nm.* recess
renfoncer: *vt.* to drive further in; to recess
renforcer: *vt.* to strengthen, to reinforce
renfort: *nm.* reinforcement; help
renfrogné: *adj.* frowning, glum
renier: *vt.* to repudiate, disown
renifler: *vt.* to sniff, snuffle
renne: *nm.* reindeer
renom: *nm.* renown, fame
renommée: *nf.* renowned, famed
renoncement: *nm.* renouncement; renunciation
renoncer: *vi.* to renounce, give up
renonciation: *nf.* renunciation; waiver
renouer: *vt.* to retie; to renew
renouveau: *nm.* spring; renewal
renouveler: *vt.* to renew; to revive
renouvellement: *nm.* renewal; revival
rénovation: *nf.* renovation; renewal
rénover: *vt.* to renovate
renseignement: *nm.* information; intelligence
renseigner: *vt.* to inform, give information to
rentabiliser: *vt.* to make profitable
rentable: *adj.* profitable
rente: *nf.* rent; profit; annuity
rentier: *nm.* stockholder, fundholder; rentier
rentrée: *nf.* reopening; reassembly; reappearance
rentrer: *vi.* to re-enter; to return

home; to begin again; *vt.* to bring in
renversement: *nm.* inversion; reversal; overturning
renverser: *vt.* to turn upside down; to reverse; to overturn
renvoi: *nm.* sending back; returning; dismissal
renvoyer: *vt.* to send back; to return; to dismiss
réorganisation: *nf.* reorganisation
réorganiser: *vt.* to reorganise
réouverture: *nf.* reopening
repaire: *nm.* den, lair
répandre: *vt.* to pour out; to scatter, spread
répandu: *adj.* widespread
réparateur: *nm.* repairer
réparation: *nf.* repairing; restoration
réparer: *vt.* to repair; to restore; to make up for
repartie: *nf.* retort
repartir: *vi.* to set off again; to start up again
répartir: *vt.* to share out; to distribute
répartition: *nf.* sharing out; allocation
repas: *nm.* meal
repassage: *nm.* ironing; grinding, sharpening
repasser: *vt.* to iron; to cross again; to resit
repêcher: *vt.* to fish out, retrieve
repeindre: *vt.* to repaint
repenti: *adj.* repentant
repentir: *nm.* repentance, contrition
repentir (se): *vr.* to repent
répercussion: *nf.* repercussion
répercuter: *vt.* to reverberate
repérer: *vt.* to spot, pick out; to mark out
répertoire: *nm.* index, catalogue; repertory
répertorier: *vt.* to itemise; to index
répéter: *vt.* to repeat; to rehearse

répétitif: *adj.* repetitive
répétition: *nf.* repetition; rehearsal
repiquer: *vt.* to plant out, transplant
répit: *nm.* respite, rest
repli: *nm.* fold, coil, meander; withdrawal; downturn
replier: *vt.* to fold up; to withdraw
réplique: *nf.* reply, retort; counter-attack
répliquer: *vt.* to reply; to retaliate
répondant: *nmf.* guarantor; bail, surety
répondeur: *nm.* answering machine
répondre: *vt.* to answer, reply
réponse: *nf.* response, reply
report: *nm.* postponement, deferment; carrying forward
reportage: *nm.* report; commentary; reporting
reporter: *vt.* to postpone; to carry forward; to transfer
reporter: *nm.* reporter
repos: *nm.* rest; tranquillity; landing
reposant: *adj.* restful, refreshing
reposer: *vt.* to put back; to rest; to ask again
repoussant: *adj.* repulsive; repellent
repousser: *vt.* to push back; to repel
reprendre: *vt.* to retake, recapture; to resume
représailles: *nfpl.* reprisals; retaliation
représentant: *nm.* agent, representative; *adj.* representative
représentation: *nf.* representation; performance
représenter: *vt.* to represent, depict; to perform; to symbolise
répressif: *adj.* repressive
répression: *nf.* repression
réprimande: *nf.* reprimand, rebuke
réprimander: *vt.* to reprimand, rebuke
réprimer: *vt.* to repress; to quell

reprise: *nf.* resumption; recapture, taking back
repriser: *vt.* to darn
réprobation: *nf.* reprobation
reproche: *nm.* reproach; objection
reprocher: *vt.* to reproach, blame
reproduction: *nf.* reproduction; copy; duplicate
reproduire: *vt.* to reproduce, copy; to repeat
reptile: *nm.* reptile
repu: *adj.* full, satiated
républicain: *nmf.* republican; *adj.* republican
république: *nf.* republic
répudier: *vt.* to repudiate; to renounce
répugnance: *nf.* repugnance, disgust
répugnant: *adj.* repugnant, disgusting, revolting
répulsion: *nf.* repulsion, repugnance
réputation: *nf.* reputation; character; fame
réputé: *adj.* reputable, renowned; supposed, reputed
requérir: *vt.* to call for, request
requête: *nf.* petition, request
requin: *nm.* shark
requis: *adj.* required, requisite
réquisition: *nf.* requisition; conscription
réquisitionner: *vt.* to requisition; to conscript
rescapé: *nmf.* survivor
réseau: *nm.* network, net
réseau: network
réservation: *nf.* reservation, booking
réserve: *nf.* reserve; reservation, caution
réservé: *nf.* reserved
réserver: *vt.* to reserve, save; to book; to lay by
réservoir: *nm.* tank; reservoir
résidence: *nf.* residence; apartment

block
résidentiel: *adj.* residential
résider: *vi.* to reside, dwell
résidu: *nm.* residue
résignation: *nf.* resignation
résigner (se): *vr.* to resign
résilier: *vt.* to terminate; to annul
résine: *nf.* resin
résistance: *nf.* resistance
résistant: *adj.* resistant; tough, unyielding
résister: *vi.* to resist, withstand
résolu: *adj.* resolved, determined; -ment = *adv.* resolutely
résolution: *nf.* resolution, determination
résonner: *vi.* to resound, resonate
résorber: *vt.* to reduce; to absorb
résoudre: *vt.* to solve; to resolve; to annul
respect: *nm.* respect, regard, deference
respectable: *adj.* respectable; sizeable
respecter: *vt.* to respect; to comply with
respectif: *adj.* respective
respectivement: *adv.* respectively
respectueusement: *adv.* respectfully
respectueux: *adj.* respectful
respirable: *adj.* breathable
respiration: *nf.* breathing, respiration
respiratoire: *adj.* respiratory
respirer: *vi.* to breathe, respire
resplendissant: *adj.* shining, radiant
responsabilité: *nf.* responsibility; liability
responsable: *adj.* responsible; liable
resquiller: *vi.* to sneak in; to take a free ride
ressaisir (se): *vr.* to regain one's self-control
ressemblance: *nf.* resemblance, likeness; similarity

ressemblant: *adj.* lifelike
ressembler: *vi.* to resemble, be like
ressemelage: *nm.* soling, resoling
ressentiment: *nm.* resentment
ressentir: *vt.* to feel, experience
resserrement: *nm.* contraction, tightening; narrowing
resserrer: *vt.* to tighten; to strengthen
ressort: *nm.* spring; motivation
ressortir: *vi.* to go out again; to stand out
ressortissant: *nmf.* national
ressource: *nf.* resource, resort, expedient
ressusciter: *vi.* to revive, re-awaken; to come back to life; *vt.* to resuscitate; to revive
restant: *adj.* remaining; *nm.* rest, remainder
restaurant: *nm.* restaurant
restaurateur: *nmf.* restaurateur; restorer
restauration: *nf.* restoration, rehabilitation; catering
restaurer: *vt.* to restore; to feed
reste: *nm.* rest, left-over, remainder
rester: *vi.* to remain, stay; to be left; to continue; to pause
restituer: *vt.* to return, restore; to refund
restitution: *nf.* restoration; restitution
restreindre: *vt.* to restrict, curtail
restreint: *adj.* restricted, limited
restrictif: *adj.* restrictive
restriction: *nf.* restriction, limitation; reserve
restructurer: *vt.* to restructure
résultat: *nm.* result, outcome; profit
résulter: *v.* to result, follow from, ensue
résumé: *nm.* summary, recapitulation
résumer: *vt.* to sum up
résurrection: *nf.* resurrection
rétablir: *vt.* to re-establish, restore

rétablissement: *nm.* re-establishment, restoring

retard: *nm.* lateness; delay; être en - = to be late; to be behind; to be backward

retardataire: *nmf.* latecomer; *adj.* obsolete

retardé: *adj.* backward, slow

retarder: *vt.* to delay; to hinder; to put back; *vi.* to be out of touch

retenir: *vt.* to hold back, retain; to remember

retention: *nf.* retention; withholding

retentir: *vi.* to resound; to ring

retentissant: *adj.* resounding; ringing

retenue: *nf.* discretion; deduction, stoppage; reservoir

réticence: *nf.* reticence

réticent: *adj.* reticent

retiligne: *adj.* straight; rectilinear

rétine: *nf.* retina

retiré: *adj.* remote, isolated

retirer: *vt.* to take off; to take out, withdraw; to redeem

retirer de l'argent: to withdraw money

retombée: *nf.* fallout; repercussions

retomber: *vi.* to fall again; to have a relapse

rétorquer: *vt.* to retort

retouche: *nf.* touching up; alteration

retoucher: *vt.* to touch up; to alter

retour: *nm.* return; recurrence; vicissitude, reversal; être de – = to be back

retournement: *nm.* reversal; turnaround

retourner: *vt.* to reverse, turn over; to return

rétracter: *vt.* to retract, take back

retrait: *nm.* ebb; retreat; withdrawal

retraite: *nf.* retirement

retraite: *nf.* retreat; retirement; refuge

retraité: *nmf.* pensioner; *adj.* retired

retranchement: *nm.* curtailment; entrenchment

retrancher: *vt.* to curtail; to entrench

retransmettre: *vt.* to retransmit

retransmission: *nf.* retransmission

rétrécir: *vi.* to narrow; to shrink; *vt.* to take in, make narrower

rétrécissement: *nm.* narrowing; shrinking

rétribuer: *vt.* to remunerate

rétribution: *nf.* retribution

rétroactif: *adj.* retrospective; retroactive

rétroaction: *nf.* retroaction; retrospective action

rétrograder: *vi.* to go backward, regress

rétrograder: *adj.* reactionary, backward

rétroprojecteur: *nm.* overhead projector

rétrospectif: *adj.* retrospective

rétrospective: *nf.* retrospective

rétrospectivement: *adv.* retrospectively

retrousser: *vt.* to roll up, hitch up

retrouvailles: *nfpl.* reunion

retrouver: *vt.* to find again, to regain; to recover; to recognise

rétroviseur: *nm.* rearview mirror

réunifier: *vt.* to reunify

réunion: *nf.* reunion, gathering

réunir: *vt.* to unite; to collect, gather; to combine

réussir: *vi.* to succeed, be a success; *vt.* to make a success of

réussite: *nf.* success, successful outcome

revanche: *nf.* revenge; en - = on the other hand

rêvasser: *vi.* to daydream

rêve: *nm.* dream, dreaming; illusion

réveil: *nm.* waking, awaking; alarm clock

réveiller: *vt.* to wake; se - *vr.* = to awaken

réveillon: *nm.* midnight feast

révélation: *nf.* revelation, disclosure; developing

révéler: to disclose

révéler: *vt.* to reveal, disclose; se *vr.* to be revealed; to prove to be

revenant: *nmf.* ghost

revendeur: *nm.* retailer; dealer

revendication: *nf.* claiming; claim; demand

revendiquer: *vt.* to claim; to demand

revendre: *vt.* to resell

revenir: *vi.* to come back, reappear; to happen again

revenu: *nm.* income, revenue

rêver: *vi.* to dream; to muse; *vt.* to dream of

réverbération: *nf.* reverberation

réverbère: *nm.* street lamp

révérence: *nf.* bow, curtsey

révérend: *adj.* reverend

révérer: *vt.* to revere

rêverie: *nf.* reverie, musing

revers: *nm.* back, reverse; counterpart

réversible: *adj.* reversible

revêtement: *nm.* coating, surface

revêtir: *vt.* to don; to assume

rêveur: *nmf.* dreamer; *adj.* dreamy

revigorer: *vt.* to invigorate; to revive

revirement: *nm.* change of mind; reversal; turnaround

réviser: *vt.* to review; to revise

révision: *nf.* review; auditing; revision

revivre: *vt.* to relive; *vi.* to live again, come alive again

révocation: *nf.* removal; dismissal; revocation

revoir: *vt.* to see again

révoltant: *adj.* revolting, appalling

révolte: *nf.* revolt, rebellion

révolter: *vt.* to revolt, outrage

révolu: *adj.* past, bygone

révolution: *nf.* revolution

révolutionnaire: *nmf.* revolutionary; *adj.* revolutionary

révolutionner: *vt.* to revolutionise; to upset

revolver: *nm.* revolver

révoquer: *vt.* to revoke; to dismiss

revue: *nf.* review; inspection

rez-de-chaussée: *nm.* invar ground floor

rhabiller: *vt.* to dress (sb) again; to fit (sb) out again

rhésus: *nm.* rhesus

rhétorique: *nf.* rhetoric; *adj.* rhetorical

rhinocéros: *nm.* rhinoceros

rhododendron: *nm.* rhododendron

rhubarb: *nf.* rhubarb

rhum: *nm.* rum

rhumatisme: *nm.* rheumatism

rhume: *nm.* cold

riant: *adj.* smiling; cheerful

ribambelle: *nf.* swarm, herd

ricanement: *nm.* snigger, sniggering

ricaner: *vi.* to snigger, giggle

riche: *adj.* rich, wealthy; abundant

richesse: *nf.* richness; wealth; abundance

ricochet: *nm.* ricochet; rebound

rictus: *nm.* grin; grimace

ride: *nf.* wrinkle; ripple; ridge

ridé: *adj.* wrinkled

rideau: *nm.* curtain

ridicule: *adj.* ridiculous

ridiculiser: *vt.* to ridicule

rien: pron. nothing

rieur: *adj.* cheerful; laughing

rigide: *adj.* rigid; -ment = *adv.* rigidly

rigidité: *nf.* rigidity, stiffness

rigole: *nf.* channel; rivulet

rigoler: *vi.* (fam) to have a good laugh

rigoureusement: *adv.* harshly, rigorously
rigoureux: *adj.* rigorous, harsh
rigueur: *nf.* rigour; harshness, severity
rime: *nf.* rhyme
rimer: *vi.* to rhyme (with)
rince-doigts: *nm.* invar finger-bowl
rincer: *vt.* to rinse out; to rinse
ring: *nm.* boxing ring
riposte: *nf.* riposte, retort
riposter: *vi.* to answer back, retaliate
rire: *vi.* to laugh; to smile; to joke; *nm.* laughter, laugh
risée: *nf.* laugh; ridicule; mockery, derision
risible: *adj.* laughable, ridiculous
risque: *nm.* risk, hazard
risqué: *adj.* risky, hazardous; risqué
risquer: *vt.* to risk; to venture
ristourne: *nf.* discount, rebate
rite: *nm.* rite
rituel: *adj.* ritual
rivage: *nm.* shore
rival: *nmf.* rival; sans - = unrivalled
rivaliser: *vi.* to rival, compete with; - de = to vie with
rivalité: *nf.* rivalry
rive: *nf.* shore, bank
river: *vt.* to clinch; to rivet
riverain: *nmf.* lakeside resident
rivière: *nf.* river
riz: *nm.* rice
robe: *nf.* dress; gown; - de chambre = dressing gown
robinet: *nm.* tap
robot: *nm.* robot
robotique: *nf.* robotics
robuste: *adj.* robust
robustesse: *nf.* robustness
roc: *nm.* rock
rocaille: *nf.* loose stones; rocky ground
rocailleux: *adj.* rocky

roche: *nf.* rock
rocher: *nm.* rock, boulder
rodage: *nm.* grinding; running in, breaking in
roder: *vt.* to grind; to run in
rôder: *vi.* to roam; to prowl about
rôdeur: *nm.* prowler
rogner: *vt.* to pare, prune, clip
rognon: *nm.* kidney
roi: *nm.* king
rôle: *nm.* role, character; roll, catalogue
roman: *nm.* novel; romance
romancier: *nm.* novelist
romanesque: *adj.* fabulous; storybook; fictional
romantique: *adj.* romantic
romantisme: *nm.* romanticism
rompre: *vt.* to break; to snap; to dissolve; *vi.* to break; to burst
ronce: *nf.* bramble
rond: *nm.* circle, ring; slice, round; *adj.* round; chubby, plump; frankement
ronde: *nf.* patrol; round; beat: *adv.* briskly, frankly
rondelle: *nf.* slice, round; disc
rondeur: *nf.* plumpness; roundness
rondin: *nm.* log
rond-point: *nm.* roundabout
ronflement: *nm.* snore, snoring; humming; roaring
ronfler: *vi.* to snore; to hum; to roar
ronger: *vt.* to gnaw
ronronner: *vi.* to purr; to hum
rosbif: *nm.* roast beef
rose: *nf.* rose; *adj.* pink; *nm.* pink
roseau: *nm.* reed
rosée: *nf.* dew
rosier: *nm.* rosebush
rossignol: *nm.* nightingale
rot: *nm.* belch, burp
rotation: *nf.* rotation; turnover
roter: *vi.* to belch, burp

rôti: *nm.* joint, roast
rotin: *nm.* rattan
rôtir: *vt.* to roast
rôtisserie: *nf.* rotisserie, steakhouse
rotonde: *nf.* rotunda; roundhouse
rotule: *nf.* kneecap, patella
rouage: *nm.* cog; gearwheel
roucouler: *vi.* to coo; to bill
roue: *nf.* wheel
rouge: *adj.* red; *nm.* red; - à lèvres = lipstick
rouge-gorge: *nm.* robin
rougeole: *nf.* measles
rougeur: *nf.* redness, blushing
rougir: *vi.* to blush, go red; *vt.* to make red, redden
rouille: *nf.* rust
rouiller: *vi.* to rust; *vt.* to make rusty
roulage: roll on; roll off system
roulant: *adj.* on wheels; moving
rouleau: *nm.* roll; roller
roulement: *nm.* rotation; movement; rumble, rumbling
rouler: *vt.* to wheel, roll along; *vi.* to go, run (train); to drive
roulette: *nf.* castor; trundle; roulette
roulis: *nm.* rolling
roulotte: *nf.* caravan
rouquin: *nmf.* redhead; *adj.* redhaired
route: *nf.* road; way; course, direction
routier: *adj.* road; *nm.* lorry driver; transport café
routine: *nf.* routine
routinier: *adj.* humdrum, routine
roux, rousse: *adj.* red, auburn
royal: *adj.* royal, regal; -ement = *adv.* royally
royaliste m: *nf.* royalist; *adj.* royalist
royaume: *nm.* kingdom
royauté: *nf.* monarchy
ruade: *nf.* kick (horse)
ruban: *nm.* ribbon; tape, band
rubéole: *nf.* rubella
rubis: *nm.* ruby

rubrique: *nf.* column; heading, rubric
ruche: *nf.* hive
rude: *adj.* rough; hard; unrefined; -ment = *adv.* roughly, harshly
rudesse: *nf.* roughness; harshness
rudiment: *nm.* rudiment; principle
rudimentaire: *adj.* rudimentary
rudoyer: *vt.* to treat harshly
rue: *nf.* street
ruée: *nf.* rush, stampede
ruelle: *nf.* alley
ruer: *vi.* to kick (horse); se - *vr.* = to pounce on
rugby: *nm.* rugby
rugbyman: *nm.* rugby player
rugir: *vi.* to roar
rugissement: *nm.* roar, roaring
rugueux: *adj.* rough; coarse
ruine: *nf.* ruin; wreck
ruiner: *vt.* to ruin
ruineux: *adj.* ruinous; extravagant
ruisseau: *nm.* stream, brook
ruisseler: *vi.* to stream, flow
ruissellement: *nm.* streaming; cascading
rumeur: *nf.* rumour; murmur; hum
ruminer: *vt.* to ruminate; to brood over
rupture: *nf.* break, rupture; breach; split
rupture de stock: stock shortage
rural: *adj.* rural, country
ruse: *nf.* cunning, slyness
rusé: *adj.* cunning, crafty
rustique: *adj.* rustic
rutilant: *adj.* gleaming, rutilant
rythme: *nm.* rhythm; rate, speed
rythmique: *adj.* rhythmic

S

sabbat: *nm.* Sabbath
sabbatique: *adj.* sabbatical
sable: *nm.* sand
sablé: *nm.* shortbread biscuit;
adj. sandy, sanded
sablier: *nm.* hourglass, sandglass
sabot: *nm.* clog; hoof
sabotage: *nm.* sabotage
saboter: *vt.* to sabotage; to mess up
saboteur: *nm.* saboteur; bungler
sabre: *nm.* sabre
sac: *nm.* bag, sack; - à main =
handbag; - de voyage = travelling bag
sac à dos: backpack
sac de couchage: sleeping bag
saccade: *nf.* jerk, jolt
saccadé: *adj.* jerky, broken, staccato
saccager: *vt.* to sack; to wreck,
devastate
saccharine: *nf.* saccharin
sacerdoce: *nm.* priesthood
sacerdotal: *adj.* priestly, sacerdotal
sachet: *nm.* bag; sachet; packet
sacoche: *nf.* saddlebag, satchel
sacre: *nm.* coronation; consecration
sacré: *adj.* sacred, holy; damned,
confounded
Sacré-Cœur: *nm.* Sacred Heart
sacrer: *vt.* to crown; to consecrate
sacrifice: *nm.* sacrifice
sacrifier: *vt.* to sacrifice; to give up
sacrilège: *nm.* sacrilege
sacristie: *nf.* sacristy
sacrum: *nm.* sacrum
sadique: *adj.* sadistic; mf sadist
sadisme: *nm.* sadism
sadomasochiste: *adj.*
sadomaso-chistic; *mf.* sadomasochist
safari: *nm.* safari
safran: *nm.* saffron
saga: *nf.* saga
sagace: adj sagacious, shrewd
sagacité: *nf.* sagacity, shrewdness

sage: *adj.* wise, sensible; well-
behaved
sage-femme: *nf.* midwife
sagesse: *nf.* wisdom, sense; good
behavior
sagittaire: *nm.* archer; Sagittarius
saignant: *adj.* bleeding; underdone
saignement: *nm.* bleeding
saigner: *vi.* to bleed; *vt.* to bleed; to
stick
saillant: *adj.* prominent, protruding
saillie: *nf.* projection; sally; flash of
wit
saillir: *vi.* to gush out; to project, jut
sain: *adj.* healthy; sound; sane
saindoux: *nm.* lard
saint: *nm.* saint; *adj.* holy
sainteté: *nf.* saintliness; holiness
saisie: *nf.* (jar) seizure, distraint;
capture
saisir: *vt.* to take hold of; (jur) to
seize, distrain; to capture
saisissant: *adj.* gripping, startling,
striking
saison: *nf.* season
saisonnier: *adj.* seasonal
salade: *nf.* salad; jumble, miscellany
saladier: *nm.* salad bowl
salaire: *nm.* salary, pay; reward
salamandre: *nf.* salamander
salarié: *nm.* salaried employee;
adj. salaried
sale: *adj.* dirty
salé: *adj.* salty, salted; savoury
saler: *vt.* to salt, add salt
saleté: *nf.* dirtiness, dirt; rubbish;
obscenity
salie: *adj.* dirty, filthy; obscene; nasty
salière: *nf.* saltcellar
salin: *adj.* saline
salir: *vt.* to make dirty, soil;
se - vr. = to get dirty
salissant: *adj.* dirty; that gets dirty
easily

salive: *nf.* saliva
salle: *nf.* room; hall; theatre; audience
salle à manger: dining room
salle d'attente: waiting room
salle de bains: bathroom
salle de séjour: living room
salliver: *vi.* to salivate; to drool
salon: *nm.* lounge, sitting room; exhibition
salopette: *nf.* overalls
salpêtre: *nm.* saltpetre
salsifis: *nm.* salsify
salubre: *adj.* healthy, salubrious
saluer: *vt.* to greet; to salute
salut: *nm.* safety, salvation; welfare; wave (hand); salute
Salut!: inter Hi!
salutaire: *adj.* salutary; profitable; healthy
salutation: *nf.* salutation, greeting
samedi: *nm.* Saturday
Sanatorium: *nm.* sanatorium
sanctifier: *vt.* to sanctify, bless
sanction: *nf.* sanction, penalty; approval
sanctionner: *vt.* to punish; to sanction, approve
sanctuaire: *nm.* sanctuary
sandale: *nf.* sandal
sandwich: *nm.* sandwich
sang: *nm.* blood; race; kindred
sang-froid: *nm.* sangfroid, cool, calm
sanglant: *adj.* bloody, gory; bloodshot; bloodred
sangle: *nf.* strap; girth
sanglier: *nm.* wild boar
sanglot: *nm.* sob
sangloter: *vi.* to sob
sangsue: *nf.* leech
sanguinaire: *adj.* sanguinary, bloodthirsty
sanitaire: *adj.* health, sanitary
sans: *prep.* without
sans-abris: invar homeless person

sans-gêne: *adj.* inconsiderate; *nm.* invar inconsiderate type
santal: *nm.* sandalwood
santé: *nf.* health, healthiness
saper: *vt.* to undermine, sap
sapeur-pompier: *nm.* fireman
saphir: *nm.* sapphire
sapin: *nm.* fir tree, fir
sarcasme: *nm.* sarcasm
sarcastique: *adj.* sarcastic
sarcler: *vt.* to weed; to hoe
sarcophage: *nm.* sarcophagus
sardine: *nf.* sardine
sardonique: *adj.* sardonic
sarrasin: *nm.* buckwheat
sas: *nm.* airlock; sieve
satanique: *adj.* satanic, diabolical
satellite: *nm.* satellite
satiété: *nf.* satiety, satiation
satin: *nm.* satin
satiné: *adj.* satiny, satin-smooth; glazed
satire: *nf.* satire, lampoon
satirique: *adj.* satirical
satisfaction: *nf.* satisfaction; gratification; appeasement
satisfaire: *vt.* to satisfy; to gratify; to appease
satisfaisant: *adj.* satisfactory; satisfying
satisfait: *adj.* satisfied
saturation: *nf.* saturation
saturé: *adj.* saturated; overloaded, jammed
saturer: *vt.* to saturate; to surfeit; to congest
satyre: *nm.* satyr
sauce: *nf.* sauce, dressing
saucière: *nf.* sauceboat
saucisse: *nf.* sausage
saucisson: *nm.* large sausage; salami
sauf: *prép.* save, except; unless; *adj.* safe, unhurt
sauf indications contraires: unless

otherwise agreed
sauge: *nf.* sage
saugrenu: *adj.* preposterous, absurd
saule: *nm.* willow
saumon: *nm.* salmon
sauna: *nm.* sauna
saupoudrer: *vt.* to sprinkle; to dust
saut: *nm.* jump, bound; waterfall
sauté: *adj.* sauté
sauter: *vi.* to jump, leap; to blow up; to get sacked
sauterelle: *nf.* grasshopper
sautiller: *vi.* to hop, skip
sauvage: *adj.* savage, wild; unsociable
sauvegarde: *nf.* safeguard; backup
sauvegarder: *vt.* to safeguard
sauver: *vt.* to save, rescue; to preserve
sauvetage: *nm.* rescue; salvage
sauveteur: *nm.* rescuer
savant: *adj.* learned; expert; skilled; *nm.* scientist, scholar
savate: *nf.* old shoe
saveur: *nf.* flavour; savour
savoir: *vt.* to know; to be aware; to understand; to be able; *nm.* learning, knowledge
savoir-faire: *nm.* know-how
savoir-vivre: *nm.* good manners, good breeding
savon: *nm.* soap
savonner: *vt.* to soap, lather
savonnette: *nf.* bar of soap
savoureux: *adj.* tasty, savoury
saxophone: *nm.* saxophone
saxophoniste: *nmf.* saxophonist
scabreux: *adj.* scabrous; dangerous; improper
scalpel: *nm.* scalpel
scandale: *nm.* scandal
scandaleux: *adj.* scandalous
scandaliser: *vt.* to scandalise
scanner: *nm.* scanner

scaphandre: *nm.* diving suit
scarabée: *nm.* beetle, scarab
scarlatine: *nf.* scarlet fever
sceau: *nm.* seal
scélérat: *nm.* villain, rascal; *adj.* villainous, wicked
sceller: *vt.* to seal
scénario: *nm.* scenario; screenplay
scénariste: *nmf.* scriptwriter
scène: *nf.* stage; scenery, scene
scepticisme: *nm.* scepticism
sceptique: *adj.* sceptical; *mf* sceptic
sceptre: *nm.* sceptre
schéma: *nm.* diagram, sketch; outline
schématique: *adj.* diagrammatic, schematic
schématiquement: *adv.* diagrammatically
schématiser: *vt.* to schematise
schisme: *nm.* schism; split
schiste: *nm.* schist, shale
schizophrène: *nmf.* schizophrenic; *adj.* schizophrenic
schizophrénie: *nf.* schizophrenia
sciatique: *nf.* sciatica
scie: *nf.* saw; bore
sciemment: *adv.* knowingly, on purpose
science: *nf.* science; skill; knowledge
science-fiction: *nf.* science fiction
scientifique: *adj.* scientific
scientifiquement: *adv.* scientifically
scierie: *nf.* sawmill
scinder: *vt.* to split, divide up
scintillant: *adj.* sparkling, glistening
scintillement: *nm.* sparkling, glistening
scintiller: *vi.* to sparkle, glisten
scission: *nf.* split, scission
sciure: *nf.* sawdust
sclérose: *nf.* sclerosis
scléroser (se): *vr.* to become sclerotic
scolaire: *adj.* school; academic
scolariser: *vt.* to send to school; to

provide schools
scolarité: *nf.* schooling
scoliose: *nf.* scoliosis, curvature of the spine
scooter: *nm.* scooter
score: *nm.* score
scorie: *nf.* slag, scoria
scorpion: *nm.* scorpion
scout: *nm.* scout, boy scout
script: *nm.* printing; script
scrupule: *nm.* scruple, qualm, doubt
scrupuleusement: *adv.* scrupulously
scrupuleux: *adj.* scrupulous
scruter: *vt.* to scrutinise, scan
scrutin: *nm.* ballot, poll
sculpter: *vt.* to sculpt; to carve
sculpteur: *nm.* sculptor
sculpture: *nf.* sculpture
se: *pron.* oneself, himself, herself, itself, themselves
se conformer à: to comply with
se renseigner: to inquire; enquire about
seance: *nf.* meeting, sitting, session; seat
seau: *nm.* bucket, pail
sécateur: *nm.* secateurs
séchage: *nm.* drying; seasoning
sèche-cheveux: *nm.* invar hairdrier
sèchement: *adv.* dryly; curtly
sécher: *vi.* to dry, dry out; *vt.* to dry, wipe
sécheresse: *nf.* drought; dryness
séchoir: *nm.* drying room
second: *adj.* second, in second place; *nm.* second
second ordre: second order
secondaire: *adj.* secondary
seconder: *vt.* to assist, help
secouer: *vt.* to shake, toss
secourir: *vt.* to help, assist
secouriste: *nmf.* first-aid worker
secours: *nm.* help, assistance; relief; rescue

secousse: *nf.* jolt, bump
secret: *nm.* secret; privacy; mystery; *adj.* secret; private; discreet
secrétaire: *nmf.* secretary
secrétaire de direction: executive secretary
secrétariat: *nm.* office of secretary; secretariat
secrétariat général: general office
secrètement: *adv.* secretly
secréter: *vt.* to secrete, exude
sécrétion: *nf.* secretion
secte: *nf.* sect
secteur: *nm.* sector, section, district
section: *nf.* section, division; branch
section de capture: cross section
section efficace: cross section
sectionner: *vt.* to sever; to divide into sections
séculaire: *adj.* secular, century-old, once a century
sécurisant: *adj.* reassuring, lending security
sécuriser: *vt.* to make sb feel secure
sécuritaire: *adj.* security
sécurité: *nf.* security; safety
sédatif: *nm.* sedative; *adj.* sedative
sédentaire: *adj.* sedentary; *nm.* sedentary
sédiment: *nm.* sediment
sédimentation: *nf.* sedimentation
séducteur: *nm.* seducer
séduction: *nf.* seduction; captivation
séduire: *vt.* to seduce; to charm, captivate
séduisant: *adj.* seductive; enticing, attractive
segment: *nm.* segment
segment conjugué: tie line
segmenter: *vt.* to segment
ségrégation: *nf.* segregation
seigle: *nm.* rye
seigneur: *nm.* lord, nobleman; master
sein: *nm.* breast, bosom; womb

séisme: *nm.* earthquake, seism
seize: *adj.* sixteen
seizième: *adj.* sixteenth
séjour: *nm.* stay, sojourn; abode
séjourner: *vi.* to stay, sojourn
sel: *nm.* salt; wit
sélecteur: *nm.* selector; gear lever
sélectif: *adj.* selective
sélection: *nf.* choosing, selection
sélectionner: *vt.* to select, pick
sélectivement: *adv.* selectively
self-service: *nm.* self-service
restaurant
selle: *nf.* saddle
selon: *prép.* according to; pursuant to
semaine: *nf.* week
semblable: *adj.* like, similar, alike;
such
semblant: *nm.* appearance, look;
pretence
sembler: *vi.* to seem, appear
semelle: *nf.* sole
semence: *nf.* seed; semen
semer: *vt.* to sow; to scatter, strew
semestre: *nm.* half-year; semester
semestriel: *adj.* half-yearly; semestral
semi-conducteur: *nm.* semiconductor
séminaire: *nm.* seminary; seminar
semi-remorque: *nf.* trailer,
semitrailer
semis: *nm.* seedling; sowing; seed-
bed
semoule: *nf.* semolina
sénat: *nm.* senate
sénateur: *nm.* senator
sénile: *adj.* senile
sénilité: *nf.* senility
sens: *nm.* sense; judgement;
consciousness; meaning; direction
sensation: *nf.* sensation, feeling
sensationnel: *adj.* fantastic,
sensational
sensé: *adj.* sensible
sensibiliser: *vt.* to make sensitive to,

heighten awareness of
sensibilité: *nf.* sensitivity,
sensitiveness
sensible: *adj.* sensitive; perceptive;
appreciable
sensiblement: *adv.* approximately;
noticeably
sensoriel: *adj.* sensory
sensualité: *nf.* sensuality
sensuel: *adj.* sensual
sentence: *nf.* sentence; maxim
sentencieux: *adj.* sententious
sentier: *nm.* path, track
sentiment: *nm.* feeling, sentiment;
emotion
sentimental: *adj.* sentimental
sentimentalisme: *nm.* sentimentalism
sentinelle: *nf.* sentry, sentinel
sentir: *vt.* to feel; to perceive, guess;
to smell
séparation: *nf.* separation; division;
pulling apart
séparatiste: *nmf.* separatist
séparément: *adv.* separately
séparer: *vt.* to separate, divide; to
pull off; to split
sept: *adj. nm.* seven
septembre: *nm.* September
septième: *adj.* seventh
sépulture: *nf.* sepulture, burial
séquelle: *nf.* after-effect
séquence: *nf.* sequence
séquestre: *nm.* sequestration,
confiscation
séquestrer: *vt.* to sequester, impound
serein: *adj.* serene, calm
sérénade: *nf.* serenade
sérénité: *nf.* serenity, calmness
sergent: *nm.* sergeant
série: *nf.* series, string; class; rank
série de lyman: lyman series
séries radioactives: radioactive series
sérieusement: *adv.* seriously,
responsibly

sérieux: *adj.* serious; responsible; *nm.* seriousness, reliability
seringue: *nf.* syringe
serment: *nm.* oath; pledge
sermon: *nm.* sermon
sermonner: *vt.* to lecture, reprimand
séropositif: *adj.* HIV positive, seropositive
serpe: *nf.* billhook, bill
serpent: *nm.* serpent, snake
serpenter: *vi.* to meander, wind
serpentin: *nm.* coil; streamer
serre: *nf.* greenhouse; claw
serré: *adj.* tight; close, compact
serrer: *vt.* to tighten, fasten; to clench
serrure: *nf.* lock
serrurerie: *nf.* locksmithing
serrurier: *nm.* locksmith
sérum: *nm.* serum
servante: *nf.* servant, maidservant
serveur: *nm.* waiter
serveuse: *nf.* waitress
serviable: *adj.* obliging, helpful
service: *nm.* service; function; department; operation
service après-vente: after-sales service
service comptable: accounts department
service contentieux: legal department
service de comptabilité: bookkeeping, accounts department
service des archives: records department
service des expéditions: shipping department
service du personnel: staff department
service publicité: advertising department
services fiscaux: tax authorities
serviette: *nf.* towel; serviette, napkin
servile: *adj.* servile, slavish;

servilement: *adv.* servilely, slavishly
servilité: *nf.* servility
servir: *vi.* to be of use, be useful; *vt.* to serve, attend to
servitude: *nf.* servitude; (jar) easement
sésame: *nm.* sesame
session: *nf.* session, sitting
seuil: *nm.* threshold
seul: *adj.* alone; single; sole;
seulement: *adv.* only; but; solely
sève: *nf.* sap; pith, vigour
sévère: *adj.* severe, austere
sévèrement: *adv.* severely; strictly
sévérité: *nf.* severity; strictness
sévir: *vi.* to deal severely; to rage, hold sway
sevrer: *vt.* to wean; to deprive
sexe: *nm.* sex; genitals
sexiste: *nmf.* sexist; *adj.* sexist
sexualité: *nf.* sexuality
sexuel: *adj.* sexual, sex
sexuellement: *adv.* sexually
sexy: *adj.* sexy
seyant: *adj.* becoming
shampooing: *nm.* shampoo
shooter: *vt.* to shoot, make a shot
shopping: *nm.* shopping
short: *nm.* shorts
si: *adv.* so, so much, however much; yes; *conj.* if; whether
siamois: *adj.* Siamese
SIDA: *nm.* AIDS
sidéral: *adj.* sidereal
sidérer: *vt.* to flabbergast, stagger
sidérurgie: *nf.* steel metallurgy
sidérurgiste: *nmf.* steel maker
siècle: *nm.* century; period
siège: *nm.* seat, bench; head office
siège social: head office, registered office
siéger: *vi.* to sit; to be located
sieste: *nf.* nap, snooze; siesta
sifflement: *nm.* whistling; hissing

siffler: *vi.* to whistle; to hiss; *vt.* to whistle for; to hiss, boo
siffler: *nm.* whistle; catcall
sigle: *nm.* abbreviation; acronym
sign emend: description, particulars
signal: *nm.* signal, sign
signaler: *vt.* to signal, indicate; to point out
signalisation: *nf.* signalling system; installing signs
signature: *nf.* signature; signing
signe: *nm.* sign; mark; indication; symptom
signer: *vt.* to sign; to hallmark
signet: *nm.* bookmark
significatif: *adj.* significant, revealing
signification: *nf.* significance; meaning
signifier: *vt.* to mean, signify; to make known; to serve notice
silence: *nm.* silence; stillness
silencieusement: *adv.* silently
silencieux: *adj.* silent; still
silhouette: *nf.* silhouette, outline
silice: *nf.* silica
silicone: *nf.* silicone
sillage: *nm.* wake; slipstream; trail
sillon: *nm.* furrow; fissure
sillonner: *vt.* to plough, furrow; to crisscross
silo: *nm.* silo
similaire: *adj.* similar
similarity: *nf.* similarity
similitude: *nf.* similitude
simple: *adj.* simple; mere; single; common
simplement: *adv.* simply, merely
simplicité: *nf.* simplicity; simpleness
simplification: *nf.* simplification
simplifier: *vt.* to simplify
simpliste: *adj.* simplistic
simulation: *nf.* simulation
simuler: *vt.* to simulate, feign
simultané: *adj.* simultaneous

simultanément: *adv.* simultaneously
sincère: *adj.* sincere, honest
sincèrement: *adv.* sincerely
sincérité: *nf.* sincerity, honesty
singe: *nm.* monkey
singulariser: *vt.* to singularise; make conspicuous
singularité: *nf.* singularity; peculiarity
singulier: *adj.* singular; peculiar; remarkable
singulièrement: *adv.* singularly; remarkably
sinistre: *nm.* disaster; accident; *adj.* sinister
sinistré: *nm.* disaster victim; *adj.* disaster-stricken
sinon: *conj.* otherwise, if not; except
sinueux: *adj.* sinuous, winding
sinus: *nm.* sinus; (math) sine
sinusite: *nf.* sinusitis
siphon: *nm.* siphon
sirène: *nf.* mermaid; siren, hooter
sirop: *nm.* syrup
sirupeux: *adj.* syrupy
sismique: *adj.* seismic
site: *nm.* setting, beauty spot
site web: website
sitôt: *adv.* so soon, as soon
situation: *nf.* situation, position; state of affairs
situer: *vt.* to site, situate
six *adj.*: *nm.* six
sixième: *adj.* sixth
sketch: *nm.* sketch
ski: *nm.* ski, skiing
skier: *vi.* to ski
skieur: *nm.* skier
slalof: *nm.* slalom
slip: *nm.* briefs, panties, swimming trunks
slogan: *nm.* slogan
snack (-bar): *nm.* snack bar
snob: *adj.* snobbish

snobisme: *nm.* snobbery, snobbishness
sobre: *adj.* sober, temperate
sobriété: *nf.* sobriety, temperance
sobriquet: *nm.* nickname
sociable: *adj.* sociable; social
social: *adj.* social;
socialement: *adv.* socially
socialisme: *nm.* socialism
socialiste: *nmf.* socialist; *adj.* socialist
sociétaire: *nmf.* member
société: *nf.* society; company; partnership
société anonyme: public company
société de capitaux: joint-stock company
société de personnes: partnership
société en commandite: limited partnership
société en nom collectif: general partnership
socio-économique: *adj.* socio-economic
sociologie: *nf.* sociology
sociologique: *adj.* sociological
sociologiquement: *adv.* sociologically
sociologue: *nmf.* sociologist
socle: *nm.* pedestal, plinth; base
socquette: *nf.* ankle sock
sodium: *nm.* sodium
sodomie: *nf.* sodomy
soeur: *nf.* sister; nun
sofa: *nm.* sofa
soi: pron. oneself; self
soie: *nf.* silk
soif: *nf.* thirst
soigné: *adj.* neat, well-kept
soigner: *vt.* to look after, care for
soigneusement: *adv.* neatly; carefully
soigneux: *adj.* neat; careful
soin: *nm.* care; attention; trouble
soir: *nm.* evening; night
soirée: *nf.* evening; evening party

soit: *conj.* either; or; whether
soixantaine: *nf.* about sixty
soixante: *adj.* sixty
soixantième: *adj.* sixtieth
soja: *nm.* soya
sol: *nm.* ground; floor; soil
solaire: *adj.* solar
soldat: *nm.* soldier
solde: *nf.* pay; *nm.* balance; clearance sale
solder: *vt.* to pay; to settle, discharge
sole: *nf.* sole; hearth
soleil: *nm.* sun, sunshine; sun-flower
solennel: *adj.* solemn
solennellement: *adv.* solemnly
solfège: *nm.* musical theory
solidaire: *adj.* jointly liable; interdependent
solidairement: *adv.* jointly
solidarité: *nf.* solidarity
solide: *adj.* solid; stable; sound
solidifier: *vt.* to solidify
solidité: *nf.* solidity; soundness
soliste: *nmf.* soloist
solitaire: *nmf.* recluse, hermit; *adj.* solitary, lone
solitude: *nf.* solitude; loneliness
sollicitation: *nf.* entreaty, appeal
solliciter: *vt.* to seek, solicit; to appeal to
sollicitude: *nf.* solicitude, concern
solo: *nm.* solo
solstice: *nm.* solstice
soluble: *adj.* soluble, solvable
solution: *nf.* solution; solving; answer
solvable: *adj.* solvent; creditworthy
solvant: *nm.* solvent
somatique: *adj.* somatic
sombre: *nf.* dark; gloomy, dismal
sombrer: *vi.* to sink, founder
sommaire: *nm.* summary, argument; *adj.* basic, brief
sommation: *nf.* summons; demand
somme: *nm.* nap, snooze

sommeil: *nm.* sleep; sleepiness, drowsiness
sommeiller: *vi.* to slumber, doze
sommelier: *nm.* wine waiter
sommet: *nm.* summit; top; crest; apex
sommier: *nm.* springs, divan base; ledger
sommité: *nf.* leading light, eminent person
somnambule: *nmf.* sleepwalker; *adj.* sleepwalking
somnifère: *nm.* sleeping pill, soporific
somnolent: *adj.* sleepy, drowsy
somnoler: *vi.* to doze, drowse
somptueux: *adj.* sumptuous, lavish
son: *nm.* sound
sonate: *nf.* sonata
sondage: *nm.* drilling; probing; sounding
sonde: *nf.* sounding line; probe; drill
sonder: *vt.* to sound; to probe; to drill
songe: *nm.* dream
songer: *vt.* to dream; to imagine; to consider
songeur: *adj.* pensive
sonner: *vi.* to ring; to go off; *vt.* to ring, sound
sonnerie: *nf.* ringing, bells; chimes
sonnette: *nf.* small bell; house-bell
sonochimie: *nf.* sonochenistry
sonore: *adj.* resonant, deep-toned
sonorisation: *nf.* sound recording
sonorité: *nf.* sonority, tone; resonance
sophistiqué: *adj.* sophisticated
soporiphique: *nm.* sleeping drug; soporific; *adj.* soporific
soprano: *nmf.* soprano
sorbet: *nm.* sorbet, water ice
sorcellerie: *nf.* witchcraft, sorcery
sorcier: *nm.* sorcerer
sorcière: *nf.* witch, sorceress
sordide: *adj.* sordid, squalid
sortant: *adj.* outgoing, retiring

sortie: *nf.* exit, way out; trip; sortie; outburst; export
sortilège: *nm.* spell
sortir: *vi.* to go out, emerge; to result; to escape
sosie: *nm.* double, second self
sot: *adj.* silly, foolish
sottise: *nf.* stupidity; stupid remark, action
sou: *nm.* five centimes; cent
soubresaut: *nm.* jolt; start
souche: *nf.* stump; stock
souci: *nm.* worry; concern
soucier (se) de: *vr.* to care about
soucieux: *adj.* concerned, worried
soucoupe: *nf.* saucer
soudain: *adj.* sudden, unexpected
soudainement: *adv.* suddenly
soude: *nf.* soda
soudeur: *nm.* solderer; welder
soudier: *vt.* to solder; to weld
soudoyer: *vt.* to bribe, buy over
soudure: *nf.* soldering, welding
souffle: *nm.* blow, puff; breath
soufflé: *nm.* soufflé; flabbergasted
souffler: *vi.* to blow; to breathe; to puff
soufflerie: *nf.* bellows
soufflet: *nm.* slap in the face; affront; bellows
souffrance: *nf.* suffering; pain
souffrant: *adj.* suffering; in pain
souffrir: *vi.* to suffer, be in pain
souhait: *nm.* wish
souhaitable: *adj.* desirable
souhaiter: *vt.* to wish for, desire
souiller: *vt.* to soil, dirty; to tarnish
soulager: *vt.* to relieve, soothe
soulèvement: *nm.* uprising
soulever: *vt.* to lift, raise; to excite, stir up
soulier: *nm.* shoe
souligner: *vt.* to underline
soullagement: *nm.* relief

soumettre: *vt.* to subdue, subjugate; to submit, deliver
soumis: *adj.* submissive
soumission: *nf.* submission
soupape: *nf.* valve; safety valve
soupçon: *nm.* suspicion, conjecture; hint
soupçonner: *vt.* to suspect, surmise
soupçonneux: *adj.* suspicious
soupe: *nf.* soup
souper: *nm.* supper
soupeser: *vt.* to feel the weight of; to weigh up
soupière: *nf.* soup tureen
soupir: *nm.* sigh; gasp
soupirail: *nm.* basement window
soupirer: *vi.* to sigh; to gasp
souple: *adj.* supple; pliable
souplement: *adv.* supply, flexibly
souplesse: *nf.* suppleness; flexibility
source: *nf.* source; origin; spring
sourcil: *nm.* eyebrow
sourd: *nm.* deaf person; *adj.* deaf; muted; veiled
sourdine: *nf.* mute
souriant: *adj.* smiling, cheerful
sourire: *nm.* smile, grin
souris: *nf.* mouse
sournois: *adj.* deceitful; sly
sournoisement: *adv.* deceitfully
sous: *prép.* under, beneath, below
sous condition: on approval
sous douane: in bond
sous-alimenté: *adj.* undernourished
sous-bois: *nm.* undergrowth
sous-chef: *nm.* second-in-command
souscrire: *vi.* to subscribe
sous-développé: *adj.* underdeveloped
sous-directeur: *nm.* sub-manager
sous-entendre: *vt.* to imply, infer
sous-entendu: *nm.* innuendo, understood
sous-estimer: *vt.* to underestimate
sous-facturé, être: to be undercharged
sous-jacent: *adj.* subjacent, underlying
sous-louer: *vt.* to sublet
sous-marin: *nm.* submarine; *adj.* underwater
sous-multiple: *nm.* submultiple
sous-officier: *nm.* non-commissioned officer
sous-préfecture: *nf.* sub-prefecture
sous-préfet: *nm.* sub-prefect
soussigné: *adj.* undersigned
sous-sol: *nm.* subsoil; basement
sous-titre: *nm.* subtitle
sous-titrer: *vt.* to subtitle
soustraction: *nf.* subtraction
soustraire: *vt.* to subtract; to remove
sous-traitance: *nf.* subcontracting
sous-traitant: *nm.* subcontractor
sous-traiter: *vi.* to subcontract
sous-vêtement: *nm.* undergarment
soutane: *nf.* cassock, soutane
soute: *nf.* hold; baggage hold
soutenir: *vt.* to hold up; to sustain; to endure
souterrain: *nm.* underground passage; *adj.* underground
soutien: *nm.* support
soutien-gorge: *nm.* bra
soutirer: *vt.* to extract from
souvenir: *nm.* memory; recollection; reminder
souvenir (se): *vr.* to remember, recollect
souvent: *adv.* often, frequently
souverain: *nm.* sovereign; *adj.* sovereign; supreme
souverainement: *adv.* supremely
soyeux: *adj.* silky
spacieux: *adj.* spacious, roomy
spaghetti: *nmpl.* spaghetti
spamme: *nm.* spasm
sparadrap: *nm.* sticking plaster
spasmophilie: *nf.* spasmophilia

spatial: *adj.* spatial; space
spatule: *nf.* spatula
spécial: *adj.* special, particular
spécialement: *adv.* specially
spécialisation: *nf.* specialization
spécialiser: *vt.* to specialise
spécialiste: *nmf.* specialist
spécialité: *nf.* speciality; specialism
spécieux: *adj.* specious
spécification: *nf.* specification
spécifier: *vt.* to specify, determine
spécifique: *adj.* specific
spécifiquement: *adv.* specifically
spécimen: *nm.* specimen; sample
spécimen, sur: by type
spectacle: *nm.* spectacle, scene
spectaculaire: *adj.* spectacular
spectateur: *nm.* spectator
spectre: *nm.* ghost
spectrométrie de masse: mass
spectrometry
spéculateur: *nm.* speculator
spéculation: *nf.* speculation
spéculer: *vi.* to speculate
spéléologie: *nf.* speleology; caving
spermatozoïde: *nm.* sperm;
spermatozoon
sperme: *nm.* sperm, semen
sphère: *nf.* sphere
sphérique: *adj.* spherical
sphinx: *nm.* sphinx
spirale: *nf.* spiral
spiritualité: *nf.* spirituality
spirituel: *adj.* witty; spiritual
spirituellement: *adv.* wittily;
spiritually
splendeur: *nf.* splendour, brilliance
splendide: *adj.* splendid, magnificent
spongieux: *adj.* spongy
sponsoriser: *vt.* to sponsor
spontané: *adj.* spontaneous
spontanément: *adv.* spontaneously
sporadique: *adj.* sporadic
sport: *nm.* sport

sportif: *nm.* sportsman; *adj.* sports;
competitive; athletic
square: *nm.* square
squatter: *vi.* to squat in
squelette: *nm.* skeleton
squelettique: *adj.* skeleton-like,
scrawny
stabiliser: *vt.* to stabilise, consolidate
stabilité: *nf.* stability
stable: *adj.* stable, steady
stade: *nm.* stadium; stage
stage: *nm.* training course; probation
stagiairre: *nmf.* trainee
stagnation: *nf.* stagnation
stagner: *vi.* to stagnate
standard: *nm.* standard; switchboard; *adj.* standard
standardiser: *vt.* to standardise
standardiste: *nmf.* switchboard
operator
starter: *nm.* choke
station: *nf.* station; stage, stop; resort;
posture
stationnaire: *adj.* stationary
stationnement: *nm.* parking
stationner: *vi.* to park
station-service: *nf.* service station
statique: *adj.* static
statistique: *nf.* statistics; *adj.*
statistical
statu quo: *nm.* status quo
statue: *nf.* statue
statuer: *vt.* to rule, give a verdict
statut: *nm.* statute, ordinance; status
statutaire: *adj.* statutory
statutairement: *adv.* statutorally
statuts de la société: articles of
partnership
stencil: *nm.* stencil
sténodactylo: *nmf.* shorthand typist
sténographie: *nf.* shorthand
steppe: *nf.* steppe
stère: *nm.* stere

stéréophonique: *adj.* stere-ophonic
stéréotype: *nm.* stereotype
stérile: *adj.* sterile, infertile
stérilet: *nm.* coil, IUD
stériliser: *vt.* to sterilise
stérilité: *nf.* sterility
sternum: *nm.* breastbone, sternum
stéroïde: *adj.* steroidal; *nm.* steroid
stigmate: *nm.* mark, scar; stigmata
stimulant: *adj.* stimulating; *nm.* stimulant, stimulus
stimulateur cardiaque: pacemaker
stimulation: *nf.* stimulation
stimuler: *vt.* to stimulate, spur on
stipuler: *vt.* to stipulate, specify
stochiométrie: *nf.* stochiométry
stock: *nm.* stock, supply
stock invendable: unsaleable stock
stockage: *nm.* stocking; stockpiling
stocker: *vt.* to stock, stockpile
stoïcisme: *nm.* stoicism
stoïque: *adj.* stoical
stop: *nm.* stop; stop sign; brake-light
stopper: *vt.* to stop, halt; *vi.* to stop, halt
store: *nm.* blind, shade
strabisme: *nm.* squinting; strabismus
strapontin: *nm.* foldaway seat
stratégie: *nf.* strategy
stratégique: *adj.* strategic
stratégiquement: *adv.* strategically
stratifié: *adj.* stratified
stress: *nm.* stress
stressent: *adj.* stressful
stresser: *vt.* to cause stress to
strict: *adj.* strict, severe
strictement: *adv.* strictly
strident: *adj.* strident, shrill
strié: *adj.* streaked, striped, ridged
stroboscope: *nm.* stroboscope
strophe: *nf.* verse, stanza
structural: *adj.* structural
structure: *nf.* structure
structurel: *adj.* structural

structurer: *vt.* to structure
stuc: *nm.* stucco
studieux: *adj.* studious
studio: *nm.* studio; film theatre
stupéfaction: *nf.* stupefaction, amazement
stupéfait: *adj.* astounded, dumb-founded
stupéfiant: *adj.* astounding, amazing; drug, narcotic
stupéfier: *vt.* to stupefy; to astound
stupeur: *nf.* amazement; stupor
stupide: *adj.* silly, stupid
stupide: *adj.* stupid, foolish, silly
stupidement: *adv.* stupidly
stupidité: *nf.* stupidity
style: *nm.* style; stylus
stylet: *nm.* stiletto
styliste: *nmf.* designer; stylist
stylo: *nm.* pen
su: *nm.* knowledge
suave: *adj.* suave, smooth
subalterne: *nmf.* subordinate; *adj.* subordinate
subconscient: *nm.* subconscious; *adj.* subconscious
subdiviser: *vt.* to subdivide
subdivision: *nf.* subdivision
subir: *vt.* to sustain; to support; to undergo; to suffer
subir une perte: to incur a loss
subit: *adj.* sudden
subitement: *adv.* suddenly
subjectif: *adj.* subjective
subjectivement: *adv.* subjectively
subjectivité: *nf.* subjectivity
subjonctif: *nm.* subjunctive; *adj.* subjunctive
subjuguer: *vt.* to subjugate; to captivate
sublime: *adj.* sublime
sublimer: *vt.* to sublimate
subliminal: *adj.* subliminal
submerger: *vt.* to submerge, flood; to

engulf

submersible: *nm.* submersible; *adj.* submersible

subordination: *nf.* subordination

subordonné: *nmf.* subordinate; *adj.* subordinate

subordonner: *vt.* to subordinate

subreptice: *adj.* surreptitious

subside: *nm.* grant

subsidiaire: *adj.* subsidiary

subsistance: *nf.* subsistence, maintenance, sustenance

subsister: *vi.* to subsist; to live on

substance: *nf.* substance

substantiel: *adj.* substantial

substantiellement: *adv.* substantially

substantif: *nm.* noun, substantive; *adj.* substantival, nominal

substitumerc: *vt.* to substitute, replace

substitut: *nm.* substitute

substitution: *nf.* substitution

subterfuge: *nm.* subterfuge

subtil: *adj.* subtle

subtilement: *adv.* subtly

subtiliser: *vt.* to steal, spirit away subtilité

subvenir (à): *vi.* to provide for

subvention: *nf.* grant, subsidy

subventionner: *vt.* to subsidise

subversif: *adj.* subversive

suc: *nm.* sap; juice

succéder (à): *vi.* to succeed, follow

succès: *nm.* success; hit

successeur: *nm.* successor

successif: *adj.* successive

successivement: *adv.* successively

succinct: *adj.* succinct

succinctement: *adv.* succinctly

succomber: *vi.* to succumb, give way

succulent: *adj.* succulent, delicious

succursale: *nf.* branch

sucer: *vt.* to suck

sucette: *nf.* lollipop; dummy

suçon: *nm.* love bite

sucre: *nm.* sugar

sucrer: *vt.* to sugar, sweeten

sucrerie: *nf.* sugar refinery

sucrier: *nm.* sugar bowl

sud: *nm.* south

suer: *vi.* to sweat, perspire

sueur: *nf.* sweat

suffire: *vi.* to suffice, to be sufficient

suffisamment: *adv.* sufficiently, enough

suffisant: *adj.* sufficient, adequate

suffoquer: *vi.* to choke, suffocate; to choke, to stifle

suffrage: *nm.* suffrage; vote; commendation, approval

suggérer: *vt.* to suggest, put forward

suggestion: *nf.* suggestion

suicidaire: *adj.* suicidal; *nm.* person with suicidal tendencies

suicide: *nm.* suicide

suicider (se): *vr.* to commit suicide

suie: *nf.* soot

suif: *nm.* tallow

suintement: *nm.* oozing; sweating

suinter: *vi.* to ooze; to sweat

suite: *nf.* rest; sequel; continuation; series; connection; progress

suivant: *nm.* next one; attendant; *adj.* following, next; *prép.* according to

suivi: *adj.* steady, regular; widely adopted; *nm.* follow-up

suivre: *vt.* to follow; to attend; to accompany; to exercise

sujet: *nm.* subject, topic; ground; reason

sujétion: *nf.* subjection; constraint

sulfate: *nm.* sulphate

sulfater: *vt.* to apply copper sulphate

sulfure: *nm.* sulphur

sulfureux: *adj.* sulphurous

sulfurique: *adj.* sulphuric

sultan: *nm.* sultan

summum: *nm.* climax, height

super: *nm.* super, four-star petrol; *adj.* ultra, super
superbe: *adj.* superb, splendid
superbement: *adv.* superbly
supercarburant: *nm.* high-octane petrol
supercherie: *nf.* trick, trickery
superficie: *nf.* area, surface
superficiel: *adj.* superficial
superficiellement: *adv.* superficially
superflu: *adj.* superfluous
supérieur: *adj.* upper; superior; higher, greater
supériorité: *nf.* superiority
superlatif: *nm.* superlative; *adj.* superlative
supermarché: *nm.* supermarket
superposer: *vt.* to superpose, stack; to superimpose; se - *vr.* = to be superimposed
superposition: *nf.* superposing; superimposition
supersonique: *adj.* supersonic
superstitieux: *adj.* superstitious
superstition: *nf.* superstition
superviser: *vt.* to supervise
supplanter: *vt.* to supplant, oust
suppléant: *nm.* substitute, understudy; *adj.* substitute
supplément: *nm.* supplement; extra charge
supplémentaire: *adj.* supplementary, additional
suppliant: *adj.* beseeching, entreating
supplication: *nf.* supplication; entreaty
supplice: *nm.* corporal punishment; torture
supplier: *vt.* to beseech, entreat
support: *nm.* support; stand
supporter: *nm.* supporter
supporter: *vt.* to support; to endure; to bear
supports publicitaires, médias: advertising media
supposer: *vt.* to suppose; to assume; to imply
supposition: *nf.* supposition, surmise
suppositoire: *nm.* suppository
suppression: *nf.* suppression; deletion; cancellation
supprimer: *vt.* to suppress; to cancel
suppurer: *vi.* to suppurate
supraconductivité: *nf.* superconductivity
suprématie: *nf.* supremacy
suprême: *adj.* supreme
sur: *prép.* on; over, above; into; out of, from
sûr: *adj.* positive, sure safe
surabondance: *nf.* overabundance
suranné: *adj.* outmoded, outdated
surcharge: *nf.* overloading; excess; surcharge
surcharger: *vt.* to overload
surchauffe: *nf.* overheating
surcroît: *nm.* surplus, excess
surdité: *nf.* deafness
sureau: *nm.* elder
surélever: *vt.* to raise, heighten
surenchérir: *vi.* to outbid
surestimer: *vt.* to overestimate; to overvalue
sûreté: *nf.* safety; guarantee, surety
surexcité: *adj.* overexcited
surface: *nf.* surface
surfacturé, être: to be overcharged
surgeler: *vt.* to deep-freeze
surgénérateur: fast breeder reactor
surgir: *vi.* to rise, appear; to arise, crop up
surhomme: *nm.* superman
surintendant: *nm.* superintendent
surlendemain: *nm.* day after tomorrow
surmenage: *nm.* overwork; overtaxing
surmener: *vt.* to overwork

surmonter: *vt.* to overcome
surnager: *vi.* to float
surnaturel: *adj.* supernatural
surnom: *nm.* nickname
surnommer: *vt.* to nickname
surpasser: *vt.* to surpass, outdo
surplomb: *nm.* overhang
surplomber: *vt.* to overhang
surplus: *nm.* surplus, remainder, excess
surpopulation: *nf.* overpopulation
surprenant: *adj.* surprising, amazing
surprendre: *vt.* to surprise, amaze
surprise: *nf.* surprise
surproduction: *nf.* overproduction
surréalisme: *nm.* surrealism
surréaliste: *nmf.* surrealist; *adj.* surrealistic
sursaut: *nm.* start, jump
sursauter: *vi.* to start, jump
sursis: *nm.* reprieve; deferment
sursitaire: *adj.* deferred; suspended
surtaxe: *nf.* surcharge
surtout: *adv.* especially; above all
surveillance: *nf.* surveillance; supervision; inspection
surveillant: *nm.* warder, guard
surveiller: *vt.* to watch; to supervise; to inspect
survenir: *vi.* to take place, occur
survêtement: *nm.* tracksuit
survie: *nf.* survival
survivant: *nm.* survivor; *adj.* surviving
survivre: *vi.* to survive
survoler: *vt.* to fly over
susceptibilité magnétique: magnetic susceptibility
susceptible: *adj.* sensitive; susceptible; capable; likely
susciter: *vt.* to arouse, incite
suspect: *nm.* suspect; *adj.* suspicious, suspect
suspecter: *vt.* to suspect

suspendre: *vt.* to hang up; to suspend; to defer
suspendu: *adj.* hanging; suspended
suspens m: en - in abeyance; shelved
suspense: *nm.* suspense
suspension: *nf.* suspension; deferment; adjournment
suspicieux: *adj.* suspicious
suspicion: *nf.* suspicion
susurrer: *vt.* to whisper
suture: *nf.* suture
svelte: *adj.* svelte, slim
syllabe: *nf.* syllable
sylvestre: *adj.* forest
symbole: *nm.* symbol
symbolique: *adj.* symbolic; token; nominal
symboliquement: *adv.* symbolically
symboliser: *vt.* to symbolise
symbolisme: *nm.* symbolism
symétrie: *nf.* symmetry
symétrique: *adj.* symmetrical
symétriquement: *adv.* symmetrically
sympathie: *nf.* liking; fellow feeling; sympathy
sympathique: *adj.* likeable, nice; friendly
sympathisant: *nm.* sympathiser; *adj.* sympathising
sympathiser: *vi.* to get on well with
symphonie: *nf.* symphony
symphonique: *adj.* symphonic
symptomatique: *adj.* symptomatic
symptôme: *nm.* symptom
synagogue: *nf.* synagogue
synchronisation: *nf.* synchronisation
synchroniser: *vt.* to synchronise
syncope: *nf.* blackout, syncope
syncopé: *adj.* syncopated
syndic: *adj.* trade-union
syndicalisme: *nm.* trade unionism
syndicaliste: *nmf.* trade unionist; *adj.* trade union
syndicat: *nm.* trade union;

association
syndiquer: *vt.* to unionise
syndrome: *nm.* syndrome
synonyme: *nm.* synonym;
adj. synonymous
syntaxe: *nf.* syntax
synthèse: *nf.* synthesis
synthétique: *adj.* synthetic
synthétiser: *vt.* to synthesise
synthétiseur: *nm.* synthesiser
syphilis: *nf.* syphilis
systématique: *adj.* systematic
systématiquement: *adv.*
systematically
système: *nm.* system

$\mathcal{T}$

tabac: *nm.* tobacco
tabagisme: *nm.* nicotine addiction
tabatière: *nf.* snuffbox; skylight
table: *nf.* table; - de nuit = bedside
table; - ronde = round-table
conference
tableau: *nm.* table; chart; timetable;
scene; - de bord = dashboard
tablette: *nf.* bar; tablet; block
tablier: *nm.* apron; pinafore; overall
tabou: *nm.* taboo
tabouret: *nm.* stool
tache: *nf.* mark; stain; spot
taché: *adj.* stained, blemished
tâche: *nf.* task, assignment; work
tâcher: *vi.* to endeavour
tacheté: *adj.* spotted; freckled
tachycardie: *nf.* tachycardia
tacite: *adj.* tacit
taciturne: *adj.* taciturn, silent
tact: *nm.* tact; avoir du - = to have
tact, be tactful
tactile: *adj.* tactile
tactique: *nf.* tactics; *adj.* tactical
taffetas: *nm.* taffeta
tagliatelles: *nfpl.* tagliatelli
taie d'oreiller: pillowcase
taillader: *vt.* to slash, gash
taille: *nf.* waist; height, stature, sizet
taille-crayons: pencil sharpener
tailler: *vt.* to cut; to carve; to sharpen
tailleur: *nm.* tailor; cutter, hewer
taillis: *nm.* copse, coppice
taire: *vt.* to hush up; to conceal
talc: *nm.* talc, talcum powder
tale: *nf.* sheet metal
talent: *nm.* talent, ability
talentueux: *adj.* talented
talisman: *nm.* talisman
talon: *nm.* heel; end; pile
talonner: *vt.* to follow closely; to
hound
talquer: *vt.* to put talcum powder on

talus: *nm.* embankment
tambour: *nm.* drum; barrel
tambourin: *nm.* tambourine
tambouriner: *vi.* to drum; to beat, hammer
tamis: *nm.* sieve; riddle
tamiser: *vt.* to sieve; to sift
tampon: *nm.* stopper, plug; tampon; buffer
tamponner: *vt.* to mop up; to stamp
tam-tam: *nm.* tom-tom; row
tandem: *nm.* tandem; duo
tandis: *conj.* - que = while; whereas
tangent: *adj.* tangent, tangential
tangible: *adj.* tangible
tango: *nm.* tango
tanguer: *vi.* to pitch (ship)
tanière: *nf.* den, lair
tank: *nm.* tank
tanné: *adj.* tanned; weathered
tanner: *vt.* to tan, weather
tanneur: *nm.* tanner
tant: *adv.* so much
tante: *nf.* aunt
tantôt: *adv.* sometimes; this afternoon; shortly
taon: *nm.* horsefly, gadfly
tapage: *nm.* din, uproar, racket
tapageur: *adj.* noisy, rowdy; showy
tape: *nf.* slap
taper: *vi.* to hit, tap, stamp; to beat down; *vt.* to beat; to slap; to type
tapioca: *nm.* tapioca
tapir: *nm.* tapir
tapir (se): *vr.* to crouch; to hide away
tapis: *nm.* carpet; rug; cloth
tapisser: *vt.* to wallpaper; to cover; to carpet
tapisserie: *nf.* tapestry; tapestry-making; faire tapisserie = to be a wall-flower
tapoter: *vt.* to pat; to tap; to strum
taquin: *adj.* teasing
taquiner: *vt.* to tease; to plague

tarauder: *vt.* to tap; to torment
tard: *adv.* late
tarder: *vi.* to delay, put off; to daily
tardif: *adj.* late; tardy; slow; backward
tardivement: *adv.* late; tardily tare; *nf.* tare; defect, flaw
taré: *adj.* tainted, corrupt; sickly
tari: *adj.* dried up
tarif: *nm.* tariff price-list
tarif dégressif: tapering rate
tarifs douaniers: customs tariffs
tarir: *vt.* to dry up; to exhaust; se *vr.* to dry up
tarot: *nm.* tarot
tartare: *adj.* Tartar
tarte: *nf.* tart, flan
tartelette: *nf.* tartlet, tart
tartine: *nf.* slice of buttered bread
tartiner: *vt.* to spread with butter, jam
tartre: *nm.* tartar; fur, scale
tas: *nm.* heap, pile; lot, set
tasse: *nf.* cup
tassement: *nm.* settling, sinking
tasser: *vt.* to heap up
tata: *nf.* auntie
tâter: *vt.* to feel, try
tâtonnement: *nm.* trial and error; experimentation
tâtonner: *vi.* to feel one's way, grope along
tatouage: *nm.* tattooing; tattoo
tatouer: *vt.* to tattoo
taudis: *nm.* hovel, slum
taupe: *nf.* mole
taureau: *nm.* bull
tauromachie: *nf.* bullfighting
taux: *nm.* rate; ratio; - de change = exchange rate
taux d'escompte: rate of discount
taverne: *nf.* tavern
taxation: *nf.* taxation, taxing
taxe: *nf.* tax; duty; rate

taxer: *vt.* to tax; to fix the price of
taxi: *nm.* taxi
te: *pron.* you, yourself
technicien: *nm.* technician
technique: *nf.* technique; *adj.* technical
techniquement: *adv.* technically
technocrate: *nm.* technocrat
technocratie: *nf.* technocracy
technologie: *nf.* technology
technologique: *adj.* technological
téflon: *nm.* teflon
teigne: *nf.* moth; ringworm
teindre: *vt.* to dye
teint: *nm.* complexion, colouring
teinte: *nf.* tint, colour, shade
teinter: *vt.* to tint; to stain
teinture: *nf.* dye; dyeing
teinturerie: *nf.* dyeing; dye-works; dry cleaner's
teinturier: *nm.* dyer; dry cleaner
télé: *nf.* TV, telly
télécarte: *nf.* phonecard
télécommande: *nf.* remote control
télécommunication: *nf.* telecommunication
téléconférence: *nf.* teleconferencing
télécopie: *nf.* facsimile transmission; fax
télécopieur: *nm.* fax machine
télédiffusion: *nf.* television broadcasting
télégramme: *nm.* telegram; cable
télégraphier: *vt.* to telegraph, cable
téléguider: *vt.* to radio-control
télématique: *nf.* telematics
téléobjectif: *nm.* telephoto lens
télépathie: *nf.* telepathy
téléphérique: *nm.* cableway; cable-car
téléphone: *nm.* telephone
téléphoner: *vi.* to telephone
téléphonique: *adj.* telephone; telephonic

télescope: *nm.* telescope
télescopique: *adj.* telescopic
télésiège: *nm.* chairlift
téléski: *nm.* lift, ski tow
téléspectateur: *nm.* television viewer
téléviseur: *nm.* television set
télévision: *nf.* television
télex: *nm.* telex
tellement: *adj.* so, so much; de so many, so much
téméraire: *adj.* rash, reckless
témérairement: *adv.* rashly; recklessly
témérité: *nf.* rashness; recklessness
témoignage: *nm.* testimony; evidence; certificate
témoigner: *vi.* to testify
témoin: *nm.* witness; evidence; proof
tempérament: *nm.* constitution; temperament; character
tempérance: *nf.* temperance
température: *nf.* temperature
tempéré: *adj.* temperate; tempered
tempérer: *vt.* to temper; to assuage, soothe
tempête: *nf.* tempest
temple: *nm.* temple
tempo: *nm.* tempo, pace
temporaire: *adj.* temporary
temporairement: *adv.* temporarily
temporel: *adj.* worldly, temporal
temporiser: *vi.* to temporise, delay
temps: *nm.* time; while; tense; beat; weather
tenace: *adj.* tenacious, stubborn, persistent
ténacité: *nf.* tenacity; stubbornness
tenaille: *nf.* pincers; tongs
tenailler: *vt.* to torture; to rack
tendance: *nf.* tendency; leaning; trend
tendancieux: *adj.* tendentious
tendinite: *nf.* tendinitis
tendon: *nm.* tendon, sinew

tendre: *adj.* tender, soft; delicate
tendrement: *adv.* tenderly, affectionately
tendresse: *nf.* tenderness; fondness
tendu: *adj.* tight; stretched; concentrated; delicate, fraught
ténèbres: *nfpl.* darkness, gloom
ténébreux: *adj.* dark, gloomy
teneur: *nf.* terms; content; grade
tenir: *vt.* to hold, keep; to stock; to run
tenir les livres: to keep the books
tenir une réunion: to hold a meeting
tennis: *nm.* tennis
ténor: *nm.* tenor; leading light
tension de surface: surface tension
tension interfaciale: interfacial tension
tentacule: *nm.* tentacle
tentant: *adj.* tempting, inviting
tentation: *nf.* temptation
tentative: *nf.* attempt, bid
tente: *nf.* tent
tenter: *vt.* to tempt
tenture: *nf.* hanging; curtain
tenue: *nf.* holding; session; deportment, good behaviour; dress, appearance
tergal: *nm.* terylene
tergiverser: *vi.* to procrastinate, beat about the bush
terme: *nm.* term; termination, end; word, expression
terminaison: *nf.* ending
terminaison de chaîne: termination step, termination of chain
terminal: *adj.* terminal; *nm.* terminal
terminer: *vt.* to terminate; to finish off
terminologie: *nf.* terminology
termite: *nm.* termite
terne: *adj.* colourless; lustreless, drab; spiritless
ternir: *vt.* to tarnish, dull

terrain: *nm.* ground, soil, earth; plot; position; site; field
terrasse: *nf.* terrace
terrasser: *vt.* to floor, knock down; to strike down, overcome
terre: *nf.* earth; world; ground, land
terre à terre: *adj.* down to earth, commonplace
terreau: *nm.* compost
terre-plein: *nm.* terreplein; platform; central reservation.
terrer (se): *vr.* to crouch down; to lie low, go to ground
terrestre: *adj.* land; terrestrial
terreur: *nf.* terror, dread
terreux: *adj.* earthy;dirty; ashen
terrible: *adj.* terrible, dreadful
terrien: *nm.* countryman; earthling
terrier: *nm.* burrow; earth; terrier
terrifiant: *adj.* terrifying, fearsome
terrifier: *vt.* to terrify
terrine: *nf.* earthenware dish, terrine
territoire: *nm.* territory, area
territorial: *adj.* land, territorial
terroir: *nm.* land
terroriser: *vt.* to terrorise
terrorisme: *nm.* terrorism
terroriste: *nmf.* terrorist; *adj.* terrorist
tertiaire: *adj.* tertiary
test: *nm.* test
testament: *nm.* will, testament
tester: *vt.* to test; to make out one's will
testicule: *nm.* testicle, testis
tétanos: *nm.* tetanus; lockjaw
têtard: *nm.* tadpole
tête: *nf.* head; face; front; top; sense, judgment
tête à tête: *nm.* private conversation
tétée: *nf.* feeding; nursing
téter: *vt.* to suck
tétine: *nf.* teat; udder; dummy
téton: *nm.* breast
têtu: *adj.* headstrong, stubborn

texte: *nm.* text
textile: *adj.* textile
textuel: *adj.* textual, literal, exact
textuellement: *adv.* literally; word for word
texture: *nf.* texture
thé: *nm.* tea
théâtral: *adj.* theatrical, dramatic
théâtre: *nm.* theatre; drama
théière: *nf.* teapot
thématique: *adj.* thematic
thème: *nm.* theme
théologie: *nf.* theology
théorème: *nm.* theorem
théoricien: *nm.* theoretician, theorist
théorie: *nf.* theory
théorie cinétique des gaz: kinetic theory of gas
théorie du complexe activé: activated complex theory
théorique: *adj.* theoretical
théoriquement: *adv.* theoretically
thérapeute: *nmf.* therapist
thérapie: *nf.* therapy
thermal: *adj.* thermal; hydropathic
thermique: *adj.* thermal; thermic
thermomètre: *nm.* thermometer
thermos: *nm.* thermos
thermostat: *nm.* thermostat
thésaurus: *nm.* thesaurus
thèse: *nf.* thesis
thon: *nm.* tuna
thoracique: *adj.* thoracic
thorax: *nm.* thorax
thrombose: *nf.* thrombosis
thym: *nm.* thyme
thyroïde: *nf.* thyroid
tibia: *nm.* tibia
ticket: *nm.* ticket
tie: *nm.* twitch, tic; mannerism
tiède: *adj.* lukewarm, tepid
tiers: *adj.* third
tige: *nf.* stem, stalk
tigre: *nm.* tiger

tilleul: *nm.* lime, linden
timbale: *nf.* kettledrum
timbre: *nm.* stamp; postmark; bell; tone, timbre
timbré: *adj.* stamped; resonant
timbrer: *vt.* to stamp; to postmark
timide: *adj.* timid, shy
timidement: *adv.* timidly
timidité: *nf.* timidity, shyness
timonier: *nm.* helmsman
tintamarre: *nm.* hubbub, uproar
tintement: *nm.* ringing; chiming; toll
tinter: *vi.* to ring, toll; to chime
tique: *nf.* tick
tiquer: *vi.* to wince
tir: *nm.* shooting, firing, fire; shot
tirade: *nf.* tirade; monologue
tirage: *nm.* drawing, drawing off
tiraillement: *nm.* tugging; pulling
tirailler: *vt.* to tug; to plague; to pester
tire-bouchon: *nm.* corkscrew
tire-fesses: *nm.* ski tow
tirelire: *nf.* moneybox
tirer: *vt.* to pull; to draw; to extract
tirer à découvert: to overdraw
tirer une traite: to draw a bill
tiret: *nm.* dash; hyphen
tireur: *nm.* gunner, sharp-shooter; printer; drawer
tiroir: *nm.* drawer
tison: *nm.* brand
tisonnier: *nm.* poker
tissage: *nm.* weaving
tisser: *vt.* to weave
tissu: *nm.* texture, fabric; tissue
titan: *nm.* titan
titane: *nm.* titanium
titanesque: *adj.* titanic
titre: *nm.* title; heading; denomination; claim, right; deed
tituber: *vi.* to stagger
titulaire: *nmf.* incumbent, holder; *adj.* titular; entitled

titulaire, porteur: *nm.* holder
toast: *nm.* slice of toast; toast
toboggan: *nm.* toboggan
toc: *nm.* tap, knock
toi: pron. you
toile: *nf.* cloth; canvas; sheet
toilette: *nf.* cleaning, grooming; washstand
toison: *nf.* fleece
toit: *nm.* roof; home
toiture: *nf.* roof, roofing
tolérable: *adj.* tolerable, bearable
tolérance: *nf.* tolerance
tolérant: *adj.* tolerant
tolérer: *vt.* to tolerate; to put up with
tomate: *nf.* tomato
tombe: *nf.* tomb; grave
tombeau: *nm.* tomb
tomber: *vi.* to fall; to sink; to decay
tombola: *nf.* tombola
tome: *nm.* book; volume
tomme: *nf.* ton
ton: *adj.* ta, pl tes your
tonalité: *nf.* tonality; key
tondeuse: *nf.* clippers, shears; mower
tondre: *vt.* to shear, clip; mow
tonifiant: *nm.* tonic
tonifier: *vt.* to tone up; to invigorate
tonique: *adj.* tonic; fortifying; invigorating; *nm.* tonic
tonitruant: *adj.* thundering
tonnage: *nm.* tonnage; displacement
tonneau: *nm.* barrel, cask
tonnelle: *nf.* bower, arbour
tonnerre: *nm.* thunder
tonton: *nm.* uncle
tonus: *nm.* tone; energy
top: *nm.* pip, stroke
topaze: *nf.* topaz
topographie: *nf.* topography
toquade: *nf.* infatuation; fad, craze
toque: *nf.* fur hat; cap
toquer: *vi.* to tap, rap
torche: *nf.* torch

torcher: *vt.* to wipe, mop up
torchon: *nm.* cloth; duster
tordre: *vt.* to twist, contort; se or to bend, twist; to sprain
tordu: *adj.* twisted, crooked, bent
tornade: *nf.* tornado
torpeur: *nf.* torpor
torpille: *nf.* torpedo
torpiller: *vt.* to torpedo
torréfaction: *nf.* roasting; toasting
torrent: *nm.* torrent
torrentiel: *adj.* torrential
torride: *adj.* torrid; scorching
torsade: *nf.* twist; cable moulding
torse: *nm.* chest; torso
torsion: *nf.* twisting; torsion
tort: *nm.* fault; wrong; prejudice
torticolis: *nm.* stiff neck; torticollis
tortiller: *vt.* to twist; se - *vr.* = to wriggle; to squirm
tortionnaire: *nmf.* torturer; *adj.* pertaining to torture
tortue: *nf.* tortoise
tortueux: *adj.* tortuous, winding, meandering
torture: *nf.* torture
torturer: *vt.* to torture
tôt: *adv.* early; soon, quickly
total: *adj.* total; absolute
totaliser: *vt.* to totalise, add up
totalitaire: *adj.* totalitarian
totalitarisme: *nm.* totalitarianism
totalité: *nf.* totality; whole
totem: *nm.* totem
touchant: *adj.* touching, moving
touche: *nf.* touch; trial; stroke; key
toucher: *vt.* to touch; to feel; *nm.* touch, feeling
touffe: *nf.* tuft, clump
touffu: *adj.* bushy, thick

toujours: *adv.* always; still; all the same

toupet: *nm.* qui , tuft; cheek

toupie: *nf.* spinning top

tour: *nf.* tower; turn

tourbe: *nf.* peat

tourbillon: *nm.* whirlwind, whirlpool

tourbillonner: *vi.* to whirl, eddy

tourerelle: *nf.* turtledove

tourisme: *nm.* tourism

touriste: *nmf.* tourist

touristique: *adj.* tourist

tourment: *nm.* torment, agony

tourmente: *nf.* storm, tempest

tourmenter: *vt.* to rack, torment

tournage: *nm.* turning

tournant: *nm.* bend; turning point; *adj.* revolving, swivel; winding

tournedos: *nm.* fillet steak

tournée: *nf.* tour; round

tourner: *vt.* to turn; to round; *vi.* to turn; to work; to change

tournesol: *nm.* sunflower

tourneur: *nm.* turner

tournevis: *nm.* screwdriver

tourniquet: *nm.* tourniquet; turnstile

tournis: *nm.* sturdy, staggers; avoir le - = to feel giddy

tournoi: *nm.* tournament

tournoyer: *vi.* to whirl, swirl

tournure: *nf.* turn; turn of phrase

tourte: *nf.* pie

tourtière: *nf.* pie tin

tousser: *vi.* to cough

tout: *adj.* all; whole; every

toutefois: *adv.* however

tout-puissant: *adj.* all-powerful

toux: *nf.* cough

toxicomane: *nmf.* drug addict; *adj.* drug addicted

toxicomanie: *nf.* drug addiction

toxine: *nf.* toxin

toxique: *adj.* toxic

trac: *nm.* nerves, stage fright

tracas: *nm.* bustle, turmoil; worry

tracasser: *vt.* to worry; to harass

trace: *nf.* track, impression; outline, sketch; vestige

tracer: *vt.* to draw, trace; to open up

trachée: *nf.* trachea, windpipe

tract: *nm.* leaflet, tract

tractation: *nf.* transaction; bargaining

tracteur: *nm.* tractor

traction: *nf.* traction; pulling

tradition: *nf.* tradition

traditionaliste: *nmf.* traditionalist; *adj.* traditionalist

traditionnel: *adj.* traditional

traducteur: *nm.* translator

traduction: *nf.* translation

traduire: *vt.* to translate

trafic: *nm.* traffic; trading; dealings

trafiquant: *nm.* trafficker

trafiquer: *vi.* to fiddle, tamper with

tragédie: *nf.* tragedy

tragédien: *nm.* tragedian, tragic actor

tragique: *adj.* tragic

tragiquement: *adv.* tragically

trahir: *vt.* to betray

trahison: *nf.* betrayal, treason

train: *nm.* train; pace, rate

traînasser: *vi.* to dawdle

traîneau: *nm.* sleigh, sledge

traînée: *nf.* trail, track; drag

trainer: *vi.* to lag, dawdle; to drag on

trainer: *vt.* to plot; to weave

train-train: *nm.* humdrum routine

traire: *vt.* to milk

trait: *nm.* trait, feature; deed

traite: *nf.* trade; draft, bill; milking

traite de complaisance: accommodation bill

traite documentaire: documentary draft

traitement: *nm.* treatment; salary; processing

traiter: *vt.* to treat; to process; to treat; negotiate

traiteur: *nm.* caterer; trader
traîtrise: *nf.* treachery, treacherousness
trajectoire: *nf.* trajectory
trajet: *nm.* distance; journey; course, path
trampoline: *nm.* trampoline
tramway: *nm.* tram, tramway
tranchant: *adj.* sharp, cutting
tranche: *nf.* slice; edge; section
trancher: *vt.* to cut, sever; to conclude
tranférer: *vt.* to transfer
tranquille: *adj.* quiet, tranquil
tranquillement: *adv.* quietly, tranquilly
tranquillisant: *nm.* tranquilliser; *adj.* soothing, tranquillising
tranquilliser: *vt.* to reassure
tranquillité: *nf.* tranquillity
transaction: *nf.* transaction, arrangement
transatlantique: *nm.* transatlantic
transcendant: *adj.* transcendent; transcendental
transcender: *vt.* to transcend
transcription: *nf.* transcription; copy
transcrire: *vt.* to transcribe; copy out
transe: *nf.* trance
transept: *nm.* transept
transférer: *vt.* to transfigure
transfert: *nm.* transfer; conveyance

transfert, réaction de: transfert reaction
transfiguration: *nf.* transfiguration
transformateur: *nm.* transformer
transformation: *nf.* transformation
transformer: *vt.* to transform, change
transfuge: *nmf.* defector
transfuser: *vt.* to transfuse
transfusion: *nf.* transfusion
transgresser: *vt.* to transgress, infringe

transgression: *nf.* transgression, infringement
transi: *adj.* numb, paralysed
transiger: *vi.* to compromise, come to terms
transistor: *nm.* transistor
transit: *nm.* transit
transitaire: *nmf.* the forwarding agent
transiter: *vi.* to pass in transit
transitif: *adj.* transitive
transition: *nf.* transition
transitoire: *adj.* transitory
translucide: *adj.* translucent
transmettre: *vt.* to transmit; to pass on, hand down
transmissible: *adj.* transmissible
transmisssion: *nf.* transmission; passing on; handing down
transmuter: *vt.* to transmute
transparaître: *vi.* to show through
transparence: *nf.* transparency
transparent: *adj.* transparent
transpercer: *vt.* to pierce; to penetrate
transpiration: *nf.* transpiration; perspiration
transpirer: *vi.* to perspire; to come to light
transplanter: *vt.* to transplant
transport: *nm.* carrying; transport; conveyance; transfer
transport maritime: sea freight
transport routier: road haulage
transportable: *adj.* transportable
transporter: *vt.* to carry; to transport
transporteur: *nm.* haulier; carrier
transposer: *vt.* to transpose
transposition: *nf.* transposition
transsexuel: *adj.* transsexual
transvaser: *vt.* to decant
transversal: *adj.* transverse
transvider: *vt.* to pour into another container

trapèze: *nm.* trapeze
trapéziste: *nmf.* trapeze artist
trappe: *nf.* trap door
trappeur: *nm.* trapper
trapu: *adj.* squat; thickset
traquer: *vt.* to track; to hunt down
traumatisant: *adj.* traumatising
traumatiser: *vt.* to traumatise
traumatisme: *nm.* traumatism
travail: *nm.* work; job, occupation; labour
travailler: *vi.* to work; to endeavour
travailleur: *nm.* worker; *adj.* diligent; hard-working
travers: *nm.* breadth; irregularity; fault
travers (à): *prep.* across (cross-wise); through
traversée: *nf.* crossing, going through; traverse
traverser: *vt.* to cross, traverse
traversin: *nm.* bolster
travesti: *nm.* drag artist; transvestite; *adj.* disguised
trébucher: *vi.* to stumble, trip up
trèfle: *nm.* clover
tréfonds: *nm.* subsoil, bottom
treille: *nf.* climbing vine
treillis: *nm.* trellis; wire mesh
treize: *adj.* thirteen
treizième: *adj.* thirteenth
tréma: *nm.* dieresis
tremblant: *adj.* trembling, shaking
tremblement: *nm.* trembling; shiver; vibration
trembler: *vi.* to tremble, shake
trembloter: *vi.* to tremble slightly, flicker
trémousser: *vr.* to wriggle
tremper: *vt.* to soak; to dip
tremplin: *nm.* springboard; ski-jump
trentaine: *nf.* about thirty
trente: *adj.* thirty
trentième: *adj.* thirtieth

trépasser: *vi.* to pass away
trépidant: *adj.* pulsating, quivering
trépied: *nm.* tripod
trépigner: *vi.* to stamp one's feet
très: *adv.* very; most; very much
trésor: *nm.* treasure
trésorerie: *nf.* treasury
trésorier: *nm.* treasurer
tressaillir: *vi.* to thrill; to shudder
tressauter: *vi.* to start, jump
tresse: *nf.* plait, braid
tresser: *vt.* to plait, braid
tréteau: *nm.* trestle
treuil: *nm.* winch
trêve: *nf.* truce; respite, rest
tri: *nm.* sorting out; selection; grading
triage: *nm.* sorting out
triangle: *nm.* triangle
triangulaire: *adj.* triangular
triathlon: *nm.* triathlon
tribal: *adj.* tribal
tribord: *nm.* starboard
tribu: *nf.* tribe
tribunal: *nm.* court, tribunal
tribune: *nf.* gallery, stand; rostrum
tribut: *adj.* dependent, tributary
tribut: *nm.* tribute
tricher: *vi.* to cheat
tricheur: *nm.* cheater
trichloréthylène: *nm.* trichlo-rethylene
tricolore: *adj.* three-coloured, tri-colour
tricot: *nm.* jumper; knitting
tricoter: *vt.* to knit
tridimensionnel: *adj.* three-dimensional
triennal: *adj.* triennial; three-yearly
trier: *vt.* to sort out; to pick over
trifouiller: *vi.* to rummage; *vt.* to rummage about in
trigonométrie: *nf.* trigonometry
trilingue: *adj.* trilingual
trilogie: *nf.* trilogy

trimer: *vi.* to slave away
trimestre: *nm.* quarter; term
trimestriel: *adj.* quarterly
tringle: *nf.* rod
trinité: *nf.* trinity
trinité: *nm.* treaty; treatise, tract
trinquer: *vi.* to toast; to booze
trio: *nm.* trio
triomphal: *adj.* triumphal
triomphalement: *adv.* triumphantly
triomphant: *adj.* triumphant
triomphe: *nm.* triumph, victory
triompher: *vi.* to triumph
triparti: *adj.* tripartite
tripe: *nf.* tripe; guts
tripler: *vi.* to triple
tripoter: *vt.* to play with, speculate with
trips le: *adj.* triple, treble
trique: *nf.* cudgel
triste: *adj.* sad, melancholy
tristement: *adv.* sadly
tristesse: *nf.* sadness; melancholy
triton: *nm.* triton; triton
triturer: *vt.* to grind up, triturate
trivial: *adj.* mundane, trivial; coarse, crude
trivialité: *nf.* triviality; crudeness
troc: *nm.* exchange; barter
troglodyte: *nm.* cave dweller, troglodyte
trognon: *nm.* core; stalk
trois: *adj.* three
troisième: *adj.* third
troisième corps: third body
trombone: *nm.* trombone
trompe: *nf.* trumpet; trunk, snout
trompe-l'oeil: *nm.* in var trompe l'oeil
tromper: *vt.* to deceive, trick
tromperie: *nf.* deception, deceit
trompette: *nf.* trumpet
trompettiste: *nmf.* trumpet player
trompeur: *adj.* deceitful; deceptive

tronc: *nm.* trunk, shaft
tronçon: *nm.* section, part
tronçonner: *vt.* to cut up, cut into sections
tronçonneuse: *nf.* chain saw
trône: *nm.* throne
trôner: *vi.* to sit on the throne
tronquer: *vt.* to truncate, curtail
trop: *adv.* too; too much, unduly
trophée: *nm.* trophy
tropical: *adj.* tropical
tropique: *nm.* tropic
trop-plein: *nm.* overflow; excess
troquer: *vt.* to barter, swap
trot: *nm.* trot
trotter: *vi.* to trot; to run about; to toddle
trottiner: *vi.* to jog along; to trot along
trottinette: *nf.* scooter
trottoir: *nm.* pavement
trou: *nm.* hole; gap; cavity
troublant: *adj.* disturbing, disquieting
trouble: *adj.* unclear; murky, suspicious
trouble-fête: *nmf.* spoilsport, killjoy
troubler: *vt.* to disturb, disconcert; to cloud, to darken
trouer: *vt.* to make a hole in; to pierce
troupe: *nf.* troupe; troop, band
troupeau: *nm.* herd, drove
trousse: *nf.* case, kit; wallet
trousseau: *nm.* trousseau; outfit
trouvaille: *nf.* windfall; inspired idea
trouver: *vt.* to find
trouver: *vt.* to find, detect; to think
truand: *nm.* gangster; tramp
truc: *nm.* trick; gadget, thingummy
truculent: *adj.* truculent; colourful, vivid
truelle: *nf.* trowel
truffe: *nf.* truffle

truie: *nf.* sow

truite: *nf.* trout

truquage: *nm.* rigging, fixing; fiddling

truquer: *vt.* to rig, fix; to fiddle

tsar: *nm.* tsar

tu: pron. you

tuant: *adj.* exhausting; exasperating

tuba: *nm.* tuba, snorkel

tube: *nm.* tube, pipe; duct

tube à choc: shock tube

tuberculose: *nf.* tuberculosis

tuer: *vt.* to kill

tuerie: *nf.* slaughter

tueur: *nm.* killer

tuile: *nf.* tile

tulipe: *nf.* tulip

tulle: *nm.* tulle

tuméfié: *adj.* puffed-up, swollen

tumeur: *nf.* tumour

tumulte: *nm.* tumult, commotion

tumultueux: *adj.* tumultuous, stormy

tungstène: *nm.* tungsten

tunique: *nf.* tunic; smock

tunnel: *nm.* tunnel

turban: *nm.* turban

turbine: *nf.* turbine

turbo: *nm.* turbo

turbulence: *nf.* turbulence; excitement

turbulent: *adj.* turbulent

turpitude: *nf.* turpitude, baseness

tutelle: *nf.* guardianship, supervision

tuteur: *nm.* guardian

tutoyer: *vt.* to address sb as 'tu'

tuyau: *nm.* pipe

tuyauterie: *nf.* piping

tympan: *nm.* eardrum, tympanum

type: *nm.* type; model; sample; bloke, chap

typé: *adj.* typical

typhoïde: *nf.* typhoid; *adj.* typhoid

typhon: *nm.* typhoon

typhus: *nm.* typhus

typique: *adj.* typical; -ment = *adv.* typically

tyran: *nm.* tyrant

tyrannie: *nf.* tyranny

tyrannique: *adj.* tyrannical

tyranniser: *vt.* to tyrannise

U

ulcère: *nm.* ulcer
ulcérer: *vt.* to sicken; to embitter
ultérieur: *adj.* later, subsequent
ultérieurement: *adv.* later, subsequently
ultimatum: *nm.* ultimatum
ultime: *adj.* ultimate, final
ultraviolet: *nm.* ultraviolet ray; *adj.* ultraviolet
unanime: *adj.* unanimous
unanimement: *adj.* unanimously
uni: *adj.* plain, self-coloured; close; smooth
unification: *nf.* unification; standardisation
unifier: *vt.* to unify; to standardise
uniforme: *adj.* uniform, regular; *nm.* uniform
uniformément: *adv.* uniformly, regularly
uniformité: *nf.* uniformity; regularity
unilatéral: *adj.* unilateral
union: *nf.* union; combination, blending
unions douanières: customs unions
unique: *adj.* only, single; unique
uniquement: *adv.* only, solely, exclusively; merely
unir: *vt.* to unite; to join; to combine
unisson: *nm.* unison
unitaire: *adj.* unitary, unit
unité: *nf.* unity; unit
univers: *nm.* universe; world
universalité: *nf.* universality
universel: *adj.* universal; all-purpose
universellement: *adv.* universally
universitaire: *adj.* university; *nmf.* academic
université: *nf.* university
uranium: *nm.* uranium
urbain: *adj.* urban, city
urbanisation: *nf.* urbanisation
urbaniser: *vt.* to urbanise

urbanisme: *nm.* town planning
urbaniste: *nmf.* town planner
urée: *nf.* urea
urgence: *nf.* urgency; emergency
urgent: *adj.* urgent
urinaire: *adj.* urinary
urine: *nf.* urine
uriner: *vi.* to urinate
urinoir: *nm.* urinal
urne: *nf.* ballot box; urn
urticaire: *nf.* hives, urticaria
usage: *nm.* use; custom; usage; practice; wear
usagé: *adj.* worn, old
usager: *nm.* user
usé: *adj.* worn; threadbare; banal, trite
user: *vt.* to make use of, enjoy; to wear out
usine: *nf.* factory
usiner: *vt.* to machine; to manufacture
usité: *adj.* in cou mon use, common
ustensile: *nm.* implement; utensil
usuel: *adj.* ordinary; everyday
usure: *nf.* usury
usurier: *nm.* usurer
usurper: *vt.* to usurp
utérus: *nm.* womb, uterus
utile: *adj.* useful
utilisateur: *nm.* user
utilisation: *nf.* use, utilisation
utiliser: *vt.* to use, utilise; to make use of
utilitaire: *adj.* utilitarian
utilité: *nf.* usefulness; use; profit
utopie: *nf.* utopia
utopique: *adj.* utopian

v

vacance: *nf.* vacancy, holiday, vacation
vacancier: *nm.* holidaymaker
vacant: *adj.* vacant, unoccupied
vacarme: *nm.* racket, row
vaccin: *nm.* vaccine
vaccination: *nf.* vaccination
vacciner: *vt.* to vaccinate
vache: *nf.* cow; cowhide
vachement: *adv.* damned, bloody
vacher: *nm.* cowherd
vacherie: *nf.* rottenness
vaciller: *vi.* to sway, totter; to falter
va-et-vient: *nm.* invar comings and goings; to and fro
vagabond: *nm.* tramp, vagabond
vagabondage: *nm.* wandering, roaming; vagrancy
vagabonder: *vi.* to wander, roam
vagin: *nf.* vagina
vaginal: *adj.* vaginal
vague: *adj.* vague, hazy, indistinct
vaguer: *vi.* to wander, roam
vaillamment: *adv.* bravely, courageously
vaillant: *adj.* brave, courageous
vain: *adj.* vain; empty, hollow; shallow
vaincre: *vt.* to defeat, overcome
vaincu: *adj.* defeated, beaten
vainqueur: *nm.* conqueror, victor
vaisculaire: *adj.* vascular
vaisseau: *nm.* vessel; ship
vaisselle: *nf.* crockery; dishes
valable: *adj.* valid, legitimate; worthwhile
valet: *nm.* valet; servant
valeur: *nf.* value, worth; security, share; meaning
valide: *adj.* able, able-bodied
valider: *vt.* to validate
validité: *nf.* validity
valise: *nf.* suitcase

vallée: *nf.* valley
vallonné: *adj.* undulating, hilly
valoir: *vt.* to be worth; to be valid
valoriser: *vt.* to valorise
valse: *nf.* waltz
valser: *vi.* to waltz
valve: *nf.* valve
vampire: *nm.* vampire
vandalisme: *nm.* vandalism
vanille: *nf.* vanilla
vanité: *nf.* vanity, conceit
vaniteux: *adj.* vain, conceited
vanne: *nf.* gate, sluice
vannerie: *nf.* basketry; wicker-work
vantard: *adj.* boastful, bragging
vantardise: *nf.* boastfulness; boast
vanter: *vt.* to praise, vaunt;
se *vr.* to boast, brag
vapeur: *nf.* haze, vapour
vaporeux: *adj.* filmy, vaporous
vaporisateur: *nm.* spray, atomiser
vaporiser: *vt.* to spray; to vaporise
varappe: *nf.* rock-climbing
variable: *adj.* variable, changeable
variante: *nf.* variant; variation
variation: *nf.* variation, change
varice: *nf.* varicose vein
varicelle: *nf.* chickenpox
varié: *adj.* varied; variegated; various
varier: *vi.* to vary, change; *vt.* to vary
variété: *nf.* variety, diversity
variole: *nf.* smallpox
vase: *nm.* vase, bowl; *nf.* silt, mud
vaseline: *nf.* vaseline
vaseux: *adj.* woolly, muddled; muddy, silty
vasistas: *nm.* fanlight
vaste: *adj.* vast, huge
vaudeville: *nm.* vaudeville
vaudou: *nm.* voodoo
vaurien: *nm.* good-for-nothing
vautour: *nm.* vulture
vautrer (se): *vr.* to wallow in
veau: *nm.* calf; veal

vecteur: *nm.* vector
vécu: *adj.* real, true-life; lived
vedette: *nf.* star; launch
végétal: *adj.* vegetable
végétarien: *nm.* vegetarian; *adj.* vegetarian
végétatif: *adj.* vegetative
végétation: *nf.* vegetation
végéter: *vi.* to vegetate; to stagnate
véhémence: *nf.* vehemence
véhément: *adj.* vehement
véhicule: *nm.* vehicle
véhicule semi-remorque: articulated vehicle
veille: *nf.* wakefulness; watch; eve
veillée: *nf.* evening; evening meeting
veiller: *vi.* to stay up, sit up
veilleur: *nm.* watchman
veinard: *nm.* lucky person; *adj.* lucky, jammy
veine: *nf.* vein, seam; inspiration; luck
vêler: *vi.* to calve
velléité: *nf.* vague desire, vague impulse
velleuse: *nf.* night light; sidelight
vélo: *nm.* bike
vélodrome: *nm.* velodrome
vélomoteur: *nm.* moped
velours: *nm.* velvet
velouté: *adj.* velvety, downy
velu: *adj.* hairy
vénal: *adj.* venal, mercenary
vendange: *nf.* wine harvest
vendanger: *vt.* to harvest grapes from; *vi.* to harvest the grapes
vendangeur: *nm.* grape-picker
vendetta: *nf.* vendetta
vendeur: *nm.* seller, sales-person
vendre: *vt.* to sell
vendredi: *nm.* Friday
vénéneux: *adj.* poisonous
vénérable: *adj.* venerable
vénération: *nf.* veneration

vénérer: *vt.* to venerate
vénérien: *adj.* venereal
vengeance: *nf.* vengeance, revenge
venger: *vt.* to avenge
venimeux: *adj.* venomous, poisonous; vicious
venin: *nm.* venom; poison
venir: *vi.* to come; to happen; to grow
vent: *nm.* wind; breath; emptiness
vente: *nf.* sale; selling; auction
vente liquidation: clearance sale
vente par correspondance: mail-order business
ventilateur: *nm.* ventilator, fan
ventilation: *nf.* breakdown
ventiler: *vt.* to ventilate; to divide up
ventouse: *nf.* sucker; suction disc
ventre: *nm.* stomach, belly; womb
ventricule: *nm.* ventricle
ventriloque: *nmf.* ventriloquist; *adj.* ventriloquous
venue: *nf.* coming
ver: *nm.* worm; grub
véracité: *nf.* veracity; truthfulness
véranda: *nf.* veranda
verbal: *adj.* verbal
verbalement: *adv.* verbally
verbe: *nm.* verb; language, word
verbiage: *nm.* verbiage
verdeur: *nf.* vigour, vitality
verdict: *nm.* verdict
verdir: *vi.* to go green; *vt.* to turn green
verdure: *nf.* greenery, verdure
verge: *nf.* stick, cane
verger: *nm.* orchard
verglacé: *adj.* icy
verglas: *nm.* black ice
véridique: *adj.* truthful, veracious
vérification: *nf.* check; verification
vérifier: *vt.* to verify, check; to audit
vérifier les comptes: to audit the accounts
véritable: *adj.* real, genuine

véritablement: *adv.* really, genuinely
vérité: *nf.* truth; truthfulness, sincerity
vermicelle: *nm.* vermicelli
vermillion: *nm.* vermilion; scarlet
vermine: *nf.* vermin
vermisseau: *nm.* small worm
vermoulu: *adj.* worm-eaten
verni: *adj.* varnished
vernis: *nm.* varnish; glaze; shine
vernissage: *nm.* varnishing; glazing
verre: *nm.* glass; lens; drink
verrerie: *nf.* glassworks, glass-making
verrière: *nf.* window; glass roof
verrou: *nm.* bolt
verrouillage: *nm.* bolting; locking
verrouiller: *vt.* to bolt; to lock
verrue: *nf.* wart, verruca
vers: *prép.* towards; around; about; *nm.* line, verse
versatile: *adj.* versatile
verser: *vt.* to pour, shed; to pay
verset: *nm.* verse
version: *nf.* version
verso: *nm.* back
vert: *nm.* green; *adj.* green
vertébral: *adj.* vertebral
vertèbre: *nf.* vertebra
vertical: *adj.* vertical
verticalement: *adv.* vertically
vertige: *nm.* vertigo; dizziness
vertigineux: *adj.* vertiginous, breathtaking
vertu: *nf.* virtue; courage
vertueux: *adj.* virtuous
verve: *nf.* verve, vigour
verveine: *nf.* verbena
vésicule: *nf.* vesicle; gall bladder
vessie: *nf.* bladder
veste: *nf.* jacket
vestiaire: *nm.* cloakroom; changing-room
vestibule: *nm.* hall, vestibule

vestige: *nm.* relic; trace, vestige
veston: *nm.* jacket
vêtement: *nm.* garment
vétéran: *nm.* veteran
vétérinaire: *nmf.* veterinary surgeon; *adj.* veterinary
vêtir: *vt.* to clothe, to dress
veto: *nm.* veto
vêtu: *adj.* dressed; clad, wearing
vétuste: *adj.* dilapidated, ancient
veuf: *nm.* widower; *adj.* widowed
veule: *adj.* spineless
veuve: *nf.* widow; *adj.* widowed
vexant: *adj.* annoying, vexing
vexer: *vt.* to annoy; to hurt
viable: *adj.* viable
viaduc: *nm.* viaduct
viande: *nf.* meat
vibration: *nf.* vibration
vibrer: *vi.* to vibrate; to quiver
vibromasseur: *nm.* vibrator
vicaire: *nm.* curate, vicar
vice: *nm.* vice; fault, defect
vice-président: *nm.* vice-president; deputy chairman
vice-versa: *adv.* vice versa
vicieux: *adj.* licentious; dissolute; incorrect
vicissitude: *nf.* vicissitude, change; trial
vicomte: *nm.* viscount
victime: *nf.* victim, casualty
victoire: *nf.* victory
victorieusement: *adv.* victoriously
victorieux: *adj.* victorious
vidange: *nf.* emptying; waste outlet
vidanger: *vt.* to empty; to drain off
vide: *adj.* empty, vacant, devoid
vidéo: *nf.* video
vidéocassette: *nf.* videocassette
vide-ordures: *nm.* invar. rubbish chute
vider: *vt.* to empty; to drain; to vacate; to gut

videur: *nm.* bouncer
vie: *nf.* life; living
vieillard: *nm.* old man
vieillesse: *nf.* old age; the elderly; oldness
vieillir: *vi.* to get old; *vt.* to age; to put years on
vieillissement: *nm.* ageing; obsolescence
vierge: *nf.* virgin; *adj.* virgin; blank; unexposed
vieux: *adj.* old; ancient; obsolete
vif: *adj.* alive, lively; quick; eager, passionate
vigilance: *nf.* vigilance
vigilant: *adj.* vigilant
vigile: *nm.* vigil
vigne: *nf.* vine; vineyard
vigneron: *nm.* wine grower
vignette: *nf.* vignette; illustration; seal
vignoble: *nm.* vineyard
vigoureusement: *adv.* vigorously, energetically
vigoureux: *adj.* vigorous
vigueur: *nf.* vigour, strength, energy
vil: *adj.* vile; lowly
vilain: *nm.* naughty boy
villa: *nf.* villa, detached house
village: *nm.* village
villageois: *nm.* villager, rustic
ville: *nf.* town, city
villégiature: *nf.* holiday; vacation
vin: *nm.* wine
vinaigre: *nm.* vinegar
vinaigrette: *nf.* vinaigrette, oil and
vindicatif: *adj.* vindictive
vingt: *adj.* twenty
vingtaine: *nf.* about twenty; score
vingtième: *adj.* twentieth
vinicole: *adj.* wine, wine-growing
vinyl: *nm.* vinyl
viol: *nm.* rape
violation: *nf.* violation; transgression

violemment: *adv.* violently
violence: *nf.* violence; force, duress
violent: *adj.* violent; considerable, excessive
violer: *vt.* to violate, desecrate; to rape
violet: *adj.* purple, violet
violette: *nf.* violet
violeur: *nm.* rapist
violon: *nm.* violin
violoncelle: *nm.* cello, violoncello
violoncelliste: *nmf.* cello player
violoniste: *nmf.* violinist
vipère: *nf.* viper, adder
virage: *nm.* turn, bend; tacking
viral: *adj.* viral
virement: *nm.* turning, tacking; transfer, clearance
virer: *vt.* to transfer; *vi.* to turn, tack
virevolter: *vi.* to spin round, pirouette
virginité: *nf.* virginity; purity
virgule: *nf.* comma; point
viril: *adj.* virile; male, masculine
virilité: *nf.* virility
virtuose: *nmf.* virtuoso, master
virulence: *nf.* virulence, viciousness
virulent: *adj.* virulent, vicious
virus: *nm.* virus
vis: *nf.* screw
visa: *nm.* stamp, visa
visage: *nm.* face; expression
vis-à-vis: *prép.* opposite
viscéral: *adj.* visceral; deep-rooted
viscère: *nf.* viscera; intestines
viser: *vt.* to aim, target; to visa
viseur: *nm.* sight; viewfinder
visibilité: *nf.* visibility
visible: *adj.* visible; evident, obvious
visiblement: *adv.* visibly; obviously
visière: *nf.* peak; eyeshade; visor
vision: *nf.* eyesight; vision
visionnaire: *nmf.* visionary; *adj.* visionary
visite: *nf.* visit; visiting, inspection;

visitor
visiter: *vt.* to visit; to examine, inspect
visiteur: *nm.* visitor; representative
vite: *adv.* fast; quickly
vitesse: *nf.* speed
vitesse angulaire: angular velouter
vitesse de réaction: rate reaction
vitesse, en grande: by passenger train
vitesse, en petite: by goods train
vitesses moléculaires: molecular speed
vitrine: *nf.* window (store)
vivre: *vi.* to live
vocabulaire: *nm.* vocabulary
voeu: *nm.* vow
voie ferrée: railroad
voile: *nf.* sail
voilier: *nm.* sailboat
voir: *v.* to see
voisin: *nm.* neighbor; adj next
voiture: *nf.* car
voix: *nf.* voice
vol: *nm.* flight; robbery; theft
volaille: *nf.* poultry
volant: *nm.* steering wheel
voler: *vt.* to fly; to steal, to rob
volet: *nm.* shutter
voleur: *nm.* thief
volonté: *nf.* will, wish; willingness; willpower
volontiers: *adv.* willingly; gladly
voltage: *nm.* voltage
volte-face: *nf.* invar volte-face, about-turn
voltige: *nf.* acrobatics; trick riding
voltiger: *vi.* to flutter about
volubile: *adj.* voluble
volume: *nm.* volume
volumineux: *adj.* voluminous, bulky
volupté: *nf.* voluptuousness, sensual pleasure
voluptueux: *adj.* voluptuous

volute: *nf.* volute, scroll; wreath
vomi: *nm.* vomit
vomir: *vi.* to vomit, be sick; to vomit, bring up
vomissement: *nm.* vomiting
vorace: *adj.* voracious
voracité: *nf.* voracity, voraciousness
votant: *nm.* voter
vote: *nm.* vote; voting
voter: *vi.* to vote
votre: *adj.* vos your, your own
vôtre: pron. yours
vouer: *vt.* to vow; to devote; to dedicate
vouloir: *vt.* to want, wish; to require
voulu: *adj.* required; deliberate
vous: pron. you, yourself
voûte: *nf.* vault
voûté: *adj.* vaulted
voyage: *nm.* journey, trip; travelling
voyager: *vi.* to travel, journey
voyageur: *nm.* traveller, passenger
voyageur de commerce: travelling salesman
voyant: *nm.* visionary, seer
voyelle: *nf.* vowel
voyeur: *nm.* voyeur
voyou: *nm.* lout, loafer, hoodlum
vrai: *adj.* true, genuine
vraiment: *adv.* truly, really
vraisemblable: *adj.* likely, probable
vraisemblablement: *adv.* probably
vrombir: *vi.* to roar, hum
vue: *nf.* sight, eyesight
vulgaire: *adj.* vulgar, crude
vulgariser: *vt.* to popularise; to coarsen
vulgarité: *nf.* vulgarity, coarseness
vulnérable: *adj.* vulnerable
vulve: *nf.* vulva

W'

wagon: *nm.* wagon, truck, freight car; wagonload
wagon-citerne: *nm.* tanker
wagon-lit: *nm.* sleeper
wagon-restaurant: *nm.* restaurant car
wagons scellés: sealed wagons
water-polo: *nm.* water polo
watt: *nm.* watt
week-end: *nm.* weekend
western: *nm.* western
whisky: *nm.* whisky

X

xénophobe: *nmf.* xenophobe
xénophobie: *nf.* xenophobia
xylophone: *nm.* xylophone

y

yacht: *nm.* yacht
yang: *nm.* yang
yard: *nm.* yard
yin: *nm.* yin
yoga: *nm.* yoga
yogi: *nm.* yogi
yogourt: nm yogourt
yo-yo: *nm.* yo-yo
yucca: *nm.* yucca
yuppie: *nmf.* yuppy

z

zèbre: *nm.* zebra
zébu: *nm.* zebu
zélé: *adj.* zealous
zèle: *nm.* zeal
zen: *nm.* zen
zénith: *nm.* zenith
zéolithes: molecular sieves
zéro: *nm.* zero, nought, nothing
zéro absolu: absolute zero
zézayer: *vi.* to lisp
zigzag: *nm.* zigzag
zigzaguer: *vi.* to zigzag
zinc: *nm.* zinc
zizanie: *nf.* ill-feeling
zizi: *nm.* willy
zodiaque: *nm.* zodiac
zona: *nm.* shingles
zone: *nf.* zone, area
zone piétonne: pedestrian zone
zoo: *nm.* zoo
zoologie: *nf.* zoology
zoologiste: *nmf.* zoologist
zoom: *nm.* zoom; zoom lens
zoophile: *adj.* zoophilic, zoo-philous
zozoter: *vi.* to lisp